A BERTOLT BRECHT
REFERENCE COMPANION

A BERTOLT BRECHT REFERENCE COMPANION

Edited by
SIEGFRIED MEWS

GREENWOOD PRESS
Westport, Connecticut • London

1997

Library of Congress Cataloging-in-Publication Data

A Bertolt Brecht reference companion / edited by Siegfried Mews.
    p.   cm.
   Includes bibliographical references and indexes.
   ISBN 0–313–29266–3 (alk. paper)
   1. Brecht, Bertolt, 1898–1956—Criticism and interpretation.
I. Mews, Siegfried.
PT2603.R397Z5655   1997
832'.912—dc20   95–44785

British Library Cataloguing in Publication Data is available.

Library of Congress Catalog Card Number: 95–44785
ISBN: 0–313–29266–3

First published in 1997

Greenwood Press, 88 Post Road West, Westport, CT 06881
An imprint of Greenwood Publishing Group, Inc.

Printed in the United States of America

The paper used in this book complies with the
Permanent Paper Standard issued by the National
Information Standards Organization (Z39.48–1984).

10 9 8 7 6 5 4 3 2 1

06/297-8360K8

Copyright Acknowledgments

Grateful acknowledgement is hereby made to the following persons and publishers for permission to quote from the works and editions below:

Copyright for those Brecht materials translated into English from *Gesammelte Werke in 20 Bänden* by Bertolt Brecht © Suhrkamp Verlag, Frankfurt am Main 1967, and *Werke, Große kommentierte Berliner und Frankfurter Ausgabe* by Bertolt Brecht, published by Aufbau Verlag, Berlin und Weimar and Suhrkamp Verlag, Frankfurt am Main (for copyright notices see the individual volumes), is held by Stefan S. Brecht © 1997 by Stefan S. Brecht.

Brecht on Theatre: The Development of an Aesthetic, by Bertolt Brecht. Edited and translated by John Willett. Translation and notes © 1964 and renewed 1992 by John Willett. Reprinted by permission of Hill and Wang, a division of Farrar, Straus & Giroux, Inc., and by permission of Methuen, London as publishers.

Collected Plays, Volume 1 and Volume 2. Edited by Ralph Manheim and John Willett. Copyright © by Stefan S. Brecht 1966, 1972, 1974, 1976, 1977. Reprinted by permission of Stefan S. Brecht and Arcade Publishing, Inc., New York, N.Y.

Journals 1934–1955, by Bertolt Brecht (1993). Courtesy of Stefan S. Brecht and reprinted by permission of the publisher, Routledge: New York and London.

Poems 1913–1956, by Bertolt Brecht (1976). Courtesy of Stefan S. Brecht and reprinted by permission of the publisher, Routledge: New York and London.

The Jewish Wife and Other Short Plays, by Bertolt Brecht. *The Measures Taken* translated by Eric Bentley. Copyright 1956, 1960, 1965, by Eric Bentley. New York: Grove Press, eighth printing 1978. *The Exception and the Rule* translated by Eric Bentley. Copyright 1954 by Eric Bentley. New York: Grove Press, eighth printing 1978.

Jungles of Cities and Other Plays by Bertolt Brecht. *Roundheads and Peakheads* translated by N. Goold-Verschoyle. New York: Grove Press 1966. Reprinted by permission of Grove Press.

Tales from the Calendar by Bertolt Brecht. Translated by Yvonne Kapp and Michael Hamburger. Methuen: London 1961. Reprinted by permission of Methuen, London, and Routledge, New York.

Saint Joan of the Stockyards, by Bertolt Brecht. Translated by Frank Jones 1969. Bloomington: Indiana University Press, 1971. Courtesy of Frank Jones.

Life of Galileo, by Bertolt Brecht. Copyright © 1940 by Arvid Englind Teaterforlag, a.b., renewed June 1967 by Stefan S. Brecht; copyright © 1955 by Suhrkamp Verlag, Frankfurt am Main. Translation copyright © 1980 by Stefan S. Brecht. Reprinted from *Life of Galileo* by Bertolt Brecht, published by Arcade Publishing, Inc., New York, New York. Also by permission of Methuen, London, publishers.

Letters, 1913–1956, by Bertolt Brecht. Translated by Ralph Manheim. New York: Routledge, 1990. Courtesy of Stefan S. Brecht.

"Brecht's Theater of Alienation," by Reinhold Grimm reprinted from *Halcyon: A Journal of the Humanities* 13 (1991). Courtesy of The Nevada Humanities Committee.

"Brechts Dialektik vom Fressen und von der Moral." English version by Herbert Knust. *Brecht heute/Brecht Today. Brecht Yearbook* 3 (1973). Courtesy of Professor Maarten van Dijk, Editor, *Brecht Yearbook.*

Brecht in America, by James K. Lyon. Courtesy of Princeton University Press.

Towards a Philosophy of Photography, by Vilém Flusser 1983. Göttingen: European Photography, 1984. Courtesy of European Photography.

Bertolt Brecht: Political Theory and Literary Practice, edited by Betty Nance Weber and Hubert Heinen. Revised version of "Brecht's Marxist Aesthetic: The Korsch Connection" by Douglas Kellner. © by the University of Georgia Press, 1980. Reprinted by permission of The University of Georgia Press and by permission of the authors.

"The Evolution of the Feminine Principle in Brecht's Work: Beyond the Feminist Critique" by Laureen Nussbaum. Revised and updated. *German Studies Review* 8 (1985). By permission of Professor Gerald R. Kleinfeld, Editor, *German Studies Review.*

Adam's Dream: A Preface to Translation, by Ben Belitt. New York: Grove, 1978. Reprinted by permission of Grove/Atlantic, Inc.

Contents

Prefatory Note   xi

Reference Guide to Works Cited in Abbreviated Form   xiii

Introduction   1
    SIEGFRIED MEWS

PART I: THEORY AND PRACTICE OF THE THEATER   33

1. Alienation in Context: On the Theory and Practice of
   Brechtian Theater   35
    REINHOLD GRIMM

2. Brecht and the Problem of Influence   47
    CHRISTINE KIEBUZINSKA

3. Brecht's *Lehrstücke*: A Laboratory for Epic and
   Dialectic Theater   70
    KARL-HEINZ SCHOEPS

4. First Comes the Belly, then Morality   88
    HERBERT KNUST

PART II: POETRY AND PROSE FICTION   113

  5. Poetry, History, and Communication   115
       CHRISTIANE BOHNERT

  6. War-Poetry, Photo(epi)grammetry: Brecht's *Kriegsfibel*   139
       STEFAN SOLDOVIERI

  7. Dialectics and Reader Response: Bertolt Brecht's
     Prose Cycles   168
       SABINE GROSS

PART III: FILM AND MUSIC   195

  8. Brecht and Film   197
       MARC SILBERMAN

  9. Brecht, New Waves, and Political Modernism in Cinema   220
       BARTON BYG

 10. Brecht contra Wagner: The Evolution of the
     Epic Music Theater   238
       VERA STEGMANN

 11. Brecht and His Musical Collaborators   261
       THOMAS R. NADAR

PART IV: MARXISM AND FEMINISM   279

 12. Brecht's Marxist Aesthetic   281
       DOUGLAS KELLNER

 13. The Evolution of the Feminine Principle in Brecht's Work:
     An Overview   296
       LAUREEN NUSSBAUM

PART V: TRANSLATION, RECEPTION, AND APPROPRIATION   319

 14. Negotiating Meanings: Thoughts on Brecht and Translation   321
       MICHAEL MORLEY

 15. Brecht and the American Theater   339
       CARL WEBER

 16. Brecht in Latin America: Theater Bearing Witness   356
       MARINA PIANCA

Contents   ix

17. Brecht in Asia: New Agendas, National Traditions,
    and Critical Consciousness   379
       MICHAEL BODDEN

    Annotated Bibliography   399
       SIEGFRIED MEWS

    General Index   405

    Title Index of Works by Brecht   419

    About the Editor and Contributors   427

Prefatory Note

In view of the proliferating studies on Brecht, the attempt to achieve inclusiveness with regard to covering all facets of Brecht's life and work must be considered an elusive goal. Hence the contributions in the present volume do not seek to replicate information easily available elsewhere. Rather than adding to the abundance of readings of individual plays, for example, *A Bertolt Brecht Reference Companion* offers in its first part a general assessment of Brecht's theater theory and practice as well as an analysis of ''influence''—an issue that has lost none of its relevance for Brecht studies. In addition, there are essays on a group of plays and on a central motif in Brecht's plays. Further contributions discuss topics that are less prominently represented in the literature on Brecht, such as poetry and prose fiction, Brecht and film, the role of music in his works, and the topical issues of feminist and Marxist approaches to Brecht. The fairly substantial concluding part deals with the problems of translating Brecht into English as well as the reception and/or appropriation of his plays and theories from various aspects and in various countries; the historical perspective of these contributions is supplemented by a demonstration of the continuing relevance of Brecht in general and the Brechtian theater in particular in the 1990s.

Quotations from texts in German by Brecht and others are generally given in English translation; the texts of the German originals by Brecht are those to be found in *Gesammelte Werke in 20 Bänden* (*GW*) and *Werke. Große kommentierte Berliner und Frankfurter Ausgabe* (for bibliographical and other details see both the "Reference Guide to Works Cited in Abbreviated Form" and the "Annotated Bibliography"). The assistance of Mr. Jerold L. Couture, New York City, in securing permission to translate passages from the works mentioned is hereby gratefully acknowledged.

The Annotated Bibliography lists the most important English translations of Brecht's works—regrettably, there is no comprehensive standard translation—as well as major works on Brecht in English. If no source for a specific translation is given, the translation is that of the respective contributor. Parenthetical and other references by name(s) of author(s)/editor(s) and/or short title of the work referred to point to the specific sources listed in the Works Cited section of each contribution. However, works by Brecht and others that are referred to frequently throughout *A Bertolt Brecht Reference Companion* have been included in the Reference Guide to Works Cited in Abbreviated Form with full bibliographical details and will not be cited in the Works Cited sections.

Titles by Brecht are generally cited in English and, if there is no extant translation of a specific title, in both German and English. One technical feature of *GW* that may cause confusion may be mentioned: pages with an asterisk (*) in the respective volumes are pages with editorial commentary rather than text by Brecht. English titles of Brecht's plays are cited according to the American (and the more inclusive English) editions of *Collected Plays* (*CP*); a listing of the titles in the American edition is found in the Annotated Bibliography. Although, apart from *Manual of Piety*, Brecht's major collections of poetry have not been published independently in English renderings, usually the title of the respective collection is given as it appears in *Poems*.

Reference Guide to Works Cited in Abbreviated Form

The following frequently cited works are given in abbreviated form in the text of the individual contributions and do not appear in the respective Works Cited sections—except for essays in collections by several authors and special issues of journals. In general, extant English translations have been used for quotations from Brecht's texts; however, since not all of Brecht's writings are available in English (or, in some cases, specific translations were found wanting), some passages have been translated from the German originals by the respective contributors; quotations from the secondary literature on Brecht in German have likewise been translated into English by the respective contributors. Further details may be found in the Bibliography.

WORKS BY BRECHT (AND OTHERS) IN GERMAN

GW	*Gesammelte Werke in 20 Bänden*. Frankfurt am Main: Suhrkamp, 1967.
Me-ti	*Prosa*. Vol. 4, *Me-ti. Buch der Wendungen*. Edited by Werner Mittenzwei. Berlin: Aufbau, 1975.
Theaterarbeit	*Theaterarbeit. 6 Aufführungen des Berliner Ensembles*. Edited by Ruth Berlau et al. 1952. Rpt. Berlin: Henschel, 1967.

Versuche   *Versuche* 1-8. Berlin: Kiepenheuer, 1930–1933.
                                             Versuche 9-15. Berlin: Suhrkamp, 1949-1956.
                                             Rpt. *Versuche* 1-15. 4 vols. Frankfurt am Main:
                                             Suhrkamp, 1959.

Werke   *Werke. Große kommentierte Berliner und
                                             Frankfurter Ausgabe.* 30 vols. Edited by Werner
                                             Hecht, Jan Knopf, Werner Mittenzwei, and
                                             Klaus-Detlef Müller. Frankfurt am Main:
                                             Suhrkamp/Berlin: Aufbau, 1988–.

WORKS BY BRECHT IN ENGLISH TRANSLATION

CP   *Collected Plays.* 9 vols. Edited by Ralph
                                             Manheim and John Willett. New York: Vintage,
                                             1971–.

Diaries   *Diaries 1920–1922.* Edited by Herta Ramthun,
                                             translated by John Willett. New York: St.
                                             Martin's Press, 1979.

Jewish Wife   *The Jewish Wife and Other Short Plays.*
                                             Translated by Eric Bentley. New York: Grove,
                                             1965. 8th ed. 1978.

Journals   *Journals 1934–1955.* Translated by Hugh
                                             Rorrison, edited by John Willett. New York:
                                             Routledge, 1993.

Letters   *Letters 1913–1956.* Translated by Ralph
                                             Manheim, edited by John Willett. New York:
                                             Routledge, 1990.

Manual of Piety   *Manual of Piety/Die Hauspostille. A Bilingual
                                             Edition.* Translated by Eric Bentley, notes by
                                             Hugo Schmidt. New York: Grove, 1966. Rpt.
                                             1991.

Plays 1   *The Threepenny Opera. Baal. The Mother.*
                                             Translated by Ralph Manheim and John Willett,
                                             Peter Tegel, and Steve Gooch, introduction by
                                             Hugh Rorrison. New York: Arcade, 1993.

Plays 2   *The Good Person of Szechwan. Mother
                                             Courage and Her Children. Fear and Misery of
                                             the Third Reich.* Translated by John Willett,
                                             introduction by Hugh Rorrison. New York:
                                             Arcade, 1993.

Plays 3   *Life of Galileo. The Resistible Rise of Arturo
                                             Ui. The Caucasian Chalk Circle.* Translated by
                                             John Willett, Ralph Manheim, and James and
                                             Tania Stern with W.H. Auden, introduction by
                                             Hugh Rorrison. New York: Arcade, 1994.

Poems	*Poems 1913–1956.* Edited by John Willett and Ralph Manheim with the cooperation of Erich Fried. London: Methuen, 1976. 2d ed. New York: Methuen, 1987.
Poems & Songs	*Poems & Songs from the Plays.* Edited and translated by John Willett. London: Methuen, 1990.
''Short Organum''	''A Short Organum for the Theatre.'' *Brecht on Theatre. The Development of an Aesthetic.* Edited and translated by John Willett. New York: Hill, 1964.
Stories	*Short Stories 1921–1946.* Edited by John Willett and Ralph Manheim. London: Methuen, 1983.
Tales	*Tales from the Calendar.* Translated by Yvonne Kapp and Michael Hamburger. London: Methuen, 1961.
Theatre	*Brecht on Theatre. The Development of an Aesthetic.* Edited and translated by John Willett. New York: Hill, 1964.

WORKS BY OTHER AUTHORS (IN GERMAN OR ENGLISH)

Benjamin, *Illuminations*	Benjamin, Walter. *Illuminations. Essays and Reflections.* Edited by Hannah Arendt, translated by Harry Zohn. New York: Harcourt, 1968. Rpt. New York: Schocken, 1969.
Bentley, *Commentaries*	Bentley, Eric. *The Brecht Commentaries: 1943–1980.* New York: Grove, 1981.
Berlau, *Memoirs*	Berlau, Ruth. *Living for Brecht: The Memoirs.* Edited by Hans Bunge, translated by Geoffrey Skelton. New York: Fromm, 1987.
Bloom, *Mind*	Bloom, Allan. *The Closing of the American Mind.* New York: Touchstone, 1987.
Bohnert, *Lyrik*	Bohnert, Christiane. *Brechts Lyrik im Kontext. Zyklen und Exil.* Königstein/Taunus: Athenäum, 1982.
Brooker, *Dialectics*	Brooker, Peter. *Bertolt Brecht. Dialectics, Poetry, Politics.* London: Croom, 1988.
Brustein, *Theatre*	Brustein, Robert. *The Theatre of Revolt.* Boston: Little, 1964.

Eisler, *Brecht*

Eisler, Hanns. *Fragen Sie mehr über Brecht. Gespräche mit Hans Bunge.* Edited by Hans Bunge. Darmstadt: Luchterhand, 1986. First published as Bunge, Hans. *Fragen Sie mehr über Brecht—Hanns Eisler im Gespräch.* Munich: Rogner, 1970.

Eisler, *Composing*

Eisler, Hanns, and Theodor Adorno. *Composing for the Films.* Oxford: Oxford University Press, 1947 [Adorno not mentioned as coauthor]. Rpt. London: Athlone, 1994.

Esslin, *Brecht*

Esslin, Martin. *Brecht: A Choice of Evils.* London: Eyre, 1959. 4th rev. ed. London: Methuen, 1984.

Freire, *Pedagogy*

Freire, Paulo. *Pedagogy of the Oppressed.* Translated by Myra Bergman Ramos. New York: Continuum, 1970. Rev. ed. 1993.

Fuegi, *Brecht*

Fuegi, John. *Brecht and Company: Sex, Politics, and the Making of the Modern Drama.* New York: Grove, 1994.

Grimm, *Struktur*

Grimm, Reinhold. *Bertolt Brecht: Die Struktur seines Werkes.* Nuremberg: Carl, 1968.

Knopf, *Lyrik*

Knopf, Jan. *Brecht-Handbuch: Lyrik, Prosa, Schriften.* Stuttgart: Metzler, 1984.

Knopf, *Theater*

Knopf, Jan. *Brecht-Handbuch: Theater.* Stuttgart: Metzler, 1980.

Korsch, *Theory*

Korsch, Karl. *Revolutionary Theory.* Edited by Douglas Kellner. Austin: University of Texas Press, 1977.

Lyon, *Brecht*

Lyon, James K. *Brecht in America.* Princeton: Princeton University Press, 1980.

Lyon, *Kipling*

Lyon, James K. *Bertolt Brecht and Rudyard Kipling.* The Hague: Mouton, 1975.

Mueller, *Media*

Mueller, Roswitha. *Bertolt Brecht and the Theory of Media.* Lincoln: University of Nebraska Press, 1989.

Münsterer, *Brecht*

Münsterer, Hanns Otto. *The Young Brecht.* Translated and introduction by Tom Kuhn and Karen J. Leeder. London: Libris, 1992.

Piscator, *Theatre*

Piscator, Erwin. *The Political Theatre.* Translated and edited by Hugh Rorrison. New York: Avon, 1978.

Schoeps, *Shaw*

Schoeps, Karl-Heinz. *Bertolt Brecht und Bernard Shaw.* Bonn: Bouvier, 1974.

Tatlow, *Mask*	Tatlow, Antony. *The Mask of Evil. Brecht's Response to the Poetry, Theatre and Thought of China and Japan: A Comparative and Critical Evaluation*. Berne: Lang, 1977.
Völker, *Brecht*	Völker, Klaus. *Brecht. A Biography*. Translated by John Nowell. New York: Seabury, 1978.
Völker, *Chronicle*	Völker, Klaus. *Brecht Chronicle*. Translated by Fred Wieck. New York: Seabury, 1975.
Willett, *Brecht*	Willett, John. *The Theatre of Bertolt Brecht: A Study from Eight Aspects*. 1959. 3rd, rev. ed. New York: New Directions, 1968.
Willett, *Brecht in Context*	Willett, John. *Brecht in Context: Comparative Approaches*. London: Methuen, 1984.
Wöhrle, *Versuche*	Wöhrle, Dieter. *Bertolt Brechts medien-ästhetische Versuche*. Cologne: Prometh, 1988.
Wright, *Brecht*	Wright, Elizabeth. *Postmodern Brecht. A Re-Presentation*. London: Routledge, 1989.

COLLECTIONS OF ESSAYS BY SEVERAL AUTHORS AND SPECIAL ISSUES OF JOURNALS

Kleber/Visser, *Re-interpreting Brecht*	Kleber, Pia, and Colin Visser, eds. *Re-interpreting Brecht: His Influence on Contemporary Drama and Film*. Cambridge: Cambridge University Press, 1990.
Mews, *Critical Essays*	Mews, Siegfried, ed. *Critical Essays on Bertolt Brecht*. Boston: Hall, 1989.
Mews/Knust, *Essays*	Mews, Siegfried, and Herbert Knust, eds. *Essays on Brecht: Theater and Politics*. Chapel Hill: University of North Carolina Press, 1974.
Munk, *Brecht*	Munk, Erika, ed. *Brecht*. New York: Bantam, 1972.
Text + Kritik 1	*Text + Kritik. Sonderband Bertolt Brecht 1*. Edited by Heinz Ludwig Arnold. Munich: Boorberg, 1972.
Text + Kritik 2	*Text + Kritik. Sonderband Bertolt Brecht 2*. Edited by Heinz L. Arnold. Munich: Boorberg, 1973.
Thomson/Sacks, *Cambridge Companion*	Thomson, Peter, and Glendyr Sacks, eds. *The Cambridge Companion to Brecht*. Cambridge: Cambridge University Press, 1994.

Weber/Heinen, *Brecht*   Weber, Betty Nance, and Hubert Heinen, eds.
                                          *Bertolt Brecht. Political Theory and Literary
                                          Practice*. Athens: University of Georgia Press,
                                          1980.

Introduction

SIEGFRIED MEWS

As the centennial of Bertolt Brecht's birth on 10 February 1998 approaches, the contradictory impulses that have influenced this controversial writer's reception in general and in this country in particular come clearer into focus. On the one hand, one may argue that publications such as the 1994 *The Cambridge Companion to Brecht*, edited by Peter Thomson and Glendyr Sacks, tend to enshrine him in the pantheon of illustrious, but very dead, white male writers and place him in the company of Dante, Chaucer, Shakespeare, Milton, and their modern equivalents Henrik Ibsen, James Joyce, and Samuel Beckett. On the other hand, the controversies that have fueled the Brecht discourse for the last fifty years or so have really never quite subsided and continue to gain momentum whenever new challenges to Brecht's reputation arise.

As a consequence of the momentous event of 9 November 1989—the opening of the Berlin Wall and the East German-West German border—the political map of Europe has drastically changed, and the post–World War II world as Brecht knew it has been fundamentally altered. The changes in the political and economic realms have also cast their shadow on the cultural sphere; given the context of Germany's forty-odd years of division and unexpected reunification in 1990, the lifting of the Iron Curtain, and the end of the Cold War led to an intense scrutiny of especially those writers who appeared to have supported a system that was in disarray and whose remnants were to vanish quickly.

The disappearance of communism in Eastern Europe and the apparent victory of capitalism posed the question as to the writers' functions and roles in their respective societies; this questioning extended also to Brecht. Although dead since 1956, he was and is perceived as an ardent proponent of social change, an avid advocate of a just world that he defined in terms of socialism/communism, and an adamant foe of capitalism for whose demise he hoped. Hence the legitimate question as to whether the failure of communism in Central and Eastern Europe has not completely outmoded the theater theory and practice of one of its chief defenders is being addressed in several contributions of the present volume. While this question may seem more relevant in the German context, the American cultural agenda of the late 1980s and 1990s has also contributed to the probing of Brecht's position and reputation from the perspectives of postmodernism, feminism, political correctness, and multiculturalism. It appears that in the climate of the 1990s' cultural wars, Brecht bashing rather than the attempt to provide a dispassionate reassessment has asserted itself. For example, John Fuegi's widely noticed *Brecht and Company: Sex, Politics, and the Making of the Modern Drama* (1994) purports to offer profoundly new insights and a "revolutionary portrait of one of the world's greatest theater artists" (dust jacket) by resorting to a curious mixture of arguments drawn from the arsenals of feminism and political correctness as well as those of political conservatism. Although ultimately untenable as a scholarly work (Willett, et al.), Fuegi's biography demonstrates both the continuing interest in one of the most influential figures of twentieth-century drama and the multiplicity of conflicting perspectives in the post-Wall world that pose the challenge of charting a course through the substantial body of literature devoted to Brecht. The contributions in this volume seek to provide the reader with information about various aspects of Brecht studies without aiming for comprehensiveness; the following introductory sketch of life and work seeks to establish the context in which Brecht operated and to draw attention to—albeit highly selectively—the vagaries of the reception process.

AUGSBURG AND MUNICH (1898–1924)

Contrary to the claim in his stylized autobiographical poem "Of [On] Poor B.B." in the 1927 *Manual of Piety* (246–49), Brecht did not come from "the black forests" (*Poems* 107); rather, Eugen Berthold Brecht was born on 10 February 1898 in Augsburg, a city located about forty miles northwest of Munich. His father's rise from clerk to manager of a paper mill enabled Brecht to grow up in comfortable middle-class circumstances, and his devoted mother encouraged his artistic inclinations. He began writing at an early age and in 1913 published poems in *Die Ernte* (The Harvest), the student newspaper at the Augsburg Realgymnasium that Brecht attended from 1908 to 1917. His first drama, the one-act play "Die Bibel" (The Bible) also appeared in *Die Ernte* in 1913; the play attests to the lasting influence that Luther's translation of the Bible made upon him. In 1928, when Brecht was steeped in Marxism, he received a magazine inquiry as to the most pervasive literary influence in his life.

His deliberately provocative response: "You will laugh: the Bible!" (*GW* 18: 12*).[1]

At the outbreak of World War I, young Brecht temporarily got caught up in the patriotism and chauvinism that swept the country and gave it literary expression in contributions to the local newspaper *Augsburger Neueste Nachrichten*. Yet in 1916 he was almost expelled from school for writing a "defeatist" essay that criticized the Horatian dictum "Dulce et decorum est pro patria mori" (It is sweet and proper to die for the fatherland). Brecht voiced his antiwar sentiments in the radically satirical "Ballad [Legend] of the Dead Soldier" (*Manual of Piety* 222–29; *CP* 1: 369–71), written in 1918 and supposed to have caused the Nazis to put Brecht's name on their blacklist in the early 1920s. But Brecht's pacifism was not of the militant variety; in order to obtain a deferment from the draft in May 1918 he enrolled in a medical course at the University of Munich, where he had begun studying in the fall of 1917 after passing his *Notabitur* (emergency school-leaving certificate) in early 1917. He ended up as an orderly in the venereal disease ward of an Augsburg military hospital. Compared to his close friend and collaborator Caspar Neher, who had volunteered in June 1915 and spent several years in the trenches on the Western Front, Brecht's brief stint in the military—he was discharged in January 1919— can surely not be considered a hardship. Presumably Brecht's uncanny survival instinct manifested itself in his attempts to avoid the life-threatening dangers to which his friends at the front were exposed.

World War I then did not have as profound an impact on Brecht as it did, for example, on future fellow playwright Carl Zuckmayer who, like Neher, was involved in the fighting on the Western Front—nor did it radically alter the lifestyle the adolescent Brecht had enjoyed during the prewar years. To a large extent, this lifestyle was characterized by his propensity for gathering a circle of friends around him and to engage in "delighted, sometimes obsessive . . . collective activity" (Thomson 23) devoted both to pleasurable pursuits and to literary activities. Brecht clearly played the dominant role in the group of young people, and we may see in these activities the beginning of the process of collective productivity that was to become the hallmark of Brecht's creativity. Brecht's friend Hanns Otto Münsterer reports that "Bert was always writing. Everyone who knew him must have been amazed at this constant stream of ideas and plans, and at the apparent effortlessness of his writing" (Münsterer, *Brecht* 79). Yet young Brecht and his clique lived a comparatively carefree existence in Augsburg and its bucolic environs; for their own enjoyment and with the intent of provoking the comfortable and content Augsburg burghers—a class to which most of them belonged—Brecht and his circle of friends and followers sang songs that Brecht had composed and that he accompanied on the guitar in the manner of the balladeer, actor, and dramatist Frank Wedekind. Brecht had met Wedekind, whose plays were heavily censored during World War I, at the farewell party of a seminar held by University of Munich "theater professor" Artur Kutscher in January 1918; when Wedekind, who was in his fifties, died unexpectedly in March 1918 from complications resulting from a hernia operation, Brecht wrote an obituary for the *Augsburger Neueste Nachrichten* in which he praised Wedekind's vitality and called him, along with Leo Tolstoy and August Strindberg, a "great educator of the new Europe" (*Werke* 21: 36).

The paucity of young men at home during the war is likely to have facilitated Brecht's "flattering access to young women." Rather than a rarely faltering "sexual confidence" (Thomson 24), however, Brecht displayed insecurity, jealousy, occasional despair, and resorted to the help of his friends in his several youthful erotic entanglements that he characteristically was engaged in simultaneously (Völker, *Brecht* 14–16). One of these entanglements resulted in Paula (Bi or Bie) Banholzer's giving birth in 1919 to Brecht's illegitimate son, who was named Frank in tribute to Frank Wedekind.

In 1918 Brecht began and completed his first major play, *Baal,* within a few months. Repeatedly revised in subsequent years—revisions as a mode of production were to serve the playwright, who subscribed to the notion of change in all realms of human endeavor, throughout his career—the play originated as a *Gegenentwurf* or counterplay to Hanns Johst's expressionist drama *Der Einsame* (The Lonely One). *Der Einsame* features as protagonist the early nineteenth-century dramatist Christian Dietrich Grabbe. The figure of Grabbe is portrayed as an individualistic genius who perishes because he is not appreciated by his philistine fellow citizens. In contrast, Brecht depicts a highly unconventional, crassly materialistic, and voraciously promiscuous poet, who is the antithesis to the idealistic artist figures favored by Johst and other expressionist dramatists before, during, and immediately after World War I. Despite Fuegi's claim that "the dark, brilliant, misogynist, violent, homoerotic, extended poem of a play" constitutes a "highly stylized self-portrait" (*Brecht* 39, 40), it is a self-portrait only in a very remote sense. *Baal* nevertheless conveys the strong antibourgeois sentiments of its young author. Not produced until 1923 in the city of Leipzig, *Baal* has since served some critics as psychobiographical evidence for Brecht's anarchic tendencies that were later harnessed by his embracing Marxism (Speirs)—a thesis that has not remained unchallenged (Tatlow).

After the death of his beloved mother—Brecht was reticent to confess his love for her during her lifetime—in 1920, Brecht's ties to his family and his hometown began to weaken. In 1921 he gave up his studies at the University of Munich without having obtained a degree. In the same year, the aspiring writer attracted the attention of critics and publishers after a short story written in 1919, "Bargan Gives Up" (*Stories*), had appeared in the Munich magazine *Der Neue Merkur*. The publication of the story, which exhibits some of the traits that are also characteristic of Brecht's early plays and poetry such as a nonbourgeois life style, exoticism, and the theme of homoerotic love, was followed by the Munich premiere of *Drums in the Night* (completed in 1919) on 29 September 1922, the first production of a Brecht play. The drama had successful runs in Munich and Berlin in the same year—despite then Munich resident

Thomas Mann's reservations. Mann informed his American readers that *Drums in the Night* was "the bitter story of a soldier returning from the war, [the play] has two good acts but then falls flat" (375). Kragler, the returning soldier, has a far less voracious appetite for life than the protagonist of *Baal*. But he is determined to claim his share after the deprivations of war. Confronted with the choice of fighting on the barricades for the revolutionary Spartacus movement in Berlin during the uprising of January 1919 or of obtaining a modicum of domestic bliss by going home with his former girl friend who is expecting a child by another man, he denounces revolutionary idealism and opts for the "big, white, broad bed" (*CP* 1: 106). Brecht, whose involvement in the revolutionary events at the end of World War I and immediately thereafter had been that of an interested observer rather than an active participant, made a half-hearted attempt to assuage potential critics in East Berlin in the 1950s. While he refused to suppress the play, he conceded that Kragler's turning his back on the revolution was the "shabbiest" of all possible outcomes (*Werke* 23: 239). Even if, in retrospect, Brecht found his play wanting in terms of a clear political message, *Drums in the Night* featured a number of anti-illusionistic devices that he developed more fully later on.

The lack of dramatic structure in *Drums in the Night* that was noted by Mann—although it externally conformed to the conventional five-act structure—was a criticism that was echoed by other reviewers. Yet the drama was awarded the prestigious Kleist Prize in 1922 by the influential Berlin critic Herbert Ihering. Ihering praised *Drums in the Night* effusively and singled out the young writer who was eventually to become one of the most innovative and successful playwrights of the 1920s: "The poet Bert Brecht, twenty-four years old, has changed Germany's poetic face overnight. With Bert Brecht a new tone, a new melody, a new vision has arisen" (Ihering 5). Ihering's emphasis on the poetic quality of Brecht's writings was supported by contemporaries such as Elias Canetti. Canetti had a series of encounters with Brecht in 1928; despite his professed "hostility toward him," Canetti was "enchanted" by the poems of the *Manual of Piety* (Canetti 274). Post–World War II critics tended to be equally laudatory. Martin Esslin stated unequivocally: "Brecht was a poet, first and foremost a poet" whose dramatic productions lived "above all through the grace of their language and the poetic vision of the world it conveys" (*Brecht* 59). In a similar vein, John Willett, editor of *Poems*, considers Brecht a "poet beneath the skin" (Willett, "Poet" 88). Other critics provide a modification and elaboration of Brecht's poetic faculty. Jan Knopf, for example, compares Brecht favorably to Rainer Maria Rilke and Gottfried Benn, the foremost twentieth-century poets in the German language. Knopf claims that Brecht's substantial poetic *oeuvre* quantitatively surpasses that of both Rilke and Benn—but it forms only part of Brecht's total work. More importantly, Knopf attributes Brecht's pioneering role to his departure from the bourgeois tradition of the lyric as an expression of innermost feelings and subjective states of mind (*Lyrik* 10–11).[2] To be sure, poetic diction is evident in all of Brecht's plays; yet overemphasizing the omnipresent manifestations of his poetic gifts ignores the fact that Brecht considered himself primarily a playwright and very deliberately used the stage as a means to promote both his concept of a new theater and his own fortunes.

In the fall of 1919, Brecht completed a number of one-act plays; some of them show the influence of the Munich folk comedian Karl Valentin, "whose twisted logic and involved dialectics impressed Brecht" (Völker, *Brecht* 36), and in whose shows he occasionally participated. The most important of these one-act plays, *The Wedding*, demasks the young newlyweds' pretensions to middle-class respectability as ill-founded in the face of the disintegrating homemade furniture, a process that accompanies and underscores the gradual revelation of the couple's illusions.

In the Jungle of Cities, Brecht's third major play, serves up homoerotic love as a means of overcoming the individual's isolation and alienation in the big and cold city of Chicago. Inspired among other sources by the German translation of Upton Sinclair's *The Jungle*, which was published in 1906 and translated into German the same year, the play presents, as the prologue states, the "inexplicable [figurative] wrestling match" (*CP* 1: 108) between the Malay lumber dealer Shlink and the lending library clerk Garga in Chicago. But Chicago, which appears here for the first time as the setting of one of Brecht's plays, resembles Berlin where Brecht had spent some time in 1921–1922. Rudyard Kipling's "jungle" has been transposed to the big city that causes the disintegration of Garga's family from the "prairies" (*CP* 1: 108). Yet in accordance with the laws of the urban jungle, it is the younger and physically stronger Garga who emerges as the victor over Shlink. The latter had sought in vain to establish human contact by means of homoerotic love. Perhaps Brecht's most inaccessible play because of the lacking integration of dialogue, which includes verbatim quotations from Arthur Rimbaud, general atmosphere, and deliberately unmotivated action—the spectators are adjoined in the prologue not to worry about the "motives of the fight" (*CP* 1: 108)—the play has moments of great poetic intensity and depicts the precarious situation of the individual in the jungle of the city.

In the Jungle—the full title *In the Jungle of Cities* was not used until the revised 1927 version—premiered in May 1923 at the Munich Residenztheater. The stage design was by Brecht's friend Neher; although the production was officially directed by Erich Engel, Brecht was also involved in directing. The teamwork of Neher, Engel, and Brecht was to continue—despite the fact that the premiere caused a scandal. In dubious taste, Thomas Mann approved the "popular conservatism" of the Munich audience that reacted against Brecht's presumed "Bolshevist art"—a term used without specific political connotations—by throwing gas bombs in the theater.

In 1919 Brecht had met the older, established writer Lion Feuchtwanger, who became his mentor and collaborator. Feuchtwanger provided a slightly ironic portrait of a "thinly disguised Brecht as an angry young man and poet who provocatively flaunts his anti-bourgeois sentiments by means of his unkempt appearance, proletarian garb, and disregard of conventional sexual mores'' (Mews, ''Portraits'' 247) in his 1930 novel *Erfolg* (Success). A notable result of the Feuchtwanger/Brecht collaboration was the translation and adaptation of Christopher Marlowe's *Edward II* under the title *The Life of Edward the Second of England*. The adaptation premiered at the Munich Kammerspiele in March 1924 under the direction of Brecht; in retrospect it is considered an important step toward what Brecht was later to call the epic theater: it is devoid of the inevitability of tragedy, neither the king nor his favorite Gaveston are presented as particularly heroic, and the narrative element is emphasized by scene titles that specify the time and place of events and provide a brief summary of what is to follow—thus diminishing suspense. The brief appearance of a ballad-seller anticipates the introduction of figures with a pronounced narrative function in later plays.

BERLIN (1924–1933)

Although it was in Munich where Brecht first attracted attention as a serious writer and dramatist, he considered the Bavarian capital merely a stepping-stone on his way to Berlin, a metropolis that in the 1920s was to become a major cultural and artistic center. Brecht had visited Berlin several times since his first trip of February/March 1920; during his extended stay from November 1921 to April 1922 he attempted doggedly to promote his interests with publishers and theater directors. Yet the conquest of Berlin proved difficult and elusive, and the alliance Brecht had formed with fellow playwright Arnolt Bronnen to accomplish the conquest did not yield immediate results. On the contrary, in January 1922 Brecht was admitted to the Charité hospital because of undernourishment; in the spring of the same year he began directing rehearsals for the production of Bronnen's *Vatermord* (Patricide) with a famous cast of actors, among them the renowned Heinrich George, for the matinée performances of the noncommercial Junge Bühne, an enterprise that labored under difficult conditions in that it did not have a permanent home. Yet Brecht's unrelenting criticism of the actors' work—perhaps surprising for a novice—resulted in the production being taken over by another director.

Playwright Carl Zuckmayer, who had met Brecht in Munich, reports: ''Brecht said we had to go to Berlin. That was where the theatrical battles were being fought'' (Zuckmayer 273). When Engel was appointed artistic director of the Deutsches Theater in Berlin, he offered both Brecht and Zuckmayer one-year appointments (from 1924 to 1925) as play reader and dramaturg—a position that was neither very demanding nor influential but provided a modicum of subsistence and time for pursuing projects and developing contacts.

Brecht settled permanently in Berlin in the fall of 1924 and remained there until 1933, the beginning of his exile. He adapted easily to the anonymous existence in the ''asphalt city,'' as he called Berlin in ''Of Poor B.B.''; in *Reader for Those Who Live in Cities* (*Poems* 131–50), he provided instructions as to how survive in the big city and suggested to his fellow city dwellers that they should not succumb to the illusion about man's autonomy in a mass society. Brecht's sharpened awareness of social processes and problems is evident in the comedy *A Man's a Man* (1927). Although plans for this play go back to Brecht's time in Augsburg, major revisions took place in 1924/1925. In the play, Brecht posits the social conditioning of human beings and their ultimate exchangeability in mechanistic, montage fashion—a procedure that allows the "transformation" of the soft-natured docker Galy Gay into Jeraiah Jip, "the human fighting machine" (*CP* 2: 69). But, as one critic has argued, *A Man's a Man* does not only present the presumed farewell to Western civilization's cherished notion of individuality, it also parodies and dismisses tragedy as a viable dramatic genre by emphasizing playfulness and epic elements. For example, for the first time in one of his plays, Brecht has "actors step out of their roles" as a reminder to the spectators "that they are watching a theatrical event" (Lyon, "*Mann*" 516).

The fact that the play takes place in a setting inspired by Kipling and that was, for German spectators, curiously remote, draws attention to another facet of Brecht's mode of production. From Kipling, whom Brecht had read before he settled in Berlin, he "derived his central image of an exotic-military-imperial world somewhere between Suez, Hong Kong and the South Pacific" (Willett, "Kipling" 47). But it was Elisabeth Hauptmann who, on account of her better command of English, further acquainted Brecht with Kipling's work and collaborated on *A Man's a Man*. Hauptmann, an aspiring writer, whom he met in the fall of 1924, had come to Berlin in 1922 and supported herself by doing secretarial work and translations. She became the first of the three important female collaborators and lovers—the two others were Margarete Steffin and Ruth Berlau—who made substantial contributions to Brecht's work and/or furthered his career—although Fuegi's claims as to their share in Brecht's output and their significance for his work must be deemed excessive.

Brecht's "polygamous" nature has been the subject of much comment; by the age of twenty-six he had fathered three children with three different women: son Frank with Paula Banholzer (born 30 July 1919); daughter Hanne (born 12 March 1923) with opera singer Marianne Zoff, to whom Brecht was married from November 1922 to November 1927; and son Stefan (born 3 November 1924) with Austrian actress Helene Weigel (he married Weigel in April 1929 and remained married to her until his death; daughter Barbara was born on 18 October 1930). Although Brecht had relied on cooperative efforts from his youth, his association with Hauptmann initiated a new phase of close cooperation with his women collaborators. As Zuckmayer remarked, the "concept of literary and theatrical 'collectives' became fashionable" (267) in Berlin in the late 1920s, and critics have interpreted Brecht's cooperative method as an indication of a new concept of the author who is no longer perceived—or perceives him- or herself—as the sole originator of works and who challenges—at least in part—the traditional notions of the "initiative, autonomy, inventiveness, creativity, authority, or originality" (Pease 105) emanating from a single source.[3] Yet Brecht's challenge to traditional notions of the author was offset by his dominant position in the collective that resulted to some degree in the exploitation of the ideas and the work of its other members. But, motivated by love as well as their adherence to the ideas of socialism/communism that they shared with Brecht, most of his female collaborators remained loyal to him. Portraying these women as helpless victims probably misses the point in that it precludes the option of an existence independent of Brecht, which is posited by Elaine Feinstein in her novel *Loving Brecht* (1992) in which the heroine, who bears some resemblance to Lotte Lenya, liberates herself from Brecht's influence and strikes out on her own. Such attempts at liberation were not confined to fiction; aspiring playwright Marieluise Fleißer, whom Brecht knew in Munich, eventually broke with Brecht in 1929–1930 because she feared being completely dominated by him, both personally and artistically. Fleißer attempted to come to terms with her hard-won independence in several texts, notably the drama "Der Tiefseefisch" (The Deepsea-fish), a revised version of which was not published until 1972.

An important development in Brecht's biography occurred in 1926, when he began to read Karl Marx in order to fathom the transactions at the Chicago Wheat Exchange for his projected play, eventually entitled "Joe Fleischhacker." Brecht's turning to Marxism has been the subject of considerable debate by critics and biographers. Esslin has advanced the psychologizing thesis about Brecht's "divided nature" (*Brecht* x) and—as he put it in the title of his book— Brecht's being confronted with a "choice of evils" that entailed a choice between anarchy and hedonism in the manner of *Baal* on the one hand, and stern, authoritarian party discipline on the other. Conversely, it has been argued that Brecht's study of Marx was the outgrowth of his endeavors to find an adequate form of representation for a complex social reality. Biographer Klaus Völker, for instance, devotes an entire section to Brecht's "Marxist Studies" and asserts that Brecht turned to Marxism-Leninism as a means of imparting a new quality to his writing that would enable him to render social processes more effectively on stage (*Brecht* 87–169).

Brecht's study of Marxism was preceded by and coincided with his more clearly focused criticism of contemporaneous drama and staging practices that eventually evolved into his theory of the epic theater. The term *Verfremdungs-effekt*, central to Brecht's theory and now a commonplace in drama theory, does not appear in Brecht's writings until the 1935 essay "Alienation Effects in Chinese Acting" (*Theatre* 91–99).[4] Nevertheless, it has caused some confusion on account of its various translations into English. On its simplest level, the *Verfremdungseffekt* means "gaining new insights into the world around us by glimpsing it in a different and previously unfamiliar light" (Willett, "Brecht" 218). There is no unanimity among critics as to whether the *Verfrem-dungseffekt* should be seen in the philosophical-historical context of the Hegelian-Marxist concept of *Entfremdung*, correctly translated as "alienation," or simply as a staging device, a formal technique in the service of conveying a message. Yet apart from the origin of the term and from the pre-Marxist Brecht's tendency to use devices for which the term had not yet been invented, divorcing the *Verfremdungeffekt* entirely from Brecht's Marxist convictions seems problematic inasmuch as aesthetics and philosophical method combine to raise the audience's level of consciousness to the point of new and liberating insights to which others such as director Erwin Piscator aspired by means of a pronounced political theater.

Before Brecht's Marxism asserted itself vigorously in his *Lehrstücke,* mostly written between 1928 and 1931, he achieved an enormous popular success with *The Threepenny Opera,* a collaboration with composer Kurt Weill that premiered on 31 August 1931 in the Berlin Theater am Schiffbauerdamm, home of Weigel and Brecht's Berliner Ensemble after World War II. Not an opera in the strict sense of the word, Brecht in retrospect deemed the 1928 production—''the most successful demonstration of the epic theatre'' and ''the first use of theatrical music in accordance with a new point of view'' (*Theatre* 85).[5] Yet the advances in the aesthetic realm came at a price: bourgeois audiences tended to enjoy *The Threepenny Opera* as pure entertainment rather than as an attack on capitalist society. For example, the intended message of Mac the Knife and Low-Dive Jenny's song ''What Keeps Mankind Alive?'' at the end of the second act was largely ignored. The song, which addresses the audience directly, includes the most famous line of Brecht's entire work, ''Food is the first thing. Morals follow on'' (*CP* 2: 201–202),[6] which proceeds from the perhaps overly optimistic assumption that human depravity is caused by social injustice and that human beings will be allowed to indulge in their propensity for kindness once a just society has been established.

After the publication of *Die Songs der Dreigroschenoper* (The Songs of *The Threepenny Opera*) in 1929, the renowned theater critic Alfred Kerr, the antipode of Brecht's supporter Ihering, noticed that the name of K.L. Ammer, translator of the ballads by François Villon used in *The Threepenny Opera,* had been omitted. As a consequence, he charged Brecht with plagiarism, but Brecht provocatively responded by professing his ''fundamental laxity in matters of intellectual property'' (*Werke* 21: 315), a statement that implicitly rejected traditional notions about the author and the mode in which artistic works are produced and substituted the concepts of montage and collective production. As mentioned previously, the concept of collective production has come under attack by Fuegi, who claims that Hauptmann not only translated John Gay's ballad opera *The Beggar's Opera* (1728), but also contributed significantly to its transformation into *The Threepenny Opera* (*Brecht* 145, 196)—albeit without offering solid proof (Willett et al., 285). At the same time, it does not detract from the stature of Brecht to acknowledge that his political views and innovative production methods did not necessarily produce harmonious personal relationships. As Canetti writes: ''He did not care for people, but he put up with them; he respected those who were persistently useful to him; he noticed others only to the extent that they corroborated his somewhat monotonous view of the world'' (274).

Brecht sought to sharpen his social and political messages when in 1930 he was asked to produce a film treatment of *The Threepenny Opera*. Yet he was rebuffed by the film producers who had expected a treatment along the ''culinary'' lines of the original play. They did not realize that in the two years following the premiere Brecht had intensified his studies of Marxism; furthermore, he had witnessed the stock market crash that resulted in the Great Depression—an event that appeared to confirm his Marxist beliefs. When an agreement with Brecht could not be reached, the film company produced a film that used only some elements of Brecht's script. Brecht insisted on his individual and artistic rights and sued the film company for breach of contract; in December 1931 he settled out of court for a considerable sum.[7]

The abortive cinematic project is an indication of the difficulties involved in changing the thrust of *The Threepenny Opera*, which had acclaimed runs all over Europe but in 1933 closed after only twelve performances in New York City. For example, the successful post–World War II revival of *The Threepenny Opera*, which opened in July 1945 in the Hebbel Theater in war-ravaged Berlin, confronted Brecht with the problem of unintended and undesirable audience reaction—a problem that was not limited to the unfocused indictment of the capitalist order in *The Threepenny Opera*. Berliners, who had no choice but to subsist on exceedingly small rations, considered the line about food and morals, quoted above, ''a welcome form of protest against the occupying powers who wanted to de-Nazify them without feeding them properly'' (Lyon, *Brecht* 311). Brecht, then in faraway California, deplored the lack of a revolutionary movement in postwar Germany that rendered the message of *The Threepenny Opera* ''pure anarchism'' (*Journals* 355).

The singular position of *The Threepenny Opera* in terms of its appeal to different audiences is also attested to by the Marc Blitzstein version that opened on 10 March 1954 in the Theatre de Lys in New York City; it ran for seven years with a total of 2,611 performances and featured Weill's wife Lotte Lenya as Jenny. Yet conservative culture critic Allan Bloom discerned a hidden political agenda and cited as a conspicuous example of the ''astonishing Americanization'' of German value relativism—a consequence of the Nietzschean revaluation of values—''the smiling face of Louis Armstrong as he belts out the words of his great hit 'Mack [sic] the Knife' '' and viewed *The Threepenny Opera* as ''a monument of Weimar popular culture, written by two heroes of the artistic Left, Bertolt Brecht and Kurt Weill'' (Bloom, *Mind* 151, 154). Bloom elevated the play to the status of a cultural icon that greatly contributed to that ''strange nostalgia among many of the American intelligentsia for this moment just prior to Hitler's coming to power'' (155). But Bloom's stern condemnation of the morally ambiguous climate of Berlin in the late 1920s, which was allegedly promoted by Brecht and Weill, rests on shaky foundations inasmuch as he bases his argument on a single play or, rather, a single song. The song alludes to the parallel between the openly rapacious shark and knife-concealing Mac, whose threatening nature and deadly intent—like those of capitalist exploiters—are not obvious at first glance.

Brecht and Weill's second major cooperative venture was the opera *Rise and Fall of the City of Mahagonny*, which opened in March 1930 in the Leipzig opera house and caused a scandal because it corresponded not at all to the traditional concept of opera in general or that of Wagnerian opera in particular. Thus lumberjack Jim MacIntyre's warning against the seductive power of false hopes (*CP* 2: 111) refers both to the deceptive promises of Mahagonny, which is located in a vaguely American setting and offers unrestricted consumption and pleasures for those who can afford them, and the seductiveness emanating from Richard Wagner's music. In his "Notes to the Opera *Rise and Fall of the City of Mahagonny*," published in 1930 and revised in 1938 (*Theatre* 33–42), Brecht provided his first systematic statement of the epic theater and epic opera that he contrasted to the "dramatic" theater and "dramatic" opera, respectively.

Although several of the *Lehrstücke*—"plays for learning" attempting a new form of participatory communication by spectator involvement rather than doctrinaire "didactic plays"—also were set to music,[8] they lack the "culinary" element of the operas. Notably *The Measures Taken*, which was performed in Berlin in December 1930, turned out to be Brecht's most controversial work. It was intended as a demonstration of politically incorrect behavior by the young comrade who was unable to subordinate his emotions to party discipline and thereby endangered the mission of the agitators who, in the early 1930s, had been sent to China to instigate a revolution. The play was rejected by both sides of the political spectrum. In particular, the death of the young comrade, who agreed to be killed to enable his comrades to avoid being captured, tended to overshadow the fact that the play strove for teaching politically correct behavior by means of presenting a stylized trial situation in which the three returning agitators defend their action by alternately assuming the role of the young comrade and pointing out his mistakes. *The Measures Taken* did not find favor with the functionaries of the Communist party. In a 1930 review, Alfred Kurella castigated the "petty-bourgeois writer" (82) Brecht for deviating from the party line and for virtually supporting the ideas of "right-wing opportunism" (79); he found the play to be revolutionary in style rather than substance. Conversely, Ruth Fischer, sister of composer Hanns Eisler, who wrote the music for *The Measures Taken*, in 1944 accused Brecht of having "approved and glorified the [Stalinist show] trials before they were conceived in their perfect form in Stalin's brain" (Fischer 89). Apparently unaware of Fischer's allegations, in October 1947 the members of the House Un-American Activities Committee (HUAC) also referred to *The Measures Taken*; they were particularly interested in Brecht's presumed advocacy of human sacrifice for the sake of political expediency and his pro-Communist sympathies. The record of the hearings shows, however, that the committee members did not pursue this line of questioning very vigorously.

The austerity of the *Lehrstücke* is mitigated in *Saint Joan of the Stockyards*, a powerful and complex play about a modern-day Joan of Arc in the stockyards of Chicago that, apart from Sinclair's *The Jungle* and other sources, is also indebted to George Bernard Shaw's *Major Barbara* (1905) and *Saint Joan* (1924). From the former play, Brecht presumably derived the notion of the Salvation Army's role as an instrument to uphold the establishment. Although Brecht's *Saint Joan* is unequivocal in its indictment of the capitalist system that found its prototypical expression in America—in the end the dying heroine Joan Dark denounces the inhuman society in which she lives and advocates its violent overthrow—Brecht created a fascinating counterpart to good but naive Joan Dark (who shares some characteristics with the guileless young comrade in *The Measures Taken*) in the "giant of [meat] packers / king of the stockyards" (*Saint Joan* 27) Pierpont Mauler. He is a Faustian character who, befitting his station as the modern equivalent of erstwhile powerful kings and rulers, is given to speaking in Shakespearean blank verse and is an eminently theatrical figure. The beginnings of the play go back to the mid-1920s, and a stage version was completed in 1931. However, the play could not be produced during the waning years of the Weimar Republic. A shortened version was broadcast on Berlin radio in April 1932; the play premiered in Hamburg after Brecht's death, in 1959.

A new member joined the Brecht collective in 1932. Margarete Steffin, a young women in her early twenties, soon proved indispensable because of her linguistic and editorial skills. Of frail health—she suffered from severe tuberculosis from which she was eventually to die—she nevertheless made great efforts to promote Brecht's work and to fulfill the many demands that he made on her. Because of her working-class origins and commitment to the Communist cause, she became Brecht's "Soldier of the Revolution" (*Poems* 279–84; Völker, *Brecht* 186) whose loss ten years later profoundly affected him.

Brecht had become acquainted with Steffin when he was directing *The Mother*, in which she had a minor role. An adaptation of Maxim Gorky's novel by the same name, *The Mother* premiered in January 1932; it features one of the resilient, resourceful mother figures that were beginning to occur with increasing frequency in Brecht's work.[9] The play is sometimes classified as a *Lehrstück* in that it shows the transformation of widowed Pelagea Vlasova from "a worker's mother" (*Plays* 1: 145) into a true revolutionary after the death of her son; in addition, the play is intended to teach the audience how to become involved in the political struggle—a timely, if not belated effort in view of the fact that *The Mother* was the last Berlin production of a play by Brecht before Hitler came to power. Brecht's earlier attitude of "bemused contempt and fascination" (Rosenhaft 16) with the mass spectacles organized by the Nazis had given way to deep concern about the threat posed by them. In July 1932 the Nazis had become the largest party in the Reichstag (the German parliament) and had taken to the streets to terrorize their opponents. Brecht tried in vain to promote an antifascist front of Communists and Social Democrats, as for example in his 1932 poem "When the Fascists Kept Getting Stronger" (*Poems* 205–206).

On 30 January 1933, Hitler was appointed Chancellor of a coalition government, and less than a month later the Reichstag was set afire—a pretext for the Nazis to step up their terror, particularly against the Left. On 28 February, one day after the Reichstag fire, Brecht, accompanied by Weigel and son Stefan, left Germany; he was not to return permanently until more than a decade later.

EUROPEAN EXILE (1933–1941)

Brecht traveled to Prague, Vienna, Zurich, and Paris where his (and Weill's) first work written in exile, the ballet *The Seven Deadly Sins,* had its premiere in June 1933. Thematically related to the later play *The Good Person of Szechwan*, especially in its dramatization of the self-exploitation of woman, the libretto does not have any specific bearing on the contemporary political situation. According to Völker, writing the lyrics provided an opportunity for Brecht to earn some cash (*Brecht*, 180)—a motivation that does not render *The Seven Deadly Sins* invalid as genuine Brechtian theater. An invitation by the Danish writer Karin Michaelis eventually enabled Brecht and his family, including his collaborator Steffin, to settle in Skovbostrand near the city of Svendborg on the Danish isle of Fyn (in German: Fünen), where they lived from December 1933 to April 1939. Brecht and other exiles' initial expectations that a return to Germany would be possible within a short time were not fulfilled. In the wistful poem "Thoughts on the Duration of Exile" (*Poems* 301–302), the persona's assumed certainty of being able to go home "tomorrow" is contradicted by his activity of watering the "little chestnut tree." Its anticipated growth forecasts the long duration of exile.

Among other hardships, exile entailed limited access to publishing opportunities and stage productions; furthermore, the exile years were overshadowed by the threat of Nazism. Hence it was a "Bad Time for Poetry" (*Poems* 330–31), but Brecht continued writing. Occasional doubts about the efficacy of his writings in the service of "liberation" (*Poems* 302) did not keep him from attacking the "house-painter" (*Poems* 331)—his favorite term of contempt for the would-be artist Hitler. Yet Brecht's first major project in exile was a novel—the only one he ever completed—a genre that offered the advantage of not being dependent on the medium of the stage apparatus to find a public. With the novel Brecht returned to the subject matter of his greatest theatrical hit, *The Threepenny Opera. Threepenny Novel* was first published in 1934 in a German-language edition in Amsterdam and in 1937 in an English translation as *A Penny for the Poor*, a title that was changed in postwar issues to emphasize its affinity with the successful play. The intensification of social and political conflicts as the result of the Wall Street crash, the Nazis' rise to power, and his experiences with the abortive film project, referred to above, motivated Brecht to use the novel as a vehicle for an unambiguously critical stance vis-à-vis the evils of capitalism.

Set in the then financial capital of the world, London, during the time of the Boer Wars around the turn of the century, *Threepenny Novel* is not concerned with individual conflicts and psychological states of mind; rather, the focus in the two separate and intermittently intertwining plots about Macheath and Peachum is on business deals. Macheath has become a ruthless entrepreneur whose final victory in the ferocious fights of the capitalist jungle is compared with Napoleon Buonaparte's campaigns—an indication that for Brecht the decisive battles take place in the realm of economics. Moreover, Macheath is characterized as a "born leader" with an "unshakeable determination" (Brecht 175) who invokes "the mutual attachment between a leader and his followers" (169)—a phrase that, particularly in the wording of the German original, alludes to the Nazis' attempt to detract from socioeconomic differences and from the class struggle. These attempts were aided by the middle class's susceptibility to believing in the strong man who would set things right and uphold traditional values. The pointed references to the political situation around 1933 draw attention to Brecht's belief, shared by other leftist intellectuals, that the Nazis merely served as a front for capitalism—a belief that is also evident elsewhere in Brecht's work.

In March 1934 Brecht, Steffin, and Eisler, who was on a visit in Denmark, reworked *Roundheads and Pointed Heads,* a play that was begun as an adaptation of Shakespeare's *Measure for Measure.* It was completed in 1932, but its publication was halted when the Nazis came to power. In his parable play, Brecht depicted the divisive effects of racial theories on the revolutionary uprising of the Sickle movement, whose members are exploited tenant farmers in the mythical country of Yahoo. The figure of Callas, derived from the protagonist of Heinrich von Kleist's nineteenth-century novella *Michael Kohlhaas,* for selfish reasons becomes a follower of the racist Iberin and refuses to join the revolutionaries. He does not realize until it is too late that it is not the shape of one's head (the exaggerated physical characteristics of Roundheads and Pointed Heads signify racial differences) but whether one is rich or poor that determines one's fate. Hence the demagogue Iberin, who bears some resemblance to Hitler, appears as a tool of the ruling classes—a questionable assessment of the causes and purveyors of racism and anti-Semitism.

Roundheads and Pointed Heads was produced in Copenhagen in November 1936; critics took exception to its "undramatic" quality. Ruth Berlau, former actress and wife of a prominent Danish physician, had introduced Brecht to theater circles in Copenhagen. Called "Red Ruth" because of her Communist leanings, she soon became Brecht's lover after they met in the fall of 1933; she was resented by both Weigel and Steffin for her histrionic flair that contrasted with the self-effacing service to Brecht they engaged in both to secure his comfort and to promote his cause.

In both *Fear and Misery of the Third Reich,* first translated by Eric Bentley

as *The Private Life of the Master Race* (1944), and *Señora Carrar's Rifles*
Brecht temporarily abandoned the parable form and made concessions to "Aristotelian drama" so as to be able to intervene more directly in the fight against
fascism. *Fear and Misery* consists of twenty-seven self-contained scenes, the
longer ones of which resemble one-act plays. In retrospect, the Nazi terror that
is depicted in these scenes appears to be comparatively mild; particularly the
spineless bourgeois intellectuals such as the judge in "In Search of Justice,"
the teacher in "The Informer," and even the Jewish wife of a non-Jewish physician in "The Jewish Wife" (these scenes have been printed separately in *The
Jewish Wife and Other Short Plays*, edited by Bentley) tend to be comical in
their futile attempts to accommodate the new rulers; according to Brecht, true
resistance to the Nazis was only to be found among the workers.

Whereas *Fear and Misery* takes place inside Nazi Germany, *Señora Carrar's
Rifles* is set in Spain at the time of the Civil War in the mid-1930s. Like the
protagonist of *The Mother*, Señora Carrar undergoes the transformation from a
passive, nonviolent figure to a fighter against the counterrevolutionary forces
under General Francisco Franco. Both *Fear and Misery* and *Señora Carrar*, in
which Weigel played the leading role, were performed by and for German exiles
in Paris, in 1938 and 1937, respectively.

Beginning in 1937, those plays that contributed more than any others to
Brecht's reputation and became part of the Brecht repertory originated in comparatively short succession in Denmark, Sweden, and Finland: the first version
of *Life of Galileo, Mother Courage and Her Children, The Good Person of
Szechwan*, and *Puntila and Matti, His Hired Man*. These plays considerably
enlarged the extant body of Brecht plays and their range; unlike *Fear and Misery*
and *Señora Carrar*, they are not explicitly related to contemporary events and
resort, in varying degrees, to the epic mode that enhances their theatricality. The
perception that these plays lacked an overt, "coldly rational and inevitably cruel
ideology" (Esslin, *Brecht* 232) no doubt facilitated their gradual acceptance in
the West—hardly a smooth process, one that began with the premieres of
Mother Courage (April 1941), *The Good Person* (February 1943), and *Galileo*
(September 1943) in Zurich during World War II when Brecht was no longer
in Europe.

Galileo in particular has served some critics to build a "case against Bertolt
Brecht," as the title of the English translation of Gerhard Szczesny's book puts
it. These critics tended to point out the alleged parallels between the protagonist's private, sensuous pleasures on the one hand and his public cowardice as
expressed in his renunciation of the heliocentric theory of the solar system on
the other. In this view, Brecht's submitting to the doctrine of Marxism, a doctrine that in its encompassing demands requires a loyalty similar to that expected
by the Catholic Church, corresponds to the case of Galileo who likewise submitted to authority so as to be able to indulge his private vices. A modification
of this argument has recently been advanced by Fuegi, who claims that
"Galileo's caving in before the Inquisition" (*Brecht* 585) is related both to

Nikolai Bukharin's confessing his deviations from Stalin's line during the Moscow show trials of the 1930s and Brecht's own unheroic appearance before the House Un-American Activities Committee. Yet readings that use texts for the theater as biographical evidence are contradicted by the appreciation of the play as "Brecht's masterpiece" (Esslin, *Brecht* 273) and "theatre on the grandest scale" precisely because, according to Bentley, it displays "Brecht's own divided nature" ("Galileo" 85).

Whereas in *The Good Person* the prostitute with a golden heart Shen Teh is forced to adopt a false identity as her ruthless male cousin Shui Ta in order to survive, and the impotent gods are unable to promote and reward goodness, the protagonist of *Mother Courage* does not make any pretensions of being good. Conceived as a "hyena" of the battlefields, the audience perceived her as a tragic mother figure who had lost her children in the Thirty Years' War and had become a victim of war from which she made her living as a camp follower. Hence it may be doubted whether the play persuaded post–World War II audiences to view camp follower Mother Courage's efforts to live off the war as reprehensible and to conclude that "no sacrifice is too great for the struggle against war" (*CP* 5: 339).

Although in a letter of January 1934 Brecht referred to his exile as "Danish Siberia" (*Letters* 167), he did not spend his time in isolation under what he later, in the motto to his collection *Svendborg Poems*, called more charitably his "Danish thatched roof" (*Poems* 320). Apart from the company of "the whole Brecht inner entourage" that Willett describes as a "mixture of family, harem, and producers' co-op" ("Englishman" 18), Brecht enjoyed visits by friends from the Berlin years such as Walter Benjamin and Brecht's Marxist teacher Karl Korsch,[10] both of whom spent extended periods of time with him. Nor was Brecht bound to Skovbostrand: he traveled to London (fall 1934 and spring/summer 1936), where he pursued film projects and participated in an international writers' congress; to Moscow (spring 1935), where he saw the Chinese actor Mei Lan-fang, whose impressive performance inspired him to the aforementioned essay "Alienation Effects in Chinese Acting"; to Paris (June 1935, summer 1937), where he participated in the international writers' congresses; and to New York City (October–December 1935) on the occasion of the leftist Theatre Union's staging of *The Mother*. Brecht's problems with the play's producers and director about the proper staging led to Brecht and Eisler being barred from the rehearsals—an experience that did not augur well for the playwright's prospects in the United States.

Brecht's productivity in his European exile is also attested to by two major prose projects that, however, remained unfinished. His reactions to both private and political events found their way into the collection *Me-ti. Buch der Wendungen* (The Book of Twists and Turns), which was not published until after his death.[11] Brecht made comparatively little use of his Chinese sources, and the fictitious, Chinese-sounding names are not designed to hide the identity of, for example, Karl Marx (Ka-meh), Stalin (Ni-en), and Brecht himself (Kin-jeh

and other names). Many of the short prose pieces are concerned with the *Große
Methode* (grand method) or a materialistic, dialectical way of thinking, and the
Große Ordnung (grand order) or the concept of a socialist order and society. But
Brecht also singles out the difficulties that the Soviet Union (Su) under Stalin encounters in establishing this great order on account of the fact that the great
method has fallen into disrepute: the social practice of the Soviet Union that does
not permit freedom of expression and engages in a Stalin personality cult.

Although Brecht attributed many of the Soviet Union's shortcomings to Stalin's baleful influence, he never spoke out publicly against Stalin's regime of
terror for fear of supporting the enemies of the only socialist country in existence
at that time. Brecht's occasional criticism of Stalin in *Me-ti* appears muted and
even apologetic. His silence may have been motivated in part by concerns for
his own personal safety after the disappearance and death in the Soviet Union
of friends such as actress Carola Neher and Soviet dramatist Sergei Tretyakov—
although he wrestled, for example, with his doubts about the allegation that
Tretyakov was a spy in the poem (unpublished during his lifetime) "Is the
People Infallible?" (*Poems* 331–33). Ultimately, however, it is reasonable to
assume that Brecht persuaded himself that Stalin's Soviet Union—and not the
Western democracies—was the only bulwark against Nazi aggression, and that
the Soviet Union was the only country capable of instituting the great order.
Hence he tolerated Stalinism and did not criticize Stalin or the Soviet Union
publicly. Clearly his assessment of Stalin constituted one of the playwright's
most serious errors (Müller 119).

Brecht was less reticent to speak out in defense of his plays and the theory
underlying them. His drama deviated considerably from the doctrine of Socialist
Realism that was propagated in Moscow by exiles such as Georg Lukács and
Kurella. Based on the mimetic representation of reality, Socialist Realism was
inimical to Brecht's aspirations for an epic theater that shunned surface realism
and naturalistic productions. In the climate of the Stalin show trials, the realism
debate was not exclusively a matter of aesthetics; Brecht, who posited the
"Weite und Vielfalt der realistischen Schreibweise" (Breadth and Abundance
of the Realistic Mode of Writing) (*Werke* 22.1: 424–33), and thereby implicitly
rejected the officially sanctioned aesthetic doctrine, was put in danger of being
cast in the role of traitor.

Comparatively safe in his Scandinavian exile, Brecht worked on a second
project for a major novel from approximately 1937 to 1939. But *Die Geschäfte
des Herrn Julius Caesar* (The Business Dealings of Mr. Julius Caesar) remained
a fragment and was not published until after his death. The historical novel was
a favorite vehicle of exiled writers for commenting on the contemporary situation. Brecht used his novel in the same way and showed Caesar as the prototypical dictator who, as the title indicates, has risen to power because of his
business dealings. Yet there was no facile comparison of Hitler's fascist dictatorship and that of Caesar in the class society of ancient Rome; rather, Brecht
perused a host of historical sources in order to insure the factual accuracy of

his novel. The perspective from which Caesar is depicted—the narrator counts among his sources the diaries of Caesar's secretary, a slave—counteracts all attempts at hero worship. Caesar is revealed as thoroughly corrupt. Constantly beset by enormous debts, he uses politics as a tool to further the business interests of his creditors and to increase their political influence. Brecht's deliberate, single-minded concentration on economics and politics caused his friends Benjamin and Fritz Sternberg to recommend the injection of more "human interest" (*Journals* 23–24) in the vein of the traditional novel.

When the Nazi invasion of Denmark became a distinct possibility, Brecht and family left for Sweden in April 1939. There they found a house on the small island of Lidingö near Stockholm. After the German occupation of Denmark and Norway, in April 1940, Brecht and his family left Sweden for Finland, their last European refuge before setting out on the voyage to the United States. As Brecht stated with but little exaggeration in his well-known poem "To Those Born Later" (*Poems* 318–20), during the "dark times" of exile, he was engaged in changing his country of residence more often than his shoes.

Inspired by the tales of and a comedy by Hella Wuolijoki, a Finnish writer who had invited Brecht and his entourage to spend some time at her country estate, Brecht began and completed *Puntila and Matti, His Hired Man,* his only *Volksstück* (popular play). The play deals with the master-servant relationship that has a long tradition in European literature. The class-conscious proletarian Matti—he is not, however, a revolutionary—is the opponent of his master Puntila. Because of Matti's economic dependence on Puntila, there can be no real confrontation between the two main characters; furthermore, their relationship is complicated by Puntila's propensity for wanting to overcome class barriers and to establish genuine communication with Matti—albeit only in his euphoric, drunk state. Puntila, a crass exploiter when sober, generous and expansive when intoxicated, is a dual character with great theatrical potential. Hence his attempts at communication tend to overshadow the fact that the display of his human qualities does not vitally affect the existing social inequality between master and servant. In the end, Matti leaves Puntila and proclaims the moral of the play that servants will be their own masters only if there are no more masters.

In his Finnish exile Brecht worked fairly consistently from October through December 1940 on his last major European prose project, *Flüchtlingsgespräche* (Refugee Conversations), a work that remained unfinished and was published posthumously. In this series of dialogues involving two German refugees in Helsinki—a bourgeois intellectual, the physicist Ziffel, and a worker named Kalle—the dialectic relationship of master and servant from *Puntila and Matti* has been retained in modified form. But in Ziffel and Kalle's bleakly humorous and self-deprecatingly ironic reflections on the state of the world, the bourgeois intellectual undergoes a change in consciousness and appears to adopt the position of the class-conscious worker. Apart from autobiographical experiences such as living through the food scarcity in Helsinki, Brecht used, as was his wont, a variety of sources, among them Denis Diderot's novel *Jacques le*

Fataliste et son maître (Jacques the Fatalist and His Master) and Jaroslav Ha-šek's *The Good Soldier Švejk*, whose tone and idiosyncratic diction pervade the dialogues. For example, Kalle's wistful remark that passports are the noblest part of a human being gained particular poignancy because of the exile situation. Brecht himself was anxiously waiting for the visas that would allow him and his circle to embark on the journey to the United States.

As Brecht stated in the poem "1940," in his flight from his "fellow-countrymen" after the outbreak of World War II in September 1939, Europe increasingly had begun to resemble a trap, and only a "small door" (*Poems* 349) remained open for escape—if one ignored the then-formidable escape hatch formed by the Finnish/Soviet border (Esslin, *Brecht* 148). The question why Brecht, given his political loyalties and ideological persuasion, did not make any serious attempt to settle in the Soviet Union and chose the United States instead, has been repeatedly raised by critics. But in view of the prevalent artistic climate in Stalin's Soviet Union, which was completely inimical to his stylized theater, and in view of the fate of the aforementioned Neher and Tretyakov, which did not bode well for the prospects of an untroubled life in Moscow, Brecht's "uncanny shrewdness" (Esslin, *Brecht* 147) in matters of survival asserted itself once again.

After obtaining the necessary papers in May 1941, Brecht's party left Finland and, because Finnish ports were controlled by German troops, went by train via Moscow to Vladivostok in Siberia, the embarkation point for the West coast of the United States. The journey through the Soviet Union took place before Hitler's June 1941 attack, at a time when the Soviet Union was the ally of Nazi Germany. Among other complications, there were difficult negotiations "with the complex and xenophobic Soviet bureaucracy" (Fuegi, *Brecht* 401) to be conducted. In Moscow, Brecht had to leave Steffin behind; she died of consumption shortly afterwards, and Brecht keenly felt the loss of a devoted and tireless collaborator who, before her death, had contributed significantly to *The Resistible Rise of Arturo Ui*.

The play, which was completed in March and April 1941, was intended for American audiences and designed to elucidate the connections between capitalism, gangsterism, and Nazism. As it did for *In the Jungle* and *Saint Joan*, Chicago provided the setting for Brecht's attempt to demonstrate that Hitler's rise to power was by no means inevitable but that, in the face of insufficient resistance, he merely seized his chance for gaining power. *Arturo Ui* parallels and reflects important moments in Hitler's career such as the burning of the Reichstag in February 1933, which provided the pretext for the wholesale arrest of all those affiliated with the political opposition, and the annexation of Austria, the *Anschluß*, of March 1938. Brecht used as his Hitler figure a gangster whom he endowed with features of Al Capone in order to expose Hitler and ridicule him as a perpetrator of "great political crimes" rather than as a great political leader and master criminal (*CP* 6: 456). The choice of Chicago during the Capone era, a subject that Brecht had carefully researched, was then projected to enable American spectators to grasp the danger caused by the political gangster Hitler when he was at the height of his power. But "the grand style of the Elizabethan theater, of classical German plays, and the perverted grand style of the dictator, as shown by Chaplin" (Schürer, "Revolution" 147) tended to blunt the analogy between Hitler and Al Capone. After the German declaration of war on the United States in December 1941, an American production of the play seemed no longer necessary or opportune; although Brecht revised the play extensively in America, it was not performed until 1958.

EXILE IN THE UNITED STATES (1941–1947)

Brecht, family, and Berlau arrived in San Pedro, the port of Los Angeles, on 21 July 1941. Aided by friends such as the Feuchtwangers, who had arrived in California the preceding year, he and his family were eventually able to settle in Santa Monica. Brecht's seven-year American sojourn turned out to be a period of considerable productivity for the tireless worker. But America yielded little in terms of publications, film projects, or stage productions of his plays. Brecht initially suffered profound "culture shock" that affected virtually all facets of his existence, but that was ultimately directed against the manifestations of "consumer-oriented capitalism . . . its superficiality and the underlying commercial ethos" (Lyon, *Brecht* 30). The necessity of making a living, however— and, perhaps, his genuine interest in film as a significant new medium—induced Brecht to attempt selling his film stories to the Hollywood studios in spite of his hatred of their unadulterated commercialism and low regard of the writer. In the pensive poem "Hollywood" he expressed his ambivalent feelings about being forced out of economic necessity to be a seller of lies—albeit a seller who "[h]opefully" takes his place among others offering their products (*Poems* 382).

The conduct of some of his fellow exiles in California, among them the Frankfurt School scholars Theodor W. Adorno, Max Horkheimer, and Herbert Marcuse, caused Brecht to further reflect on the role of bourgeois intellectuals. Brecht designated them as *Tuis*, a neologism derived from *Tellekt-uell-ins*, a pun on *Intellektuelle* or intellectuals. For Brecht, *Tuis* represented a class of people who "lend" their intellects to the highest bidder. But Brecht believed that in America his projected *Tui* novel (which did not advance beyond the conceptual stage) would lose its satirical thrust because the sale of opinions and theories went on publicly without any pretense of intellectual independence at a time when everything, including intellect, had become a salable commodity. After his return to Germany, Brecht was to write *Turandot, or The Whitewashers' Congress,* a play based on some of the *Tui* materials and set in a mythical China. It satirizes the intellectuals who serve as apologists of an unjust order.

The only notable film project in which Brecht was involved, that of Fritz Lang's *Hangmen also Die,* brought Brecht little recognition but a considerable sum of money. Conceived as a response to the assassination by Czech resistance fighters in May 1942 of Reinhard Heydrich, the feared henchman of Nazi-occupied Czechoslovakia, the writing turned into a controversy about credits for the screenplay that involved Lang and screenwriter John Wexley. This controversy did nothing to enhance Brecht's opinion of Hollywood and of Lang who, in Brecht's opinion, had sold out to the film industry.

Beginning in February 1943, Brecht undertook almost annual journeys to the East coast in order to promote his theatrical projects. When in New York City, he stayed with Berlau who had moved there in May 1942. But his efforts to have his plays produced proved futile: "Just as the sight of Broadway failed to overwhelm him, so Brecht failed to overwhelm Broadway, though it was not for lack of trying" (Lyon, *Brecht* 121). The first of the plays he completed in America evolved from a collaborative effort with Feuchtwanger who in 1940 had escaped from a French internment camp and whose memoirs provided a valuable source. *The Visions of Simone Machard* is set in wartime France of 1940 and features a young heroine who, in a series of dream sequences, identifies with Joan of Arc and hears voices that inspire her to resist the invading Germans. But it is the people's voices, not those of angels, that urge her to engage in patriotic deeds and undermine the collaboration of the French upper classes, among whom is her boss, the hotel proprietor in a small town on one of the main highways leading from Paris to the South of France. In accordance with Brecht's view that the war victimized the working people whereas the ruling classes tended to collaborate with the enemy in order to retain their possessions, Simone Machard is punished for her patriotic deed of burning the gasoline supplies, which she does not wish to fall into the hands of the Germans. Although she is confined to an asylum operated by cruel nuns, the play ends optimistically: the people have been motivated by her example and are beginning to engage in acts of resistance.

Unlike the unsuccessful planned adaptation of John Webster's *The Duchess of Malfi* (1614), which actress Elisabeth Bergner and her husband Paul Czinner had commissioned, Hašek's *The Good Soldier Švejk* seemed to offer the promise of a stage success. In the late 1920s Brecht had worked on the script for Piscator's production of *Schweyk*. Švejk is the quintessential little man with a shrewd, unheroic instinct for survival that manifests itself in subversive folk wisdom and idiosyncratic tales. Brecht transposes him from the Austro-Hungarian Empire of World War I to the Prague of Nazi occupation and the Russian front of World War II. Hitler and other Nazi leaders appear in the play as oversized caricatures who pursue their pernicious plans of conquering the world at the expense of the little man, but the Flagon, Mrs. Kopecka's Prague inn, provides an atmosphere of hospitality and kindness and represents a counterpart to the destructive ambitions of great leaders. "The Song of the Moldau" in particular poetically heralds the inevitable changing of times and the demise of those in power. *Schweyk in the Second World War* was not produced until after Brecht's death; when working on the project, both Weill and Piscator were profoundly irritated by the playwright's notorious pursuit of several avenues and simultaneous negotiations with several collaborators.

Among the plays that originated in America, it is without doubt *The Caucasian Chalk Circle* that gradually achieved highest praise from critics in the West. Esslin lauded the aesthetic qualities of the play and judged it to be "the outstanding example of the technique of the 'epic' drama . . . [and] one of Brecht's greatest plays" (*Brecht* 279) because of its poetry, its use of the Singer who narrates the successive rather than parallel stories of Grusha and Azdak, and its stylization that requires the evil characters to wear masks. Other critics were similarly effusive about a play that in several respects may be considered Brecht's most "American." Although he had been familiar with the *Chalk Circle* materials since the 1920s, Brecht wrote the drama during 1944 in Santa Monica. Furthermore, it was intended for an American Broadway premiere— rather than for Northfield, Minnesota, where it opened in March 1948. Finally, the play is concerned with "motherhood and justice" (Watts)—topics conceived of as genuinely American. Yet the emphasis on the aesthetic qualities of the play tended to obscure the radical questioning of traditional concepts of motherhood, property rights, and justice. After all, it is the socially productive Grusha, whom Brecht did not want to appear as a "sucker" (*CP* 7: 297), who is awarded custody of the child rather than the child's biological—albeit callous— mother. Social justice can only be served because the class system has been temporarily suspended in feudal Caucasian Georgia during a period of revolutionary unrest. Wily and idiosyncratic Azdak, according to Brecht a "disappointed revolutionary" (*CP* 7: 298–99), seizes the moment and, based on the famed chalk circle test, gives the child to the mother who is both good herself and good for the child. The acceptance of the play was facilitated by the fact that in the first productions the "Prologue," which Brecht considered an integral part, was omitted. The "Prologue" features the members of two collective farms in then Soviet Georgia at the end of World War II who amicably and rationally settle their conflicting claims to a fertile valley and in doing so drastically deviate from the norms of settling property disputes prevalent in America.

In the short story "The Augsburg Chalk Circle" (1940), first published in the enormously successful collection *Tales from the Calendar* (1948), a both learned and popular judge in Brecht's home town of Augsburg during the Thirty Years' War similarly proceeds from the child's interests and implicitly postulates a new definition of motherhood that is based on the bondage created by work and suffering rather than that based on biological factors.

Brecht did achieve a success of sorts with the second, American, version of *Galileo*, an extraordinarily productive cooperative effort with actor Charles Laughton, who served as a congenial translator despite his extremely limited knowledge of German. Eventually there were performances in Beverly Hills (July 1947) and, after Brecht's departure from the United States, in New York City (December 1947). The dropping of the atomic bombs on Hiroshima and

Nagasaki in August 1945 lent topicality to *Galileo* in that the role of science and the scientist appeared in a new light. In Brecht's view it was no longer sufficient to pursue scientific research without considering the consequences, and Galileo's recantation when faced with the sight of torture instruments now appeared as an abject act of cowardice rather than a cunning move to deceive the church authorities about the smuggling of Galileo's papers out of Italy. Hence Galileo condemns his recantation as the betrayal of his profession, a profession whose true goal it was to serve humankind, not to be at the disposal of those in power. Perhaps, as biographer Ronald Hayman suggests, "blaming Galileo for Hiroshima was a naïve mistake Marx would never have made, believing as he did, with Hegel, that individual virtues and vices never determine the course of history" (296–97).

But it was Brecht's political persuasion rather than the discrediting of Galileo and his alleged failure as a responsible scientist that was at the center of the playwright's interrogation by HUAC and that prompted the closing of the New York production after one week. Laughton who, in keeping with Brecht's conception of the character, had portrayed Galileo with a rare combination of "intellectual brilliance" and "physical self-indulgence" (Bentley, "Galileo" 193), was persuaded that, as his biographer wrote, "he was playing into Communists' hands" (Singer, quoted in *CP* 5: xvi)—reason enough for him to withdraw from the production and doom the play.

HUAC was investigating the assumed Communist infiltration of the movie industry. Brecht's appearance on 30 October 1947 had been preceded by that of his friend and collaborator, composer Hanns Eisler. In contrast to the questioning of Eisler, Brecht's statements turned out to be an uneventful affair in that he was praised for his testimony, which he had rehearsed well and was considered an exemplary witness by the committee. Brecht is generally credited with outwitting his ill-prepared interrogators; in fact, Esslin reports that Brecht's interrogation was compared to the cross-examination of a zoologist by apes (*Brecht* 73). As indicated previously, one critic has resorted to reviving the argument that Galileo's cowardice parallels that of Brecht before HUAC: "Like Galileo before the Inquisition, Brecht helped strengthen the hand of his inquisitors" (Fuegi, *Brecht* 483)—but apart from the dubious practice of reading plays as autobiographical accounts, the factual basis for this critic's assertions is slim indeed (Willett, et al. 340). At the same time, the resurrection of such charges shows the longevity of biases that were to impede Brecht's reception in this country even after his permanent departure for Europe on 31 October 1947, one day after his testifying before HUAC.

RETURN TO EUROPE: ZURICH (1947–1949) AND EAST BERLIN (1949–1956)

Brecht left New York City and landed in Paris but soon went to Zurich, where three of his plays had premiered during World War II. There he met his old friends from Augsburg, stage designer Neher, playwright Zuckmayer, who had likewise returned from the United States, and Swiss architect and writer Max Frisch. Although Brecht, who was joined by Weigel, daughter Barbara (son Stefan remained in the United States), and, in January 1948, Berlau, was planning to return to Berlin, he proceeded with caution. As a preparatory step for future productions in the German-language theater, he collaborated with Neher on the adaptation of Sophocles's *Antigone* in Friedrich Hölderlin's German translation. *Antigone* premiered in February 1948 in the Swiss city of Chur, but it had only a short run.

The Zurich Schauspielhaus continued its tradition of bringing out Brecht's plays by staging *Puntila and Matti* in June 1948. Although Brecht's name was not officially mentioned, he participated in directing the play, which had an excellent cast. Ironically, in part based on the mistaken assumption that *Puntila and Matti* lacked the antagonistic class conflicts of other Brecht plays, the play became a favorite with West German directors and audiences alike in the late 1940s and 1950s. Stage productions were accompanied by the refinement of theory; in Zurich Brecht completed one of his most important theoretical works whose title is derived from Renaissance scientist Francis Bacon's *Novum organum*: "A Short Organum for the Theatre" (*Theatre* 179–205). First published in 1949, the treatise was intended as a summary of the unfinished *The Messingkauf Dialogues*. "Short Organum" defines the aesthetics of the "theatre of the scientific age" (*Theatre* 205) and opposes the "Aristotelian" theater, which dulls the spectators' critical faculties by inviting them to empathize with the respective protagonists as well as the naturalistic theater of mimetic representation. Despite its stress on enlightening the spectators, the new Brechtian theater was not supposed to be devoid of entertaining aspects.

After having obtained the necessary travel permits, in October 1948 Brecht and Weigel traveled to Berlin via Salzburg in Austria. In East Berlin Brecht noted with disappointment that few people realized that socialism imposed from above was better than no socialism at all (*Journals* 404) and commented on the provincial attitude that complicated the negotiations for a theater of his own. Yet in January 1949 *Mother Courage* opened at the Deutsches Theater with Weigel in the title role. Although dramatist Friedrich Wolf, a Communist representative of "Aristotelian" cathartic theater, and critic Fritz Erpenbeck—like Wolf a returnee from the Soviet Union and a strong proponent of the offical doctrine of Socialist Realism—toed the party line and criticized the play as lacking optimism, in due course *Mother Courage* became an international success and was probably "the decisive event for the authorities' consideration of Brecht's Berliner Ensemble project" (Weber 167). The reception of the play highlights the dilemma Brecht faced in East Berlin: on the one hand, he was claimed to be the chief artistic representative of the soon-to-be-established German Democratic Republic (GDR); on the other, he was in constant danger of being criticized for deviating from the aesthetic norms of Socialist Realism.

Brecht returned once more to Zurich, but in May 1949 he settled permanently in East Berlin, the city that became his home until his death. Brecht's German citizenship had been revoked by the Nazis, but he had not become an American citizen. In Zurich, Brecht vigorously pursued the acquisition of Austrian passports for Weigel—who was Viennese by birth—and himself on the grounds that, as he wrote to Austrian composer Gottfried von Einem in spring 1949, he did not wish to be claimed by one part of Germany only and wanted to have access to all German-language theaters (*Letters* 473). Whereas Hayman implies that Brecht's "manoeuvering simultaneously for an East German theatre and Austrian citizenship" amounted to "double-dealing" on a par with his deceiving Paula Banholzer and Marianne Zoff (337) and was morally reprehensible, Esslin takes a more pragmatic view and posits that an Austrian passport could function as a "safeguard [against restrictions] and a means to travel in the West" (*Brecht* 81). In retrospect, Brecht's choice—he did obtain an Austrian passport in the autumn of 1950, after the GDR had been founded in October 1949—seems to have been a shrewd move. After all, the awarding or withholding of travel privileges was used by the GDR as an instrument to reward writers' loyalty and punish their oppositional tendencies until unrestricted travel became possible after the fall of the Berlin Wall. In any case, exile had taught Brecht to appreciate valid papers; Kalle's wistful remark in *Flüchtlingsgespräche*—cited above—about passports as the noblest part of a human being is a case in point.

Pragmatic considerations notwithstanding, one should perhaps not dismiss Brecht's envisioning a representative role, which transcended the political division of Germany, for himself and his theater. The vehicle for assuming this role was the Berliner Ensemble, headed by Weigel, which became one of the GDR's premier cultural institutions. The Berliner Ensemble officially and successfully opened its season in November 1949 with *Puntila and Matti*; Brecht's efforts to make the play more palatable to those who considered it a relic of the semi-feudal agrarian past that had been overcome in the GDR had paid off. Brecht saw his main task as rebuilding the repertory from the ruins of a war that had not only destroyed theater buildings but, more importantly, devastated the aesthetic and philosophical foundations of theater culture. The traditions Brecht wanted to pursue with the Berliner Ensemble were dramas that were concerned with social revolutions, plays that "critically probed class society," and comedies that were in notoriously short supply in Germany (Weber 170). In critically adapting plays from the German and international stage, Brecht resorted to "the collective working method . . . which became a hallmark of the Berliner Ensemble" (Weber 171). In 1952 he collaborated with Berlau, Peter Palitzsch, and Claus Hubalek to compile the volume *Theaterarbeit*, "probably the most thorough investigation of a company's working practice ever published" (Weber 173), that documented the productions of the Berliner Ensemble.

While Brecht enjoyed having at his disposal a financially well-endowed troupe with virtually unlimited time for rehearsals, its advantages were, to some extent, outweighed by continuing difficulties with the cultural apparatchiks. For example, the March 1951 trial run of the opera *The Trial of Lucullus*, originally a radio play with music by Paul Dessau[12] (who also cooperated on the opera), caused massive interference by party functionaries because they sensed both formalist and pacifist tendencies at a time when the GDR supported North Korea—the self-styled victim of imperialist aggression—in the Korean war. Brecht and Dessau accepted part of the criticism by making changes; they also retitled the opera, now called *The Condemnation of Lucullus*, to emphasize the point that the wars of aggression the Roman general Lucullus had waged were to be condemned. In 1954 the Berliner Ensemble was able to move into its new permanent home, the Theater am Schiffbauerdamm, site of the triumph of *The Threepenny Opera* in 1933. The theater opened with a production of Molière's *Don Juan* in an adaptation by Benno Besson, Hauptmann, and Brecht.

Brecht's ascendancy to the position of "modern classic" in the West proceeded slowly and was hampered by politics. In the wake of Stalin's death on 5 March 1953, Brecht's actions contributed to the serious questioning of his politics that, as Willett observes, have been "resented with a virulence quite spared to more orthodox communist writers like Aragon or Neruda or Aimé Césaire, earning him a leading place in the cold war propagandists' Pandaemonium" (Willett, "Politics" 178). Brecht made merely a "stonewallingly ambiguous comment" that was in stark contrast to poet and minister of culture Johannes R. Becher's "fulsome verse panegyric" (Hayman 365) and that casts serious doubts on Hannah Arendt's assertion in her 1968 assessment that Brecht had written an "ode to Stalin" and praised "Stalin's crimes" (207–10). Brecht responded in similarly ambiguous fashion to the workers' uprising. On 17 June 1953 he addressed a brief note to Walter Ulbricht, General Secretary of the SED, the Sozialistische Einheitspartei Deutschlands (Socialist Unity Party), in which he suggested that an open discussion about the "tempo of socialist construction" (*Letters* 515–16) might be called for. Since only the last sentence of the note, in which Brecht confirmed his support of the SED, was published by the party organ, *Neues Deutschland*, on 21 June 1953, it appeared that he had expressed contemptible servitude to the regime against which the workers rebelled.

Günter Grass posited that "Brecht emerged without visible harm from the workers' revolt" (xxxv) by retiring to Buckow, the country house near Berlin that he acquired in 1952, and writing the *Buckow Elegies*. The work of the Berliner Ensemble was not affected, Grass avers, and Brecht "continued to be the cultural property and advertisement of a state to which, according to his passport, he did not belong" (xxxv). In his play *The Plebeians Rehearse the Uprising* (1966) Grass presents a Brecht-like figure, the "Boss," who prefers to remain in the lofty realm of aesthetics instead of dirtying his hands in practical politics, that is, helping the workers who have come to ask him for moral support as well as assistance in formulating a call for a general strike. In using the workers as extras in his rehearsal of Shakespeare's *Coriolanus* until the uprising has been crushed, Brecht remains a "man of the theater, serene and untroubled" (xxxvi) and ignores one of the central tenets of his drama theory, the application of the insights gained in the theater to social practice. Grass's criticism of Brecht's clinging to abstract theoretical models for social progress that do not have any relevance for his personal conduct is not entirely without justification; however, poems such as "Nasty Morning" and "The Solution" from the *Buckow Elegies* (*Poems* 440) are not indicative of Brecht's unperturbed serenity.

1956 AND AFTER

Brecht's health had begun to deteriorate during 1955 and 1956; he developed heart trouble and showed signs of fatigue. During the night of 13–14 August 1956 his condition became critical, and he died of a coronary thrombosis late on 14 August. Of the women who had played such an important part in his life, Weigel remained head of the Berliner Ensemble until her death in 1971. Hauptmann, who had returned to East Berlin from America, lived until 1973 and edited the twenty-volume edition of his works that appeared in 1967 (*GW*). Berlau, to whom Brecht had devoted "Geschichten von Lai-tu" (Stories about Lai-tu) in *Me-ti*, had ultimately not managed to follow Brecht's prescriptions and regard love as a relationship in which the two partners change by cooperating in order to attain a friendly disposition toward that which is socially productive. Her relations with Brecht had become strained during the last years of his life; she died in 1974. Her *Memoirs* under the title *Living for Brecht* were published posthumously.

Grass's critical portrayal of the Brecht figure in *The Plebeians Rehearse the Uprising* is but one indication that Brecht continued to be a provocation even after his death. Boycotts of his plays in West German theaters ensued following the Hungarian uprising in 1956 and the construction of the Berlin Wall on 13 August 1961. These boycotts were apparently based on the curious assumption that Brecht would most likely have endorsed repressive measures perpetrated by the Soviet Union or its satellite, the GDR. The intolerant Cold-War climate of the 1950s fostered the polarization of convictions: Brecht tended to be acceptable to those who appreciated his craft at the expense of his politics; conversely, he was condemned by those who regarded him chiefly as a purveyor of Communist ideas in poetic guise.

In the 1960s, however, the wholehearted reception of Brecht's plays resulted in "a golden age for Brecht" (Völker, "Today" 427). A new generation of directors began staging his plays along the lines suggested by the "model" productions of the Berliner Ensemble that performed Brecht's plays in London, Moscow, and Paris. In the 1971–1972 season, Brecht advanced to the position of being the author whose plays were most frequently performed in the Federal Republic—even if the entertainment aspects tended to predominate over social analysis and political message in productions that featured "culinary" works such as *The Threepenny Opera*. The preference for theatrical spectacles at the expense of the playwright's underlying sociocritical intent caused Frisch to remark in 1964 that Brecht had reached the "penetrating ineffectiveness of a classic" (quoted in Völker, "Today" 427), a phrase eagerly used by those who no longer believed that Brecht's theater could provide vital impulses.

It was specifically Austrian writer Peter Handke who challenged Brecht's theater by positing that it only insufficiently reflected complex states of consciousness and tended to offer simplistic solutions. Instead of Brecht, he implicitly recommended playwright Ödön von Horváth as a model worthy of emulation. Handke's sentiments were echoed by British playwright Christopher Hampton in his play *Tales from Hollywood* (1983). Hampton imaginatively used the figure of Horváth as his spokesperson for a post-Brechtian theater by having the play's character inveigh against Brecht's notion of the theater as a potential vehicle for societal change that is to be achieved by setting in motion the audience's process of reflection.[13] Hampton's criticism, which focuses on Brecht's mode of presentation and its underlying assumptions, may be seen as an expression of European *Brechtmüdigkeit* (Brecht fatigue) that, however, was not universally shared. For example, in the 1960s and early 1970s, the United States witnessed the appropriation of Brecht, carried on mostly by college and regional theaters in their desire for experimental and innovative productions. Brecht, in the words of one critic, evolved into a minor cult figure, and "enthusiasm for his work became a kind of badge of radicalism, a sign that you favored free speech, opposed the war in Vietnam and the Nixon administration. He was at least part of the package—and at the most, to some, the touchstone of radical authenticity" (Cook 217). The radicalism of the student protest movement is no longer in vogue, and Brecht's status as a patron saint of the radical Left was short-lived.

But the reception of Brecht's works is not confined to Europe and the United States; it is in less developed regions of the globe where Brecht's influence can be clearly observed.[14] Owing to the prevalence of easily discernible patterns of social and economic divisions, patterns that differ significantly from the complex social reality in most industrialized, Western countries, Brecht's plays seem to offer a cogent analysis of societal problems rather than simplistic explanations.

The impact that is achieved through the staging of his plays is, without doubt, an important facet in the attempt to assess the significance of Brecht. But his significance is also attested to by the thriving scholarly enterprise of the international Brecht "industry" that has not noticeably suffered from "Brecht fatigue" and that seems to become invigorated when controversies such as those caused by Fuegi's *Brecht and Company* erupt. Commemorative events likewise serve as stimuli for scholars' and publishers' initiatives; on the occasion of the ninetieth anniversary of Brecht's birth, Brecht's West German publisher Suhrkamp and his East German publisher Aufbau jointly published a comprehensive and annotated thirty-volume edition of the works (*Werke*), which is being followed by the joint planning by the cities of Augsburg and Berlin for the centennial celebration in 1998. The awarding of the first Brecht Prize to Bavarian playwright Franz Xaver Kroetz in March 1994 signals that Brecht's desire to be considered a representative German writer has at last been officially acknowledged in reunited Germany.

What then remains of Brecht and his works in the 1990s? If we subscribe to the notion that, as British novelist David Lodge wrote about Graham Greene, "revelations about a writer's life should not affect our independently formed critical assessment of his work. They may, however, confirm or explain reservations about it" (28), then we may dismiss Fuegi's poorly substantiated claims as largely inappropriate for the assessment of Brecht. Although there may be little inclination to consider Brecht a sage whose life's work was devoted to finding proper responses to humankind's fundamental problems (*Welträtsel*) such as poverty, exploitation, and injustice—as the subtitle of Werner Mittenzwei's voluminous biography (1987), which was published before the fall of the Berlin Wall, suggests—he remains one of the great innovators as well as practitioners of the theater, and his "most truly revolutionary legacy" is perhaps "his effect on our understanding of the relationship between performer and spectator" (Patterson 283–84). Nor should Brecht's political insights be entirely discarded; for instance, the May 1995 production of *Arturo Ui* at the Berliner Ensemble under the direction of the late Heiner Müller—who was both perpetuator of and rebel against the Brecht tradition—may serve as a timely reminder of the dangers that Brecht warned against and that are still with us even more than fifty years after the end of World War II.

NOTES

1. Apart from the sources acknowledged in the text and in Works Cited, I have also drawn on "Introduction." In Mews, *Critical Essays* 1–17.

2. See also Christiane Bohnert, "Poetry, History, and Communication," in this volume.

3. See also Christine Kiebuzinska, "Brecht and the Problem of Influence," in this volume.

4. See also Reinhold Grimm, "Alienation in Context: On the Theory and Practice of Brechtian Theater," in this volume.

5. See Vera Stegmann, "Brecht contra Wagner: The Evolution of the Epic Music Theater," in this volume.

6. See also Herbert Knust, "First Comes the Belly, then Morality," in this volume.

7. See Marc Silberman, "Brecht and Film," in this volume.

8. See Karl-Heinz Schoeps, "Brecht's *Lehrstücke*: A Laboratory for Epic and Dialectic Theater," in this volume.

9. See also Laureen Nussbaum, "The Evolution of the Feminine Principle in Brecht's Work: An Overview," in this volume.

10. See Douglas Kellner, "Brecht's Marxist Aesthetic," in this volume.

11. See also Sabine Gross, "Dialectics and Reader Response: Bertolt Brecht's Prose Cycles," in this volume.

12. See also Thomas R. Nadar, "Brecht and His Musical Collaborators," in this volume.

13. See Mews, "Ohnmacht."

14. See, e.g., Michael Bodden, "Brecht in Asia: New Agendas, National Traditions, and Critical Consciousness"; and Marina Pianca, "Brecht in Latin America: Theater Bearing Witness," both in this volume.

WORKS CITED (SEE ALSO REFERENCE GUIDE TO WORKS CITED IN ABBREVIATED FORM)

Arendt, Hannah. "What Is Permitted to Jove." *New Yorker* (5 November 1966): 68–122. Rpt. "Bertolt Brecht: 1898–1956." In Arendt, *Men in Dark Times*. New York: Harcourt, 1968. 207–50.

Bentley, Eric. "The Science Fiction of Bertolt Brecht." In *Galileo: A Play by Bertolt Brecht*. New York: Grove, 1966. 7–42. Rpt. "Galileo (I)." In Bentley, *Commentaries* 183–208.

Brecht, Bertolt. *Threepenny Novel*. Translated by Desmond I. Vesey and Christopher Isherwood, with introduction by John Willett. London: Granada, 1958.

Canetti, Elias. *The Torch in My Ear*. Translated by Joachim Neugroschel. New York: Farrar, 1982.

Cook, Bruce. *Brecht in Exile*. New York: Holt, 1982.

Feinstein, Elaine. *Loving Brecht*. 1992. London: Sceptre, 1993.

Feuchtwanger, Lion. *Erfolg. Drei Jahre Geschichte einer Provinz*. 2 vols. Berlin: Kiepenheuer, 1930.

Fischer, Ruth. "Bert Brecht, Minstrel of the GPU." *Politics* 1 (April 1944): 88–89.

Fleißer, Marieluise. "Der Tiefseefisch." In *Gesammelte Werke*, vol. 1. Edited by Günther Rühle. Frankfurt am Main: Suhrkamp, 1972.

Grass, Günter. "The Prehistory and Posthistory of the Tragedy of *Coriolanus* from Livy and Plutarch via Shakespeare Down to Brecht and Myself." In *The Plebeians Rehearse the Uprising. A German Tragedy*. Translated by Ralph Manheim. New York: Harcourt, 1966. vii–xxxvi.

Handke, Peter. "Horváth ist besser als Brecht." *Theater heute* 9.3 (1968): 28.

Hayman, Ronald. *Brecht. A Biography*. New York: Oxford University Press, 1983.

Ihering, Herbert. Review of *Drums in the Night*. *Berliner Börsen-Courier*: 5 Oct. 1922. In *Brecht in der Kritik*. Edited by Monika Wyss. Munich: Kindler, 1977. 4–6.

Kurella, Alfred. "What Was He Killed For? Criticism of the Play *Strong Measures* [*The Measures Taken*] by Brecht, Dudov and Eisler." *Literature of the World Revolution*. No. 5. Moscow: State Publishing House, 1931. Rpt. In Mews, *Critical Essays* 77–82.

Lodge, David. "The Lives of Graham Greene." Review article. *New York Review of Books* (22 June 1995): 25–28.

Lyon, James. "Brecht's *Mann ist Mann* and the Death of Tragedy in the 20th Century." *German Quarterly* 67 (1994): 513–20.

Mann, Thomas. "German Letter (September, 1923)." *The Dial* (Oct. 1923): 375.

Mews, Siegfried. "Introduction." In Mews, *Critical Essays* 1–17.

———. "Portraits of the Artist as Committed Writer: Brecht in the Context of Literature." In *Exile and Enlightenment: Studies in Honor of Guy Stern on His 65th Birthday*. Edited by Uwe Faulhaber, et al. Detroit, MI: Wayne State University Press, 1987. 247–55.

————. "Von der Ohnmacht der Intellektuellen: Christopher Hamptons *Tales from Hollywood.*" *Exilforschung. Ein internationales Jahrbuch* 3 (1985): 270–85.

Mittenzwei, Werner. *Das Leben des Bertolt Brecht, oder der Umgang mit Welträtseln.* 2 vols. Frankfurt am Main: Suhrkamp, 1987.

Müller, Klaus-Detlef. "Brecht und Stalin." In *Von Poesie und Politik. Zur Geschichte einer dubiosen Beziehung.* Edited by Jürgen Wertheimer. Tübingen: Attempto, 1994. 106–22.

Patterson, Michael. "Brecht's Legacy." In Thomson/Sacks, *Cambridge Companion,* 273–87.

Pease, Donald E. "Author." In *Critical Terms for Literary Study,* edited by Frank Lentricchia and Thomas McLaughlin. Chicago: University of Chicago Press, 1990. 105–17.

Rosenhaft, Eve. "Brecht's Germany: 1898–1933." In Thomson/Sacks, *Cambridge Companion* 3–21.

Schürer, Ernst. "Revolution from the Right: Bertolt Brecht's American Gangster Play *The Resistible Rise of Arturo Ui.*" In Mews, *Critical Essays* 138–54.

Shaw, Bernard. *Saint Joan: A Chronicle Play in Six Scenes and an Epilogue.* London: Constable, 1924.

————. *John Bull's Other Island, and Major Barbara.* New York: Brentano's [c.1907].

Sinclair, Upton. *The Jungle.* New York: Doubleday, 1906.

Singer, Kurt. *The Laughton Story. An Intimate Story of Charles Laughton.* Philadelphia: Winston, 1954.

Speirs, Ronald. "Baal." In *Brecht's Early Plays.* Atlantic Highlands, NJ: Humanities Press, 1982. Rpt. In Mews, *Critical Essays* 19–30.

Szczesny, Gerhard. *The Case against Bertolt Brecht with Arguments Drawn from His Life of Galileo.* New York: Ungar, 1969.

Tatlow, Antony. "Mastery or Slavery? [On Brecht's Early Plays]." *Colloquia Germanica* 17.3/4 (1984): 289–304. Rpt. In Mews, *Critical Essays* 30–45.

Thomson, Peter. "Brecht's Lives." In Thomson/Sacks, *Cambridge Companion* 22–39.

Völker, Klaus. "Brecht Today: Classic or Challenge." *Theatre Journal* 39 (1987): 425–33.

Watts, Richard, Jr. "Brecht, Motherhood, and Justice." *New York Post* (25 March 1966).

Weber, Carl. "Brecht and the Berliner Ensemble—The Making of a Model." In Thomson/Sacks, *Cambridge Companion* 167–84.

Willett, John. "Brecht, Alienation and Karl Marx." In *Brecht in Context* 218–21.

————. "The Case of Kipling." In *Brecht in Context* 44–58.

————. "The Changing Role of Politics." In *Brecht in Context* 178–210.

————. "An Englishman Looks at Brecht." In *Brecht in Context* 9–20.

————. "The Poet Beneath the Skin." *Brecht heute/Brecht Today: Brecht Yearbook* 2 (1972): 88–104.

Willett, John, James Lyon, Siegfried Mews, and H. C. Nørregaard. "A Brechtbuster Goes Bust: Scholarly Mistakes, Misquotes, and Malpractices in John Fuegi's *Brecht and Company.*" *Brecht-Jahrbuch/Brecht Yearbook* 20 (1994): 259–367.

Zuckmayer, Carl. *A Part of Myself. Portrait of an Epoch.* Translated by Richard and Clara Winston. New York: Harcourt, 1970.

PART I

THEORY AND PRACTICE OF THE THEATER

1

Alienation in Context: On the Theory and Practice of Brechtian Theater

REINHOLD GRIMM

It will come as no great surprise that I consider Bertolt Brecht the most important German playwright of the first and, possibly, the second half of the twentieth century; his influence extended far beyond Germany. What distinguishes Brecht above all is his unique combination of dramatist and practitioner of the theater— mainly as a director, but also as a musician; as playwright/practitioner he is comparable only to such dramatists as Sophocles, Shakespeare, and Molière. In addition, Brecht is no less important and influential as a theoretician of drama and the theater.

None of Brecht's contemporaries can compete with him in this regard. For example, the famous Frenchman Antonin Artaud, the propagator of a "theater of cruelty," was surely a kind of theoretician—or, to be more precise, a visionary—of the theater and likewise a practitioner of sorts; but he was in no way a playwright. In fact, his sole full-fledged drama is an adaptation of Shelley's *The Cenci*. Brecht's friend and collaborator, Erwin Piscator, the advocate of a "political theater," was chiefly a director, and a most innovative one to boot; but he was neither a dramatist nor a theorist proper. His programmatic book of 1929, *The Political Theatre*, is not a theory but a report on his theatrical activities. The great Russian, Constantin Stanislavsky, was also a magnificent director, no doubt, and a brilliant trainer of his actors as well, but again, he was not really a theorist, and certainly not a dramatist. His famous productions with the Moscow Art Theater were based on the plays of his compatriot Anton Chekhov, or on those of the German Naturalist Gerhart Hauptmann. Similar observations could be made, for instance, with regard to George Bernard Shaw and his fellow countryman Samuel Beckett. The only representative of modern theater who comes somewhat close to Brecht's universality is perhaps that towering Swede, August Strindberg.

To be sure, Brecht did not suffer from any excess of modesty, either. Allegedly, he once proclaimed, "I am the Einstein of the new stage form" (Gorelik, quoted in Fuegi 214). Yet similarly, he declared, "I am the last catholic writer" (quoted in Melchinger 174). The latter statement, seemingly paradoxical, is actually rather easy to decipher. Doubtless, the term "catholic" is being used here by Brecht in its original, literal Greek sense, meaning "all-embracing," which makes the statement indeed true. For not only was Brecht a prolific playwright, theoretician, and practitioner of the theater; he was also a fine poet, an incisive critic, and a superb storyteller. He even wrote three novels, although two of them remained unfinished. In other words, Brecht was a "catholic writer" insofar as he covered all literary genres and modes of expression with equal, or near equal, mastery. He also devoted his efforts to the opera and the ballet, as his "grand opera" *Rise and Fall of the City of Mahagonny* and his lesser known but no less accomplished ballet *The Seven Deadly Sins* attest. Both works were composed in collaboration with Kurt Weill, who also wrote the score of *The Threepenny Opera*.

Brecht's claim to be "the Einstein of the new stage" was, of course, a provocative exaggeration, since he knew full well that his theory and practice of the theater had absorbed and made use of a great many ideas and devices from the past. And yet, in his fascinating and highly effective combination of them, as well as in his anti-Aristotelian stance, Brecht was unique and did in fact usher in a new concept of the theater that, in his terminology, was called "non-Aristotelian," "epic," "dialectical," theater of "alienation"—a theater based on his own dramatic output. Significantly, he also termed it a "theater of the scientific age" (*Theatre* 276).

In sheer quantity, Brecht's theory is truly formidable. There are no fewer than seven volumes of his theoretical writings in the authoritative twenty-volume *Gesammelte Werke* (1967), which are being superseded by the thirty-volume *Werke* (1988–). Let me briefly characterize the most important of these theoretical contributions, beginning with the two that either appeared, or were conceived of, as independent publications. The first is one of the most widely read and most wildly debated of all Brechtian publications: "A Short Organum for the Theatre" of 1948. However, this text does not constitute an exhaustive treatment of Brecht's theorizing; rather, it is a concise, indeed compact, summary of his main theoretical thoughts. Interestingly enough, its form is modeled after that of the *Essayes* of Sir Francis Bacon, the great British scientist of the early seventeenth century. The other major theoretical work of Brecht's is entitled *The Messingkauf Dialogues* and was published posthumously in 1963 as a vast fragment of several hundred pages. This text amounts to the author's most ambitious attempt at summarizing and systematizing his theoretical insights. *The*

Messingkauf Dialogues are a discussion, a huge dialogue—or, more correctly, a "tetralogue" (*Viergespräch*), as Brecht called it (*GW* 16: 1*)—among four people: the playwright, the director, the actress, and the philosopher. Its form is derived from the writings of yet another great scientist—this time, an Italian—who lived during the early seventeenth century: the *Discourses* of Galileo Galilei. Incidentally, one may wonder why Brecht chose so cryptic a title as "buying brass" (the literal translation of *Messingkauf,* whose meaning is not readily apparent). Brecht used to liken his attitude toward the old, traditional, mainly bourgeois theater to that of a man who wants to buy a trumpet—not, however, because it is a costly, carefully wrought musical instrument fit for playing the classics, but simply because it consists of brass. He is interested merely in the metal it is made of, in its "material value" (*Materialwert*) (*GW* 15: 105), a favorite and most telling term of the theoretician. This, precisely, was also Brecht's attitude toward the bourgeois theater: he was interested solely in the material it offered, the stuff it supplied—not a bit in its artistry.

Other such Brechtian contributions, if on a more minor scale, include the following articles or essays, talks or reports: notes to the opera *Rise and Fall of the City of Mahagonny*, translated as "The Modern Theatre Is the Epic Theatre" (*Theatre* 33–42); "Theatre for Pleasure or Theatre for Instruction?" (*Theatre* 69–77); "Alienation Effects in Chinese Acting" (*Theatre* 130–35); and "On Experimental Theatre" (*Theatre* 91–99). These texts could be augmented almost at will; among them, Brecht's notes to the opera, which date from 1930, constitute the first and the most daring, most provocative formulation of his theory. They culminate in the juxtaposition of two columns of key terms and notions: on the one hand, those pertaining to the "dramatic"—that is, the old, the traditional—theater; on the other, those referring to the new, the "epic" or Brechtian theater. This listing culminates in the contrasting of two basic concepts: that of emotion (*Gefühl*) for the dramaturgy Brecht sought to overcome, and that of reason (*Ratio*) for the one he propounded and strove to effect. The latter contrast in particular has caused a lot of misunderstanding among critics, for they have interpreted with great carelessness Brecht's juxtaposition as being an absolute opposition. Invariably, they have overlooked a footnote (*Theatre* 37) that decreed, clearly and unequivocally, that the distinction between emotion and reason did not signify an absolute opposition but just a shift of emphasis (*Gewichtsverschiebung*). In short, Brecht—contrary to a widespread opinion among scholars as well—did not wish to do away with emotion in the theater altogether and to substitute plain reason instead; all he wished to achieve was a sound reduction and curtailment (or, at least, a firm control) of the former.

As to the remaining contributions here mentioned, I think I can be fairly brief. For instance, "Theatre for Pleasure or Theatre for Instruction?" is, quite naturally, a blatantly rhetorical question, since pleasure, or enjoyment, and instruction, or learning, were in no way mutually exclusive of each other in Brecht's view; rather, they supplemented and complemented each other. This essay, composed in the mid-1930s, testifies to the permanence of the European Enlightenment in Brecht's thought, especially to the ideas of Lessing and Diderot, both of whom he admired, and to the Horatian *prodesse et delectare* they had maintained. His next essay, the aforementioned "Alienation Effects in Chinese Acting," which was written shortly afterwards, reports on, and pays homage to, the greatest Chinese actor of the twentieth century, Mei Lan-fang, and thus attests to another weighty heritage gratefully and creatively assumed by the German playwright: that of East Asian theater. Last but not least, "On Experimental Theatre" (*Theatre* 130–35), which originated as a talk Brecht gave in Sweden and Finland during the years 1939–1940, can safely be said to provide, even though it fills but a few pages, the most easily accessible and intelligible introduction to his theorizing that can be recommended to the Brecht neophyte.

In the following, I shall discuss the most important aspects of Brecht's theory. However, one has to bear in mind from the very beginning that theory and practice in his work are inextricably linked. Tellingly enough, the favorite maxim he cherished was that well-known English proverb, "The proof of the pudding is in the eating." Which is to say that Brecht, unlike some of his doctrinaire disciples, was anything but an austere and dogmatic theorist; whenever he was confronted with a choice between theory and practice—if they can be separated at all—he would opt for the practical theater. "We are not staging an alienation effect but a play," he once told an overly zealous actress, "and if you don't stop your ludicrous antics, I'll kick you in the ass" (Müller/Semmer 57).

Our first Brechtian term to be considered is the concept of a "non-Aristotelian drama" (*nichtaristotelisches Drama*). It implies a threefold rejection, first and foremost of which is Aristotelian catharsis, seen as the result of total "empathy" (*Einfühlung*), which calms, even paralyzes, the spectators instead of activating them; it is dismissed in favor of critical distance and detachment. (Whether this is in effect a tenable interpretation of Aristotle's notion is quite a different matter, but it need not concern us here.) At any rate, in order to arrive at said attitude, the spectators are advised by Brecht to light up, to smoke in the theater. People who are smoking, he held, are cool as cucumbers; they cannot work up any passions or lose themselves in the events or in the characters by empathizing with them. Brecht, himself an avid smoker of cheap, stinking cigars, surely knew what he was talking about. Second, Brecht also dismisses the Aristotelian notion of organic unity. It is rejected in favor of a technical, indeed artificial, construct: the montage and collage of heterogeneous elements are to replace the homogeneous "living organism" (which is, as will be remembered, Aristotle's metaphor, or simile, for the work of art, reading in full, "like one whole living organism" [*Poetics* 23.1]). The third Brechtian rejection here involved—closely related to the foregoing one, if somewhat contradictorily—eliminates the precept of a tight tectonic structure for the drama, with its absolute interdependence of parts; this tectonic structure (often pictured as a pyramid) is broken down by Brecht into a loose sequence of more or less independent scenes, or little pieces within the piece (*Stückchen im Stück*) according to his terminology, to be arranged and rearranged in a nearly unlimited fashion. In point of fact, scenes may even be added or left out. It goes without saying that all of this is entirely impossible according to Aristotle's *Poetics*. Aristotle taught that the whole dramatic edifice will inevitably collapse and crumble should even the smallest dramaturgical particle be removed. Or to vary that difference once more, if in exaggerated fashion: in Brecht's drama, the events on stage simply follow each other, rather than logically and cogently following *from* each other as prescribed by Aristotle. Among other things, the Brechtian approach entails the possibility—decidedly non-Aristotelian—of a "dramatic biography," that is, the depiction of the entire life of a given protagonist, pitted against anonymous societal or historical forces. *Mother Courage and Her Children* and the Thirty Years' War or *Life of Galileo* and the institutions of feudalism and the Catholic Church provide examples of such dramatic biographies.

There is only one single instance where Brecht openly and unmistakably avowed his adherence to Aristotelian principles: that is, he maintained the predominance of plot over character portrayal. Indeed, Brecht, the materialist, deigned to employ the word "soul" (for plot) he found in the *Poetics*. To him, the story—the interaction of the characters with other characters or their struggle with blind societal and historical forces—is much more relevant than any subtle probing into the depths of an individual psyche. This also explains, needless to say, the impressive array of so-called split characters populating Brecht's plays. An excellent case in point is the heroine and double figure of Shen Teh/Shui Ta in his Chinese parable *The Good Person of Szechwan*. As Shen Teh, she embodies the good-natured, kindhearted prostitute who cannot say no; as Shui Ta, she embodies the mean, ruthless entrepreneur and exploiter, her alleged cousin. Both characters are impersonated by the same actress, albeit in totally different costumes and masks as a means of disguise. The male protagonist of Brecht's ribald folk comedy *Puntila and Matti, His Hired Man* is a wealthy Finnish landowner who does not alternate between two persons, yet he certainly has two sharply contrasting faces. For as long as he is drunk, he is kind, indulgent, generous, and humane—a really nice chap—and even prone to giving away not only his daughter but also his possessions; as soon as he has sobered up, however, he is again the brutal capitalist and slave driver, sucking the blood of his farmhands and servants. And a similar split in character can be observed in Brecht's chronicle of the Thirty Years' War: its protagonist, too, plays a double role, now appearing as the loving, selfless mother and now, in jarring contrast, as the shrewd and reckless business woman. But the most spectacular duality of that sort is, in all likelihood, the one we encounter in the Brechtian ballet mentioned earlier, *The Seven Deadly Sins*. The story told in this beautiful, unduly neglected piece deals with the various branches of exploitative American show business and the desperate attempts of a young girl trying to succeed in it. All its episodes and occurrences are related by the singer, Anna I, who is backed up by the orchestra and a chorus; all are acted out, simultaneously and expressively, by Anna II, the dancer. Everything is highly theatrical as well as thoroughly nonpsychological, and the singer does not mince words. We are actually one person, she bluntly informs the audience, and we have "one heart and one bank account" (*GW* 7: 2860).

The second key notion of Brecht's that has to be analyzed is his apparent contradiction in terms, "epic theater" (*episches Theater*). What is this term supposed to convey? Let me put it this way: Brechtian theater does not form a closed sphere having "no exit"; it is not a Sartrean hell as in his play by the same name, where the figures are imprisoned forever. Rather, it is a wide open space which allows free movement on all levels and in all directions. The stage in its entirety—in fact, the entire production in all its complexity and multiplicity—serves to unfold a loosely knit story instead of centering on a few tightly knit events. The adjective "epic," in Brecht's usage, just as in German aesthetics and poetics in general, has very little to do with a lofty heroic epic; what it normally refers to is the narrative genre as such. "Epic" (*episch*) is then more or less synonymous with the adjective "narrative," whether in verse or in prose.

Obviously, Brecht's concept of an "epic theater," or "epic drama," has a good deal in common with his concept of an "Aristotelian" or "dramatic" drama or theater. Amusingly, he liked to spell the hateful term "dramatic" with three r's and to pronounce it accordingly in the manner of his native region of Swabia; as a Swabian, he was able to trill his r's on the tip of his tongue, he could thereby give voice to his utter contempt and loathing. There is, as might be expected, much more emphasis on the actual production in Brecht's "epic theater," for all its affinity with his "non-Aristotelian drama." The hybrid term mentioned above, "epic drama" in lieu of "epic theater," occurs very rarely indeed; as a matter of fact, it appears only in the mid-1920s, during the incubation period, so to speak, of Brecht's theorizing. Later on, he would carefully differentiate between "epic theater" on the one hand and "non-Aristotelian drama" on the other. Hence, even though an epic structure is mandatory for the script of the play, hosts of additional stage devices are introduced—devices that, each in its own way, aid the theater in telling a story in that specific Brechtian manner.

As an additional "epic" consequence, the narrator himself, the storyteller in person, emerges on Brecht's stage. It abounds with such figures, Anna I being a pertinent case. Yet the best and the most convincing example in both theatrical and poetical terms is, without fail, the "singer" (*Sänger*) in Brecht's moving and charming, grave and hilarious play of 1944–1945, *The Caucasian Chalk Circle*. Once again, all the events of the story—or, more exactly, of Azdak's and Grusha's stories, respectively—are gradually unfolded by a narrative agent who relates them with the help of musicians. Doubtless, the agent must be viewed as a reincarnation of the omniscient, indeed omnipotent, almost godlike narrator dominating the "authorial novel" (*auktorialer Roman*) as described by F. K. Stanzel; for not only can the narrator hark back to the past as well as anticipate the future, he can even penetrate the minds and hearts of the characters present to disclose and express what they are thinking and feeling. These genuinely "epic" capacities, near boundless in nature, are further increased and intensified by the use of projections, posters, songs, commentaries in verse or prose, prologues and epilogues, interludes and choruses, and so on. Every conceivable aspect of the production is employed as a means of telling, on and through the stage, a story about human society and history in as effective a way as possible.

The very core of Brecht's theorizing is his famous—or notorious—concept of "alienation" (*Verfremdung*), along with his equally noted "alienation effect" (*Verfremdungseffekt*). Citing the catchword coined for the latter, Brecht curtly remarked on his *The Messingkauf Dialogues*: "In the midst [of it all,] the A-effect" (*In der Mitte der V-Effekt*; *GW* 16: 1*). Evidently, the concept of "alienation" is, to all intents and purposes, not just the central, most relevant and important category but likewise the thorniest and most difficult aspect of Brecht's theory and practice. No wonder that it has caused even more turmoil and confusion among critics than the previously discussed "reason vs. emotion" dichotomy. In large measure, the confusion has arisen from the fact that the term "alienation" carries a very specific, clearly defined, philosophical and/or sociological meaning in most Western languages (compare French *aliénation*, Italian *alienazione*, etc.), which, as a result, tends to blur and distort the one envisaged by Brecht. "Estrangement," that other popular translation of *Verfremdung*, does not work either; nor does—for different reasons—the less frequent rendering of "distanciation." So why not adopt the German term as it is, and incorporate it for good in dramaturgical criticism and scholarship? For such an appropriation there are precedents; for example, the terms *lied* and *leitmotif* have become current in English. I am sure that such an appropriation would facilitate our discussions a great deal. Until this happens, we will have to continue using the most widely accepted of those *ersatz* terms, that is, "alienation." First, I shall try to explain its essence; second, its origins; and third, its application and effects.

Brecht's concept and device of alienation are essentially based on the assumption that the world in general and society and its workings in particular are too familiar to be really understood. In other words, we take too many things for granted and do not question them any more, or we do not question them sufficiently. What we therefore need, Brecht argues, is a method, or procedure, that makes us see the world afresh, that virtually forces on us a process or experience of understanding. In order to achieve this goal, he proceeds along dialectical lines. That is to say, he makes what is all too familiar appear strange, and what is seemingly self-evident, he renders unfamiliar and thus questionable (*merkwürdig* and *fragwürdig*). In the beginning, Brecht specifies, we naively believed that we had understood; then, all of a sudden, we experienced a shock of alienation, of profound estrangement. Ultimately, by combining and critically comparing these attitudes or experiences, we shall arrive at a renewed, a concrete, a real understanding. This tripartite and triadic process is—beyond dispute—also "dialectical." (The much-abused notion and term of "dialectic[s]" are truly indispensable, not just apposite or legitimate.) Brecht formalized the dialectical process accordingly. Our initial, both imperfect and incomplete, comprehension equals a Hegelian thesis; this gives way, if only temporarily, to a total incomprehension equaling a Hegelian antithesis; and this, in turn, provokes the final and genuine comprehension, which is tantamount to a Hegelian synthesis or a Hegelian "sublation" (*Aufhebung*) in the triple sense of negation, preservation, and elevation to a higher level. Or to add yet another dialectical definition dear to Brecht: alienation is the act of laying bare, or exposing, the contradictions inherent in human society and history, indeed in the world in its entirety.

So much for the essence of Brecht's alienation. As to its origins, they are threefold: (1) in Hegelian philosophy, as indicated; (2) in Marxian sociology; and (3) in the aesthetic theory of the Russian Formalists.

Hegel, then, provides the philosophical formula for Brechtian alienation. It is to be found, phrased pithily and poignantly, in the preface to his *Phenomenology*: "Das Bekannte ist darum, weil es bekannt ist, nicht erkannt" (28). Which might be paraphrased as follows: That which is well-known or familiar is, precisely because it is so well-known or familiar, not really known, or recognized, or understood. Such is the dialectical formula, the philosophical "discourse of method" (*discours de la méthode*) of any and all Brechtian alienation. As is well known, Marx supplied the sociological content for this Hegelian method. Pursuant to his teachings, man is alienated from his true self, his work and world, especially in a capitalist society, because of the division of labor and the existence of various classes, with the concomitant exploitation of man by his fellow man. According to Marx as well as to Brecht, man has to be made aware of his state of alienation in order to be able to change his conditions, that is, society at large.

The least known of those three roots is (or has been for a long time) the aesthetic theory of the Russian Formalists. Let me merely submit this much: Russian Formalism was a school of critics that flourished in the wake of the Russian Revolution, alongside Russia's avant-garde movements as represented by, for example, Vladimir Mayakovsky. Yet Formalism was brutally crushed by Stalin and his aesthetic henchman, Andrei Zhdanov, when they proclaimed the doctrine of Socialist Realism in the early 1930s. Ever since, terms such as "formalist," "formalism," and "formalistic" have meant an absolute anathema in each and every discussion of Marxist aesthetics. It goes without saying that the consequences for the members of that school of critics were dire indeed. Most of them were either "liquidated" during the infamous Stalinist purges or disappeared and perished in the concentration camps of the Archipelago Gulag. Only very few managed to survive; one of them was the prolific writer and theorist, Victor Shklovsky, who is of primary interest here. In my opinion, no study of Brechtian alienation can do without mentioning him and his contribution. For Shklovsky advanced—in 1917 or, perhaps, as early as 1914—a theory of the poetic metaphor that bears a striking resemblance both to the Hegelian and Marxian concepts of alienation as well as to their Brechtian counterpart. In point of fact, it was none other than Shklovsky who, in an essay and speech called "Art as Technique," coined the term "alienation effect" about two decades before Brecht ever used it. Shklovsky's slogan, *ostranenie*, corresponds almost literally to Brecht's *Verfremdungseffekt*. Admittedly, there are certain differences between their respective theories; however, those are immaterial in our context and can, therefore, be disregarded, particularly in view of further similarities such as a discernible kindred sociological application as well as the aesthetic and gnoseological, or epistemological, thrust of Shklovsky's thought in his literary criticism.

These, then, are the three roots of Brechtian alienation; and the way they converge in Brecht's theory and practice ought to be manifest by now. The following summary definition may be appropriate: Brechtian alienation is an aesthetic device to make us aware, by means of a philosophical method, of our sociological and historical condition and situation. The act of alienation or estrangement produces, dialectically, a bewildered insight into the state of alienation.

German is capable of disentangling, clarifying, and expressing this whole complex cluster of multifarious relations by virtue of one etymological root, plus an identical suffix and varying prefixes. The word in question is, not surprisingly, the adjective *fremd* (strange, alien); and my explanation, which should be regarded as a corollary to my definition above, is as follows: *Entfremdung* denotes the state of alienation, of being estranged; it stands for a passive experience. *Verfremdung* denotes the device or act of alienation, of making strange; it stands for an active experience. And *Befremdung* designates the result of alienation: that is to say, a momentary "bewilderment" (as the exact English equivalent reads) that is conducive, on the part of the audience, to new insights and, in the long run, even actions; clearly, it stands for both a passive and an active experience.

It is true that Brecht did use the term *Entfremdung* (borrowed directly from Marx and Hegel) when he first sketched his theory of *Verfremdung* during the mid-1930s; only after his visit to Moscow in 1935 did he employ the latter term. It is likely that he received it from the Russian Formalists despite the stubborn protestations by stern proponents of Socialist Realism; in all probability, it was passed on to him by Sergei Tretyakov, his Russian friend and fellow writer who was soon to become yet another victim of Stalin's reign of terror. Because Brecht had demonstrably used the term *Befremdung* as well as the basic idea of alienation several years before his visit to Moscow—most notably, in his *Lehrstück* of 1930, *The Exception and the Rule*—we may conclude in good faith that he had developed his theory (or, at the least, its decisive core) rather independently. It was, so to speak, germane to his innermost thought; indeed it was innate, in a way, in his entire intellectual makeup. Whatever he detected afterwards, both in Hegel and/or Marx and in Russian Formalism, was but a wealth of supplements and welcome confirmations. The same holds true, of course, for his encounter with the Chinese actor Mei Lan-fang, which also took place in Moscow in 1935. All Mei offered Brecht was a brilliant demonstration of the applicability of the principle of alienation to the stage and, specifically, the art of acting.

There are countless examples that illustrate the last of our three aspects of Brechtian alienation, its application and effects. The principle of alienation permeates and impregnates the whole production of a Brechtian play, from the dramatist's first scribbled notes to the finished product of the first night, the premiere, and, sometimes, even beyond. On closer scrutiny, however, it all boils down to a fundamental threesome once more. For we have to distinguish among three areas, or levels, of applied alienation and its respective effects; and they relate to, or rest on, one another (if I may avail myself of a simile) like geological layers or strata. At the bottom, we find the non-Aristotelian structure as characterized previously, but also the texture, the wording as such, of the play: everything in the script, to the minutest detail of punctuation, is imbued with alienating devices. In the middle, needless to stress, there extends the "epic" production proper, as prepared by the combined efforts of the director, the scene designer, the composer, and so on: staging, set, music, choreography, pantomime, costumes, masks, lighting, and whatever else could possibly be listed. And on the surface—in broad daylight, as it were—of this threefold stratification, we face the actual work of the cast, the miens and voices and movements of the actors and actresses: the actual delivery of the lines and acting out of the business during a given performance. In short, Brecht, in his theatrical endeavors, drew upon all the "sister arts" (*Schwesterkünste*, as he called them) in order to create a "total work of art," a *Gesamtkunstwerk* (as propagated and practiced by Richard Wagner). Yet this Brechtian totality is a far cry from a Wagnerian one, for instead of welding everything together, as Wagner had done, Brecht set everything apart. For him, the stage was not a melting pot but a place of experimentation, demonstration, and observation. Picture, text, and music do not merge in Brecht's theater, as they do in Wagner's; quite to the contrary, they "alienate each other" (*sie verfremden sich gegenseitig*; GW 16: 699). Such a view entailed, of necessity, a thoroughgoing "retheatricalization" (Gassner) of the stage, as opposed to the total illusion once advocated by Naturalism; but, all the same, Brecht's stagecraft never even bordered on what might be labeled the pompous or the fantastic or, worse yet, on both. Though it made use of all kinds of devices, including exaggeration and, as often as not, grotesqueness, it was and remained based on solid realism.

In conclusion, we have to consider—however briefly—Brecht's "theater of a scientific age," since it is this term that delineates the historical framework for his theatrical endeavors. Constantly, in situating them, he harked back to the time around 1600, the dawn of our modern age, and to the scientists promoting it, like Galileo and Francis Bacon. The latter (about whom he also wrote an enlightening short story, "The Experiment") gave him the cue for his "A Short

Organum for the Theatre,'' for both its title and its method are derived from the Englishman's seminal treatise of 1620, *Novum organum scientiarum*, itself an anti-Aristotelian ''discourse of method'' expounding the new experimental approaches in the natural sciences. The former, on the other hand, the hero of the Brechtian *Life of Galileo*, looms large within the text of Brecht's own ''Short Organum,'' serving, among other things, as one of the prime examples of his principle of alienation. Just as the Italian, according to a well-known if apocryphal story, contemplated the swinging chandelier in the Cathedral of Pisa, and thus, by questioning that all-too-familiar sight, discovered the laws of gravity, so, too, is the theater called upon to produce such effects and results on the stage and in the house. In sum, the advent of new concepts in the natural sciences marks the beginning of our modern age; and the advent of new concepts in sociology and history signals the culmination of our modern age. It is high time, declares Brecht, to introduce these new scientific methods and insights as they pertain to nature as well as to society into the realm of art, of literature, of the theater: in brief, into the entire aesthetic sphere. This is why Brechtian theater claims to be ''of the scientific age.'' And it also follows that learning and pleasure, didacticism and enjoyment, cannot be mutually exclusive in Brecht's thought; rather, they complement each other. In fact, learning for him was a pleasurable experience and one of the most gratifying. Brecht for one delighted in the acquisition of knowledge, in new insights and ideas, indeed in change and transformation as such. Nothing, he held, is permanent, much less eternal. Everything is historical, is in continuous flux. In an almost Nietzschean—or Heraclitean—fashion, Brecht derived boundless joy from the ever-changing, never-ceasing interplay of contradictions as they emerge, clash, and dissolve into each other, only to create another such series of contradictions. Not only does this explain why he was able to use the terms ''epicize'' (*episieren*), ''dialecticize'' (*dialektisieren*), and ''historicize'' (*historisieren*) as near synonyms, but it also suggests that his concept of the theater, as of art at large, frequently tended to transcend the narrow boundaries of his self-imposed ideology. Although Brecht clearly was a Marxist playwright, without a doubt he was also a Marxist heretic. For instance, Brecht's beloved teacher, the Marxist philosopher and politician Karl Korsch,[1] was a lifelong foe of Lenin's as well as Stalin's; he was expelled from the Communist party as early as 1926, but he simultaneously left it of his own accord. What more can one demand as proof of radical disassociation? This happened at the same time when the young Brecht set out seriously to study Marxism—with none other than Korsch.

May I conclude with a both brief and Brechtian anecdote that I was told by one of Brecht's former collaborators. Time and again, critics (especially Western critics) asked Brecht what would happen to his theater and its theories once he had achieved what he was fighting for, socialism. Was his work not geared, indeed tied, to capitalism and a bourgeois audience? Would it not become useless and obsolete, and, as a consequence, be discarded, under socialism? To which Brecht replied, calmly and with a grin: ''My dear fellow, you do not know how to think dialectically. My theater and its theories are valid under capitalism and in a bourgeois society; and they will be valid under the dictatorship of the proletariat, under socialism, communism, in a classless society . . . and in all societies to follow.''

NOTE

This is a revised version of my essay, ''Brecht's Theater of Alienation,'' *Halcyon: A Journal of the Humanities* 13 (1991): 51–66.

    1. See also Douglas Kellner, ''Brecht's Marxist Aesthetic,'' in this volume.

WORKS CITED (SEE ALSO REFERENCE GUIDE TO WORKS CITED IN ABBREVIATED FORM)

Aristotle. *Aristotle's Poetics*. Translated, introduction, and notes by James Hutton. New York: Norton, 1982.

Artaud, Antonin. *The Cenci. A Play*. Translated by Simon Watson Taylor. New York: Grove, 1970.

Bacon, Francis. *Advancement of Learning. Novum Organum. New Atlantis*. Chicago: Encyclopaedia Britannica, 1955.

———. *The Essayes or Counsels, Civill and Morall*. Cambridge, MA: Harvard University Press, 1985.

Fuegi, John. *The Essential Brecht*. Los Angeles, CA: Hennessey, 1972.

Galilei, Galileo. *Dialogues Concerning Two New Sciences*. Translated by Henry Crew and Alfonso de Salvio. Evanston, IL: Northwestern University Press, 1950.

Gassner, John. *Form and Idea in Modern Theatre*. New York: Dryden, 1956.

Hegel, Georg Wilhelm Friedrich. *Phänomenologie des Geistes*. Edited by Johannes Hoffmeister. 6th ed. Hamburg: Meiner, 1952.

Horace. *The Art of Poetry*. Translated by Barton Raffel and James Hynd. Albany: State University of New York Press, 1974.

Melchinger, Siegfried. *The Concise Encyclopedia of Modern Drama*. New York: Horizon, 1964.

Müller, André, and Gerd Semmer. *Geschichten vom Herrn B. 99 Brecht-Anekdoten*. Frankfurt am Main: Insel, 1967.

Sartre, Jean-Paul. *No Exit (Huis clos). A Play in One Act, and The Flies (Les Mouches), A Play in Three Acts*. Translated by Stuart Gilbert. New York: Knopf, 1947.

Shelley, Percy Bysshe. *The Cenci*. Leipzig: Insel-Verlag, 1930.

Shklovsky, Victor. ''Art as Technique.'' *Russian Formalist Criticism: Four Essays*. Edited by Lee T. Lemon and Marion J. Reis. Lincoln: University of Nebraska Press, 1965. 3–24.

Stanzel, F. K. *A Theory of Narrative*. Translated by Charlotte Goedsche. Cambridgeshire, NY: Cambridge University Press, 1984.

2

Brecht and the Problem of Influence

CHRISTINE KIEBUZINSKA

Verwisch die Spuren!
(Obliterate the traces)

—*GW* 2: 157

In writing on Bertolt Brecht and the problem of influence, one is faced with the daunting task of examining the proliferation of studies alleging the primacy of Brecht's precursors on the development of his *Weltanschauung*, the development of his dramatic style, and his theatrical theories.[1] Many critics writing on Brecht and the problem of influence persist in the notion that an author has proprietary rights over his work, and anyone who transgresses and borrows from the work either lacks originality or, even worse, is denounced as a plagiarist. The attacks on Brecht, which have continued through the decades, use the romantic concept of creativity as something uniquely personal bestowed on the individual of rare sensibility, and the dilemma posed by these value judgments is that authors and texts are treated as products of something called the "literary imagination." Any evidence to the contrary is taken as evidence of the lack of creativity, originality, and imaginative vision. From this perspective, the literary artifact is important not only in itself but also as an encapsulation of the creative energies of the unique creative spirit (Eagleton, *Theory* 19).

In many of the studies exploring the debts that Brecht owes to William Shakespeare, Bernard Shaw, François Villon, and others, the arguments are based on the idea that art is the product of some spontaneous, mysterious faculty known as the aesthetic process developed according to purely individual aesthetic inspiration. Consequently, the privileging of artistic creativity totally ignores the work of art as a signifying system, both deriving from and directed to an organized collective that determines aesthetic evaluation. At the same time, the endless tracing of Brecht's *Urväter* or intellectual predecessors tends to reduce the nature of the author; consequently, as Eric Bentley mentions, Brecht thereby becomes "that most passé of all creatures, a leader of a former avant-garde, hero of yesterday's tomorrow" ("Influence" 189).

While the majority of studies attempt to situate Brecht in a relationship to the past, a number of studies also focus on the exploration of the debt Brecht owes to his contemporaries, such as Lion Feuchtwanger, Max Reinhardt, Erwin Piscator, Walter Benjamin, and Karl Korsch; or to his collaborators such as Elisabeth Hauptmann, Helene Weigel, Kurt Weill, Marieluise Fleißer, Margarete Steffin, Hanns Eisler, and Caspar Neher (Fuegi 41). The problem with studies arguing that so-and-so influenced Brecht and therefore plays a significant role in Brecht's creativity is to deny that Brecht was as much a participant in the same cultural discourse as his contemporaries. Conversely, one could maintain that Brecht had a profound reciprocal influence on his contemporaries as well, an approach that would ultimately prove to come full circle privileging one influence over the other. At the same time, in examining this rather limited list, one can easily determine just from the juxtaposition of Reinhardt and Piscator as potential influences on Brecht's theory and practice that an inherent contradiction exists, particularly since Reinhardt's theater has a substantially different method and intent from that of Piscator's agit-prop theater. What emerges from Brecht's engaged involvement as a student director for both Reinhardt and Piscator is his dialogic attempt to think himself out from what Mikhail Bakhtin calls the monologism of conceptual glue, in this case the study of theatrical tradition and influence. Bakhtin's dialogism may be helpful in liberating Brecht from the dominance of literary or theatrical tradition since, as Bakhtin explains, "the contexts of dialogue are without limit," and even meanings emerging from dialogues of the past "will never be finally grasped once and for all, for they will always be renewed in later dialogue" (Clark/Holquist 349–50).

The list of "others" with whom Brecht participated in dialogue in his formative years in Berlin can be extended indefinitely, as John Fuegi mentions (41), and includes encounters with luminaries from both high and low culture. The artist George Grosz; the writers Heinrich Mann, Arnolt Bronnen, Hanns Johst, Carl Zuckmayer, and Gerhart Hauptmann; the composers Paul Hindemith, Kurt Weill, Arnold Schoenberg, and Igor Stravinsky; the architect Walter Gropius; the actors and directors Peter Lorre, Carola Neher, Lotte Lenya, Emil Jannings, Marlene Dietrich, Leni Riefenstahl, Georg Willhelm Pabst, and Josef von Sternberg; visiting "others" Sergei Eisenstein, Isadora Duncan, Christopher Isherwood, Asja Lacis, Bernhard Reich, and Sergei Tretyakov, and the representative of the sports world, boxer Paul Samson-Körner—all belonged to Brecht's circle.

Similar problems arise when one addresses Brecht's influence on contemporary theater. Though Brechtian theory and theatrical models have had an incalculable effect on contemporary dramatists, theatrical directors, and critics—this influence is sometimes openly acknowledged by playwrights such as Edward Bond or critics such as Roland Barthes—to a large extent Brecht's influence is something imposed on dramatists and directors by critics who seek in that particular text or that particular *mise-en-scène* evidence of what can be designated as "Brechtian." But the label "Brechtian" excludes the problem of reception in which Brecht's theatrical practices, particularly Brecht's techniques of *Verfremdung* and *Gestus,* have entered the universal language of contemporary theater, irrespective of ideological contexts in which montage, epic narration, or foregrounded theatricality are practiced. As Herbert Blau observes, "since Brecht, and his assault on illusion, the lights are not always hidden now" (*Audience* 212). In theatrical practice, however, Brecht's unmasking of theatrical illusion is dispersed amid other theatrical methods or approaches—along with Antonin Artaud's theater of cruelty, the theater of the absurd, performance art, musicals, and mainstream Broadway productions. This paradox in the reception of Brecht's theory and practice suggests, as Marc Silberman mentions, an "epistemological decentering" of what has been designated as Brechtian ("Postmodernized" 2). Consequently, the contradictory nature of the displacement in contemporary theater and criticism of Brechtian theory and practice as employed by Brecht creates a situation that Andrzej Wirth pertinently describes as "Brecht reception without Brecht" (16). This reception of Brecht without Brecht suggests that Brecht's texts, as Patrice Pavis writes, are no longer used as building materials that a committed Brechtian reading "would shape in obedience to a specific ideological project" ("Classical" 19). Instead, Brecht's texts have become part of the many theatrical enunciators constituting a multiplicity of points of view and the infinite variations of interpretations that link them together.

In the attempts to resolve the dilemma of the significance of both influence on Brecht or Brecht's influence on others, perhaps one should turn to Brecht's observations on historical processes, for in "A Short Organum for the Theatre" Brecht writes that the stage image should above all reveal contradictions between the different responses or interpretations of historical periods presented in that image. According to Brecht, the image that provides a historical definition "will retain something of the rough sketching" indicating "traces of other movements and features" in the completed picture. To bring out the simultaneity of the "traces of other movements" Brecht suggests that one should imagine a man making a speech while standing in a valley, at times changing his views or uttering thoughts that contradict one another, "so that the accompanying echo forces them into confrontation" (*Theatre* 191). Brecht's decidedly Derridean observation may, as a result, be applied to the analysis of his own work, which echoes and shows traces of the influence of others as sketched on theater in general. These echoes reappear in his work as "traces of other movements and features" and provide his theater with its "fully worked figure" or character.

In the light of contemporary poststructuralist critical theory regarding authorship and its proprietary adjunct, the literary work of art, the notions of both
author and work have been found to be inadequate. Brecht himself serves as a
precursor to the poststructuralist dismantling of authorship as spiritual property
when he observes that originality is related to "worn out notions of what constitutes property" (*GW* 15: 202). Brecht feels that the notion of the literary
masterpiece as private property is outmoded since art essentially belongs to the
field of collective reception. In the 1930s, when Brecht was overturning the laws
that constitute literary property, members of the Prague Linguistic Circle, in
particular Jan Mukařovsky, were revolutionizing literary theory by calling attention to the fact that influence is not a hierarchical process that gradates several
influences, allowing one to prevail over the other. Instead they posited that
infuence functions by "penetrating" and "colliding" with the tradition of local
literature to whose conditions and needs it is subordinated. The local artistic and
ideological tradition can thus "create dialectic tensions among the influences"
(Mukařovsky, *Structure* xxi).

Brecht understood that quotability was the hallmark of the "collision" of one
text with another, and he foregrounded the "quoted, narrated, anticipated, reminded" through estrangement of the original (*GW* 1: 65, translated in Szondi
72). Consequently, in his theatrical practice, his stage decor no longer represents
the world of the original but merely quotes it, or refers to it through such
Verfremdungseffekte as the actor's technique of the *Gestus* as part of the quotation, the half-curtain that announces a new way of looking at representation,
stage decor that uses projections on a screen of either documentary material or
of announcements of upcoming events in the play, and the use of choruses,
songs, and frequently interrupted action. Brecht's use of these effects deflects
the spectator's expectations of traditional interpretations, which, if they were to
be catered to, would produce a theater that would be "boring, a cliché." Instead,
according to Mukařovsky, artists like Brecht "violate norms, however slightly,
in order to provoke interest" (*Aesthetic* 99). The violation of norms on Brecht's
part is not a purely aesthetic endeavor, for in exposing naturalistic illusion, he
also wants to problematize the illusion-making capacity of theater as well. In
particular, Brecht wants to expose "the public side of role behavior behind
which the technique of staging is hidden" (Jauss, *Aesthetic* 138), and by exposing the theatrical mechanism he wants to expose the mechanism of social
roles as well.

At the same time, Brecht further estranges the sanctity of the original text by
introducing elements from popular entertainment forms such as the cabaret,
vaudeville, revues, the circus (especially clown acts in the style of Karl Valentin
or Charlie Chaplin), film, radio plays, detective fiction, cowboy films, jazz,
sports events, and children's theater. In particular he admires the economy of
Chaplin's strictly nonpsychological performance technique and frequently refers
to Chaplin as the ideal actor for his epic theater because Chaplin's reflexes are
not just biological but "already social" (Weber 55–56). Even before he has a

chance to put his theory into practice, he envisions hiring two clowns to engage in an *entr'acte* commentary on the outcome of the play (Völker, *Brecht* 69). From film, Brecht borrows the term "montage," specifically from Eisenstein's use of montage in such films as *Potemkin*. He does so in order to show that the sequences of interrupted scenes in his plays were not just a "piling up" of fragments without a goal, but a very purposeful juxtaposition to foreground the *Gestus* of each scene (Mueller 474–75). Similarly, Brecht recognizes that although the radio as a broadcast medium could potentially operate as a democratic and political public organ, "bourgeois society uses the medium to isolate and passify the listener." Brecht understands that, as in theater and film, new methods must be introduced in order to "make visible the functions which insert themselves between real things and images of things" (Silberman, "Politics" 450). At the same time, the *Gebrauchsmusik* or applied music, practiced by Weill, Hindemith, and Eisler, gives Brecht the opportunity to extend the power of entertainment and allows him to introduce songs into his plays that with their ease of execution and accessibility to the untrained ear demolish the existing barriers between grand opera and popular music. And the kinship of *Gebrauchsmusik* to the "dynamic rhythms and unsnobbish popular appeal of jazz" encouraged the actor "to adopt an attitude, either for or against" the surface sentimentality of the songs (Willett, *Brecht in Context* 153–57).

Brecht also includes the spectators in the process by suggesting that they observe the action as if at a sports event or boxing match, a process that would allow them to interrupt the action by siding with one side or another. In addition, smoking would allow the spectator further opportunity to interpose detached judgment on the outcome. Brecht envisions a theater that would combine the effect of the planetarium, a space in which the spectator would adopt the "quietly contemplative, balanced and controlled attitude" that has led technologists and scientists to their discoveries and inventions (*GW* 15: 221). Though it is difficult to imagine a disengaged spectator at a boxing match, Brecht envisions Samson-Körner's "matter-of-fact boxing" as a springboard for the scientific, cool attitude of the spectator (*Theatre* 16). An intertextual precedent exists for Brecht's fascination with boxing in Shaw's description of the matches of his favorite boxer Gene Tunney; Shaw describes the boxers as aware that "they are paid to fight for the amusement of the spectators," so that the success of the outcome serves as "conclusive proof of the superfluity of the conventional hypocrisies of fiction" (quoted in Schoeps, *Shaw* 68). As in Shaw's plays, in which a boxing match of ideas is made visible, Brecht's dramatic theory uses the boxing match as a metaphor to reveal "the intellect lurking in the background" (*Theatre* 16).

Thus, Brecht's aesthetics not only thematize role distance as the function of the actor but also create the possibility for the spectator to experience oneself through the doubling process that role enactment presents. In some plays, this construct is already built in, as for example in the double figure of Shen Teh/ Shui Ta in *The Good Person of Szechwan,* or in the figure of Puntila, who is good when he is drunk and bad when he is sober. In other plays, it is the actor's and spectator's function to provide "otherness" to characters through the process of the double alienation technique. To make this understanding between spectators and actors possible, the structures that lie behind the roles have to be uncovered. Simultaneously, the devices of the theater are also exposed so that "the naturalistic illusion concerning social determinants" can be exposed (Jauss, *Aesthetic* 139).

The notion of displaying historical contradictions that is so central in Brecht's own approach to both his drama and theatrical practice has become a major concern in rethinking, as Pavis explores, "the classical heritage of modern drama" ("Classical" 1). In attempts to evaluate the heritage or influence of past traditions, one is confronted by defining notions that are both imprecise and archaic, since each of these notions "recalls its opposite, or at least a corrective or a different point of view that relativizes its meaning" (Pavis, "Classical" 1). The evaluation of the role of historicity in Brecht's texts depends on factors of reception. Frequently, this point of view denies Brecht, or any other reader, the playful activity of interpreting Christopher Marlowe, William Shakespeare, John Gay, J.M.R. Lenz, or Bernard Shaw according to one's own aesthetic and cultural values and in light of individual concerns. Since all literary works are "rewritten" by the societies that read them, as Terry Eagleton observes, "different historical periods have constructed a 'different' . . . Shakespeare for their own purposes" and have found in his plays different elements "to value or devalue" (*Literary* 12).

Roland Barthes, who finds the literary work in its formalistic, almost sacred, concreteness inadequate in explaining what occurs when the reader approaches a text, suggests that the problem may lie in the idea that when reading is reduced to consumption, the consequence is often "boredom": "to suffer from boredom means that one cannot produce the text, open it out, make it go" (Barthes, "Work" 80). However, in examining Brecht's reception or readings of the classics, one sees that he is not bored and instead opens up what he has read in order to produce his version of the reading. What is omitted from the devaluation of the role that reception plays in studies of influence is that a variety of different receptions or readings of literary texts is possible. These readings range from inspiration, the recognition of similar values, the questioning of systems of values and beliefs to reactions that evoke strong negative responses, provocation, and so on.

Nor should influence as such be restricted to the giants of literary tradition. As is well known, Brecht probably read more detective fiction than great classics, and the detective novels of Edgar Wallace were his particular favorites. According to Brecht, when you open a detective novel, you know precisely where you are because you have learned the "rules of the game" in the same manner as one learns the rules of the game in order to enjoy a soccer game. Brecht envisioned his epic theater as a theater in which the spectators would at all times know where they were in the same way as they do in the detective

novel, the Western, the revue, the operetta, and the soccer game. Brecht felt that
the epic theater model would only work if all plays "resembled one another as
one egg resembles another" (*Werke* 21: 227); standardization of form rather
than originality were to be the features of what Brecht envisioned as the theater
of the future.

It could be argued that Brecht in his reading of the classics was giving them
the same kind of scrutiny that the reading of detective fiction demanded. However, in reading the classics, Brecht was searching for clues that might fit the
construction of his solution to the problems of history and economics. In reading
Shakespeare, much as in reading Wallace, Brecht was examining the construction of something Jan Kott describes as the "grand mechanism," an image of
history as a "great staircase," in which every step, like the progress of a detective novel, "is marked by murder, perfidy, treachery" (10). At the same time,
as Willett points out, Shakespeare interested Brecht not as a classic but as a
practical man of the theater. In particular, he liked Shakespeare's lack of obvious
manipulation of effect on the spectator. According to Brecht, everything in
Shakespeare "takes a natural course" without obvious connections between the
acts to show the "lack of connection in a man's fate." Brecht admires Shakespeare as someone who has no need to "tidy up" the plot in order to strengthen
an idea "which can only be a prejudice by an argument which is not derived
from life" (*GW* 15: 119, translated by Willett, *Brecht in Context* 27).

From the very beginning, Brecht challenged the concept of originality, and
when accusations of plagiarism were made against him for having used Villon's
ballad in *The Threepenny Opera* without giving credit, he defended this omis-
sion as having been due to forgetfulness. The source of his forgetfulness, he
explained in 1929, was that he felt that the "creations of the intellect belong
on a similar plane as do the products of roadside gardens" (*Werke* 21: 315,
quoted in Völker, *Brecht* 132–33). According to Brecht, the history of literature
is a history of appropriations, and literature like property is theft. In other words,
the cumulative literary heritage from all ages are there to be plucked for use in
much the same way as the fruit from a roadside garden. Unlike the plagiarist,
who usually attempts to "obliterate the traces," Brecht openly reveals his
sources, calling attention to the very elements that mark the questions he addresses to the original text.

In addition, Brecht usually makes his reading a public event to which many
participants contribute; some of the participants in his reading are other authors
whom he is reading at the same time. Such is the case of Brecht's reading of
Villon, whom he read from his earliest formative years along with Frank Wedekind, Georg Büchner, Rudyard Kipling, Arthur Rimbaud, Paul Verlaine, and
others.[2] For example, Brecht's first play *Baal* seems to have been directly inspired by the somewhat wild lives of Verlaine and Rimbaud, whose wanderings
through Holland Brecht knew of. But the play also contains traces of Wedekind
and Knut Hamsun, who represented a kind of vitalism and romantic realism that
Brecht admired. Since Brecht was not a solitary reader, much of his reading

took place in the collective circle of childhood friends and later in study groups. Thus, his reading belonged to a public shared space, and he relied on the collective interpretation of his friends and colleagues—who brought their own insights, references, and experiences—for his own frequently inspired reading. From the very beginning then, Villon, much as Wedekind or Kipling, belonged to the intertextual texture of Brecht's literary persona.

The question that should be asked is whether Brecht's appropriation from Villon was merely a passive culinary consumption. Perhaps attention to Julia Kristeva's observation that "any text is constructed as a mosaic of quotations; any text is the absorption and transformation of another" (*Desire* 66) may elucidate the complicated process whereby "the one who writes is the same as the one who reads" (86–87). The writer as reader of another text becomes "no more than a text rereading itself as it rewrites itself" (Kristeva, *Revolution* 59–60). Barthes also advances the theory that any writer is primarily a reader whose reading serves as the organizing center of interpretation since any text is "composed of multiple writings, drawn from many cultures," entering into mutual relations with each other in the form of "dialogue, parody or contestation" ("Death" 148).

Nor is Brecht necessarily the kind of reader who merely dresses up what he has read in "modern" clothes. Brecht would agree with Pavis's observation that often interpretations of classics on stage have approached the text "as if time had done no more than cover the text with layers of dust," a process that describes "dusting" as "dehistoricizing," or denying history by reducing it to outside particles that, when removed, present a clean, dehistoricized surface. On the other hand, a refusal to "dust off" involves a consciousness that foregrounds the historicized dust "instead of ignoring it or covering it up" (Pavis, "Classical" 5). For Brecht, the fascination of reading the classics has to do with exposing the mechanism of history in such a manner—he himself mentions Piscator's production of Schiller's *The Robbers*—that people leaving the performance might remark that the passage of 150 years is "no small matter" (Pavis, "Classical" 6).

Brecht learned from Piscator that the dramatic work is rooted in the actuality of its time; however, succeeding ages shift the play's meaningfulness from one aspect to another according to changing circumstances by throwing into relief the elements they find relevant to their own conditions (Piscator, *Theatre* 132–34). Brecht echoes Piscator's observations in his complaint that when theaters perform plays from other periods "they like to annihilate distance, fill in the gap, gloss over the differences," thereby eliminating the spectator's "delight in comparisons, in distance, in dissimilarity" and also delight "in what is close and proper to ourselves" (*Theatre* 276). In his productions, Brecht repudiates the hollow externals of modernization, and in his stagings of adaptations of Marlowe's *Edward II*, Lenz's *The Tutor*, Gerhart Hauptmann's *The Beaver Coat*, and Shakespeare's *Coriolanus*, he attempts instead to make them relevant by having them present life that had significance to their own times.

Brecht's attitude toward historicity foregrounds the conclusion that contradictions in contemporary readings of classics echo similar contradictions already inhering in a text such as Marlowe's *Edward II*. In his staging of *Edward II*, Brecht attempts to free the theater from the ill-founded assumption that "only a full mimetic representation," authentic in every detail, can truthfully display Marlowe's text (Fuegi 33). Brecht's catchwords in his theorizing of the epic theater—written a few years following his production of *Edward II* in Munich in 1924—suggest a consistent approach marked by intellectual distance, objectivity, and cool rationality in contrast to the awe-inspiring and emotion-wringing practices of naturalism. Thus, Brecht's production of Marlowe's *Edward II* illustrates in embryonic state the contradictions that were to mark Brecht's theatrical practice in general. An examination of the description of the *mise-en-scène* of the "hanging scene" in *Edward II* reveals Brecht's application of a complex, often contradictory mixture of naturalistic effects with "self-conscious, non-realistic 'theatre theatrical' elements" (Fuegi 33). Brecht insists on a technically realistic "working gallows and a realistically appropriate rope"; however, the "real" gallows is placed within a set whose backdrop calls attention to the obviously painted canvas, while the actors playing the soldiers are made up in whiteface "so stark as to suggest the makeup worn by clowns" (Fuegi 33).

Brecht's attenuation of the emotion-provoking elements in *Edward II* to the whiteface as *Gestus*, or sign, reduces to one striking image Constantin Stanislavsky's complex building of the given circumstances of characters and their subtextual exploration of emotional significance. At the same time, Brecht's use of the whiteface as the *sign* of the fear and cowardice of the soldiers simultaneously refers both to the whiteface used by clowns such as Valentin as well as to Chaplin's mask of pale pathos. Similarly, Brecht's use of the "real" gallows with its "realistically appropriate rope" forces the spectator to ponder the fact that the reality of the gallows, despite technological improvements, has not changed significantly since Marlowe's time. Consequently, Brecht's construction of the working gallows demonstrates to the actor and spectator a "realistic grasp of the 'craft of hanging' " (Fuegi 33) and effectively historicizes that which is already historicized in Marlowe's text. The juxtaposition of Brecht's techniques of realistic representation and his techniques foregrounding the presentation of self-conscious theatricality exposes simultaneously both the "inside" and "outside" of the scene (Fuegi 33).

In the vast mass of Brecht's writings on the theater from his first definitions of "non-Aristotelian drama" to "Short Organum," one can trace the shifting stages of Brecht's aesthetics as he formulates and reformulates his critique of modern theater. However, as Pavis writes, in Brecht's journey toward a theory of dialectical theater, one key notion that remains "particularly resistant to thematic and terminological variations" is that of the *Gestus*, which remains a veritable pillar of Brecht's theoretical structure (Pavis, "Brecht's Notion" 40–41). All of the references to the *Gestus* appearing from the term's first usage in

"On the Use of Music in an Epic Theatre" (1935; *Theatre* 84–90) to "Short Organum" (1948; *Theatre* 179–205) have a common social dimension of "characterizing relations among people" (*GW* 16: 753, translated in Pavis, "Brecht's Notion" 41). The *Gestus*, unlike conventional gestures that are primarily expressive or aesthetic, serves as an index of a social attitude, an intentional sign used by the actor to indicate the character's social attitude. Essentially, the *Gestus* appears to be a kind of prelanguage, giving a direct presentation of social relationships; at the same time it serves as an alienating mask rather than as a medium of true expression. As in the tradition of Shakespeare's theater, such a nonnaturalistic, irreal style of acting allows the actor to call upon moments of direct communication with the audience. Thus, the *Gestus* demonstrates over and over that the signs of social forces can be discovered and made legible.

Even Brecht's early reviews written between 1918 and 1921 for the Augsburg *Volkswille* reveal the depth of his concern for acting technique, and his review of a 1919 production of Henrik Ibsen's *Ghosts*, for example, shows attention to the delicate harmony between word and action (*Werke* 21: 39). Though in this review the concept of the *Gestus* is not yet articulated, it is evident that Brecht is thinking about the "bodily posture, accent, and facial expression" that display the *Gestus des Zeigens* or, self-referentiality, a style of performance that is "always linked with the performer's self-presentation as the possessor of special skill" (Esslin, "Reflections" 138). Brecht insists that the mastery of the *Gestus* necessitates a renunciation of the dramatic style in favor of epic narrative. In epic theater, the events unfolding on stage no longer completely fill out the performance in the way dramatic events had previously done, and the concern for the dramatic outcome of the play is replaced by "the epic freedom to pause and reflect" (Szondi 71).

The road to Brecht's aesthetic of the *Gestus* is very winding, and it is difficult to trace all the footpaths that intersect it. However, some of the footpaths have not been obliterated, and one can explore the intersection between Brecht's aesthetics and those of Russian constructivism, Eisenstein's montage, and Shklovsky's theory of *ostranenie*, or the "making strange" effect and Brecht's epic theater. The work of Vsevolod Meyerhold, who in the 1920s did away almost entirely with traditional illusionist conventions of the stage, has particular relevance for Brecht's theater. Instead of a curtain or naturalistic props, Meyerhold's theater used nothing but stage "constructions" such as scaffoldings, cubes, and gangplanks on which the actors, using an acting system called "biomechanics," presented the play. Biomechanics directly assaulted the naturalistic acting style developed by Stanislavsky by assuming the form of depersonalized, stylized, and symbolic gestures, each signifying, but not imitating, a different emotion. Actors and stage constructions were in almost continual motion, while the dramatic plot was repeatedly "interrupted" by spotlights, projected film sequences, and musical accompaniment by a jazz band that was made visible on stage. Unlike Stanislavsky's carefully rehearsed performances at the Moscow Art Theater, Meyerhold's theatrical presentations were not finished products, but

open-ended creations of actors and spectators alike. While the stage constructions suggested the contemporary industrial world, the audience was never allowed to forget that what they were seeing was a theatrical workshop.
Meyerhold's attention to the process of production had an effect on his student
Eisenstein, who later in his films sought to demonstrate through the architectural
composition (involving editing of "constructed" elements, or montage) the dialectical collision of economic classes in the social process. According to Brecht,
the very same sort of complicated montage with which the filmmaker creates
his text also takes place on the stage when specific scenes are juxtaposed to
other scenes. Rather than the linear development found in naturalistic drama,
Brecht proposes that each scene stand for itself and that the unity emerge from
juxtaposition rather than from the causal connections of traditional dramatic plot.

Though the intent of the Russian formalists' technique of *ostranenie*, or defamiliarization, was purely aesthetic, Shklovsky's observation that an art object
must be defamiliarized and pried loose from the facts of life is an important
strategy of Brecht's *Verfremdungseffekt*, a term that comes into use in Brecht's
vocabulary at the time he first discovers the Russian formalists' work. Shklovsky
writes that in order to shake up the reader/spectator's perception, it is necessary
to tear the aesthetic object out of the context of habitual perception, to "deau-
tomatize" the seeing of it, "to turn it like a log in a fire" (81). In this manner,
the object is converted into something "palpable," something "capable of becoming the material of art." The spectator is thus struck by the novelty resulting
from placing the object in a new ambiance, of seeing it in "new dress" (Shklovsky 81).

The theories of the Russian formalists were not confined to the borders of
the Soviet Union, and the interaction of the Berlin intellectual scene with that
of the Soviet Union can be documented from visits of poets such as Vladimir
Mayakovsky, who gave poetry readings in Berlin in 1925, 1927, and 1928;
Meyerhold's traveling production of Sergei Tretyakov's *Roar China* in 1930;
Tretyakov's frequent visits to Berlin; Asja Lacis's—she was Brecht's assistant
in his *Edward II* project—frequent visits to Moscow and her reports of the
theatrical scene there; and by the translation into German of Alexander Tairov's
Notes of the Director. Although Brecht himself did not use the term *ostranenie*
or his version *Verfremdungseffekt* until after his visit to the Soviet Union in
1935, the attitude of "making strange," of breaking conventional perceptions,
hung in the air in the 1920s. This can be seen in the highly unnaturalistic
stagings of the plays of the German expressionists with whom Brecht shared
the common heritage of Wedekind, the first staging of Büchner's *Woyzeck*, the
first German staging of Pirandello's *Six Characters in Search of an Author*; as
well as the political concerns of Georg Kaiser and Ernst Toller, the political
cartoons of George Grosz, the analysis of social and political discourse by Karl
Kraus, Reinhardt's theater for a mass audience, and Piscator's staging of *The
Good Soldier Schweik* in his agit-prop theater.

While the various aesthetic theories proliferating in the Berlin of the 1920s

allowed Brecht to clarify his version of theatricality, Brecht's sociological studies led him to Marxism and a clarification of the function of his theater. It is
then important in the study of influence in Brecht not only to trace the many
aesthetic practices that anticipate much of Brecht's practice of breaking down
fourth-wall illusionism through the foregrounding of theatricality but also to
trace his study of sociology and political economy. Marxism provided Brecht a
framework for crystallizing the negative elements he saw in the 1920s' German
society into positive patterns that would prove to be aesthetically satisfying.
Marxism, as Esslin mentions, "provided the dramatist with a splendid picture
of conflict, a ready-made tragic pattern of history" (*Brecht* 151). Once exposed
to the Marxist dialectic, with its rational, intellectual approach to the solution
of the world's economic problems, Brecht became fascinated with it, to the point
that for him Marx was to become "the only spectator" for his theater.

From Marx, Brecht learned to focus on the paradox of ends and means, and
unlike in his early plays such as *Baal* or *In the Jungle of Cities*, in his later
plays he did not begin with the individual but with the problem. He wrote in
1926, "When I read Marx's *Das Kapital,* I understood my plays." It is not that
Brecht recognized that he had "written a whole pile of Marxist plays without
knowing it," but that he felt that because of Marx's intelligence, his plays
"would have made food for his [Marx's] thought" (*Werke* 21: 256–57). However, Brecht never claimed to have become a systematic Marxist doctrinaire, for
fascination and enthusiasm are reflections of a reader's reception, and Brecht's
fascination with Marx is also mitigated by the innate cynicism of the romantic.
Thus Brecht's inclination toward Marxism is less a substitute for his early dis-
illusioned romanticism, an attitude that binds him intertextually to Büchner and
Wedekind, than a layer superimposed on top of his essential pessimism. As
Robert Brustein writes, Brecht's "rational ideology emerges as the dialectical
counterpart of his irrationalism and despair" (251). At the same time, as Fritz
Sternberg—one of Brecht's first teachers of Marxist dialectics—recounts, systematic thought that is considered so essential to the study of Marxism "just
didn't suit" Brecht. Brecht considered linear thought unproductive, and as Sternberg's comment to Brecht reveals, Brecht's method was based on associations:
"You don't think in straight lines, but in leaps. You think in associations which
nobody else would think of" (12).

Nor does Marxism provide Brecht a way out of his essential pessimism. Brustein observes that Brecht responded more to the critical than to the utopian side
of Marxism (253). Marxism, in effect, provides Brecht with a social frame of
reference within which he would continue to write plays marked with a strong
sense of the power of aesthetics, particularly the *Verfremdungseffekt* and the
Gestus. Blau comments that Brecht was primarily interested in the "*structure*
of appearances and the historical *gestus*: *what's* happening and *why* and *who* is
paying for it at one end or the other of a scale of victimization" (*Eye* 177).

But one must not forget that much of Brecht is also rooted in Hegel's insights
into the nature of the split between the role of the individual as a citizen of the

state and his private desires as an individual living in a bourgeois society. In Brecht's early plays *Drums in the Night* (1920), *In the Jungle* (1923), and *A Man's a Man* (1926), he argues against the uniform, socially constructed assembly-line version of humanity in favor of the private desire of buying a fish for one's private pot. In particular, the dramatic quality of the Hegelian dialectic with its coexistence of opposites and the merging of thesis and antithesis appeals to Brecht's aesthetic sense of the ambiguity of all things. The Hegelian oppositions between speculative and intuitive thought, between reality and idealism, between emotion and intellect, between pleasure and learning, are extended by Brecht to the subject matter for his didactic theater (Voigts 29). For Brecht, as he stated in *Flüchtlingsgespräche* (Refugee Conversations), Hegel extended ambiguity by denying that one equals one, not only because everything that exists is continually turning into something else, namely its opposite, "but because generally nothing is identical with itself" (quoted in Esslin, *Brecht* 152). In addition, Hegel's discourse on the detail assigns to the epic the description of "what is there, where and how deeds have been done" (Hegel 1: 254); Hegel's emphasis on the detail contributes immensely to Brecht's own observation on the important place for realistic detail in his own theatrical practices. The detail as aesthetic category undergirds the entire edifice of Hegel's *Aesthetics* and enables him to draw generic as well as period distinctions. Brecht echoes Hegel's attention to the "fullness and detailing of external fact" (1: 254) in his own delineation of realism: "There are a few generally recognized criteria of realism, such as the true detail" (*Werke* 22.2: 637).

If we take Borges's observation that "each writer *creates* his own precursors" to heart (201), we can determine that for Brecht Hegel is such a precursor. As Brecht later attempts to situate *In the Jungle* within his collected works, he recognizes in the play's "boxing match" between Garga and Shlink an illustration of Hegelian oppositions of idealism versus pragmatism even before he had read "a single line of Hegel" (Völker, *Brecht* 79). Even though Brecht was to become a devoted student of Marxist dialectics, his acknowledgment of Hegel's influence is significant, for in his theatrical practice, Brecht's use of the play of oppositions suggests an interest more in the means than in the end, a method that is ultimately more Hegelian than Marxist.

It is significant that Brecht undertook his study of Marx and revolutionary theory in 1929 with Korsch, with whom he was to maintain a lifelong friendship, and it was through Korsch that Brecht first made contact with workers' groups, trade unionists, and members of the Communist party. Korsch was one of the first to develop a neo-Marxist theory of revolutionary and democratic socialism. He provided a critique of the sort of state socialism, centralized bureaucracy, and new forms of domination that he saw developing in the Soviet Union. For Korsch, the workers' councils best represented political and economic fusion, and hence he suggested that the councils were to be the focus for renewed revolutionary struggle.[3] When one examines Brecht's *The Measures Taken* (1930), one can see that he is less concerned with teaching the immediate political lessons of Marxism than with exploring Marxism's wider implications as an account of human conduct and as an embodiment of the spirit of detached scientific inquiry whose importance for constantly rethinking Marxism he had learned from Korsch.

It was also Korsch who called Brecht's attention to the necessity of developing a historicist version of Marxism. Korsch was convinced that there was an inner connection between Hegel's German idealism and Marxism on the grounds that both were expressions of the same revolutionary process. Korsch understood that Marxism, in order to be considered as scientific methodology, must use self-reflexivity in order to stand aside and judge its historical development. In both the early *Lehrstück* period and in his later plays written in exile, one can see that Brecht well understood the lessons of his former teacher, and one can discern in Brecht's attention to historicism a similar self-reflexive impulse. Korsch's understanding of the changing ground rules as revolution is confronted by counterrevolution is also reflected in Brecht's plays in which it is impossible to determine the rules, the strategy for winning, or the probable outcome of the conflict.

Korsch also served as a catalyst in the relationship between Brecht and Benjamin. Although it is likely that Brecht first met Benjamin through Asja Lacis and not through Korsch, Benjamin and Brecht's mutual position as outsiders with ambivalence toward joining the Communist party becomes an important link. In his writings on Brecht, Benjamin calls attention to the playwright's uncanny sense that ideological positions, as if pieces of a chess game, are changeable since "the function of each piece changes after it has stood in the same square for a while" (Benjamin, *Brecht* 108). Brecht's relationship to Benjamin differs significantly from that to Korsch, for the exchange of ideas between Brecht and Benjamin is much more reciprocal. Not only is Marxism relevant to their discussions, but both Brecht and Benjamin feel strongly that changes in society brought about by revolution require a revolution in aesthetics as well.

The association of Brecht and Benjamin arose out of their common rejection of the traditional view of art as an autonomous object, and like Georg Lukács and Theodor Adorno, they looked to art as a means of uncovering social contradictions. Benjamin plays a significant role in validating Brecht's epic theater aesthetics. In the confrontation of the four Marxist theorists—Lukács, Adorno, Brecht, and Benjamin, each of whom focuses on his own version of the role of the artist at a time of imminent social change—Benjamin sides with Brecht and supports Brecht's views of promoting an aesthetic of contradiction against the more conservative, though differing theories, of Lukács and Adorno. Thus, only Brecht and Benjamin were in agreement about the positive ideological function of avant-garde techniques as important contributions to demystifying the notion of art as an autonomous practice in "the age of mechanical reproduction" (Benjamin, "Art" 217). According to Benjamin, "the technique of reproduction detaches the reproduced object from the domain of tradition" and substitutes "a plurality of copies for the unique experience" (223). The aesthetic object is thus no longer invested with traditional norms and values such as uniqueness, and hence the spectator's perception is pried loose from the "secular cult of beauty" (226). As Elizabeth Wright mentions, Benjamin and Brecht hoped with the help of avant-garde techniques to break up the continuity of the historical world and thus "reveal the contradictions under capitalism as a first step in the de-reification of modern mass urban life" (*Brecht* 76). The extent to which Brecht's conversations with Benjamin on the reproducibility of art objects validated his own ideas of the practices of the artistic marketplace is evident in his conclusions that originality is related to "worn out notions of defining property, or ownership" (*GW* 15: 202).

What is also relevant to the discussion of Brecht's dramatic theory is Benjamin's conclusion that human conditions are not governed by individual fate but by external conditions that are enacted upon a community. For Benjamin, while death in tragedy represents "individual destiny," the *Trauerspiel* (mournful drama) "takes the form of a communal fate" (*Origin* 136). Though in Brecht's epic theater manmade social conditions are presented as being potentially alterable, the attention to the ruptures of representation characteristic of the epic point to the similarity between the *Trauerspiel* and Brecht's epic theater. Benjamin's conclusions on the similar nature of the *Trauerspiel* and Brecht's epic theater reveal that the role of the epic in dramatic texts has a particular function of pointing to the gap between the demands of the social order and individual experience.

Concurrently, Benjamin describes the baroque allegory in terms that reproduce his reflections on Brecht's theater. In particular, he pays attention to the allegory's tendency to lay bare the device, "posing motto and caption in blunt, obtrusive relation to the visual figure" (Benjamin, *Origin* 22) and describes the *Trauerspiel* as fragmented, device-baring, nonhierarchical, and densely encoded, all characteristics he is later to champion in Brecht's drama. In turn, Benjamin's distillation of the characteristics of Brecht's theater serves as a stimulant for Brecht to refine his theory and move beyond the early stages of epic theater. At the same time, the rather heated ideological debate between Brecht and Lukács was to provide Brecht with further material for his theoretical explorations. Lukács, in his championing of bourgeois culture to the Stalinists as an approriate model for Socialist Realism forces Brecht to assume a counterposition and to address such issues as the conflict between "realism" and experimentation.

The dispute between Brecht and Lukács takes place in 1938 in the course of a debate on expressionism that was waged in the columns of *Das Wort*, a review founded by Germans in exile. The debate soon focuses on their differing conceptions of Socialist Realism, which had become the official aesthetic of the Soviet Union since A. A. Zhdanov's call to the First All-Union Congress of Soviet Writers as "engineers of the human soul." According to Zhdanov, the purpose of the writer was to present artistic images whose "truthfulness " and "historical exactitude" must "be linked with the task of ideological transformation" (quoted in Esslin, *Brecht* 188). Lukács, in order to modify the simplification demanded by Socialist Realism, attempts to enlist the great bourgeois novelists to the limited canon of Socialist Realism by bringing to light their natural tendencies toward critical realism, but, in creating the link between critical realism and Socialist Realism, Lukács takes a strong position against the subjectivist and formalist tendencies of movements like expressionism, as illustrated by the "formalist" methods of writers like Brecht.

Consequently, the confrontation between Lukács and Brecht centers on their opposite conceptions of what constitutes "realism" within the context of the declared political struggle of Marxism. For Lukács, it is important that Marxist aesthetics reflect continuities of realism and rational thought in the great nineteenth-century epic novels of Honoré de Balzac, Stendhal, and the more recent ones of Thomas Mann. Lukács is concerned with providing appropriate precursors of socialist art, for he feels that modernism's irrationalist heritage has led to fascism as a "grotesque culmination" of its journey. Consequently, he assumes that "a correct epistemology and ontology will produce significant art" (Eagleton, *Benjamin* 84). Lukács believes that in critical realism the alienation of the individual is transcended by the understanding that emerges regarding social totality, and the critical-realist writer has intuitively provided a model for the future "by embodying in his work the necessary transcendence of the contradictions" (Wright, *Brecht* 74). Brecht, on the other hand, believes that realistic experience cannot be recuperated through representation since that in itself represents a false consciousness, one that ultimately does not allow the observer to see the underlying abstract connections of economic and social processes. Lukács is interested in the progress of history as it works itself through naturally from critical realism to Marxism; Brecht, however, is more interested in historicizing and demonstrating that, despite changes, nothing has changed. Brecht's method is to displace the action of his plays into a historicized—but not necessarily historical—past, and in his great epic tragedies such as *Mother Courage* or *Galileo*, Brecht purposefully sets the action into the recognizable but not real Thirty Years' War or the Renaissance in order to demonstrate, as Galileo says in his experiment of the sunspots, that we cannot take steps but crawl by inches.

In his redefinition of "realism," Brecht insists that the term must be "spring-cleaned" before "it can be applied" (*Theatre* 108). As justification for the spring-cleaning of the term, he calls attention to the conception of *Volkstum*, the broad masses of people, who respond to art that is "popular." For Brecht, "popular" means being intelligible to broad masses, and popularity is achieved by taking over the popular "forms of expression and enriching them" (*Theatre* 108). Unlike Lukács, Brecht insists that the conception of realism needs to be broad and political and free from aesthetic restrictions and independent of convention. Thus, while realism as propounded by Lukács privileges the continuities of bourgeois culture with its continuous script-endorsing progress, Brechtian theory, in order to foreground historical discontinuities, corresponds to a vast program in democratizing theater by means of including elements borrowed from popular entertainment forms such as the cabaret, the circus, the sports arena, film, radio serials, and detective fiction.

To Brecht, realist art means "laying bare society's causal network" in order to expose the problems afflicting society (*Theatre* 109). He concludes that "concreteness" and "abstraction" are essential characteristics of realist aesthetics. But the terms themselves are contradictions; mere abstraction is of no use to Brecht, but neither is mere concreteness. Benjamin recounts that when Brecht was living in exile in Svendborg, he had painted the words "truth is concrete" on one of the beams supporting the ceiling of his study (*Brecht* 108). In his theatrical practice he liked solid stage properties because they announced themselves in their concreteness and hence did not impede the spectator's freedom to speculate about the truths they represented. Brecht's training for actors was to produce a similar effect on the spectator; through attention to concreteness, the actor was expected to draw together the activity of the manual worker, the detached philosopher observing the action, and the actor commenting on the role of both. Realism for Brecht represented a scientific approach whose end was that if you are going to change the world, you have first to recognize its ways.

Brecht's conflict with Lukács in the late 1930s teaches him to reduce to reasonable proportions his natural tendencies toward avant-garde aesthetics, and his "Short Organum," written in 1948, reflects his adjustment to both Lukács's criticism and the reality of transplanting his aesthetics to the Berliner Ensemble in East Berlin. In order to make his adjustment to Socialist Realism as expedient as possible, Brecht changes the critical terms of his aesthetics. He no longer rails against Aristotelian principles, as he did in theorizing his epic theater; instead, he harnesses Aristotle and puts him into the service of promoting his theater for a "scientific age." According to Brecht, the scientific attitude includes an aesthetic framework, and he calls upon Galileo, Einstein, and Oppenheimer in support of the argument that pleasure is an important consequence to be derived from making scientific discoveries. These scientific discoveries are not unlike those to be experienced by the spectator once he has "scientifically" come to the proofs that reveal the structure of society (*Theatre* 179–205).

However, it would be imprudent to turn Brecht's theoretical writings exclusively into examples of political correctness whose sole purpose was to submit to the "influence" of external political pressures and events. Despite the adjustments Brecht made in his theory to the realities of keeping his theater free from the pressures that the aesthetics of Socialist Realism demanded, Brecht's theoretical writings from "The Modern Theatre Is the Epic Theatre" (1930) to the "Short Organum" (1948) continue to remain vaguely and contradictorily defined. The center of gravity is constantly shifting; thus one travels from a critique of the Aristotelian dramatic form, presented as a particuarly vehement reaction to the notion of identification, to Brecht's renewed interest in the possibility of imitation and critical realism. In the end, he abandons the overly stressed binary oppositions between epic/dramatic, formalism/realism, and introduces in "Short Organum" the possibility of following "the thread of Aristotelean demonstration" from the concept of imitation to the spectator's pleasure at that imitation (Pavis, "Brecht's Notion" 39–40).

Having come to terms with Lukács upon his return from the United States to East Berlin, Brecht had to accommodate another formidable theoretical opponent, in this case Constantin Stanislavsky. Unlike the Brecht/Lukács conflict, which was directly played out in the press, the Brecht/Stanislavsky conflict had more to do with the dominant influence of Stanislavsky's fourth-wall illusionism in the Moscow Art Theater, at that time promoted by the Communist party as the method for theatrical representation. This was made clear when in 1953 a Stanislavsky conference was organized in East Berlin, and actors and directors from East Germany were lectured on the absolute obligation of having to follow Stanislavsky's method. This method, according to the party organ *Neues Deutschland*, most effectively represented the "fight against formalism and cosmopolitanism on the stage." As a result, Helene Weigel was forced to defend the Brechtian practices of the Berliner Ensemble by showing the parallel approaches of both directors that consisted in their "accuracy of observation, ensemble acting, truthfulness, naturalness" (quoted in Esslin, *Brecht* 167), and Brecht himself promptly included a serious study of Stanislavsky into the program for actors at the Berliner Ensemble.

Brecht's critique of Stanislavsky dates back to the period of Zhdanov's proclamation of Socialist Realism in 1934, and though Brecht never overtly rejects the official aesthetics, his remarks on Stanislavsky in such essays as "Alienation Effects in Chinese Acting," "The Street Scene," and "On Experimental Theatre" deny by implication Stanislavsky's naturalistic practices. He sees Stanislavsky's Method pervading the practices of the "left" theater in New York and simultaneously becoming the method in the new Soviet orthodoxy. According to Brecht's *Journals* entry of 5 March 1939, the "great emotions racket" generated by the discovery of behaviorism and psychology results in "the souped-up petty bourgeois, a romantic character" (24). Brecht hopes that Piscator's influence in Moscow might halt the Stanislavsky Method's growing influence, but Piscator's own position in Moscow soon becomes highly uncomfortable, and he too is forced to emigrate.

Unable to stem the tide of Socialist Realism's pervasion of theater aesthetics, Brecht forms the Diderot Society to act as an international society promoting an exchange of theoretical ideas. Brecht finds support for his own theory in Diderot's observations on the paradox of the actor. It is significant that Brecht draws on Diderot as his precursor, because Diderot in his time of the Enlightenment also promoted a new type of drama whose subject was to be drawn from everyday, middle-class life to depict what he termed "social conditions." Like Diderot, writes Darko Suvin, Brecht started from the assumption that human reason can understand and master even the most unreasonable instincts and "the most complex circumstances, even the bloodiest contradictions" (65). Diderot felt that the bourgeois play would necessitate a new type of acting whereby the actor, through his art, would transmit to the audience through "tears flowing from the brain" (Suvin 65) the illusion of the emotion he does not himself feel. Diderot's description of the paradox of the actor as both actor and beholder of social roles serves as an appropriate antecedent to Brecht's epic theater and as basis for the *Gestus* and *Verfremdungseffekt*. At the same time, Diderot's ideas on the social function of the theater were promoted by Soviet scholars as representing the first stages in which "the philosophy of acting was put on a solid scientific materialist basis" (Miller 34), a paradox that Brecht surely recognized. In this manner, Brecht was able to promote Diderot's concept of the theater as a site for both learning and pleasure and as an alternative to Stanislavsky without committing ideological fallacies.

Not only does Diderot provide Brecht with an alternative for evading the strictures of Socialist Realism, but the paradoxes in Diderot's novel *Jacques the Fatalist and his Master* concerning the irreconcilable differences between the master and his servant, and between determinism and free will, allow Brecht to playfully assume Diderot's dialogic mode in his play *Puntila and Matti, His Hired Man*. This paradoxical play provides Brecht with the opportunity to both explore and possibly disclose the range of interpretations of reality. The comic distantiation of Diderot's method in *Jacques the Fatalist* inhibits Aristotelian empathy, and similarly Brecht's use of comic distantiation in *Puntila and Matti* allows the audience to "think about the action," a process that clearly involves their mental faculties. Since thinking itself is pleasurable, this does not wholly dissipate the comic effect. Brecht's observations on laughter are echoed in Benjamin's comments on Brecht's theater that there is no better starting point for thought than laughter since "spasms of the diaphragm generally offer better chances for thought than spasms of the soul" (*Brecht* 101).

Since Brecht's essays promoting the *Gestus* and *Verfremdungseffekt* and his attempts to found a Diderot Society date back to the 1930s, it is evident that he is on dangerous ground during the Stanislavsky conference, as accusations charging him with practicing "formalism" mount from all sides. The evidence is overwhelming, for indeed Brecht favored the "splendid remoteness" generated by the Chinese actor's use of alienation effects over "the creative mood" demanded by the necessity of the actor's conversion into the character of the Stanislavsky Method. While the Chinese actor's reliance on the *Gestus* produces a "coldness" akin to Diderot's paradox of the actor, who also promotes a remoteness from the character, Stanislavsky's method for actors, according to Brecht, engenders the rape of the actor "by the individual he portrays" (*Theatre* 92–93). Since the method actor always speaks in the first person and the present tense and absorbs all stage directions into a living illusion of the actual reality, Brecht instead proposes an actor who, in order to distance himself from the character, relies on the *Gestus*, and in rehearsal uses the third person and past tense, sometimes even reading the stage directions (Bentley, "Ibsen" 242). While the Brechtian actor is trained to be objective and to demonstrate the behavior of the character "in such a way that the bystanders are able to form an opinion," the Stanislavsky method actor relies on subjectivity in "the engendering of illusion." In Brecht's theater the spectator is cast in the role of a bystander in order to weigh the presented evidence; in the illusionistic theater the spectator is pulled into the story in order to "experience" the represented events (*Theatre* 121–28).

Brecht, fully aware of the fate that other formalists such as Meyerhold and his friend Tretyakov faced during the Stalinist purges, concedes that "some things can be learnt from Stanislavsky," among them the attention to a play's poetry, the responsibility to society in presenting art based on the social meaning of craft, reliance on ensemble acting, attention to the structure of the play and its supporting details, the fundamental truthfulness of the actor's observation of the character based on a methodical approach, and Stanislavsky's continuous renewal of approach in the stagings at the Moscow Art Theater (*Theatre* 236–38). Though privately Brecht later admitted to Willett that Meyerhold was "murdered of course" (*Brecht in Context* 238), publicly Brecht started building a careful defense by shoring up his situation by means of references to Swift, Voltaire, Lessing, and Diderot, all recognized as appropriate precursors of Socialist Realism. Esslin ironically states that Brecht "just manage[d] to secure the all-important epithet 'realist' " (*Brecht* 197) and was rewarded with the Stalin Peace Prize in 1955.

A paradoxical consequence of Brecht's rehabilitation as an important Communist writer is that upon Khruschev's dismantling of Stalin's ideological framework, including that of Socialist Realism, Brecht himself assumed an important position as a precursor of revolutionary thought. Consequently, a study on Stanislavsky and Brecht by Tamara Surina written in 1975, after the rehabilitation of Meyerhold, accords both Stanislavsky and Brecht equal prominence, and by a curious reversal attempts to justify Stanislavsky's approach as being quite similar to that of Brecht. This is a paradox that Brecht, the elusive "obliterator of traces," would have appreciated.

The Brechtian paradox leads to Barthes's conclusion that there are many Brechts: on the reactionary right his work is discredited because of his communism; on the right, while his works are accepted and "enlisted under the banners of eternal theater," the man is dissociated from them and consigned to party politics. Similarly, on the liberal left Brecht is seen, both in theory and practice, as the Marxist "humanitarian champion of man." And on the far left, in order to promote his romantic revolutionary beliefs, his theory and theatrical practice are minimized as "formalist" or "modernist" (*Critical* 272). Thus, in the end, the extreme right and left merge in their belief that literature must fit an ideology. The question that emerges for our time is what kind of re-reading "will produce another Brecht" (Silberman, "Postmodernized" 1), a Brecht more suitable for the turn of the century?

As Barthes mentions, Brecht can be approached only "through the voices that our society spontaneously employs in order to 'swallow' him." Paradoxically,

Brecht cannot be reduced to a single position for he "exposes" anyone who talks about him (*Critical* 272). What emerges from these paradoxes is that Brecht was himself not a unified man but a veritable committee of mixed tendencies, a colloquium all to himself, in which different voices spoke up at different times. The proliferation of Brecht refutes, as Michel Foucault writes, the notion of "author" as constituting the "privileged moment of *individualization* in the history of ideas" (141). Instead we should look to Brecht as a producer "of the possibilities and the rules for the formation of other texts" (Foucault 154), a process of continuous mediation of past and present art and an attitude that requires abandonment of convenient paradigms established by tradition. The process, as I have tried to show, is ultimately continuous, for the past, as Jauss writes, needs the productive work of understanding in order "to be taken out of the imaginary museum and appropriated by the interpretative eye of the present" (*Toward* 72).

NOTES

1. A brief and incomplete overview of the studies on Brecht and influence includes Baum; Berg-Pan; Buck; Eaton; Grimm; Lyon, *Kipling*; Oba; Schoeps; *Shaw*; and Surina.

2. I have drawn on a number of sources for biographical background on Brecht; among them Esslin, *Brecht*; Fuegi; Voigts; Völker, *Brecht*; and Willett, *Brecht in Context*.

3. See Korsch, *Theory*; and Douglas Kellner, "Brecht's Marxist Aesthetic," in this volume.

WORKS CITED (SEE ALSO REFERENCE GUIDE TO WORKS CITED IN ABBREVIATED FORM)

Barthes, Roland. *Critical Essays*. Translated by Richard Howard. Evanston: Northwestern University Press, 1972.

———. "The Death of the Author." In *Image-Music-Text*. Translated by Stephen Heath. New York: Hill, 1977. 142–48.

———. "From Work to Text." In *Textual Strategies*. Edited by Josué V. Harari. Ithaca, NY: Cornell University Press, 1979. 73–81.

Baum, Ute. *Bertolt Brechts Verhältnis zu Shakespeare*. Berlin: Brecht-Zentrum der DDR, 1981.

Benjamin, Walter. *The Origin of German Tragic Drama*. Translated by John Osborne. London: Verso, 1985.

———. *Understanding Brecht*. London: New Left, 1972.

———. "The Work of Art in the Age of Mechanical Reproduction." In Benjamin, *Illuminations* 217–51.

Bentley, Eric. "Ibsen, Shaw, Brecht." In *Commentaries* 215–47.

———. "The Influence of Brecht." In Kleber/Visser, *Re-interpreting Brecht* 186–95.

Berg-Pan, Renate. *Bertolt Brecht und China*. Bonn: Bouvier, 1979.

Blau, Herbert. *The Audience*. Baltimore, MD: Johns Hopkins University Press, 1991.

———. *The Eye of Prey*. Bloomington: Indiana University Press, 1987.

Borges, Jorge Luis. *Labyrinths*. Edited by Donald A. Yates and James E. Irby. New York: New Directions, 1962.

Brustein, Robert. *The Theatre of Revolt*. Boston: Little, 1962.

Buck, Theo. *Brecht und Diderot oder über Schwierigkeiten der Rationalität in Deutschland*. Tübingen: Niemeyer, 1971.

Clark, Katerina, and Michael Holquist. *Mikhail Bakhtin*. Cambridge, MA: Harvard University Press, 1984.

Eagleton, Terry. *Literary Theory: An Introduction*. Minneapolis: University of Minnesota Press, 1983.

————. *Walter Benjamin or Towards a Revolutionary Criticism*. London: Verso, 1981.

Eaton, Katherine Bliss. *The Theater of Meyerhold and Brecht*. Westport, CT: Greenwood, 1985.

Esslin, Martin. "Some Reflections on Brecht and Acting." In Kleber/Visser, *Reinterpreting Brecht* 135–46.

Foucault, Michel. "What Is an Author?" In *Textual Strategies* 141–60.

Fuegi, John. *Bertolt Brecht. Chaos, According to Plan*. Cambridge: Cambridge University Press, 1987.

Grimm, Reinhold. *Brecht und Nietzsche oder Geständnisse eines Dichters*. Frankfurt am Main: Suhrkamp, 1979.

Harari, Josué V., ed. *Textual Strategies*. Ithaca, NY: Cornell University Press, 1979.

Hegel, Georg Wilhelm Friedrich. *Aesthetics: Lectures on Fine Art*. Translated by T. M. Knox. 2 vols. Oxford: Clarendon, 1975.

Jauss, Hans Robert. *Aesthetic Experience and Literary Hermeneutics*. Translated by Michael Shaw. Minneapolis: University of Minnesota Press, 1982.

————. *Toward an Aesthetic of Reception*. Translated by Timothy Bahti. Minneapolis: University of Minnesota Press, 1982.

Kott, Jan. *Shakespeare Our Contemporary*. New York: Doubleday, 1964.

Kristeva, Julia. *Desire in Language: A Semiotic Approach to Literature and Art*. Edited by Leon S. Roudiez, translated by Thomas Gora, Alice Jardine, and Leon S. Roudiez. New York: Columbia University Press, 1980.

————. *Revolution in Poetic Language*. Translated by Margaret Waller. New York: Columbia University Press, 1984.

Miller, Arnold. "Diderot and Soviet Criticism, 1917–1960." *Diderot Studies* 15 (1971): 23–36.

Mueller, Roswitha. "Montage in Brecht." *Theatre Journal* 39.4 (1987): 473–86.

Mukařovsky, Jan. *Aesthetic Function, Norm and Value as Social Facts*. Translated by Mark E. Suino. Ann Arbor: Michigan Slavic Contributions, 1979.

————. *Structure, Sign, and Function*. Translated and edited by John Burbank and Peter Steiner. New Haven, CT: Yale University Press, 1977.

Oba, Masaharu. *Bertolt Brecht und das Nô-Theater: Das Nô-Theater im Kontext der Lehrstücke Brechts*. Frankfurt am Main: Lang, 1984.

Pavis, Patrice. "On Brecht's Notion of *Gestus*." Translated by Susan Melrose. *Languages of the Stage: Essays in the Semiology of the Theatre*. New York: Performing Arts Journal Publications, 1982.

————. "The Classical Heritage of Modern Drama: The Case of Postmodern Theatre." Translated by Loren Kruger. *Modern Drama* 29.1 (1986): 1–20.

Schoeps, Karl-Heinz. *Bertolt Brecht und Bernard Shaw*. Bonn: Bouvier, 1974.

Shklovsky, Viktor. "Parallels in Tolstoy." *Twentieth-Century Russian Literary Criticism*. Edited by Viktor Erlich. New Haven, CT: Yale University Press, 1975. 81–85.

Silberman, Marc. "The Politics of Representation: Brecht and the Media." *Theatre Journal* 39.4 (1987): 448–60.
———. "A Postmodernized Brecht?" *Theatre Journal* 45.1 (1993): 1–19.
Sternberg, Fritz. *Der Dichter und die Ratio*. Göttingen: Sachse, 1963.
Surina, Tamara M. *Stanislavskij i Brecht*. Moscow: Iskusstvo, 1975.
Suvin, Darko. "The Mirror and the Dynamo: On Brecht's Aesthetic Point of View." *Drama Review* 12.1 (1967): 56–67.
Szondi, Peter. *Theory of the Modern Drama*. Edited and translated by Michael Hays. Minneapolis, University of Minnesota Press, 1987.
Voigts, Manfred. *Brechts Theaterkonzeptionen: Entstehung und Entfaltung bis 1931*. Munich: Fink, 1977.
Weber, Carl. "Vaudeville's Children: The Impact of American Performance Traditions on Brecht's Theory and Practice." *Brecht-Jahrbuch/Brecht Yearbook* 15 (1990): 55–70.
Wirth, Andrzej. "Vom Dialog zum Diskurs: Versuch einer Synthese der nachbrechtschen Theaterkonzepte." *Theater heute* 1 (Jan. 1980): 16–19.
Wojcik, Manfred. *Der Einfluß des Englischen auf die Sprache Bertolt Brechts*. Berlin: Brecht-Zentrum der DDR, 1982.

3

Brecht's *Lehrstücke*: A Laboratory for Epic and Dialectic Theater

KARL-HEINZ SCHOEPS

By the end of the 1920s, Brecht had reached a new phase in his personal philosophy and artistic development. Up to that time, the rebellious bourgeois nihilist had no philosophic or artistic concept for altering those conditions in the theater that he strenuously objected to. This changed dramatically with his conversion to Marxism and his encounter with such eminent composers as Paul Hindemith, Kurt Weill, and, notably, Hanns Eisler.[1] He now attempted to revolutionize the stage with new forms of musical and theatrical productions such as the "culinary" operas *The Threepenny Opera* and *Rise and Fall of the City of Mahagonny* on the one hand, and the more austere didactic plays/plays for learning on the other.

In a sense, all of Brecht's plays are *Lehrstücke* owing to Brecht's lifelong concern with matters of pedagogy. But during the period of around 1928 to 1930, the playwright experimented with the specific *Lehrstück* form of theater and wrote plays such as *The Flight over the Ocean*, *The Baden-Baden Cantata*, *He Who Said Yes*, its counterpart *He Who Said No*, *The Measures Taken*, and *The Exception and the Rule*—all of which constitute the main body of the *Lehrstücke* texts. Although *The Horatii and the Curiatii* of 1934 and the fragment *Demise of the Egotist Johann Fatzer*, a project Brecht began in 1927, for chronological and other reasons fall somewhat outside the "canon" of *Lehrstücke*, they will be briefly considered here; however, "Der böse Baal, der asoziale" (Evil, Asocial Baal), an abortive attempt to rewrite *Baal* in the *Lehrstück* mode, has been excluded from discussion. *The Mother* (1931–1932), to be sure, was "written in the style of the *Lehrstücke*" (*Werke* 24: 115), but it is a full-length play written with an audience in mind rather than a training piece for actors without spectators—hence, for our purposes, it does not merit extensive comment.

The *Lehrstücke* "belong to the nexus of Brecht's most innovative writing" (Mueller 79); they were the laboratory for his experimentation with epic or dialectic theater that determined the rest of his career as a playwright. The *Lehrstück* experience, which entailed the representation of the relation between the individual and the collective and their respective responsibilities, remained with Brecht throughout his life. He considered this experience of such importance that when, late in life, he was asked about the theater of the future, he answered that the future belonged to his play *The Measures Taken* (Wekwerth 78).

Although the *Lehrstücke* were intended to be used for the political instruction of those participating in the production rather than for presentation on a stage before a passive audience, most of them were eventually performed before audiences. They were conceived as educational experiments in the art of dialectical thought and as points of departure for further explorations and discussions of the issues presented. Most of the *Lehrstücke* were performed by students in schools and workers in workers' organizations without spectators, and the "actors" often took turns in acting out different roles in order to develop the art of "dialectic thinking."

Brecht, like many other playwrights and composers of his time, was dissatisfied with the traditional stage and music-hall productions that demanded a passive consumer. He wanted to activate this spectator/listener and turn him/her into a producer of art. Unlike conservative traditionalists, Brecht wanted to break out of the temples of high art and make art accessible to a much broader audience. Traditional theaters were too commercialized for Brecht's goal of "develop[ing] a type of theatrical event that would influence the thinking of those participating in it" (Steinweg, "Äußerungen" 249–50). He wanted "art for the producer rather than art for the consumer" (250). In this effort, he also recognized the great possibilities of the developing technical media such as radio and film.

The first version of *The Flight over the Ocean* under the title *Der Lindbergh-flug* (Lindbergh's Flight) cannot be considered a *Lehrstück* in the strict sense of the term. When it was written in 1928–1929 in collaboration with Elisabeth Hauptmann and Kurt Weill for the Baden-Baden music festival, Brecht's Marxist views had not yet solidified; he still admired rather uncritically the technological progress as expressed in Charles Lindbergh's feat, and he did not yet use the term *Lehrstück*. In the 1930 version, Brecht, now an avowed Marxist, changed the title to *Der Flug der Lindberghs* (The Flight of the Lindberghs), added the subtitle "a radio *Lehrstück* for boys and girls" (*Werke* 3: 401), and strengthened the didactic, collective, as well as ideological aspects of the play, notably by adding a section called "Ideology" that was to be sung (or spoken) by the "collective Lindberghs" rather than a single, individualized Lindbergh. The emphasis shifted from narrowly defined technological progress to the unlimited possibilities of human advancement, particularly in the political and sociological fields. In the "ideology" section the flight represents the victory of the progressive (i.e., Marxist) over the primitive (capitalist) world view: "Disorder still reigns in the cities / Resulting from ignorance which is god. / But the machines and the workers / Will fight it, and you, too, / Should participate in / Fighting against what is primitive" (*Werke* 3: 17).

Der Lindberghflug, as it was now called, was first performed as a cantata, conducted by Hermann Scherchen, at the Baden-Baden music festival on 27 July 1929. The major portion of the score was composed by Kurt Weill, while Paul Hindemith contributed the scores for the nature pieces (Fog, Snowstorm, Sleep) and the final chorus. The performance was intended to show to the spectators and radio people present at the production how they could use the new medium of radio productively. Actors on stage demonstrated to spectators in the stalls how they, as listeners at home, could participate in a radio production. On stage, the flier (the radio listener at home) was placed opposite a radio set and posters; projections were used to enlist the participation of the audience. The audience was meant to see and learn how radio and listener can join together to produce the piece in which the radio supplies the frame the listener needs to perform his/her part. The production was well received by the press—it was labeled the most important event at this festival—as well as by the attending representatives from radio stations and from the *Schulmusikbewegung* (movement for school music) (*Werke* 3: 407). After World War II, for a radio broadcast planned by the South German Radio in December 1949, Brecht demanded that the play be broadcast with a prologue and that the name of Lindbergh be expunged because of the latter's alleged admiration for the Nazi *Luftwaffe*. Henceforth the play became known as *The Flight over the Ocean*.

While Hindemith composed only a small portion of *Der Lindberghflug*, he wrote the entire score of what was intended as a companion piece and turned out to be his final collaboration with Brecht, *The Baden-Baden Cantata,* the text of which was published under the title *Lehrstück* in 1929. Brecht wrote the first version of the text in 1929 in collaboration with Elisabeth Hauptmann and Slatan Dudov (in German, Dudow); it was first performed at the music festival in Baden-Baden on 28 July 1929, a day after *Der Lindberghflug*. Brecht himself directed, and his old friend Caspar Neher was responsible for the stage design, including film clips and projections.

The Baden-Baden Cantata presents four fliers who have crashed after soaring to ever greater heights because of their fascination with machines and technology at the expense of ignoring human concerns and the plight of ordinary people. They ask for help, and the ensuing scenes examine the question of whether man is a helper of man. In one of the most shocking scenes in any of Brecht's texts, two clowns dismantle a consenting or acquiescing Herr Schmidt by sawing off his hands, his feet, and, finally, his head in a drastic demonstration that answers the question posed in the negative. The audience is supposed to learn and realize that a society in which man does not help his fellow man and in which acceptance of inhuman conditions is the norm is in desperate need of change. As in several of Brecht's plays, the learning experience is supposed to result from viewing a negative example. But as Brecht demonstrated in his early play *A Man's a Man*, the dismantling of the individual can also be seen as a positive aspect in the construction of a collectivist society (Knopf, *Theater* 79).

Unlike Brecht, Hindemith was not interested in pursuing ideological goals. He considered the score pure *Gebrauchsmusik* (applied music) "which would educate via the pleasure of performing together; it simply added a further stratum by means of an instructive text" (Willett 127): "Since the Lehrstück has the purpose of engaging all those present in the execution of the work and does not, in the first instance, wish to create a particular impression as a musical and poetic utterance, the form of the piece is, if possible, to be adapted as required" (*Werke* 24: 90; translated in Hinton 209).

In the Baden-Baden production, Hindemith and Brecht also intended to activate the audience. A "gelernter Chor" (professional choir), lead by a speaker, was placed opposite the audience and sought to involve it in the action on stage by leading a kind of "antiphonic" singing (Knopf, *Theater* 80). The parts intended for the audience were kept simple and were projected on screens; the audience was helped along by professional singers placed in its midst.

Initially, Brecht seems to have agreed with Hindemith's intentions that the performance would have primarily a formal function (see Hinton 208–209), but he soon abandoned this view and opted for a more didactic approach. As he noted in his annotations to the 1930 version, he definitely wanted to create a particular impression that performing and acting were no longer ends in themselves but served specific purposes: "Even if one expected . . . that here certain spiritual, formal congruencies come about on a musical basis, it would never be possible for such an artistic [artificial] and shallow harmony, even for a few minutes, to create on a broad and vital basis a counterbalance to the collective formations which pull apart the people of our times with a completely different force" (*Werke* 24: 91; translated in Hinton 209). Therefore, Brecht's revisions of 1930 served to strengthen the ideology of the play that no longer served "a vaguely Utopian technological paradise" but "the socialist state of the future" (Milfull 73). In view of their artistic and ideological differences, it came not as a surprise that soon after the music festival of Baden-Baden Brecht broke with Hindemith, mainly on political grounds. Brecht's association with Weill lasted somewhat longer but came to an end for similar reasons; their rivalry was exacerbated by the quarrel over the primacy of text or music, a quarrel that was intensified by their respective groups of supporters.

Whereas for Brecht Hindemith had not gone far enough by merely composing *Gebrauchsmusik* instead of Brecht's *angewandte Kunst* (art for a purpose), Hindemith's concept was also criticized from another quarter. Arnold Schoenberg, the great innovator of twentieth-century music, vigorously defended the autonomy of art and the inviolability of the work. He rejected Hindemith's concept of *Gebrauchsmusik* as incomprehensible and morally wrong (Hinton 210). While Schoenberg bemoaned the end of traditional art, Brecht welcomed it (Hinton 211). In this context, the reaction of two Schoenberg students to Brecht/Hindemith's *Lehrstück* is significant. Anton Webern found it "horrible," while Hanns Eisler, who had broken with his teacher and was on the verge of becoming Brecht's most important and most congenial musical collaborator, thought the premiere "splendid" and the music "magnificent" (Hinton 211). In general, Hindemith's music was favorably received as an example of a new kind of *Gemeinschaftsmusik* (communal music), while the reactions to Brecht's text were mixed at best, and the clown scene in particular attracted little praise.

In the wake of their successful *Der Lindberghflug*, Brecht and Weill collaborated on another *Lehrstück* for a 1930 Berlin festival devoted to new music. Elisabeth Hauptmann had translated the Japanese *No* play *Taniko (The Valley Hurling)* from a 1921 English translation by Arthur Waley and showed it to Kurt Weill, who was looking for a text that could be used as the basis for a *Schuloper* or an opera for schools and/or for schooling or training. Inasmuch as the original Japanese play took place in a pedagogical environment, it proved useful for Weill's intentions, and he turned Hauptmann's translation over to Brecht for an adaptation that was called *He Who Said Yes*.

Weill's idea for a *Schuloper* was closely related to his new concept for operas, as he explained in the program for the premiere. According to Weill, the concept of *Schuloper* allowed for a number of possibilities. To begin with, such an opera could be used for the training of individual composers or for an entire generation of composers. Weill emphasized the importance of creating basic forms (*Urformen*) of opera particularly during times such as the late 1920s when the genre of opera was being redefined. He considered his teacher Ferruccio Busoni's *Arlecchino* (1917), Hindemith's *Hin und Zurück* (1927; Back and Forth), Darius Milhaud's *Der arme Matrose* (1926; The Poor Sailor), and his own collaborative effort with Brecht, *The Threepenny Opera*, as models.[2] Second, the *Schuloper*, in Weill's view, could serve as a training ground for the performance of operas. For this reason, the operas should be "simple and natural" so that even children could perform them. But they could also serve to train opera singers in the art of simplicity and naturalness so sorely lacking in contemporary opera houses. Third, *Schuloper*, as the term indicates (*Schule* means "school"), was a form of opera to be performed in schools. Weill intended to extend the traditional realm of music production and consumption—radio, concert, theater—to include schools and workers' choirs. For that reason, he insisted that works had to be created in such a way that they could be performed in those new arenas. His (and Brecht's) *He Who Said Yes* was conceived for performance in schools with students as performers and as set and costume designers. But for Weill, simple did not mean simplistic; he insisted on a certain level of musical difficulty that required careful study on the part of the performers. The aspect of training and rehearsing—rather than the final product, the performance—was of greatest importance. In other words, it was the educational effect that mattered most: "*It is, therefore, extremely desirable that a schoolpiece present the boys with an opportunity to learn something beyond giving the pleasure in performing*" (Weill 62; Weill's italics). While the schooling process was intended to start with the music, the performers' intensive study of music could, in Weill's opinion, also lead to their intensive study of an idea.

The Japanese *No* play is a highly stylized form of theater that employs few actors, who are portrayed as types rather than psychologically developed characters; deals with myths and legends; and makes use of dance, music, masks, and stylized gestures. Since Brecht and Weill had no use for the mythical and legendary elements of the original *Taniko* play, they made a number of changes, although they left the bulk of Hauptmann's translation (around 90 percent) unchanged. In the Japanese play, a student at a temple school, whose mother has fallen ill, accompanies a teacher on a pilgrimage to pray for his mother's recovery. When the student is unable to continue the dangerous and arduous journey through the mountains, he is hurled into the valley in accordance with an ancient custom. In the Brecht/Weill version, the school is no longer a temple school, the journey is now a scientific expedition, and the boy wants to obtain medication for his mother and instruction from the doctors beyond the high mountains. Most important, before he is hurled into the valley he is asked to give his consent: "Most important of all is to learn consent" (*Werke* 3: 49). This emphasis on consent, with which *He Who Said Yes* opens, closely links it to the *Baden-Baden Cantata* and to *The Measures Taken*, to be discussed later. The main lesson to be learned by the students is the realization that joining a group or a community entails accepting certain duties and obligations (Weill 68).

He Who Said Yes was first performed by students of various Berlin schools on 23 June 1930. Discussions after this performance and a subsequent student performance at a secondary school in Berlin-Neukölln caused Brecht, at the end of 1930, to revise *He Who Said Yes* and add a counterplay, entitled *He Who Said No,* in which the boy refuses to consent. In the new version of *He Who Said Yes*, Brecht strengthened the motivation for the trip and the boy's death; the trip was of vital importance for the community, and the sick boy endangered the mission of the collective. *He Who Said No*, on the other hand, retained much of the original version of the first version of *He Who Said Yes* (the ancient custom as reason for killing the boy) but questioned the conditions that lead to the boy's death. The boy challenged the validity of the old custom that condemns him to death: "I demand a new custom which we should introduce immediately, namely the custom to think anew in each new situation" (*Werke* 3: 71). Since the two plays complement each other in a dialectical fashion, Brecht insisted that they be performed together. There is no music for the two new plays, and Brecht never witnessed a production during his life time.

The Measures Taken, a collaborative effort with Eisler, is Brecht's best known but also his most controversial *Lehrstück*. According to Albrecht Betz, it is "the most advanced outpost of political art of the late Weimar Republic. In it, Eisler and Brecht fused the genre each had evolved in his own field into a synthesis which possesses a lasting power to disturb'' (Betz 93–94). As in *He Who Said Yes*, the main theme is consent and self-sacrifice in the service of a higher goal. In fact, Brecht worked on the first version of *The Measures Taken* while revising *He Who Said Yes*; the first scene of *The Measures Taken* was originally entitled ''Der Jasager (Konkretisierung)'' (He Who Said Yes: Concretization).

Essentially, *The Measures Taken* takes the central issue, consent and self-sacrifice, from *He Who Said Yes* and places it in the political context of the revolutionary phase of the civil war in China 1927–1937, when the Communists fought against Chiang Kai-shek's Kuomintang party for control of the country. In the play, four agitators have returned from China and demonstrate to a control choir (the party) why they were forced to kill one of their comrades. Against the explicit advice of the agitators, the comrade had endangered their revolutionary mission through well-intended but misplaced compassion. Instead of convincing the coolies to band together and demand better shoes for their arduous task of pulling boats through canals, he helped individual coolies when they slid in the mud and fell. Instead of distributing leaflets urging workers to strike, he attacked a policeman who mistreated workers and had to flee and hide. Instead of enlisting the aid of a Chinese merchant in the common struggle against the English, he refused to sit down to dinner with the exploiter of the coolies. Instead of waiting for the right moment to start a general uprising, he could not bear injustice and oppression any longer and revealed himself as an agent from Moscow who had come to help the downtrodden. When this spontaneous act threatened the premature exposure of the agitators and gravely endangered their mission, they had no choice but to kill their comrade. The young comrade agreed that there was no other way and consented to his execution and elimination in a chalk pit ''in the interest of communism'' (*Werke* 3: 125). The control choir approves the measure taken by the agitators; in an addition to the 1931 version, the control choir concludes the play by pointing to the resourcefulness and the sacrifices that are necessary to change the world:

> But your report also shows us how much
> Is necessary to change the world:
> Rage and toughness, knowledge and indignation
> Rapid action and serious consideration
> Cold patience and endless perseverance
> Comprehending the details and comprehending the whole:
> Instructed only by reality we are able
> To change reality.
>
> (*Werke* 3: 125)

The young comrade's mistake was not his compassion but his penchant to place individualism above collectivism and his refusal to heed the advice and guidance of the Communist party that derives its wisdom from the Marxist classics, as the control choir states:

> For the individual has two eyes
> The party has a thousand eyes
> . . . . .
> The individual can be destroyed
> But the party cannot be destroyed
> For it is the vanguard of the masses
> And conducts its struggle
> With the methods of the classics which are taken
> From their knowledge of reality.
>
> (*Werke* 3: 120)

With contemporary hindsight after the downfall of communism, this infinite trust in the wisdom of the Communist party appears seriously misplaced, but around 1930, during the time of the Great Depression, communism seemed to provide the only hope for the future of great numbers of people in different countries.

The first version of the play was written in the spring of 1930 in collaboration with Slatan Dudov and Eisler; further versions followed throughout the 1930s. The central theme in the different versions remained basically the same; the differences lie mainly in Brecht's attempts to clarify the agitators' actions. In the first two versions, for example, the agitators travel to Urga (today's Ulan Bator) rather than to Mukden. In the later versions, direct references to the plot of *He Who Said Yes* were eliminated. In the 1931 version, the agitators no longer seek to build up the Chinese Communist party but do attempt to support it. In addition, Brecht made a few small but significant changes in three of the four tests given to the young comrade in order to demonstrate more clearly the nature of his failure and to justify his elimination—although these changes did not placate all critics.

All versions are written in a highly poetic language with liturgical qualities inspired by the Lutheran Bible. Scene 8, ''Die Grablegung'' (The Internment), is a clear reminder of the passion of Jesus Christ. *The Measures Taken* is a model of epic or dialectic theater in which the possibility of emotional identification is minimized and perhaps excluded by means of the highly stylized language and the structure of the play. The action has the character of a demonstration; it is frequently interrupted by the chorus, which is reminiscent of Greek drama, and its generalizing comments such as praising the party. The spectators' identification with the young comrade is made difficult by the stipulation that the four agitators should alternate taking his part—a process that robs the young comrade of a distinct identity, including that of gender (Knopf, *Theater* 98). Thus, the young comrade never emerges as a genuine character but serves as a point of departure for the discussion of correct behavior in revolutionary situations and the moral dilemmas fostered by revolutions; the play is an experiment to probe patterns of revolutionary behavior.

The first performance did not take place in the Neue Musik Berlin (a place devoted to the performance of new music) as planned because its directors, including Hindemith, objected to the "low quality" (i.e., the obvious political bent) of the play (Knopf, *Theater* 93). Brecht and Eisler protested this blatant attempt at censorship but to no avail; the work premiered instead in a different Berlin location in a midnight performance on 13–14 December 1930, in which three combined workers' choirs and a small orchestra participated. Directed by Dudov and conducted by Karl Rankl, a Schoenberg student who became musical director at Covent Garden, the production featured Eisler among the singers, and Helene Weigel, Ernst Busch, and Alexander Granach among the actors. The audience rewarded the performance with "friendly applause" (*Werke* 3: 440), but the critics' reaction was decidedly mixed. Heinz Stuckenschmidt, one of the few objective critics, in his review in the *Berliner Zeitung* of 15 December 1930 called the work "prophetic" and the production "a huge success." Without judging the political implications of the play he felt that "the attempt at instructing the people through artistic means has never found a more appropriate and more inspired but less demagogic form" (Steinweg, "Äußerungen" 325). The reviewer for the *Berliner Tageblatt* of 15 December 1930, on the other hand, called it "a didactic play of communist militarism [*Militarismus*], miserable, longwinded and boring" (Steinweg, "Äußerungen" 335). However, more disturbing for Brecht and Eisler were the attacks from their new friends of the Left. The critic of the Communist paper *Rote Fahne* rejected the text as "not Marxist," and Otto Biha from the paper *Linkskurve* found the play too idealistic, too theoretical, and the portrayal of the party dead wrong. According to Biha, the real party would never have condemned the young comrade to death.

The criticism most damaging to Brecht and Eisler came from Alfred Kurella, who would later become an important cultural functionary in East Germany. He called Brecht a "bourgeois poet" and the play "an experiment with inappropriate means," representing "typically petit bourgeois intellectualism." In his view, the young comrade, not the agitators, demonstrated correct political behavior; the Brecht/Eisler version constituted a "deviation to the right" and "opportunism on the right" (Kurella 77–82).

With the rise of National Socialism in Germany, the right-wing attacks on *The Measures Taken* increased in frequency and severity. In January 1933, shortly before the Nazis came to power, a performance in the city of Erfurt was interrupted and closed by the police. The organizers were accused of high treason for staging a play that "teaches strategy and tactics of communist subversion, especially in the army and in the police" (Steinweg, "Äußerungen" 416). The right-wing press was elated: "It is high time that our theaters again become temples of true German art" (Steinweg, "Äußerungen" 415). A few weeks later, Brecht and Eisler left Germany; all experiments to break out of these "temples of true German art" came to an abrupt halt. After the war, the play became a tool of the Cold War. In 1948, Ruth Fischer, Eisler's sister, who had played a prominent role in the German communist party in the 1920s, denounced Brecht as "the minstrel of the GPU [Stalin's secret police]" (Fischer 615) and the play as a prefiguration of the Stalinist terror that was to erupt in the Moscow trials. *The Measures Taken* also figured prominently in Brecht's hearing before the House Un-American Activities Committee in October of 1947. Fearing that during the years of the Cold War the play would be used for anti-Communist propaganda, Brecht and Eisler refused to give permission to produce it, as Brecht made clear on 21 April 1956 in a letter to Paul Patera, a Swedish teacher who wanted to stage it in Uppsala: "*The Measures Taken* was not written for an audience but for the instruction of the performers. As we know from experience, productions before an audience usually cause nothing but morally negative reactions. For a long time, therefore, I have not given permission to produce the play" (Steinweg, "Äußerungen" 258).

As a collaborative effort between playwright Brecht and composer Eisler, *The Measures Taken* represented their endeavors to reform—if not revolutionize and politicize—existing art forms. Both came from bourgeois backgrounds; they had come to the theater metropolis of Berlin to make their mark, and they had converted to Marxism at approximately the same time. Thus they were ideally suited for each other in cooperating on a project of an obviously political nature such as *The Measures Taken*—a project that most likely would not have found the support of either Hindemith or Weill.

Brecht and Eisler first met in the summer of 1929 at the music festival in Baden-Baden where Eisler was represented with his *Opus 9*, entitled *Tagebuch* (Diary), a "little cantata for three female voices, tenor, violin, and piano." A "counter-provocation addressed to his teacher" Schoenberg, Eisler wrote the piece in 1926, half a year after he had broken with Schoenberg and moved from Vienna to Berlin (Betz 49). Schoenberg's former star student Eisler joined the proletarian movement in 1927, became the music critic for the Communist paper *Rote Fahne*, and composed for workers' choirs and communist agit-prop troupes such as *Rotes Sprachrohr* (Red Mouthpiece) that engaged in agitation and propaganda. Brecht and Eisler's interests coincided in that both were dissatisfied with the exclusivity of art in drama and music, respectively. Eisler searched for new forms in music that could serve the proletariat. In an October 1927 article in *Rote Fahne*, Eisler bemoaned the isolation of modern music from the people and the community:

The result of this "timelessness" and restrictiveness of music is that modern music has no public—no one wants it. As a private concern of well-educated people, it leaves the proletariat cold. The bourgeoisie hankers after stronger stuff for their diversion and entertainment. Like virtually no other art, modern art is leading an illusionary existence which can only be maintained by artificial means.

The disintegration of bourgeois culture is expressed more markedly by music than by any other of the arts. Despite all its technical refinements it is an empty vessel, for it is devoid of ideas and of a common language. An art which loses its sense of community thereby loses itself. (quoted in Betz 66)

Eisler demanded that the proletariat "forge for itself a new music out of the expertise and artistic methods of the bourgeoisie" (quoted in Betz 66). Art was supposed to break out of its isolation and assume a "militant and educational character" (quoted in Betz 67) that, in terms of music, demanded *angewandte Musik* (applied music). His militant songs and political ballads, as well as his collaboration with Brecht on *The Measures Taken*, constituted such efforts to create militant art. Eisler had a strong influence on Brecht; it was Eisler who turned Brecht away from bourgeois leftist radicalism and toward the workers' movement. "Eisler acted as the latter's 'emissary.' He brought the organizational connection and his practical experiences with it to his association with Brecht" (Betz 91). Moreover, Eisler was more experienced than Brecht in "reflection on revolutionary categories in Leninist thinking such as organization, class conflict and material power" (Betz 92). *The Measures Taken*, therefore, marked a turning point in Brecht's career and philosophy. At the same time when Brecht, in *Der Lindberghflug*, had uncritically admired technological progress during his brief phase of "technological optimism" (Milfull 71), Eisler, in collaboration with Robert Gilbert, had written a radio cantata entitled *Tempo der Zeit* (The Speed of Our Time), which features airplanes. But Eisler/Gilbert came to conclusions that Brecht reached only after his collaboration with Eisler, that is, that technical progress had far outstripped social progress (Betz 93). *Tempo der Zeit* included characteristic traits of the "Brechtian" *Lehrstück*; it was Eisler's first attempt "to create a form of musical theater that teaches the dialectical interaction of thought and behavior" (Lucchesi 146). Eisler, therefore, exercised considerable influence on Brecht's political development and his concept of the *Lehrstücke*.

Eisler took frequent recourse to musical forms of early church music of the sixteenth and seventeenth centuries (Betz 79, 85). The model for *The Measures Taken* is the Christian oratorio; in fact the music begins "with an almost literal quotation from the beginning of Bach's *St. Matthew Passion*" (Andriessen 364), a work that represented exemplary epic theater for Brecht. Yet the Christian positions of the oratorio are reversed, secularized, and politicized. It is no longer the individual saving the masses but the masses saving the individual. The suffering of the young comrade is shown to be avoidable; his example is a model *not* to be imitated. The Christian model with Christ on top and the masses at the bottom is inverted: the collective is on top and the individual at the bottom. Accordingly, Eisler gives the greatest weight to the choruses. In order to avoid emotional involvement, *The Measures Taken* included all the new forms of proletarian music Eisler had developed: "complicated polyphonic choruses, monodic militant songs, speaking choruses, aggressive chansons and ballads" (Betz 94). Like Brecht, Eisler opposed "beautiful singing," as he stated in his advice for rehearsals of *The Measures Taken*. Instead, he recommended that the singing should be "extremely taut, rhythmical, precise, and expressionless" (quoted in Betz 96). The presentation should be clear so that it can be understood by the audience at all times. The basic tempo of *The Measures Taken* should be march-like; it should not drag. In keeping with the basic requirements for *Lehrstücke*, the performers should not take the text for granted but discuss it in rehearsals, so that every participant will understand its message (Eisler 248). The Russian writer Sergei Tretyakov summarized Eisler's concept of the *Lehrstück* as follows: "The Lehrstück ... is a seminar of a special kind for questions of strategy and tactics of the party" (Tretjakov 248).

The Exception and the Rule, written between 1930 and 1932 in collaboration with Elisabeth Hauptmann (who provided the textual base with her translation of a Chinese play from a French source) and Emil Burri, "is centered around the ironic fact that a good deed, if it occurs, must necessarily be misunderstood in a society where the bad deed is the rule" (Schoeps 182). Although conceived for music from the outset, it was not until 1948 that Paul Dessau composed music for the introduction, the finale, the songs, and the pantomimes representing the race through the desert and the river crossing. Between 1934 and 1936, Brecht worked on a revised version, which included choruses, that was intended to be linked to then-current events in Germany. However, this version was never completed (*Werke* 24: 490).

In the first part of the play, a merchant in pursuit of a lucrative oil deal races through the Mongolian desert to reach the city of Urga (Ulan Bator) in order to beat his competitors. He is accompanied by a coolie whom the merchant murders when he feels threatened as the coolie approaches him with a water bottle in his hand that the merchant mistakes for a stone. In the second part, a law court rules that the merchant acted in justifiable self-defense since the coolie had every reason to murder him because of the mistreatment he had suffered at the hands of the merchant.

Following the *Lehrstück* mode, the play is written in the epic style. Before presenting "the story of a journey," the actors admonish the audience:

> Watch closely the conduct of these people
> Find it strange but not unfamiliar
> Inexplicable, even if widespread
> Incomprehensible but the rule.
> . . . . .
> We beseech you, do
> Not find natural that which occurs all the time!
>
> (*Werke* 3: 237)

The action is frequently interrupted by songs to prevent the spectators' emotional involvement and to make room for intellectual reflection. One of the most thought-provoking songs, for example, is that in praise of victory of the strong over the weak. "Taken from at least two separate Kipling sources" (Lyon,

Kipling 97), it is one of Brecht's strongest indictments of capitalism and imperialism via the time-honored principle of inversion (i.e., expressing the opposite of the intended meaning) in order to challenge the audience:

> The sick man dies and the strong man fights
> And that is good.
> The strong man is helped and the weak man not
> And that is good.
> Let fall what falls, even give it a kick
> And that is good.

(Werke 3: 248)

Because Brecht had to leave Germany shortly after the completion of the play,
there was no chance for a production of *The Exception and the Rule* or its
publication in Germany before the Nazi takeover. The play was first published
in 1937 in *Internationale Literatur*, Moscow, and, in a slightly revised form, in
1938 by Malik in London; it was first produced on 1 May 1938, in Hebrew, at
the kibbutz Givath Chajim in Palestine.

When he began working on *The Exception and the Rule* in 1930, Brecht
originally intended to follow the model of the dual play he had developed with
He Who Said Yes and *He Who Said No*. He planned to write two plays; one
emphasizing the rule and the other stressing the exception. In 1934, he also
developed the idea of a ''musical commentary'' with a choir on the right of the
stage representing the exploiters and a choir on the left representing the exploited. Brecht dropped both ideas, however. In its present form, the text of the
play can easily be adapted as a parable for the stage (Knopf, *Theater* 115). Of
all the *Lehrstücke*, *The Exception and the Rule* is the most easily accessible,
especially when performed by amateurs before an audience. This play was also
the first of the *Lehrstücke* Brecht published after World War II, and he recommended this play rather than *The Measures Taken* for performance in amateur
theaters (Steinweg, ''Äußerungen'' 258). Although it took a long time before
The Exception and the Rule appeared in print and on stage, it has become the
most frequently produced of Brecht's *Lehrstücke*.

The *Lehrstücke* discussed above mark a certain period in Brecht's career as
a playwright, but he returned to the *Lehrstück* model time and again until the
end of his life. Brecht employed the *Lehrstück* technique for his first play in
exile, *The Horatii and the Curiatii*, a collaborative effort with Margarete Steffin.
The plot derives from the Roman writer Titus Livius and his Roman history in
which he describes a war between Rome and a rival city state. The war is not
fought by large armies; rather, three brothers on each side, the Roman Horatians,
and their opponents, the Curiatians, represent their respective communities.
Brecht added a social component to the plot; the Horatians and the Curiatians
are no longer on equal footing. The Curiatians are rich, and in order to divert
attention from internal strife and the class struggle, they wage war against the

poorer Horatians to capture their lands and their possessions. Initially, the Horatians suffer one defeat after another but through collective cooperation, clever use of tactics, and a strategic retreat, the Horatians manage to divide and defeat the Curiatian armies and win the war. The first publication in *Internationale Literatur* (1936) is based on the second version of the play; for the Malik edition of his works in 1938, Brecht added the term *Schulstück* (play for schools or for schooling), and for the publication in *Versuche* (1955) he supplied the subtitle *Lehrstück über Dialektik für Kinder* (*Lehrstück* on Dialectics for Children).

The play is classic Brechtian epic and dialectic theater. Each side consists of three armies: archers, lancers, and swordsmen. The leaders of the respective units are delegated to do the actual fighting. A chorus of Horatians and a chorus of Curiatians accompany the action; the choruses serve as narrators and commentators. In 1938, Brecht suggested that in the style of Chinese theater each leader carry a small wooden ledge on his back. The small flags attached to the ledges represented the individual army units; for each defeated unit the respective flag was to be removed. Brecht envisioned a miniature stage design with a slanted stage and knee-high wings; obstacles such as crevices in the rocks and snowdrifts were to be marked by small signs. In the battle of the archers, the movement of the sun from dawn to dusk was to be indicated by an actor carrying a spotlight on a pole from one side of the stage to the other. The stylized, slow motions of the fighters were supposed to correspond to the slow motions of the actor carrying "the sun" (see *Werke* 24: 221).

The intended lesson of the play is the need for flexibility and adaptability to changing circumstances. Each new situation requires new analysis and different reactions. In this way, even a superior but inflexible enemy can be beaten, as the Horatians demonstrate.

Brecht wanted Eisler to compose the music for this play, but to Brecht's chagrin Eisler declined because of other commitments. As a consequence, Brecht wrote in 1938 that a production of the play was possible without music, and recommended the use of drums as a substitute (*Werke* 24: 222). Only in 1955 did Kurt Schwaen compose a score for this play (see Lucchesi 121–27). The play was first performed in 1958 in Halle, East Germany. Although Walter Benjamin called it "the most complete of all of Brecht's *Lehrstücke*" (quoted in Wyss 352), *The Horatii und the Curiatii* has remained one of the least known of Brecht's plays.

The fragment *Demise of the Egotist Johann Fatzer* offers proof that the *Lehrstück* is more than just an episode in Brecht's career as a playwright. Brecht worked intensively on *Fatzer* from 1927 to 1931, and he returned to it throughout his life. Although portions of *Fatzer* have been published and staged, the approximately 550 pages—mostly handwritten—constitute the largest fragment in the Brecht Archives. John Milfull called *Fatzer* "the most nearly complete, the most significant and the most important for an understanding of his [Brecht's] development" (65); according to the same critic, the fragment is closely connected to *Baal* and his character Herr Keuner in the "Anecdotes of

Mr. Keuner'' (Milfull 66). The plot of *Fatzer* centers on Fatzer and three German army deserters during World War I who go into hiding but are endangered by Fatzer's selfish and individualistic actions. In analogy to *The Measures Taken*, his comrades plan to execute Fatzer in order to save the collective. In 1939 Brecht noted in his *Journals* that his play *Life of Galileo* represented "technically, a great step backwards," and that the fragments *Fatzer* and "Der Brotladen" (The Breadshop) were of "the highest technical standard" (*Journals* 23). He implied that *Galileo* ought to be rewritten in the style of *Fatzer*. In the early 1950s, when Brecht wanted to write a play about the East German model worker Hans Garbe, he noted in *Journals* of 10 July 1951 (438) that he planned to do it in the verse of the *Fatzer* model. However, like *Fatzer*, the Garbe project remained a fragment; in 1956 Heiner Müller, initially a student of Brecht's, completed a version under the title *Der Lohndrücker* (The Scab). *Fatzer* was to be part of Brecht's vision of the socialist theater of the future and was intended to teach correct collective behavior; it belonged to what Brecht called "Große Pädagogik" (Grand Pedagogy) rather than "Kleine Pädagogik" (Lesser Pedagogy) designed to enlighten bourgeois societies.[3]

Brecht's idea of using plays for didactic purposes is not new; his *Lehrstücke* are part and parcel of a long tradition. During the religious strife in the sixteenth and seventeenth centuries, for example, didactic plays were commonly used in schools by both Protestants and Catholics to gain converts. One of the most successful examples of this kind is the Jesuit play *Cenodoxus* by Jakob Bidermann (1578–1639). He wrote the play during his tenure as a teacher in Brecht's home town Augsburg (1600–1602), where it was also first performed. Brecht's *Lehrstücke* continued this tradition of using plays for the purpose of ideological indoctrination, albeit in a secularized, political context rather than a religious one.

In the 1920s, Brecht's *Lehrstücke* were also part of a larger effort to reform the theater and the concert hall in particular and the arts in general. A large number of artists searched for new forms of theater and music as well as painting, design, and architecture—as evidenced, for example, by the Bauhaus movement—in order to break out of the confining parameters of the nineteenth century. In music and theater, specifically, numerous attempts were made to bridge the gap between life and art and to bring music and theater closer to the people. Seen in this context, Brecht's voice was but one among many voices, and he was greatly aided in his efforts by the composers with whom he collaborated and who shared his ideas about the function of art. In fact, since Brecht's *Lehrstücke* are so closely linked to the idea of *Gebrauchsmusik*, Klaus-Dieter Krabiel goes so far as to argue that they pertain "to the musical genre in origin, form, and purpose" (16) rather than the dramatic genre.

Brecht was not the only playwright who worked in the *Lehrstück* mode during the last phase of the Weimar Republic's existence, but he and his collaborators served as trailblazers and pioneers in this form of political drama. Following in the wake of the *Lehrstück* performances at the Baden-Baden music festival in

1929, a number of composers and writers teamed up to write *Lehrstücke*,[4] and a broad discussion pertaining to the *Lehrstücke* took place in the pages of the journal *Musik und Gesellschaft* (Music and Society). For example, Gerhart Scherler, dramaturg at a provincial theater, questioned whether *Lehrstücke* were at all suitable for professional theater productions under the then-prevailing conditions, because the *Lehrstücke* offered "a new and great movement capable of thoroughly reforming the condition and the kind of today's theater" (277).

The *Lehrstück* mode benefited from the special attention that was given to the education of young people through theatrical and musical means by such movements as the lay actors' movement (*Laienspielbewegung*), the youth music movement (*Jugendmusikbewegung*), the youth movement (*Jugendbewegung*), and the reform pedagogy (*Reformpädagogik*). Brecht's endeavors aimed at teaching and learning through performing was a basic tenet of *Reformpädagogik*; Brecht learned about the practice and goals of reforming education from his friend and, beginning in the 1950s, publisher Peter Suhrkamp, whom he had first met in 1919. Brecht developed his ideas about the *Lehrstück* in close co-operation with Suhrkamp, who contributed to the annotations Brecht wrote in 1929–1930 for *Der Flug der Lindberghs* and *Mahagonny*. Suhrkamp had ample experience in both theater and education: from 1921 to 1925, he was dramaturg and director at the Darmstadt theater, and from 1925 to 1929, he taught at the reform school in Wickersdorf both as a teacher and assistant principal (Unseld/ Ritzerfeld 67–73).

When the Nazis came to power in Germany in 1933, Brecht and most of his collaborators had to flee the country, but the Nazis continued to use music and theater for didactic and propaganda purposes in order to forge a *deutsche Volks-gemeinschaft* (a community of the German people) and overcome the internal divisions of German society during the Weimar Republic. What distinguishes Brecht's *Lehrstücke* not only from the Nazi appropriation but also from other, less politically overt efforts is their artistic mastery and their Marxist-oriented political content. In their attempt at political instruction and indoctrination they are comparable to the agit-prop theater that eschewed traditional modes of presentation. However, while the agit-prop plays presented quick and immediate reactions to daily events, Brecht's *Lehrstücke* aim at more fundamental issues in a refined poetic language. Their legacy tends to be more durable, especially in those cases in which Brecht collaborated with eminent musicians such as Hindemith, Weill, and Eisler.

NOTES

1. See also Thomas R. Nadar, "Brecht and His Musical Collaborators," in this volume.

2. See also Vera Stegmann, "Brecht contra Wagner: The Evolution of the Epic Music Theater," in this volume.

3. See also Douglas Kellner, "Brecht's Marxist Aesthetic," in this volume.

4. For example, Hermann Reutter and Robert Seitz, *Der neue Hiob* (The New Hiob); Ernst Toch and Alfred Döblin, *Das Wasser* (The Water); Paul Hindemith and Robert Seitz, *Wir bauen eine Stadt* (We Are Building a City); Paul Dessau and Robert Seitz, *Tadel der Unzuverlässigkeit* (Censure of Unreliability) and *Das Eisenbahnspiel* (The Railroad Game).

WORKS CITED (SEE ALSO REFERENCE GUIDE TO WORKS CITED IN ABBREVIATED FORM)

Andriessen, Louis. "Komponieren für *Die Maßnahme.*" In *Brechts Modell der Lehrstücke: Zeugnisse, Diskussion, Erfahrungen.* Edited by Reiner Steinweg. Frankfurt am Main: Suhrkamp, 1976. 362–82.

Betz, Albrecht. *Hanns Eisler. Political Musician.* Translated by Bill Hopkins. Cambridge, MA: Cambridge University Press, 1982.

Brecht, Bertolt. *Die Maßnahme: Kritische Ausgabe mit einer Spielanleitung.* Edited by Reiner Steinweg. Frankfurt am Main: Suhrkamp, 1972.

Eisler, Hanns. "Einige Ratschläge zur Einstudierung der *Maßnahme.*" In Bertolt Brecht, *Die Maßnahme: Kritische Ausgabe mit einer Spielanleitung.* Edited by Reiner Steinweg. Frankfurt am Main: Suhrkamp, 1972. 248–49.

Fischer, Ruth. *Stalin and German Communism: A Study in the Origins of the State Party.* Cambridge: Harvard University Press, 1948.

Hinton, Stephen. *The Idea of Gebrauchsmusik: A Study of Musical Aesthetics in the Weimar Republic (1919–1933) with Particular Reference to the Works of Paul Hindemith.* New York: Garland, 1989.

Krabiel, Klaus-Dieter. "Das Lehrstück—ein mißverstandenes Genre." *Der Deutschunterricht* 46.6 (1994): 8–16.

Kurella, A[lfred]. "What Was He Killed For? Criticism of the Play *Strong Measures* [*The Measures Taken*] by Brecht, Dudov and Eisler." In Mews, *Critical Essays* 77–82.

Lucchesi, Joachim, and Ursula Schneider, eds. *Lehrstücke in der Praxis: Zwei Versuche mit Bertolt Brecht's "Die Ausnahme und die Regel," "Die Horatier und die Kuriatier."* Berlin: Akademie der Künste der Deutschen Demokratischen Republik, 1979.

Milfull, John. *From Baal to Keuner: The "Second Optimism" of Bertolt Brecht.* Berne: Lang, 1974.

Mueller, Roswitha. "Learning for a New Society: the Lehrstück." In Thomson/Sacks, *Cambridge Companion* 79–85.

Scherler, Gerhart. "Lehrstück und Theater." In *100 Texte zu Brecht.* Edited by Manfred Voigts. Munich: Fink, 1980. 276–78.

Schoeps, Karl H. *Bertolt Brecht.* New York: Ungar, 1977.

Steinweg, Reiner. "Die Äußerungen der Autoren zur Maßnahme (Theoretische Texte)." In Bertolt Brecht, *Die Maßnahme: Kritische Ausgabe mit einer Spielanleitung.* Edited by Reiner Steinweg. Frankfurt am Main: Suhrkamp, 1972. 233–504.

———, ed. *Brechts Modell der Lehrstücke: Zeugnisse, Diskussion, Erfahrungen.* Frankfurt am Main: Suhrkamp, 1976.

Tretjakov, Sergei. "Eisler referiert von Tretjakow." In Bertolt Brecht, *Die Maßnahme: Kritische Ausgabe mit einer Spielanleitung.* Edited by Reiner Steinweg. Frankfurt am Main: Suhrkamp, 1972. 248.

Unseld, Siegfried, and Helene Ritzerfeld. *Peter Suhrkamp: Zur Biographie eines Verlegers in Daten, Dokumenten und Bildern.* Frankfurt am Main: Suhrkamp, 1975. Revised and enlarged edition. Frankfurt am Main: Suhrkamp, 1991.

Voigts, Manfred, ed. *100 Texte zu Brecht.* Munich: Fink, 1980.

Weill, Kurt. *Ausgewählte Schriften.* Edited by David Drew. Frankfurt am Main: Suhrkamp, 1975.

Wekwerth, Manfred. *Schriften.* Berlin: Henschel, 1973.

Willett, John. *The Theater of the Weimar Republic.* New York: Holmes, 1988.

Wyss, Monika, ed. *Brecht in der Kritik: Rezensionen aller Brecht-Uraufführungen, sowie ausgewählter deutsch- und fremdsprachiger Premieren.* Munich: Kindler, 1977.

4

First Comes the Belly, then Morality

HERBERT KNUST

"Literature will remember me as the man who wrote 'First comes the belly, then morality.' " If Brecht sighed when he spoke these words (Mayer 44), it was because that saucy line "Erst kommt das Fressen, dann kommt die Moral" was among the many (in)famous verses from *The Threepenny Opera* that were parroted time and again with culinary relish by a raucous audience. Such parroting was not to the taste of the eager proponent of an anticulinary theater theory of estrangement. The line about *Fressen* (gorging, devouring) and *Moral* (morality) became proverbial in Brechtian criticism as well. It is frequently (and often uncritically) quoted in contexts that seem similar to the passage in *The Threepenny Opera* without differentiating between variants of the motif that range from the early one-act piece *Die Bibel* (The Bible) to Brecht's last play, *Turandot*. Critic Hans Bänziger calls *Fressen* the asocial thesis of the early work *Baal*, and *Moral* the Marxist antithesis of the subsequent *Lehrstücke* or learning plays[1]; he concludes that in the late plays a synthesis of culinary and moral food is offered, especially in dinner scenes that bear an unmistakable similarity to the biblical Last Supper (Bänziger 496–503). Conversely, theater director Alf Sjöberg stresses the pagan-faunlike sensuality in Brecht's work that is apparent in—among other things—the vitality of characters with a lust for eating and drinking. In Sjöberg's opinion, such sensuality serves to activate political morality. Brecht's tremendous hunger for life only needs to be properly staged to effectively bring out the untenable situation of the suffering and the needy, thereby intensifying the battle against unworthy conditions of life (Sjöberg 143–

48). Another commentator calls *Fressen* "one of the most important activities in Brechtian drama"—an expression of anarchic, amoral appetites accompanied by "a hint of nausea" (Brustein, *Theatre* 256).

These sporadic interpretations offer some noteworthy, albeit contradictory suggestions for a closer examination of the reciprocal ties between *Fressen* and *Moral* that obsessed Brecht the dramatist and moralist *par excellence* throughout his life. The essence of the two concepts, and the perspectives from which they are presented, may vary; but they are always inextricably connected. In other words, whatever is expressed by *Fressen* and *Moral* is never just a sequence of two independent entities but always an interplay of two variables conditioning each other—a central constellation in Brecht's view of life. These variables often represent extreme opposites such as those of the optimist, who is always eating, and the pessimist, who is always prophesying doom. Both of them lose their appetites when they see each other—a response that must bring them closer to reality (*GW* 7: 2851). Alternately, these variables balance each other and suggest a utopian condition that Brecht often enough called for but rarely gave shape to because he knew that such portrayal of utopia would result in a diminution of the theatrical and its dramatic effects of contrasts.

In Brecht's youthful work, *Fressen* appears as existential lust and *Moral* as unexpressed challenge. This constellation explains his early figures' rebellious concern with the self, and his biting cynicism. The greed for life of *Fresser* Baal who, in rhythm with vegetative dynamics, grazes off the world, is soon satiated by his experiences and yet remains unsatiable. This greed is a private lyrical expression of Brecht's own immense hunger for life, of his sympathy for sensualist figures such as Frank Wedekind, Paul Verlaine, and Arthur Rimbaud, as well as his antipathy toward the thinblooded notion of "genius" as portrayed by Hanns Johst, with whose play *Der Einsame* (The Lonely One) he takes issue. But this boundless claim on life, tantamount to self-deification, springs from the threatening loss of the self, from the reaction against nothingness. His lust is kindled by a relentless antithesis; his soul is like "the gleam in the eyes of two insects that want to devour each other" (*CP* 1: 29); he gains a sense of heightened existence from devouring what would devour him:

> Baal will watch the vultures in the star-shot sky
> Hovering patiently, waiting for Baal to die.
> Sometimes Baal plays dead. The vultures swoop.
> Baal, without a word, will dine on vulture soup.
>
> (*CP* 1: 4)

His sensualism battles to the hilt: he even wants to swallow death, just so that he can hear the explosion when he bursts from overeating. But this idol of a god, who devours the world in order to discharge it as excrement, falls himself into nature's digestive process and must spit out again the life that he held in his teeth like prey. His voracious biological poetry, the expression of his self, ends in the world's cesspit. His self-deification is followed by atheism; his self-elevation, nourished by the debasement of others, ends in solitary extinction. It seems that even the early *Baal* is a variation of Brecht's aphorism: "People act according to their hunger and receive their lesson by death" (*GW* 18: 46).

What conclusions can be drawn? From the perspective of Brecht's later sociomoral view, it is easy to condemn Baal's individualist, amoral indulgence as essentially immoral, and to maintain that the play lacks wisdom. Nonetheless, Baal remains an ambiguous figure. For at the same time that Brecht excused Baal's asocial behavior by pointing to the asocial world in which he lived, he also compared him with the fat Chinese god who symbolizes man's yearning for happiness. Brecht has left open the question to what extent divine happiness may be realized individually; he only mentions that the god's disciples have transformed a personal striving for happiness into a social concern. Thus Baal's egoistic, materialistic lust for pleasure may be seen as both prototypical of individualistic exploitation and the source of a Communist promise. With death as the ultimate test case of all morality in life—Brecht did not believe in an afterlife—pleasure and happiness are confirmed as life values as long as they do not come at the expense of others. Baal shares this ambivalence with later figures such as Galileo, Puntila, or Azdak, whose vitality and sensual indulgence are fused, to various degrees, with guilt.

Fressen as a sign of social corruption was criticized by Brecht not just in retrospect. In the introductory dinner scene of *Baal* he ridiculed the false morals and the parasitic pleasures of the bourgeoisie. The one-act play *The Wedding* is an exposure of a blindly eating, pseudomoral society that smothers in food and cream any possibility for self-recognition. In *Drums in the Night*, a play dealing with the 1918 revolution in Berlin, the engagement feast celebration of the *petit bourgeois* Balickes, who had sponged off war deals, is dubbed *Fressen*. The celebration is marred by the returning soldier Kragler who pops up like a phantom, yet the emaciated soldier wants nothing but his piece of the pie, which, however, remains incomparably smaller than Baal's mighty "portion" (*GW* 17: 954). Kragler prefers limited but certain sensual pleasures to uncertain political morals by turning his back on the Spartacus uprising and going to bed with his reclaimed though "damaged" bride as his sorry booty. The playwight's apparent approval of Kragler's action is contradicted not only by the later Brecht, but also by the parodistic technique of the play. An echo of the first scene in *Baal* may be seen in the confrontation of the decadent lust of the profit hunters and the existential lust of the individual who does not wish to be ground into mincemeat—yet there is a notable difference in that the revolution posits a moral alternative that is dictated by social consciousness. The war has introduced a causal relationship between the appetite of the Balickes and the appetite of Kragler. This conflict forms a basic model for Brecht's later confrontation of the "great ones" (whose *Fressen* has enlarged their appetites) and their victims (the "little ones" whose hunger, brought on by deprivation, must snatch at the next-best bite without hope for a change).[2] Brecht here presents an elaboration

of the dialectic relationship of these contradictory appetites: the distinction between *Fressen* as an expression of lust and *Fressen* resulting from want follows
from the development of his socioeconomic thinking.

The potential social explosiveness obtaining from hunger, poverty, and the
needs of the masses is not yet tested in Brecht's early plays and disappears
behind a forced individualistic selfishness that manifests itself in sensual greed
and animal-like lust for prey. In *Baal*, poverty appears as something grotesque.
In *Drums in the Night*, poverty as a threat remains in the shadowy background.
In the Jungle of Cities gives more profile to misery and poverty as the result of
reckless power struggles, but physical hunger is not yet a social cause for battle.
Rather, the merciless, rapacious duel between Shlink and Garga looks like a
progressively absurd duel of principles that is conducted with ever-changing and
increasingly complicated methods. This struggle is motivated by sheer lust, passion, and extravagance; morality is only a means to an end. The appetite of
Baal's lyrical monologues has given way to a dramatic baring of teeth in dialogue—conditioned but also limited by man's infinite solitude. The metaphysical
battle turns into butchery and yields neither communication nor a clear victory.
At the end it is simply the biologically younger man who survives—and the
reader/audience is left with the impression of a tremendously wasteful, gradually
stagnating deployment of energy on the wrong object. The conflict in *In the
Jungle of Cities* reveals a new situation: if the "great ones" tear each other to
pieces, the "little ones" are devoured as well. This model is to point to a new
primary goal of moral endeavor: the struggle against the exploitation of the
hungry masses by the selfish greed of the voracious few.

A parallel to *In the Jungle of Cities* is the jungle of history in *The Life of
Edward the Second of England*, a wild bestiary in which the "great ones" act
like lustful, rabid tigers and wolves. The reversibility of all values is demonstrated in this play in exemplary fashion—especially in morality. Homer's *Iliad*,
which tells of lust, ten years of war because of a woman, and of "human lips
/ turned into tiger jaws" (*CP* 1: 182), does not serve as a warning but as a
model for the lustful relationship between the king and his favorite Gaveston,
between the queen and Mortimer, and, similar to the duel between Shlink and
Garga, also between Edward and Mortimer. This violent coveting produces thirteen years of mutual slaughtering and lays waste the whole country. The extravagance of these cravings and murderous urges is expressed in bestial images
of devouring, slaughtering, and dismemberment that swallows up the rational,
social motif of nourishment for the people. For the sake of his catamite, Edward
willfuly squanders the millet supplies in Ireland and promises a pound of meat
to each beggar. Mortimer's concern about food supplies for London fades before
his concern about his own greatness: "But don't / Fling me down headlong
between dinner and mouthwiping / Because a cub that's lost his jackal father /
Is yapping for blood" (*CP* 1: 253). Even the people's concern for food is made
relative by their craving for the man who willfully denies them their nourishment: "People of London, come and feast your eyes: / Behold King Edward

with his pair of wives'' (*CP* 1: 180). The soldier Baldock criticizes the King's mismanagement, then becomes his cupbearer, but betrays him in the pantry of an abbey so that his mother in Ireland may eat some bread. He finally wagers all of his money in a public bet as to which of the two great butchers of the people—Edward or Mortimer—will prevail. Baldock's example, which has its counterparts in the higher ranks of society, illustrates how reason is devoured by cancerous passions in an absurd world. Physical and intellectual lust, one turning into the other, wastes life and perpetuates a vicious circle by demanding ''an eye for an eye'' and ''a tooth for a tooth.''

Even the *Lustspiel* or comedy *A Man's a Man* is a new variation of man's only constant: his lust for cutting his slice of meat. The play demonstrates with almost mathematical precision how the little docker Galy Gay, who has almost no passions and only wants to buy a small private fish for dinner, is transformed—through calculable manipulation of his cupidity that does not allow him to say ''no''—into an insatiable war machine who grabs his comrades' portions and whets his growing appetite for slaughter:

> Already I feel within me
> The lust to sink my teeth
> In the enemy's throat
> The instinct to kill
> The breadwinner
> To carry out the orders
> Of the conquerors

> (*CP* 2: 70)

Significantly, this chameleon-like Galy Gay can take the place of the soldier Jip, who has been transformed on the same basis: for a piece of steak he is turned into a temple god who can be used for the exploitation of the pious. As in *The Life of Edward the Second,* the transformability and interchangeability of figures has negative results.

Nevertheless, Brecht's moral intentions become more evident. In *The Life of Edward the Second* young Edward the Third, after his father's and Mortimer's devastating reign of terror, starts a third cycle of rulership and passes sentences reflecting cold morals and dehumanized justice. This chain of events forces the question upon us of what kind of morality could lead to a change of conditions in such a vicious cycle. Brecht's negative examples are based on scientific-behaviorist grounds; they show the transformability of Galy Gay into a monstrous war machine and that of Jip into an exploiting god. Both examples are interchangeable in their rapacious destructiveness; they imply that the natural appetites of mankind may be whetted and directed to other functions as well. The question of new morals, drawn from negative examples, Brecht will answer positively as his sociological perspective grows. Brecht's developing social conscience sharpened his criticism of an amoral, individualist sybaritism that can be manipulated for exploitation. In his portrayals of clearly defined causal connections between abundance and dearth, riches and poverty, the haves and have-nots, the upper and lower classes, the big and the little ones, *Fressen* increasingly becomes the typical mark of the exploiters, while hunger becomes the main symptom of the exploited. The symbolism of the bestiary in *The Life of Edward the Second* is transferred to the brutalities of capitalism. Under the sign of the tiger, the wolf, the crocodile, the vulture, and especially the shark, the exploiter seizes his prey. All great and fat figures become suspect. The insatiability of these beasts of society increases the hunger of the little creatures who have been reduced to extreme misery. Brecht, who had once been taken to the Berlin Charité Hospital because of undernourishment, knew what he was talking about when he called hunger insufferable—not only for moral reasons (*GW* 15: 287). So he set hunger in its extreme, vital need as a main force against greedy crapulence. Beginning in 1926, Brecht's plays and theoretical writings began to reflect the confrontation of these contrary appetites within a socioeconomic context.

The Threepenny Opera, in which the reciprocal relationship of *Fressen* and *Moral* is emphasized as a main theme, represents a transitional stage in Brecht's development that gives cynical expression to this conflict of appetites. The shark Mac the Knife, the police officer Tiger Brown, and the fat exploiter Peachum are the predatory beasts of society, who either share their prey or fight over it. What is so dangerous about them is brought to our attention by Brecht's estrangement technique: unlike natural beasts of prey they cannot be recognized by their openly shown teeth, fins, and claws—they hide them behind moralizing talk and kid-gloved manners.[3] They perform their robberies under moral disguise: Peachum according to the Bible, Mac according to public etiquette, and Brown according to the law. But while they, under the pretense of such morals, land their big steaks, catch the best fish, feast on stolen goods (e.g., in the wedding scene), and victimize people in business and in war as their ''beefsteak tartare'' (*CP* 2: 167–68), others who are subject to the dictates of such morality must eat stones instead of bread, have nothing in their stomachs, and live in shacks at which rats are gnawing. A morality allowing sustenance to some but not to others, permitting man to torture, attack, ravage, strangle, and devour his fellow man by thoroughly forgetting his humanity, has lost all meaning. The logical consequence and provocative countermorality directed at those in charge has a double ring:

> First you must give us food, our proper slice—
> That's the beginning! Then go preach and moralize
> . . . . .
> There's one thing you must learn and clearly see,
> No matter how you always try to twist and cheat:
> First comes the belly, then morality.

First make it possible for those who're well-nigh dead
To cut their decent share from life's big loaf of bread.

(GW 2: 457–58)

These lines are sung by Mac *and* by Jenny, by the bourgeois exploiter *and* by the rebellious bar girl. Both subscribe to the same motto. Both place *Fressen* against *Fressen*. The "upper" circles behave like the "lower" circles, and the "lower" circles will behave like the "upper" circles. This anarchic-absurd morality of the belly points to a heightened confrontation, not to an improvement of corrupt social conditions. The parodistic complementary feast and trial scenes suggest the same. The wedding feast in the stable, an innovation compared to Gay's *The Beggar's Opera*, Brecht's source, not only shows that religion (Pastor Kimball), law (Brown), and bourgeois criminality (Mac) are in league, but also alludes to the biblical manger scene, suggesting that the message of salvation has been turned into a message of theft and exploitation, while Mac's last treat consists not of vinegar and gall but of a delicate asparagus dish. In a parody of mankind's salvation through Christ's crucifixion, Mac is saved from the gallows by a riding messenger, only to live on as mankind's plague, for as a banking magnate he will become a big-style exploiter. In the irreconcileable confrontation between the great and the small, the motto about the priority of *Fressen* no longer suffices, as *Saint Joan of the Stockyards* demonstrates most clearly. The anarchic antithesis of *Fressen* against *Fressen* will have to be modified by a new morality—but Brecht has not yet reached that point.

His next step consisted of fortifying one position by weakening the other. In the conflict between the *Freß*-urge of the exploiters and the hunger of the exploited, Brecht set his hopes as much on the decadence of those who overstuff themselves as on the strengthening of new appetites among their opponents. The corruption of capitalism extended to its art form, which Brecht called "culinarism"—consequently he used the simile of greedy ingestion (as a sign of decadent consumerism) for his criticism of current art forms as well.

"Culinarism," a word derived from the Latin *culina* (kitchen), refers to the pleasures of eating—which Brecht uses as a pungent metaphor for the corrupt pleasures of art consumption on the part of a parasitic bourgeoisie that "gobbles up" individuals on the theater stage and pays no attention to action. Such an audience "creeps into" their heroes, eats, drinks, and feels with them, consumes their joys and their pains as amusement. The drama of great individual experiences thus is a drama for cannibals who devour everything: Shakespeare's Richard III is consumed with pleasure, and Gerhart Hauptmann's Drayman Henschel is consumed with pity—and this habit of swallowing everything is worse than taking in only the bad stuff. Dramatic art interested only in consumption through sentimental participation, shared feelings, self-identification, produces merely cannibalistic theater. And what the parasitic audience does not swallow on its own will be spoon-fed to them by culinary theater critics such as Alfred Kerr or Bernhard Diebold (*GW* 18: 164), whose interpretive words have turned into a mere collection of primitive culinary sounds, a smacking of lips or belching.

What Brecht so cynically terms a theater of cannibalism is a theater of empathy that eats up, or swallows—by way of self-identification with their objects of pleasure—the audience's own, most human quality, namely its ability to think. The capacity for critical thought is made impossible by mere parasitic participation, which is nothing but an unnerving pleasure, a fruitless act of consumerism, discharging the viewer as a surfeited object without an appetite to think or the ability to make decisions.

In the opera *Rise and Fall of the City of Mahagonny*, Brecht takes aim at culinarism and the society that indulges in it. The decadence of devouring, overstuffing oneself, and being devoured, is portrayed on two levels that are linked by "gold." Mahagonny, the golden city of nets for edible birds, has been founded by sharks around a fishing pole called "Rich Man's Hotel," which functions as bait for the discontented who are ready to buy their pleasure:

> For it is a man's greatest pleasure
> Not to suffer and do what he feels like.
> That is what money gets you.

> (CP 2: 88)

Cash breeds passion: those who have money, want pleasures; and those who want money, offer pleasures. Such is Brecht's image of the capitalistic world theater, in which culinary pleasures are traded as commodities:

> First, don't forget the joys of eating
> Second, comes the sexual act.
> Third, go and watch the boxers fighting
> Fourth comes drinking as per pact.
> But mainly get it through your head
> That nothing is prohibited.

> (CP 2: 115)

Man in search of his "fun" is terrible, however—more terrible than the hurricane and the typhoon. Capitalism's uncurbed lust for devouring and culinarism's greed for pleasure lead to self-destruction. Jake the Glutton eats three calves, would like to eat himself, and falls dead. In a boxing match with Trinity Moses (who, too, may do everything for money, including unfair fighting), Joe is punched until he is dead. Paul Ackermann (Jim MacIntyre in the *CP* version), who through the worst of all sins, lack of money, has ended up on the electric chair, must recognize that the piece of meat he carved out for himself for his money, was rotten: "I ate and was still hungry, I drank and was still thirsty" (CP 2: 140).[4] At long last, Mahagonny falls in a battle of all against all.

The moral of the story is that a system of unleashed greed stuffs itself to death.[5] This was a step beyond *The Threepenny Opera*, but remained unsatisfactory inasmuch as Brecht's "epic theater," whose tenets he began to develop in connection with the *Mahagonny* opera, was not to *satisfy* demands but to *activate* them. He contrasted culinary pleasure with a different kind of pleasure that did not satiate or overstuff the recipient but strengthened his appetite in the sense of the Latin *appetere* (to strive toward, desire, obtain). Brecht did not want a consuming, digestive pleasure, but a productive, critical pleasure. To move criticism away from indulging in gormandizing, culinary aesthetics had to be replaced by socioscientific aesthetics. This critical-intellectual appetite would not be brought about by sumptuous delights for eyes or ears but rather by instructive food for thought; not by sensual empathy, but by searching observation.[6] Only then a moral perspective would arise. True, already in his early plays, especially in *The Threepenny Opera* and in *Mahagonny*, Brecht endeavored to create a critical "scientific" awareness by way of satire, parody, cynicism, and other means of provocation. But he also had learned that even parody and cynicism were liable to be digested as culinary pleasures in various quarters. Besides, he still had not given a distinct goal to the social appetites he wanted to sharpen. So he decided to thematize, after *Fressen* and culinarism, the new moral appetite and the instruction it would yield. It was an instruction he himself had just received through his recent studies of Marxism.

In his *Lehrstücke*, Brecht no longer emphasized the clash of *Fressen* against *Fressen*; rather, he played out *Wissen* (knowledge) against *Fressen*—not knowledge for its own sake, but practical knowledge that would be helpful in changing unsatisfactory conditions and would lead to a just distribution of the necessities of life. Such a distribution would enable not just a few but the people at large to enjoy life. As before, *Moral* focuses on nourishment (food) as the quintessential material substance for life and as the prerequisite for life's enjoyment. Indeed, the fight of the hungry for food becomes the most ethical of battles, all the more so since ruling ideologies branded physical needs as lowly.[7] But as Brecht had begun to emphasize intellectual pleasure rather than culinary pleasure, he now tended to let abstract thought processes prevail over sensual portrayals, hoping that instruction as theme and method would suffice in stimulating productive appetites. Sensual imagery and especially scenes of *Fressen* or hunger now give way to stylized expressions in songs or didactic chorus passages in which socioeconomic processes are succinctly analyzed, for example:

> The food from down there
> Feeds people up here
> Those who bring it up for them
> Have not fed
>
> *(The Measures Taken* 87)

> The first emerges with a smile from the dangerous water
> Onto the opposite bank which he has conquered:
> He now sets foot on his property and eats new food.

The second emerges from the dangerous water
Into nothing . . .

(The Exception and the Rule 124)

The corn is seized by the enemy.
The farmer
Wipes the sweat from his brows
But the bread is eaten
By the man with the sword.

(The Horatii and the Curiatii; GW 3: 1053)

A line such as "That won't make the flour any cheaper" was so insignificant in *The Life of Edward the Second* that it was omitted in the play's second version (Grimm 117). Reworded as "That didn't make the bread any cheaper," it becomes a refrain, spoken by the chorus in *The Baden-Baden Cantata* (*GW* 2: 592–93), demonstrating that people, in whatever they achieve, fail to help each other. Thus "helping" as a moral act must eventually be discarded in favor of changing the world—a new morality that would include the equitable provision of bread. In *The Measures Taken* this morality is underlined by the antithetical motifs of food and honor. The table-and-belly song of the businessman, who "cooks up" misery for the poor and is "nourished" by their misery (*GW* 2: 650–51), is contrasted with three examples of *Eßmoral* (morality governing eating), only one of which is honorable. This genuine morality is neither expressed in the refrain of the hungry coolies dragging the rice boats up-river: "Pull faster / We want our dinner" (*The Measures Taken* 86) nor by the young comrade's refusal to sit at the table with the exploitative businessman—although the young comrade might have gained concessions for the poor coolies. Rather, the action of those who at their sparse table are preparing their liberation meets the code of honor:

Yet the impoverished host invites Honor to supper
And out of the tiny and tumble-down hut steps irresistibly
Greatness

(The Measures Taken 83)

Compared to this morality everything else becomes relative or must be refuted. The rule of individual self-service—"Who wins the battle / Can sit down to dine" (*The Exception and the Rule* 127)—or the exceptional offer of individual help—"You give a man something to drink / And it's a wolf that drinks" (*The Exception and the Rule* 141)—are no longer acceptable. Brecht exposes especially the deceitful gift of honor to the hungry, for example: "How generously those who have eaten apportion honor to those who feed them but who themselves are starving!" (*GW* 18: 232), or: "What use is honor as my treat / If it provides no bread to eat?" (*GW* 3: 1023).

In the plays *Saint Joan of the Stockyards* and *The Mother*, Brecht returns to the scenic portrayals of the belly/morality complex and adds enhanced visual imagery to the formulaic demonstrations. Although Brecht frequently stressed the importance of drawing abstractions from processes, he also saw the need for sensory perception. Once he even compared critical art appreciation to the process of eating (*GW* 18: 274). As a man of the theater, he could not do without imagery meant to appeal to the senses. He knew that the viewers he wanted to address did not just bring their intellect but their senses as well. The appetites he wanted to instill in them ought not lose their sensual taste. In order to better communicate with the common people, Brecht had studied their speech in the vein of Martin Luther, translator of the Bible into the German vernacular, and he had studied Luther's own diction as well. In Luther he found an abundance of colorful idioms, among them many striking similes referring to eating that he found useful for the mediation of morality. As early as 1922 Brecht had termed his interest in similes one of his important concerns (*GW* 15: 62); surely, there were lessons to be drawn from culinary similes for the people. In Brecht's theoretical writings, especially in his excursions on realism, the increasing emphasis on sensuality in the cognitive process becomes evident.

Brecht continued to formulate stylized expressions of economic interdependencies by appealing to the audience's sensuality in general and their sense of taste in particular. As sensual objects of demonstration, however, realistic details become more frequent. For example, a pointed sentence from *Roundheads and Peakheads*, "one shall sit down to eat / The other slave to furnish him with meat" (275), uses elaborate imagery supported by the gestures of bending down and placing food and drink on the table:

> The landlord ponders day and night
> On how to satisfy each whim.
> And when he thinks of it, presto,
> The tenant runs and fetches it for him.
> He brings him a dish
> Of meat or fish
> And at a sign
> pours him wine

(Roundheads and Peakheads 222)

Not only thin soup, potatoes, bran, and breadcrusts may be used for building up an appetite, savory morsels as well as Lucullian delicacies may serve the same purpose (in *The Trial of Lucullus*):

> Your lamb with bay leaves and dill!
> Cappadocian venison! Those lobsters from Pontus
> And those Phrygian cakes with bitter berries!

(CP 5: 109)

But Brecht does not serve these delicacies up as culinary tidbits; rather, he uses them as bait to draw attention to paradoxes that are to help control appetites and steer them into promising directions. He finds it especially useful to pose unusual questions about the origin and supply of food, for instance: "Did they know where the corn grew that they ate? Were they familiar with the name of the ox whose tenderloins they dined on?" (*GW* 15: 210), or: "Will it lead to a tragic effect, when a spectator ponders whether the food Lear demands from his daughter for one hundred courtiers is really available at the place from where it might have to be taken?" (*GW* 15: 333). Through the paradoxical use of colloquialisms as well as punning that is difficult to translate, Brecht turns gastronomic and gastric effects into moral points. For example: the little ones are without their meal while the big ones cut their deal; starved workers hear that God's word is sweeter than cream, but the soup does not become fat through the service to God; the telescope (that could help to bring about a better life) is hawked for a sandwich (or "for a song"); soldiers lusting for a capon, mustard sauce, carrots, and red cabbage are fed up on peace already; eager for prey they must bite the dust; people are dying to serve no-good gods; the stomach does not stop rumbling on the emperor's birthday. On the other hand, Brecht endeavors to make lessons palatable by appeals to the taste buds. For example: Marxism is gobbled up like warm rolls; the people eagerly snatch and swallow the truth; compared to the tasteless, fruitless dispute among the court scientists, Galileo's appetizing findings are devoured like the apple of knowledge.

In his scenic imagery, Brecht focused the central problem of finding justice and finding nourishment in complex images of demonstrative emblematic quality. The dialectic structure of this imagery points, time and again, to the reciprocal relation of belly and morality ([*Fr*]*Essen* and *Moral*). There are the juxtapositions of dishes and book, cooking pot and Bible in *The Mother*; of milk jug and book, fat geese and scientific tract in *Galileo*. Galileo's telescope wrapped in a table cloth parallels the food wrapped in the political pamphlets that are carried by Pelagea Vlasova. Other such juxtapositions are the throwing of rolls, bread loaves, and cakes in "Der Brotladen" (The Breadshop) and in the story "Eßkultur" (*GW* 11: 337–43; Dining Culture); the rifles and bread loaves of Señora Carrar; the bread impaled on bayonets in *The Days of the Commune*. Especially complex is the final scene of *Roundheads and Peakheads*, in which the submissive tenant-farmer Callas ladles his soup at the feet of the feasting landlords while the other, rebellious tenant-farmers are lined up at the gallows. Realizing his mistake too late, Callas dumps his plate while "the barrel of a large cannon is lowered over the table" (279), and a large red sickle appears on the wall like the *mene, mene, tekel, upharsin* at Belshazzar's feast. No less striking is the visual impact of *Fear and Misery of the Third Reich*, in which the majority of the twenty-four scenes present emblematic variations on the theme of (*Fr*)*Essen* and *Moral*. Many other culinary-didactic demonstration objects may be listed: Mauler's canned meat, Joan's soup of salvation, Galileo's and Andrea's apple, Mrs. Sarti's bread cringle, Mother Courage's capon, Lucullus's cherry tree, Shen Teh's rice, Mr. Puntila's whiskey bottle, Matti's herring, Arturo Ui's cauliflower, Simone Machard's food baskets, Anna Kopecka's inn the "Flagon," Schweyk's dog, Baloun's meal, Grusha's goose, Azdak's cheese, Nu Shan's bread basket, and so on. The examples are too numerous to be fully analyzed here; a brief sketch of how in Brecht's masterworks eating is indicative of either too big or too small an appetite may suffice. In fact, Brecht once described the content of his plays in terms of those appetites (*GW* 15: 70).

In no other play has Brecht portrayed the reciprocal relation of *Fressen* and *Moral* as sharply as in *Saint Joan of the Stockyards*. Under the impact of the economic crisis of 1929 and his reading of *The Capital*, Brecht turned to Upton Sinclair's Chicago novel *The Jungle*, which he had recommended ten years earlier as an antidote to Friedrich von Schiller's ideology of freedom. In *Saint Joan*, one of his bitterest counterplays, Brecht demonstrated the dehumanizing force of hunger and the human powers that cause it. Schiller had idealized the alliance between the king of France and the god of battle, brought about by the noble, self-sacrificial spirit of the saintly Joan of Arc on the battlefields. Brecht counters this by the commercial alliance between the king of the Chicago slaughterhouses and the Salvation Army, brought about by the well-meaning naiveté of Joan Dark, angel of the stockyards. In contrast to *The Threepenny Opera*, in *Saint Joan* Brecht did not stop at the cynical-parodistic demasking of the alliance between capitalist *Fressen* and perverted Christian ethics to which the hungry and suffering fall victim; rather, he now puts Marxist morality on stage—with which he had experimented somewhat abstractly in his learning plays. The brutality of the fight for spoils, pitched to "basest gluttony, beastliest / habituation" (*Saint Joan* 60) among the hungry, clashes in powerful, contrasting images. The world is a bloody slaughterhouse: cattle, abatoir bosses, workers, and even God are labeled as consuming and consumable goods—unified by the central symbol of the bellowing ox (whose muzzles should not be gagged) destined for slaughter. This motif reaches its horribly grotesque climax in the fate of the worker Luckerniddle, who falls into a boiling vat, is processed as if he were meat, and ends up in cans. His place is desperately seized by a jobless worker, while Mrs. Luckerniddle, in a crass example of degradation caused by hunger that elevates eating over morality, is forced to an agreement bordering on cannibalism: in exchange for twenty meals she is to forget that her husband ever lived.

Into this slaughterhouse world, in which the greed of exploiters and the hunger of the exploited clash, steps Joan and urges both sides to place Christian morality above the belly (*Essen*). The contradictions in her sayings, which Brecht cannibalized from the Bible, only prove that Christian morality does not work. The sharks of the stock exchange will profit from the morals Joan is preaching to them: "You might consider helping your neighbor simply as serving a customer. Then you'll understand the New Testament in a flash, and see how basically modern it is, even to-day!" (*Saint Joan* 59). She wards off the hungry with thin moral soup, according to the biblical motto: "Man does not live by bread alone." However, she has to find out by her own example that the power of hunger is greater than "higher" concerns. Failure and privation cause her to approach Mauler, who has recovered from his pseudomoral fainting spell by eating a rare steak, an act that revives his pleasure in skinning his victims. As

Mauler feeds on her morals, Joan, starved like Mrs. Luckerniddle before her, gulps down the food from his hand, although she has just compared him to sinful Adam "with his arms in a doe again, up to the elbows, as it were" (*Saint Joan* 79). Mauler, however, looks at morals not from Adam's but from God's perspective: he is interested in reinstating the sacrifice-demanding God of the hungry, so that the sacrifice-devouring God of the slaughterhouses may continue to exist. When Joan gradually comprehends these connections, she turns to the Communists but betrays their cause because she dreads violence. She has not yet reached the lowest level of humiliation—she knows that there is still some merciful soup waiting for her. Only when hope no longer remains, when the great blizzard envelops her like a shroud in which voices call out her failure, does she realize that nothing but complete self-denial can lead to a change. She cannot prevent the new contract between the king of the slaughterhouses and the god of the Salvation Army. She had been the instigator, but now becomes the victim of that alliance which will provide just enough soup to the tired and oppressed to keep them from breaking their tools and trampling on their bread baskets. Such a plot is necessary, say the Black Strawhats, because all achievements would remain "but patchwork, lacking soul / if matter make not spirit whole"; and the bosses of the stockyard readily agree: "And ever 'tis a glorious sight / when soul and business unite!" (*Saint Joan* 120). This means that in religious practice *Fressen* is the soul of *Moral*, and in business practice *Moral* is the soul of *Fressen*, but to both the dictum "First comes the Belly, then Morality" applies. Against these two sibling souls in man, dying Joan, in a last demonstrative gesture, sets the demand for a new morality. With Hosannas on their lips, her pious allies try to spoon her a merciful soup. Twice she rejects the plate; the third time she grasps it, holds it up high like a sacred monstrance—and empties it. No other image could more pointedly translate Christian into Marxist morals of salvation; in the former the host represents the body of the Lord as symbol of divine sacrifice for the sake of mankind; in the latter the spilled soup serves as symbol of human sacrifice for the sake of mankind.

Yet this image's radical message in the service of a new humanity that has its root in early Christianity also contains the problem of Marxist utopia. Only in the face of death can Joan embrace a dogma that is to lead to enjoyment of life. In *The Trial of Lucullus* the voices of the dead, who can no longer be seduced by their senses, speak on behalf of a posterity eager to rejoice in life. In the earlier learning plays Brecht experimented with the individual's readiness for death as a prerequisite for a change warranting society's future happiness. Did he really presume to strengthen the collective appetite for a worldly life by negating the individual's appetite—a stance tantamount to asking for a degree of self-denial that is more demanding than Christian virtue? Was there not a morality *for* life that could be guided by life rather than by death and that could combine the individual's appetite more palatably with the collective's appetite?

The importance of this problem is brought home in Brecht's extended work on *Life of Galileo*, in which he merges sensuality and teaching, individualism and social consciousness in provocative patterns. Galileo's sensuality is not pure culinarism—it is wedded to reason in that he thinks because of his sensuality. Knowledge to him is passion, research is voluptuousness. He does not eat his olives "absentmindedly," gets his best ideas over a good meal, and wants the "fleshpots" while collecting his "proofs." We gain the impression that eating and learning go hand in hand not only for Galileo but for society at large. Galileo trusts that scientific discoveries will bring about a change in society that will lead to a new age with the promise of a great life for all.

When confronted with torture, the unity of his sensual and intellectual appetite is split apart. Pressed by the Inquisition, Galileo revokes his teachings but smuggles a copy of his *Discorsi* out of the country. Later he reproaches himself and blames his recantation on his concern for his physical self-interest—an act that he now condemns as a betrayal of humanity. This rationalizing view and Andrea's view of the recantation as a deceptive maneuver—which suggests a new ethics in the service of mankind—do not exclude each other. Members of an audience who, in given circumstances, were inclined to draw practical lessons from either argument would be committed to the social cause in different ways but would eventually work into each other's hands. In this context, it is noteworthy that in the last (fifteenth) scene, Brecht suggests a synthesis of Galileo's and Andrea's ethics.

The courage to face death, then, is not an absolute precondition for changing the world. The hypothesis that if Galileo had not feared death, the world would have been changed more quickly, can be countered by another hypothesis. If Galileo had acted differently in certain situations (without sacrificing himself and his teachings), the Inquisition might have been avoided. For Galileo's "crime" lies not primarily in his recantation but rather in his optimistic view that he, far ahead of his times, expected a spontaneous union of senses and reason from his compatriots as well. This faith, an oddity on the part of a man who teaches doubt, is proven wrong by the revolutionary chaos of the carnival procession and by the reaction of the Church. Galileo deceives himself when he expects people to assume that food will result from reason—without allowing for the probability that reason will result from food. Such contradictions are brought out even in casual arguments. Galileo's remark: "And you know I despise men whose brains are incapable of filling their stomachs" (*CP* 5: 26) is seconded by Mrs. Sarti's comment: " 'I knew what I was saying when I told him to give the gentleman a good dinner first, a nice piece of lamb, before they start in on his tube. Oh no!' (*She imitates Galileo*) 'I've got something better for them' " (*CP* 5: 29). These contradictions can only be bridged when interest in the "Milky Way" and other stellar constellations goes hand in hand with the interest in daily milk and the necessities of life—as Galileo himself comes to realize in his last big speech. But Andrea, adjusting to the situation, shows a practical way.

Andrea demonstrates this by the use of two objects, which in Galileo's opening words appeared as central concepts for food and knowledge, that is, milk jug and book. Andrea's crossing of the border signifies the transition to a new epoch, synthesizing science and concern for the people. With his eyes he devours Galileo's *Discorsi*, and at the same time he overhears the children's superstitious talk. They believe that the old woman Marina can obtain a jug of milk only through witchcraft. Andrea's last action, which concludes the play, consists of disseminating knowledge among the boys and providing a jug of milk for old Marina; that is, he fuses the teaching of youngsters who are thirsty for knowledge with his readiness to help the hungry of the older generation. This scene is not an isolated incident in Brecht's works; there are other examples of an attitude that bases the improvement of living conditions on circumspect, gradual education through knowledge and kindliness rather than on a plan for a violent reversal.

The attempted synthesis of sensuality and reason, of hunger for life and thirst for knowledge in *Life of Galileo* splits apart into a seemingly hopeless antithesis in *Mother Courage and Her Children*. Just as in *Galileo*, Brecht's central Janus-like motif is introduced provocatively at the outset: "How can you have morality . . . ? Everybody eats what they like" (*CP* 5: 235). In *Galileo* the children are the hope of the new generation; in *Mother Courage* they are the victims of the old. But Brecht does not glorify dumb Kattrin's self-sacrifice by which she warns a city of the approaching enemy. Instead, he calls for a moral conscience that would overcome paradoxes rather than allow unbridgeable polarizations in which a stone must begin to speak because man has turned into a beast and become silent. Bestial devouring as the metaphor for man-turned-animal by war borders on cannibalism (Boeddinghaus 81–88). In her conversations with the cook and the priest, who embody the paradoxical combination of *Fressen* (from war) and *Moral* (for war), Mother Courage comes close to realizing that greed and the "ethics" of self-sacrifice are reciprocal conditions. Yet as hyena of the battlefield she tears her bread from war loot and bites the coin earned from the war—which contributes to her family being devoured by the war. The lesson Mother Courage does not learn is demonstrated in numerous scenes suggesting alternatives; the dialectics of lust (through metaphors of eating) and reason (through moral arguments) keep recurring in such demonstrations and are evident in small particles of language structure. For example, a word beginning with *Fl* triggers not only the lust for *Fleisch* (meat) but the appetite for *Fluß* (i.e., the flow of things, change) as well (*GW* 4: 1364). The most conspicuous symbol of the culinary-didactic complex is the capon the Cook wants to buy from Mother Courage. The bird, praised as fat by the seller, belittled as wretched by the buyer, is peppered with telling associations: nutrition and extortion; revelry and starvation, rats, cooked leather straps, and stinking oxen meat; feast of honor and marauding; the miracle of five hundred breads and humans chopped to mincemeat; rolls, wine, and moldy bread. Such a treat of combined flavors is difficult to stomach and calls for food that is more palatable for body and soul.

Brecht repeatedly invoked the double meaning of *Gericht* (dish and judgment) to bespeak the well-being of body and mind. Ideally, *Gericht* as "food" and *Gericht* as "justice" form a harmonious balance or are congruous—as in the prologue of *The Caucasian Chalk Circle*. The people of two opposed villages come together and, while consuming moderate quantities of cheese and wine, peacefully resolve their disagreements on the most efficient cultivation of food in their valley. They then merrily join each other for a festive dinner. This optimistic scene is contrasted by others in which the two meanings of the word *Gericht* are split asunder, juxtaposing food without justice and a demand for justice without food—as in the confrontation of the fat farmer couple at dinner and the exhausted Grusha, who collapses from privation. Another example is the artful portrayal of dissimilar, yet interconnected, simultaneous scenes such as that of Yussup's death chamber and that of the feasting guests in an adjacent room at Grusha's wedding. The cake trays wandering back and forth between the two rooms are a symbolic commentary on the paradoxical relationship of morality and belly.

Brecht used the ambiguity of *Gericht* provocatively in scenes, images, and word plays. The song about *Gerichte* in *The Exception and the Rule* states that legal courts that slay justice feed the vultures (*GW* 2: 812–13). At the end of *Roundheads and Peakheads* the landlords prepare for the great banquet-and-gallows-scene, at which they will feed on their injustice towards the tenant farmers. The criminal Viceroy proclaims:

> And now to dinner, friends.
> I think we'll take this judge's bench [*Richtertisch*], on which
> Justice has so often been administered,
> And let it serve us as a dinner table [*Eßtisch*].

(276)

The field commander Lucullus "reports at eventide, when Rome sits down above the graves to eat / To the highest court [*Gericht*] in the realm of shades" (*CP* 5: 111). For the dual meaning of *Gericht*, Brecht coins a great many syntactic variants echoing the motif, "First comes the Belly, then Morality." Most of these variations point to the injustice of insisting on moral precepts without heeding the demands of the stomach. The split concept is also expressed in metaphors, as in the frequently used biblical phrase: "You shall not muzzle an ox when it is treading out the grain." Among Brecht's figures we encounter, time and again, eating judges and judging eaters. Eating and kitchen scenes, in which injustice is revealed or justice is much talked about, and trial scenes, in which food is discussed as a basic material prerequisite or as metaphor of mankind's existential needs at large, recur frequently in Brecht's plays.

I have mentioned the satirical nature of the eating scenes in Brecht's early works and the table (eating) and trial scenes, which complement each other; examples include such as those in *The Threepenny Opera*, with its parody of Christian morality, or that in *The Trial of Lucullus*, in which the culinary banquet is contrasted with the judgment pronounced by the dead. Brecht's most famous trial (*Gericht*) scene, however, is in the parable play *The Good Person of Szechwan*. Here the well-nourished gods, who cannot feed humanity, are sitting in judgment of Shen Teh/Shui Ta, who on the one hand gives rice to the poor but on the other hand must be unjust to survive. At the same time, these gods are exposed to human judgment. The *Gericht* dialectic, culminating in this final scene, works as a poignant structural element throughout the play. In a provocative twist, judges, whose stomachs get upset from consuming fat geese, and fat gods, who pronounce poor verdicts, are interchangeable. One must conclude that such contradictions would disappear only if god, eater, judge, and the person being judged, would become one and the same. Or, to put this utopian vision in other words: *Gerichte* (law courts, trials) would be unnecessary if people would not have to fight over *Gerichte* (food). Provocative paradoxes, according to Brecht, are to influence human actions; these paradoxes are evident in double meanings and punning:

The Wife: ... Throw a piece of meat in your garbage pail, and all the mongrels in the neighborhood will be at each other's throats in your backyard. What are law courts [*Gerichte*: law courts, meals] for?

Shen Teh: The courts [*Gerichte*, see above] won't support [nourish] him if his work doesn't. (*CP* 6: 15)

But similarly to Mother Courage, Shen Teh understands her own observation only as a fact of determinism, not as a provocation for change. Otherwise she would not subscribe so unreservedly to that endearing yet also questionable goodness that makes her give away food which she must provide through Shui Ta's hardened practices. She would not have to relentlessly pursue the boy's theft of bread by calling in the police; she would not have to become the victim of a parasitic wedding party; she would not have to teach her yet unborn child both how to steal cherries and how to shun the punishment of the law; she would not—when seeing a hungry child search for food in a trash can—have to turn into a tiger fighting for her own cub. In short, she would not need to fall from pure compassion into wolfish anger that changes her lips to fangs,[8] irreconcilably splitting her feeling and her reason apart rather than allowing her to use both faculties in a balanced way that might help bring about solidarity among the downtrodden.

In the folk play *Puntila and Matti, His Hired Man*, the *Gericht*-dialectic finds expression in real and imaginary table gatherings. In the opening scene a judge, who gets drunk while carousing with the landowner, falls off his chair and becomes nonfunctional or superfluous, as it were. Indeed, it seems as if in this scene, in which master and servant explore each other's humanity, they also find justice without the intervention of the judge. Puntila gives Matti boiled beef, scolds the wealthy farmers who deprive their domestics of food, and proclaims that he would like nothing better than to give roast beef to all his employees.[9] Matti, too, does not beat around the bush. He tells how he raised rebellious spirits that fomented rebellion on his former landlord's estate. The landlord had only given his servants measly rations, but the "spirits" quieted down at the smell of meat. However, unlike judge Azdak, who disappeared during the dance of the peacefully united couples, the judge has not disappeared during Puntila and Matti's conversation—he is only dead drunk. Indeed, Puntila's justice becomes evident only during his own inebriation. When sober he sees things differently:

No employer can stomach a servant whose eyes start popping out when he sees what the masters eat. But when a servant contents himself with what he's got, they'll keep him on forever. Why wouldn't they? When you see a servant working his fingers to the bone, you're willing to forget his faults. But when all he wants is time off and roasts as big as toilet seats, he makes you good and sick, and out he goes. (CP 6: 126)

Thus it is not surprising that Matti, who wants to help Puntila's hungry "brides," carries aquavit to his master rather than smuggling milk to the enslaved brides. But Matti's clever ruse, countering Puntila's game, is still a questionable method for a seemingly good cause inasmuch as it is a service to Puntila as well. For the master's aquavit (i.e., "water of life" or "fountain of life") springs precisely from the fact that the lower ranks cannot obtain any milk without him. Thus the comparison between the biblical and the worldly lord— the former walks on water and the latter on aquavit—has its common denominator in the faith of the people, who hope that through such miracles they will find nourishment for soul and body. Puntila's brides lose their faith when a keg of butter, a slaughtered pig, and two barrels of beer are hauled into Puntila's house, and they have to content themselves with the smell of food and with Matti's speeches about a yearned-for lunch with the judge who would surely give them justice (Recht) if they are not given anything to eat (Gericht). Having dissolved their engagement with Puntila, they continue to be concerned with the Gericht problem in two contrary examples. In one case, a servant maid waives her right to justice because of love and forfeits alimony from a farmer's son. In another case, "red" Athi, who in jail must "eat grass," refuses out of a sense of justice the buttered fish his mother brings to him from her landlady. The brides consider the maid's behavior stupid, but they deem Athi's conduct clever because it makes an impression. Yet both the "justice" on account of love and the "justice" for the sake of opposition remain breadless and do not change a thing. Would a well-dosed fusion of both attitudes lead to more practical action? Is this the question pondered by the women when they stand up and, silently, walk on? Then follows that ambiguous Gericht scene in Puntila's house that is reminiscent of the wedding banquet in The Threepenny Opera. Judge, lawyer, and priest, the representatives of worldly and religious law, convene once again at a lavish buffet. But compared to the rough, cynical stable scene in The Threepenny Opera, the engagement scene in Puntila's dining room sparkles with fireworks of culinary-moral dialectics. It culminates in a demonstration of the incompatibility of those gathered around the table because of the unbridgeable social differences that make this engagement—a union between the upper and the lower ranks—illusory. Matti rubs it in with his "salted herring" speech that not only contrasts Puntila's appetite for sandwiches and the clergyman wife's indulgence in buttered mushrooms, but also contains a bitter lesson about social (in)justice:

(*He picks up a herring by the tail.*) Welcome, O herring, thou sustenance of the poor! Appeaser of hunger at all times of day, salty twister of the bowels! From the sea thou hast come, into the earth wilt thou go. Thou art the power that fells the pine forests and sows the fields, the power that moves the machines known as hired hands, who have not yet achieved perpetual motion. O herring, you dog, if it weren't for you, we'd start asking the boss for pork, and what would become of Finland then? (*He puts it back, cuts it up and gives each of the guests a little piece.*) (*CP* 6: 172)

Bänziger calls this episode a formal analogy to the Last Supper, but it looks more like a parallel to the biblical feeding of the four (five) thousand,[10] to which Brecht refers in several of his plays. Pertinent to *Puntila and Matti* is the fact that right after the miracle of feeding the five thousand with bread and fish there occurs another miracle: Christ's walking on water,[11] which is the model for Puntila's walking on aquavit. These two allusions have one thing in common: the miraculous. But there is a twist in that in the New Testament it is through a miracle that the Lord feeds the people; in Brecht's folkplay it is a miracle that the people feed the lord. No wonder, then, that to Puntila the salty herring, which keeps the people from asking the boss for pork, "tastes like a delicacy" (*CP* 6: 172). Thus it is difficult to agree with Bänziger's point (501) that Matti's herring sermon suggests a secularized blessing of the bread. More likely, Matti's herring here has a function similar to Joan's soup. Both feedings are put offs, as they invert the holy communion between the Lord and His people into an unholy communion between factory boss and his workers, landlord and his hired hands. Similar to Joan, Matti breaks with his master: "It's time your hired hands showed you their rears. / They'll quickly find good masters when / The masters are the working men. / (*Goes out quickly*)" (*CP* 6: 191).

But in order to be one's own master, one first has to become one's own master, and not just economically. In *Mother Courage* and in *The Good Person of Szechwan*, the apparently hopeless human abasement was left unresolved, and in *Puntila and Matti* the hired man simply leaves—as if that were to dispose of the landlord. However, in *The Caucasian Chalk Circle* and in *Schweyk in the Second World War*—both plays were written at about the same time with an eye to postwar reconstruction—the progressive self-determination of the lower class becomes a constructive force. According to his conviction that an improvement of conditions is an affair of the "little ones," Brecht here focuses his attention primarily on significant processes among the little ones themselves, especially in the climactic concluding scenes showing the encounter between Grusha and Azdak, and the confrontation of Schweyk and Baloun, respectively. Metaphors of nourishment, trial and table (supper) scenes as the poetic medium of the food/morality problem are once again of central significance.

The servant maid Grusha and the village scribe Azdak, the two main figures in *The Caucasian Chalk Circle*, embody two different and paradoxical forms of behavior of the "little ones"; each attitude is doomed to failure in an unjust world. Grusha, who chooses the fattest geese for the slave-driving governor's table, is moved—influenced by her betrothal to the soldier Simon Chachava—to adopt the governor's helpless child, Michael, who was left behind by her callous mother when she fled from the beleaguered palace. In the service of the "big ones," abused by fat farmers, persecuted by fat princes, for all of whom *Fressen* comes before *Moral*, Grusha's morality consists of her self-sacrifice for little Michael. But this Christian morality of love appears to be in vain. The food metaphor in the memorable wedding/wake scene symbolizes perhaps most clearly that Grusha, by nourishing others, eats her own heart out. Everyone gets a piece of the cake: Michael, the sponging guests, and even war-dodger Yussup, thought to be dead; but the cake pan falls from Grusha's hands when she hears that the soldiers are returning from the war. Instead of picking up the cakes, she pulls out the symbolic love token she received from Simon, *"the silver cross and chain from her blouse, kisses the cross and begins to pray"* (*CP* 7: 188). Yet the fruits of her selfless acts of love come to nothing. Simon turns his back on her, the ironshirts of the fat prince capture the child, the marriage contract with "dying" Yussup, intended as a love contract for others, now becomes a forced labor contract for herself. Thus Grusha does not receive her share of the sweet cake of life—neither does Simon or Michael.

Azdak's attitude does not spring from selfless love of his neighbors but from rather egocentric slyness. Yet his calculations become problematic for him and his social concern for the people, just as as Grusha's goodness of heart becomes problematic for her and her familial interests in Simon and the child. When Azdak sees a hungry fugitive eat greedily, smacking his lips like a grandduke or a pig (both comparisons hit the mark), he merely tries to teach him the eating habits of a poor man rather than hand him over to the police. This reinforces the subsequent passage to the effect that Azdak will remain a cowardly catcher/ eater of rabbits rather than act as a heroic catcher/devourer of feudal lords (*CP* 7: 196–97). But his opportunistic anticipation of advantages due to political reversals is disappointed, as Azdak's dangerous career between the gallows and the seat of justice shows. His "Song of Chaos" demonstrates the exchangeability of the gorging of the "big ones" and the grabbing of the "little ones," the role reversal from judge to blackguard and blackguard to judge. The judge indicts others such as Ludovika for "eating too much, especially sweet things" (*CP* 7: 210), a crime of which he himself becomes guilty in that for him "it all goes into eating and drinking" (*CP* 7: 224). In this kind of reversal, where an eye for an eye, a tooth for a tooth become synonyms for justice, the lines "So he broke the laws like bread that it might nourish them'' (*GW* 5: 2086) can only suggest a precarious, unstable transitional stage in a vicious circle.

This is brought out in the symbolism of the chalk circle scene. Only through the synthesis of Grusha's morality-before-eating and Azdak's eating-before-morality, of the unselfish goodness of heart and the calculated self-interest, can the vicious circle of injustice be broken. For it is the conjunction of both forces that pulls little Michael out of this circle into a new realm, a new life. And so Michael is not just a child of love, as Grusha says to Simon, but also a child of love and of reasoning. Azdak himself assumes the role of father of a new generation when he requests that the governor's estates be turned into a park for children and be named after himself. As in *Galileo*, Brecht sets his hope on the child as the product of an educational process that emphasizes the heart and the mind alike; the child functions as the secular savior for the future, as the being in whom evolution and revolution condition each other.[12]

A similar prospect is offered by the last (eighth) scene of *Schweyk in the Second World War* in connection with the hopeful Moldau song that promises changing times: ''The great will not remain great, nor will the little remain little / The night has twelve hours, then follows the day'' (*GW* 5: 1994). The ''little man'' Schweyk finds himself between two ''big'' ones: his enemy Hitler and, on a different scale, his friend Baloun. Hitler's country-devouring hunger for power and Baloun's gluttony—''Food is his vice'' (*CP* 7: 68)—are comparable in the threat they pose to the little man. Schweyk points out this parallel in his comments on the ''big'' ones in the first act: ''to a great man the common people are a ball and chain. It's like offering Baloun here, with his appetite, a small Hungarian sausage for supper, what good is that?'' (*CP* 7: 75). Brecht emphasizes the parallels between the political and social situations at the end of the play in the bizarre encounter between Hitler and Schweyk and the subtle juxtaposition of Baloun and Schweyk. As embodiment of the ''little man,'' Schweyk succeeds in undermining the plans of the ''great'' by his deceptive collaboration; he also succeeds in surviving the war by having a keen eye on the grub dispensed on the battlefield. But survival counts for little if it means falling back on miserable living conditions. Here, again, the chances for the future are in the hands of the ''little man.'' In the synoptic juxtaposition of the two interdependent scenes among the ''little ones,'' Brecht shows the threat of death for one man and a feast of life for the other and points toward the necessity of a synthesis of behavior. While the forlorn Schweyk is wandering over the icy Russian steppes, the insatiable glutton Baloun is sitting in the warm, cozy ''Flagon'' back home. Despite his clever dialectics, Schweyk finally finds himself in a state of exhaustion and close to freezing to death because of his undaunted, self-sacrificing intercession for his compatriots. At the very moment when the selfish glutton Baloun, who is in part responsible for Schweyk's dilemma, stops eating and, in an almost Schweykian twist, recognizes the need for moderation, the endangered Schweyk is suddenly reinvigorated and raises himself from the snow that threatens to engulf him. This symbolic scene suggests that the "little ones" will only gain a chance to strengthen each other and stop being little when self-interest and altruism are joined together; when the care for one's own stomach and the care for the other's well-being balance and strengthen each other. Only the development of such socially conscious solidarity can lead to a viable means to curb the appetites of the would-be "greats."

In view of the large number of examples (proverbial phrases, contrastive imagery, scenic portrayals) in which Brecht's major concern with hunger and eating finds expression, tracing the ramifications of this central motif could be amplified. There is hardly any other modern playwright who focused as much and as consistently on the abysmal inequalities between the wealthy and the wretched of the earth as did Brecht. As we have seen, the continuous interplay of *Fressen* and *Moral* serves both a contrastive and an analytical purpose and poses the unceasing question whether a world run by those in power cannot be changed into a more just and more livable world. If we reflect on the many associations prompted by Brecht's key metaphor of eating, which is based on his moral views and present from his early beginnings through the various stages of his development to his late masterworks, we must conclude that he had no reason to sigh when he said: "Literature will remember me as the man who wrote 'First comes the Belly, then Morality.' "

NOTES

This is an adapted English version of my essay, "Brechts Dialektik vom Fressen und von der Moral," *Brecht heute/Brecht Today. Brecht Yearbook* 3 (1973): 221–50.

1. See Karl-Heinz Schoeps, "Brecht's *Lehrstücke*: A Laboratory for Epic and Dialectic Theater," in this volume.

2. This problematic "cutting-your-slice-of-the-pie" or "piece of flesh" is a recurrent motif accompanying Brecht's developing concept of *Moral*. See *A Man's a Man* (*GW* 1: 332); *The Threepenny Opera* (*GW* 2: 457–58); *Mahagonny* (*GW* 2: 560); *The Mother* (*GW* 2: 840); *Roundheads and Peakheads* (*GW* 4: 1437); *Turandot* (*GW* 5: 2249–51).

3. The women in *Puntila and Matti, His Hired Man* are deceived by similar methods: "We're too dumb for all their tricks. They fool us every time. The trouble is they look the same as we do, that's what fools us. If they looked like bears or snakes, we'd be more careful" (*CP* 6: 161).

4. Apparently an inverse allusion to justice in Christ's sermon on the mountain: "Blessed are those who hunger and thirst for righteousness, for they shall be satisfied" (Matthew 5:6; see also Luke 6:21), or to Jesus as the bread of life: "I am the bread of life; he who cometh to me shall not hunger, and he who believes in me shall never thirst" (John 6:35).

5. Brecht attached importance to the moral effects of his renewal of opera: "In the opera *Mahagonny* these are the innovations that allow theater to portray moral behavior (by revealing the mercantile nature of pleasure and of its consumers); and innovations that turn the viewers into moral spectators" (*GW* 17: 1016, n. 1).

6. Brecht criticized the abuse of scientific findings for culinary purposes not only in his theory of theater but also in his theory of radio: "It was a colossal triumph of technology to dish up a Viennese waltz and a kitchen recipe to the whole world" (*GW*

18: 119). Compare the culinary and scientific use of the telescope in *Life of Galileo* (*CP* 5: 16–17):

Senator: Mr. Galilei, I can see the fortifications of Santa Rosita.—Over there on that boat they're having lunch. Fried fish. I'm getting hungry.

Galileo: I tell you, astronomy has been marking time for a thousand years for lack of a telescope.

Senator: Mr. Galilei!

Sagredo: You're wanted.

Senator: One sees too well with that thing. I'll have to warn my ladies to stop bathing on the roof.

Galileo: Do you know what the Milky Way consists of?

Sagredo: No.

Galileo: I do.

    7. See the following examples for Brecht's emphasis on "lowly" concerns: "Times of extreme suppression are usually times when there is much talk about great and noble things. In those times, amidst great clamor that sacrifice is the main thing, it takes courage to speak about such base and small concerns like food or workers' living conditions" (*GW* 18: 223); "What is useful for the suppressed is called lowly by the suppressors. The constant concern about filling one's stomach is considered lowly" (*GW* 18: 235); "For the realist the needs of the body are of huge importance. To him it is detrimental how far he will be able to detach himself from those ideologies and moral preachings that brand the demands of the body as 'lowly.' . . . In our time of man's exploitation by man, sensuality takes the form of concern with hunger, poor housing, social diseases, perversion of sexuality" (*GW* 19: 371).

    8. As early as *The Life of Edward the Second* Brecht had used the image of man turned beast: "Instead they feel human lips / Turned into tiger jaws" (*CP* 1: 182).

    9. Ironically, Puntila's first name is "Johannes," that is, "the Lord giveth," "the Lord is merciful."

    10. Matthew 14:13–21 (15:32–39); Mark 6:31–44 (8:14–21); Luke 9:10–17; John 6: 1–14.

    11. Matthew 14:22–36; Mark 6:45–56; John 6:15–21.

    12. The child Michael ("Who is like God?") is persecuted by the princes like Christ by Herod. Analogous to Christ's resurrection (symbol of hope for heavenly bliss), Michael, on "that Easter Sunday when the great uprising took place" (*CP* 7: 195), becomes the symbol of hope for secular bliss. See the scene "Das Hohe Kind" (*GW* 5: 2008–2025), translated as "The Noble Child" (*CP* 7: 145–61), in which the oppressed people want to see the governor's heir. See also Grusha's suggestive song: "Your father is a bandit / And your mother is a whore / Every noble man and honest / Will bow as you pass. / The tiger's son will / Feed the little foals his brothers / The child of the serpent / Bring milk to the mothers" (*CP* 7: 177).

WORKS CITED (SEE ALSO REFERENCE GUIDE TO WORKS CITED IN ABBREVIATED FORM)

Bänziger, Hans. "Zuerst kommt das Fressen, dann kommt die Moral." *Reformatio* 9 (1962): 496–503.

Boeddinghaus, Walter. "Bestie Mensch in Brechts Mutter Courage." *Acta Germanica* 2
      (1968): 81–88.
Brecht, Bertolt. *The Exception and the Rule*. In *The Jewish Wife* 75–108.
———. *The Measures Taken*. In *Jewish Wife* 109–43.
———. *Saint Joan of the Stockyards*. Translated by Frank Jones. 1969. Bloomington:
      Indiana University Press, 1971.
———. *Roundheads and Peakheads*. Translated by N. Goold-Verschoyle. In *Jungle of
      Cities and Other Plays*. New York: Grove, 1966. 167–280.
Grimm, Reinhold, ed. *Leben Eduards des Zweiten von England. Vorlage, Texte und
      Materialien*. Frankfurt am Main: Suhrkamp, 1968.
Mayer, Hans. *Brecht und die Tradition*. Pfullingen: Neske, 1961.
Sjöberg, Alf. "Sensuality in Brecht." *Drama Review* 12 (1967): 143–48.

PART II

POETRY AND PROSE FICTION

5

Poetry, History, and Communication

CHRISTIANE BOHNERT

Brecht's general political stance was that of an activist intellectual who supported the workers' social struggle with his pen. The conviction that society and environment can be engineered permeates his work; this conviction finds especially powerful expression in the lengthy epic poem "Die Erziehung der Hirse" (*Werke* 15: 228–38; The Education of the Millet) and in the much more compact poem from his cycle *Buckow Elegies* "Reading a Soviet Book" (*Poems* 444). His plays, too, such as his indictment of scientists in *Life of Galileo* and his parable of *The Caucasian Chalk Circle*, affirm his unshakeable, optimistic belief that society, the human mind, and the environment can be engineered. Readers of today, who are familiar with the results of this belief, the appalling environmental disaster in the industrial areas of East Germany and Eastern Europe, may find Brecht's optimism hard to swallow—particularly if one considers how thoroughly that belief's philosophical foundation, Marxism-Leninism, has been discredited when it proved to be insufficient as the basis for a humane state. But politically and ideologically, Brecht was very much a product of his time; in a sense, he belonged to Hemingway's lost generation that in Weimar Germany faced a society too preoccupied with the past and unable to offer a grand vision of the future.

Nonetheless, Brecht's poetry, while most of its content is locked in the past, refers to the present and future in its innovative use of the lyric. In a manner of speaking, Brecht turned theoretical thoughts and intellectual associations into a respectable subject matter for a genre that until then had demanded emotions generated by moods, events, and states of mind. Perhaps unsurprisingly, Brecht's achievements, while exerting their influence on poets during the decades from the 1950s to the 1970s, have not been recognized by traditional critics. Whether middle-class or Marxist, these critics tended to look for the traditional "beauty" that they found in the poems of what Brecht called "the in-between-time" (*Journals* 91), that is, the period of exile when, for the most part, he lacked an audience and publishers, and his texts survived in dark cupboards and suitcases. These critics overlook Brecht's hints that even during these "dark ages" he aimed at activism, at the reader's response, and at relating those times directly to his work. Rather than being personal, Brecht's poetry concerns possible historical change. Its "production and function" is "historici[z]ed" (Brooker, *Dialectics* 97). Even when his Californian exile temporarily cut him off from publishing opportunities, in August 1943 Brecht insisted: "a lyrical oeuvre must have an (inner) history, which may chime harmoniously with or stand in contrast to external history" (*Journals* 291).

Brecht's collections of poems and his *Journals* reflect how subjective and objective history interweave on the individual level. The subjective history of poetry centers upon a prototypical individual that includes but is not confined to the author. Brecht's poetry depicts the individual as a mere cog in a huge machinery such as the capitalist system or the technological mobilization spawned by World War II. Brecht's *Kriegsfibel* (War Primer) is perhaps the most representative work in terms of relating subjective literary concerns to social history. It consists of sixty-seven photographs cut out from newspapers with their captions as well as historical explanations and "epigrams" by Brecht. For example, in referring to Hitler's first *Blitzkrieg*, the invasion of Poland, Brecht comments on a photograph showing a long line of vehicles occupied by soldiers:

> My friends, if you hear somebody say
> A great empire he had swept away
> In just eighteen days, ask him about me.
> Of those eighteen days, I lived for seven, you see.
>
> (*Werke* 12: 139)[1]

Brecht ironically labels Poland "a great empire." The Poles had partly fought German tanks on horseback and had been no match for the German war machine. Brecht juxtaposes the heroic braggadocio with the anonymous death of the anonymous individual driver of one of those imposing tanks.

In his *Journals*, Brecht creates the same effect when in April 1941 he connects his activities as an exiled writer in Finland with the war going on in other areas of Europe: "grete [Steffin] tortures me with scorpions because of the iambics in [*The Resistible Rise of Arturo Ui*]. . . . the slick (!) iambus is a retrograde step, compared with the syncopated one I usually use. but here it is right, i think. these are good exercises. yesterday, the war between germany and serbia and germany and greece began" (*Journals* 138). Based on his belief that the author is a partner in the struggle for historical change and literature a "practical activity," Brecht in exile is acutely aware of his geographical and mental distance from the "decisive events" that are taking place elsewhere (*Journals* 97).

In a similar manner, his poems juxtapose individuals and historical contexts. In the poem "1940," for instance, human beings and nature become backdrops of an ever more destructive technology. When the Battle of Britain seems about to be won by the Germans, the war threatens the survival of humanity in every sense of the word. Brecht hovers on the brink of despair regarding his and his contemporaries' present, whereas his long-term perspective remains buoyed by Marxist-Leninist theories and his own hopes for the human potential. In part VI of the poem, these perspectives form a thesis and antithesis. Learning seems unimportant given the impending destruction of the world as Brecht knew it. Instead of studying mathematics and languages, acquiring simple survival skills such as sign language will be sufficient to obtain "bread" and to make oneself understood. And instead of learning history as a guide to future actions, keeping one's head down is the proper strategy for survival. But hope reasserts itself as the antithesis to despair when the poet's persona addresses his son:

> Yes, learn mathematics, I tell him
> Learn French, learn history.

(*Poems* 348)

Only educating young people in sciences, languages, and history will produce a new generation capable of overcoming the societal conditions that led their parents into World War II. Individual and historical perspectives oppose each other. By keeping his or her eye on the larger context, individuals can rise above despair.

In a similar manner, all of Brecht's poems and collections of poems are cycles assembled in dialectic fashion. Brecht's cycles do not appeal to the reader's emotions by a unifying mood, theme, or place, as traditional cycles do. Instead, they collect diverse poems to create a dialectic structure of meaning that embraces thesis, antithesis, and synthesis. *Lieder, Gedichte, Chöre* (Songs, Poems, Choruses) appeared in 1934, the *Svendborg Poems* were published in 1939, *Hundert Gedichte* (A Hundred Poems) came out in 1951, and *Kriegsfibel* was published in 1955. These years were indeed "dark times for lyrics." Exile, National Socialism, impending World War II, and the Cold War necessitated the immediate publication of the poems. In January of 1934, Brecht's chief impetus had been to participate in the resistance against the Nazis. In March of 1939, his poems were geared toward "those born later." Their publication seemed to ensure the survival of a work that had been threatened by the confiscation of the third volume of a planned four-volume edition of Brecht's collected works when the Germans marched into Czechoslovakia. Yet in 1951, Brecht was hardly known as a poet in Germany; the *Manual of Piety* of 1927 was then his last volume of poetry published in Germany. In 1955, Brecht thought it necessary to intervene directly in what he perceived as dangerous remnants of fascism in his fellow country persons' behavior and attitudes. Because of the experimental nature of the *Kriegsfibel*, it was not received as a work of poetry.

Furthermore, Brecht's publishers such as Marxist Wieland Herzfelde or "bourgeois" capitalist Peter Suhrkamp were prompted by considerations of how to succeed in attracting the widest possible audience. They did not want to alienate potential readers by imposing upon them Brecht's formal experiments such as his cherished idea of disposing of capital letters or offering them dialectically constructed cycles rather than those assembled by criteria of mood. Not until 1988, when the first volumes of the *Werke* edition began to appear, were the cycles published intact and without omissions. Hence, owing to the circumstances of the poems' first publication, the dialectic structure of the cycles was not recognized until decades after Brecht's death. In the following, Brecht's major cycles will be discussed in chronological sequence.

I

Brecht's first cycle, *Tachenpostille* (1926; Pocket Manual), parodies traditional expectations of poetry. It encountered resistance from a board member at the Kiepenheuer publishing house, but it was brought out by Propyläen as *Manual of Piety* (1927). Pocket Manual was published by Kiepenheuer, however, as a limited, private edition in the form that Brecht had originally intended. Pocket Manual parodies the Bible and other works of religious edification by imitating their format and printing verses in both black and red ink. The reader was thus alerted to the fact that this was no ordinary collection of poems and that the book was to be used rather than revered as the exquisite product of a poetic genius. The term *Hauspostille* (*Manual of Piety*) is reminiscent of Martin Luther's inspirational *Hauspostille* ("Devotions for the Home") that the master of the house was to read aloud to his extended family—a family that included relatives and servants.

The inner structure of both Pocket Manual and *Manual of Piety* imitates religious texts. There are "Five Lessons," a "Guide to the Use of the Individual Lessons," and a "Concluding Chapter" that, the author recommends, ought to be read after each lesson as a kind of refrain. An "Appendix" parodies the reverence that traditional poetry and its creators were accorded by showing the author and his friends as marginal figures in bourgeois society.

Finally, the *Manual of Piety* contains tunes for several poems. The tunes work in two ways. First, they enhance the parody of the repetitiveness of religious edification by encouraging the reader to sing as if in church. Second, they contribute to the usability of the poems. Readers can sing along with the poems if they feel like it. In adding music to the poems, Brecht anticipates his later

Marxist theory that poems must have "practical value," that is, they must relate to practical concerns via propaganda or enjoyment.

From the beginning, the voices and heroes of Brecht's poetry are human beings shown either to suffer from enforced conditioning by religion and bourgeois habits or to have freed themselves from such conditioning. The goal of the *Manual of Piety* is to demonstrate how the liberation from conditioning can lead to a rich and meaningful existence. The prototypical Baal figure, who appears both in the cycle and in Brecht's first play by the same title, returns to a natural state that celebrates life. Death is regarded as a part of life, and the heavens merge with the sky to form the human horizon. At this stage of his career, Brecht's critique of society is based upon a strictly materialistic view of the individual as evidenced by the "Legend of the Dead Soldier"—also called "Ballad of the Dead Soldier" (1918; *CP* 1: 369–71)—one of the few of his early poems that he reused in later cycles and that contributed to his difficulties in getting the Pocket Manual published.

In the *Manual of Piety*, the "Legend" (*Manual* 222–29) is a statement against the abuse of individuals. In later cycles, it acquires a social dimension because it is put in the context of socially aggressive, Marxist poems. The "Legend" offers a good example of the effect that the construct of a cycle has on the meaning of single poems.

In the spring of 1918, the German imperial general staff faced a personnel shortage in the unending trench warfare. As shown in the final scene of Erich Maria Remarque's *All Quiet on the Western Front* (1928) and its movie adaptation of 1930, even soldiers who had managed to survive for four years started dying because of fatigue, despair, or simply bad luck—as Brecht's first stanza intimates:

> And when the war was in its fourth spring
> Not slowing at all down for breath
> The soldier did the only possible thing
> And died a true hero's death.
>
> (*GW* 8: 256)

Brecht's soldier attains his status as a dead hero not, as war propaganda would have it, because of patriotic fervor. Rather, he despairs of ever seeing peace that would allow him to go home. He dies from exhaustion and a feeling of futility.

The second stanza refers to the general staff's desperate move to encourage review boards to certify men fit for active service who had been previously rejected for health reasons:

> The war it seemed was not yet done.
> The Kaiser said, "it's a crime.

> To think my soldier's dead and gone
> Before his appointed time.''
>
> (GW 8: 256)

The war takes on its own life. Death is not subject to humane considerations, such as mourning a premature end to a promising life. From the individual's perspective, it is a salvation from further futile service. From the establishment's perspective, the war ended prematurely for the individual.

Brecht uses the rhetoric device of hyperbole, or paralogic, to show the absurdity and inhumanity of enforced conscription. In the ''Legend,'' physicians from a review board dig up the dead soldier's decomposing body and certify him ''A-1.'' The poem depicts an anachronistic jingoist parade, in which the dead soldier who is propped up by societal and clerical establishment figures and cheered on by the crowds, continues on his way to an infinite number of heroic deaths.

The soldier as a puppet on display demonstrates how individual soldiers have become alienated and cannot lead a fulfilling life. Brecht expresses this alienation in a recurring metaphor. The soldier's helmet blocks his view of the stars when he begins his march:

> Right away they took the soldier off.
> The night was soft and warm.
> With no helmet on your head, you'd see,
> The stars they see at home.
>
> (GW 8: 257)

Unlike Brecht's Baal figure, whose vision is only limited by the endless sky, the dead soldier wears a helmet that prevents him from seeing the sky. He has become part of the hysterical crowd and an invisible victim: ''One can only see him from above / Which only stars can do'' (GW 8: 259). The relationship between individual and nature is destroyed both by the crowds that force the soldier to conform and the uniform that forces him to die for something in which he has no vested interest. The helmet, a device designed to protect the soldier from head injuries, becomes a symbol of his dehumanizing confinement.

Apart from ''Legend,'' there are other reflections on death and the individual in *Manual of Piety*. Each of these emphasizes that humans are primates for whom death is the final end. There is no afterlife, and therefore life must be lived to the fullest. Brecht's early poetry is concerned with human rights, but it claims these rights from an anarchicistic-individualistic perspective. The inevitability of death gives rise to the demand that life must be free of physical and mental exploitation. The *Manual of Piety* does not suggest societal solutions to the loss of individuality a person faces in the modern world. Individuals must change their consciousness, so to speak, to extricate themselves from religious or societal demands that are in conflict with their enjoyment of life in the here-and-now. According to Brecht, the concept of sin and redemption has been superimposed upon humans just as have been other ideas espoused by religion and the society that it supports. Rather than helping the individual to cope with life, these ideas obscure the basic fact of the individuals' primal nature.

While some aspects of Brecht's world view that can be deduced from his early poems and plays may be called vitalistic, he is not a nihilist. Brecht regards individuals as oppressed by the church and society, institutions whose interests are at variance with the individual's interests. Brecht uses rhetorical devices in a poetic and constructed cycle to convey his criticism.

II

It is noticeable how much Brecht's world view corresponds to the concerns of Marxism-Leninism. Thus, when Brecht began to read Marx in 1926, his paradoxical statement that he found Marx to be "the only spectator of his plays" (*Werke* 21: 256) is plausible. Rather than "converting" to Marxism-Leninism because of nihilist angst, as has been alleged, Marxism-Leninism added a historical dimension to Brecht's opinions that had been lacking before. The exploitation of the individual that Brecht observed in his early period he begins now to explain in terms of the class struggle in which the interest of bourgeoisie and proletariat clash and in which the bourgeoisie, which represents the established order, seeks to prevent humanity from developing in its natural way by suppressing the workers. This suppression warps the characters of both the oppressors and the oppressed. Although the bourgeois exploiters would be expropriated in the course of a proletarian revolution, their or their descendants' humanity would gain from such a revolution.

Brecht did not have to change his means of literary communication when he studied Marxism's philosophical and aesthetic dimensions. He added a dialectic component to his rhetoric when he began to see dialectics as governing the infinite process of history, a process that was shaped by individuals. The workers' hopes for success were sustained by the knowledge that history was constantly in a state of flux. But in order to bring about change, the workers' active participation in an uprising and revolution was required.

In his poetry, Brecht felt able to rely on subjective dialectics, that is, the readers' consciousness, for conveying his message of objective dialectics, that is, historical necessity. Instead of having to rely on repetition (as he does in *Manual of Piety* by asking readers to read the "Concluding Chapter" after each lesson) Brecht now relies on a direct relationship between sender and receiver. It is from the Marxist concept of the mirrored relationship between subjective and objective dialectics that Brecht gains new confidence in his ability to persuade. His goal is to make readers "see" by writing poems that are eye-openers, as one of his last poems shows:

> And I always thought: the very simplest words
> Must be enough. When I say what things are like

Everyone's heart must be torn to shreds.
That you'll go down if you don't stand up for yourself
Surely you see that.

(Poems 452)

Between his slow appropriation of Marxism from 1926 to 1929 and the beginning of his exile in February 1933, Brecht developed poetic and dramatic forms of direct intervention. Whereas the *Manual of Piety* had largely relied on emotions, Brecht's new "directly intervening" poems and plays try to reason that readers should accept both his views and their respective roles as workers or intellectuals allied with the workers. He wrote operas, texts for song plays, *Lehrstücke*, radio adaptations, and worked with the workers' choirs in film, for example, *Kuhle Wampe* (1932). He also began forays into epic theater by dramatizing Maxim Gorky's *The Mother* (1930).

Brecht's "dialectic poetry" (Abusch 344) is assembled in *Lieder, Gedichte, Chöre*, a collection that appeared in January 1934 in Paris. Its first part begins with the "Legend of the Dead Soldier" and depicts the immediate past of the Weimar Republic, the second part deals with contemporaneous events such as the resistance against Nazism and the future of a socialist/Communist society, and the third part consists of songs from the plays *The Mother* and *The Measures Taken*.

A fourth part presents the history of the intellectual in the Weimar Republic and reflections on the writer/intellectual in a class society. Intellectuals must decide between the middle class that caused the Nazi devastation and the working class that alone can give back Germany to its rightful heirs. Brecht transforms the autobiographic element of traditional poetry into an address to his peers. It is the "disgrace" of every intellectual, including himself, when "Germany, [the] pale mother" (*Poems* 218) sits "among the peoples / A mockery or a threat!" (*Poems* 220). Brecht allied himself with the working class, but many other intellectuals straddled the fence trying to be humanitarian without committing themselves to a cause. Nonetheless, even intellectuals who allied themselves do not escape the accusation that they may have done too little too late to prevent Hitler's resistible rise.

Brecht had been in exile for almost a year when the collection was published. He hoped that the edition would find readers in Germany and contribute to the anti-Nazi resistance. Like most exiles in 1933 and 1934, Brecht underestimated the effectiveness of Nazi suppression that made direct intervention impossible. One example for Brecht's interventionist style is the "Burial of the Trouble-Maker in a Zinc Coffin" (1933):

Here in this zinc box
Lies a dead person
Or his legs and his head
Or even less of him

Or nothing, for he was
A trouble-maker.

(Poems 216)

This first stanza relies on the reader's knowledge of the fact that dead victims of the Storm Troopers' terror in the concentration camps were returned to their loved ones in sealed zinc coffins and that the family received a document certifying that the respective victim had died of illness. The "or" sequence in the first stanza emphasizes the relatives' lack of control over the remains since they cannot view the deceased.

The last clause seems to say that the dead person got what he deserved. But "person" (*Mensch*, human being) and "trouble-maker" (*Hetzer*) seem antagonistic. The second noun negates the first one in that the speaker conveys the inhumane viewpoint of those who closed the zinc coffin to hide the victim's remains:

He was recognised as the root of all evil.
Dig him in. It will be best
If his wife goes alone to the knacker's yard with him
Because anyone else going would be a marked man.

(Poems 216)

The dehumanizing of the dead individual continues. Rather than a man, he was "the root of all evil" who must be dug in or *verscharrt*, that is, buried without rites, papers, and/or a marked grave. The second stanza alludes to the pervasive oppression that makes everyone who accompanies the coffin to the grave a "marked man." The question as to who is marked by whom is answered in the very next stanza:

What is in that zinc box
Has been egging you on [*verhetzt*] to all sorts of things:
Getting enough to eat
And having somewhere dry to live
And feeding one's children
And insisting on one's exact wages
And [on] solidarity with all
Who are oppressed like yourselves. And
Thinking.

(Poems 216)

The line "What is in that zinc box" is the climax in the process of dehumanization. Rather than being considered the corpse of a human being, the dead man is reduced to an object. At the same time, the third stanza points to a contradiction. The dead person, who fought for humanitarian causes, receives a dehumanizing treatment from his enemies and perhaps even from those of his friends who do not dare accompany him to his grave. In the last stanza, the murderers who put the dead individual into the zinc coffin resort to a direct threat:

> And because what is in the zinc box said that
> It was put into the zinc box and must be dug in
> As a trouble-maker who egged you on.
> And whoever now . . .
> . . . thinks and proclaims his solidarity
> With all who are oppressed—
> From now on through eternity
> He will be put into a zinc box like this one
> As a trouble-maker and dug in.

> (*Poems* 217)

Contrary to Brecht's usual practice, the role playing of the persona and the seeming identification with the oppressors is not resolved in the final stanza. Nonetheless, the demands that the man in the zinc box had made amount to basic human rights such as subsistence, shelter, equality, and freedom of thought. Withholding these rights argues against those who claim to have "eternity" on their side. Contrasting dehumanization and humanitarianism is supposed to make the reader see murder and oppression for what they actually are—despite deceptive Nazi rhetoric.

The "Burial of the Trouble-Maker" is placed between two poems dedicated to the Communist resistance. Together these three poems emphasize that a temporary defeat such as the imprisonment or murder of a considerable number of Communists constitutes a temporary setback, but that the fight must go on. The concluding songs from *The Mother* and *The Measures Taken* provide a hopeful reminder of a better future. The Nazi claim to an eternal empire that would last a thousand years is refuted by a reminder of dialectic progress in "In Praise of Dialectics," a song marking both the end of *The Mother* and of the third part of *Lieder, Gedichte, Chöre*. It encapsulates both past and present by recapitulating the contemporaneous situation in the first stanza:

> Injustice walks today with a firm step.
> The ruling class is settling in for ten thousand years.
> Violence asserts: Things will stay as they are.
> No voice is heard but the voice of the ruling class
> And on the markets, Exploitation shouts: I am just beginning.
> But many of those repressed say now:
> We will never reach our goals.

> (*GW* 9: 467)[2]

The workers may lose confidence in the future in view of the overwhelming odds against any improvement. They may get the idea that the oppressors hold all the aces. Such thoughts lead to a vicious circle in that retreat is a self-fulfilling prophecy. It spells the end of all hopes because only the oppressed themselves can improve their lot:

> While you're alive, don't say never!
> Certainty isn't certain
> And things will not stay as they are.
> When the ruling class finishes speaking
> Those they rule will start to answer.
> Who dares to answer: never?
> Who is to blame, if oppression stays? We are!
> Who is responsible for its destruction? We are, again!
> He who is struck down, will rise again!
> He who thinks he has lost, will fight on!
> He who has recognized his situation, how is he to be held back?
> For the defeated ones of today will be the victors of tomorrow
> And "never" turns into "today"!
>
> (GW 9: 468)

"In Praise of Dialectics" works with a question-and-answer format that traditionally is used in the art of persuasion. The last part refutes the seeming invincibility of a stagnant empire. Workers who move and think, who "rise," "fight," and recognize their lot, have the potential to overcome oppression that seems solid like a wall. But walls can be battered down.

Clearly, *Lieder, Gedichte, Chöre* was assembled with a view to an immediate victory, a mood that also sustained many Communists during the last years of the Weimar Republic. Considering the state of Germany, as described in the very last poem of the collection—a "gory" sight among the peoples, "a mockery or a threat" (*Poems* 218–20)—human dignity, historical necessity, and patriotism demand an immediate decision to join the fight against the Nazis.

"In Praise of Dialectics" demonstrates that Brecht differed from Stalinist views of dialectics and revolution. Unlike Stalin with his truncated dialectics, according to which history automatically will usher in socialism upon the breakdown of capitalism, Brecht envisions revolutionary success as contingent upon the workers' active participation. The inexorable pull of objective dialectics does not lead to automatic historical progress that one can await in one's armchair. Rather, it buoys the workers' confidence in the successful outcome of their revolutionary commitment and reassures them that they are doing the right thing.

It is this activist view that makes it easier for Brecht than for other Marxist writers to rationalize the Communist failure to resist Hitler. After World War II, Brecht's activist view would make him distrustful of the "revolution" in East Germany, a Soviet import. Unlike others, he considered the fight of workers a prerequisite to a true revolution—a key element that was missing in East Germany.

III

In 1934 and 1935, Brecht recognized that an immediate, or even midterm, revolution was highly unlikely. Consequently, he planned for a long exile. Rather than creating directly intervening poems, he began to write poems that would last and retain their meaning in the post-Nazi era. Again, Brecht's view of dialectics as expressing a potential rather than certain historical necessity stood him in good stead, as did his theory of the reader/audience as active participant in the creative process.

Brecht's poetic course correction was prompted by a shift in his political outlook, yet it was not entirely unpremeditated. He had first formulated his thoughts on such a contingency in 1932 when exile seemed only a remote possibility. In "About the Way to Construct Enduring Works," he enumerated potential reasons for writing for posterity. These reasons sound prophetic; they include the fear of "man's infirmity," the "perseverance of enemies," and "all-shattering cataclysms" (*Poems* 195). The first part of the poem is concerned with the interaction between author and reader. Not the author but rather the reader writes enduring works as long as s/he is challenged to complete the work, to participate in its staging or reciting. In this perspective,

Wise works
Require wisdom
Those devised for completeness
Show gaps.
. . . . .Those planned on a really big scale
Are unfinished.
. . . . .Work for endurance must
Be built like
A machine full of shortcomings.

(Poems 193–94)

Brecht's view that the reader provides closure corresponds to present-day views; it is at odds with the contemporaneous traditional literary theory that held that readers were reacting to rather than interacting with texts written. At the same time, Brecht's view implies that enduring, future-oriented poems must work for the poet's and reader's present, too. In April 1941, he wrote:

[T]o equip works to stand the test of time, on the face of it a "natural" aim, becomes a more serious matter when the writer has grounds for the pessimistic assumption that his ideas (ie the ideas he advocates) may find acceptance only in the long term. the measures, incidentally, that one employs to this end, must not detract from the topical effect of the work. the necessary epic touch applied to things which are "self-evident" at the time of writing [makes for valuable defamiliarization effects for this time]. the conceptual autarky of a work contains an element of criticism: the writer is analysing the transience of the concepts and observations of his own time. (*Journals* 146)

Beginning in 1935 Brecht developed a poetic language composed of meta-phorical images of nature and material possessions. He also began to write short poems that he called epigrams; they succinctly commented upon the difficulty of describing a world plunged into oppression, torture, murder, and war.

The cycle *Svendborg Poems* (published in Copenhagen in 1939) is constructed both of poems that directly intervene and of poems written to last. The cycle's motto addresses the resistance fighters—both those at large and those in con-centration camps. These are the "friends" whose "struggle" the poet follows from abroad, from the comparative security provided by his "Danish thatched roof" (*Poems* 320). While this dedication establishes the historical space of the cycle, it also refers to the remote chance of Germans getting to read the cycle.

The *Svendborg Poems* consist of six sections and an appendix. As in the two previous cycles, the appendix contrasts the poet's intellectual concerns with the external history outlined in the main part. In *Svendborg Poems* Brecht's lyrical "I" serves as the point of departure to depict the intellectual in exile. The first section, "Deutsche *Kriegsfibel*" (German War Primer), is perhaps the most top-ical in view of the fact that World War II was only six months away when the cycle appeared. Here Brecht's epigrams come to the fore, as for example in the poem "The House-Painter Speaks of Great Times to Come":

> The forests still grow.
> The fields still bear.
> The cities still stand.
> The people still breathe.

> (*Poems* 287)

The "house-painter" is Hitler who engages in whitewashing and a kind of window-dressing. The expression "great times" imparts a sense of bitter irony in that these times will not arrive for those people who will die in World War II while their country is being devastated. Brecht's natural and material images, together with the repetition of "still," create an impression that forces the con-temporaneous reader to think beyond immediate circumstances.

Among the *Svendborg Poems*, we find some of Brecht's most lyrical texts. The "Legend of the Origin of the Book Tao-Tê-Ching on Lao-Tsû's Road into Exile" occupies a central position in the cycle's pivotal third chapter. It is a parable on how an intellectual bound for exile can intervene in the affairs of his country. Lao-Tsû encounters a customs officer, a member of the working class, who asks questions of Lao-Tsû that lead to the philosopher's writing a book that he leaves behind in the care of the customs officer. The customs officer facilitates the philosopher's writing by providing shelter, food, and quiet. The intellectual and the member of the working class cooperate and therefore share in the resulting book:

> But the honour should not be restricted
> To the sage whose name is clearly writ.

For a wise man's wisdom needs to be extracted,
So the customs man deserves his bit.
It was he who called for it.

(Poems 316)

"To Those Born Later," the last poem of the collection, corresponds to the "Legend of the Origin" in that it describes a German intellectual's past, present, and future struggles in three parts. In the first part the refugee is faced with the horrors of Nazi Germany, the starvation and degradation that are taking place in concentration camps. Having escaped appears as a stroke of luck, but luck can run out, and survival is not to be taken for granted:

Truly, I live in dark times!
The guileless word is folly. A smooth forehead
Suggests insensitivity. The man who laughs
Has simply not yet had
The terrible news.
. . . By chance I have been spared. (If my luck breaks, I am lost.)
They say to me: Eat and drink! Be glad that you have it!
But how can I eat and drink if I snatch what I eat
From the starving, and
My glass of water belongs to one dying of thirst?
And yet I eat and drink.

(Poems 318)

Human rights have been canceled, and laughter signals either ignorance or insensitivity. Chance is the only ally left. Against the backdrop of an inhumane present and a warlike past (depicted in the second part), Brecht introduces the concept of friendliness. The fight he and others are engaged in is not a heroic myth, a shoot-out after which the good guys ride proudly off into the sunset. Rather, the necessity of waging the fight requires apologies to those born later:

You who will emerge from the flood
In which we have gone under
Remember
When you speak of our failings
The dark time too
Which you have escaped.
For we went changing countries more often than our shoes
Through the wars of the classes, despairing
When there was injustice only, and no rebellion.
And yet we know:
Hatred, even of meanness
Contorts the features.
Anger, even against injustice
Makes the voice hoarse. Oh, we

> Who wanted to prepare the ground for friendliness
> Could not ourselves be friendly.

> *(Poems* 319–20)

The fighters, however benevolent their intentions, are tainted by the inhumanity of war. They cannot build a society based on ''friendliness'' that manifests itself in attitudes, behavior, and human interaction. Hence, they hope for understanding rather than admiration from those born later:

> But you, when the time comes at last
> And man is a helper to man
> Think of us
> With forbearance.

> *(Poems* 320)

In *Hundert Gedichte*, the first cycle Brecht published in the German Democratic Republic (GDR), ''To Those Born Later'' again concludes the collection. This positioning of the poem is hardly a coincidence; rather, it seems to serve as a subtle reminder that those in the GDR who were about to build a socialist Germany, men like Walter Ulbricht and Erich Honecker, had been just as tainted by the wars of the classes as Brecht and his fellow intellectuals. Therefore, they were equally unsuited to promote the attitude of friendliness that in Brecht's view was the cornerstone of a truly Communist society.

IV

In his metaphorical poetry, Brecht reflects frequently upon the dialectic view of history that he had addressed in ''In Praise of Dialectics.'' Rather than appealing to the workers in straightforward fashion, he now works with imagery taken from his daily life in the poems of a cycle that he constructed in 1944, *Poems in Exile*. The title of ''Reading the Paper while Brewing the Tea'' juxtaposes the world news concerning the ruling class with a domestic image:

> In the early hours, I read in the paper of epoch-making projects
> On the part of pope and sovereigns, bankers and oil barons.
> With my other eye I watch
> The pot with the water for my tea
> The way it clouds and starts to bubble and clears again
> And overflowing the pot quenches the fire.

> *(Poems* 382)

Contrary to using symbols or allegories that stand for something else, Brecht's point of departure is the matter at hand. On one level of the poem, the domestic scene he is describing must be taken seriously. The juxtaposition of ''paper'' and ''tea'' is joined by other pairs, such as ''epoch-making events'' and ''watch-

[ing] the water," "pope and sovereigns, bankers and oil barons" and "I," "water" and "fire."

The seeming insignificance of the lyrical "I" and the act of boiling water for tea is opposed by the seeming importance of ruling figures and the events they inspire. The potential effect of water on fire—its ability to extinguish fire if available in sufficient quantity—alludes to Marx's famous statement that quantity at one point in history turns into quality, that is, in sufficient numbers ill-equipped workers can overwhelm the well-equipped armed forces of the middle class.

In "Of Sprinkling the Garden," the relationship between the point of departure in daily life and the poem itself can be traced more closely. Brecht wrote in October 1942 about the pleasure that sprinkling the garden gave him. Clearly, the political implications of certain seemingly innocuous activities are never far from his mind:

what i enjoy doing is sprinkling the garden. curious how all such everyday occupations are affected by one's political awareness. why else should one mind about the possibility of some part of the garden getting neglected, the little plant over there might not get enough or get less, that old tree might be neglected because it looks so strong. weed or not, anything that is green needs water, and one discovers so much green in the soil once one starts watering. (*Journals* 261)

Of course, in Southern California, as Brecht noted in August 1941 after his arrival, nothing will grow if not watered: "but they tell you that all the greenery is wrested from the desert by irrigation systems. scratch the surface a little and the desert shows through: stop paying the water bills, and everything stops blooming" (*Journals* 159).

In the desert climate of Southern California the neglect of a plant will condemn it to almost certain death. This dramatic consequence, however, does not explain why Brecht's "political consciousness" demands that he care for weeds as well as for flowers or trees. In fact, in the poem he goes one step further by telling the reader not to forget the "naked soil":

> O sprinkling of the garden, to [encourage][3] the green!
> Watering the thirsty trees. Give them more than enough
> And do not forget the shrubs
> Even those without berries, the exhausted
> Niggardly ones. And do not neglect
> The weeds growing between the flowers, they too
> Are thirsty. Nor water only
> The fresh grass or only the scorched.
> Even the naked soil you must refresh.

                                                                                          (*Poems* 382)

Brecht's political consciousness refers to acts of "friendliness," that is, to a humane society that treats human beings, animals, and even plants with a profound awareness of each living entity's dignity. Brecht himself reflects upon similar concerns regarding his dog, and his friend Salka Viertel reports that Brecht treated her dog with unwavering, ritual courtesy (Viertel 298). Correspondingly, in sprinkling the garden, the addressee must "encourage" the green. S/he must give "more than enough" water to the trees; must not forget "niggardly" shrubs that take water without giving berries in return; must care for the weeds, the "scorched" grass, and "the naked soil," aspects of a garden that a gardener usually would eliminate, and turn them into a productive part of the garden. In order to be watered in the average Southern Californian garden, a plant or a piece of soil would usually have to provide the gardener with some kind of return.

In his poem as well as in his *Journals* entry, Brecht advocates a garden that is based upon "encouragement." A spot of "naked soil" that is regularly watered may produce something in the end. "Exhausted, niggardly shrubs" may hold another batch of berries after a while. Acts of "friendliness" are ends in themselves that make for a better garden, that is, a better society. When sprinkling the garden, Brecht's "political consciousness" relates the garden to a society and an economy that is based upon a feeling of community rather than the law of give and take.

In a market economy, everything, including friendliness, often carries a price. By contrast, Brecht pleads with the reader to regard friendliness as an end in itself. The basis for his plea is not the Christian faith that preaches "it is more blessed to give than to receive" (Acts 20: 35). Rather, Brecht's vision encompasses a truly Communist society that would include the weak, exhausted, and unproductive members of society, just as his sprinkling includes the weak, exhausted, and unproductive plants. All of them would live their lives in accordance with their abilities and wishes. Through images like the tea water and the garden, Brecht continues to communicate with his readers by inviting them to decode the image and see the vision behind it.

At a time when Brecht was a refugee from Hitler's Germany, such a vision resembled a concrete utopia in the common-sense meaning of the word, a utopia that Brecht thought of as a realistic expectation. His poetry was a tool to argue in favor of conditions that would make the vision come true.

Relying on the contact with readers, his poetry depended on a market, even the limited market constituted by other German-speaking refugees. When he began his Californian exile in 1941, this contact was completely severed, and, as he wrote in April 1942, Brecht faced a crisis of poetic production: "to write poetry, even topical poetry here [in California] amounts to withdrawing into an ivory tower. it is like plying the art of the goldsmith. there is something quaint, something oddball, something limited about it. it is like putting a message in a bottle. the battle for smolensk is a battle for poetry too" (*Journals* 218).

At the end of the *Steffin Collection*[4]—the first cycle that was completely oriented toward his exile— he had discussed this very problem in the sonnet "Finnish Landscape":

> Those fish-stocked waters! Lovely trees as well!
> Such scents of berries and birches there!
> Thick-chorded winds that softly cradle the air
> As mild as though the clanking iron churns
> Trundled from the white farmhouse were all left open!
> Dizzy with sight and sound and thought and smell
> The refugee beneath the alders turns
> To his laborious job: continued hoping.
>
> He notes the corn stooks, spots which beasts have strayed
> Toward the lake, hears moos from their strong lungs
> But also sees who's short of milk and corn.
> He asks the boat that takes logs to be sawn:
> Is that the way that wooden legs are made?
> And sees a people silent in two tongues.

(*Poems* 353)

The first five lines describe a rich, peaceful, romantic, and beautiful countryside. But the first discordant note is struck by the sixth line. Rather than enchanted or impressed, the speaker is "dizzy," not only from nature but also from "thought." He is a refugee, and his thoughts continuously turn toward hope— although hope is difficult to maintain. The last six lines reveal the beauty of nature to be a cover for a dark underside. In the midst of plenty, there are people who starve and who are in need of artificial limbs as a consequence of World War II. Yet the sale of Finnish wood flourishes because of the war. Whereas "On Sprinkling the Garden" had stayed within the realm of the parable and left the reader to deduce its other level of meaning, this sonnet is more typical of Brecht's poetical communication in the early 1940s in that it provides clues for the reader.

The reader knows or is able to deduce that Finland (and Sweden) supplied Nazi Germany with raw materials such as wood and ore. Moreover, Finland shed all pretensions of being a democratic country in the wake of the 1940– 1941 war with the Soviet Union when it adopted a friendly stance toward Nazi Germany. The Finnish people suffered in enforced silence in their two official languages, Finnish and Swedish. As Brecht showed in his play *Puntila and Matti, His Hired Man* (1941), Finland is a repressive capitalist state.

V

In Brecht's poetry, comments on the countries of his exile (Denmark, Sweden, Finland and the United States) occurred occasionally, but the affairs of these countries never distracted his attention from Germany. As soon as the possibility of Hitler's defeat appeared on the horizon in 1944, he inquired about ways and means to return (Lyon, *Brecht* 120–21). After an exploratory stay in Switzerland from 1947 to 1949, he moved to the Soviet zone of occupation that in October 1949 became the German Democratic Republic, five months after the Western allies had created the Federal Republic of Germany. Brecht acquired Austrian citizenship and put the money from the Stalin Peace Prize (later renamed the Lenin Prize) that he received in 1951 into a Swiss bank account. With the Cold War raging and brinkmanship being practiced by both superpowers, the experience of poverty and of being stateless during his exile years presumably served as a strong incentive to diversify his assets and to obtain the passport of a neutral country.

His production of poetry took a back seat to his efforts to promote his plays through productions of the Berliner Ensemble. Although he published *Hundert Gedichte*, he temporarily abandoned his plans to bring out the *Kriegsfibel* when it no longer seemed topical.

On 17 June 1953, the East German workers rebelled against their government. Although fomented by the West, this rebellion was the result of genuine grievances. In Brecht's view, it also demonstrated a lack of understanding on the part of workers. Officials of the SED (the Socialist Unity Party) as well as intellectuals had to be held responsible because they had neither managed to overcome the Nazi influence within the populace nor had they been able to explain the necessity of socialism. In the 1990s, Brecht's criticism seems especially topical when the crimes against foreigners in East Germany show that the GDR failed signally in helping its young people to come to terms with Nazism. Brecht tried to address this lack of understanding on the part of the workers in three works, the play *Turandot, or the Whitewashers' Congress*, the *Kriegsfibel,* and *Buckow Elegies*—works he published despite his intense involvement with the Berliner Ensemble.

His *Kriegsfibel* (1955) was to remind readers that capitalism and Nazism meant war. It features World War II in all its horrors—whether in Europe, Asia, Australia, or Africa. For instance, the caption of a photograph of a dead soldier from "desert fox" Erwin Rommel's Africa Corps reads:

> O fanfares of War and storm of pennants!
> O mythical Swastika crusade of the Germans!
> At the end, just one thing was on your mind
> Finding a hole to hide! Something you didn't find.
>
> (*Werke* 12: 198–99)

The epigram points to the fact that grandiloquent talk and ideas become meaningless for the individual who faces death as the only reward for believing in them. The *Kriegsfibel* also attacks certain individuals, among them German Social Democrat Gustav Noske, the cabinet minister responsible for crushing the workers' uprising in 1919, and Winston Churchill, whom Brecht considered an arch-capitalist and colonizer.[5] Elsewhere Brecht expressed the hope that the younger generation would facilitate the change from a capitalist-fascist to a socialist society.

The *Buckow Elegies* are an entirely new cycle that Brecht wrote at his country house in Buckow in the vicinity of Berlin, where he spent his summers. Six of these elegies he published in volume thirteen of his series *Versuche* in 1954.[6] It is perhaps indicative of how "alienated" (*Journals* 454) Brecht felt after the uprising of 17 June 1953 that the *Buckow Elegies* combine two techniques that are intended to ensure the poems' survival beyond the moment of their composition. Nature and objects are referred to in an almost epigrammatical form, but pivotal to Brecht's argument is the topic of friendliness.

Like the title *Svendborg Poems*, the heading *Buckow Elegies* alludes ironically to the traditional concept of cycles. It suggests a harmonious mood that is fostered by a tranquil locality. However, according to traditional standards, elegies are considered poems of lament. Brecht had used the term elegy for his poems "Germany" and "To Those Born Later," and in 1941 he had written "Hollywood Elegies" (*Poems* 380–81). The implicit lament in these poems does not concern doubts about the possibility of change. Rather, Brecht laments the historical role of the intellectual whose task of contributing to the change of behavioral patterns in his fellow citizens will take much longer than he had assumed. As during his exile, he faces the possibility that he himself will not be around to see real changes taking place. The carefully constructed six poems of *Buckow Elegies* show the desirability of this change.

In "The Flower Garden," Brecht juxtaposes his garden and his wishes for his art in two four liners:

> By the lake, deep amid fir and silver poplar
> Sheltered by wall and hedge, a garden
> So wisely plotted with monthly flowers
> That it blooms from March until October.
>
> Here in the morning, not too frequently, I sit
> And wish I too might always
> In all weathers, good or bad
> Show one pleasant aspect, or another.

(*Poems* 439)

A "sheltered" garden presents the picture of an undisturbed, intact nature, quite unlike Brecht's nature images from his Californian exile, when nature represented something wanting. The garden is "plotted," that is, it owes its peace to its human owner. Faced with this self-made image of nature, the poet wants to write accordingly, showing "pleasant" rather than ugly sights.

The next elegy, however, shows that the past continues to dominate the attitudes of GDR citizens. In "Still at It," Brecht observes his children in a summer camp from his garden, and he is struck by the unfriendly treatment they are accorded by adults. In view of the fact that Brecht sees children as the true claimants to a new society, this perpetuation of militaristic gestures is deeply disturbing inasmuch as it may adversely affect the children's future behavior:

> The plates are slammed down so hard
> The soup slops over.
> In shrill tones
> Resounds the order: Now eat!
>
> The Prussian eagle
> Jabbing food down
> The gullets of its young.

(Poems 441)

The next poem "Paddling, Talking" reports a future-oriented interaction. Both activities and conversation are undertaken in a spirit of equality:

> It's evening. Two canoes
> Glide past, inside them
> Two naked young men: paddling abreast
> They talk. Talking
> They paddle abreast.

(Poems 443)

The nakedness of the two young men supports the argument that they are absorbed in each other's humanity rather than distracted by social trappings as manifested by clothing.

The fourth poem emphasizes that nature is not an end in itself; it breaks with the tradition of nature lyrics, a genre assiduously cultivated by mostly second-rate poets who wrote and were published in Germany during the Nazi era. "The Smoke" reads:

> The little house among trees by the lake.
> From the roof smoke rises.
> Without it
> How dreary would be
> House, trees and lake.

(Poems 442)

The smoke indicates that the house is inhabited. Unlike the human beings of Brecht's exile poetry, the human being in this poem is neither the destroyer of other human beings nor the victim of war. Instead, the human's presence points to the priority human beings have over nature.

The development of a friendly vision, however, remains endangered by attitudes from the past, as evidenced in "Hot Day":

Hot day. My writing case on my knee
I sit in the summer-house. A green boat
Appears through the willow. In the stern
A stout nun, stoutly clad. In front of her
An elderly person in a bathing-costume, probably a priest.
At the oars, rowing for all he's worth
A child. Just like old times, I think
Just like old times.

(Poems 441)

Despite the socialist society's denunciation of the churches as servants and prof-
iteers of middle-class society, even children who carry the hope for a changed
society continue to be deferential to the members of institutionalized religion.
The child's exploitation by the two clerics is unrelieved by any human contact.
It stands in sharp contrast to "Paddling, Talking," in which the work is shared
in a spirit of togetherness.

In contrast to the relationship of exploitation that precludes communication,
the last poem, "Reading a Soviet Book," shows how civilization can profit
from the fully developed human spirit:

To tame the Volga, I read
Will not be an easy task. She will call
On her daughters for help, on the Oka, Kama, Unsha, Vyetluga
And her granddaughters, the Chussovaya, the Vyatka.
She'll summon all her forces, with waters from seven thousand tributaries
Full of rage she'll crash down the Stalingrad dam.
That genius of invention, with the devilish cunning
Of the Greek Odysseus, will make use of every fissure
Deploy on the right flank, by-pass on the left, take cover
Underground—but, I read, the Soviet people
Who love her, sing songs about her, have recently
Studied her and no later
Than 1958
Will tame her.
And the black fields of the Caspian plains
The arid, the stepchildren
Will reward them with bread.

(Poems 444)

Although Brecht knew that there were many problems in the Soviet Union and
opted for the United States as his country of exile, he elects to treat Soviet
society as a myth. Such a treatment does not constitute an unambiguous endorsement. The U.S. Western Frontier with its violence, diseases, and high mor-
tality rate became mythicized in the figure of John Wayne and others who rode
into town, shot the villains, and rode off to new adventures. These Western
heroes came to epitomize the American who is self-reliant, fearless, and on the

side of the good guys. In the same spirit, Brecht uses the image of the Soviet Union to encapsulate the potential of a socialist society. All the people work together to build a dam against the mighty forces of nature so that they might improve their food supply.

"Reading a Soviet Book," the last poem, corresponds to the first poem, "The Flower Garden," in that it also shows something "plotted." This time, however, the plotted object is a societally responsible project rather than a place of leisure. The fourth poem, "Smoke," bridges these two by emphasizing the importance of the human being vis-à-vis nature.

The second and fifth poems also correspond. Both show old habits that are hard to abandon. They not only make the GDR vulnerable to another 17 June, but they also endanger the children, the members of a generation Brecht had hoped would grow up untainted by the class wars of his own generation. Again, the fifth poem is more explicit than the second one in that it features specific figures rather than anonymous voices. The third poem relates to these two as an antithesis, a model of how behavior would have to change.

The third and fourth poem are the pivot of the cycle. They celebrate life lived according to a person's own human needs and dignity—life without oppression and without a hierarchical structure. In the background of this vision is the concept of "friendliness" that encapsulates both Brecht's utopian intention and his criticisms of both capitalist and "real" socialist society. Today, we know that Brecht was right in doubting the ability of war-tainted leaders such as Stalin, Walter Ulbricht, and Erich Honecker to deliver on their promises for a socialist society—not to mention a Communist one. Moreover, at present, utopias in general are considered of dubious value. Brecht's poetic work remains important, however, because of the unique manner in which he transformed traditional poetic forms and contents. His "dialectic poetry" is a rhetorically as well as metaphorically rewarding combination of poetry and history that had a considerable effect on post-Brechtian poets—even if they did not share Brecht's political views.

NOTES

1. See also Stefan Soldovieri, "War-Poetry, Photo(epi)grammetry: Brecht's *Kriegsfibel*," in this volume.

2. In *The Mother* (*Plays* 1: 206), only the last part of the poem in *Lieder, Gedichte, Chöre* is recited, but see *Poems & Songs* (240–41).

3. Brecht uses *ermutigen* (encourage) rather than "enliven" (*beleben*), as in *Poems*. It is important for my interpretation that Brecht uses an anthropomorphism when talking about the green.

4. The collection is named after Margarete Steffin, Brecht's lover from 1930 to 1941, the year of her death. She collaborated with him on a number of plays and was the first reader of virtually everything he wrote during this time.

5. The fact that Franklin D. Roosevelt escapes such a stricture suggests that Brecht viewed the New Deal as a positive development (Lyon, *Brecht* 253). This is all the more

remarkable as Brecht tended to view capitalism as a softer version of fascism, as for instance in his 1944 poem "Hakenkreuz und Double-Cross" (Hook-Cross [swastika] and Double-Cross).

6. It has been suggested that Brecht encountered censorship regarding his *Buckow Elegies*, and that this is the reason for including only six of the twenty-four poems he wrote in *Versuche*. There is no evidence for this theory, however, and Brecht was generally very selective with regard to the publication of his poems.

WORKS CITED (SEE ALSO REFERENCE GUIDE TO WORKS CITED IN ABBREVIATED FORM)

Abusch, Alexander. *Der Deckname: Memoiren*. Berlin: Dietz, 1984.

Bohnert, Christiane. "Brecht: Rhetorische Gedichte im Spannungsfeld der Geschichte. Kriege der Klassen und Freundlichkeit." In *Brecht-Journal*, vol. 2. Edited by Jan Knopf. Frankfurt am Main: Suhrkamp, 1986. 114–47.

Buhl, Barbara. *Bilder der Zukunft–Traum und Plan: Utopie im Werk Bertolt Brechts*. Bielefeld: Aisthesis, 1988.

Fahrenbach, Helmut. *Brecht: Zur Einführung*. Hamburg: Junius, 1986.

Hartinger, Christel. *Bertolt Brecht: Das Gedicht nach Krieg und Wiederkehr*. Berlin: Brecht Zentrum der DDR, 1982.

Kamath, Rekha. *Brechts Lehrstück-Modell als Bruch mit den bürgerlichen Theatertraditionen*. Frankfurt am Main: Lang, 1983.

Mennemeier, Franz-Norbert. *Bertolt Brechts Lyrik: Aspekte, Tendenzen*. Düsseldorf: Bagel, 1982.

Müller, Klaus-Detlef. "Utopische Intention und Kritik der Utopien bei Brecht." In *Literatur ist Utopie*. Edited by Gert Ueding. Frankfurt am Main: Suhrkamp, 1978. 335–67.

Schlenstedt, Sylvia. "Lyrik im Gesamtplan der Produktion." *Weimarer Beiträge* 24.2 (1978): 5–29.

Viertel, Salka. *The Kindness of Strangers*. New York: Holt, 1969. Translated into German as *Das unbelehrbare Herz: Ein Leben in der Welt des Theaters, der Literatur und des Films*. Translated by Helmut Degner. Reinbek bei Hamburg: Rowohlt, 1979.

6

War-Poetry, Photo(epi)grammetry: Brecht's *Kriegsfibel*

STEFAN SOLDOVIERI

The *Kriegsfibel* is one of Brecht's most fascinating experiments and occupies a unique place in his lyric production. Literally a "war primer," in the sense of a reader or ABC book, the *Kriegsfibel* is a series of poem-photograph composites whose vigorous critique of World War II aspires to nothing less than a retraining of vision. Poetry plays a constitutive role in Brecht's attempt to facilitate an active, questioning gaze. In the confrontation between poem and photograph, the *Kriegsfibel* projects an operative reading praxis as an antidote to the passive logic of reception elicited by the media image. The issues of perception and representation raised by Brecht's reader of critical war poems remain relevant today in light of the technical image's increasing saturation of the social space.

A MARGINAL TEXT?

Brecht's ostensibly simple procedure of mounting four-line epigrams to newspaper photographs of war subjects frustrates generic classification. It compels us to reconsider the tools and presuppositions of conventional textual exegesis. Is this poetry? photography? or visual art? The *Kriegsfibel* certainly does not conform to our familiar ideas about what a poetry collection or cycle ought to look like. The genres of photojournalism and photomontage do not seem to apply in this case very well either: Brecht neither took the photographs in the *Kriegsfibel* himself nor did he fracture the photographic image using montage techniques like his contemporary John Heartfield.

It is no use searching the literary tradition for predecessors to the *fotoepi-gramm(e)* (photoepigram(s)), the term Brecht coined to refer to his poem-image hybrids in his *Journals* (319).[1] The Baroque emblem, with its tripartite structure of *lemma* (motto), *pictura* (picture), and *subscriptio* (epigram), was suggested as a model by an early interpreter of the *Kriegsfibel* (Grimm, "Emblematik"). But despite a similarity with at least a few of the photoepigrams—a number of which incorporate the original newspaper titles and captions that stand in for the emblematic *lemma* and *subscriptio*—and a broadly shared pedagogical impetus, the emblem form leaves the media-critical impulse of the text wholly unaccounted for. Nor can the text be read as a collection of epigrams with appended photographs, that is, as a simple visual variation and Marxist-humanist interpretation of this well-established lyric form (see Wagenknecht). Brecht's appeal to the epigram is more complex; classical poetic categories will only get us so far in attending to the specificity of the *Kriegsfibel*.

The history of the *Kriegsfibel* poses problems as well: spatial and temporal discontinuities mark the course of the text's production. Berlin and the Weimar Republic provide the backdrop for Brecht's prewar reflections on photography from the late 1920s to the early 1930s. These short fragments constitute a context of theoretical concerns that exert a structuring effect upon the territory of the *Kriegsfibel* without comprising its theory. Brecht's textual practice in the *Kriegs-fibel* is more productive than any concept that can be derived from his scattered theoretical considerations regarding the photographic medium.

The text's sixty-nine photoepigrams form an inner topography of war scenes spanning the twelve years of fascism in Germany from Hitler's war preparations to the war's end. These *Kriegsschauplätze* (*Krieg* = "war," and *Schauplätze* are "scenes" or, literally, "looking places"), the equivalent of the rather cynical but revealing idea of a "war theater" in English, include Berlin, Liverpool, Sweden, Norway, France, London, Singapore, Italy, Moscow, the United States, and other locations. This geographical terrain intersects with the stations of Brecht's exile that was, of course, impacted by the war's expanding periphery. Brecht's exile began in 1933—one day after the burning of the Reichstag on 27 February. When the war commenced with Hitler's invasion of Poland, Brecht had already been in exile for over five years. German troops occupied Denmark and Norway on 9 April 1940, but Brecht was able to keep a step ahead of Hitler's army, fleeing to Sweden, Finland, and finally California.

The text cannot be so easily mapped onto these geographies, however. The *Kriegsfibel* is perhaps more than a "satisfactory literary report on my years in exile," as Brecht rather laconically described the text in a *Journals* entry in June of 1944 (321). The *Kriegsfibel*'s final phase of construction had less to do with his exile than with the cultural and political exigencies of the German Democratic Republic. Nearly banned for its supposedly vague pacifism and insufficient critique of the West, the text was finally published in East Berlin in 1955 by Brecht's editor Ruth Berlau—almost twenty years after Brecht began assembling the first photoepigrams (see Bohnert, *Lyrik* 243–49).

The *Kriegsfibel* is one of Brecht's less well-known works. In both parts of Germany, fewer than 4,000 copies were sold in its first six months of publication (Bohnert, *Lyrik* 248). Although the reprint licensed by the GDR's Eulenspiegel publishing house for distribution in the Federal Republic, Austria, and Switzerland in 1978 caused a new flicker of interest and sold well, the text remained relatively unstudied by Brecht scholars. This can be attributed at least in part to the fact that older editions of Brecht's collected poems and works excluded the images altogether and only printed the four-line poems. The most recent critical edition of Brecht's works is the first to print Brecht's poem-image composites as they were intended, albeit in a necessarily reduced format (*Werke* 12: 127–267). Nor has the *Kriegsfibel* been translated into English. The most widely available and complete collection of Brecht's poems in English addresses the issue of the *Kriegsfibel* in the introduction but wisely chooses to leave the task to an edition that can provide an adequate presentation of the photographs as well (*Poems* xxiii).

Needless to say, the *Kriegsfibel* has posed somewhat of a dilemma for Brecht studies, and the text's idiosyncratic juxtaposition of poem and newspaper image has rarely been appreciated in its full complexity. While Brecht the poet has enjoyed increasing attention since the late 1970s, and while his relationship to the media is the object of two recent monographs (Wöhrle, *Versuche*; Mueller, *Media*) there are still only a few article-length treatments of the *Kriegsfibel*. Of the sparse academic literature on the text, little has appeared outside of Germany.[2] The territory staked out by the *Kriegsfibel* on the outer confines of the Brechtian canon and its complex positionality with respect to aesthetic, generic, geographical, and historical boundaries makes the text "marginal" in a contemporary and immanently theoretical sense. The *Kriegsfibel*'s suitability for an introduction to Brecht's poetry lies as much in its important links to Brecht's more conventionally lyric production as in the way that it problematizes notions of the classical "work."

The *Kriegsfibel* is very much concerned with margins and frames. The "reframing" of the newspaper image that the text stages raises the general question of where the site of reading begins and ends. For it is the margin—that which is by definition not a part of the image "proper"—that constitutes the territory of the visual text in the first place. In its function as commentary on the photographic image and as an appeal to writing in an increasingly visual, image-oriented world, poetry contributes significantly to the *Kriegsfibel*'s productive displacement and "re-vision" of the photograph. This introduction hopes to encourage an active reading and rereading of Brecht and Brecht's poetry—a process of reading that the *Kriegsfibel* itself suggests.

BRECHT AND PHOTOGRAPHY

Trust not your eyes
Do not trust your ears

You see darkness
Perhaps it is light.

(*Werke* 14: 163)

Before the term *fotoepigramm* became the accepted designation, commentators on the *Kriegsfibel* shifted between different forms, but Brecht's neologism for his poem-image hybrids invites speculation.

In the history of the photographic medium, the "photogram" refers to a cameraless image created by exposing objects placed directly on a photographic surface to light. The use of this technique to produce abstract images began around 1918 and was soon picked up on by Man Ray and the Hungarian-born painter, graphic artist, and experimental photographer László Moholy-Nagy. At about the same time that Brecht began experimenting with photographic images and poetry, Moholy-Nagy was using his photograms as a way to exploit the most rudimentary functions of the camera. His short article of 1929, "Photogram and Frontier Zones" (translated in Passuth 305–306), suggests an understanding of the photogram as a new territory of perception that recalls the *Kriegsfibel*'s own intervention in the process of seeing. While Brecht was generally skeptical about what he viewed as abstract art's neglect of content, his own reflections on photography and his experiments with image and written text in the *Journals* and the *Kriegsfibel* also aimed at an interrogation of the medium.

Brecht's reflections on photography are rather sparse and unsystematic. His most sustained attempt in the area of the visual media was *Der Dreigroschenprozeß* (1931; The Threepenny Trial)—an important text dealing specifically with the institution of the cinema and the court case surrounding the filmic adaptation of his successful *The Threepenny Opera* (1928). Nevertheless, there are a few short texts from the prewar period that point to the political and aesthetic concerns that bear on the *Kriegsfibel* as well. While they do not project a theory of the *Kriegsfibel*, they stake out the theoretical, aesthetic, and political territory of Brecht's later appropriation of the technical image. They shed light on the text as a space for experimenting with visual perception and anticipate the photoepigram's articulation of the photographic image and poetry.

Brecht's interest in photography is a part of a historical response to the mass reproduction of the photographic image that began in the late 1880s. Technological developments making it possible to print photographs in the same press with the newspaper type coincided with advances in photographic technology such as dry plates and cellulose nitrate film, allowing photographs to be reproduced cheaply and in great quantities. By the mid-1920s, Dresden's Leitz company had introduced its first Leica, which was quickly followed by even smaller cameras, better lenses, and flash bulbs.

The course of the photographic image's proliferation in newspapers, advertising, and film was commented upon by intellectuals of all stripes. One of the most sophisticated and best-known treatments of this historical transformation from a culture of writing to a culture of images is Walter Benjamin's "The

Work of Art in the Age of Mechanical Reproduction'' (1936). In this influential essay, Benjamin described how the reproduction of the photographic image undermines its status as an aesthetic object and how the photograph becomes a part of the media's process of producing meaning. Benjamin saw this fundamental shift in perception in largely positive terms as an expansion of visual experience and the possibility of breaking with bourgeois concepts of art and authorship.

While Brecht was interested in the immense possibilities lying in mass media such as film and radio, he greeted the increasing hegemony of the technical image with considerable skepticism. In an often-cited text written upon the occasion of the tenth anniversary of the *Arbeiter-Illustrierten-Zeitung* (The Worker's Illustrated) in 1930, a magazine to which John Heartfield often supplied his political photo-montages, Brecht observed:

The *truth* regarding the prevailing conditions in the world has profited little from the frightening development of photo-journalism: photography has become a terrible weapon *against* the truth in the hands of the bourgeoisie. The immense amount of photo-material that the presses spew out on a daily basis and which does have the appearance of truth really only serves to obscure the facts. The camera can lie just like the typesetting machine. (*Werke* 21: 515)

Registering the sheer volume of images flooding the social space in a general way, Brecht's critique in this place is primarily ideological and institutional. The photographic image in the conventional illustrated press is the bearer of class interests; in passing off a particular representation of reality as a generally binding truth, bourgeois values appear as universally human values. Brecht's emphasis is more on the insertion of the photograph in social and material discourses than on the photographic medium's specific mode of representation.

While the passage is perhaps more concerned with the problem of the ''misrepresentation'' of political contents and class interests than of language or the image *as* representation, the manner in which Brecht points to the limits of vision opens up the possibility of questioning the photograph's seeming transparency. The photographic image is a fundamentally signifying surface. Images can ''lie'' because, like language, the camera is a technology of representation and not a presencing machine. Words and images are a part of the meaning they produce in the process of signification. The newspaper photograph's connection to information and its implicit claim of ''objectivity'' obscure the fact that the black/white image is the product of a highly abstract coding process with an unclear relationship to that which it represents. As Vilém Flusser notes: ''The naive observer sees color and black/white situations in the photographic universe, but are there corresponding color and black/white situations 'out there?' And if not, how is the photographic universe related to the world?'' (Flusser, *Philosophy* 29).

But what to do with these ''abstract'' photographic texts? One of the things that the *Kriegsfibel* does very well, in fact, is to deny a facile, "black/white" view of the war in the media images that it takes up. Brecht's epigrams complicate the photographs in the interest of a material and political critique of the war, while the framing operation of the photoepigrams draws attention to the camera in interrupting and activating the reader's gaze.

In the *Kriegsfibel*, the Americans appear as welcome but calculating liberators who did too little to prevent the decimation of the Soviet army; without obscuring the line between victim and victimizer, soldiers are shown as brutal oppressors and fear-driven implements of power; the military machine is connected to the interests of industrial and political elites; a rather brief reference to the plight of the Jews addresses not only Hitler's politics of genocide but the world's reluctance to intervene. In photoepigram no. 50, the object of Brecht's critique is the United States' self-representation in the media. Referring both to the image and the accompanying newspaper caption (in English) "Restoring the normal flow of life. AMG officers selling flour to Italian civilians," the epigram points to the trade in a particular ideology as well. The poem's first two lines read: "We bring flour and a king, take! / But he who accepts flour must also accept the king" (*Werke* 12: 228). These are but a few examples in the range of issues with which Brecht deals in the *Kriegsfibel*.

Brecht's interest in photography dates back at least to the mid-1920s. In 1926, his favorite books of the year included two photographic works, Ernst Friedrich's *War against War* and Erich Mendelsohn's *Amerika*. Brecht's praise of Mendelsohn's book is guarded. A collection of one hundred photographs paired with short prose commentary texts on the facing pages, *Amerika* documents the mixture of fascination and disdain with which European intellectuals regarded the United States in these years. A photograph entitled "NEW YORK The Beginning of Broadway—Closeup," for example, is accompanied by a text commenting on the architecture's human toll and the economic forces behind it. "Admire the greatest dimensions in the smallest space," he writes, "as the work of man—but at the same time it takes away your faith in human worth" (Mendelsohn 36).

Although its political critique was probably not radical enough for his taste, Brecht's reservations regarding *Amerika* would seem to stem less from a rejection of the political content of Mendelsohn's commentary, which he does not address specifically in his brief remarks, than from the text's failure to break with a certain photographic aesthetic. Brecht writes: "[These are] outstanding photographs, almost all of which could be pinned up on the wall and which lend the great cities the (no doubt deceitful) appearance of inhabitability" (*Werke* 21: 176).

Brecht's parenthetical comment on the ominous aesthetic appeal of the photographic image characterizes his cautiousness regarding the photographic medium in general and points to the problems he anticipated in appropriating the medium for his political and artistic purposes. For Brecht, *Amerika* runs the risk of succumbing to the very danger acknowledged by its author in the text's introduction when he describes Europe's transatlantic perspective on America: "The reality of the U.S.A.—the United States of America—is usually seen in Europe through admiring rather than conscientious eyes" (Mendelsohn ix). Brecht's qualifying remark on *Amerika*, cited above, suggests that this is precisely the relationship of and to viewing that the text reproduces. He raises the question of whether the text succeeds in interrupting the phatic character of the photograph: its tendency to fix the viewer's gaze and arrest the eye's active and potentially creative capacity.

Brecht's dissatisfaction with the photographic practices of his contemporaries led him to consider the photographic image in the period before its technical reproduction. In the fragment "Über Photographie" (On Photography), written around 1928, he writes: "The historical perspective demonstrated by a number of photographs from the early period . . . appears to be extinguished. I do not only mean the selection of objects, although I mean these as well, but above all a certain expression of singularity, a temporal specificity that artists who know what a document is are able to lend their images. But this involves an interest in the objects themselves and not just the lighting" (*Werke* 21: 264).

Struck by the "historical perspective" inhering in the early photograph, Brecht's gesture to the beginnings of the medium is not a demand for a return to some supposedly more authentic photographic aesthetic. The commercial photographs of the advertising industry and the illustrated magazine provide the foil for the terms in which Brecht describes the photographs of the medium's early period. Singularity, originality, and a genuine attention to the object are the pendants to the fleeting, superficial character of the technically reproduced photograph.

Brecht is not alone in his critique of the mass reproduced image, and a number of photography volumes from the late 1920s and early 1930s display a similar gesture to photography's beginnings. Heinrich Schwarz's tribute to David Octavius Hill (1802–1870) is but one example. Brecht's description of the early photograph will be familiar to those acquainted with Benjamin's notion of "aura." Like Brecht, Benjamin singles out the uniqueness and historical specificity of the early photograph against the photographic practices of his own time. In an essay text entitled "Kleine Geschichte der Photographie" (Short History of Photography, 1931), parts of which were later incorporated into the art work essay, Benjamin sets up the opposition in the auratic *Bild*, as picture or image, and the *Abbild*, its technically reproduced copy. He, too, associates singularity and duration with the former and transience and repetition with the latter (Benjamin 379).

The relationship between the *Bild* and the *Abbild* suggests a distanciation from a supposed origin. The prefix "ab" indicates not only a separation but also negation and diminution. The apparent essentialism of this rhetoric should not distract from the fact that neither Benjamin nor Brecht recommend a return to the practices of early photography and the aesthetic categories of authorship and authenticity. For Benjamin, aura is primarily the sign of a historically specific relationship between technology and technique that has become displaced with the rapid developments in photographic technology, reproduction, and distribution. Critical of Benjamin's formulation of the concept of aura, Brecht nevertheless locates a similar incongruence between technology and technique when he chides contemporary photographers for their preoccupation with form and scorn of content. "Über Photographie" continues: "Photography really ought to be beyond the point where artists only keep on trying to demonstrate everything one can do with a camera—especially when all they want to prove is that you can do what you can also do with a paint brush. This is far too little" (*Werke* 21: 264).

Brecht's interest in photography lies in the specificity of the medium and the possibility of harnessing its potential in a particular historical constellation. Having criticized the relationship of the photographer to the photographic apparatus, he turns to the question of the camera's relationship to its object: "Professional models are not irritated enough by the apparatus, they present themselves to the camera differently than they would later to an observer, the result is a tasteless, harmless atmosphere" (*Werke* 21: 265). All of Brecht's reflections on photography involve drawing attention to the concealed "irritation" of the camera in an effort to destroy the image's apparent innocuousness. Almost an anticipation of the function of *Kriegsfibel*'s epigrammatic captions, the text breaks off abruptly with an appeal to writing as a corrective to the duplicity of the photograph.

A second short text entitled "Fotografie" from the same period suggests Brecht's interest in the photograph as a space for experimentation. The text outlines two investigations into vision aimed at exploring "not only what things are like, but just as importantly what they do, how things behave" (*Werke* 21: 265). The first investigation envisions a collection of portrait photographs of men and women taken over the course of years. Not without irony, Brecht outlines the experiment as a gamelike exercise whose object is to assign husbands and wives to their respective partners, the assumption being that "physiognomic adaptations" (*Werke* 21: 265) occur between partners who have been married for a long time. A second experiment dealing with "functional images" proposes a collection of hands: workers' hands holding hammers and various machine parts; the hands of intellectual workers, *Kopfarbeiter*, holding the tools of their trade; workers holding pens and design plans; finally, photos of intellectuals' hands holding the tools of manual laborers.

Both experiments, and the context of "experimentation" in general, appeal to the nature of the camera as a scientific tool, a technology of magnification, miniaturization, acceleration, and deceleration that expands the field of visual perception. This is particularly apparent in the first experiment where the photograph assists a measuring procedure—the gradual accommodation of two physiognomies over time—by solving a spacio-temporal problem, namely how to assemble people inhabiting different points in time in one visual plane. The exercise involving the confrontation of hands and tools, on the other hand, suggests a sensitivity to the photographic image's fundamentally symbolic surface structure and an interest in its artistic potential. Whereas the first experiment appeals more to what one might call the "denotation drive" of the photograph—the manner in which it denies its own rhetoricity in showing "how things are"—the staged contrast between hands and manual implements is already a deliberate act of interpretive construction.

This constellation of art, perception, and photography crystallizes in an often cited passage from the *Der Dreigroschenprozeß* in which Brecht comments on the difficulty of the photographic representation of social and material relationships. Pointing to the absent context of reified human relations, he writes: "A photograph of the Krupp factory or the AEG says almost nothing about these institutions" (*Werke* 21: 469). As a compensation for the limits of the photograph's signifying surface, Brecht proposes an artistic intervention much in the spirit of the second photographic experiment described above: "So it is that there really is 'something to construct,' something 'artistic,' 'artificial.' Thus art is in fact necessary" (*Werke* 21: 469).

The proximity of art and technology in Brecht's writings on the photographic medium points to an understanding of art as *techne*. Not unlike the German *Kunst*, *techne* encompasses both the notion of "skill" as well as "art." Brecht's interest in photography's artistic potential is informed by a concept of art that is very much a part of modern art's preoccupation with vision and recalls a pre-Romantic notion of aesthetics in the sense of a science of perception.

THE *FIBEL* FRAME

The refunctionalization of traditional dramatic and poetic forms is a characteristically Brechtian maneuver and the common denominator of his entire literary production. The frame of the *Fibel*—defined as a primer, above—offers a first approach to the text's formal construction.

The appropriation of the *Fibel* form links the conception of the *Kriegsfibel* to Brecht's early poetry collections, *Manual of Piety* (1927) and *Reader for Those Who Live in Cities* (1930). In the former, Brecht transforms the *Hauspostille*, a traditional instrument of religious education in the home, by replacing its exemplary sermons with poems grouped into five *Lektionen* (Lessons) designated for different purposes. So it is that the poems of the first lesson entitled "Bittgänge" (Processions) have little to do with the supplication prayers and invocations of Catholic ritual. Instead, Brecht uses the "Bittgänge" as an occasion to point to the rather profane matters of infanticide, parricide, and robbery. The protagonists of these poems are not held up as negative examples; there is no appeal to divine grace or moral instances. Instead, the language of these poems suggests obscure and uncontainable social and psychic forces—something that led Brecht to distance himself from the *Manual of Piety* in later life for what he considered to be its exaggerated fascination with bourgeois society's decline.

Without wanting to press the connection between the two texts, both are indebted to a notion of "use value" that is fundamental to the concept of reading that informs the *Kriegsfibel*. The *Manual of Piety* is introduced by a kind of user guide that begins by emphasizing that the text is intended for practical use and "not meant to be unreflectingly swallowed without thought" (*Poems* 456). Suggestions for the proper occasions for reading the different lessons follow this distinction between use and consumption in relation to reading.

Brecht brings up the term "use value" within the specific context of poetry in a brief text, written in 1927, entitled "Kurzer Bericht über 400 (vierhundert) junge Lyriker" (Short Report on 400 [Four Hundred] Young Poets), in which he responds to the vehement public criticism of his performance as juror in a poetry competition. In his verdict, Brecht had taken contemporary lyric to task for its preoccupation with matters of form. Polemicizing against Rainer Maria Rilke, Stefan George, and Franz Werfel, he nominated an obscure young versifier whose poem, "He! He! Iron Man!," was a rather parodic tribute to a popular Australian bicycling champion. The poem about the "Iron Man," which Brecht claimed to have found in a cycling magazine, had not even been submitted.

Despite the ironic tone in which Brecht lauds the poem's "singability" and "documentary value," the call for an operative poetry is earnest (*Werke* 21: 192–93). Recalling his remarks on Mendelsohn's *Amerika*, in "Kurzer Bericht" Brecht constructs the opposition between the aesthetically spurious photographs of great cities, that is, the aesthetic appeal that the photograph can lend the most desolate and sterile urban landscape, and the notion that "All great poems have the value of documents" (*Werke* 21: 191). The result is an intriguing chiasma that ties poetry to "objectivity" on the one hand, and suggests the actual "subjectivity" of the photographic image on the other. Brecht uses this inversion to criticize what he considers to be the "sentimentality, falseness, and unworldliness" (*Werke* 21: 192) of bourgeois concepts of autonomous lyric.

The term "use value" is borrowed from the Marxist economic critique, where it is privileged over "exchange value." In Brecht's writings on poetry, use value becomes the sign of a certain relationship between reader and poem not subject to the logic of consumption to which he also refers in the preface to the *Manual of Piety*. The use value of poetry implies an engaged process of reading that finds an echo in Roland Barthes's notion of *re-reading*, which he defines as "an operation contrary to the commercial and ideological habits of our society, which would have us 'throw away' the story once it has been consumed" (Barthes, *S/ Z* 15).

The *Kriegsfibel* is outfitted with instructions of its own. Unlike the occasional directions of the *Manual of Piety*, the *Kriegsfibel* presents itself as a primer for retraining our reading of the photograph—a project of enormous scope, given the preponderance of technical images in our experience of the world. Taking her cue from Brecht's critique of the illustrated press in his short texts on photography, editor Ruth Berlau writes: "He who forgets the past remains its captive. This book seeks to teach the art of reading images. For reading images is as difficult as reading hieroglyphs for the untrained. The ignorance of social relations that capitalism seeks to maintain makes the thousands of photographs spewed out by the illustrated press truly seem like hieroglyphs to the unsuspecting reader" (*Werke* 12: 129).

The constellation of reading, history, social and material forces, and the media image signals a highly complex intersection of concerns. It marks the territory of the *Kriegsfibel* as a juncture or articulation, itself already suggested by a secondary meaning of the word *Fibel*, whose root lies in the Latin *fibula*, meaning clasp. Inhering in the figure of a clasp, of course, is the notion of a corresponding operation of decoupling that secures the territory of the *Kriegsfibel* as a privileged artistic space for reconstituting and activating the gaze of the reader.

THE COMPOSITIONAL FRAME

Brecht was closely involved with the design of the *Kriegsfibel* and followed the preparations for the book's printing with great care (Bohnert, *Lyrik* 309). The text's overall composition contributes in important ways to the author's attempt to stimulate an active reading posture. The *Kriegsfibel* is in folio format. Each page encompasses a large amount of seemingly "empty" space, a feature that Brecht regarded highly as a formal device. A brief text on Chinese painting, written in 1935, reads like a formal manifesto for the *Kriegsfibel*:

Chinese artists also have a lot of space on their paper. Many sections of the surface appear to be unused; but these sections play an important compositional role; they appear to be just as scrupulously conceived in terms of form and proportion as the outlines of the objects. In these openings the paper or canvas itself emerges as a very specific value. The artist does not simply negate the background in covering it over. The mirror in which something is reflected in this space maintains its integrity as a mirror. This means among other things a laudable refusal to subjugate the observer whose sense of illusion never quite becomes complete. (*Werke* 22.1: 134)

The broad black borders framing the images in the photoepigrams and the expanses of paper on the opposing pages suggest the same effort to draw attention to the context and constructedness of the images and epigrams taken up in the *Kriegsfibel*. In the spaces between image, frame, and epigram, "The eye," Brecht remarks, "can go out exploring" (*Werke* 22.1: 134).

The *Kriegsfibel*'s front cover is a possible point of departure for the reader's venturing eye. It consists of a black/white photograph of a group of soldiers clearly exhausted and struggling against the cold. Photoepigram no. 61, which incorporates the same image, includes the accompanying caption identifying the haggard soldiers as "The Face of the German Army in Russia" (*Werke* 12: 251). The enlargement of what must have been a much smaller original photograph magnifies the coarse resolution that characterizes all of the images of the *Kriegsfibel*. The rhetoric of the newspaper photo is central to the conception of the text's critique of the media and the photographic image.

The exclusion of the images in early editions of the *Kriegsfibel* published in Brecht's collected works is indicative of a fundamental misunderstanding characterizing most scholarly treatments of the text. The evident resistance to taking seriously the images in the *Kriegsfibel* goes back to its immediate reception in the GDR. When the book finally appeared in November 1955, it was entered in the competition for the most attractive book of the year. Despite Brecht's attention to the book's printing, it received only an honorable mention. Among the grounds given were the poor concept realization, type choice, and inferior print quality (Bohnert, *Lyrik* 309).

As reproductions of clipped newspaper images, the images are clearly not art-photograph quality. One could, perhaps, attribute the conspicuously "low-tech" images to Brecht's enthusiasm for the "historical" quality of the photograph in its early period. But Brecht was generally too interested in new technologies and disinclined to nostalgia to have seriously considered the possibility of a return to an older photographic praxis. His interest in the specific visual texture of the daguerreotype, too, is in the obstacles it presents to identification and not in its purely aesthetic appeal (*Journals* 913). If Brecht had been interested in producing a glossy coffee-table book, on the other hand, he surely could have taken recourse to negative archives in the process of preparing the *Kriegsfibel* for publication after the war. It seems plausible enough that the images contained in the text are meant to be recognizable as reproductions of newspaper material. The themes, camera perspectives, and especially the numerous captions, headings, dates, page or volume numbers (nos. 4, 6, 22, 38, 42, 66, 69), and references to the Associated Press (nos. 25, 39, 55) all belong to the easily identifiable rhetoric of the illustrated newspaper.

The features that mark the photoepigram images as belonging to the illustrated newspaper are the precondition for the double function of the accompanying epigrams. The epigrams can function both as *commentary* on the images and as a mechanism of *displacement* vis-à-vis the media in which they are constituted. The epigrams offer both a reinterpretation or "re-vision" of the images and remove them from the newspaper's economy of signification. In the *Kriegsfibel*, the photographic image is no longer subjected to the logic of consumption informing "fast" visual media. Instead, the text opens up the reader's "symbolic eye" (Wright, *Brecht* 56–57) whereby the photograph loses the illusion of transparency as the object of a rereading.

The outer design of the *Kriegsfibel* introduces a number of other compositional elements whose recurrence contribute to the overall artistic composition of the text. The torn line that symbolically divides the title on the title page diagonally into black and white halves signals the disharmony of war and picks up on the incision created by Brecht's signature on the cover photograph. It sustains a graphic mark that becomes a motif in the rest of the text. In the pages of the *Kriegsfibel*, it can be rediscovered, for example, in the contrast between the white left hand pages and the dark photoepigrams on the right. This same pattern structures a number of photoepigrams as well.

In no. 5 the page is bisected vertically so that the image depicting a Jeep convoy takes up the entire right side, while the left remains black. In nos. 13 and 24 the relationship between black and white in the images themselves creates the compositional tension. Photoepigram no. 13 shows the author Lion Feuchtwanger behind barbed wire in an internment camp. A large, dark doorway opening in the background accomplishes the chromatic contrast between light and shadow that separates the image into two halves. The division of the image, the creation of a border, contributes to the motif of division and imprisonment signalled by the barbed wire and Feuchtwanger's gaze beyond its confines.

A shadow falling across the face of the Social Democrat Gustav Noske in a portrait photograph creates a similar effect in photoepigram no. 24. The quatrain reads:

> I was the bloodhound, mates. I gave
> This name to myself, I, the people's son
> They approved of it: when the Nazis came
> They granted me abode and sustenance.
>
> (*Werke* 12: 176)[3]

The contrast between the two halves of his face underscores Brecht's critique of the Weimar Defense Minister's ''two-faced'' politics as representative and traitor of the working class. It is striking how often diagonal lines of contrast slash through the images. Additional examples of this compositional feature can be found in photoepigram nos. 2, 7, 8, 9, 12, 19, and 29. The visual motif of separation and estrangement recurs in any number of places in the *Kriegsfibel*— not surprising given the text's theme of war. But this should not distract from the text's imperative to attend to the fundamentally symbolic nature of the photographic image. The reader has been forewarned: ''images are like hieroglyphs.''

The *Kriegsfibel*'s sixty-nine photoepigrams consist of reproductions of newspaper photographs collected by Brecht while in exile from different print media sources, including *Life* and various American and Swedish newspapers. With one important exception, all of the photoepigrams in the *Kriegsfibel* contain a photographic image and a four-line epigram and are accompanied by a white facing page. The actual number of differing photoepigram forms, however, is surprising. Many incorporate original newspaper titles, captions, or both, most often in English or Swedish, in which case the German translation appears on the facing page. Most of the photoepigrams include some type of frame, although here as well the variations are numerable, once again pointing to the importance of the *Kriegsfibel*'s ''reframing'' function. The majority of the images have a ''classical'' frame: a broad black border on all four sides. Variations include one-, two-, and three-bordered frames with the image running off the page on the top and/or sides. In two cases (nos. 6 and 65) the image takes up the entire page.

The various photoepigram forms suggest a number of different text-image relationships and reading strategies. The epigrams can often be read as rather straightforward ''commentaries'' on the images. In other cases the images ''explain'' the epigrams more than critique them, and there are all manner of possibilities in between—especially in those cases where captions and titles further complicate the text. The fact that there is, strictly speaking, no ''prototypical'' photoepigram only underscores the photoepigram's integration into the text's overall composition. In addition to the photoepigrams, the text is accompanied by an appendix containing explanatory notes that supply historical information. Brecht seems to have made this addition willingly in response to official criticism that not all of the photoepigrams were still understandable in the context of the mid-1950s. The appended information not only serves to contextualize the photoepigrams, however: it also adds another moment of delay or complexity that requires the reader to maintain a mobile reading posture.

The arrangement of photoepigrams in the *Kriegsfibel* follows a loose chronology beginning with Hitler's rise to power and concluding with the war's end. The first shows Hitler in profile standing at a podium. Arms outstretched toward an invisible audience, the microphones, pose, and text before him suggest that he is giving a speech:

> Like one who had already ridden the course in my sleep
> Chosen by fate, I know the way
> The narrow path leading into the abyss:
> I'll find it in my sleep. Won't you follow?

The epigram circumscribes the temporal expanse of the *Kriegsfibel* from Hitler's solicitation ''Won't you follow?'' to the ''abyss'' of war and Germany's destruction.

The narrative that is announced in this first photoepigram accrues in the rest of the text in a number of ways. Photoepigram no. 42, for example, depicts a Thai woman seeking safety in a primitive shelter dug into the ground. Like a large number of images in the *Kriegsfibel*, this one stems from the cover of the illustrated magazine *Life*, whose title appears in large white letters on the upper part of the image. The date of the issue, 17 March 1941, is clearly visible. The photoepigram's position in the *Kriegsfibel* is not unmotivated: located two-thirds of the way into the series, it corresponds roughly to the date's place in the years between 1933–45.

One should not overemphasize the linearity of the text's narrative structure. Like the scenes in Brecht's epic drama, the assembly of photoepigrams in the *Kriegsfibel* is montage-like. The text's ''reader'' character—with its commentary, epigrams, titles, and captions—serves to interrupt a narrative flow that would offer an oversimplified and completed view of the war. The individual "scenes" in the *Kriegsfibel* are largely interchangeable and meaningful apart from the overarching narrative frame. Barthes's description of Brecht's epic scenes as tableaus applies equally well to the *Kriegsfibel*. In their arrangement and structure, the photoepigrams both signify and point to the process of signification (Barthes, "Diderot" 34–35). The interplay of text and image in the photoepigrams is open to readings that intersect with Brecht's materialist critique in productive ways. Photoepigram no. 3, for instance, contains an excerpt-like image of a woman seated on a rocky shore whose soiled hands and feet (as the epigram informs the reader) are covered with oil. The photoepigram offers little narrative information:

> On Spanish shores women often find
> After bathing among the cliffs
> Black oil on arms and breasts:
> The last traces of sunken ships.

The reference to oil and destroyed ships has less to do with a materialist critique in a narrow, economic sense—although the oil supply was certainly an economic and strategic concern—than with the material effects of war on the body. While one could argue that Brecht relies on notions of the inviolability of the female body for his critique, the photoepigram's grainy texture and the somewhat obscure framing of the bather are not especially conducive to a voyeuristic spectator position. In its attention to the corporeal effects of the Nazi regime, the photoepigram signals the extensive functionalization of women for the war, from physical labor in armaments factories to programs obliging biological reproduction.

The emphasis on the notion of the margin warrants another look at the text's "periphery." Brecht's signature, a facsimile in white lettering on the cover photograph, represents an initial sanctioning gesture: traditionally, a signature authorizes a work of art. We need not read this appeal to art as an authorizing procedure securing the originality of the *Kriegsfibel* as a "work," however. Brecht's poem "Why Should My Name Be Mentioned?" (*Poems* 264–65) and his well-known "laxity regarding intellectual property" (*Werke* 21: 315) attest to his critical appraisal of conventions of authorship, originality, and copyright.

Brecht's answer to the bourgeois work of art, reproduction, montage, and the quote holds linked concepts. In a short text on plagiarism, Brecht writes of literary adaptations: "This is where the quote realizes its naturally elevated status. It is the most important stylistic feature. Quotability. Finding potential 'plagiarisms' means art in this context" (*Werke* 21: 318). Based upon the possibility of reproduction, the newspaper photographs appropriated by Brecht in the *Kriegsfibel* are "quotes" of another order, since the idea of an original newspaper image that could be the precondition of a citation is nonsensical. Nevertheless, Brecht's recontextualization of the image in the photoepigram is part of an operation of montage that he describes in a different context as a method of destroying the unity of the work (*Journals* 21). This process of destruction bears on the unity and hence the *authority* of the author as well: "The 'Author' is unimportant, he endures in that he disappears" (*Werke* 21: 318). This brings us back to Brecht's signature as the sign of the author's absence or distance from the location where meaning is produced in the process of reading.

Brecht's intriguing remark on the disappearance of the author resonates with additional meaning in terms of the *Kriegsfibel* as the opening of an aesthetic terrain. His signature marks an artistic territory and not authorship. The return to the rhetoric of territories and geography is predetermined. As Deleuze and Guattari note: "The signature, the proper name, is not the constituted mark of the subject, but the constituting mark of a domain, an abode. The signature is not the indication of a person; it is the chancy formation of a domain. . . . One puts one's signature on something just as one plants one's flag on a piece of land" (316).

In the case of the *Kriegsfibel*, Brecht's signature marks an aesthetic terrain for questioning vision and retraining the eye. It recalls Benjamin's photography essay, in which the rhetoric of the signature intersects with matters of perception in his characterization of aura's decline. He writes of the shattering of aura as the "signature of a mode of perception" (Benjamin, "Geschichte" 379). The *Kriegsfibel* bears Brecht's own perceptual signature: a new mode of seeing operating on the very logic of images that Brecht and Benjamin credit with the photograph's loss of singularity and historical specificity.

The eccentricity of the signature is, of course, paradoxically related to its reproducibility; the convention of the signed endorsement can only function because it is repeatable (see Derrida 315). The same paradox inhabits Brecht's signature on the cover of the *Kriegsfibel*. The mark of an interruption of particular mode of perception and logic of reproduction, it is itself indebted to duplication. But it is also a gesture to writing itself; it signals a reinscription of the cover photograph and an intervention in the expanding universe of images.

This notion is picked up in the text's flap that includes a photograph of Brecht sitting at his writing desk. Printed below it are the first two lines of the poem that serve as the motto of his *Svendborg Poems*: "Refuged beneath this Danish thatched roof, friends / I follow your struggle" (*Poems* 320). While reference to the author's exile in Denmark signals a historical and geographical positionality, this initial constellation of photograph and poetic text in the inner jacket prefigures the photoepigrams to come in which the epigram functions not only as commentary to the images—an important function for Brecht's war critique—but also as a mechanism of re-inscription. In this way, the *Kriegsfibel* can be seen as an intervention in the history of the relationship between writing and the technical image that is also the history of a certain relationship to reading. On the threshold of a postmodern media society, Brecht's war and media critique make a final appeal to an operative reading praxis under the sign of writing.

EPIGRAM AND INSCRIPTION

That which you are reading here is written in verse!
I say this because you may no longer know
What a poem and also: what a poet is!
Truly, you have not treated us well!

> From "Lied der Lyriker" (*Werke* 11: 250; The Poets' Song)

The engraving stylus is a carnassial tooth,
and one who writes inscriptions is a slashing tiger:
a shredder of images.

> (Flusser, *Die Schrift*)

What motivates the choice of verse over prose text? If the epigrams in the *Kriegsfibel* function primarily as "commentary," as editor Berlau suggests in the cover flap text, why take the detour through rhyme and meter? While the specificity of the text lies precisely in the complex linkage between poetic text and image, Brecht's understanding of the epigram offers an important insight into the way in which the epigrams function in the *Kriegsfibel*.

For the most part, the text's sixty-nine epigrams follow an a/b/a/b rhyme scheme; the rest either rhyme internally (as in nos. 10, 11, 13, 14, 66, and 68) or conform to an a/a/b/b scheme (as in nos. 5, 34, and 36). At first glance, the use of the epigram in the *Kriegsfibel* appears as a somewhat unaccustomed gesture to traditional poetics. Brecht's scattered reflections on the lyric form and his lyric practice in collections like the "German Satires" (sampling in *Poems* 294–300) in particular, represent a decided departure from traditional rhyme schemes and meter. Brecht the poet is better known as an innovator than as an imitator.

In the well-known text "On Rhymeless Verse with Irregular Rhythms," Brecht refers to "the oily smoothness of the usual five-foot iambic meter" (*Poems* 464)—the very form in which he cast many of the epigrams in the *Kriegsfibel*. But while Brecht was interested in a type of poetry that subverted what he considered to be the "disagreeably lulling, soporific" effect of regular rhyme and meter, he never stopped writing in traditional lyric idioms (*Poems* 470). Even the most traditional forms such as the epigram remained relevant.

Brecht could take recourse to older lyric forms because he approached form in general from the perspective of its function. In a text entitled "Underrating the Formal Aspect," he writes: "At one time or another I have studied the old forms of poetry, the story, the drama and the theatre, and I only abandoned them when they started getting in the way of what I wanted to say" (*Poems* 471; *Journals* 11). The emphasis on function reminds us of Brecht's early demand for a utilitarian lyric and points once again to the *Kriegsfibel*'s "reader" character. The strict rhyme and simple form of the epigrams do, in fact, recall the verse of the traditional *Fibel*, aimed at fostering memorization and the absorption of knowledge (Knopf, *Lyrik* 214).

But the rhyme scheme and meter of poems in the *Kriegsfibel* seldom add up to the regularized and consuming reading rhythm that Brecht believed would arrest the activity of the reader. The text's important and more narrowly didactic interest in the transmission of political contents—the critique of the Second World War and the solemn warning to future generations—is coupled with a more comprehensive lesson that has little to do with rote memorization. To quote once again from the introduction, the *Kriegsfibel* "seeks to teach the art of reading images." Brecht is interested in enabling an alert reading praxis, a reorganization of reading conceived of in its broadest sense as perception. In a short passage on a poem by Wordsworth, Brecht brings poetry into connection with perception in an unambiguous way. Insisting that poetry cannot be reduced to "mere expression," he notes: "The reception of a poem is an operation just like seeing or hearing, i.e. much more active" (*Poems* 483; *Journals* 91).

Brecht's literary production relies heavily on a communicative, often dialogic textual practice that also characterizes much of his poetry. One of his main critiques in the aforementioned "Kurzer Bericht" was that the poems that he had judged "distance themselves too far from the original gesture of the communication of an idea" (*Werke* 21: 191). A number of the epigrams that appear in the *Kriegsfibel* are, in fact, written in a dialogic mode, addressing either the reader or constructing an internal dialogue. The latter is the case in photoepigram no. 2, which thematizes the contradictory logic of the war economy. The image depicts workers maneuvering a heavy sheet of iron using thick cables; Brecht's accompanying epigram:

> "What are you building, brothers?"—"An iron wagon."
> "And what about these sheets lying close by?"
> "Shells that pierce through iron walls."
> "And what is all of this for, brothers?"—"In order to live."

In photoepigram no. 61, the poem's initial line gestures directly to the reader: "See our sons, deaf and blood bespattered." In other cases, the epigrams engage persons and objects that are a part of the images. The effect is a complex play of referentiality that is not fully described by the poem-image relationship informing the notion of the epigrams as commentary.

Brecht's definition of the reception of poetry is quite radical. Reading poetry, we are told, "is an operation like seeing or hearing." This conflation of reading and perception results in a revaluation by which the poem acquires new importance as an extension of experience. On the other hand, the fundamental role of interpretation in Brecht's expansive concept of reading displaces the familiar notion of perception as the unmediated absorption of visual, tactile, acoustic, and other stimuli. Brecht's remark implies that on a fundamental level, our perception of the world is always already an interpretation.

The connection between poetry and perception points once again to the *Fibel* character of the text and hints at why verse could represent an option for Brecht in his critique of the photographic image. Brecht does not construct a poetry-prose opposition based upon the notion of the former's "subjectivity" and the latter's supposed "objectivity." Instead, the appeal of verse in the context of the photographic image is that it draws attention to writing itself. The particular functionality of the epigram form remains to be explained, however. For while the specificity of the text lies precisely in its confrontation of poem and newspaper photograph, the fact that Brecht refers to both photo- and *epigrams* has important implications for the text's displacement of the media image and re-organization of reading.

Brecht's understanding of the epigram is highly indebted to its classical conception. He writes: "The sonnet and the epigram were forms that I took over as they stood" (*Poems* 472; *Journals* 12). Traditionally, epigrams have been engraved on gravestones, monuments, and works of art, the primary requirement being the succinct and poetic expression of an idea. Epigrammatic brevity characterizes a large part of Brecht's wartime and subsequent lyric production. To varying degrees, and with varying concessions to rhyme and rhythm, the poems of his exile in Sweden and Finland—among them the *Svendborg Poems* (1939) and the poems of the *Steffin Collection* (1940)—as well as his later *Buckow Elegies* (1953) all tend toward the economy and clarity of expression typical of the classical epigram.

In September 1940 Brecht laments the difficulty of reconstituting an epigrammatic "poetry of objects" (*Journals* 94) during a time when the available objects were so closely associated with war and destruction. He continues, "The beauty of an airplane has something obscene about it." In a situation in which an airplane is always a potential bomber, Brecht was well aware of the danger of assisting an aestheticization of the war machine. In another place, he notes: "Interestingly, it is not only dangerous, but difficult to represent the war accurately. Simply reporting or copying what one sees is by no means sufficient" (*Werke* 23: 63). Perhaps in recognition of this problem, during the course of the *Kriegsfibel*'s construction, Brecht omitted a photoepigram incorporating the visually arresting image of a bomber plane caught in the play of dazzling search lights (see *Werke* 12: 276).

Insofar as the *Kriegsfibel* might be said to represent a poetry of objects, the war machine is continuously subject to disturbances. In photoepigram no. 15, for example, the top half of the photoepigram is occupied by the image and the bottom half is black: like a film halted in midframe. The image depicts the tight quarters of a *Luftwaffe* plane's cockpit and its three-man crew. The reader's gaze is denied the associations of speed, flight, and technological supremacy that characterized the Nazi propaganda effort to represent the war as a *Blitzkrieg* that would be quickly and easily won. One's attention is drawn to the rather enigmatic expressions of the crew, whose eye's betray the fear thematized in the epigram's last line:

> We're the ones who came over your city
> O woman, anguishing about your children!
> We've fixed our sights on you and them
> And if you ask us why, then: out of fear.

Brecht consistently links the war apparatus to human agents with very human apprehensions, thereby leaving open the possibility for opposition despite the war machine's self-perpetuating logic and apparent anonymity.

In another place in the *Journals*, Brecht turns once again to the materiality of Greek epigrams, describing their "marvelous concreteness" (80), and is reminded of one of his own poems. Following an a/b/a/b rhyme scheme in the German original, the first two strophes of the poem read:

> Why not inscribe the beautiful structures
> That you're building there, guns slung about?
> Sunk into stone, they ought to bear
> The handwriting of their founding classes.
>
> Record also its use and: heed you it well!
> And so that it be commonly known, chisel it in!
> Building for yourselves for the first time
> Record it in the lasting stone!

> *(Werke* 14: 301–302)

It is no coincidence that the poem takes up the rhetoric of writing and the signature under the sign of engraving and inscription. The notion of the epigram as inscription appeals to the Greek roots of the word in the verb *epigraphein*, meaning "to write on." In the German original, Brecht uses the word *Schriftzug*, whose literal meaning can be rendered as a "stroke of writing," linked here to the image of striking words into stone. Brecht composed a number of such epigrams for public buildings. His inscription for a building at Weberwiese, the first high-rise in East Berlin after the war, also appeals to the idea of the working class's signature handwriting:

> And having then decided
> To finally trust in our own strength
> And to build a more beautiful life
> We were not daunted by toil and struggle.

> *(Werke* 23: 203)

In the "German War Primer"—a part of the *Svendborg Poems* that is not to be confused with the *Kriegsfibel* itself—Brecht implements the poems as a literal "writing on the wall," as is the case with a concise quatrain that begins with the words "On the wall was chalked." The poem ends with the solemn notice that the writer of the graffiti thematizing war preparations has already fallen in battle (*Poems* 288). First published in 1937 and written as a warning and anticipation of the war, in the epigram it is writing that perseveres as a caution to the future. The fact that chalk can be washed away, however, introduces a moment of uncertainty in light of the rhetoric that coalesces around the opposition between superficiality and depth that Brecht develops.

The notion of the enduring inscription and the perseverance of writing over time informs the *Svendborg Poems* to no small degree. When Brecht mocks Hitler as the *Anstreicher* or "house painter" in the "German War Primer," for example, playing on the Nazi leader's early artistic aspirations, he does so not only in the interest of satirical critique but also as part of a coherent figural language. The image of Hitler as the house painter who merely paints over the fissures in German society while ignoring the true sources of social and political rifts is the theme of "Das Lied vom Anstreicher Hitler" (The Song of Hitler, the House Painter), a poem from about the same period. The first two of the poem's four strophes are:

> Hitler the house painter
> Said: Good people, let me have a go!
> And he took a fresh bucket of whitewash
> And gave Germany's house a new coat.
> The whole German house a new coat.
>
> Hitler the house painter
> Said: in a flash the renovation will be over
> And the holes and cracks and crevices
> He simply painted it all over.
> The whole shit he painted over.

(*Werke* 11: 215)

In the third strophe, Brecht queries: "O house painter Hitler / Why weren't you a mason?" creating the opposition between the mere covering of a surface and the work of the mason—one who not only builds but whose chisel also cuts inscriptions deep into stone.

Hitler's superficiality is a motif that extends throughout the "German Satires" in particular, as, for example in "Wenn der Anstreicher durch die Lautsprecher über den Frieden redet" (As the House Painter Talks over the Loudspeakers about Peace). The poem juxtaposes the concrete proof of the construction of military roads with Hitler's inflated radio speeches and promises of peace. The first two strophes are:

> As the house painter talks over the loudspeakers about peace
> The street workers on the highways watch
> And see
> Knee-deep cement, meant for
> Heavy tanks.

The house painter talks about peace.
Straightening their aching backs
Large hands on cannon barrels
The cement pourers listen.

(*Werke* 12: 11)

Brecht's privileging of the inscription, the epigrammatic marking of a surface over and against Hitler's lies and empty phrases, finds programmatic expression in a poem from the *Svendborg Poems*' third section entitled "Chroniken" (Chronicles). The poem "Die unbesiegliche Inschrift" (The Undefeatable Inscription), tells the story of a socialist soldier imprisoned in Italy who scratches the words "Long Live Lenin" into the wall of his cell. The prison guards' efforts to paint over the illicit inscription only serve to make it larger and more visible—the painter had merely followed the lines of the lettering with his paint brush. Nor can a second coat applied in broad, concealing strokes prevent the words from eventually bleeding through. The poem's final verse relates the eventual triumph of the inscription over the injustice of the prison walls:

So the guards sent a mason with a mason's knife to counter the inscription
And he scratched out letter for letter an hour long
And when he was finished, the cell wall above displayed, faded
But engraved deeply into the wall the undefeatable inscription:
Long live Lenin!
Now remove the wall! said the soldier.

(*Werke* 12: 39–40)

While the figural language of inscription is not taken up in the *Kriegsfibel* as it is in the previous examples, the epigrams retain their inscriptive moment. The poems in photoepigram nos. 7 and 10, both of which were taken over from the *Steffin Collection*, appeal to the epigram in its traditional function as an engraved epitaph. The first, accompanying an image of surf breaking on a rocky coast, commemorates those lost near Kattegat, the area between Jutland and Sweden belonging to Denmark, where the Germans lost a number of light ships and converted fishing cutters in the campaign against Norway. Its four lines read:

We're eight thousand in Kattegat.
Freighters took us down.
Fishermen, if your nets have caught many fish here:
Remember us and let one go.

Photoepigram no. 10 takes an even more pronounced recourse to the epigram's link to the epitaph—if only as an occasion to replace the epigraph's commemorative tone and third-person address with the accusation of the one who has fallen. "That he may die a miserable death is my last will" is the epigram's unforgiving first line. The image, which Brecht clipped from an American newspaper, depicts a simple cross marking a grave. In contrast to the majority of the epigrams in the *Kriegsfibel*, the quatrains in this photoepigram are not mounted below the image but "inscribed" onto the surface of the photograph itself. In other cases, the epigrams accompany photographs of buildings—many nearly completely destroyed by repeated bombings—in another appeal to their traditional function.

As compared to the "constituting" operation of Brecht's epigrams for public buildings—the social and historical marking of an abode—the epigrams in the *Kriegsfibel* have a reconstituting function with a specific media-critical potential. Seen from the perspective of the displacement of writing with the proliferation of the technical image in the form of photographs, video, television, and film, the epigrams read like an appeal to writing itself. Beyond their commentary function and contribution to Brecht's war critique, the epigrams stand for a "re-inscription" of the image in the name of an eroding writing culture.

PHOTO(EPI)GRAMMETRY

Photogrammetry means "picture measuring." It is the science of constructing maps by using photographs taken from different positions over a given terrain and subjecting them to triangulation, plotting, and various other measuring procedures. Having obvious military applications, photogrammetry exploded with the advances in aerial photography that accompanied the two world wars and marked a further stage in the technical image's expansion of perception that Brecht and Benjamin had already identified in the late 1920s.

But what might "photo**epi**grammetry" be? The intersection of war and photography that characterizes the history of photogrammetry is complicated by poetry, writing, in the *Kriegsfibel*. Brecht not only stages a visual reframing in taking up and disrupting the territory opened up by the media photograph. His "photoepigrammetry" involves an operation based upon the word's relationship to the Greek root *gramma*, with its connotations of both linguistics and measurement (*gramma*="letter" and "a small weight"). Both war and media critique, the *Kriegsfibel* involves a linguistic remapping and re-inscription that functions in different ways in the various photoepigrams. The variety of photoepigram types reflects the complex convergence of historical and theoretical concerns that come together in the *Kriegsfibel*. As a consequence, the following, closing, interpretations are not "exemplary" analyses, but reading suggestions.

Photoepigram No. 21

The image in photoepigram no. 21 is an aerial view of what appears to be an industrial or military port complex with its storage tanks arranged in neat rows. Smoke billows upwards in ominous clouds: an apparent "hit." Brecht's epigram adds:

A plume of smoke betrays that they have been there:
Sons of fire, but not of light.
And where did they come from? Out of darkness.
And where are they going from here? Into nothingness.

In its commentary function, the epigram reinforces the assumption—given the general context of war—that the image shows the aftermath of a bombing raid. "Smoke" can be read as the sign of the invisible enemy and identifies the perpetrators as the subject of the first line. The second line's "sons of fire" extends the metaphor and at the same time raises the issue of the perversion of technological mastery: "Sons of fire, but not of light." In the final two verses, "darkness" and "nothingness" suggest an ethical void, namely the moral vacuum of Hitler's war machine that is underscored by the darkness of the photoepigram's frame.

The rhetoric of light and darkness and the questions of the bombers' origin and destination—"And where did they come from? . . . And where are they going from here?"—signal the issues of visibility and invisibility that inform the rhetoric and tactics of military conflict. Military success depends upon both a superior knowledge of a terrain and the ability to disguise one's own tactical maneuvers. The approach and departure of the camera, whose lens captures the image that Brecht takes up, motivates the epigram's reference to the approach and departure of the bombers in the epigram. Both for the military and the public, it was increasingly the photographic image that mediated the war experience.

The Nazis' sophisticated manipulation of the visual media is well known. In the Nazi newsreels depicting the attack on Norway, however, the camera was apparently almost too successful in staging the speed and efficiency with which the *Luftwaffe* defeated the small country. An internal SS report recommended supplying additional information to the viewers to emphasize the distances that the planes had to cover during the course of the air attack (Welch 192). Apparently, the victory had come across as being too easy and lacking in heroic effort.

Although a long way from the kind of hyperaestheticized and antiseptic video representation of war that has become familiar since the Gulf War and the United States' attack of Panama, the image in photoepigram no. 21 nevertheless points to an earlier stage in the relationship between the military apparatus and the camera. Few types of photographic image draw attention to the camera as explicitly as the aerial photograph. Its rhetoric is a military one. Inviting the spectator to participate in the surveying of the bombed target, the eye becomes a charting instrument assessing the damage to an enemy terrain. More than a mere extension of the human eye, the aerial perspective contributes to the collapse of distance and the eclipse of time that characterizes the confluence of military and photographic technology described by Paul Virilio in terms of a new "logic of perception" in his *War and Cinema*.

The alliance between photographic and military technology accelerates the evaporation of time from the photographic image. The image is produced, consumed, and disposed of quickly. The images are transmitted quickly for rapid distribution. Two of Brecht's photoepigrams, in fact, make use of "wirephoto" images. Credited to the Associated Press wirephoto service, which was established in 1935 and was relatively widely used in World War II, the poor resolution and strange contrast in images of Goebbels and a grieving Malaysian woman in nos. 25 and 39, respectively, stand out in the *Kriegsfibel*.

Brecht's epigram and his framing of the photographic image in photoepigram no. 21 point to the camera and interrupt the eye's targeting gaze. The dialogic form of the quatrain's last two lines—a feature of a number of epigrams—enjoins the reader to question both the origin and destination of the enemy, which in turn allows us to consider the origin of the image as well. The black margin borders the image on three sides, but allows the image to run off the page where one might expect the upper border to be in a "classical" frame. Decentering the official media representation of the war, the spectator's gaze is drawn out of the frame, pointing, perhaps, to the historical contingencies and causalities outside the margin of the photographic image. The surprising number of framing variations in the *Kriegsfibel* suggest once again the importance of the notion of a "marginal vision" in the text's conception. Brecht's appropriating operation in the photoepigram both occupies the visual terrain of the war image and demonstrates the limits of vision.

Photoepigram No. 33

Questions of visibility and looking play a role in a number of other photoepigrams, as is the case in no. 8 depicting soldiers looking out from under the shelter of a railroad car. A caption in English identifies them as German assault troops. The epigram reads:

> I see you keeping a lookout for your enemy
> Before you charge out into battle:
> Was it the Frenchmen at whom your gaze was directed?
> Or was it your captain who guards you?

Taken together, poem and image thematize a play of watching and being watched that is a part of the logistics of war already mentioned. In this example, Brecht employs the motif of observation to point to the instrumentalization of the common infantryman caught between enemy fire and his own military apparatus.

The image in photoepigram no. 33 appears to present an aerial view similar to that in no. 21. It depicts the crater-pocked contours of a battlefield with a white road cutting through the dark background. Brecht supplies the following epigram to the image:

Brothers, here in distant Caucasus
I now lie buried, a Swabian farmer's son
Felled by the shot of a Russian farmer.
I was defeated long ago in Swabia.

On the one hand, Brecht's epigram performs a redefinition by which the soldier is re-inscribed in terms of class or social position. No longer enemies by political decree, the poem suggests that Russian and Swabian share a common background. The final line places responsibility for the war and the death of the latter not with the Russian soldier but with Germany and the war's historical roots: "I was defeated long ago in Swabia." Brecht's commentary text to the photoepigram in the back of the *Kriegsfibel* offers a precise context by giving the date of the German invasion of the Soviet Union and the material interests behind the invasion: land, wheat, minerals, and oil (*Werke* 12: 420).

The title on the facing page has a different function. It does not so much contribute to the historical and political recontextualization accomplished by epigram and commentary text as point to the literal constructedness of the depicted scene: "Attack of the Soviet Union (prepared in a sand box)." A comment on the medium in general, the image is in fact a photograph of a model. Once again, Brecht's interest in destabilizing the gaze of the reader is apparent. Beyond the appeal to take a "closer look"—it is in fact difficult to identify the image as a model battle—is the suggestion of the role of visual representation and simulation in warfare. In the U.S. attack of Iraq, for example, video images were used both in the military technology itself (in bomber cockpits and surveillance systems) and later on television as a way to reduce the bloodshed to an abstract and harmless video game. Brecht's choice of image addresses in a seemingly accidental way what has become an integral part of modern warfare.

Photoepigram No. 31

Whereas the other photoepigrams incorporate newspaper photographs, photoepigram no. 31 reproduces a newspaper text stemming from an unidentified source. Written in Swedish, the somewhat blurred print is translated into German on the left-hand page in the *Kriegsfibel*. Entitled "Motorized German Churches," the blurb reports dryly on the Catholic Church's effort to reach small towns with altar-bearing automobiles. The brief text closes with the information that the priests drive themselves in most cases—it is not difficult to imagine why the idea of a motorized priest might have appealed to Brecht. The epigram's four lines can be rendered in the following way:

O joyous missive: God mobilized!
Hitler advanced and God could not follow.
Let us hope that God does not lose the war
Because in the end he, too, ran out of oil!

The poem clearly polemicizes against the role of the Church in the war. The mixture of military and religious rhetoric in the phrase "God mobilized" suggests the complicity of the Church in the functioning of the war. The second line extends the military rhetoric in describing God, while the connection to Hitler may be read as an ironic remark on the latter's pretensions to infallibility. A biblical allusion to Matthew 25:1–13 and the virgins who forget to bring oil for their lamps (*Werke* 12: 429) links both to economic concerns in the increasing scarcity of oil during the war.

In photoepigram no. 31, Brecht's political and material critique of the war once again collides with fundamental issues of perception and interpretation. The relationship between epigram text and image text is not exhausted by situating the epigram exclusively as a critique of the newspaper text. We can see the reproduction of newspaper text as a gesture to writing and a reminder of the "legibility" of all of the images in the *Kriegsfibel*. Images are to be "read" in the encompassing sense of the project announced in the text's short introduction. Complicating the idea of the "deciphering" or translation of images, however, is the inherent act of interpretation involved in such a procedure.

The fact that Brecht chooses to take up a text that is not written in German can be attributed to several factors, including, most obviously, the newspaper sources available to him while in exile. But perhaps there is more to it than this: it would have been simple enough to replace the Swedish caption with a translation. The Swedish text and its German counterpart on the facing page is a reminder of the fundamental operation of doubling involved in reading. In a more straightforward way than the other photoepigrams' articulation of epigram and photographic image, photoepigram no. 31 signals the reader's own position between readings in a succession of nonidentical repetitions. The constellation of newspaper clipping, epigram, and the translation on the left-hand page facilitates the movement of the eye and an operative reading praxis that allows the reader to arrive at new readings and meanings.

As opposed to the media image that it appropriates, the *Kriegsfibel* is "slow text." It takes time to read, and it is designed for re-reading, a process that it teaches. The interplay between text and image that Brecht stages in the *Kriegsfibel* creates the kind of artistic space for reading that Brecht believed to have discovered in Chinese painting, a space in which "The eye can go out exploring" without coming to rest at one reading (*Werke* 22.1: 134).

Brecht's "quote" of newspaper print can also be read in relationship to the historical shift in our relationship to writing, one aspect of which can be described as the weakening of the written word's privileged status as the bearer of information in favor of the condensed form of the technical image. Writing before the advent of digitalized information, video, and the symbolic surface of the user-friendly terminal, Brecht described the development of the mass media in terms of the growing distance between sender and receiver and the degeneration of writing's communicative function. In "Writing the Truth: Five Difficulties," he characterizes this shift as the movement from "writing for someone'' and an abstract ''writing'' subject to the laws of the media market (Brecht 140).

In photoepigram no. 31, writing itself appears as image or ''quote,'' circulating in the media's marketplace of meaning. Appearing to fade into the photoepigram's dark background, the blurry print marks writing's receding profile. Seen from the other side of ''real-time'' satellite transmission and ''virtual reality,'' the *Kriegsfibel*, a response to an earlier stage in the history of the technical image, appears to us something like the photographs of the medium's early period appeared to Brecht. In his war critique and poetic interrogation of the photographic image, we can see an appeal to a ''historical perspective'' and an attempt to reclaim a space for writing and the reader.

NOTES

1. Brecht's *Journals* are closely linked to the *Kriegsfibel*. Brecht pasted a number of photographs and newspaper clippings onto the pages of the *Journals* in different combinations with text. Photoepigram no. 6, for example, can be found in nearly identical form in *Journals* (319).

2. Recent studies of Brecht's poetry in general include Brooker, *Dialectics*; des Pres; Thompson; and Whitaker. The history of the *Kriegsfibel*'s reception begins with Grimm, ''Emblematik.'' For further studies see Wagenknecht; Grimm (''Antinomik''; ''Gehupft''); Bohnert (*Lyrik* 235–85), Wöhrle (*Versuche* 163–89); Knopf (*Lyrik* 204–216); Heukenkamp; Howald; Lang; and Brady.

3. Since the photoepigrams can be easily located by number (see *Werke* 12: 127–83), no further references to the *Werke* edition will be given where individual photoepigrams are cited in the text.

WORKS CITED (SEE ALSO REFERENCE GUIDE TO WORKS CITED IN ABBREVIATED FORM)

Barthes, Roland. *S/Z*. Translated by Richard Howard. New York: Hill, 1974.
———. ''Diderot, Brecht, Eisenstein.'' *Screen* 15. 2 (1974): 33–39.
Benjamin, Walter. ''Kleine Geschichte der Photographie.'' *Gesammelte Schriften*. Frankfurt am Main: Suhrkamp, 1978. 2.1: 368–85.
———. ''The Work of Art in the Age of Mechanical Reproduction.'' In *Illuminations* 217–52.
Brady, P. V. ''From Cave-Painting to 'Photogramm': Brecht, Photography and the *Arbeitsjournal*.'' *Forum for Modern Language Studies* 14.3 (July 1978): 270–82.
Brecht, Bertolt. ''Writing the Truth: Five Difficulties.'' Translated by Richard Winston. In *Galileo*. Translated by Charles Laughton, edited by Eric Bentley. New York: Grove, 1966. 133–50.
Deleuze, Gilles, and Félix Guattari. *A Thousand Plateaus. Capitalism and Schizophrenia*. Translated by Brian Massumi. Minneapolis: University of Minnesota Press, 1987.
Derrida, Jacques. *Margins of Philosophy*. Translated by Alan Bass. Chicago: University of Chicago Press, 1982.
des Pres, Terrence. *Praises & Dispraises*. New York: Viking, 1988.

Esslin, Martin. "Brecht's Poetry in English." In *Mediations*. London: Sphere, 1983. 66–67.

Flusser, Vilém. *Die Schrift*. 1987. Frankfurt am Main: Fischer, 1991.

———. *Towards a Philosophy of Photography*. 1983. Göttingen: European Photography, 1984.

Friedrich, Ernst. *Krieg dem Kriege! Guerre à la Guerre! War against War! Oorlog aan den Oorlog!* Berlin: Freie Jugend, 1926.

Grimm, Reinhold. "Marxistische Emblematik. Zu Bertolt Brechts *Kriegsfibel*." In *Wissenschaft als Dialog. Festschrift für Wolfdietrich Rasch*. Edited by Renate Heydebrand and Klaus Günther Just. Stuttgart: Metzler, 1969. 351–79.

———. "Forcierte Antinomik." In *Emblem und Emblemrezeption*. Edited by Sibylle Penkert. Darmstadt: Wissenschaftliche Buchgesellschaft, 1978. 560–63.

———. "Gehupft wie gesprungen." *Brecht-Jahrbuch 1977*: 177–83.

Heukenkamp, Ursula. "Den Krieg von unten ansehen. Über das Bild des Zweiten Weltkrieges in Bertolt Brechts *Kriegsfibel*." *Weimarer Beiträge* 31 (1985): 1294–1312.

Howald, Stefan. "Notiz zur *Kriegsfibel*." In *Aktualisierung Brechts*. Edited by Wolfgang Fritz Haug, Klaus Pierwoß, and Karen Ruoff. Berlin: Argument, 1980. 208–215.

Lang, Joachim. "Brechts Sehschule. Anmerkungen zur *Kriegsfibel*." In *Brecht-Journal*, vol. 2. Edited by Jan Knopf. Frankfurt am Main: Suhrkamp, 1986. 95–114.

Mendelsohn, Erich. *Erich Mendelsohn's Amerika. 82 Photographs*. 1926. Translated by Stanley Appelbaum. New York: Dover, 1993.

Passuth, Krisztina. *Moholy-Nagy*. London: Thames, 1985.

Penkert, Sibylle, ed. *Emblem und Emblemrezeption*. Darmstadt: Wissenschaftliche Buchgesellschaft, 1978.

Schwarz, Heinrich. *David Octavius Hill. Der Meister der Photographie*. Leipzig: Insel, 1931.

Thomson, Philip J. *The Poetry of Bertolt Brecht: Seven Studies*. Chapel Hill: University of North Carolina Press, 1989.

Virilio, Paul. *War and Cinema. The Logic of Perception*. 1984. New York: Routledge, 1988.

Wagenknecht, Christian. "Marxistische Epigrammatik. Bertolt Brechts *Kriegsfibel*." In *Emblem und Emblemrezeption*. Edited by Sibylle Penkert. Darmstadt: Wissenschaftliche Buchgesellschaft, 1978. 543–549.

Welch, David. *Propaganda and the German Cinema*. 1983. Oxford: Oxford University Press, 1990.

Whitaker, Peter. *Brecht's Poetry. A Critical Study*. Oxford: Clarendon, 1985.

7

Dialectics and Reader Response: Bertolt Brecht's Prose Cycles

SABINE GROSS

The critical and popular reception of Brecht's work has been uneven in that, by and large, the plays and theoretical writings on the theater have drawn most of the attention, and most critical articles and books have consistently focused on his work for the stage. Brecht's poetry has also been fairly widely noticed— although not to the extent that its quality and significance would seem to demand.[1] Brecht's prose, finally, has been not so much underrated as largely neglected. While a considerable number of studies, particularly in German, have treated individual and selected prose works, much of the secondary literature has been more pedagogical than scholarly in approach and has tended to concentrate on stories deemed suitable for use in German secondary schools (e.g., Hasselbach/Hasselbach, Wöhrle).

Brecht's prose can be grouped into the three categories of (1) short stories; (2) the prose cycles "Anecdotes of Mr. Keuner" (in part included in *Tales from the Calendar*), *Me-ti. Buch der Wendungen* (Me-ti. Book of Changes), *Flüchtlingsgespräche* (Refugee Conversations), and *Tales from the Calendar*; and (3) the novels and novel projects, foremost among them the *Tui-Roman* (Tui Novel), *Threepenny Novel*, and *Die Geschäfte des Herrn Julius Caesar* (The Business Dealings of Mr. Julius Caesar).

Critical attention has seemed to mirror Brecht's own attitude towards his prose works. Even though he wrote prose during most of his career, he apparently considered it somewhat marginal compared with his concurrent work in other genres. No systematic, comprehensive study of his prose works is yet available in either German or English. Mews gives an overview for English-language readers; a commentary on Brecht's narrative prose (Müller, *Kommentar*) and the sections on prose in Knopf's handbook (*Lyrik*) provides useful information on dates, origins, manuscripts, the circumstances under which texts originated, and occasional interpretations of individual texts. Müller and Knopf also conveniently summarize much of the existing literature on Brecht's prose.

One obvious reason for the paucity of English-language criticism on Brecht's prose is that so few of these works have been translated into English. *Tales from the Calendar* (1961) is a translation of Brecht's 1949 publication *Kalendergeschichten*; the collection *Short Stories 1921–1946* offers a substantial selection from the short prose fiction in collected works (*GW* 11). Another obstacle for critics is the fact that so much of Brecht's prose remained either unfinished or unpublished during his lifetime. This is particularly true of his novels, with the notable exception of *Threepenny Novel*, which was finished in 1933, published in 1934, and translated into English as *A Penny for the Poor* in 1937.

The generally accepted three phases of Brecht's artistic development—the pre-Marxist Brecht until 1926, the dogmatic Marxist of the *Lehrstücke* period (which marks a decisive and conspicuous change in style), and the "mature" Brecht who began to emerge after 1933—also apply to his literary prose, although the second phase is less relevant and not as easily distinguishable from the third phase. His early, pre-dialectical stories frequently combine the anarchic posture and anti-bourgeois thrust characteristic of the early plays with a style reminiscent of newspaper reporting, but they do not yet show the distinctively "Brechtian" tone, precision, and dialectical structure that make the mature works instantly recognizable. The language of Brecht's early works reflects expressionist influences and—especially after he settled in Berlin in 1924—frequently incorporates aspects of metropolitan life and mass culture (such as sports) that fascinated him. His short stories are seldom plot driven, and a number of them betray a certain disdain for the conventional kind of plot structure that would provide a climax or denouement for the reader. This lack of plot orientation anticipates the more conspicuous renunciation of plot in Brecht's later prose works—a characteristic of his prose work in general. One might speculate that his failure to complete most of his novels can be traced to his consistent refusal to subordinate other elements to an overarching plot structure or to an outright lack of interest in traditional plot development. Instead, a loose arrangement of short, episodic prose passages seems to have suited him best. This is certainly in keeping with his theory of the epic theater, more specifically his assertion that each scene must be taken by itself, not as a means to an end.

Brecht's prose cycles form a substantial and representative portion of his fictional prose work. Brecht was an excellent prose writer, and the literary merit of his prose is sufficient reason for critical attention. While each of the four prose cycles has its specific purpose, program, and coherence, all four show both the diversity and homogeneity of Brecht's prose, his skillful and innovative use of prose forms, subgenres, and traditions. Specifically, Brecht's prose cycles present themes and structures that recur throughout his work. The four cycles discussed here were produced over the course of three decades. Only the *Tales from the Calendar* and a number of the "Anecdotes of Mr. Keuner" were published while Brecht was alive. The majority of the texts were written during his years of exile; they reflect this experience and thematize Hitler's rise to power, the dynamics of German fascism, and the political situation in a number of ways. The circumstances under which these prose texts were written may also account for their somewhat experimental form and for the way in which they blur traditional genre boundaries. Hermsdorf has surmised that writing in exile, with little prospect of publication, may have offered Brecht "a particular 'freedom' of writing that develops when a text has to end up in the desk drawer or targets an indefinite 'posterity' " (35).

A characteristic feature of Brecht's work, especially of his fictional and non-fictional prose, is that genre boundaries as well as the borders between the literary and the theoretical, between narrative and expository texts, are permeable; this makes some of his texts difficult to classify. The social engagement of Brecht's writing shows clearly in the sociopolitical pedagogy to which he subordinates his works; the application of dialectical thinking in these texts goes back to his studies of philosophy, in particular Marxism. *Me-ti* is a case in point; more than any of Brecht's other works, this prose cycle is situated in the border zone where literature and political-philosophical analysis meet, which makes it difficult to categorize the work. Knopf treats it as part of Brecht's theoretical writings and places it between his philosophical writings and his writings on literature and art (*Lyrik* 447–76); Brecht's collected works (*GW* 12) include it with his prose; Müller (*Kommentar*) also considers it part of Brecht's narrative prose. *Me-ti* is rather similar in structure to the "Anecdotes of Mr. Keuner" in that it consists of a number of short, independent texts that share one central character who is a thinker/philosopher/teacher. The texts combine aspects of anecdote, aphorism, apophthegm, and parable; they straddle the division between literary prose and analytical essay in presenting philosophical mininarratives or philosophy narrativized and illustrated by case studies. The stories in the "Anecdotes of Mr. Keuner" and *Me-ti* dispense with plot and extensive setting; instead, they employ dialogue in a pedagogical attempt to convey insights. Both address similar topics: philosophy, society, politics, and the arts. The "Anecdotes of Mr. Keuner," *Me-ti*, and the *Flüchtlingsgespräche*, in particular, display Brecht's philosophical thinking to an extent that situates them in a tradition of philosophical-literary writing in the manner of both ancient Chinese and Western philosophers. Brecht's short texts are examples of the revival of this form. Berghahn points out that a number of such texts—"a combination of observation and reflection, a rare cross between literature and philosophy" (200)—were written around 1930 by authors such as Ernst Bloch, Siegfried Kracauer, and Robert Musil as well as by Brecht's friend, philosopher Walter Benjamin. Berghahn uses Benjamin's term *Denkbild* (thought-image) to place these texts in the emblematic tradition; his characterization of a Bloch story as "image and thought mediated by critical theory, and a utopian vision" (Berghahn 209) similarly applies to Brecht's short prose texts.

Brecht employed this form of literary prose to explain his political views as well as his artistic aims in terms of the role of literature and art in society. *Me-ti* is probably the most programmatic and self-referential text Brecht wrote. Both *Me-ti* and the "Anecdotes of Mr. Keuner" are also reflexive in their focus on the role of the teacher/philosopher, a role in which Brecht clearly saw himself. Indeed, all four prose cycles have autoreferential elements. Brecht did not shy away from referring to himself and his theories in his literary texts and citing his own works: the "Anecdotes of Mr. Keuner," *Me-ti*, and the *Flüchtlingsgespräche* all contain oblique or explicit references to his theories. In the Keuner story "Form and Substance," Mr. K objects to art—and philosophy—because they neglect substance in favor of form; he launches into a parable of an apprentice gardener whose attempts to prune a laurel tree into the shape of a sphere or ball result in a very small tree. The gardener's disappointed reaction: " 'Yes, that's a ball, but where's the laurel?' " (*Tales* 111) can be read as an orthodox affirmation of content-centered art over formalist experiments in the context of the formalism-realism debate of the 1930s. Conversely, in its pointed exaggeration the absurd question can be read as subverting the ostensible message of the story: without content, there would be no form.

Several "Anecdotes of Mr. Keuner" as well as a number of texts in *Me-ti* deal with ways of representing reality through art. Brecht himself appears repeatedly in *Me-ti* as Kin-jeh. "Über reine Kunst" (*GW* 12: 509; On Pure Art) is strongly reminiscent of the poem "Bad Time for Poetry" (*Poems* 330–331) in its insistence that it is impossible to produce "pure art" as long as social injustices exist to prevent its enjoyment. And another of the *Me-ti* stories offers one of the most succinct definitions as well as several examples of what Brecht called "gestic" language, a language that is "stylized and natural at the same time." It is said about Brecht's fictional alter ego that "he merely put attitudes into sentences and always let the attitudes show through the sentences" (*GW* 12: 458). Mr. K also comments on originality in a way that reflects the ease with which Brecht appropriated the work of others. Far from praising originality, Mr. K interprets it as a lack of ability, an avoidance of genuine intellectual effort in a reversal of the usual praise accorded original work: "They know no larger edifices than those one man can build by himself" (*Tales* 115).

According to Knopf, "it has become apparent that the poet cannot be separated from his so-called world view" (*Grundkurs* 57). That is certainly true insofar as this world view has shaped the subject matter and, even more importantly, the structure of Brecht's texts. Grouping *Me-ti*, in particular, with Brecht's theoretical and philosophical writings can be justified on the grounds that there is considerable overlapping. But while *Me-ti* "resists being read as fictional prose" (Knopf, *Grundkurs* 57), neither should it be regarded as a direct statement by the author Brecht. In *Me-ti*, Brecht presents his views in mediated form, having transformed them into a literary text that combines traditional and experimental elements. The narrativization, the parable structure, the fictionalization of characters all distinguish the text from the status of a treatise.

Me-ti provides clear examples of how Brecht circulates material in his work, fitting it into different slots, as it were, trying out different forms, and creating intersections with a number of other texts. *Me-ti* shares with *Flüchtlingsgespräche* the extensive discussions and analyses of the dynamics of fascism and a focus on Hegel's dialectics. The section on ''writing'' appended to the *Flüchtlingsgespräche* was originally intended for inclusion in *Me-ti*. Brecht initially planned to combine stories from *Tales from the Calendar* and the dialogues of *Flüchtlingsgespräche* into one book, interspersing dialogical form with narrative. This mixing of different genres is carried out in *Tales from the Calendar*, which alternates poems and stories. Mr. K made a first appearance in other works before he found a place in the aphoristic ministories named after him.

Brecht's work shows a unity that transcends genre boundaries. Motifs, phrases, and structures are constantly circulated, varied, and repeated, as a closer look at some of his lesser-known prose texts will demonstrate.

''ANECDOTES OF MR. KEUNER''

Brecht wrote Keuner stories from 1926 until his death in 1956. Few are longer than one page, and several consist only of two brief sentences. Many cannot be dated and were published at different times in various combinations. Altogether, there are eighty-seven stories; the collected works (*GW* 12) follow the order of publication and include all stories found among Brecht's manuscripts after his death. Thirty-nine of these stories have been translated as part of *Tales from the Calendar*.

The title has an element of intentional ambiguity; it can be translated as stories about, of, or by Mr. Keuner. While Brecht apparently did not attribute any special significance to the name Keuner, which is frequently shortened to K in the stories in a move from eponymity to anonymity, as early as 1930/1931 Benjamin linked the name to the Greek *koinos* or ''that which is general/belongs to all'' (662). Benjamin also developed the parallel to Odysseus's encounter with Polyphemus under the name *utis* (nobody): Keuner, like Odysseus, is resourceful, experienced, and endowed with both cunning and wisdom (523). To the first allusion we might add the Greek *koine* (colloquial language, comprehensibility); the second fits in nicely with the near-homonym *keiner* (nobody).

In the stories, Keuner is frequently referred to and defined as *der Denkende*, that is, ''he who thinks'' or ''the thinking one.'' Rather than use the noun ''thinker,'' Brecht chooses the gerund, thereby emphasizing that thinking is not a state but a process, an ongoing activity. Keuner's function, however, goes beyond dispensing wisdom: he gains as well as imparts insights, and he learns from events and the behavior of others as he expects them to learn from his words and actions. Keuner is characterized by his attitude, his way of interacting and imparting information, rather than as a "rounded" psychological character. In seventy-eight of the eighty-seven stories, Keuner is engaged in dialogue with others, speaking to them or telling stories, and most of the remaining stories have communicative elements. While Mr. K does most of the talking, fifty of the stories present an exchange, mostly in the form of question and answer. In eighteen instances, a question is posed to Keuner, in sixteen cases he is the one asking the question (Krusche 191–92).

The Keuner character has been traced to the *Lehrstücke* or learning plays where(Haack/Huge; Häußler), and he appears in Brecht's *Lehrstück* fragment "Untergang des Egoisten Johann Fatzer" (Demise of the Egotist Johann Fatzer). Several of the earliest stories (those published in 1930 and 1932) can be linked to *He Who Said Yes* and *The Measures Taken*, *Lehrstücke* that were written around the same time. They share a dogmatic insistence that in order to survive adversity and propagate what is politically necessary, one may have to ignore moral values such as honesty and compassion. Mr. K expresses this conviction repeatedly. A later story, "Über den Verrat" (On Betrayal), argues that when conditions change, promises change with them. The story ends: "He who thinks betrays. He who thinks only promises that he will remain one who thinks" (*GW* 12: 404). Yet the arrogant certainty of this statement is called into doubt by another story that offers a pointed criticism of the Communist party's apparent monopoly on knowledge and insight. "Convincing Questions" not only contests certainty, but it actually raises doubt about the value of certainty and the effect it has: " 'I've noticed, said Mr. K, that a lot of people are put off by our teaching because we know the answer to everything. Couldn't we, in the interest of propaganda, draw up a list of questions which appear to us quite unresolved?'' (*Tales* 124). The title of this story offers a paradox; the story drives home the point that an open question can be more convincing than a supposedly authoritative answer. This kind of revaluation with a surprising twist plays a role in a number of "Anecdotes of Mr. Keuner." Here it is the concept of "propaganda" that is undercut with psychological insight. Conversely, the attempt to make a list of what defies solution defeats the attempt to escape preset categories. As in some other texts, it is hard to tell whether the irony is intentional.

Häußler subdivides "Anecdotes of Mr. Keuner" into the following thematic groups: "philosophy and religion," "sociological-political subjects," "art," "virtues," and—the largest category—"(dialectical) attitude of the thinker." Even in the earliest stories, there is a repeated emphasis on *Haltung* (attitude/posture/position). Mr. K listens to a professor of philosophy and then diagnoses his shortcomings: "You sit awkwardly, you talk awkwardly, you think awkwardly." Mr. K counsels the professor that moving clumsily, he will never reach his destination, and he concludes: " 'I see your bearing [posture/attitude] and so I am not interested in your goal [destination]' " (*Tales* 113). The deceptive appearance of attitudes is highlighted in another very brief story in which Mr. K explains that he, too, once adopted an aristocratic posture: he did so when the rising waters reached his chin. What is supposedly a stance of social superiority is revealed under the circumstances to be a desperate measure. The story works as a parable on both the psychological and sociopolitical levels: the aristocratic posture/position is a last-ditch effort to survive and constitutes a social anachronism. Brecht's dialectical view of *Haltung* anticipates and parallels his attention to *Gestus* (gesture, stance), a term he coined to denote "social attitude."

One of the most popular "Anecdotes of Mr. Keuner," "If Sharks Were People," has Mr. K answer a question posed by his landlady's young daughter: "If sharks were people, would they be nicer to the little fishes?" Mr. K answers in a parable, an extended subjunctive that enumerates what exactly sharks would do if they were human. They would provide medical care for any injured fish "so that the sharks should not be deprived of it by an untimely death." They would also organize parties, "for happy little fishes taste better than miserable ones." In order to prepare their fishes for war they would emphasize the differences between them and their opponents. Although all little fishes shared the characteristic of being unable to speak, "they are silent in quite different languages and therefore cannot possibly understand each other." All the supposedly considerate and morally commendable actions that characterize human society are exposed as profoundly ideological, exploitative, and self-serving. Mr. K's conclusion—"In short, the sea would only start being civilized if sharks were people" (*Tales* 120–21)—sums up the ironical structure of the parable. Culture, supposedly the pinnacle of human development, is devalued so thoroughly that it makes sharks seem decidedly decent creatures when compared with humans. Other stories such as "The Natural Instinct for Property" are organized around similar tongue-in-cheek premises.

Precision of thought and economy of language are thematized by Mr. K himself in "Organisation," one of the earliest stories, in which he says that he who thinks uses no light, no piece of bread, and no thought beyond what is necessary. Mr. K's attitude toward thinking is defined from the outset in comparison with and opposition to the "professional thinker" (Wöhrle 77), even though Mr. K's own dogmatism and superciliousness seem to characterize him as an exemplary "orthodox philosopher perpetuating the status quo" (Klingmann 169). But Mr. K not only imparts wisdom, he also frequently revises his views, makes his statements more precise when he recognizes their shortcomings in dialogue with others, and accepts the lessons he is taught. This is exemplified in "Herr Keuner und die Zeichnung seiner Nichte" (Mr. K and his Niece's Drawing), in which Mr. K notices that the chicken shown in the drawing has three legs. His niece explains that since a chicken cannot fly, it needs a third leg to push off from the ground. The story ends with Mr. K's answer: "I am glad I asked" (*GW* 12: 400). Clearly, the brief exchange has not given him additional information about chickens; but instead of looking at an incorrect picture and assuming that his niece perhaps did not know better, he now realizes that an act of reasoning has gone into producing it. Mr. K does not use words unnecessarily, and neither did

Brecht. The inclusion of Mr. K's reaction shifts the emphasis and highlights his insight into and appreciation of his niece's thought process, even if the result is "objectively" wrong.

ME-TI. BUCH DER WENDUNGEN (ME-TI. BOOK OF CHANGES)

Brecht worked on his *Me-ti* between 1934 and 1942, but he did not finish the cycle, and the texts were left in no discernible order. First published in 1965, each of the three editions of *Me-ti* followed different sequencing principles, including one that highlights the "philosophical-aesthetic principle of composition" by arranging the texts thematically in five different "books"—"Book of the Grand Method," "Book of Experience," "Book on Disorder," "Book of Revolution," and "Book of the Grand Order." As Müller (*Kommentar*) points out, however, Brecht did not group the "Anecdotes of Mr. Keuner" according to their thematic coherence, and it is therefore questionable whether he would have imposed that kind of order on *Me-ti*, especially since Me-ti himself offers repeated warnings against the simplification of systematic thought and "the construction of overly complete world views" (*GW* 12: 463).

One of the most important sources of the book is Alfred Forke's German translation of the writings of the Chinese philosopher Mo-tzu (also Me-tse or Me-ti), a copy of which was one of Brecht's most highly prized possessions in exile and is now kept in the Brecht Archives. The apophthegmatic form used by Mo-tzu served as a model that Brecht adopted for his *Me-ti* as well as for the "Anecdotes of Mr. Keuner." The Chinese influences and stylization are obvious in *Me-ti*, so much so that an early critic called *Me-ti* Brecht's "Chinese quarry" (Knopf, *Grundkurs* 37, 49). A short preface offers the facetious claim that the book is based on a translation from the Chinese with additions in the same style; it emphasizes its eclecticism by claiming that while "modern thoughts" have been inserted, the book is still a presentation of the "basic thoughts" of an ancient Chinese philosopher. In accordance with Brecht's definition of defamiliarization as a form of historicization, the Chinese "disguise" defamiliarizes the subject matter. The subtitle is ambiguous and may be translated in various ways: "Book of Phrases/Turns/Changes." The allusion to the classical Chinese *I Ching. Book of Changes* is no doubt intentional, though it is not borne out by the content of *Me-ti*. Also, Brecht interprets "changes" in a specific way in that the German term *Wendungen* refers both to a turn of events and to phrases. The term then denotes twists or turns, that is, specific and possibly unexpected changes including dialectical reversals, as well as phrases, idioms, or figures of speech. This ambiguity implies a relation between actual social events and linguistic means—in Brechtian terminology "operative sentences." The latter are required to pinpoint and analyze the former and to initiate changes. Presumably Brecht was aware of the irony of linking in his title one of the canonical works of Confucian philosophy—the *Book of*

Changes—with the name of a philosophical pragmatist considered a heretic by Confucianism.

When reading the historical Mo-tzu (480–400 B.C.), it is obvious why his writings appealed to Brecht. Mo-tzu defines and practices dialectics as an art of thinking, differentiation, and judgment. He was a social philosopher and pragmatist who emphasized the practical use of thoughts and based his ethics on man's existence as a social and political being. For example: "Making the people play musical instruments has three drawbacks: Those who are hungry do not get fed that way, those who are cold are not clothed, and those who are tired get no rest" (*Me-ti* 366).

Mr. K's emphasis on the significance of attitudes is echoed by Brecht's Me-ti character in the story "Tu Wants to Learn how to Fight and Learns how to Sit" (*GW* 12: 576). In the original Mo-tzu, Brecht had read the following story: "Several disciples told Master Me-tse that Kao-tse stood out because of his virtue. But Master Me-tse remarked: 'That is not correct. Kao-tse exercises virtue like someone who stands on tiptoe to be tall or who rests his arms on something to appear wide. It does not last long' " (*GW* 12: 577). Some of Mo-tzu's statements come very close to Brecht's definitions of thinking, as in: "Master Me-tse said: 'One may constantly utter words that can lead to actions, but if they do not result in actions, one must not perpetually talk about it' " (*GW* 12: 554). This is one of the passages Brecht himself marked with a thick pencil stroke in the margin.

Brecht's Me-ti is a fictional character loosely based on the Chinese philosopher. Like Mo-tzu, he refuses to accept statements at face value, emphasizing instead the need to question and review thoughts and actions. Witness the way Brecht's Me-ti expresses his allegiance to dialectics: "There is only one thing that entitles me to call myself a supporter of the *Grand Method*; I have doubted it often enough" (*GW* 12: 527). He also points out that accepted rules can get into the way of finding solutions and advocates as productive those ways of thinking that, if necessary, transgress boundaries. For instance, the story "Die Spielregeln verletzen" (Violating the Rules of the Game) relates that after his mathematics students have failed in their attempts to calculate the surface area of a piece of paper that has been cut into a highly irregular shape, the master succeeds by using a scale to weigh the sheet. Me-ti's comment: "He had solved the task as an actual task, irrespective of any rules" (*GW* 12: 464).

Me-ti has been called "Brecht's most comprehensive reflexion on and investigation of Marxism," featuring "aphoristic debates in which Leninism, Stalinism, and the construction of socialism in the Soviet Union are measured against the ideas of Marx and Engels, Korsch, Luxemburg, and Trotsky" (Kellner 37).[2] The text has been analyzed and criticized extensively in terms of the political opinions it reveals (Kellner; Pike). True, on one level it represents an inquiry into Marxism and constitutes an expression of Brecht's ambivalence toward the implementation of socialism in the Soviet Union and his attempt to come to terms with it. On another level, in the manner of the *Tui-Roman*, it is also an investigation of German fascism (Wagner) in that a number of *Me-ti* stories deal with Hitler's rise to power and the contemporary situation in Germany. Characters who appear under Chinese names include Lenin (Mi-en-leh), Stalin (Ni-en), Trotsky (To-tsi), Marx (Ka-meh), Hegel (Hü-jeh), Hitler (Hi-je), and Brecht himself as Kin-jeh (*GW* 12: 420). Brecht uses this device also in the *Tui-Roman*, where the derogatory term of TUI (Tellect-Ual-In) for "mind-workers" is based on a reversal of "intellectual" (*GW* 12). *Me-ti*, however, cannot be reduced to a philosophical tractatus, a new form of "political reasoning" (Wirth), or a manifesto on Marxism, Leninism, or Stalinism. Müller affirms that "*Me-ti* is not a theoretical treatise and should not be cited as a source of views that Brecht held" and describes the text instead as "a literary, consciously entertaining manual of dialectic thought" (55).

Indeed, the *Me-ti* texts keep returning, either explicitly or implicitly, to dialectics, or the "Grand Method." *Me-ti* has been called an "introductory course on dialectics" (Knopf, *Grundkurs*), an " 'exercise for suppleness' in dialectical thinking" (Mittenzwei 193), and a collection of "practice pieces on dialectics" (Koch 167). Haug addresses the different levels on which dialectics is found in *Me-ti* when he defines it as "a casuistic manual of objective dialectics and of dialectics as a method of comprehension and expression and as political strategy of behavior" (Haug 2). Dialectical thinking is indeed one of Brecht's major preoccupations in these texts. Not only do many of them exemplify dialectics, they also offer definitions and discussions of the Hegelian dialectic and its axioms and principles. They occasionally use Hegel's own examples, as when Me-ti explains: "For a [dialectical] thinker, the concept of the bud is already the concept of something which strives not to be what it is" (*GW* 12: 493). Me-ti argues against undialectical ways of "arresting"—and ultimately invalidating— experiences by turning them into world views, and he cautions against approaching complicated processes as if they could be verbally pinned down once and for all. For Me-ti, as for Hegel, dialectics is not only a philosophical or intellectual approach, but above all an inherent quality of reality, be it natural or social: "You cannot find anything which you can cause to remain true to itself for long; nor can you find a term that is willing to stick to the matter at hand even while you speak, if you say more than one sentence" (*GW* 12: 548). That is why Me-ti advocates caution in transforming experiences into finished insights. Insights, he argues, should be handled like snowballs; they are good weapons that do not keep well and must be used at once (*GW* 12: 452).

FLÜCHTLINGSGESPRÄCHE (REFUGEE CONVERSATIONS)

Flüchtlingsgespräche, most of which was written in Finland during 1940–1941, consists of eighteen dialogues with very brief narrative introductions and transitions resembling stage directions. In fact, *Flüchtlingsgespräche* has been staged successfully a number of times. Two German emigrants, the intellectual Ziffel and the worker Kalle, meet in a railway station in exile, in a town named

Helsingfors that is modeled on Helsinki. Brecht's own years in exile as well as earlier experiences provided material for *Flüchtlingsgespräche*. The conversation moves back and forth easily between concrete details of life in exile, political issues, and philosophical reflections. The last dialogue ends with Kalle and Ziffel furtively toasting socialism. The situation of two refugees philosophizing in a railway station has its own absurd logic. As Ziffel remarks: "The best school of dialectics is emigration. Refugees are the most astute dialecticians. . . . From the smallest signs they deduce the most profound events . . . and they have a fine eye for contradictions" (*GW* 14: 1462).

Dialogue as pedagogical technique is one of the oldest philosophical forms, as exemplified in the Western tradition by the Platonic dialogues, in which Socrates practices his "midwifery" as teacher. His questions help others to clarify their thoughts and develop understanding. In ancient Chinese philosophy, dialogue was popular as well (Wang 191). Brecht uses the conversation/dialogue form in his philosophical-pedagogical treatise on the theater, *The Messingkauf Dialogues*. Both the "Anecdotes of Mr. Keuner" and those in *Me-ti* incorporate dialogical elements; in *Flüchtlingsgespräche*, Brecht uses this form to its full potential. Kalle and Ziffel come from different social backgrounds, but they meet as equals. Neither has a privileged "Socratic" position, and each learns from the other in areas where he lacks expertise or knowledge, a more dialectical constellation than the hierarchy of knowledge and wisdom that defines the roles in most Socratic dialogues.

In addition to the philosophical tradition, Brecht had a number of more immediate literary models for *Flüchtlingsgespräche*: Goethe's *Unterhaltungen deutscher Ausgewanderten* (Conversations of German Refugees, 1794/1795), Diderot's novel *Jacques le Fataliste et son Maître* (Jacques the Fatalist and his Master, 1775/1780), and Diderot's satirical dialogue *Le Neveu de Rameau* (Rameau's Nephew, 1774). Brecht was also inspired by the Finnish author Aleksis Kivi (1834–1872), who is referred to in the fourth conversation and whose use of dialogue Brecht admired. Another possible source is Lessing's *Ernst und Falk: Gespräche für Freimäurer* (Ernst and Falk: Conversations for Freemasons, 1778/1780), which closely follows the model of Socratic dialogue.

Like *Me-ti*, *Flüchtlingsgespräche* is an investigation and application of Hegelian dialectics. Kalle and Ziffel discuss Hegel explicitly, pointing out that humor is required to understand him. Ziffel attributes a sense of humor to Hegel; after all, "he couldn't think of something like order without disorder," and "he disputed that one equals one" (*GW* 14: 1460). In *Flüchtlingsgespräche*, dialectics is applied with wry humor to everything from the lack of decent coffee, beer, and cigarettes to national and international politics. Dialectical reasoning allows Kalle and Ziffel to make pointed yet veiled references to their situation, including the impossibility of speaking openly: "To live in a country where there is no humor is unbearable, but it is even more unbearable to be in a country where humor is necessary" (*GW* 14: 1459). They make subtle distinctions: "When nothing is in the right place, that is disorder. When in the right place there is nothing, that is order'' (*GW* 14: 1390). The definition of order as lack reflects the war situation as well as the potential destructiveness of certain forms of order. Ziffel emphasizes that meaningless tasks, in particular, require strict order, since otherwise those forced to carry them out will go mad. Both Kalle and Ziffel point out "the gigantic advantages of sloppiness" (*GW* 14: 1389) that can save lives. The extent to which Nazi cruelty is dependent on order is illustrated with examples; Kalle describes a concentration camp guard from Dachau as extremely organized and conscientious, even when he is whipping inmates: "His love of order was so deeply ingrained in him that he would rather not beat up [the inmates] than do it in a disorderly fashion." Ziffel concludes: "I feel that humans are not mature enough for a virtue such as love of order. Their mind is not sufficiently developed for this virtue. Their endeavors are idiotic, and only a slovenly and disorderly execution of their plans can save them from major damage" (*GW* 14: 1386).

In the course of the dialogues, Ziffel begins to write his memoirs. In what is without doubt a reference to the author's situation in exile, he stops working on them when he cannot find Kalle, since Kalle is the only speaker of German he knows in exile, and without at least a single potential reader/listener his work will serve no purpose. When assessing his secondary school education, at the beginning of his memoirs, he recounts the famous strategy used by his fellow student B.—allegedly Brecht himself—to avoid flunking a test. Less sophisticated students tried to improve their grade by erasing some of the teacher's red marks. But they would be caught because the procedure left traces. B., on the other hand, added red marks to a number of correct passages and then complained. The teacher had to admit that there was nothing wrong in the underlined passages, erased the "erroneous" marks himself, and emended the final grade. Ziffel points out that school had certainly taught this student how to think (*GW* 14: 1403–1404).

Exaggeration in the form of reversal is much more pronounced in this text than, for example, in the "Anecdotes of Mr. Keuner." Its frequent use results in a sustained ironic structure; despite their serious subject matter, in these dialogues much is said tongue-in-cheek. Schools are praised for preparing students for reality by giving them the opportunity "to study cruelty, malice, and injustice four to six hours every day" (*GW* 14: 1402). Frequently, Kalle and Ziffel comment on their precarious situation by extracting the logic that seems to govern it. For example, Kalle states that "a passport is the noblest part of a human being," and then reasons that it is much easier to make a human being than to make a passport (*GW* 14: 1383). Rather than diagnose the situation itself as twisted and degrading, Kalle and Ziffel offer ironic logic as a seemingly adequate appraisal of a time when persecuted individuals and refugees were not treated as humans. Priorities appear reversed in order to reveal the perversity and inhumanity of war. A military expert is quoted as complaining that "the civilian population has become a serious problem for the military" because civilians flee from air strikes "without considering at all that this would significantly interfere with military operations'' (*GW* 14: 1426). Ziffel's conclusion, ''Either one gets rid of the population, or war will become impossible'' (*GW* 14: 1428), is both logical and absurd; it is also a scathing indictment of the disastrous effects of war and the mindset of those who wage it.

TALES FROM THE CALENDAR

The texts included in this collection were written between 1926 and 1946 and arranged by Brecht specifically for the volume *Kalendergeschichten* that was published in 1949. *Tales from the Calendar*, a title that could also be translated as Tales for the Calendar, is the only prose cycle that was published during his lifetime. Although in the West German Federal Republic of the 1960s it was still considered politically inopportune to teach Brecht, *Tales from the Calendar* turned out to be one of Brecht's most popular publications. The edition published by Rowohlt had sold 880,000 copies by 1992, and several of the stories in *Tales from the Calendar* have become classics that are now regularly included in textbooks and anthologies.

The term ''prose cycle'' must be used with a qualification here. While poems are occasionally included or quoted in Brecht's other prose collections, they are fully integrated and of equal importance in *Tales from the Calendar*. Brecht's original arrangement alternates eight tales and a number of ''Anecdotes of Mr. Keuner'' (the latter are grouped together as one unit) with eight poems. Interpreting the tales and poems separately is to miss part of their significance.

In choosing the title *Tales from the Calendar*, Brecht consciously took up a tradition that dates back to the sixteenth century. Popular calendars included dates, religious holidays, astronomical and astrological data, and weather rules based on farmers' experiences; but they also increasingly included essays, anecdotes, and brief tales that were written with a view toward providing useful information and a ''moral'' serving both education and entertainment. In many households, such an almanac would be one of the few books besides the Bible. (Brecht had once before used the title of a moral-educational volume for his collection of poems, *Manual of Piety*.) In the nineteenth century, collections of stories were frequently published as ''Tales from the Calendar,'' regardless of whether they had actually appeared in calendars first or simply emulated the type of story that was traditionally included in a calendar. Taking up this popular tradition was in keeping with Brecht's insistence that writing ''for the people'' need not be simplistic and ''folksy.'' In 1938, he defined ''popular'' (*volkstümlich*) as: ''comprehensible to the masses, taking up and enriching their form of expression / taking their position, affirming and correcting it / representing the most progressive section of the people in such a way that they can take the lead, . . . / continuing traditions and developing them'' (*GW* 19: 325).

Calendars continued the democratic Enlightenment tradition; calendar tales represent ''stories about history'' (Knopf, *Geschichten*). Brecht's texts emphasize history; they suggest possible ways of approaching history and of viewing historical figures. Many of them present fictional events involving actual historical characters. For Brecht, calendar stories were a way of providing a critical perspective on "monumentalist" history and advancing a democratic view that would make sense of history for all those who participate in shaping it yet never find a place in traditional historical accounts.

Unlike *Me-ti*, the "Anecdotes of Mr. Keuner," and *Flüchtlingsgespräche*, which are unified through form and use of the same character(s), in *Tales from the Calendar*, texts of different genres and lengths with their variety of subjects are united by a common orientation and purpose. Among the forms Brecht used are ballad, legend, anecdote, and parable. The following analyses of individual texts are intended to show how each text fits into and contributes to the overall purpose of the collection.

The poem "Questions from a Worker Who Reads" can be considered programmatic for the entire collection by virtue of the perspective it offers on history. With its "complementary or alternative representation of history from below and with new standards for what constitutes historical achievement" (Müller, *Kommentar* 309), it not only corrects but attempts to replace a traditional view of history as the sum of achievements of great men. Moving from famous historical sites such as Thebes, the Wall of China, Rome, and Byzantium to famous historical figures such as Alexander, Caesar, Philip of Spain, and Frederick the Great, the poem asks increasingly direct questions to draw attention to those who have been left out: the builders, masons, slaves, and cooks. The poem concludes: "Every ten years a great man. / Who paid the bill?" (*Tales* 82).

Stripping traditional heroes of glory or showing them from a new angle is another recurrent strategy in these texts. The story "Socrates Wounded" is a good example (*Tales* 83–99). When Socrates's attempt to flee from battle is thwarted by a thorn in his foot, his only resort is to frighten away the enemies. His apparent courage in battle results in a flood of praise and celebration. In a dialectical twist, Socrates finally shows true courage by admitting his lack of courage.

In other tales, Brecht offers us a "view from below" of historical figures through the choice of narrative perspective. In "The Heretic's Coat" (*Tales* 45–53), Giordano Bruno owes money for a winter coat which he had ordered and received before learning that he would soon be thrown into prison for heresy. But the tailor and his wife, whose narrative point of view we share, have little sympathy for his plight and no comprehension of his ideas. They are poor and need the money. Bruno's humanity is shown when, in spite of his desperate fight for his life, he counters the resentment of his creditors with patience and consideration. While he is involved in the "great history" we know from history books, we see him making every attempt from his position of powerlessness to set things right. He returns the coat to them as restitution shortly before his execution.

In the tale "The Experiment" (*Tales* 33–43), the point of view of the tailor's wife is paralleled by that of a stable boy in whom Sir Francis Bacon takes sufficient interest to train him in the foundations of scientific thought. Bacon succeeds in developing the boy's natural curosity and teaching him to replace belief by knowledge. The tale starts out with an omniscient narrator's negative description of Bacon as a power-hungry and corrupt political figure. The narrative point of view then shifts to the stable boy, who knows little about Bacon's political life and is interested in his thoughts not for their "scientific significance" but because of the "manifest utility" (*Tales* 35) and applicability of what Bacon teaches him. The tale presents Bacon in a number of different roles: for history, he is the manipulative Lord Chancellor as well as the humanist and philosopher; for his servants, he is the master; for the boy, he is the teacher as well as a frail old man who catches a fatal cold because his scientific interest is aroused by a frozen bird. In opposition to accepted and "proper" notions of mourning, the boy—even when threatened with punishment—accepts the old man's legacy; despite, or perhaps because of, his genuine sadness and sense of loss, he continues the experiment, thereby confirming the value of the old man's curiosity and proving himself a worthy disciple. Scientific curiosity, as the tale points out, is not restricted to the domain of philosophers and scholars. On the contrary, the learned doctors whom the boy approaches take no interest in his discovery. In keeping with the message of the "Anecdotes of Mr. Keuner" that knowledge may have to dispense with other virtues and social niceties, the boy lies to his grandmother so that he may complete his experiment by eating the bird—hoping to demonstrate what we already know: that a frozen bird will keep fresh. By the time we leave the boy sitting expectantly by the boiling chicken to return to the historical, omniscient, impersonal narrative perspective in the final sentence, we have been forced to somewhat reassess our view of Bacon's character because of his interaction with the boy. While this interaction does not cancel out Bacon's political manipulations and deceit, we have come to see that there is another side to him that enables others to seek useful knowledge. The tale opens up a dialectical perspective on Bacon as a contradictory character.

The meticulous construction of this tale is characteristic of Brecht's prose. Brecht's stories are crafted to convey insights by means of narrative, not to provide atmosphere or involve the reader in a plot. "The Experiment" is also typical in the way it engages readers by appealing less to their emotions than to their knowledge. The tale does not include the outcome of the experiment. Rather, it goes back to a historical stage of discovery and lets the reader supply its conclusion.

We find another, even more striking example of this technique of historicizing progress in the poem "At Ulm, 1592" (*Tales* 44). The poem presents a tailor's attempt to fly, Icarus-like, from the cathedral roof by means of wings he has made himself. The bishop's reaction to this challenge appears at the end of the first stanza: "No man will ever fly." In the second stanza, the attempt fails, and the bishop repeats his conclusion verbatim to the gathered crowd—the "people" who are accustomed to following his authority. The poem ends at this point;

history does not. The appeal to the reader to "complete" the poem is so effective that when students in a literature class had to summarize the poem, they were convinced that they had actually read a third stanza of the poem—a stanza in which the bishop was proved wrong and the tailor right: "The poem explicitly demands a critical commentary by the reader on the narrated events. He, not the poet, has to supply the missing third stanza. The students had 'inadvertently' written it" (Mayer 249).

"At Ulm, 1592" is based on an actual occurrence, and it is instructive to note how Brecht changed the facts to "historicize" the situation and polarize the social conflict, bringing it in line with the general thrust of *Tales from the Calendar*. The real tailor, Albrecht Ludwig Berblinger, made his flight attempt in 1811 from a castle wall in Ulm, and he survived it, merely incurring ridicule after he landed in the Danube. Brecht shifts the attempt to 1592, thereby placing it in the Renaissance, the age of discovery that rejected established authority in its quest for knowledge. The desire for discovery is further emphasized by the placement of the poem between two stories with a similar tendency, "The Experiment" and "The Heretic's Coat." The deployment of the bishop—the representative of established authority that is based on belief rather than knowledge—and the setting at the cathedral (the site at which the Church's power and control over the people manifested itself) contribute to investing the tailor's experiment with symbolic significance. Progress has to be wrested from the hands of those in power by defying reactionary teachings that effectively preserve the *status quo*, and it will have to come from the people whom the poem portrays as adversaries of church authority. Finally, the tailor's death makes him a martyr of progress.

As the tale of "The Unseemly Old Lady" illustrates, liberation from preconceived notions can be found not just in memorable and historically significant deeds but also in seemingly insignificant lives as well. Along with "The Augsburg Chalk Circle," which Brecht later reworked and extended into the play *The Caucasian Chalk Circle*, this is arguably one of Brecht's most popular tales; it is both touching and beautifully constructed, and every detail makes a specific point that contributes to its overall effect. Here Brecht used a first-person narrator, the grandson of the protagonist mentioned in the title. The "Old Lady" is called *Greisin* in German, a term that does not convey any "ladylike" features, but merely emphasizes the woman's advanced age. The narrator starts with factual information about his grandmother who had spent her life raising children, working for her family, and conscientiously fulfilling her duties as a thrifty wife and mother. Aged seventy-two when her husband died, she declined offers to live with any of her children and also refused to share her house with her son, a printer by trade and the narrator's uncle, and with his family who lived in cramped quarters. The printer's point of view—as relayed by the narrator—provides a counterpoint to the narrator's gradually emerging perspective on the old woman as she upsets her children's expectations by progressively violating gender assumptions and the norms of lower middle-class life. Her

"luxuries," the narrator remarks, are modest. While the printer becomes increasingly upset by his mother's "unseemly" behavior, the narrator's report on
details of his grandmother's life gradually moves away from an initially objective stance to an endorsement of her process of liberation. He points out that
"she lived two lives in succession. . . . The first life lasted some sixty years; the
second no more than two." (*Tales* 105). The circumstances of her death are
significant; she does not die a lonely woman in keeping with the expectations
of bourgeois respectability that she had violated, but suddenly and unexpectedly,
sitting in a chair ready to go out and in the company of a girl she has befriended.
In the final sentence the narrator waxes poetic: in his effusive endorsement of
his grandmother's process of individuation he closes with a metaphor, something
we rarely find in Brecht's prose: "She had savoured to the full the long years
of servitude and the short years of freedom and consumed the bread of life to
the last crumb" (*Tales* 106). The old woman remains modest and thrifty when
she embarks on her second life; she keeps her house scrupulously clean—evidence that the changes she makes are not an aberration but in keeping with her
basic character. The relatively small steps she takes in her successful attempt to
enjoy the rest of her life in her own fashion are invested with symbolic and
social significance; her liberation from the confining, subservient female role
goes hand in hand with a shift away from the hidebound petit bourgeois class
and its reactionary views of working-class individuals and their leisure-time
activities such as going to the cinema or the races, eating, drinking, and playing
cards at the inn. In order to link socially progressive ideas unequivocally with
the working class, the cobbler whose company the old woman keeps is identified
as a Social Democrat.

The poems included in the collection are of the narrative kind, and a number
of them are structured around questions or dialogue. The final poem in the cycle,
"Legend of the Origin of the Book Tao Te Ching on Lao Tzu's Way into Exile"
brings us back to dialectics. It also weaves together concerns and motifs found
repeatedly in Brecht's work. Brecht preferred the Taoist to the Heraclitan image
of flux because the Taoists taught not only that everything flows but also how
it flows and how it can be made to flow (Tatlow, *Mask* 457). Here Lao-tzu,
creator of the *Tao-te Ching* and the Taoist form of dialectics, is placed in a
setting that emphasizes the sociopolitical relevance of Taoism, ascribes its origin
to an exchange between a teacher and one who wants to learn, and relates two
attitudes that figure prominently in Brecht's work, that is, inquisitiveness and
courtesy. Lao-tzu is polite in complying with the request for knowledge; he
interrupts his flight into exile to accept the customs official's hospitality and
says: " 'Those who ask a question / Deserve an answer' " (*Tales* 109). He
writes down his teachings for an exploited member of the lower classes who
realizes that the dialectics of strength and weakness can be applied to his specific
situation, discerning in a general description of change an application to the
question of who wins and who loses in social power struggles.

A SYNOPTICAL VIEW: TEXTUAL STRATEGIES AND
READER RESPONSE

Having discussed the individual cycles separately, it is time to return to their position within the overall context of Brecht's literary work. The way Brecht employs dialectical thinking to engage readers—a central and characteristic feature of his writing—is illustrated more clearly by his prose than in any other part of his work; sufficient reason to reevaluate the marginal role frequently assigned to it. Not surprisingly, we end up with yet another dialectical relationship: the prose reveals its full significance only in the context of Brecht's work as a whole, and our understanding of the basic principles that govern Brecht's writing in any genre would be incomplete without a close scrutiny of the prose.

Brecht repeats and varies motifs, phrases, and structures throughout his work. For example, two stories from the "Anecdotes of Mr. Keuner" and another one from *Me-ti* take up the same subject and treat it in similar ways. In the Keuner story "The Helpless Boy" (*Tales* 112), a passerby finds out that the boy is crying because some of his money has been stolen. His apparent concern instills hope in the boy. However, when the passerby learns that the boy is unable to shout for help loudly enough, he takes the rest of the money from him without any qualms. The story with its seemingly callous moral is told by Mr. K to illustrate "the bad habit of suffering injustice in silence." It is interesting to note that in the original 1932 version of this story (*Versuche* vol. 5), the man taking the money from the boy was Mr. K himself. Brecht subsequently removed Keuner from the position of the cruel stranger because this was not in keeping with the character of thinker/teacher that Mr. K was to become.

Brecht varies this short scene in the later story "Die Rolle der Gefühle" (The Role of Emotions), in which Mr. K finds his son crying. After a while, he returns to discover that his son is still crying, and admonishes him: "It doesn't make sense to cry with this wind blowing, because nobody can hear you" (*GW* 12: 412). The son takes the advice and returns to his playing. The logic of the latter story is by no means convincing; after all, Mr. K did hear his son; moreover, the sudden, insightful maturity of the young boy is fairly implausible. But many of Brecht's stories are constructed rather than credible; Brecht placed instructive value that could be generalized above plausibility, and the story is constructed around a rather complex set of implicit points such as that a mere display of emotions is futile, that it should be directed at a purpose, and that one should make sure that one's behavior has an effect on others and causes them to react.

The version of the second story found in *Me-ti* is rather similar but the title introduces an additional level of abstraction by shifting attention from the actual event to its instructive relevance: "Auf einen Hauptpunkt hinweisen" (Drawing Attention to a Major Point). In this version, Me-ti finds a boy crying and tells him "indifferently" and "in passing": "Nobody can hear you, the wind is too strong." This time, Brecht clarifies Me-ti's attitude without resorting to additional cruelty, as in the first version above. The man's "unconcerned" attitude appears in Me-ti as pedagogy rather than lack of sympathy. Me-ti's role is to teach, not to empathize, and the responsibility of accepting the insight offered is shifted to the boy. This is reinforced by the final sentence, in which the narrator not just highlights the boy's actual insight, but also emphasizes his ability to recognize useful information and to extract the relevant part of an utterance: "The boy had recognized the reason Master Me-ti gave for his crying, namely, to be heard, as a major point" (GW 12: 463). Brecht has further didacticized his story. In the second Keuner version, the boy learns something. In the *Me-ti* story, the reader learns something about learning from the way the boy's insight is represented. While the first two stories present an insight, the third one downplays the actual insight, turning it into an illustration of the dynamics of teaching and learning.

Brecht wanted his readers to learn, and he frequently portrayed acts and attitudes of learning. The texts discussed provide ample evidence that Brecht did not limit his emphasis on teaching to his *Lehrstücke* or to his theater work. Asking questions and questioning answers is probably the most important *Gestus* in his work, and considerable emphasis is placed on learning and acquiring knowledge. Several of the examples cited bear out this insistence on questioning "final" insights and encouraging fresh thinking and unconventional ways of solving problems. Many of Brecht's poems and prose texts portray "productive attitudes" such as curiosity ("The Experiment," "Legend of the Origin of the Book Tao Te Ching"), doubt (the poem "The Doubter"), skepticism, surprise, and questioning. Many of them present teacher characters, and the question of how best to enact teachings plays a large role. For example, several of Me-ti's disciples deliberate on what to give to him. Each tries to come up with a gift that will show the usefulness of their master's teachings. Their friendly one-upmanship ends when one of them suggests giving Me-ti something he can give away, that is, a warm vest which he can then present to a needy acquaintance (GW 12: 521). By changing the meaning of "gift" as something the recipient will keep or use himself, the disciple's gift best accomplishes the purpose of pleasing their teacher by being useful. The poem "The Carpet Weavers of Ku-yan-Bulak Pay Tribute to Lenin" is in a similar vein. The poor carpet weavers in a small village realize that the best way to honor their teacher is to use the hard-earned money they have collected for improving their own living conditions and thereby applying his teaching rather than to follow convention and dedicate a bust. In addition, they put up a plaque reporting their action—a procedure that both combines the application and commemoration of Lenin's teaching and is of instructive value. It would be difficult to find a more convincing illustration of the Hegelian three-step of thesis-antithesis-synthesis.

Brecht's texts are intended to produce precisely those reactions they so frequently convey, that is, to make readers question knowledge that is taken for granted. Knowledge, for Brecht, is not a fixed entity. It is changeable, adjustable, and something that can and must always be called into doubt. This emphasis on the limits of knowledge is borne out by the Keuner story "Who Knows Whom," in which Mr. K asks two women whether they know their husbands. The first one never doubts that she knows him fully; she is, after all, familiar with his business, his parents, his friends, and his diseases. The second woman answers precisely, but tentatively; she is clearly unable to pin down her husband and is very much aware of the limits of her knowledge: "When he comes, sometimes he is hungry, but sometimes he has eaten. But he doesn't always eat when he is hungry, and doesn't refuse a meal if he has eaten." While the first woman can sum up her knowledge of her husband in a few neat sentences, offering predictable and conventional indices of knowing another person, the second woman struggles to do justice to her husband and what she knows about him. When she expresses her uncertainty as to whether she loves him, Mr. K interrupts her: "I see you know him. No human being knows another better than you know him" (GW 12: 408). Compared with the second woman's testimony, the first woman's statement sounds complacent and superficial. Knowledge, it becomes clear, is largely constituted by knowing its own limits. The mysterious figure of the second husband—the "dark lord" who seems to be engaged in shady dealings—is reminiscent of Brecht's works from the 1920s and his interest in anarchic, antisocial outlaw figures. But the story includes this character in a structure of opposing attitudes that is typical of the more "mature" Brecht in its didactic tendency. Brecht was interested in constructing examples, not in creating naturalistic or psychologically plausible characters. A variation on this skepticism toward "firm" knowledge is Brecht's insistence, expressed repeatedly by Me-ti, that insights age quickly and that truth is valid only for a limited time and in a specific situation. In *Flüchtlingsgespräche*, the two exiles take this insight to an extreme as they discuss plans for a symbolic alphabet in which the sign for "eternal truth" would at the same time denote "intellectual fraud" (GW 14: 1513).

Brecht's texts challenge the reader to make sense of them by intervening in them, and Brecht applied dialectical strategies to this end. Me-ti's definition "Thinking is something that follows from difficulties and precedes action" (GW 12: 443) can be taken as a rephrasing of the concept of "operative" or "intervening" thinking (*eingreifendes Denken*) that is not only a political concept for Brecht but also at the heart of his aesthetic-pedagogical views. Brecht's ideal, one that has repeatedly come under criticism, was a way of thinking directed toward social reality with the goal of changing it (Knopf, *Lyrik* 442–46; Pike). But before this can be accomplished, readers are called upon to perform a certain kind of "operative thinking" in engaging the texts and making sense of their contradictions. Reading and understanding them, however, does not automatically cause readers to change their own attitudes or the world (Ter-Nedden 367–68). Brecht's texts display a contradiction: while they support and encourage critical thinking, they are authoritarian by virtue of predetermining the reader's contribution to establishing meaning. Beginning in the late 1920s, Brecht developed an extraordinary talent for shaping readers' reactions and achieving certain effects by using language and logic in particular ways. His texts are brilliantly and precisely engineered for interaction with the reader's cognitive strategies of reading, strategies that are automatically activated when we try to make sense of texts. Brecht uses twists (*Wendungen*) and inversions to control the reader's expectations and patterns of thinking and to influence them. In order to solve difficulties, escape from textual aporias, and undo logical paradoxes, the reader has to rewrite and complete the texts in ways that are already written into the textual structure. Perhaps it is this double form of dogmatism in Brecht's texts—the way in which they always know better, prescribing both the insight and the cognitive path toward attaining insight, permitting and simultaneously restricting cognitive play—that ultimately limits their political effectiveness. The texts become caught up within the dialectics of openness and closure, questioning and dogmatic certainty that characterize them. First, the pleasure derived from his texts does not necessarily translate into implementing changes; rather, Brecht's texts provide an intellectual challenge to readers, the solution of which can easily turn out to be its own reward and produce its own satisfaction. Second, his textual strategies leave the reader little choice. While his early texts genuinely baffle readers, in his later texts the bafflement is often temporary, factored in as a necessary step toward the predetermined insight. It is not surprising if the readers' pleasure at rising to a challenge becomes tinged with a certain resentment at the ultimately authoritarian way in which the text frequently engages them.

Nevertheless, Brecht was quite successful at turning dialectics into a rhetorical and textual strategy. His study of Marxism did more than provide him with a message; it also profoundly influenced the structure of his texts. While Grimm (*Struktur* 77) correctly states that Brecht's work from the very outset evinces a "basic structure of consciously or unconsciously making contradictions visible," the pointed dialectical twists and turns are not found before the late 1920s. In particular, a comparison of the first versions and later reworkings of the early plays—these versions are available in the new *Werke* edition—reveals that the dialectical defamiliarizations (*Verfremdungen*) were added later.

There is a close relationship between *Verfremdung*, according to Grimm the most basic and pervasive structure in Brecht's work, and dialectics.[3] *Verfremdung* is most frequently an effect brought about by the application of dialectics in a way that momentarily baffles the reader and brings out unexpected aspects. In Brecht's words: "To defamiliarize an event or a character means in the first instance simply to strip away what is self-evident, familiar, plausible about it and to generate surprise and curiosity" (*GW* 15: 301). The examples cited above demonstrate that many of his texts are meant to make a point that carries a surprise, a new insight, or a reversal of an established judgment. As indicated, *Me-ti* weighing a piece of paper as a way of measuring its surface is an excellent example of *Verfremdung* and its uses; looking at something in a new light is generally a productive attitude. Brecht's statements show that for him *Verfrem-*

dung had a dialectical structure. His brief note "Defamiliarization as comprehension (to comprehend—not to comprehend—to comprehend), negation of negation" (*GW* 15: 360) must be understood as meaning that the aim of *Verfremdung* was to make the obvious incomprehensible in order to make its comprehension easier ("Short Description of a New Technique of Acting"). *Verfremdung* distances readers from the text and from what it presents by first negating the initial, naive comprehension. An apparent contradiction or opposite element is presented. Solving the contradiction and mediating the opposites is the second step of negation that leads to comprehension. The structure of the text and the process of reading that follows it are dialectical. Meaning is created through a temporary collapse of meaning. Contradictions are productive, then, in the immediate sense of making the reader produce meaning. Establishing "productive" gaps and twists is part of a *Verfremdung* that is anchored in the text and takes effect in the reader who is temporarily forced outside the text in a moment of incomprehension. In bridging the gaps and undoing surprising conjunctions, the reader frequently has to draw on extratextual reality. In the second step of defamiliarization, the world to which the text refers is made to appear unfamiliar through the devices employed in the text.

"At Ulm, 1592" provides an explicit illustration of a strategy that Brecht employed in many of his texts, that is, calling upon the reader to set the text straight. Here it is history, or progress, that supplies the irony and turns the configuration presented by the text upside down: the tailor is vindicated by history, the bishop proven wrong and made ridiculous. The statement made in the text is the opposite of the statement made by the text. In a truly dialectical move, the text forces readers to distance themselves from it, to mediate it. By pretending to a historical immediacy that has been by-passed by history, it challenges readers to supply the historical perspective that it seemingly lacks.

While *Verfremdung* is most frequently associated with Brecht's works for the theater, his prose works and poetry likewise offer an abundance of instances where the use of dialectical strategies engenders *Verfremdung*. In the Keuner story, "On Meeting Again," a phrase that is normally used automatically and unthinkingly, is taken literally and "made strange" or defamiliarized. When an old acquaintance greets Mr. K with: " 'You haven't changed at all,' " he responds in a surprising fashion: " 'Oh!' said Mr. K and turned pale" (*Tales* 124). Mr. K reacts to a politely reassuring commonplace as if it were a disturbing observation, and the reader, trying to make sense of the exchange, must interpret Mr. K's reaction as an implicit affirmation of the necessity and value of change. The first step—taking words literally—corresponds closely to the sense in which Russian Formalists such as Victor Shklovsky originally used the term "defamiliarization" (Striedter xxiii). Brecht's use of the term can be related to the positive value he assigned to change. Defamiliarization shows something in a new light in order to strip away the impression of immutability that results from the acceptance of what is familiar, opening up the possibility of personal and social change. The inevitability of change is, of course, the basic assumption behind Hegel's concept of dialectics. Brecht's texts not only present dialectical thinking as a way to insights; dialectics is written into them as a textual strategy.

Another dialectical strategy is to resituate a question or problem in order to view it in a different light. Me-ti, asked whether adultery is unethical for a married woman, implicitly invokes Kant's definition of marriage as a mutual and exclusive contract for the use of each other's genitals and then combines it with the economics of marriage (see also "On Kant's Definition of Marriage" in the *Metaphysics of Ethics*; *Poems* 312). While the husband has bought the exclusive right to his wife's genitals, the contract itself is unethical because women are forced to sell that right in order to survive. Me-ti's conclusion: "I think: In a country like ours everything is unethical, both adultery and marriage" (*GW* 12: 475). In the story "The Question, Is There a God," Mr. K begs the question by advising the questioner to think about whether his behavior would change in response to the answer. He continues: "If it would not, we can drop the question. If it would, then at least I can be of some help to you by telling you that your mind is already made up: you need a God" (*Tales* 112). Questions are only worth asking if they have practical value, that is, if the answers have an impact on reality.

Yet another characteristic dialectical strategy consists in reversing the usual perspective. For instance, Me-ti reflects on the fact that there are "many different ways of killing" and concludes: "Only a few of them are prohibited in our country" (*GW* 12: 466). This kind of reversal—a form of substituting the unexpected for the expected—can also be applied to a seemingly perfectly logical question. For example: "Tu said: How is one to fight if one strives for pleasure? Me-ti said: Why should one fight if one does not strive for pleasure?" (*GW* 12: 576). In this form of negation, the customary sequence of cause and effect is turned around, forcing the reader to reflect on the underlying assumptions of an attitude or statement. In these examples linear causality is reversed. In other cases, it is turned into a circularity of interdependence, as in the following passage on respect from *Me-ti*: "The room must be quiet when he who has much experience speaks. Whoever believes that his suggestions will be acted upon is going to think them through carefully" (*GW* 12: 465). Respect and the quality of suggestions are seen in mutual interdependence, not linear dependence.

Dialectical reversal is particularly effective when it undermines the significance of traditional values and virtues, as in dialogue seventeen of *Flüchtlings-gespräche* in which Ziffel voices his resentment of all virtues. The causal framework Ziffel establishes for the display of virtues strips them of their lofty moral value: "I tell you, I'm fed up being virtuous because nothing works, making sacrifices because of unnecessary shortages, being assiduous like a bee because of lousy organization and courageous because my government involves me in wars" (*GW* 14: 1497). *Me-ti* uses similar logic: "When I hear that a ship needs heroes as seamen, I ask whether it is rotten and old. . . . If the captain has to be a genius, apparently his instruments are unreliable" (*GW* 12: 518). This particular view of virtues circulates throughout Brecht's prose texts, writings, and plays. The same logic is used to expose virtues as ideological constructions made necessary by social injustice or employed in order to make up for short-comings. The cook in *Mother Courage* is keenly aware of the danger that virtues represent; Galileo laments the fate of countries that need heroes, and both Shen Teh in *The Good Person of Szechwan* and Grusha in *The Caucasian Chalk Circle* exemplify the danger inherent in succumbing to the temptation of being generous. On the other hand, Brecht draws attention to the effort it takes Shen Teh to maintain the harshness and anger that are dictated by adverse circumstances. Similarly, in the short poem "The Mask of Evil" (*Poems* 383) the strain of being angry elicits sympathy and pity rather than revulsion or aggression.

Commonly held views can be reduced to absurdity by taking them to their logical extreme. This strategy of exaggeration to the point of reversal is used frequently in the *Flüchtlingsgespräche*. As pointed out above, civilians are seen as obstacles to the effective waging of war, or human beings are reduced to holders of passports. Here defamiliarization lies in the switching of positions; a possible deviation is taken to the extreme and then presented as the normal case. The affirmative stance lures the reader into an acquiescence that is rendered untenable by the outrageousness of the apparently deadpan statements. A famous instance is Brecht's poem on the East German workers' uprising on 17 June 1953, in which he criticized those who condemned the people for defying the government by asking whether the government should perhaps "dissolve the people / And elect another?" (*Poems* 440).

Brecht's texts frequently present obstacles to readers, who will find it necessary to create a new text between the lines and to deviate from the overt text or subvert it as in the Keuner story "The Exertions of the Best People": " 'What are you working on?' Mr. K was asked. Mr. K replied: 'I am having [going to] a lot of trouble: I'm preparing my next mistake' " (*Tales* 124). The title is ambiguous. It can be taken to mean that even the best have to make efforts to achieve something, in which case the reader expects the story to be universally applicable and valid. The title may also refer to efforts made only or particularly by the best. In that case, the positive value of efforts or exertions would be stressed even before we know what these efforts consist of. The title, in conjunction with the use of the verb "preparing," builds up an expectation that is contradicted by "mistake." However, readers will hardly be willing to dismiss "mistake," a noun that is presented so prominently, as some kind of error, even though it seems to negate the preceding text. In order to make the text coherent and meaningful, the reader must address the tension between the expectation generated by the context and the key word "mistake." The basic positive *Gestus* of the text in combination with the verb "to prepare" prompts us to revaluate the irritating word "mistake," rather than to dismiss the text as nonsense. On the other hand, it is impossible to simply ignore the customary negative value of "mistake." As a result, the text manages to raise questions about the usual

way of defining success and mistakes as well as the apparent certainties that
govern such judgments. Furthermore, readers are called upon to doubt the optimistic assumption that efforts will always lead to the intended result and are
invited to ponder positive implications of unexpected outcomes. Actually, readers have just been taken through the experience the text articulates. They have
been confronted with an apparent mistake in the text that they have managed
to "correct" in a way that yielded an insight.

Defamiliarization does not necessarily generate both *Verständnis* (comprehension) and *Einverständnis* (consent) in accordance with Brecht's wishes. But
his prose cycles show him as a virtuoso of applied dialectics in the service of
textual strategy. They emphasize important themes and present thoughts and
attitudes that are characteristic of Brecht's work as a whole—parallels that are
lost from view if his production in any single genre is regarded in isolation.
They also show how Brecht's literary works in general are structured by his
thinking in a manner that engages readers in a particular way, and they exemplify his pedagogical use of dialectics as a way of activating readers' thought
processes. After 1926, the dialectical structure discussed here became an essential and constitutive factor in Brecht's work, in his poems and plays as well as
in his prose. Brecht's texts are of dialectics in a double sense: discourse on
dialectics through dialectics at work.

NOTES

1. See, for example, Christiane Bohnert, "Poetry, History, and Communication," and
Stefan Soldovieri, "War-Poetry, Photo(epi)grammetry: Brecht's *Kriegsfibel*," in this volume.
2. See also Douglas Kellner, "Brecht's Marxist Aesthetic," in this volume.
3. See also Reinhold Grimm, "Alienation in Context: On the Theory and Practice of
Brechtian Theater," in this volume.

WORKS CITED (SEE ALSO REFERENCE GUIDE TO WORKS CITED IN ABBREVIATED FORM)

Benjamin, Walter. "Bert Brecht." In *Gesammelte Schriften. Werkausgabe*, vol. 5. Edited
by Rolf Tiedemann and Hermann Schweppenhäuser. Frankfurt am Main: Suhrkamp, 1980. 5: 660–67.
———. "Was ist das epische Theater (1). Eine Studie zu Brecht." In *Gesammelte Schriften. Werkausgabe*, vol. 5. Edited by Rolf Tiedemann and Hermann Schweppenhäuser. Frankfurt am Main: Suhrkamp, 1980. 519–31.
Berghahn, Klaus. "A View Through the Red Window: Ernst Bloch's Spuren." In
Modernity and the Text. Revisions of German Modernism. Edited by Andreas
Huyssen and David Bathrick. New York: Columbia University Press, 1989. 200–
215.

Forke, Alfred, ed. *Me-Ti des Sozialethikers und seiner Schüler philosophische Werke.* Berlin: Vereinigung wissenschaftlicher Verleger, 1922.

Haack, Ekhard, and Eberhard Huge. "Zu Bertolt Brechts Geschichten vom Herrn Keuner." *Neue deutsche Hefte* 23 (1976): 495–516.

Hasselbach, Ingrid, and Karlheinz Hasselbach. *Bertolt Brecht. Kalendergeschichten. Interpretation.* Munich: Oldenbourg, 1990.

Häußler, Inge. *Denken mit Herrn Keuner. Zur deiktischen Prosa in den Keunergeschichten und Flüchtlingsgesprächen.* Berlin: Brecht-Zentrum der DDR, 1981.

Haug, Wolfgang Fritz. "Nützliche Lehren aus Brecht 'Buch der Wendungen.'" *Das Argument* 46 (1968): 1–12.

Hermsdorf, Klaus. "Brechts Prosa im Exil." *Weimarer Beiträge* 24 (1978): 30–42.

Kellner, Douglas. "Brecht's Marxist Aesthetic: The Korsch Connection." In Weber/Heinen, *Brecht* 29–42.

Klingmann, Ulrich. "Das Denken und das Gedachte: Zur Problematik des dialektischen Denkens in den Geschichten vom Herrn Keuner." *Acta Germanica. Jahrbuch des Südafrikanischen Germanistenverbandes* 18 (1985): 168–87.

Knopf, Jan. *Geschichten zur Geschichte.* Stuttgart: Metzler, 1973.

———. "Kleiner Grundkurs in Dialektik. Aphoristik in Brechts *Me-ti.*" *Der Deutschunterricht* 30 (1978): 37–52.

Koch, Gerd. *Lernen mit Bert Brecht. Bertolt Brechts politisch-kulturelle Pädagogik.* Hamburg: Association, 1979.

Krusche, Dietrich. *Kommunikation im Erzähltext. Analysen.* Munich: Fink, 1978.

Mayer, Hans: "Anmerkung zu einer Szene." In *Theaterarbeit.* 249–53.

Mews, Siegfried. "Bertolt Brecht." In *German Fiction Writers, 1914–1945.* Edited by James Hardin. Detroit, MI: Gale, 1987. 39–61.

Mittenzwei, Werner. "Nachwort. Der Dialektiker Brecht oder Die Kunst *Me-ti* zu lesen." *Me-ti.* 182–234.

Müller, Klaus-Detlev. "*Me-ti.*" In Weber/Heinen, *Brecht* 43–59.

———. *Brecht-Kommentar* zur erzählenden Prosa. Munich: Winkler, 1980.

Pike, David. "Brecht and 'Inoperative Thinking.'" In Mews, *Critical Essays* 253–75.

Šklovskij, Viktor. "Iskusstvo, kak priem."/"Die Kunst als Verfahren." In *Texte der russischen Formalisten.* Vol. 1: *Texte zur allgemeinen Literaturtheorie und zur Theorie der Prosa.* Edited by Jurij Striedter. Munich: Fink, 1969.

———. "Voskresenie slova."/"Die Auferweckung des Wortes." In *Texte der russischen Formalisten.* Vol. 2: *Texte zur Theorie des Verses und der poetischen Sprache.* Edited by Wolf-Dieter Stempel. Munich: Fink, 1972.

Striedter, Jurij. "Zur formalistischen Theorie der Prosa und der literarischen Evolution." In *Texte der russischen Formalisten.* Vol. 1: *Texte zur allgemeinen Literaturtheorie und zur Theorie der Prosa.* Edited by Jurij Striedter. Munich: Fink, 1969. ix–lxxxiii.

Ter-Nedden, Giesbert. "Brechts fiktive Lehren. Didaktische Poesie als hermeneutisches Problem am Beispiel der Keunergeschichten." In *Germanistik in Erlangen.* Edited by Dietmar Peschel. Erlangen: Universitätsbund Erlangen-Nürnberg, 1983. 365–88.

Wagner, Frank. *Bertolt Brecht. Kritik des Faschismus.* Opladen: Westdeutscher Verlag, 1989.

Wang, Mei-Ling Luzia. *Chinesische Elemente in Bertolt Brechts "Me-ti. Buch der Wen-dungen."* Frankfurt am Main: Lang, 1990.

Wirth, Andrzej. "Brecht: Writer Between Ideology and Politics." In Mews/Knust, *Essays* 199–208.

Wöhrle, Dieter. *Bertolt Brecht. Geschichten vom Herrn Keuner.* Frankfurt am Main: Diesterweg, 1989.

A BERTOLT BRECHT REFERENCE COMPANION

Edited by
SIEGFRIED MEWS

GREENWOOD PRESS
Westport, Connecticut • London

1997

PART III

FILM AND MUSIC

8

Brecht and Film

MARC SILBERMAN

INTRODUCTION

Many regard Brecht's interest in the cinema as secondary because his film scenarios and essays reflecting on the medium seem to be scattered and intermittent.
Brecht participated directly as writer and director in only one major film project,
Kuhle Wampe (1932), while his collaboration on Georg Wilhelm Pabst's adaptation of The Threepenny Opera (1930) and Fritz Lang's Hangmen also Die
(1943), for which he cowrote the original screenplays, was in his own eyes
highly compromised. More than forty other scenarios—some elaborately worked
out and others only short exposés—were never realized as motion pictures during his lifetime. Moreover, Brecht's many essays and notes on the cinema have
always been published among his other voluminous writings on theater, literature, and politics. Yet there is no question about Brecht's enthusiasm for the
movies. His entries in Diaries and Journals as well as reminiscences by friends
and acquaintances testify to frequent excursions to the movies and his enjoyment
of film entertainment (see Bronnen, Eisler, Leiser, ''Wahrheit,'' and Losey). In
fact, Brecht's scenarios, film notes, and film industry plans accompanied his
entire career as a dramatist, and even though the quality and quantity did not
remain constant throughout his life, his work on such projects consistently
sought unconventional solutions. Thus, ''Brecht and film'' touches the very core
of the writer's creativity: seeking ways to use a medium that not only throws
into question dominant production practices but also changes these practices and

the attitudes of the audience as well. Moreover, Brecht's ideas on such questions count among the most fundamental contributions to *the* problem of twentieth-century modernism: the dialectical relations between art, social revolution, and technological change.

At the outset there are four issues that need to be clarified. First, Brecht's interest in film comprises only one dimension of his work in various media, including theater, opera, radio broadcasting, music recording, photography, fine arts, ballet, and book printing. One might best understand his entire artistic career as an ongoing and explicit experiment in how to reach an audience by using the specific advantages of different media. The fact that his "experiments" often did not succeed led him to reflect time and again on the possibilities and limits of such undertakings. This touches a second issue. Brecht's relationship to the cinema cannot be demonstrated on the basis of his occasional notes, essays, and explanations alone but must also be considered in the context of specific projects. In other words, the boundaries between film scripts, stories, essays, plays, and the context of their publication or production should not be drawn too starkly, since all of them belong to a larger learning process and often were undertaken parallel to each other. At the same time—and this relates to the third issue—Brecht does not confront us with the transference or translation of results from one medium to another. He is an artist who never recognized the form/content split but rather played with the variables of textual material, the properties of the medium, and the historically formed audience. Both his practical work and commentaries on it were devoted precisely to articulating media-specific modes of representation and reception. Fourth and finally, Brecht never produced a theory of aesthetics or a systematic media critique. As an experimenter he was more interested in the challenges presented by the changing demands of technology and history. In this respect, "Brecht and film" can be subsumed under the goal that guided his entire creative output, that is, making the familiar strange so that the audience sees the principles governing reality and learns how to manipulate them. In summarizing Brecht's relationship to the cinema, then, it will be important to show how it fits within his more general rethinking of representation.

Not until the publication of Brecht's *Texte für Filme* (Texts for Films) in 1969 did the centrality of the cinema in his oeuvre become visible and provide the basis for serious scholarship to begin. The few familiar details known until then had suggested a love-hate relationship to a medium that had "betrayed" him. To be sure, in the second half of the 1960s New Left intellectuals in West Germany were rediscovering both Brecht's and Walter Benjamin's media critiques from the 1930s in their search for alternative, progressive models to the "culture industry."[1] But only the publication of the film texts themselves enabled a general taking of stock and led to retrospectives of the pertinent films.[2] The most comprehensive among the early scholarly contributions was cinephile Wolfgang Gersch's 1975 monograph *Film bei Brecht* (Film and Brecht), a survey of the film scenarios and essays that included detailed notes on the background and context of their development. Drawing on new material that had become available through the publication of Brecht's *Journals* in 1973 and *Diaries* in 1975, as well as on unpublished documents in the Brecht Archives, Gersch was able to demonstrate conclusively that Brecht returned again and again to sociological and artistic concerns posed by the cinema and in turn used these reflections to formulate more general aesthetic issues. Since then the scholarly discussion in Germany has largely followed a similar path, focusing on sources and institutional frameworks as well as on questions of influence and impact. Dieter Wöhrle's more recent and well-informed study (*Versuche*) proposes a new, promising approach that does not restrict itself to film alone but investigates the continuity in Brecht's various media experiments from a media theory perspective. Outside Germany, much of the discussion on Brecht and film—especially in France, England, and the United States—has concentrated on a new generation of filmmakers inspired by theoretical issues of the epic theater and *Verfremdung*.[3] Distinctive English-language contributions to the evaluation of Brecht's work in the cinema can be found in Lyon's historical detective work on Brecht in Hollywood (*Brecht*), Willett's interarts approach to Brecht (*Art and Politics*), and Mueller's collection of essays on Brecht and media theory (*Media*).

BRECHT MEETS THE CINEMA

Brecht's first published commentary on the cinema was a short article in his hometown newspaper for which he had begun writing theater reviews in the fall of 1919. After Germany's defeat in the Great War, social and political disruptions led among other things to a loosening of censorship regulations. The movie market was briefly flooded with prurient tales of fallen maidens and prostitutes under the guise of moral education. Typical for Brecht, his article addresses the negative sociological impact of such films on the audience and criticizes the hypocritical practice of marketing a false ideology of sexual emancipation to earn profits.[4] In his *Diaries* (47 et passim) of the early 1920s, Brecht's casual comments about movies and script projects suggest a more positive attitude in which he does not see the cinema as a threat but as an indisputable form of entertainment. He recognized that the sensationalism, suspense, grotesque humor, and the documentary quality of showing events and objects were cinematic effects that appealed to a broad public. Moreover, the film industry represented an outright challenge to prevailing forms of high culture production and reception, a development that the young iconoclast Brecht appreciated. Brecht's interest in the cinema at this time was stimulated as well by the success of expressionist films such as Robert Wiene's *The Cabinet of Dr. Caligari* (released 1920). Although he never commented directly on these art films (Brecht wrote no film criticism as such), he was an astute observer both of the new aesthetics and the way the audience responded. Distorted visual perspectives, stylized sets, and innovative spatio-temporal relations achieved through distinctive editing were some of the techniques that Brecht would adapt in his own early film scripts.

While Brecht's *Diaries* indicate that he was working on numerous film projects, only three scripts and a short scenario are extant, each completed in a few days between 1921 and 1922.[5] The main motivation for this sudden flurry of activity seems to have been financial need, but the romantic adventures also deal with themes and figures typical of his early poems and plays (e.g., *Drums in the Night* and *In the Jungle of Cities*). Brecht adapts genre conventions of the silent cinema—sensationalism, eccentric characters, mysterious events, intense suspense—but transforms the metaphysical soul-searching and melodrama of the expressionist period with humor and irony. The depiction of narrative events is sometimes visually striking, including descriptions of visual structures and details about image composition and editing. Of course, the texts are only preliminary sketches of films that never materialized, but they do demonstrate principles that would continue to interest Brecht in other media as well: episodic structure, aspects of rupture and distanciation, and the strong story line (or *Fabel*).

"Der Brillantenfresser" (*Texte für Filme* 43–76; The Jewel Eater), the first of the extant scripts completed in March 1921, reflects Brecht's familiarity with American gangster films. Set in a port-city dive, various small-time gangsters cook up plots to make big money. Slapstick scenes of drunken brawls and chases emphasize the physical rather than the psychological dimension of the action, and plot twists structured around mistaken identities and masquerade lend themselves to the potential of cinematic trick shots. The second script, "Das Mysterium der Jamaika-Bar" (*Texte für Filme* 77–115; The Mystery of the Jamaica Bar), was completed about a month later. The story was written specifically for the popular Stuart Webb detective series produced by a Munich film company to which Brecht had good connections, although the script was ultimately turned down. The complicated plot of disappearing party guests is constructed around a cumbersome, carousel-like set that allows the kidnappers to stage mysterious disappearances. The visual imagination inherent in this play of appearance and reality coupled with frequent gender cross-dressing again maximizes the cinematic possibilities. "Drei im Turm" (*Texte für Filme* 9–48; Three in the Tower), coauthored with Caspar Neher in July 1921, is based on a sentimental triangle plot in which an officer kills himself when he notices that his wife loves a younger lieutenant. He hides and dies in a closet and pursues the lovers as a ghost until the lieutenant, who is meanwhile unhappily married to the woman, happens to discover the half-decomposed body. The narrative ends with a drastic scene of the lieutenant raping his wife next to the skeleton of the former husband laid out on a bed. Set in an isolated watchtower, the script incorporates traits of the expressionist chamber film with its restricted number of characters, the emphasis on interior space (including corridors and winding staircases), and motifs of tortured marriage relations. But in fact it is a self-consciously amusing horror film that plays off the preoccupation with phantoms and the disastrous psycho-logical tension of the expressionist cinema.

Unlike these three film scripts, "Robinson in Assuncion" (*Texte für Filme* 307–12; Robinson in Assuncion) is a short film scenario, closer to a prose story and lacking entirely in cinematic details. Coauthored by Brecht and his friend and collaborator, Austrian dramatist Arnolt Bronnen, the plot again features two men and the woman they fight over on an island paradise that has been dev-astated by a volcanic eruption. This struggle is in counterposition to another between nature and technology, which in some of the brief descriptions antici-pates the wrath of the machines so effectively captured by Fritz Lang in *Me-tropolis* (1926). Written for a prize competition that the authors did not win, the scenario was nonetheless produced by Lothar Mendes under the title *SOS. Die Insel der Tränen* (1923; SOS. The Island of Tears), but Brecht was no longer listed as author, and Bronnen himself no longer recognized even a trace of the original idea after seeing the movie (Bronnen 146). The only film pro-duction in which Brecht actually participated at this time was a surrealistic comedy of twenty-eight minutes called *Mysterien eines Frisiersalons* (1923; Mysteries of a Hairdressing Salon). The film was directed by Erich Engel, but Brecht, together with the Munich clown Karl Valentin, probably helped script the grotesque episodes of the tortures perpetrated by the barbershop employees on their customers.[6]

When Brecht's theater career began to prosper in 1923 with the first produc-tions in Berlin and Munich, his active interest in the cinema waned. Nonetheless, various sources indicate that he considered film ideas throughout the 1920s, among them an adaptation of Franz Kafka's story *Metamorphosis* in 1926 (Gersch 39, n. 1). More substantial for understanding the role of the new me-dium in his thinking were his occasional reflections on the cinema. In September 1922, Brecht was the first to participate in the series German Authors on the Film published by the newspaper *Berliner Börsen-Courier*. The short article "Über den Film" (*Werke* 21:100; On Film) is both a polemic against the com-mercial structures of the film industry that deter the engagement of serious writ-ers and a critique of arrogant writers who reject the cinema as lowbrow entertainment. These positions were to be theoretically elaborated in *Der Drei-groschenprozeß* (The Threepenny Trial) almost ten years later. Another fruitful stimulus was Brecht's discovery of Charlie Chaplin. The impression he recorded after seeing his first Chaplin film in 1921—*The Face on the Barroom Floor*—stresses the actor's simplicity and directness, which struck Brecht because the deadpan, unsentimental earnestness elicited constant laughter from the audience (*Diaries* 140–41). The impact of Chaplin's nonpsychological acting contrasted with the introspective habits of German actors and became a major factor in the economy of expression that Brecht developed later in his notion of gestic acting. In an unpublished note written after viewing *Goldrush* in 1926, he reflected upon this simplicity as a quality of the film structure itself, but now he drew an

explicit comparison to the possibilities of stage dramaturgy. Since film as a new
medium was not burdened with the techniques that had developed over centuries
in the theater, its power, he proposed, was in the simple documentation of reality
(*Werke* 21: 135–36). This position was a revision of Brecht's own experience
as a scriptwriter in the early 1920s, when he employed a spectrum of visual and
narrative techniques that went far beyond mere documentation; in his delimi-
tation of the cinema, Brecht suggests a view that he would radically rethink and
expand in the context of *Der Dreigroschenprozeß*.

   The emphasis on the objectifying aspect of film images was symptomatic for
another tendency during these years. In 1927 Brecht recognized in Erwin Piscator's incorporation of film sequences into theater spectacles a means of presenting on stage a contrastive reality to the actors' spoken words. As an
interruptive mechanism, the use of motion pictures in the theater suggested at
this point a way of undermining the passive, consumer attitude of the audience.
This mechanism was comparable to other innovations in his developing theory
of epic theater such as songs, gestic acting, and projected titles (*Werke* 21: 196–
97). Brecht's own use of film footage, however, remained limited to the 1932
production of *The Mother*, in which a documentary sequence of the Russian
revolution was planned as a final coda.[7] One could speculate that Brecht was
sensitive to the media-specific impact of moving images on the stage and preferred to avoid the dangers of identification that would complicate his anti-
illusionistic approach in the epic theater.

   Additional evidence for his sophisticated understanding of the cinema comes
from another direction. In the highly accomplished short story "The Monster"
(1928), Brecht combines a nonpsychologizing prose style evoking the documentary perspective of the camera lens with a narrative about the difficulty of
filming a historical scene realistically.[8] Set in a Soviet film studio, a crew is
preparing to shoot the pogrom scene in which a ruthless Russian governor, the
monster of the title, signs the execution order for a group of Jews. An old man
who is standing around the set is allowed to try the role because he looks just
like the governor. The attentive reader quickly surmises that he is indeed the
historical governor, now impoverished and trying to earn some money as an
extra. All the other characters, however, prefer the effect produced by the star,
who is better able to convey the idea of monstrosity with his expressive acting.
In other words, Brecht constructs the situation around the issue of representation:
what is the value of authenticity for representing reality? How does the effect
of artistic representation (the old style of acting) conceal the real monstrosity?
The narrator's ironic closing statement that only art, not physical resemblance,
can convey a monstrous "impression" (*Stories* 111) refers to Brecht's central
concern during the next years: how to render the natural problematic.

   The importance of the cinema for Brecht can be most clearly ascertained in
the traces it left in his theater work during the 1920s. The disruptive, episodic
construction of the epic play recalls the shot-by-shot development of the early
film scripts. The use of intertitles and projected titles on stage is a technique

adapted from the silent movies. The exaggerated expressiveness of expressionist acting on stage and in the cinema provoked Brecht to devise the mechanics of gestic acting. His "behaviorist" approach to characterization derived from an inductive method of observing events and attitudes related to the documentary quality of film images. Beyond these formal aspects, however, he was also beginning to understand that the cinema was changing the way people perceived reality. The introduction of new media technology was affecting not only literary production but also audience expectations and habits. Brecht's experience with the filming of *The Threepenny Opera* provided the occasion to examine the implications of these changes.

THE *THREEPENNY* COMPLEX

Brecht was unusual among the cultural critics of the Weimar Republic in that he did not fear the entertainment industry. On the contrary, he sought out opportunities to use its mechanisms against conservative and progressive intellectuals alike who celebrated traditional art forms. Nothing illustrates this practice better than the fate of *The Threepenny Opera* in its metamorphosis from the most successful stage production of the Weimar Republic (1928) to the scenario *Die Beule* (1930; The Bruise), which was commissioned for a commercial film adaptation, to the actual film by Pabst (1931) to *Threepenny Novel* (1934). Accompanying these stages were the court trial initiated by Brecht and composer Kurt Weill against the film production company for copyright infringement (1930) and the book-length essay *Der Dreigroschenprozeß* (1932), Brecht's most incisive and sustained reflection on the conditions of cultural production under capitalism. For the context of our topic, the focus here will be on Brecht's scenario and essay in order to demonstrate his paradigmatic significance as an artist who addressed the impact of changing technology on institutional relations affecting artistic representation.

The legendary success of *The Threepenny Opera* launched Brecht's international theater career. Based on the popularity of Weill's music and the provocative but cynical decadence of the play's characters, the Nero film company bought the adaptation rights on 21 May 1930. At Brecht's insistence, Nero film negotiated a further agreement, signed on 3 August, that included details allowing Brecht to write a scenario with his theater collaborators Caspar Neher and Slatan Dudov, as well as Leo Lania, an assistant to Erwin Piscator. Although the agreement accorded Brecht the right to demand changes if the final cut did not follow his and his collaborators' scenario, it also obliged them to follow the original play's text both in style and content. Meanwhile, Brecht and his team were already writing the film treatment, and Nero film, which had resold the rights to Tobis-Klang-Film and Warner Brothers in anticipation of an international release by celebrated director Pabst, proceeded to rent studio space and hire the casts for both a German and a French version.[9] When it became clear that the treatment differed in essential points from the play, Nero film, under pressure to begin shooting on deadline, sought some kind of accommodation with Brecht. When that failed, the production began nonetheless with a new script written by Béla Belázs and Ladislav Vaida—whereupon Brecht went to court (Gersch 58–67).

The bone of contention was the text of *Die Beule*, which in comparison to the play is definitely a cinematic treatment but also substantially changed in its thrust. Not only had Brecht's own views about capitalist society become more radical through his study of Marxism, but also the didactic orientation of his *Lehrstücke* was increasingly at odds with the mix of politics and entertainment that characterized the original play. Moreover, the two years since the play had been written had witnessed the market crash and a worldwide depression, creating a politically more polarized context than was the case in 1928. (No wonder that *Saint Joan of the Stockyards* and *The Measures Taken*, the plays on which Brecht was working when he was writing the text of *Die Beule*, contained his most severe political critique up to this point.)

For the film adaptation, Brecht basically took from the play the characters and the Victorian setting in order to construct a much more radical image of struggle between class interests. This modification of the story line affected the sequence of scenes and songs as well as the play's message.[10] Everything is inflated: Macheath's gang counts 120 members, the wedding party includes a crowd of 150 guests with many dignitaries, Peachum heads a trust with a stable of lawyers, and the beggars' march needs thousands of extras. More significantly, the gang of criminals is directly equated with the bourgeoisie. Now they do not break into a bank but buy it, becoming financiers in order to engage ''legally'' in their criminal activities. To this end, an entirely new motif, the eponymous bruise, is introduced as the mediating element between the three antagonistic groups: Macheath and his gang, Peachum and his beggars, and Brown and his police. Sam, one of Peachum's beggars, is boxed around after squealing on a gang member. It is the resulting bruise as much as Macheath's marriage to Peachum's daughter Polly that motivates the struggle between the beggars' trust and Mac's gang, but it also symbolizes for Peachum an injustice that demands police intervention. Hence, he must ''help'' his case along by beating Sam to revive the bruise. Of course, ultimately Sam is sacrificed and takes the place of Macheath in prison. In a typically Brechtian interpretation of the Hollywood happy ending, the three former enemies discover their common interests when confronted with the threat of a revolt by the mass of exploited beggars. While the former join together to await the arrival of the queen, the latter wait for Sam in vain, whose role has once again changed. Awaiting his execution, he now becomes for the beggars the symbol of the justice they seek.

Brecht and his collaborators not only revamped the story to sharpen the political message but also took into account the cinematic medium for which they were writing. As in his previous film scripts, Brecht integrated in *Die Beule* conventions of the American gangster and romance film genres. But just as the play *The Threepenny Opera* ''quoted'' traditional theater dramaturgy in order to undermine its function, so does *Die Beule*: not the head gangster but his wife is the boss; the bank break-in is staged as a peaceful buy-out; the classical chase sequence does not lead to closure but to a higher level of corporate corruption, and so on. Moreover, the scenario includes important parallel montage sequences that crosscut simultaneous actions; for example, at the beginning of the third part when Mac disappears into a brothel and Polly proceeds to buy a bank, or at the end when police chief Brown and beggar king Peachum both rush to Macheath's prison cell—albeit with contradictory aims. It is important to note that "the apparatus [camera] seeks its images, so to speak, it is a sociologist" (Brecht; *Texte für Filme* 333, n. 12). The idea of this "gestic camera" was to construct each section with distinct cinematographic techniques and with a visual rhythm dictated by the action. The authors also anticipated specific visual details. The changing shape of the bruise as the central metaphor would have lent itself to humorous closeup shots; the transformation of the robbers into bankers is projected as a trick shot; and Brown's nightmare of the silent, marching masses before the conclusion promised a spectacular dream sequence playing with choreographed crowd movement, sound, and silence. Finally, there are also traces of interruptive epic dramaturgy, such as the printed titles punctuating the scenes and the contrast in the wedding sequence of a traveling shot observing the guests' behavior while a superimposed article from a newspaper society page describes the honored guests.

Since Nero film was interested in cashing in on the *Threepenny* stage hit, neither Brecht's revision nor Leo Lania's shooting script, which was adapted from Brecht's after he was fired, served the end of remaking the original.[11] The resulting film has been celebrated by cinephiles and Pabst specialists as one of his masterpieces, while Brecht scholars have largely regarded it as a betrayal (Elsaesser). In fact, the film version of *The Threepenny Opera*, which was shot from 19 September through mid-November 1930 and opened in Berlin on 19 February 1931, undoubtedly contributed to the play's international fame as well as to that of Brecht, even though it contradicted some of its most elementary structural aspects: separation of the elements, *Verfremdung*, and the anti-illusionist foregrounding of stage mechanics. Instead, Pabst concentrated on the weakest aspect of Brecht's text, the romanticized, antibourgeois world of gangsters and whores, in order to explore the illusions of the bourgeoisie through the cinema's inherent possibilities of play between the visible and the invisible. Using impressionistic lighting to recreate the underworld atmosphere and editing on movement or with dissolves that smoothes over epic disruption, Pabst shifted Brecht's cynical, political satire into a tale of power relations mediated through erotic attraction. As a result, he reproduced visually the pathos and sentimentality of Weill's music rather than working against it. Brecht and Weill filed suit against Nero film, however, not because the company had rejected the scenario but rather to regain the film rights for *The Threepenny Opera*. On the grounds that the production was not fulfilling its contractual obligation of "protecting" the integrity of the work, they threatened the entire investment of the production company. The trial lasted four days, from 17–20 October 1930, and generated an unusually large press response owing both to Brecht's own notoriety and to the fact that the case had a signal function. It touched on the sensitive question of competition between the cinema and the theater and on the speculative issue of artists' rights to control their ideas in the mass media.[12]

Brecht must have been pleased with the fact that he lost his suit, for if he had won, he would have had to recognize that the capitalist system was *not* following its own rules. The essay on the lawsuit represents Brecht's analysis of how this system functions, exposing the intersection of power, false ideas, and art. The essay sought to confirm Brecht's political victory by unmasking the justice of the bourgeois state as the justice of the ruling class that is willing to violate its own legal system in order to protect its financial interests. Although the suit was the point of departure, the text of the essay neither documents the trial nor raises the issues of cinematic adaptation surrounding *Die Beule* or, for that matter, Pabst's film. Rather, Brecht plays the role of the naive artist who goes to court to defend the inviolability of intellectual property guaranteed by the liberal, democratic constitution. There he discovers that in fact the validity of individual ownership is measured against economic consequences, for in the case of the cinema the economic risk is so great that the profit motive in producing the commodity (the film) is deemed more important than the right of the poet to his immaterial property (the ideas). In short, Brecht shows that, contrary to what many artists would like to believe, the work of art, like other commodities, is subject to market forces. *Der Dreigroschenprozeß* (*Werke* 21: 488–514) is a brilliant demonstration of the implications of this insight.

Divided into five unequal sections, the essay comprises a montage of press reports about the trial, excerpts from contracts, lawyers' explanations, reports on discussions, and polemical analyses. Brecht spells out in a brief introduction that his purpose was to ''stage'' his own experience in the film industry as an object of critical regard in order to make visible the difference between the actual practices and the ideas of how culture, law, and public opinion function. The first section sets the stage with a summary of the events leading up to the lawsuit, the court's decision, and public reactions as recorded by various newspapers. The next section, ''Von der Spekulation zum Experiment'' (From Speculation to Experiment), investigates the consequences of the lawsuit's possible resolutions only to conclude, as the court did, that the ''ideals'' of an artist— that is, the belief that contractual law protects ideas—is false. Like all property rights, they can be purchased by capital. This was, in effect, the outcome of Brecht's trial, and the echo registered in the press excerpts indicate that from this perspective Brecht's action corroborated traditional and even left-wing attitudes about the incompatability of art and commerce. If he had stopped here, he would have achieved, however, at least one important concession from the court: the public admission that the tradition of the law, oriented exclusively toward notions of individual creativity, was incompatible with the capitalist mode of production based on collective activity.

In the third section Brecht proceeds a step further. He argues that art can neither reject nor simply avoid the new mass media as "bad," since the technologically most progressive media define the standard for all other arts, including the traditional forms of poetry and drama. This is an issue not merely of collective forms of production but also of reception. The addressees of the work of art perceive reality differently, that is, they read novels knowing how the mass media represent reality. The fact that traditional forms of art still dominate the cinema (for example by filming the *stage* play *The Threepenny Opera*) results from an obsolete ideology of individualism needed for the functioning of production in a historically specific phase of capitalism. In this central and longest part, "Kritik der Vorstellungen" (The Critique of Ideas), Brecht examines fourteen typical ideological assumptions underlying the court trial: first, he addresses opinions about the relation of art and the cinema in order to characterize the specificity of the film; from these he moves to the role of art and the cinema in society as commodity forms; finally he considers how the system of law treats art and the cinema as commodities in order to make possible their production in capitalist society. Each subsection is introduced with a pertinent quote from the press as a reminder that these ideas were in circulation, but they were also intended to show that Brecht himself was engaged in a didactic process of self-instruction, a learning process about the new medium. The fourth section is a brief recapitulation, stressing once again the need to relinquish the metaphysical idea of "quality" art as the expression of the individual artist's personality for a more progressive, adequate idea of the work of art as a commodity, as a combination of discrete, interchangeable parts. The final section explains the two goals suggested by the subtitle of the essay, "Ein soziologisches Experiment" (A Sociological Experiment): to analyze how culture functions in a particular society (sociological) and to construct a controlled public framework in order to trigger a collective thought process (experiment). Like Brecht's contemporaneous *Lehrstücke*, the lawsuit essay was conceived as a model. Thus, it was less concerned with answers than with exposing contradictions, making them visible in order to explode them and to provoke new ones.

THE FILM *KUHLE WAMPE*

If *Der Dreigroschenprozeß* represents Brecht's most sophisticated contribution to cinema theory, then the film *Kuhle Wampe* (1932) can be considered his most important legacy in film history, the only example of his practical work that came close to realizing the idea of deindividualizing (aesthetic) production in the cinema. Not only the film's planning and shooting, but also its themes and structure integrate the collective experience with new ways of representing reality. In contrast to Pabst's *The Threepenny Opera* film, *Kuhle Wampe* fell outside the boundaries of commercial film production. It can be considered more pertinently within the context of ambitious efforts during the 1920s to develop in Germany an independent, noncommercial cinema aimed at serving the political and entertainment needs of the organized working class.

Early in 1931 the Bulgarian Slatan Dudov approached the Prometheus film corporation with a film sketch that he had coauthored with Brecht about the problem of unemployment in a working-class family. Dudov (in German spelled Dudow), who after studying theater in Berlin had become involved with Piscator's political stage, met Brecht in 1929 and collaborated with him on several theater projects. Prometheus film—founded in 1926 in loose conjunction with the Communist party as a distribution outlet for the new, revolutionary Soviet films by Sergei Eisenstein, Dziga Vertov, and Vsevolod Pudovkin—had gradually become interested in producing films for the working-class audience. The introduction of sound technology, however, coupled with the effects of the Great Depression, seriously undermined the existence of such an alternative, leftist cultural institution.[13] Despite its financial difficulties, the firm accepted the collaborative project suggested by Dudov and planned to combine it with an in-house project on the Communist youth movement and its sports clubs. In fact, *Kuhle Wampe* was the last Prometheus production and its first sound film before its collapse in 1932.[14] The collective structure that came together around Brecht and Dudov resulted in part from these less-than-ideal production conditions but also reflected a self-conscious attempt to counteract the hierarchical studio arrangements in the commercial industry. Dudov brought in novelist Ernst Ottwalt to help with the script because of the latter's intimate knowledge of the working-class environment.[15] The composer Hanns Eisler, who was working with Brecht and Dudov on the stage production of *The Mother* in January 1932, also joined the team. He had experience writing modernist film music and enjoyed a reputation for his popular workers' songs. Some of the actors were well known in the workers' theater movement, and the appearance of the leading agit-prop theater group, Das rote Sprachrohr (The Red Megaphone), as well as the participation of thousands of enthusiasts organized in workers' sports clubs for the film's finale, brought an unusual degree of visibility and public attention to the collective project. Indeed, the successful completion of the shooting was a significant public event in Brecht's sense because it had brought together a number of leading intellectuals of the Left with workers' organizations in a creative process.

Kuhle Wampe was a departure from the "traditional" working-class films produced by Prometheus. It does take up familiar plot elements from the social drama—including a suicide, a love affair, leisure activities, and the political emancipation of a young person—but it also thematizes petit-bourgeois behavior as a contradiction within the working class.[16] The story presents a loose sequence of episodes and events divided into three sections. The exposition, in section 1, introduces the Bönike family and its disintegration under the pressure of unemployment (the son commits suicide). Section 2 follows the complications of family life: eviction, the daughter's pregnancy, the parents' pressure on her to marry her lover. Section 3 suggests a resolution to the young couple's quandary (she has an abortion) and an alternative to the parents' resignation in the face of impoverishment when the lovers reunite at the workers' sports festival. The film problematizes, in other words, an issue that was proving to be a fertile ground for the Nazis as well. In the period of crisis characterizing the last years of the Weimar Republic, the instability of the working class, caused by unemployment and impoverishment, made it particularly susceptible to middle-brow ideologies of social harmony and classless statism proposed by the National Socialists. *Kuhle Wampe* addressed this issue not so much to clarify the causes but rather to show the powerlessness effected by the desire to escape from politics altogether. Furthermore, an alternative was portrayed in athletic competitions as an allegory for solidarity and strength in the class struggle.

Beyond its thematic and political distinction, *Kuhle Wampe* introduced a new structural approach that was influenced by the Soviet cinema. Although Soviet films had been widely distributed in Germany since 1926, their innovative film narration had less impact on the German cinema than on literature and the dramatic arts (Willett, *Art and Politics*). The Prometheus productions, for example, stressed their proletarian content as a ''class conscious'' alternative to the dominant cinema, but the films tended to imitate popular melodramas of the major studios at the expense of formal innovation. Brecht had met and corresponded with Soviet intellectuals in these years; clearly the montage principles of the Soviet cinema reveal parallel interests to his epic theater, but there is virtually no direct comment by Brecht about the new visual effects. What Brecht found congenial was the construction principle of montage, premised on the idea of interruption and collision. Montage editing brings together images or shots that do not ''fit'' and insists on them being ''read'' by the spectator. In *Kuhle Wampe*, for example, the filmmakers' attention focused on the organization of the images within the cinematic frame (the documentary quality of the image) as well as between frames (the disjointed quality of montage). This explains why the camera work itself is relatively restrained when compared to the expressivity of earlier Weimar cinematography. On the other hand, Dudov and Brecht integrated from the Soviet cinema an awareness of narrative punctuation that they exploited to the fullest. The opening sequence is a paradigmatic example. It opens not with an establishing shot but with a collage of quick takes from dynamically contrasting camera angles, localizing the action geographically in Berlin (the Brandenburg Gate), in a working-class quarter of the city (shots of a factory and tenements), and temporally during the Depression (a sequence of newspaper headlines indicating the steep rise in unemployment figures). The printed title and the overture-like opening music—highly theatrical markings of this and each subsequent section, familiar from Brecht's stage productions—cue the spectator to the film's structural pattern: a self-conscious narration has been assembled to solicit the spectator's active role in a cognitive process beyond mere watching.

Kuhle Wampe is an exceptional example of how to link questions of representation, social change, and the subject that will effect that change as suggested by Brecht in *Der Dreigroschenprozeß*. This didactic quality is most pronounced in the film's last section, where family and personal problems are subordinated to the collective spirit of the workers' sports festival. It culminates in the final scene, which transfers the lesson of solidarity from the sports events to a political discussion, from image to word. Pressed into a subway car is a sociopolitical cross-section of the city's inhabitants, each of whom comments on a newspaper report that the Brazilian government has burned millions of pounds of coffee to protect the falling commodity price. The quick, polemical argument, mirrored by fast cuts from one face to another, climaxes in the question: "Who will change the world?" Speaking face front to the camera in a direct challenge to the spectator, one of the young woman workers responds: "Those who don't like it."

The film's reception indicates the consequences of the filmmakers' untraditional approach. The conditions under which the film was conceived and produced—always with an eye to the eventuality of censorship problems and to its precarious financial backing—necessitated compromises at every level of its realization. This meant that the complicated filmic structure had to camouflage further its agitational thrust behind the relatively harmless allegory of sports and racing and the appeal of the youthful participants.[17] As Brecht himself recognized, the politically sympathetic critics understood *Kuhle Wampe* less well than the censors, who initially forbade its distribution (*Werke* 21: 548–50).[18] The latter, like Brecht, were most concerned with the film's overall impact on the spectators and identified the power of the critique in the convincing portrayal of typical behavior (i.e., the gestic acting), whereas the former reproached the filmmakers for a lack of partisanship and clarity owing to the disruptive montage style. Nonetheless, the film ran successfully but briefly until it fell victim to the elimination of the left-wing public sphere with the onset of National Socialism in March 1933. Its impact, therefore, as a model for a politically motivated revolutionary cinema and as an alternative to studio conventions was in fact negligible.[19]

BRECHT IN EXILE

Brecht was among the first writers to feel the impact of the Nazi takeover in 1933, and he left Germany immediately after the Reichstag fire on 28 February 1933. Emigration meant not only the abrupt end to collective projects in Berlin but also the loss of direct access to his audience. Yet Brecht continued to pursue cinema projects, like many other German exiles, undoubtedly for both financial and political reasons. During the exile years in Scandinavia he sought, through fellow emigrés such as Piscator in Moscow and Lania in London, opportunities to place original exposés, to negotiate contracts for film adaptations of his plays, or to obtain commissions for film scripts. Despite promising leads with directors such as Alexander Korda, Joris Ivens, and Hans Richter, nothing materialized other than the lame project for a British film of Leoncavallo's opera *I Pagliacci* in 1936, for which Fritz Kortner wrangled Brecht a contract to help with the dialogues. He was paid off, but his texts were not used (Gersch 180–90; Willett, "Motion Pictures" 119). More typical for Brecht's cinematic work was the migration and transformation of story elements, characters, and themes from one medium to another. He considered a film adaptation of the German translation of Jaroslav Hašek's *The Good Soldier Švejk*, which would later become a play, and he wrote the treatment "Der Gallische Krieg oder Die Geschäfte des Herrn J. Cäsar" (1938–1939; The Gallic War or The Business Affairs of Mr. J. Caesar) while working on his novel *Die Geschäfte des Herrn Julius Caesar* (The Business Dealings of Mr. Julius Caesar).[20] Generally, however, the film plans receded behind more intensive work on projects in other media (plays, novels, stories, poems, and political and literary essays).

Brecht arrived at the port of Los Angeles in July 1941. He decided to settle on the West Coast rather than in New York, where he also had an invitation, because of the large community of German emigré artists and because of his potential contacts to the film industry in Hollywood.[21] Brecht was encouraged by reports that German screenwriters actually enjoyed a good reputation in the industry, and during his six years in Hollywood he rubbed shoulders with many of the most important studio personalities (Lyon, *Brecht* 83). Yet obviously Brecht in no way fit the pattern of Hollywood filmmaking. He held its formula writing in contempt, criticized its immense waste, and shared none of its sensitivity to serious criticism. Brecht still considered the script to be a literary text, while Hollywood practice had already broken it into a series of separate responsibilities (of idea, treatment, scenario, script, shooting script, and so on). Furthermore, his notion of collective production did not fit the studio model of industry specialization and rationalization. Neither his aesthetics nor his temperament prepared him for the conditions in Hollywood. At the same time, Brecht's reputation in the United States was not established, despite productions of *The Threepenny Opera* and *The Mother*. Hence, he was dependent on friends and acquaintances to open doors for him; considering his disdain for the Hollywood institution, it is astonishing the degree to which they cooperated. But Brecht never lost his fascination with American movies, as the many entries in his *Journals* about screenings from these years indicate. That he mentioned or actually brought to paper at least fifty film projects offers evidence for his determination to break into the industry, especially in view of the fact that his hopes were hardly fulfilled.[22] Not one of the projects actually became the film Brecht envisioned, few found their way into more than fragmentary textual form, and they occupied Brecht's time as much as a means to earn income as to reach the mass audience with an antifascist message.

Brecht's two Hollywood "successes" are quickly summarized. The script collaboration with John Wexley for Fritz Lang's *Hangmen also Die* (1943) about the assassination in Czechoslovakia of Reinhard Heydrich, the head of Hitler's Security Office, was ultimately taken out of his hands. In an appeal brought by Brecht before the Screen Writers Guild contesting the film credits, Wexley was determined to have been the sole scriptwriter based on Brecht and Lang's original story about a modern tyrant. Brecht was paid well by United Artists for his intense work on the script during 1942, but the final cut reflects few of the distinctive cinematic qualities associated with his name.[23] Although, along with Ernst Lubitsch's *To Be or Not to Be* (1942) and Fred Zinnemann's *The Seventh Cross* (1944), the film counts among Hollywood's best antifascist features, its sensationalist gangster and action film effects mark it as a Lang classic. Brecht was also able to sell indirectly the idea of his play *The Visions of Simone Machard*. Fellow exile author Lion Feuchtwanger had written a novel based on Brecht's 1942 play about a modern-day Jeanne d'Arc in the French Resistance, for which MGM purchased the story rights in 1943. Feuchtwanger split the sizable sum with Brecht, but the film was never made because the lead actress became pregnant, and by the time shooting was again possible, France had been liberated by the Allies.

Brecht's many other projects disclose a curious mixture of willingness to adapt to the demands of the film industry and refusal to compromise on its terms. The adaptations of classical as well as modern texts emphasized the contemporary, everyday familiarity of the conflicts rather than literary "quality."[24] The bio-pics avoided heroism and sentimentality in favor of portraying the social conditions behind historical figures.[25] The topical films conformed to established genre conventions while seeking every opportunity to sharpen the social contrasts.[26] Toward the end of the war, Brecht became active in the "Council for a Democratic Germany," an emigré organization formed to prepare for the postwar transformation of the country. Together with Dieterle he wanted to produce a series of short agitational films based on scenes from his antifascist plays for use in the American POW camps to reeducate German soldiers; immediately after Germany's capitulation, he began to plan longer didactic films that could be produced in Germany for the defeated Germans. The American government refused to cooperate.

Brecht, who consistently and knowingly sought unconventional solutions for his cinematic projects, could not have been surprised by his lack of success in Hollywood. Called with other motion picture personalities before the House Un-American Activities Committee (HUAC) on 30 October 1947, he could state with a clear conscience, but not without irony: "I am not a film writer, and I am not aware of any influence I have had on the film industry, either politically or artistically" (quoted in Lyon, *Brecht* 71; *GW* 20: 305).

POSTWAR PROJECTS

Brecht left the United States for Europe following his HUAC hearing, and after almost a year's wait in Switzerland for the necessary visa papers he arrived in East Berlin prepared to form a theater ensemble. This meant the opportunity at last to produce plays under congenial conditions, to continue the theater experiments broken off in 1933, and to see his own plays come to life in the context for which they were written. It is all the more surprising, then, that he found any time for the film projects that continued to preoccupy him until he died. Ironically, though, even under the socialist regime in East Germany, Brecht found himself once again confronted with the limitations of an industrially and ideologically conservative apparatus at the newly established DEFA film studios. Although there is hardly any written record of his critical positions, the ongoing string of unrealized film projects allows some conclusions to be drawn.[27]

As mentioned above, Brecht had turned his attention in Hollywood to the reworking of classical literary texts for the cinema. This approach was also a mainstay of his directing work at the Berliner Ensemble, where adaptations of important classical plays represented a crucial aspect of the theater's experimental and model character. In consultations with the DEFA studios Brecht also recommended adaptations of literary texts (Gersch 262), and among his own first projects were plans for *Hoffmanns Erzählungen*, conceived in America, as well as a new treatment coauthored with Günter Weisenborn and based on the traditional comic Eulenspiegel figure. Both of these projects were abandoned, however, when DEFA showed interest in an adaptation of Brecht's own new play at the Berliner Ensemble, *Mother Courage and Her Children*. Work began on a script in September 1949 with director Engel, and six years and four scripts later the shooting was interrupted after ten days when unresolvable differences between Brecht and new director Wolfgang Staudte arose. The record of this and Brecht's only other contribution to the filming of his plays, Alberto Cavalcanti's 1956 adaptation of *Puntila and Matti, His Hired Man*, reveals both the continuity of his views on "refunctionalizing" the cinema as well as the resistance to them.[28] The situation was complicated in the early 1950s, when the ideological front in the cultural sphere crystallized between mimetic notions of realism and modernist experimentation, and Brecht found himself under attack in East Germany for formalist deviations.

The *Mother Courage* script, the only one Brecht completed in the late phase of his life, can be compared to the earlier *Die Beule* as an attempt to hone and sharpen the representation of social contradictions after the experience of staging the respective play.[29] In the case of the former, Brecht was aiming his antiwar drama specifically at the vicissitudes of the Cold War. Similar to the adaptation of *The Threepenny Opera*, from the beginning he proposed numerous details to emphasize the film's anti-naturalistic, stylized aesthetics. These included distancing features like specially exposed filmstock to reproduce the look of old, grainy, daguerreotype photography; the use of actors from the Berliner Ensemble, who were trained in gestic acting; disruptive intertitles; and a highly static, tableau-like dramaturgy to undermine the dramatic movement of the images.[30] The *Puntila and Matti* play seemed like a good idea for a film adaptation: its structure, based on Puntila's changing behavior according to his level of inebriation, recalled Chaplin's successes (e.g., *City Lights*), and the exaggerated, slapstick humor made it potentially accessible to a large cinema audience. After the play's critically acclaimed production at the Berliner Ensemble, DEFA considered a film adaptation, but when scheduling problems developed, the rights were sold to the Austrian company Wien-Film in 1953. Brecht proposed Joris Ivens as director, but Ivens in turn suggested Cavalcanti. Brecht's major recommendations for the first script version, which was prepared by Vladimir Pozner, included substantial cuts and a new frame story (shot in a tinted sepia color) and were intended to alleviate what he recognized as a strong naturalistic tendency, particularly in the dialogues (Brecht, *Texte für Filme* 636–40). Because of other theater engagements, Brecht was unable to attend to the actual filming, and when he finally screened Cavalcanti's *Puntila and Matti*, he considered it a vulgarization—a view shared by most critics.

CONCLUSION

This overview of Brecht's practical and critical interventions in the cinema during a period of thirty-five years demonstrates his important role in defining sites of conflict and contestation in the new mass media. At a crucial point in his artistic development he perceived that the power of the apparatus—the institutions of cultural production and reception—determined the product, the work of art. This fundamental insight led him to formulate an experimental approach that was produced by institutional realities but that also produces reality, all the while observing the practice of this "production" itself. The various representational innovations he devised in the theater and the cinema were attempts to foreground this complex activity; they served as means of *Verfremdung* that aimed at disrupting the identification between the audience and the reality represented. The goal was to demonstrate the historicity of any specific moment in order to empower the audience to change it. While Brecht's understanding of the relation of representation to power and social change is still germane, his experimental method suggests that the anti-illusionistic techniques of distanciation and disruption are dependent on the respective context in which they operate. In short, it is necessary to reinvent constantly new ways of seeing that are themselves to be problematized as means of perception. Brecht offers no abstract answers for the media apparatus, but he does model a self-reflexive practice of media representation that is aware of its function, its historicity, and its inherent social and economic interests. In the postmodern age of simulations, the notion of anti-illusionism seems almost antiquated in its reliance on the possibility of knowing reality, yet at a time when critical discourses claim their authority precisely through the theorizing of images and image production, it is worthwhile to reconsider Brecht's questions as well.

NOTES

1. Brecht's essays on radio broadcasting (*Werke* 21: 189–90, 215–17, 217–18, and 552–57) and *Der Dreigroschenprozeß* (The Threepenny Trial) as well as Benjamin's essay on the work of art were the central texts, refashioned most coherently in a New

Left model by Enzensberger ("Constituents"). The turn in the 1960s to the Critical Theory of the Frankfurt School (e.g., Theodor W. Adorno and Max Horkheimer) can in part be explained by the need to confront the growing importance of television, a new technology raising questions that paralleled those considered by Brecht and Benjamin in the early 1930s.

2. Among the most substantive reviews of *Texte für Filme* were Leiser ("Brecht") and Jenny. The first scholarly articles included Hinck, Witte, and Dieckmann. In February 1973 the Arsenal Cinema in West Berlin organized the first major retrospective of films on the topic *Brecht und das Kino* (Brecht and Cinema), documented in Gregor and Gregor. In Summer 1975 the editors of the British film journal *Screen* organized a series of screenings around the topic "Brecht and Cinema/Film and Politics," documented in an issue of the journal that appeared under the same name.

3. See Barton Byg, "Brecht, New Waves, and Political Modernism in Cinema," in this volume.

4. "Aus dem Theaterleben" (From the Theater Scene), originally printed in *Augsburger Volkswille*, 7 November 1919 (*Werke* 21: 40–41), is a commentary on two films by Richard Oswald. Brecht also treated the theme of prostitution in his early one-act absurdist comedy *Lux in Tenebris*, written around the same time as the newspaper article.

5. See "Brecht, Bertolt, (a) Film projects" (*Diaries* 174), Völker (*Chronicle* 28–34), and Gersch (20–21).

6. See Jahnke. No printed script remains, but there is a record that the original 672-meter film was passed by the censor on 14 July 1923, after cuts comprising 11.75 meters had been agreed to.

7. The two-minute sequence was forbidden by the police, however. Again in his 1951 production of *The Mother* at the Berliner Ensemble, Brecht used a similar sequence of documentary images from the Chinese revolution at the end of the play. For details on Brecht's other suggestions or plans to integrate film images into stage productions, see Gersch (152–53). Of course, projections of stills and titles were incorporated into Brecht's stage productions as early as 1928 in *The Threepenny Opera*.

8. Brecht's story, written for a competition sponsored by the *Berliner Illustrierte Zeitung*, was one of five prize-winning submissions. Brecht directed his story "against" the previously released Josef von Sternberg film *The Last Command*, starring German actor Emil Jannings in his Oscar-winning role as a Russian general who plays himself in a Hollywood film version of his wartime exploits. See Wöhrle (*Versuche* 36–40) and Knopf (*Lyrik* 255–59).

9. During the introduction of sound it was not unusual to produce versions in different languages of the same film, often with different national casts using the same sets. In this case some of the major roles in the German version drew on the original stage cast (another aspect of the attempt to piggyback on the play's theatrical success), and the French version featured two stars, Albert Préjean as Macheath and Florelle as Polly. The French cut was almost 500 meters shorter, to a large extent owing to the recut of the beggars' march in order to eliminate the German-language posters. See Gersch (327–28, nn. 1, 10).

10. *Die Beule* was published together with *The Threepenny Opera* and *Der Dreigroschenprozeß* in *Versuche 8–10* (1931). The scenario is a prose text divided into four numbered parts with subsections and only cursory indication of dialogues. Footnotes contain explanations such as which songs are to be used from the play and how some of the scenes could be cinematically structured. About halfway through, footnote 17

(dated September 1930) informs the reader that the authors ceased such commentary because they recognized that *their* text would not be made into a film (Brecht, *Texte für Filme* 329–45).

11. An English version of the "original shooting script . . . provided by the Munich Film Archive" was published in *Masterworks of the German Cinema* (179–263), although this is not the "final" shooting script. For a brief detailing of the scripts at the Munich Film Archive, see Kocks (217, n. 6). Lania's script as well as a synopsis by Pabst are reprinted in Bock/Berger (275–389). For a critical discussion of the script versions, see Wöhrle (*Versuche* 107–24).

12. Weill won his part of the suit concerning the music, and the court granted him monetary damages. Brecht lost in that Nero film was allowed to complete and distribute Pabst's film. An out-of-court settlement was reached before the appeal, however, in which Nero film paid Brecht a monetary reimbursement, returned to him the film rights, and covered the trial costs (*Werke* 21: 770–76). After Brecht's death the film rights were purchased from the Brecht estate once again by West German producer Kurt Ulrich and Gloria Film-Verleih for an adaptation by director Wolfgang Staudte in 1963. Staudte's DM 4 million production, based on a new script by Staudte and Günter Weisenborn and featuring international stars Hildegard Knef, Curt Jürgens, and Sammy Davis, Jr. (who sang "Mac the Knife") was a critical and commercial flop. See *Die Dreigroschenoper 63*.

13. Prometheus film released as many as fifteen silent film productions a year between 1927 and 1930, but cut back to only four shorts in 1931 as sound cinemas began to dominate the market. In 1932 they produced only two shorts and *Kuhle Wampe*. See Murray.

14. The technical team and cast of professional and amateur actors worked without pay in order to contain production costs. A short, unpublished fragment signed by the film collective (Brecht, Dudov, Höllering, Kaspar [Neher], Ottwalt, Eisler, and Scharfenberg) describes the difficulties in completing the film (*Werke* 21: 544–45). The title *Kuhle Wampe* refers to a summer campsite on the periphery of Berlin that by 1932 had become a popular tent city for working-class families evicted from their homes. The film was originally distributed in the United States under the title *Whither Germany?*

15. The film credits as well as the original poster list Dudov as director and Brecht and Ottwalt as scriptwriters. The censorship card, however, lists Brecht as director, assisted by Dudov. The film often runs under both Dudov and Brecht's names, and especially in its post-1960s reception it has frequently been attributed—incorrectly—to Brecht alone.

16. The original shooting script was never found; however, a detailed scene segmentation is available (*Texte für Filme* 119–87). Brecht wrote a short film exposé parallel to *Kuhle Wampe* for a project planned at the Soviet Meshrabpom Studios that treated similar petit-bourgeois attitudes in a working-class family (see *Texte für Filme* 346–48).

17. The images of a mass sports rally have led some critics to compare this film with Nazi images of sports events, for example in Leni Riefenstahl's documentary of the 1936 Berlin Olympic Games under the title *Olympia* (1938; see Pettifer 62). In my view such a comparison disregards entirely the film structure and ignores the fact that images are perceived in a context.

18. *Kuhle Wampe* was released for distribution on 25 April 1932 after several cuts were made in the original version. For documents on the censorship controversy, including examples of press responses, see Gersch/Hecht, *Kuhle Wampe* (103–67).

19. In 1955 *Kuhle Wampe* was rereleased in the German Democratic Republic. Only ten years later, in the mid-1960s, did the film become an object of interest in the Federal Republic; at least initially, it was situated almost exclusively within the scholarly reception of Brecht's artistic endeavors.

20. *Texte für Filme*, 369–71. In 1942 in Hollywood Brecht once again turned to the Caesar figure at the suggestion of William Dieterle when he wrote a long but incomplete treatment under the title "Cäsars letzte Tage" (Caesar's Last Days) (*Texte für Filme* 372–400). This later became the story "Caesar and His Legionnaire" in the *Tales from the Calendar*. Julius Caesar was, of course, a favorite figure of Brecht's for explicating the evils of dictatorship, and the later treatment reflects Brecht's understanding of Orson Welles's *Citizen Kane*, which also presents the reconstruction of a historical personality in a multiperspectival structure. See *Journals* (28 Dec. 1941).

21. Various Hollywood personalities, including already established German emigrés, supported Brecht's immigration beginning in 1939. Lyon (*Brecht* 23) mentions Fritz Lang, William Dieterle, Fritz Kortner, Dorothy Thompson, Kurt Weill, Oskar Homolka, Bruno Frank, and Lion Feuchtwanger.

22. Some of the projects never advanced beyond the naming of a title or the jotting down of a fragmentary thought; others can only be surmised from comments in the *Journals* or from correspondence that indicates Brecht was working on a film exposé. *Texte für Filme* (372–631) includes fourteen scenarios written in Hollywood as well as a number of undated fragments in an appendix. Lyon's discussion of the Hollywood years gives a complete, chronological overview (*Brecht* 48–85), while both Willett ("Motion Pictures" 120–23) and Mueller (*Media* 98–100) briefly summarize Gersch's historical research. See in particular Gersch's attempt to list all the Hollywood film projects (355–56, n. 6).

23. Many of Brecht's journal entries during the second half of 1942 mention his efforts and frustrations with the film under the working titles "Silent City" and "Trust the People." As Lang began to make changes in the original script, Brecht also referred to a second script, an "ideal script" that has never been found and that has led to much speculation about what Brecht's version may have looked like. For background on Brecht's contribution, see Lyon (*Brecht* 58–71).

24. Classical adaptations included the script based on the Macbeth story *All Our Yesterdays* and treatments for "Die Judith von St. Denis" (Judith of St. Denis) based on a play by Friedrich Hebbel, *Hoffmanns Erzählungen* (Tales of Hoffmann), and "Der große Clown Emael" (The Great Clown Emael) revolving around a stage production of *Richard III*; modern adaptations included treatments for Edgar Lee Masters's *Spoon River Anthology*, Schnitzler's *La Ronde* (under the title "Uncle Sam's Property"), and Gogol's *The Overcoat*.

25. Biographical projects included the long treatments "Cäsars letzte Tage," "Die seltsame Krankheit des Herrn Henri Dunant" (The Strange Illness of Mr. Henry Dunant) about the founder of the International Red Cross, and "Die Fliege" (The Fly) about Walter Reed's struggle against malarial fever.

26. These included treatments for the comedy "Rich Man's Friend," written for Peter Lorre, and for "Die Frau des Richters" (The Judge's Wife), set in Vichy France, as well as scripts for the detective film *Silent Witness*, set in French Resistance circles, and for the comedy *The Goddess of Victory* about an Italian grain merchant seeking his fortunes in America. The extant texts printed in *Texte für Filme* for *All Our Yesterdays* (438–75), *The Goddess of Victory* (484–537), and *Silent Witness* (538–97) are in the English of

Brecht's respective collaborators with a direct German translation. Brecht's own German versions have never been found.

27. Brecht also contributed in a minor way to film projects of others, that is, he wrote the texts for the theme song of Joris Iven's *Song of the Rivers*, produced for the World Federation of Trade Unions in 1953, and for the "Lied vom Glück" (Song of Happiness) in Dudov's 1952 DEFA feature *Frauenschicksale* (Women's Fates).

28. In 1941 Vsevolod Pudovkin shot five scenes from Brecht's play *Fear and Misery of the Third Reich*, but it was censored at the time, and Brecht did not screen it until 1955 in Moscow. Plans for Joseph Losey to shoot *Life of Galileo* in Italy came to nothing in the late 1940s.

29. The fourth and last script version prepared by Brecht, Emil Burri, and Staudte in 1955 and divided into ninety-seven sequences is included in *Texte für Filme* (183–288).

30. Three notes by Brecht, written while at work on the earlier versions of the script, explain some of these suggestions (*Texte für Filme* 289–93). Despite the fiasco with Staudte, DEFA considered a new version in early 1956 once again with director Engel, but Brecht's illness and sudden death put an end to the planning. A film of the stage version of *Mother Courage* at the Berliner Ensemble was finally completed in 1960 by Peter Palitzsch and Manfred Wekwerth.

WORKS CITED (SEE ALSO REFERENCE GUIDE TO WORKS CITED IN ABBREVIATED FORM)

Benjamin, Walter. "The Work of Art in the Age of Mechanical Reproduction." In *Illuminations* 217–51.

Bock, Hans Michael, and Jürgen Berger, eds. *Photo Casparius: Filmgeschichte in Bildern.* Berlin: Stiftung deutsche Kinemathek, 1978.

Brecht, Bertolt. *Texte für Filme.* 2 vols. Edited by Wolfgang Gersch and Werner Hecht. Frankfurt am Main: Suhrkamp, 1969.

"Brecht and Cinema/Film and Politics." Transcript of the 1975 Edinburgh Film Festival Brecht Event. *Screen* 16.4 (1975/1976).

Bronnen, Arnolt. *Tage mit Bertolt Brecht.* Vienna: Desch, 1960.

Dieckmann, Friedrich. "Brechts Filmtexte." *Weimarer Beiträge* 19.2 (1973): 174–84.

Die Dreigroschenoper 63: Staudte + Heckroth + Raguse. Werkbuch zum Film. Munich: Laokoon, 1964.

Elsaesser, Thomas. "Transparent Duplicities: *The Threepenny Opera* (1931)." In *The Films of G.W. Pabst: An Extraterritorial Cinema.* Edited by Eric Rentschler. New Brunswick, NJ: Rutgers University Press, 1990. 103–15.

Enzensberger, Hans Magnus. "Constituents of a Theory of the Media." 1970. *The Consciousness Industry: On Literature, Politics and the Media.* Translated by Michael Roloff. New York: Seabury, 1974. 95–128.

Gersch, Wolfgang. *Film bei Brecht.* Berlin: Henschel/Munich: Hanser, 1975.

Gersch, Wolfgang, and Werner Hecht, eds. *Kuhle Wampe. Protokoll des Films und Materialien.* Frankfurt am Main: Suhrkamp, 1969.

Gregor, Erika, and Ulrich Gregor, eds. *Brecht und das Kino.* Berlin: Freunde der Deutschen Kinemathek, 1973.

Hinck, Walter. "Die Kamera als 'Soziologe.' " *Brecht heute/Brecht Today: Brecht Yearbook* 1 (1971): 68–79.

Jahnke, Eckart. "Brecht schuf 'Mysterien.' " *Notate* 1 (1980): 4–5.

Jenny, Urs. "Von den Knaben an der Quelle—Bertolt Brecht und die Filmbranche." *Süddeutsche Zeitung* (4 December 1969).

Kocks, Klaus. *Brechts literarische Evolution. Untersuchungen zum ästhetisch-ideologischen Bruch in den Dreigroschen-Bearbeitungen.* Munich: Fink, 1981.

Leiser, Erwin. "Bert Brecht und der Film. Aus Anlaß der Herausgabe seiner Drehbücher und Filmschriften." *Neue Zürcher Zeitung* (22 August 1970).

———. " 'Die Wahrheit ist konkret': Notizen eines Filmemachers über Brecht und Film." *Brecht-Jahrbuch/Brecht Yearbook* 11 (1983): 29–39.

Losey, Joseph. "L'Oeil du maitre." *Cahiers du cinéma* 114 (December 1964): 21–32.

Masterworks of the German Cinema. Introduction by Roger Manvell. New York: Harper, 1973.

Murray, Bruce. *Film and the German Left in the Weimar Republic. From "Caligari" to "Kuhle Wampe."* Austin: University of Texas Press, 1990.

Pettifer, James. "Against the Stream—*Kuhle Wampe.*" *Screen* 15.2 (Summer 1974): 49–64.

Willett, John. *Art and Politics in the Weimar Period. The New Sobriety 1917–1933.* New York: Pantheon, 1978.

———. "Brecht and the Motion Pictures." In *Brecht in Context* 107–28.

Witte, Karsten. "Brecht und der Film." In *Text und Kritik* 1: 81–99.

9

Brecht, New Waves, and Political Modernism in Cinema

Barton Byg

Brecht's assertion to the House Un-American Activities Committee in October 1947 that he was unaware of any influence he may have had on the cinema was perhaps only a slight exaggeration. But posthumously Brecht has indeed exerted influence on the rise of European New Wave film movements and the development of politically engaged, independent filmmaking that began in the 1960s. Tracing this influence is difficult, however, because it is usually mediated through several layers of reception as reflected in academic debates of film theory. Hence interest in Brecht has focused on the theoretical interpretation of his avant-garde aesthetic positions rather than on the adaptation of his plays, the reception of his work in cinema, his comments on the cinema, or his theories on working with actors. Since the 1960s the discussion of Brecht in the cinema has been conducted more often in a French and Anglo-American context than in a German one.

But Brecht's relative failure in dealing with Hollywood and the dominant cinema during his lifetime has contributed to making him, after his death in 1956, an important reference figure for movements hoping to resist and trans- form those institutions. Since the 1950s, European new waves, New Cinema movements elsewhere in the world, and feminist film practice have all built on the challenge that Brecht's ideas pose to the dominant assumptions of cultural production.

In post–World War II European cinema, new waves arose in opposition both to the stagnation and denial of historical memory and political responsibility for fascism and collaboration. In the face of the domination by slick, commercial, industrial film production, which tended to continue the so-called white tele- phone films of the fascist era, and against conservative government film policies and prevalent censorship, young film critics and directors looked to Brecht as well as to other models such as Soviet filmmakers Sergei Eisenstein and Dziga Vertov as well as the Frankfurt School theorists Walter Benjamin, Theodor W. Adorno, and Herbert Marcuse for a source of avant-garde resistance (Mueller, *Media*). By the 1960s, a widespread discussion of political filmmaking had de- veloped, primarily on the basis of the French New Wave, which then was im- ported to the Anglo-American context in the 1970s. As Sylvia Harvey notes, these discussions of politics and cinema were a return to the Brecht-Lukács debates of the 1930s, even if the participants were not conscious of it (''Brecht'' 45).

Young *cinéastes* began by finding Brechtian elements in the work of previous artists before they undertook to make ''Brechtian'' films themselves. Thus we find in the film journals of the 1950s and 1960s claims for the Brechtian qualities of Kenji Mizoguchi, Ingmar Bergman, John Ford, and others. Examples of crit- icism that couched the debate in Brechtian terms were the (West) German jour- nal *Film 56* and its successor *Filmkritik*, the French essay by Marcel Martin and others, ''Brecht, le cinéma et nous'' (1973), and Roland Barthes's ''Diderot, Brecht, Eisenstein,'' originally published in 1973 and reissued in 1974.

Of the European filmmakers who became active in the 1960s, those most consistently linked to Brecht are Jean-Luc Godard, Alexander Kluge, and the team of Danièle Huillet and Jean-Marie Straub (Straub/Huillet). Originating with them, one can trace the influence of Brecht in several strains of what Harvey has termed ''political modernism'' in cinema (see also Bordwell/Thompson, *History* 646–50). These strains extend from the European new waves to the New Latin American Cinema (e.g., that of Glauber Rocha) and to the theory and practice of a significant portion of feminist filmmaking both in Europe and the United States (e.g., Yvonne Rainer). As our distance from the new waves and political films of the 1960s and 1970s increases, the Brechtian quality of the films we will examine becomes more diffuse. For example, Brecht has in- fluenced the work of such directors as Rainer Werner Fassbinder in West Ger- many and Yvonne Rainer in the United States, but the Brechtian elements have been mediated through a complex process of reception before appearing in the work. Similarly, debates since the 1980s have challenged the formalistic appro- priation of Brechtian theory that has resulted in defining avant-garde art as an entity separate from reference to or participation in sociopolitical struggles. Whereas Peter Gidal and Martin Walsh were among the most rigorous propo- nents of the formalistic version of ''political modernism,'' the formalistic Brech- tianism, which downplays political interventions and social involvement, was criticized by Dana Polan and, more recently, by Coco Fusco and others dissat- isfied with esoteric (and predominantly *white*) feminist theory. Brechtian terms thus persist in 1990s discussions among filmmakers and critics whose politics and aesthetics are directed toward the struggle for liberation, however broadly defined.

DIRECT BRECHTIAN INFLUENCE IN THE 1950s AND 1960s

The discussion of the 1980s and 1990s must not obscure the preceding, direct—if mitigated—reception of Brecht by film culture. A case in point is the admiration of French New Wave filmmakers for early *auteurs* Fritz Lang and Jean Renoir, both of whom had known Brecht and worked with him. Lang, for example, recites part of Brecht's poem *Hollywood* in Godard's film *Le mépris* (1963; *Contempt*), in which he portrays a director attempting to film Homer's *Odyssey*. Fassbinder's fascination with the films of Douglas Sirk, which is usually attributed to the former's interest in the expressive potential of melodrama, also reveals a link to Sirk's Brechtian theater productions in the Weimar Republic.

Despite the cultural policies of the German Democratic Republic (GDR) that during the Cold War entailed the Stalinist disapproval of the 1920s avant-garde tradition, Brecht's collaborators Slatan Dudov and Hanns Eisler remained influential in the GDR (Wolf; Eisler, *Brecht*). Dudov was the mentor of those young filmmakers who sought to carry on the tradition of the Italian Neo-Realists (e.g., Gerhard Klein, Heiner Carow), and one can see traces of "epic" structure and Brechtian *Verfremdung* in the banned films of 1965 or in Konrad Wolf's *Ich war 19* (1968; *I was 19*). Eisler participated in the creation of one of the milestones of the New Wave by providing the music for Alain Resnais's *Nuit et brouillard* (1955; *Night and Fog*). Eisler's book *Composing for the Films* (1947)—the name of co-author Adorno was added later—owes a great debt to Eisler's discussions with Brecht in Hollywood. Other GDR artists also introduced Brecht to the French cultural scene; Gisela May's recording of Brecht/Weill's *The Seven Deadly Sins* won the *Grand prix du disque* in 1968, and the Berliner Ensemble engaged in guest performances of Brecht plays in Paris in 1971, the one hundredth anniversary of the Paris Commune. Before the demise of the GDR, Brecht represented in that country the hopes of the avant-garde and the adherents of modernism in the arts in general, while Georg Lukács was used to defend the state-sanctioned view of Socialist Realism (Klatt; Barck/Schlenstedt/Thierse).

FRANCE AND THE NEW WAVE

The growth of interest in Brecht's work in France accompanied the explosion of political filmmaking and criticism from the 1960s into the early 1970s. This development is outlined in detail in Harvey's *May '68 and Film Culture*, the English translations from the journal *Cahiers du cinéma*, and D. N. Rodowick's *The Crisis of Political Modernism*. The interpretations of Brecht's work were elastic enough so that it could be cited by virtually all factions of the Left in

France at the time. Brecht was enlisted as an ally by both the radically militant Dziga Vertov group (see below) and by those whom the Maoists viewed as "formalist" followers of the bourgeois avant-garde, such as Straub/Huillet.

The career of Godard is perhaps paradigmatic of the development of Brecht's influence in Western European political modernist cinema. In the early 1960s, Brecht was seen by the young critics and would-be *auteurs* as a representative of the avant-garde impulses that were oppressed by the system of industrial film production. Brecht figures in such early Godard works as *Vivre sa vie* (1962; *My Life to Live*) and *Contempt* as well as in the New Wave updating of Brecht's story "The Unseemly Old Lady" under the title *La vieille dame indigne* (1964; *The Shameless Old Lady*) by René Allio. In the late 1960s and early 1970s, the Brechtian reception tends more toward political self-reflection and narrative fragmentation. The films of the Dziga Vertov group, which was formed by Godard and Jean-Pierre Gorin, reflect the militancy of the period following the student uprisings of May 1968, a period that was marked by protests of the war in Vietnam. These films include *British Sounds*, *Vent d'Est* (*Wind from the East*), *Luttes en Italie* (Struggles in Italy)—all released in 1969—and *Vladimir et Rosa* (1970; *Vladimir and Rosa*). Parallel to film practice, associates of the Dziga Vertov group developed a militant avant-garde program linking aesthetics and political action that was outlined in the journal *Cinéthique* (see Leblanc). In a practice reminiscent of Brecht's *Lehrstücke*, the group even conceived of film reception as a work of collective criticism that might result in a restaging or rewriting of the work itself. The "Program for a Public Reading" of the 1963 avant-garde film *Méditerranée*, by Jean-Daniel Pollet and Philippe Sollers, is an example.

Godard/Gorin turned to a more theatrical and entertaining form of Brechtianism in the film *Tout va bien* (1972), which was broadly distributed—perhaps owing to the fame of its stars, Jane Fonda and Yves Montand. This "prototypical Brechtian film" (Bordwell/Thompson, *History* 649) engages in playful theatrics both in presenting its plot (a strike at a French factory) and reflecting on its own production, by showing, for instance, a flurry of checks being written in the opening sequence in order to allow the filming to begin. Bordwell/Thompson point out that a leading character in the film quotes Brecht's introduction to *Rise and Fall of the City of Mahagonny* regarding the social limitations on an artist's expression (*Film Art* 360).

Of the many filmmakers whose early work arose in the context of the politics of the 1960s, Godard (along with Straub/Huillet) remains perhaps the most consistent in his Brechtian approach to cinema (and television). Often in collaboration with Anne-Marie Miéville, Godard has continued to interrogate the relation of visual images to subjectivity, gender, and imperialism, for example in *Ici et ailleurs* (1976; Here and Elsewhere) and *Six fois deux* (1976; *Six Times Two*). In carrying this critique of cinematic representation and power relations into video and broadcast television, Godard/Miéville parallel the avenue of Brechtian influence followed by Kluge in Germany (see Klawans).

BRECHT AND THIRD-WORLD CINEMA: NEW LATIN AMERICAN CINEMA

Critics have noted the importance of Brecht to the development of New Latin American Cinema, particularly in the case of Glauber Rocha and *cinema nôvo* in Brazil (Hollyman; Bordwell/Thompson, *History* 624). Bordwell/Thompson discuss the connections between the new waves and Neo-Realism of Europe and the struggles of Third World cinema (*History* 610–32). They cite as an example Rocha's film *Der Leone Have Sept Cabecas* (1970; The Lion Has Seven Heads) that was produced in the People's Republic of the Congo. In Rocha's words, the film is "a communiqué on the cinema of the 1960s"; he terms it "a dialogue with Eisenstein, Brecht and Godard" (quoted in Bordwell/ Thompson, *History* 624). Two of Rocha's films provide excellent examples of the application of Brechtian approaches in the Brazilian context: *Deus e o Diabo na Terra do Sol* (1964; *Black God, White Devil*) and *Antonio das Mortes* (1968).

In both his criticism and his films, Rocha refers to Brecht as well as to Godard, while Godard/Gorin refer to Rocha in particular and to Latin American cinema in general. The interchange reveals the similarities and differences in the enterprises of European independent cinema and related movements elsewhere in the world. The dilemma present throughout the Third World is perhaps thematized by the role Rocha plays in *Wind from the East*. He is shown standing at a dusty crossroads with arms outstretched; a young woman with a movie camera comes up one of the paths and says very politely: "Excuse me for interrupting your class struggle, but could you please tell me the way toward political cinema?" Rocha indicates two paths, one in front of him and the other behind and to the left of him as he says: "That way is the cinema of aesthetic adventure and philosophical enquiry, while this way is the Third World cinema—a dangerous cinema, divine and marvelous, where the questions are practical ones like production, distribution, training 300 filmmakers to make 600 films a year for Brazil alone, to supply one of the world's biggest markets" (quoted in Macbean 109).

In the new waves of Europe, a Brechtian critique of the prevailing film industry, deemed to be synonymous with Hollywood, expressed itself with the development of the *auteur* cinema; it intensified when radical formal experimentation with a political intent took over. But outside of Europe, independent filmmakers are confronted with the dilemma of creating a cinema that will function as an industry and be viable commercially while, at the same time, it is required to function as a vehicle criticizing the assumptions underlying the commercial model. This historical trajectory of the New Latin American Cinema has been described by Ana Lopez. Although initially inspired by Italian Neo-Realism and European new waves, New Latin American Cinema is united not by a uniform style or by its opposition to Hollywood's domination, but by its joint social project, that is, "to change the social function of the cinema in Latin America" (Lopez 94).

Rocha's appropriation of Brecht is different from that of the Europeans; the difference arises from the peculiarity of his position in regard to the film industry. But working politically to create a film industry while seeking to subvert it with "popular" gestures and characters still bears a relation to Brecht's cultural work (Lopez 112; Hollyman 72–73, 92–95).

In *Black God, White Devil* and *Antonio das Mortes*, Rocha attempts to create an alternative "national" cinema by way of both myth and distanciation. Set in the desolate expanses of the *sertão* of northeastern Brazil, the films juxtapose myths, "epic opera" (Hollyman 73), historical popular uprisings of the 1930s, and contemporary characters' attempts at political education. In a Brechtian demonstration of the dependency of character on social and historical roles, Antonio functions both as the mercenary hired gun who puts down revolts for the landowners and as a mythical embodiment of popular rebellion.

As in Europe, then, Third World cinemas have employed Brechtian devices in their attempts to create independent and national cinemas against Hollywood's international hegemony. Developments in Western Europe, as we shall see, have opposed Hollywood with a more pronounced theoretical and formalistic Brechtianism.

BRECHT AND THE YOUNG GERMAN CINEMA AND NEW GERMAN CINEMA

One might expect the so-called New German Cinema, which for a time seemed to offer an alternative to Hollywood norms, to be the most direct avenue for contemporary Brechtian influence in the United States. But the most dedicated Brechtian filmmakers in Germany have tended to be the most obscure in the United States (see Gregor). Kluge and Straub/Huillet were among the first notable artists of the 1960s who promoted the reception of Brecht by the cinema. Straub/Huillet, along with Hans Jürgen Syberberg (and the French author/filmmaker Marguerite Duras), were dubbed "three cinéastes of the text" (Bonnet), a reference to their Brechtian tendency to distance the audience from the illusion of film by introducing written language in various forms.

Kluge's films, from *Abschied von gestern* (1966; Departure from Yesterday, released in the United States as *Yesterday Girl*) to *Der Angriff der Gegenwart auf die übrige Zeit* (1985; The Assault of the Present on the Rest of Time, released as *The Blind Director*),[1] as well as his recent television work, owe much to Brecht in their fragmentation of narrative, their use of intertitles, their quoting from other texts or art forms, and their engagement with the audience, which is aimed at dialogue rather than manipulation. *Yesterday Girl* accomplished in Germany that which the New Wave films did in France: it opened up the possibilities of experiment with narrative and representation. Kluge films such as *Artisten in der Zirkuskuppel: ratlos* (1967; *Artistes at the Top of the Big Top: Perplexed*) and especially *Die Patriotin* (1979; *The Patriot*) helped to break down the barriers between fictional narrative unity and documentary that led to the ''essay film'' as an international form, a development that is ultimately indebted to Brecht.

A Brechtian concern for the role of history in cultural self-definition is central to the work of Straub/Huillet as well as to that of Kluge. Since all of the films of Straub/Huillet explore the potential of Brecht's ideas for film, they take up a substantial part of Walsh's 1981 book, *The Brechtian Aspect of Radical Cinema*. Straub/Huillet's *Geschichtsunterricht* (1972; *History Lessons*) stands as the best example of a postwar film of a Brecht text that makes productive use of a Brechtian process as well. Based on Brecht's novel fragment, *Die Geschäfte des Herrn Julius Cäsar* (The Business Dealings of Mr. Julius Caesar), the film shares the novel's project of exposing the emptiness of the narrative view of history as the exploits of great men (see Byg 117–38). Along with a ''documentary'' approach to Brecht's words—mainly the monologues of the witnesses—other documents are presented: the unstructured everyday reality of 1972 Rome, a statue of Julius Caesar erected by the Fascists, and maps of the shrinking Roman empire. If history's meaning is not to be found in an appreciation of Caesar's biography, the audience is left with the task of producing meaning from the materials presented through Brecht's words and the film's images.

Despite the volume of criticism locating the Brechtianism of Straub/Huillet in avant-garde film techniques, their use of language and methods of working with actors are perhaps Brecht's most significant legacy—despite the fact that Straub ridiculed the idea of ''distanciating'' film scenes. On the other hand, Jean Renoir reported from personal experience that the originality of Brecht was in his work with the actors. Renoir's description of the actor's relation to the text also parallels that of Straub/Huillet: ''The work only starts after absorbing the lines, after making the lines your own.'' The Brechtian influence is consistent in Straub/Huillet's work; it reaches a high point no doubt in the performances in *Antigone* (1992), in which they adopted certain aspects of Brecht's *Modell* that he developed when he was writing down some of his directorial methods in ''A Short Organum for the Theatre.''

Despite several similarities, one must distinguish between the Brechtianism of Straub/Huillet and that of Kluge. Many of their techniques are similar, to the extent that Anton Kaes's descriptions of them are almost interchangeable (19, 114). Kaes also notes the presence of printed texts in both Kluge and Straub/Huillet. But Straub/Huillet follow Brecht in treating language as part of the material basis for their film craft, while Kluge's insertion of title cards to break up the narrative calls attention to the director's subjectivity. Like voice-overs, the cards are an intrusion of the author's voice whose ''tone . . . hovers between elegy and irony'' (Kaes 131). Although apparently inviting the spectator to take apart the work, the author's position is clearly superior, if not condescending, as B. Ruby Rich has noted (32). Furthermore, Thomas Elsaesser has observed that ''Kluge's protagonists are invariably the appendages of a discourse that is rarely, if ever, capable of questioning its own authority and, instead, by letting voice-over dominate the image, subjects the characters to the tyranny of the commentary'' (*Cinema* 136).

Hans Jürgen Syberberg's connection to Brecht is biographical and aesthetic rather than political or theoretical. As a young man in the GDR, Syberberg had been allowed to make 8mm films of Brecht's rehearsals at the Berliner Ensemble; he later adapted them in his film *Nach meinem letzten Umzug* (1970; After My Last Move). He also produced other documentaries about the Brechtian actor Fritz Kortner at work. Despite his reference to Brecht as his ''foster father'' (quoted in Bordwell/Thompson, *History* 661), Syberberg's use of collage and distancing effects such as puppets and quotations from other media (radio, painting, opera) is postmodern rather than avant-garde and potentially reactionary in its political effects. A more significant antecedent is Richard Wagner, who for Syberberg is evocative of nostalgic and melancholy grandiosity. Syberberg's films that make use of Brechtian theatrical devices such as *Ludwig—Requiem für einen jungfräulichen König* (1972; *Ludwig—Requiem for a Virgin King*) and the monumental collage *Hitler—ein Film aus Deutschland* (1977; *Our Hitler*) exhibit a strong romantic longing for lost historical harmony; they turn Brecht's modernism into its aesthetic and political opposite.

The Brechtian aspects of Fassbinder's cinema—both intriguing and difficult to pin down—have been analyzed by film scholars in the United States (Gemünden; Moeller, ''Brechtian''; Shattuc). The clearest evidence of what Ben Brewster calls Brechtian theatricalization of the cinema as well as his use of alienation and *Gestus* in directing actors is found in Fassbinder's early films. Here the influence of the French New Wave, student radicals' interest in Brecht, and the model of Straub/Huillet coincided with Fassbinder's earliest projects. Straub/Huillet's original plan had been to stage *The Measures Taken* at the Munich Action Theater in 1967. Only when the rights for the play proved to be unobtainable was Ferdinand Bruckner's *Krankheit der Jugend* (Pains of Youth), a drama from the 1920s, substituted. Fassbinder had a central role in the play; in addition, his own play *Katzelmacher* ran on the same evenings in a double billing. The production of the Bruckner play (reduced to eleven minutes) then became part of the influential Straub/Huillet short *Der Bräutigam, die Komödiantin und der Zuhälter* (1968; *The Bridegroom, the Comedienne, and the Pimp*; see Byg 85–94). In the film version of *Katzelmacher* as well as in *Götter der Pest* (1969; *Gods of the Plague*) and *Der amerikanische Soldat* (1970; *The American Soldier*), however, Fassbinder was transforming Brecht rather than following his precepts. Shattuc attributes this approach to Fassbinder's being attracted to pop culture as an alternative to the Brechtianism associated with the establishment Left (37). The transformation process becomes even clearer in works that Fassbinder produced after his discovery, around 1971, of the Hollywood melodramas of Douglas Sirk. Although Sirk had directed stage productions of Brecht plays in the Weimar Republic, his melodramas show only vague traces of a political aesthetic. Yet Fassbinder's overstylization of melodramatic plots reveals two aspects that recall Brecht's critique of conventional representational forms. First, the artificiality of the plots makes it patently obvious that "things could have turned out otherwise"—in other words, Brecht's tenet that history is produced by human beings who can alter its course is validated. Second, as film scholars writing in English such as Gemünden, Moeller, and Elsaesser ("Anti-Illusionism") have demonstrated, Fassbinder goes beyond Brecht in revealing how both his fictional characters and the audience allow themselves to be duped by illusions that conceal the workings of power. Yet these illusions, as manifestations of ideology, become part of the fabric of reality of which the work is a captive.

Die Ehe der Maria Braun (1979; *The Marriage of Maria Braun*), perhaps Fassbinder's best-known film, provides an excellent example of his synthesis of Hollywood melodrama and Brecht's epic theater. The improbable plot shifts and the rags-to-riches theme lure the spectator into a conventional identification with the heroine; yet the exaggeration of her character includes speeches revealing profound materialist analyses of her situation in an almost Marxist sense. Like Brecht's figure Puntila, Maria seems to be two characters: one functioning only according to the laws of economic self-interest, and the other—who embodies the vestiges of the melodramatic *fiction*—following human and emotional motivations. Despite the appearance of conventional staging, the film's plot reversals, its arrangement of characters in screen space, and the inclusion of "documentary" elements interrupt the flow of the entertainment with moments of Brechtian *Gestus*.

A number of other directors in the New German Cinema have referred to Brecht from time to time, but usually in a manner subordinate to other narrative concerns (see Möhrmann). For instance, Helma Sanders-Brahms's *Deutschland bleiche Mutter* (1979; *Germany Pale Mother*) begins with a recitation of Brecht's poem "Germany"—the line "O Germany, pale mother" (*Poems* 218–20) gave the film its title. The poem is read in voice-over by Brecht's daughter Hanne Hiob, and the rest of the film contains other documentary fragments that also interrupt the narrative. Michael Verhoeven's *Das schreckliche Mädchen* (1988; *The Nasty Girl*) presents its ironic investigation of a town's Nazi past with an "epic" separation of the scenes, yet the distance thus achieved does not undermine the unity of the authorial point of view or the spectator's superior position. The most lasting Brechtian impact, however, remains in experimental or avant-garde films that investigate questions of authorship and subjectivity. Perhaps Jutta Brückner has concentrated on Margarete Steffin and the women around Brecht in her film *Lieben Sie Brecht?* (1993; *Fond of Brecht?*) in order to show women's desire to have "speech, writing, and a public" (Phillips-Krug 160).

FROM THE CONTINENT TO "COUNTER CINEMA"

As several critics have demonstrated, the Brechtian tradition of political film-making, which arose from the student movement and protests involving film on the Continent, next moved to the Anglo-American critical scene. This move was aided by the work of Godard, Straub/Huillet, and others, but theoretical discussions became at least as important as the reception of Brechtian films themselves. An important mediator, the British journal *Screen*, published two special issues devoted to Brecht in 1974 and 1975–1976. The critics most responsible for the adaptation of Brechtian theory into what Peter Wollen called the "counter cinema" included Brewster, Stephen Heath, and Colin MacCabe (Rodowick 52–55). Wollen's important 1975 essay "The Two Avant-Gardes" outlined the political differences between more or less "formalist" movements at the time; in a 1974 essay Claire Johnston claimed the term "counter cinema" for feminism; and Harvey provided a significant survey of these developments in the 1980s ("Brecht").

It is surely no coincidence that this new interest in radical film theory was simultaneous with a rapid and energetic development of feminist film theory. *Screen* had set out the Brechtian terms for a radical critique of film practice, and Brewster had given Brecht's name to this rejection of conventional narrative cinema in "The Fundamental Reproach." In an influential article of 1975, Laura Mulvey spelled out a feminist fundamental reproach of the manipulative basis for visual pleasure in film.

Screen and feminist film theory had returned to the idea shared by Brecht, Benjamin, and the Soviet avant-garde, that it was not enough to take over the mechanisms of cultural production, but that they also needed to be transformed. Brecht's theoretical influence offered a way of merging into the subject matter of film a critique of the process of filmmaking, its place in society, and the role of the audience. In refining the process of adaptation by including psychoanalysis and semiotics, film theory of the 1970s was adapting French Marxist theorist Louis Althusser's idea of "theoretical practice" (Rodowick 70–71). An editorial statement by Brewster/MacCabe reveals Brecht's central position: "It is above all his reflections on his own work in literature, theater and cinema and on the politico-aesthetic controversies of his day that provide the framework within which it is possible to begin to think of a revolutionary cinema" (6). The connection between Mulvey's essay and Brechtian concerns of the time is made clear by MacCabe: "It is this emphasis on the reader as producer (more obvious in *Tout va bien*, which is in some ways more Brechtian than *Kuhle Wampe*) which suggests that these films do not just offer a different representation for the subject, but a different set of relations to both the fictional material and reality" (MacCabe 18).

More than a decade later, Teresa de Lauretis took this juncture in the history of film criticism as the starting point for her work *Alice Doesn't*. In the chapter

"Semiotics and Experience," she discussed the feminist anti-Freudian criticisms of *Screen* and its hopes for a Brechtian cinema:

Unless we too want to toss the baby along with the bath water, both Marx and Freud must be retained and worked through at once, and this has been the insistent emphasis of *Screen* and its extraordinarily important contribution to film theory and, beyond it, to feminism.

    That patriarchy exists concretely, in social relations, and that it works precisely through the very discursive and representational structures that allow us to recognize it, is the problem and the struggle of feminist theory. It is also, and more so, a problem of women's life. (165)

Corresponding to this appeal to connect theory and concrete experience, which has a clear antecedent in Brecht, the "political modernism" arising in the 1970s had, according to Rodowick, a utopian dimension as well. In addition to addressing the realities of social relations, theoretically informed filmmaking would also work on the construction of subjectivity, the process that was perceived as the core of all gender oppression. Rodowick raises relevant issues by citing the German theoretician Gertrud Koch:

What is at stake is less—and at the same time more—than the most general sense of the concept of subject: in the sense that Marx could speak of the working class as the subject of the revolution, in the sense that the women's movement could be the subject of the transformation of sexual politics. The most advanced aesthetic products represent a utopian anticipation of a yet to be fulfilled program of emancipated subjectivity: neither of a class nor of a movement or a collective, but as individuals, as concrete subjects [as] they attempt to insist on their authentic experience (Rodowick 296–97).

In her book on the relation of the Frankfurt School to cinema and memory, Koch further argues that critical theory (and the Brechtian debates of the 1930s) remain relevant for feminist considerations of film in the 1990s (Koch 28–29).

    De Lauretis's emphasis on the connection between theory and experience perhaps does not go far enough in clarifying the context of *Screen*'s introduction of psychoanalysis and semiotics in the 1970s. In their attempt to create a theory of revolutionary cinema in a Brechtian sense, *Screen*'s editors did not see themselves as abandoning political involvement but as intervening on the more profound level of social manipulation, that of the construction of subjectivity. The "scientific" insights of psychoanalysis and semiotics were meant to serve as more advanced tools for the task at hand and as a safeguard against romantic, ultra-left, and other simplistic temptations (MacCabe 17). The introduction of psychoanalysis into the equation, however, was not meant to exclude explicitly political and historical considerations, as Franco Fortini's 1974 essay in *Screen* attests. Here the debates of the 1930s and the premises of Neo-Realism are subjected to political and philosophical scrutiny by having recourse to Brecht's position on aesthetic innovation and the avant-garde.

The tendency to shun politics in favor of psychoanalysis became increasingly manifest in feminist film theory after the 1970s. Perhaps because a global transformation of society by feminism or by the Left seemed less and less likely, the theoretical aspects of the discussion took on a life of their own. There has been little talk of political goals, there has been little common ground between theorists and filmmakers, and psychoanalysis is no longer considered merely a scientific tool for use in conjunction with Brechtian aesthetics.

Work such as that by Koch and de Lauretis seeks to restore a balance between a Brechtian or Frankfurt School critique of representation and the theories of psychoanalysis and semiotics. What de Lauretis stresses too little, I believe, is the political dilemma of the artist, which was clearly addressed by Brecht and later by Fortini. The difficulty of finding orientation and freedom of movement within irreconcilable contradictions exists not only for the reader/spectator but for the artist in society as well.

FROM FEMINIST FILM THEORY TO PRACTICE

It was the work of theoreticians that caused Brecht to be adopted by women filmmakers in Great Britain and the United States after the European revolts of the 1960s. Some critics have demonstrated Brecht's influence on German feature films by women—for example, on the work of Sanders-Brahms. Yet the mediated application of Brechtian theory in feminist avant-garde filmmaking is a special case that offers fascinating opportunities for further study and that continues to pose the question of the 1930s, 1960s, and 1970s, that is, whether ''high theory'' and political activism can be combined within works of art.

For instance, Martha Rosler's video *Vital Statistics of a Citizen, Simply Obtained* (1977) pursues the Brechtian question of what can be told about reality by photographs, in this case by photographs of the artist's own body. In Rosler's work the mechanisms of recording and measurement are explicitly connected to political mechanisms of domination. Rosler also has noted the importance of the Brechtian Straub/Huillet film *History Lessons* to the context of her work (Weinstock 93–94). Sally Potter's *Thriller* (1979), in its re-construction of the opera *La Bohème* from the point of view of the woman as subject, echoes both Kluge and Brecht's use of essay-like devices to foreground the staging of a canonical work as an aspect of social production (Kuhn 169–77).

Yvonne Rainer's work is most explicit among feminist filmmakers in taking feminist theory, including psychoanalysis, as part of her films' subject matter (see Rainer, *Films*). She has explored the practical and theoretical dilemmas of connecting theory, politics, and gender relations, beginning with her earliest films. The Brechtian devices that she applies include actors addressing the camera both as (multiple) fictional characters and as themselves, introducing written language or quotations from other media, and using fragments of narrative arranged in an ''epic'' form introduced by a (fictional) narrator whose gesture is that of *illustrating* or *demonstrating.* Rainer's exposure to the European

Brecht reception was perhaps more direct than that of other filmmakers in the United States. She lived in Berlin in 1971 during a highly politicized period as a fellowship recipient. Her Berlin experiences formed the basis for her 1980 film *Journeys from Berlin/1971*.

Rainer's films can be seen as a Brechtian experiment (*Versuch*) or test on several levels. Most fundamentally she is exploring and opening up the structure of relationships which make up her narrative or even authorial persona. Both the characters her actors depict and the authorial voice of the filmmaker within the film are presented as changeable constructions and not as fixed points of view. In one of her films that grew out of her career as a dancer, *Film about a Woman Who* . . . (1974), Rainer has couched this investigation of the relation between form and content in a consistent treatment of film as "performance." Her 1990 film *Privilege* shares with *The Man Who Envied Women* (1980) the themes of real-estate dynamics in New York, that is, the rivalries between the Anglo artists and the Hispanics who are competing for the same housing. The latter film continues the discussion of racial fears and prejudices and the contemplation of the author's own body as an aspect of the "material" world. In addition to being "about" authorship, racism, and property relations, *Privilege* also describes itself as "a film about menopause." Finally, while treating Anglo-American fantasies about minorities—for example the Brazilian singer with tropical fruit on her hat, Carmen Miranda—Rainer employs a fantasy reminiscent of Fassbinder's early play and film *Katzelmacher*. Rainer's alter ego, the director character making a video-within-a-film, is played by a black woman. Similarly, Fassbinder plays the foreign worker who is attacked in *Katzelmacher*—linking problematically, as Rainer does, the author and persecuted "other" in the film.

Rainer's *The Man Who Envied Women* may serve as an example of Brechtian concerns in contemporary United States feminist filmmaking and performance art. The film does have a narrative, which is provided by the female voice-over of Trisha, but parts of the film fall outside the vision of Trisha's narration. In this way, the narrator stands apart from other elements, producing the tension Brecht describes. The montage of elements introduced here expands outward from the domestic melodrama of Trisha and her husband Jack, played by two different men, but the melodrama is not acted out on the screen. Instead, we see for example Trisha's shoulder from the back as she moves things out of the apartment she is giving up in order to leave him. Jack also wants her to remove her "art work" from the wall, but the collage of photos remains to become a focal point for the wider issues Trisha's voice will consider later in the film. In presenting the photos directly to the film audience, the fiction collapses to an investigation of their value as documents and their relation to the fictional "author" who presents them in the film.

One of the photos is an ad for estrogen supplements for older women, supposedly helpless without a (male) doctor's care and prescriptions. Another is a photo of mutilated bodies of torture victims in El Salvador. Like Trisha's opening speech, these images violently confront private biological reality with world politics. Later in the film there is another juxtaposition of the two, as Trisha remarks on the photos, "The woman who has stopped bleeding and the corpses that have stopped bleeding." The investigation of photography as a medium to reveal or conceal reality has of course always been a concern of avant-garde film, as the films of Harun Farocki and Helke Sander, to be discussed below, will show.

The other partner in the domestic melodrama, husband Jack Deller, who gets to keep the loft, balances the voice-over narration of Trisha. Amid a variety of film quotations, Jack's language floods the film with confessional and theoretical monologues related to women, sex, power, and psychoanalysis. The text itself is a collage of quotations from Raymond Chandler, Frederic Jameson, Michel Foucault, and others. Although Jack is often seen in lofts, he seems oblivious to the dispute over the renovation of loft space in New York City. The film returns often to documentary footage of hearings that demonstrates the competition between artists and other low-income people for housing. But it is the female voice-over that juxtaposes the documentary reality and the fiction of her own persona, saying, "Property is profit and not shelter," and "The language troubles my New York sleep."

The plot of the woman who leaves this theorizing man, and who ponders the connection of New York housing policies to war in Central America, is not the only aspect of the film that is presented epically and that is subject to constant revision. Since Rainer was once a dancer and performance artist, there is a strong sense of performance in other aspects of her films as well. As Heath has noted, "One mode of distanciation in film has often, and centrally, been the exact reference to theater" (117). Aspects of theatricality abound: two different actors portray Jack; his text is made up of quotations; his monologues to his shrink are delivered from a stage while excerpts from Hollywood melodramas are projected behind him. A dream sequence is artlessly acted out, accompanied by Trisha's voice-over narration, and at one point Rainer bends down near the camera lens to say, "Would all menstruating women please leave the theater." Rainer also calls our attention to the materiality of the film image by including footage of widely varying technical quality.

This fragmentation of the film's material and its narrative does more than call our attention to its construction by the artist. It makes us aware that the artist's subjectivity is also constructed. When we hear the voice-over discussing with friends whether to call her character Jack Teller or Jack Deller, we cannot be sure whether to identify this voice with a fictional character or with Rainer, the filmmaker. A strong *Verfremdungseffekt* also takes place when Jack pensively or impatiently moves one of the photos pinned to the wall. As the camera singles it out, the voice-over is saying, "I have another to put up." The viewer must construct both the nature of this "I" and her own relationship to the image out of the relationships posited by the film.

There are numerous other aspects of Rainer's work with a Brechtian orientation. They include the acting styles, the use of quotations of many kinds, the disjuncture between sound and image, and the use of documentaries and various media—from still photography to film, video, and computer screens. Both Brecht and Godard are recalled by the theoretical discussion overheard on the streets and in a coffee shop. Many scenes in the film urge a return of feminist film discussions to materialist concerns. In these scenes, the "clash of ideas" J. Hoberman finds so exciting (and reminiscent of Kluge) is placed within a feminist and Brechtian transformation of the means of presentation. For instance, after a discussion about the competition for real estate in New York and long quotations from psychoanalytic theory, the female voice-over observes succinctly: "You know, this expression 'class struggle' applies to El Salvador or Guatemala, not to the U.S. In Guatemala the war against communism is in reality a war against the poor. Here in America, the war against the poor does not yet have to be masked as a war against communism." And the very last word in the film—over the credits—is not theoretical but practical: a documentary sound recording from a rally for abortion rights.

In Rainer's own words, she is "talking about films that allow for periods of poetic ambiguity, only to unexpectedly erupt into rhetoric, outrage, direct political address or analysis, only to return to a new adventure of Eddy Foot or New Perils of Edy Foot" ("Ruminations" 25). She does not reject theory, action, or traditional narrative clichés. Instead she hopes to put them into a productive relation to each other and to open up some breathing space that will allow archetypal female rivals one day to stop tearing off each other's dresses and say: "Hey, we're wearing the same dress, aren't we? Why don't we pool our energies and try to figure out what a political myth for socialist feminism might look like?" ("Ruminations" 25).

CONCLUSION

A glance at developments from the 1960s to the 1990s in the work of Farocki, Sander, and Rainer reveals the submerged yet dynamic Brechtian debates that recall those of the 1930s (Elsaesser, "Notes"). Farocki, who directly quoted *Kuhle Wampe* in his film *Zwischen zwei Kriegen* (1977; *Between Two Wars*) has continued his investigation into the phenomenological and political nature of visual representation in film, photography, and television (Silverman). Sander, like Farocki and Rainer, juxtaposed photographs with the gesture of revealing/ concealing—in regard to the Berlin Wall in *Die allseitig reduzierte Persönlichkeit—Redupers* (1977; *The All-Round Reduced Personality: Redupers*). She has continued to intervene in German political life and management of historical memory with her film *BeFreier und Befreite* (1990; *Liberators Take Liberties*). This film caused much controversy even among feminists for treating the taboo subject of the rape of German women at the conclusion of World War II. In a similar vein, Rainer has been criticized for pursuing the agenda of white middle-class feminists—even though she problematizes questions of race in her films (Fusco; Rainer/Reynaud).

While Rainer faces the contradiction between the art of the film and the academic, theoretical, and material realms that threaten to reify it, Farocki explores film innovation in the context of technology's increasing "industrialization of thought." Sander, on the other hand, continues to expose audiences to the political contradictions arising from gender differences in German society and history. These three filmmakers, whether their methods can still be termed Brechtian or not, and the unfinished business they represent, reveal the continuities between political modernism in the cinema and the dilemmas of Brechtian theory.

NOTE

1. Italicized titles in parentheses indicate that the respective foreign films have been released in an English version and/or are commonly referred to by English title in the secondary literature.

WORKS CITED (SEE ALSO REFERENCE GUIDE TO WORKS CITED IN ABBREVIATED FORM)

Barck, Karlheinz, Dieter Schlenstedt, and Wolfgang Thierse, eds. *Künstlerische Avant-garde. Annäherungen an ein unabgeschlossenes Kapitel.* Berlin: Akademie-Verlag, 1979.

Barthes, Roland. "Diderot, Brecht, Eisenstein." 1973. Translated by Stephen Heath. *Screen* 15.2 (Summer 1974): 33–40.

Bonnet, Jean-Claude. "Trois cinéastes du texte." *Cinématographe* 31 (October 1977): 2–6.

Bordwell, David, and Kristin Thompson. *Film Art: An Introduction.* New York: McGraw-Hill, 1993.

———. *Film History: An Introduction.* New York: McGraw-Hill, 1994.

Brewster, Ben. "The Fundamental Reproach (Brecht)." *Ciné-Tracts* 1 (1977): 44–53.

Brewster, Ben, and Colin MacCabe. "Brecht and a Revolutionary Cinema?" *Screen* 15.2 (Summer 1974): 4–6.

Browne, Nick, ed. *Cahiers du Cinéma.* Vol. 2 (1960–1968); vol. 3 (1969–1972). Cambridge: Harvard University Press, 1986, 1990.

Byg, Barton. *Landscapes of Resistance: The German Films of Danièle Huillet and Jean-Marie Straub.* Berkeley: University of California Press, 1995.

de Lauretis, Teresa. *Alice Doesn't.* Bloomington: Indiana University Press, 1984.

Elsaesser, Thomas. "From Anti-Illusionism to Hyper-Realism: Bertolt Brecht and Contemporary Film." In Kleber/Visser, *Re-interpreting Brecht* 170–85.

———. " 'It Started with These Images'—Some Notes on Political Filmmaking after Brecht in Germany: Helke Sander and Harun Farocki." *Discourse* 7 (Fall 1985): 95–121.

———. *New German Cinema: A History.* New Brunswick, NJ: Rutgers University Press, 1989.

Farocki, Harun. "The Industrialization of Thought." Translated by Peter Wilson. *Discourse* 15.3 (Spring 1993): 76–77.

———. "*Zwischen zwei Kriegen.*" *Filmkritik* 22.11 (November 1978): 562–606.

Fortini, Franco. "The Writers' Mandate and the End of Anti-Fascism." *Screen* 15.1 (Spring 1974): 3–70.

Fusco, Coco. "Fantasies of Oppositionality: Reflections on Recent Conferences in Boston and New York." *Screen* 29.4 (Autumn 1988): 80–93.

Gemünden, Gerd. "Re-Fusing Brecht: The Cultural Politics of Fassbinder's German Hollywood." *New German Critique* 63 (Fall 1994): 55–75.

Gidal, Peter. *Materialist Film*. London: Routledge, 1989.

Gregor, Erika, and Ulrich Gregor, eds. *Brecht und das Kino*. Berlin: Freunde der deutschen Kinemathek, 1973.

Harvey, Sylvia. *May '68 and Film Culture*. London: British Film Institute, 1978.

———. "Whose Brecht? Memories for the Eighties." *Screen* 23.1 (May/June 1982): 45–59.

Heath, Stephen. "Lessons from Brecht." *Screen* 15.2 (Summer 1974): 103–128.

Hoberman, J. "The Purple Rose of Soho." *Village Voice* (8 April 1986): 54.

Hollyman, Burnes Saint Patrick. *Glauber Rocha and the Cinema Nôvo: A Study of His Critical Writings and Films*. New York: Garland, 1983.

Johnston, Claire. "Women's Cinema as Counter-Cinema." In *Sexual Strategems*. Edited by Patricia Erens. New York: Horizon Press, 1979. 133–43.

Kaes, Anton. *From Hitler to Heimat: The Return of History as Film*. Cambridge: Harvard University Press, 1989.

Klatt, Gudrun. *Vom Umgang mit der Moderne: Ästhetische Konzepte der dreißiger Jahre*. Berlin: Akademie-Verlag, 1985.

Klawans, Stuart. "Jean-Luc Godard: Son + Image." *Nation* (23 November 1992): 642–44.

Kluge, Alexander. *Abschied von gestern. Protokoll*. Frankfurt am Main: Filmkritik, 1967.

Koch, Gertrud. *Die Einstellung ist die Einstellung: Visuelle Konstruktionen des Judentums*. Frankfurt am Main: Suhrkamp, 1992.

Kuhn, Annette. *Women's Pictures: Feminism and Cinema*. London: Routledge, 1982.

Leblanc, Gérard. "Quel avant-garde? (note sur une pratique actuelle du cinéma militant)." *Cinéthique* 7–8 (1970): 72–92.

Lopez, Ana M. "An 'Other' History: The New Latin American Cinema." In *Resisting Images: Essays on Cinema and History*. Edited by Robert Sklar and Charles Musser. Philadelphia: Temple University Press, 1990. 308–30.

Macbean, James Roy. "Wind from the East or Godard and Rocha at the Crossroads." In *Weekend and Wind from the East. Two Films*, by Jean-Luc Godard. New York: Simon, 1972. 109–19.

MacCabe, Colin. "Realism in the Cinema." *Screen* 15.2 (Summer 1974): 7–28.

Martin, Marcel, Erwin Leiser, Barthélemy Amengual, and Wolfgang Gersch. "Brecht, le cinéma, et nous." *Ecran* 13 (March 1973): 3–29.

Moeller, Hans-Bernhard. "Brecht and 'Epic' Film Medium: The Cineaste Playwright, Film Theoretician and His Influence." *Wide Angle* 3.4 (1980): 4–11.

———. "Fassbinder's Use of Brechtian Aesthetics (*The Marriage of Maria Braun, Veronika Voss, Lola*)." *Jump Cut* 35 (1990): 102–107.

Möhrmann, Renate. "The Influence of Brecht on Women's Cinema in West Germany." In Kleber/Visser, *Re-interpreting Brecht* 161–69.

Mulvey, Laura. "Visual Pleasure and Narrative Cinema." *Screen* 16.3 (Autumn, 1975): 6–18.

Phillips-Krug, Jutta. "Sprach-Gestus. Ein Gespräch mit Jutta Brückner über ihren Steffin-Film *Lieben Sie Brecht?*" *Brecht-Jahrbuch/Brecht Yearbook* 19 (1994): 140–61.

Polan, Dana. "The Politics of a Brechtian Aesthetics." *The Political Language of Film and the Avant-Garde*. Ann Arbor, MI: UMI Research Press, 1985. 79–99.

"Programme pour une lecture publique de *Méditerranée*." *Cinéthique* 13 (1972): 78–79.

"Quel front culturel?" *Cinéthique* 17 (1974): 4–18.

Rainer, Yvonne. *The Films of Yvonne Rainer*. Bloomington: Indiana University Press, 1989.

———. "Some Ruminations around Cinematic Antidotes to the Oedipal Net(les) while Playing with De Lauraedipus Mulvey, or, He May Be Off Screen, but. . . ." *Independent* 9.3 (April 1986): 22–25.

Rainer, Yvonne, and Bérénice Reynaud. "Response to Coco Fusco's 'Fantasies of Oppositionality.' " *Screen* 30.3 (Summer 1989): 79–99.

Renoir, Jean. "The Film as Art." Interview [1960]. *Pacifica Radio Archive* 1983.

Rich, B. Ruby. "She Says, He Says: The Power of the Narrator in Modernist Film Politics." *Discourse* 6 (Fall 1983): 31–46.

Rodowick, D.N. *The Crisis of Political Modernism: Criticism and Ideology in Contemporary Film Theory*. Urbana: University of Illinois Press, 1988.

Shattuc, Jane. "*Contra* Brecht: R.W. Fassbinder and Pop Culture in the Sixties." *Cinema Journal* 33.1 (Fall 1993): 35–54.

Silverman, Kaja. "What Is a Camera?, or: History in the Field of Vision." *Discourse* 15.3 (Spring 1993): 3–56.

"Texte collectif." *Cinéthique* 9 (1971): 1–70.

Walsh, Martin. *The Brechtian Aspect of Radical Cinema*. Edited by Keith M. Griffiths. London: British Film Institute, 1981.

Weinstock, Jane. "Interview with Martha Rosler." *October* 17 (Summer 1981): 77–98.

Wolf, Konrad. *Direkt in Kopf und Herz: Aufzeichnungen, Reden, Interviews*. Berlin: Henschel, 1989.

Wollen, Peter. "The Two Avant-Gardes." 1975. *Edinburgh Magazine* 1 (1976): 77–84.

———. "Counter Cinema: *Vent d'Est*." *Afterimage* 4 (Autumn 1972): 6–17.

10

Brecht contra Wagner: The Evolution of the Epic Music Theater

Vera Stegmann

Brecht, whose propensity for collaborating with talented friends is well known, was one of the great innovators in twentieth-century theater in general and music theater in particular. Brecht's works are best understood in their historical context, that is, in the light of contemporaneous European developments in literature and the arts as well as being a reaction against prevailing movements in theater and opera.

One towering figure against whom Brecht came to rebel was Richard Wagner. Wagner had revolutionized opera in the nineteenth century through his concepts of *Gesamtkunstwerk*, *Leitmotiv*, "endless melody," and the "invisible orchestra," all of which contributed to the idea of "music drama." The term *Gesamtkunstwerk* implied an encompassing art work in which each of the three elements that comprise an opera—music, language, and the visual element of stage settings—unify and blend together in order to achieve a highly poetic musical drama. This unity was also symbolized by the fact that Wagner wrote his own libretti. The use of *Leitmotive*, leading motifs—basic musical phrases that describe a character or an idea and recur in varied forms throughout a piece—helped weave the operatic texture. Unlike previous operas, which were divided into recognizable musical numbers, Wagner created endless melodies without a clear beginning or an end that aimed at embodying the infinite. Wagner's decision to locate the orchestra in his Bayreuth theater invisibly below the stage in an orchestra pit was further designed to endow music with the mysterious force of a kind of transcendental narration underlying the drama.

By the end of the nineteenth century, Wagnerian music drama had come to dominate the musical and artistic scene in central Europe to such a degree that musicians and poets of the early twentieth century began to resist Wagner's monumental influence. This anti-Wagnerian movement became even stronger in the 1920s and 1930s when Wagner's aesthetics came to be identified with Nazism, which used and abused them for political and ideological ends.

Like many of his contemporaries, Brecht can be called an anti-Wagnerian. Brecht's antagonistic though complex relationship to Wagner was anticipated by other European artists who, in their rejection of Wagner, created musico-theatrical works in the epic vein. Brecht's theory of epic music theater and one of its prominent works, *The Threepenny Opera*, can be more easily understood in this contextual background.

EUROPEAN ANTI-WAGNERISM

Brecht was by no means the only European artist in the early part of this century who searched for post-Wagnerian musico-theatrical forms. The jazz movement, Kurt Weill, Ferruccio Busoni, the French group of composers *Les Six* (with whom Jean Cocteau and Eric Satie were associated) and Igor Stravinsky consciously moved away from Wagner's music drama and contributed, directly or subtly, to Brecht's concept of epic music theater.

The American jazz movement spread rapidly in Europe after the end of World War I. It has been seen as an antithesis to Wagner (Dümling 118) inasmuch as it is playful, humorous, improvised, and based on short numbers; it allows individual players much versatility and independence, and it is unromantic. Intellectuals in the European capitals, who were steeped in Wagner, regarded jazz as a wholly new experience that shook the traditional musical canon. Brecht wrote in a note around 1926 that because of the arrival of jazz bands, he finally felt good about music and demanded that the atmosphere of the jazz concert prevail in the theater as well (*GW* 15: 69). In contrast to Wagnerian music, jazz did not induce hypnotic seduction; rather, it represented to him mere joy.

Kurt Weill, the first major composer to work with Brecht, was also strongly influenced by jazz. Weill probably met Brecht in 1927, after he had heard Brecht's play *A Man's a Man* with song compositions by Edmund Meisel on the radio. Weill wrote an enthusiastic review of the play for the weekly journal *Der deutsche Rundfunk*, to which he was a regular contributor during 1925–1928. The first result of the Brecht-Weill cooperation was *Songspiel Mahagonny*, a setting of poems from Brecht's collection *Manual of Piety*; and in spite of its brief duration of about four years, the collaboration between Brecht and Weill produced some of the most original works in twentieth-century music theater, among them *Mahagonny* (1927–1929), *The Flight over the Ocean* (1928), *Happy End* (1929), and *He Who Said Yes* (1930). *The Seven Deadly Sins* (1933) originated in Paris, when Brecht and Weill briefly resumed their cooperation during the beginning of their exile.

Weill's anti-Wagnerism was less radical in its rhetoric than that of Brecht. While Brecht understood his theater in opposition to Wagner, Weill rather perceived Wagnerian music drama as the culmination of an art form to which nothing could be added and which allowed no other art to exist beside it. His background may have contributed to this moderate view in that Weill's native city of Dessau had developed the reputation of a "North German Bayreuth" and had become a major center for the cultivation of Wagnerian art. Furthermore, in 1918 Weill studied composition with the Wagnerian Engelbert Humperdinck in Berlin. He then spent two years in the town of Lüdenscheid as conductor at that city's theater and performed several of Wagner's operas, notably *The Flying Dutchman*. It was not until the fall of 1920, when Weill returned to Berlin as a master student of the composer and conductor Ferruccio Busoni that he turned away from Wagner and looked for models in Bach and Mozart.

Under the influence of Busoni and, possibly, Brecht, Weill rejected Wagner's subject matter—his preference for mythological or superhuman heroes, gods, and kings—as well as the form of his music drama. In his 1926 essay, "Busoni's *Faust* and the Renewal of Operatic Form,"[1] Weill argued against Wagner's intention to introduce every idea or character with a *Leitmotiv*, because he feared the potential strong literary influence on the process of musical composition. Rather, Weill preferred a return to the traditional concept of opera, in which the closed musical numbers are defined by more abstract or musical principles (Kowalke 470). In this sense, the number character of a Mozart opera—in contrast to Wagnerian music drama—bears some resemblance to the jazz movement. Weill also published a euphoric "A Note Concerning Jazz" in the musicological magazine *Anbruch* in 1929 (see Kowalke 497–98).

As did Brecht, Weill perceived opera in a crisis at the turn of our century. Like Brecht, he attributed this musical crisis to the operatic apparatus, a term he may have borrowed from Brecht. But while Brecht criticized the apparatus in a philosophical and Marxist sense and reflected on the power that any means of production exerts over art, Weill, in a more realistic vein, considered the question from a practical and economic angle. In his 1932 essay "Actually an Operatic Crisis?" he defined the difficulties of operas at the time as largely financial. The most popular opera composers—Wagner and Richard Strauss—required a huge apparatus that was no longer affordable in the postdepression era (Kowalke 543). The return to smaller and more modest musical and theatrical forms was then not only an aesthetic but also a monetary necessity.

During the four years in which Weill worked as music critic for *Der deutsche Rundfunk*, he reviewed several Wagner productions such as *Tannhäuser* and the *Ring* tetralogy. A close reading of his critiques in this journal reveals a much more complex and less negative attitude toward Wagner than evinced by many contemporary composers. Weill admired Wagner's music, but he was opposed to the concept of *Gesamtkunstwerk* as well as to Wagner's aesthetics, his politics, and the dominance of his libretti over the music (Kowalke 154). While

Busoni may have opened Weill's eyes to the perceived shortcomings of Wagner, Brecht confirmed Weill's anti-Wagnerism. But only in the United States did Weill articulate his complete break with Wagner: American musical comedy, he declared in various interviews in New York in the 1940s, had nothing to do with Wagner (Weill 336, 338).

Weill had expressed some of his earliest disagreements with Wagner in essays on Busoni, his revered teacher in Berlin from 1921 to 1923. Born in Florence in 1866, this highly original composer, pianist, and thinker of German and Italian origin, founder of the "young classicism" that favored Bach and Mozart over the nineteenth-century romantics, had made Berlin his home in 1894. He remained there, apart from his sojourn in Switzerland during World War I, until his death in 1924. Busoni exerted a strong influence on Weill, an influence that Weill presumably transmitted to Brecht. Brecht, however, hardly mentioned Busoni in his writings, with the exception of a brief note of October 1940 in which Brecht claims to have turned Weill away from the style of psychological composition favored by Busoni (*Journals* 108). But Brecht was certainly familiar with Busoni's work, both his musical compositions and his theoretical writings; a 1941 edition of Busoni's ground-breaking treatise *Sketch of a New Esthetic of Music,* published in 1907 in Trieste and reissued in a slightly expanded version in Germany in 1916, was in Brecht's private library. Busoni's *Sketch* may be seen as an early outline for a model of epic theater, and especially the 1916 version contains passages that are sharply critical of Wagner. In his 1921 essay, "The Essence and Oneness of Music," he explained his differences with Wagner most succinctly: Busoni saw opera as " 'a musical work of the combined arts' as against the Bayreuth conception of it as 'a work of the combined arts' " (*Essence of Music* 7). In *Sketch*, Busoni had regarded Wagner as a closed chapter of musical history that did not allow any possibilities for further development. Any new movement in musical theater, he claimed, first needed to liberate itself from Wagner. To the "routine" of Wagner's indulging sensuality and his emotional excesses, Busoni juxtaposed the values of musical economy, taste, and style. He also insisted on the separation of the terms "feeling" and "expression." It may not be a coincidence that the "Sketch"—dedicated to the poet Rainer Maria Rilke, "musician in words"—is preceded by a quote from Hugo von Hofmannsthal's "Lord Chandos Letter," an essay that had formulated the crisis of language as a means of poetic expression at the turn of this century. Busoni's choice of an epigraph from Hofmannsthal hints subtly at the connection between the perceived inability of words to reflect meaning and the musical or operatic crisis characteristic of the post-Wagner generation.

Beyond his general rejection of Wagner, Busoni's *Sketch* anticipated in concrete ways Brecht's theory of epic music theater. Preparing the way for Brecht's theory of the "separation of the elements," Busoni's *Sketch* demanded that each art form should strive to remain strictly within its realm. Brecht's occasional suggestion that music can work against a text in order to achieve an ironic contrast in the interest of a complete and dialectical work is foreshadowed in Busoni's text. Busoni even outlined Brecht's idea of *Verfremdung* when he described the respective roles of the actor, who should always remain playful, and the spectator, who should doubt rather than believe. Like Brecht, Busoni argued against the romantic notion of identification, that is, neither the performer nor the audience should ever become fully immersed in the action presented on stage. As a passionate pedagogue, Busoni, much in the manner of Brecht, emphasized the role of the viewer in the reception and production of an art work.

In addition to Busoni's theoretical writings, one of his compositions, *Arlecchino*, figures as a precursor of epic music theater. This "theatrical caprice in one act," as Busoni subtitled it, was written between 1914 and 1916 and premiered in Zurich in 1917. Although we have little information about Brecht's knowledge of it, Weill did see a performance in 1923 in Dresden. A blend of opera, *commedia dell'arte*, and puppet play, *Arlecchino* is also a satire on World War I. Busoni, who wrote both the text and the music, created the main role of Arlecchino for a speaker, not for a singer. In commenting on events, Arlecchino takes on the role of narrator and turns alternately to the public, to the singers, and to the orchestra; but he is also a participant in the plot, who appears behind a different mask—as deceiver, warrior, husband, and winner—in each of the four movements. Arlecchino wins a duel against the aristocrat Leandro and gains the woman he desires. In its political message as well as its formal construction Busoni's caprice thus points to later epic developments by Brecht and Weill.

Another prominent anti-Wagnerian movement originated in France. It may not be a coincidence that Paris, the city in which Wagner celebrated his earliest artistic triumphs in the 1840s, became in the 1910s the center of *Les Six*. These six composers—Georges Auric, Louis Durey, Arthur Honegger, Darius Milhaud, Francis Poulenc, and Germaine Tailleferre—had met as conservatory students in Paris, and they began appearing together in regular concerts in 1918. They were united by a common search for a new and authentically French music that was receptive to innovations provided by the music hall, the circus, and jazz bands. They were opposed to the traditions of art music or grand opera; above all, they intended to liberate music from the German tradition in general and Wagner in particular. Eric Satie, creator of *Parade*, acted as intellectual patron to *Les Six*, while Jean Cocteau, author of the manifesto *Le coq et l'arlequin* (1918; The Rooster and the Harlequin), became the spokesman of the group.

Both Brecht and Weill were aware of the new movement in French music. In July 1927, they met Milhaud, one of four composers—along with Paul Hindemith, Weill, and Ernst Toch—invited to present a composition at the festival of new chamber music in Baden-Baden that year. Milhaud produced an "opéra minute," Weill and Brecht presented *Songspiel Mahagonny*. They deliberately avoided the term "opera" in order to demonstrate their departure from traditional notions (Dümling 153). Brecht wrote the names of Milhaud and Honegger on one of the copies of his 1935 essay, "On the Use of Music for an Epic

Theatre,'' an indication that he knew of their work and possibly envisioned a collaboration (Lucchesi/Shull 166). Indeed, various of Milhaud's theater works, *Le boeuf sur le toit, ou, The Nothing Doing Bar* (1919), *La création du monde* (1923; The Creation of the World), and *Christophe Colomb* (1930), bear epic traits in the Brechtian sense. Honegger's works, *King David* (1921) and *Joan of Arc at the Stake* (1934–1935), return to the form of the oratorio, an epic genre by virtue of its use of a narrator and its frequently moral or educational content. Weill presumably maintained closer contacts to members of *Les Six* than did Brecht; in 1932 Weill was invited to Paris to present a version of *Songspiel Mahagonny*, and among the audience were Cocteau, Milhaud, Auric, Honegger, André Gide, Stravinsky, and Pablo Picasso (Lucchesi/Shull 373). This visit may have prompted Weill to invite Cocteau to write the libretto for *The Seven Deadly Sins* in the following year; after Cocteau declined, Weill turned to Brecht.

As the intellectual mentor of *Les Six*, Satie was probably the most outspoken anti-Wagnerian of the group. After a youthful dalliance with the catholic Wagner cult of Joséphin Péladan and his organization *Rose Croix*, Satie left the Wagnerian fold. When he argued in his writings strongly against truth in art, this point was also directed against Wagner's need to express meaning transcending the merely musical. Around 1920, Satie developed the concept of "furniture music," which Hindemith, another collaborator of Brecht's, adopted at the festival of new music in 1927. Rather than expressing lofty ideas, music should be useful, practical, varying freely depending on the place where it was performed, and thus—although Satie never employed the term—epic. Milhaud cites an episode during a performance of Satie's pieces, in which Satie noticed that the audience stopped conversing and became quiet at the onset of his piece, upon which he shouted to the people: "Go on talking! Walk about! Don't listen!" (Milhaud, *Notes without Music* 123). Brecht's provocative poster at the 1922 Berlin premiere of *Drums in the Night*, "Stop that Romantic Gaping" (*CP* 1: 372), as well as his later suggestion that the spectator should assume the distanced and reflecting disposition of a smoker, are foreshadowed in Satie. Both Satie's and Brecht's targets were the spectators' romantic identification with a piece as demanded by Wagner. Satie's Wagner critique also had a political dimension: just as Brecht drew the parallel between Wagner and Bismarck, Satie related Wagner to the events in 1871, fearing that German music would conquer French culture. *Les Six* should produce an authentically French music, he stated, while preserving the individual style of each member, as suggested by the pluralistic name "six." Satie was adverse to the rigidly conformist idea of artistic schools, and in his search for democracy in art he would have found a partner in Brecht.

Satie's *Parade* became a model for new epic possibilities in music theater in the post-Wagner era (Weisstein 145). A collaboration between Picasso, Satie, and Cocteau, this "ballet réaliste" premiered in 1917 at the Théâtre du Châtelet in Paris and caused a scandal. The action of *Parade* takes place in a circus;

but it is a self-reflective piece, a circus performance about the subject of the circus. Like a circus performance, it is divided in numbers; the performer of each number carries a sign describing the artists, not unlike the intertitles Brecht would later use to introduce the songs of *The Threepenny Opera*. Furthermore, adjusting to the improvisational style of jazz, *Parade* permits a change in the sequence of the numbers. Satie's music for *Parade* is based on the principle of montage and mixes classical composition with jazz numbers and dances, Gregorian chants and Bach-style fugues with ragtime and cakewalk, march or waltz. Picasso's beautiful though deliberately grotesque costumes added to the humorous and playful atmosphere of the piece, but also created a distance between the spectators and the action.

In the course of the work on *Parade*, the role of Cocteau's libretto was reduced significantly, so that the final text of the piece consisted of a one-page description of the stage and the plot. Based on his experiences with *Parade*, Cocteau wrote the pamphlet *Le coq et l'arlequin*. Cocteau defended and promoted Satie as the model for a new French music (''coq'') whose style would be simple, brief, gay, humorous, yet profound and polemicized against the impressionism of Claude Debussy and that of Stravinsky's early works. Above all, he took issue with Wagner and the German romantics (''arlequin'') and used arguments from Nietzsche's critique in *The Case of Wagner*.

Cocteau was also the librettist of Igor Stravinsky's *Oedipus Rex*, a work important in this context. Its German premiere took place in 1928 in Berlin, and Weill received it enthusiastically. In a euphoric review written for *Der deutsche Rundfunk*, he praised *Oedipus Rex* as a cornerstone in the development of a new opera; he emphasized its rejection of music drama, its pure vocal style, its focus on music by keeping the text in Latin, and its oratorio-like form (Weill 277). In his ''Notes to *Mahagonny*,'' Brecht criticized Stravinsky's use of Latin but he did take notice of *Oedipus Rex*. The translation of Cocteau's libretto into an archaic language, presupposing the audience's knowledge of the text, provided a form of *Verfremdung*. But Brecht could not accept the purpose of this particular *Verfremdung*, in that it diverted attention away from word and meaning. For Brecht Stravinsky remained a *Tui*, his satirical description of an intellectual who declines to use knowledge in the service of society (*GW* 12: 673). Yet Brecht respected Stravinsky highly as a composer and an innovator in rhythm and musical form; during his exile in the United States in the 1940s he hoped that Stravinsky would collaborate on the *Lucullus* project. (After Stravinsky declined, Brecht's composer friend Paul Dessau agreed to compose the music.) In spite of mutual artistic recognition—Stravinsky was deeply impressed by Brecht's *Galileo* in a performance by Charles Laughton—there were too many ideological discrepancies separating them. The professedly apolitical, conservative Russian orthodox Stravinsky would have clashed on many issues with the Marxist and atheist Brecht.

Yet on the subject of Wagner they would have seen eye to eye. After an early infatuation with Wagner's music that led to the acknowledgment of Wagner's influence, Stravinsky began to reject him after attending a 1912 production of *Parsifal* in Bayreuth. The Bayreuth spectacle seemed to Stravinsky the equivalent of a religious ritual; he was strongly opposed to the romantic view of art as religion. His arguments in his autobiography are rather Brechtian. In contrast to a religious service, which requires blind belief from the congregation, Stravinsky demanded the very opposite—critical judgment—from the audience at a musical or theatrical performance. In his emphasis on disbelief and a critical attitude, he was in accord with Brecht. On the other hand, Stravinsky also argued strongly against the expressivity of music. Music should never express anything outside itself, he claimed, contradicting Wagner who had dedicated a whole chapter in *Opera and Drama* to "expression in music." But he also disagreed with Brecht who was always ready to convey a human or political message. Then again, Stravinsky seemed to side with Brecht in his critique of Wagner that was closely linked to his critique of opera in general, a genre that Wagner seemed to embody and that Stravinsky regarded with deep suspicion; he considered the Wagnerian fusion or marriage of several art forms akin to bigamy (White 225).

Beginning in the 1910s, Stravinsky created small works of modest scale, several of which influenced Brecht and Weill in their epic experiments. Besides *Oedipus Rex*, these pieces include the "musical fairytale" *The Nightingale* (1914), *The Soldier's Tale* (1918), and *The Wedding* (1923). Particularly *The Soldier's Tale*, for which the Swiss novelist Charles Ramuz provided the libretto, may be characterized as a forerunner of epic music theater (Stegmann 115–83). Weill reacted enthusiastically to this piece; in the 1920s he saw it at least three times, and he praised it as "the hybrid genre with the most assured future" (Kowalke 465). In his essay, "Opera in America" (1937), he placed it in the same context as *The Threepenny Opera* (Weill 117). Indeed, *The Soldier's Tale*, beyond its anti-Wagnerian characteristics, anticipates some formal innovations of *The Threepenny Opera*. In sharp contrast to Wagner's concept of the "invisible orchestra," the orchestra of *The Soldier's Tale*, consisting only of a small jazz ensemble, is located visibly on stage. Furthermore, the text is spoken, not sung, and the narrator, reading from a book, sits on stage and faces the orchestra. The music, which consists of dances and jazz numbers, rarely accompanies the spoken word. Rather, words and music alternate, creating a far more radical "separation of the elements" than was done by Brecht. Finally, *The Soldier's Tale*, composed in Switzerland during World War I, is a piece with a strong antiwar message. As Stravinsky remarked, it is his only stage work with political significance—an element with which Brecht could identify.

BRECHT CONTRA WAGNER

Brecht's attitude toward Wagner changed throughout his life, from that of cautious respect that bordered on artistic fascination in his early years to a complete and radical rejection of all Wagnerian concepts in his later life once he had formulated his own style. The young Brecht was not free from the spell of Wagner's music; he even enjoyed "conducting" Wagner in the solitude of his apartment. After intense hours of writing, he would relax by conducting silently in his room, an exercise for which music did not seem necessary; Brecht claimed that he heard it in his mind. On one such occasion, Brecht's boyhood friend Johann Harrer found a score of Wagner's *Tristan and Isolde* on Brecht's conducting stand (Frisch/Obermeier 111). Brecht's first wife, Marianne Zoff, to whom he was married from 1923 until 1927, was an opera singer at the Augsburg Stadttheater, and among the many roles she played were those in Wagner's operas *Lohengrin*, *The Valkyrie*, and *The Rhinegold*. The latter piece became the subject for Brecht's satire in a diary entry in October 1921. After attending a performance of *The Rhinegold* in Augsburg, Brecht ridiculed the "flat-footed" orchestra, the "Jurassic rock formations" of the opera, and the steam emanating from the room in which "Wotan's dirty underclothes" were washed; he applauded only the beauty of Marianne Zoff's voice (*Diaries* 140). On other occasions, Brecht ingeniously parodied Wagner. Hanns Otto Münsterer, another of Brecht's Augsburg friends, tells of a Tristanesque aria that Brecht sang, accompanied by his guitar, to his wolfhound: "Come hither Ina, my beloved" (*Brecht* 69).

These satires that Brecht created in his private life were soon replaced by Wagner parodies that Brecht integrated in his works. In an early version of *Baal* (1919), Brecht evoked the image of Wagner as a "sweating genius." The main character Baal is compared to Wagner because he blends perspiration with inspiration. The third act of *Drums in the Night* (1922) is subtitled "Ride of the Valkyries" and points ironically to Wagner's *The Ring of the Nibelung*. The final scene of the opera *Rise and Fall of the City of Mahagonny* (1927–1929) contains allusions to *Parsifal*; and as late as 1943 Brecht and Hanns Eisler worked on an operatic fragment entitled *Goliath*, in which they planned to integrate a song contest, an ironic reference to *The Mastersingers of Nuremberg*.

Brecht's early infatuation with Wagner thus turned quickly to parody and to a profound search for a countermodel. In his arguments against Wagner, Brecht may well have been influenced by Nietzsche. Among other writings by Nietzsche, Brecht owned the two volumes *The Case of Wagner* and *Nietzsche Contra Wagner*, both in editions published around 1909. Hence it is likely that Brecht read them in his youth. What Brecht disliked and distrusted most in Wagner's music was its emotional and irrational element, its tendency to make the audience indulge, dream, give in to erotic ecstasies, but forget how to think and to judge critically. "Laßt euch nicht verführen" is an important line in *Mahagonny*; the standard English translation "Let not hope confound you" (*CP* 2: 111) which, although poetic, cannot quite render all the shades of meaning. Perhaps "Don't give in to seduction" more adequately conveys the ambiguity inherent in both the false promises of Mahagonny and the seductive power of Wagnerian music that epitomized opera at the time.

In fact, Wagner's name became almost identical with opera for a while, and

Brecht's rebellion against Wagner also implied a rejection of traditional opera. In one of his prominent essays about music, "Notes to *Mahagonny*" (*Theatre* 33–42), published in 1930 and in revised form in 1938, Brecht asserted that the renewal of opera, which he envisioned, implies a radical departure from the Wagnerian *Gesamtkunstwerk*. Influenced by Marxism, Brecht began his discussion in the essay with the idea of the "apparatus." All art is seen as a commodity that is in need of a means of production. Compared to other forms of artistic expression that require apparatuses such as drama or the novel, opera, a form uniting so many arts, cannot operate without a powerful apparatus. The function of this apparatus is to provide evening entertainment, a purpose that Wagner knew to exploit more than almost any artist in the nineteenth century. His *Gesamtkunstwerk* was composed for the best and largest opera houses at the time. But Brecht, interested in a democratization of art and aware of the potentially dangerous political influences of mass media and the entertainment industry, proposed to move away not only from Wagner's art but also from the operatic apparatus as well. Brecht wanted to achieve both purposes through his concept of "separation of the elements," a formative principle of epic theater in direct contrast to Wagner's *Gesamtkunstwerk*. The separation of the elements implies a musical theater in which text, music, and visual design are equally important but independent of each other; and it rejects Wagner's attempt to fuse the individual elements so that in climactic passages text and music might be indistinguishable. By breaking the elements apart, Brecht meant to liberate opera from Wagner's "witchcraft" and "hypnosis" (*Theatre* 38). He thereby dismembered the *Gesamtkunstwerk* as well as the power of the operatic apparatus on the grounds that the theory of separation promotes thinking and reflecting rather than believing and indulging. Brecht also incorporated the spectator into his theory as one further extension of the various chains of separations, hence the "separation of the elements" is linked to the *Verfremdungseffekt* as a further form of distancing. Just as the audience should distance itself from the action presented on stage, the artistic elements are distanced from each other. Thus the theory of epic theater inevitably becomes a theory of epic music theater.

In Brecht's case, theory often followed practice, and he composed his essay after the 1930 premiere of *Mahagonny* in Leipzig and after his artistic and ideological discrepancies with Weill had become clear. Brecht and Weill had argued about the primacy of *musica* or *parola*, the classic operatic dichotomy. Weill insisted on the predominance of music in an operatic work, and wanted to proceed "according to purely musical considerations" (Weill 77), whereas Brecht would not permit himself to be reduced to the role of an operatic librettist. Actually, their disagreement led Brecht to postulate his theory of separating the elements. He hoped that, by keeping the single arts independent, the question of priority would disappear. But Weill proved to be a much more consistent anti-Wagnerian than Brecht when he defended the primacy of the music. Wagner had stated in his treatise *Opera and Drama* that music was the means and drama the purpose of expression in his music dramas; thus he placed the emphasis on the literary and the theatrical. Like Brecht, Wagner liked to see a meaning in his operas that reached beyond the purely musical. However, the difference between Brecht and Wagner lay not in their common emphasis on dramatic meaning, but in the nature of this meaning: Brecht rejected the romantic, pleasure-oriented, and passivity-promoting meaning of Wagner's "culinary" operas (*Theatre* 35) in favor of his more ideological, rational, and politically critical content.

The political orientation in Brecht's view of Wagner became sharper and more pointed in the 1930s, especially after Hitler took power in 1933. In a provocative look at German history in his 1943 essay, "On Stage Music," Brecht compared Bismarck's 1871 founding of the German Reich to Wagner's creation of the *Gesamtkunstwerk* in that both had conquered Paris; Bismarck militarily, Wagner with his operas (*GW* 15: 486). Brecht thus came to associate Wagner with imperialism, and in several other writings he drew a direct parallel between Wagner and Hitler. In referring to Hitler's dictatorship, he spoke of the "Bayreuth Republic," and in one of his satires from the *Svendborg Poems*, "Dream of a Great Grumbler," he placed Hitler in an opera house, delivering a deceitful speech to the masses (*Poems* 294). Possibly influenced by Benjamin's view of fascism as an aesthetization of politics, this poem shows Hitler choosing opera— the most "culinary," *l'art pour l'art* art form—as a means to suppress the people.

In another poem from the *Svendborg* collection, "Prohibition of Theatre Criticism," Brecht again compared Hitler and Wagner and suggested an analogy between the Nazi party meeting in Nuremberg and the festival of Wagner's operas in nearby Bayreuth. Drawing on two Wagner operas (*Parsifal* and *Lohengrin*), the poem describes theater, the only area of competence of the Nazi regime, as a political cult that allows no criticism: in the festival, near Bayreuth, called Reichsparteitag, the chancellor takes on the role of a "Parsifal-like simpleton" and sings the well-known aria "Nie sollst du mich befragen" (*Poems* 299). The "simpleton," the pure fool Parsifal, is a biting reference to Hitler, and the aria (Never shall you ask me) refers to Lohengrin, who promised to save and marry Elsa under the condition that she would never inquire about his origins. Brecht reinterprets the romantic, quasi-religious legend of Lohengrin as a prohibition of critical thinking; the Lohengrin myth then becomes the Hitler cult. *Lohengrin* occupied Brecht for decades; as early as 1926 he published an ironic note about this opera in which the protagonist does not allow his beloved to ask about his name (Lucchesi/Shull 109). Brecht considered Wagner's ultra-romantic tendency to mystify ridiculous. While he regarded Wagner's desire to hide origins rather than to provide rational explanations as a cause for humor and perfect material for satire in the 1920s, he judged it to be hypocritical and dangerous in the 1930s when Hitler rose to power. Later, in his American exile, Brecht planned a film project entitled *Lohengrin* that was to center on the question of blind confidence (Lucchesi/Shull 77).

It may have been less Wagner's *oeuvre* itself than the nationalistic and fascist reception of Wagner in the 1930s and 1940s that intensified Brecht's radical refutation of Wagner. But in the GDR in 1954, Brecht proposed a *Siegfried* film project on the Wagnerian hero that was intended as a counterproject to Wagner. Brecht adopted the Wagnerian juxtaposition of the blond Siegfried and dark Hagen, figures whom the Nazis interpreted in accordance with their dichotomous world view as the respective representatives of Germans and Jews. But Brecht reversed the Nazis' value code by relating the story to the biblical Jewish tradition, the legend of David and Goliath. The small, dark, but educated and human David wins over the primitive, blond, muscular giant Goliath. Brecht's reinterpretation, which did not advance beyond the project stage, differed sharply from the Germanic and Wagnerian myth, in which Hagen wins through the use of deceit (Lucchesi/Shull 76–77).

There are then three different periods in Brecht's reception of Wagner. The young Brecht was still fascinated by Wagner's genius. In the 1920s his cautious approval turned to satire and a skeptical attitude based on aesthetic and political reasons. Brecht moved away from romanticism and criticized the passive consumer attitude of a public that was lulled and numbed by an overwhelming entertainment machine driven by the operatic apparatus. Beginning in the 1930s and fueled by Hitler's takeover, Brecht's political criticism became concrete; he increasingly referred to Wagner as a forerunner of fascism.

MUSIC AND BRECHT'S THEORY

Theory is an essential aspect of Brecht's work; his body of theoretical writings almost comprises an *oeuvre* in itself. Much of Brecht's thinking is highly pragmatic; he claimed to value a new idea only when it was applicable or useful for his theater or for society in general. Yet, he also enjoyed the act of thinking itself; his ironic remark about the German propensity for abstract thinking in "A Short Organum for the Theatre" that "even materialism is little more than an idea with us" (*Theatre* 204) applies also to himself.

For several reasons, a close study of Brecht's theory is not unproblematic. First, Brecht's method was inductive rather than deductive; he usually wrote his theoretical analyses after he had finished the works to which they refer. Second, in his writings on works he coauthored with Weill, Brecht's theory was occasionally designed to justify his own position vis-à-vis that of Weill. Third, Brecht's theory, which evolved over several decades, was not always consistent; he did not always follow his own prescriptions. For example, in *Mother Courage and Her Children*, in an apparent deviation from his theory, he created characters of such humanity and complexity that the spectator cannot regard them without feeling or empathy. Brecht is thus great in spite of himself, as one critic has suggested (Esslin, *Brecht* 209–18); his genius resides precisely in his failure, his unwillingness to be coerced into the formula he himself created. All *caveats* aside, however, Brecht's theory of epic theater, by definition a theory of epic music theater, constitutes an important body of writings that revolutionized modern drama and allows us to identify plays as epic or Brechtian.[2]

Brecht conceived of his epic theater as a political theater, a theater that should ultimately contribute to changing and improving the world. These changes should occur through thinking and reasoning on the part of the spectator rather than through indulgence in private emotions. "Epic" theater embraces epic elements; it narrates events on stage rather than embodying them in the manner of the "Aristotelian" drama, the term used by Brecht to denote the theater he opposed. Brecht also called his theater a "theatre of the scientific age," a theater that both makes use of the latest technological advances and requires a scientific attitude on the part of its spectators—an attitude of doubt, critical distance, and rational reflection (*Theatre* 121, 196). Brecht derived this critical attitude, curiously, from the sports arena, where he professed to have found an audience of "experts" (*Theatre* 44). The scientific theater also proposes to be antipsychological in the sense that it is not interested in exploring individual personalities, a process that might lead the audience to empathize with the characters on stage; rather, this kind of theater tries to understand the workings of society as a whole.

One of the basic structural principles of the new epic theater is that of montage. The term montage, describing the activity of placing prefabricated parts together to form a new entity, is derived from technology; within the arts, it is commonly used in film and applied to editing techniques. In literature and music, montage implies a nonmimetic art, an art seen as artifice, as opposed to the idea of organic growth. Philosopher Walter Benjamin, a close friend of Brecht's, stated that two basic means of achieving montage were the insertion of quotes within a work and the act of interrupting an event (Grimm 90). Brecht's principle of *Verfremdung* is therefore related to montage, since Brecht described it also as a form of quoting. The actor should "quote" rather than fully identify the character portrayed (*Theatre* 94). Montage may also have appealed to Brecht for its capacity to promote social change: a constructed art work is more likely to reflect an active world that allows us to contribute to it, as opposed to the passivity that may result from the idea of natural growth, on which humans ultimately would have little effect. Not surprisingly Brecht considered "growth" and "montage" as fundamental opposites that distinguish the dramatic from the epic theater (*Theatre* 37).

The application of the concept of montage to the genre of music theater results in the separation of the elements:

When the epic theatre's methods begin to penetrate the opera, the first result is a radical *separation of the elements*. The great struggle for supremacy between words, music, and production . . . can simply be by-passed by radically separating the elements. So long as the expression "Gesamtkunstwerk" (or "integrated work of art") means that the integration is a muddle, so long as the arts are supposed to be "fused" together, the various elements will all be equally degraded, and each will act as a mere "feed" to the rest. (*Theatre* 37–38)

Brecht goes on to discuss the effect of this new theory on the spectator. While the fusion of the elements in the Wagnerian *Gesamtkunstwerk* can turn the spectator into a passive receiver, their separation, resulting in contrasts and internal breaks, should allow for a more critical and rational audience. Such a separation of the elements can occur in at least two ways. First, spoken words and singing can remain completely apart as in, for instance, *The Threepenny Opera*. Second, Brecht wrote: "there is a kind of speaking-against-the-music which can have strong effects" (*Theatre* 45). In this case, while text and music occur simultaneously, the ironic contrast and commentary of one art form on the other produces a dialectics that allows each of the arts to remain independent. The music expresses an emotion or a message different from that of the text. For example, in *The Threepenny Opera* Peachum introduces his exploitative business with a Lutheran chorale, and Mac and Jenny describe their bordello by means of a tender love song. The theory of separation continued to occupy Brecht throughout his life, although he slightly modified and tempered it over the years when he began emphasizing the whole work rather than its individual elements. In "Short Organum" he wrote: "So let us invite all the sister arts of the drama, not in order to create an 'integrated work of art' in which they all offer themselves up and are lost, but so that together with the drama they may further the common task in their different ways; and their relations with one another consist in this: that they lead to mutual alienation" (*Theatre* 204). The term "sister arts" here implies as much the common goal as the differences, the alienation or *Verfremdung*. In 1956, referring to a production of *The Caucasian Chalk Circle* in Berlin, Brecht went one step further, replacing the term "separation of the elements" with the socialist formulation, a "collective of independent arts" (*GW* 17: 1210).

A further vital aspect of epic music theater is the visibility of the sources of music. At the Bayreuth theater, the orchestra was hidden under the stage; its invisibility was designed to endow the music with a magical, mythical force. Conversely, Brecht appealed to the audience's rationality and intellect by having the musicians perform visibly on stage, most notably in *The Threepenny Opera*. All devices of stagecraft, including the musical instruments, were to be laid open on stage, to be perceived, analyzed, and understood by the spectators. In epic theater, the artistic process was to be foregrounded as much as the final product. Rather than ask: what happened? spectators were supposed to pursue the question: how did this happen? Brecht's interest in the process extended to the performers as well: "It helps the actor, if the musicians are visible during his performance and also if he is allowed to make visible preparation for it" (*Theatre* 45). In *The Threepenny Opera* he also introduced one further method of making artistic processes visible: the "titles and screens" (*Theatre* 43). Each scene was preceded by a short summary of its contents projected on a screen in order to reduce the spectator's fixation on the action as well as to help focus on the form of its presentation. The titles and screens, a form of "footnotes" in playwriting (*Theatre* 44), are thus showing the mechanisms of the art work and enable the spectator to question the hidden mechanisms of the workings of society as well—demanding an exercise in "complex seeing" (*Theatre* 44).

"He who is showing should himself be shown" (*Theatre* 45). To Brecht, this rule seemed especially important for singers. The act of showing rather than that of embodying or becoming is also the main principle of Brecht's theory of *Verfremdung*. Brecht insisted that not only acting but also the stage setting and music, through the use of choruses and songs, contribute to the *Verfremdungs-effekt* in theater, a term that Brecht often shortened to *V-Effekt* ("A-effect"; *Theatre* 96).

Another important element in Brecht's theory, not unrelated to his use of *Verfremdung*, is *Gestus*, a concept that Brecht probably arrived at in collaboration with Weill. In fact, Weill used the term *Gestus* before Brecht—although he referred to his work with Brecht in his definition of *Gestus*. Weill defined gestic music in his 1928 self-portrait "The Musician Weill" and then more exhaustively in his 1929 essay "Concerning the Gestic Character of Music." Both texts describe the gestic character of music in opposition to Wagner and assign different and more dominant roles, including interrupting a text, to music in the new theater. Without representing psychological states, music can not only illustrate but also create a basic *Gestus*, an attitude toward the events presented on stage. Music can therefore determine an interpretation of human interactions; and it becomes gestic through its "rhythmic fixing of the text" by providing a formal constraint, much like a fugue or a sonata (Kowalke 493).

Gestus occupies a much more central role in Brecht's writings than it does in Weill's. Brecht first mentions the term in his 1930 essay on *Mahagonny*, but the expressions *Gestus*, gestic acting, gestic language, gestic music, and gestic content recur in Brecht's writings for the following two decades. Brecht used *Gestus* as a principle for actors, who should convey in their delivery the basic gest or socially significant attitude underlying a play. Just as *Verfremdung*, *Gestus* originated as a formative acting strategy for an epic and political theater; in fact, the two terms are logically interconnected. Without having first presented the basic gest of a piece, its *Verfremdung* cannot be achieved. Both *Verfremdung* and *Gestus* are non-Aristotelian; *Gestus* "takes over, as it were, from the principle of imitation" (*Theatre* 86). One of the most important forms of *Gestus* in acting is the "gest of showing" (*Theatre* 136, 203).

From gestic acting Brecht moved to gestic language, a concept he elucidated most clearly in his essay "On Rhymeless Verse with Irregular Rhythms" (1939). In Brecht's use of language, *Gestus* often implied rhythmic syncopations and, furthermore, a technique in which a sentence structure follows the gest of a speaking person. In comparing two sentences drawn from the Bible—"Pluck out the eye that offends thee" and "If thine eye offends thee, pluck it out,"—Brecht characterized only the latter variety as gestic (*Theatre* 117).

Gestic music is best described in Brecht's essays "On the Use of Music in an Epic Theatre" (1935) and "On Gestic Music" (1937). Similarly to language, gestic music should bring out the social gests shown on stage. Although Brecht did not adopt Weill's language, a "rhythmic fixing of the text" through music could suggest such a social attitude, particularly if the musical rhythms are easily recognizable to the audience. For this reason, Brecht also considered singing actors better suited to gestic music than opera singers, and he often looked for musical models among the so-called cheap music (*Theatre* 87). One basic premise of Brecht's theory of gestic music is the belief, not universally held, that music does express meaning. When Brecht asked of the musician to comment on the text and "to adopt his own political attitude while making music" (*Theatre* 104), be it through the composition of a score or through the manner of its performance, he tacitly assumed that music, especially gestic music, is always capable of carrying extramusical, social connotations. Just as montage, *Verfremdung,* the separation of the elements, and the focus on the visibility of music, *Gestus* is thus an essential concept characterizing music in Brecht's theater.

THE THREEPENNY OPERA AS AN EXAMPLE OF EPIC MUSIC THEATER

The Threepenny Opera brought world fame to Brecht and Weill. Although by no means an opera in the conventional sense, both Brecht and Weill characterized it as an *Urtypus* or *Urform* (archetypal type or form) of opera. It is hard to prove who coined the expression and who originated the idea, although Brecht's statement on *The Threepenny Opera* was first published several months before Weill's respective essay, which appeared in January 1929. Brecht's remarks, written for the 1928 premiere of *The Threepenny Opera*, described the *Urtypus* of this opera only briefly and generally as a new formal invention, combining elements of opera and drama (*Werke* 24: 57). Weill, on the other hand, went into much greater detail in his response to questions by the editor of the Viennese musicological journal *Anbruch*. He linked the *Urform* of opera to *Zeitoper* (contemporary opera), a genre that he had previously developed. Weill argued that traditional opera had remained an aristocratic art form, which isolated itself from modernizing movements in theater. Conversely, *The Threepenny Opera* constituted a new beginning because it returned to more primitive operatic forms that assigned new and independent roles to music, addressed a contemporary audience, and placed the concept of opera as a subject on stage (Weill 55–56). Weill characterized *The Threepenny Opera* as "the most consistent reaction to Wagner" and "the complete destruction of the concept of music drama" (quoted in Hinton 27, 187).

The Threepenny Opera, which premiered on 31 August 1928 in Berlin's Theater am Schiffbauerdamm (now home of the Berliner Ensemble), is surrounded by legends, scandals, and conflicting accounts that have bestowed an almost mythical dimension on the original production. More than any other piece of music theater, by definition the work of an ensemble rather than an individual, *The Threepenny Opera* was the product of a true group effort. In the winter of 1927–1928, writer Elisabeth Hauptmann, Brecht's collaborator and close friend, received the manuscript of John Gay and Johann Christoph Pepusch's *The Beggar's Opera* from friends in London. The work had been revived with tremendous success in 1920 at the Lyric Theatre in Hammersmith (London), almost 200 years after its premiere in 1728. Hauptmann was immediately fascinated by this satire of the English prime minister Sir Robert Walpole, of corrupt London society, and of composer Georg Friedrich Händel, who was worshiped by that society. Recognizing all the possible parallels to modern-day Berlin, Hauptmann translated the work into German and, together with Brecht, adapted it for a Berlin audience. Brecht had unsuccessfully offered the manuscript to impresario/director Max Reinhardt's Deutsches Theater. He then took advantage of a chance meeting with Ernst Josef Aufricht, a wealthy impresario, who had recently rented the Theater am Schiffbauerdamm and was looking for new plays for the 1928–1929 season. In April 1928 he found Brecht in café Schlichter, working on "Joe Fleischhacker," an early version of *St. Joan of the Stockyards*. Aufricht showed no interest in this drama on wheat and the stock exchange in Chicago, and he was about to leave when Brecht dropped a casual remark about his adaptation of Gay's piece about the London underworld. Aufricht was intrigued: "The story smelled of theatre" (quoted in Hinton 17).

Brecht had titled the first version of his adaptation "Gesindel" ("scum"); he then suggested the title "Die Ludenoper" ("Lude" means "pimp" in Berlin jargon), and finally, following a suggestion by writer Lion Feuchtwanger, he settled on *Die Dreigroschenoper*. Only after Aufricht had accepted the manuscript did Brecht propose Weill's participation in the project. Aufricht hesitated at first, because he found Weill's two one-act operas, *The Czar Has His Photograph Taken* and *Protagonist* (texts by Georg Kaiser), that were then playing at the Charlottenburg Opera, "too atonal" (quoted in Hinton 17). Although "atonal" does not describe the score of either opera, Aufricht may have been intimidated by the music's complexity. He therefore asked musical director Theo Mackeben to prepare Pepusch's original music for *The Beggar's Opera* as a possible alternative. Weill knew nothing about this backup plan; he and his wife Lotte Lenya as well as Brecht and his family went to Le Lavendou on the French Riviera to spend six weeks writing intensively. When they returned in early July of 1928, neither the music nor the text were quite finished. Time was running short, since Aufricht wanted the premiere to take place on his birthday, on 31 August. But when Weill played his songs for him on the piano, Aufricht was moved and discarded his plans to use Pepusch's original music as a substitute.

The Berlin premiere of *The Threepenny Opera*, now a legendary moment in theatrical history, was marred by disasters that threatened to prevent it from ever taking place. Practically everything went wrong for a while, and almost everybody threatened to cancel at one point or another. Carola Neher, the actress cast in the role of Polly, needed to leave for Davos (Switzerland), where her husband, the poet Klabund, was dying of tuberculosis. When she returned after her husband's death in mid-August, she found that many of her best lines had been given to other characters, and in spite of Brecht's efforts to gain her back, she quit and was replaced by Roma Bahn. Helene Weigel, Brecht's wife, suddenly suffered from an attack of appendicitis, and her role was dropped completely. Brecht himself was incensed when he learned that he would not receive the giant mechanical horse for the messenger who should announce Macheath's pardon at the end; he too, for a while, vowed not to continue. Erich Ponto, the actor who was to play Peachum, complained about substantial cuts in his part and threatened to leave; so did the operetta star Harald Paulsen, given the role of Macheath. He insisted on the costume of his personal choice, an expensive black suit with a bright blue necktie. Paulsen's vanity gave birth to the most famous song of *The Threepenny Opera*, ''The Ballad of Mac the Knife,'' because Brecht and Weill were forced to come up with a *Moritat* (ballad) that made the crimes of the elegantly dressed Mac more heinous. Finally, even Weill, who was known for his pleasant and balanced personality, became furious when he noticed that the name of Lotte Lenya, in the role of Jenny, was missing in the program. But Lenya was able to appease him by assuring him that the audience would remember her performance even without her being mentioned in the program. Lenya eventually proved to have been right; after a slow beginning, the ''The Cannon Song'' brought the house down. The show became a complete success, it was sold out for months, and to this day *The Threepenny Opera* enjoys a popularity matched only by classics in musical and operatic literature.

The term ''montage'' appropriately describes the production process of *The Threepenny Opera*, both in a literal and a euphemistic sense. As the adaptation of an eighteenth-century model it was not the product of organic creation, but of translation, cutting, and pasting. While Weill composed almost entirely new music—he retained Peachum's ''Morning Hymn'' from Pepusch—Brecht adapted many lines from Gay's text, although the play differs significantly from *The Beggar's Opera*. The montage process also allowed Brecht to edit and rewrite the text after the 1928 premiere; the standard version from 1931 incorporates many additions and changes that reflect Brecht's increasingly Marxist convictions. The play is constructed in such a way that characters may exchange lines or entire songs. During rehearsals Brecht freely shuffled lines from one character to another; for example, the ''Pirate Jenny'' song, originally written for the character of Polly, could easily be performed by Jenny (Lotte Lenya) in the film version. Montage is then both a formal device as well as part of the contents in Brecht's theater. He shunned the belief in individual personalities or character continuity, as evinced in *A Man's a Man*, in which a simple and innocent worker is transformed into a war-mongering beast through the process of montage.

At the euphemistic level, ''montage'' becomes a pseudonym as well for plagiarism, or, in Brecht's words, his ''fundamental laxity in matters of intellectual property'' (*Werke* 21: 315). In 1929, the theater critic Alfred Kerr noticed that Brecht had not acknowledged K.L. Ammer, translator of the ballads by François Villon that appear in *The Threepenny Opera*. Recently, John Fuegi (*Brecht*) has advanced the thesis that Hauptmann not only translated Gay but also wrote major portions of the text of *The Threepenny Opera*. Brecht acknowledged her in the original playbill as translator and in successive versions of the published play as collaborator (Hinton 9).

Despite its title, *The Threepenny Opera* is not an opera in the conventional sense; "a play with music," Weill's subtitle of the musical score (Vienna: Universal-Edition, 1928) characterizes the work more aptly. Brecht opined in his 1936 essay "On the Use of Music in an Epic Theatre" that the 1928 production of *The Threepenny Opera* was "the most successful demonstration of the epic theatre" and "the first use of theatrical music in accordance with a new point of view" (*Theatre* 85). The strict separation of music from other elements is further emphasized by the special golden song lighting and by screens on which the song titles are projected during the singing. In the published text, major songs are introduction by stage directions such as: "Song lighting: golden glow. The organ is lit up. Three lamps are lowered from above on a pole" (*CP* 2: 195 *et passim*), and a sign indicates the respective title of each song. The sources of light become visible, and so do the musical instruments. In the Berlin premiere the orchestra was placed on stage; its centerpiece was a large country fair organ at the back of the stage that had been elevated on a staircase. Its lights blinked colorfully when the orchestra played, evoking memories from Brecht's youth at the Augsburg *Plärrer* or local fair. The orchestra of *The Threepenny Opera* had little in common with our conception of a symphony orchestra; rather, a jazz band consisting of a small ensemble of about ten instruments sufficed. Weill's score called for a tenor saxophone, an alto saxophone, two trumpets, a trombone, a banjo, a kettledrum, percussion, a harmonium, and a piano. The songs do not derive from the classical tradition; they are mostly modern dances, frequently lifted from North and South American popular music. Fox-trot, tango, waltz, march, and chorale are represented in the twenty songs of *The Threepenny Opera*. The songs were composed not for professional singers but for singing actors. Weill's new approach to music, for example, departed radically from operatic practice in general and that of Wagner in particular. In some instances, the operatic parody bordered on the grotesque—for example, in the carnivalesque illumination of the country fair organ and its deliberate play with kitsch. It may be argued that *The Threepenny Opera* was just as successful in breaking down Wagner's musical predominance in Europe as *The Beggar's Opera* had been in destroying Händel's popularity among his contemporaries two hundred years earlier.

The epic qualities of *The Threepenny Opera* are evident from the introduction of narrator figures such as Peachum; from the songs that form independent entities, interrupt the action, do not further the plot, and provoke the audience to think, and from the titles and screens used. Each of the nine scenes of the three-act play is preceded by a projection of the title and a brief summary of the scene on a screen. Thus the spectators already know the content while watching events unfold, and they can participate in the estranging "literarization of the theatre" (*Theatre* 43).

As a work that introduces new techniques, *The Threepenny Opera* is also highly self-referential; it may be viewed as an opera on the subject of opera. The final scene in particular satirizes grand opera; the "Third Threepenny Finale," which follows the arrival of Brown as a royal messenger who announces Mac's reprieve, ridicules the cliché endings of many operas and comedies by adopting operatic conventions while simultaneously pointing out their illusionary character.

The wedding scene in act 1, scene 2 has been described as a model epic scene (Knopf, *Theater* 61), and it includes several references to music and opera. The scene takes place in a horse stable; all utensils, food, and furniture have been stolen by Mac's gang. The wedding—for Brecht a social ritual as worn out as the musical ritual of opera—serves as a vehicle of operatic criticism. Musical instruments play an important role—for example, Mac criticizes the presence of a luxurious rosewood harpsichord and the absence of basic furniture; the harpsichord was an essential part of the orchestra for Händel's operas that *The Beggar's Opera* had parodied. Generally speaking, it represents classical music, and Mac proposes to replace the worn-out status symbol with something more useful, a table and chair. His gang proceeds to turn the harpsichord into something useful by sawing off its legs so that it becomes a bench, all the while singing a laconic wedding song. Later, Mac demands more music: "Couldn't somebody sing something? Something delectable?" (*CP* 2: 161). He then qualifies his request: "I'm not asking you to put on an opera" (*CP* 2: 161–62). The word "delectable" parodies the *l'art pour l'art* function of traditional opera; Mac the robber, who throughout the play exhibits bourgeois qualities, here becomes also a bourgeois art critic. As it turns out, the piece that comes closest to Mac's notions of "opera" is not the wedding song sung by his gang but Polly's song "Pirate Jenny." The gang receives her song with great applause, but Mac's reaction is more ambiguous: he publicly praises Polly's delivery as "art," but in "an undertone" he reminds her that he disapproves of her play-acting (*CP* 2: 166). This afterthought shows Mac's growing insecurity about his wife-to-be Polly; it may also be read as an example of bourgeois art criticism that idolizes high art, while distrusting and disliking its political potential at the same time. The *l'art pour l'art* facade that Macheath assumes expresses then also an *antiart* sentiment, a fear of the social power of art.

"Pirate Jenny" is one of the masterpieces in *The Threepenny Opera*. Polly introduces this song in the epic manner. She begins by telling Mac's crew about the cleaning girl in a small dive in Soho, then, as if in a dress rehearsal, she teaches the men how to ask the right questions that will lead up to her song, and finally she sings her number accompanied by the golden glow. The audience thus witnesses the performance of her song as well as its rehearsal; it is invited to watch the spectators on stage, Mac's bandits, who participate in a play within a play and help destroy the illusions through the process of showing them.

Performed in lieu of an appropriate wedding song addressed to Polly, "Pirate Jenny" has little to do with love or marriage, but rather with anarchy, the apocalypse, or even world revolution. The material is gestic; Polly expresses a social attitude by rising beyond the role of wife and assuming a different identity. Her song tells the story of a cleaning maid in a cheap hotel by the harbor who lives on the miserly wages she receives for washing dishes and making beds. But one day a pirate ship arrives whose cannons destroy the entire town except her shabby little hotel. The pirates arrest everybody in town, and when Jenny is asked whom they should kill, she responds: all of them. She then disappears in the ship.

Ernst Bloch has detected ironic references to Wagner's *Lohengrin* or *The Flying Dutchman* in this song, comparing Jenny to Elsa or Senta, but their savior has now become a revolutionary, a red terrorist (quoted in Hecht 79–80). This song may also be seen as foreshadowing the end of the Weimar Republic five years after the premiere of *The Threepenny Opera*. But the momentary vision of impending disaster in Polly's song offers only a brief interruption; the mock wedding continues as if nothing had occurred. Nor does the song anticipate the play's ending. Just as Jenny is in the song, Mac will be saved—not by means of a revolution but, in the most traditional manner, through the queen's pardon. Society remains unchanged, and it is not clear how many viewers took this sour-sweet, parodistic reality of opera as a signal and challenge to alter the world, as Brecht had wished. Years after the premiere, in a fictional self-interview in 1933, Brecht expressed his disappointment in the audiences who considered the work primarily as entertainment while neglecting its social critique. But the Nazis presumably understood its subversive potential and felt threatened. They denounced *The Threepenny Opera* and prohibited all performances after Hitler seized power; the 1938 exhibition on "Degenerate Music" in Düsseldorf dedicated an entire room to it.

Weill's music for "Pirate Jenny" represents one of the most memorable and magnificent compositions of the play; it prompted Bloch's tongue-in-cheek suggestion that the song be used as a national anthem on joyful occasions (Hecht 77). Its 2/4 rhythm suggests a march, an ironic contrast to the revolutionary content of the song. Parts of the melody derive from Brecht's own composition, transcribed and arranged by composer and collaborator Franz Bruinier. Brecht's note of 1940 asserting that he had whistled or dictated melodic patterns to Weill (*Journals* 108) may be true, although there can be absolutely no doubt that Weill was responsible for the major part of the music.

The Threepenny Opera is one of the many works, not only in Germany but throughout Europe, that can be characterized as a step toward renewal of the operatic genre after Wagner in the 1920s; indeed, it certainly represents a climax. Its anti-Wagnerism is evident most notably in its application of the montage principle, the complete separation of the songs from the spoken text, the presence of various narrator figures as well as narrating devices such as the titles and screens, the use of singing actors rather than trained singers for the songs, and the placement of the jazz orchestra on stage so that music becomes demasked as a visible participant in the artifice. Wagner remained a dominant counterpole for both Brecht and Weill—albeit to a slightly lesser extent for the latter. Yet Brecht's antagonism to Wagner is coupled with much respect for and even admiration of Wagner's musicianship. In addition, Brecht was not entirely immune to the highly emotional effects of his music. It stands to reason that Brecht rejected Wagner so profoundly in his later years because he had studied him so intensely in his youth. Such a hypothesis gains credence by the fact that Brecht chose to ignore other composers of quality who, however, did not attain Wagner's stature. Ultimately, Brecht's critique of Wagner is productive rather than destructive, and for this reason it remains a rich and complex subject to this day.

NOTES

1. Weill's essays "Busoni's *Faust* and the Renewal of Operatic Form" (1926), Concerning the Gestic Character of Music" (1929), "A Note Concerning Jazz" (1929), and "Actually an Operatic Crisis?" (1932) are included in Kowalke (468–544).

2. Among the many texts by Brecht on the subject of theater and music, some of the most prominent are "The Modern Theatre Is the Epic Theatre: Notes to the Opera *Rise and Fall of the City of Mahagonny*" (1930; "Notes to Mahagonny"), "The Literarization of the Theatre: Notes to *The Threepenny Opera*" (1931), "On the Use of Music in an Epic Theatre" (1936), "On Gestic Music" (1937), "A Short Organum for the Theatre" (1948), and "From the *Mother Courage* Model" (1949). These texts are included in *Theatre*; a complete collection of Brecht's texts on music in English will be available upon publication of the translation of Lucchesi and Shull's encyclopedic *Musik bei Brecht*, to be published by Pendragon Press.

WORKS CITED (SEE ALSO REFERENCE GUIDE TO WORKS CITED IN ABBREVIATED FORM)

Busoni, Ferruccio. *Arlecchino: A Theatrical Caprice in One Act.* Vocal Score: English and German. Wiesbaden: Breitkopf, 1968.

———. *The Essence of Music, and Other Papers.* Translated by Rosamond Ley. Westport, CT: Hyperion, 1979.

———. "Sketch of a New Esthetic of Music." In Debussy, Claude, Ferruccio Busoni, and Charles Ives. *Three Classics in the Aesthetic of Music.* Translated by Theodore Baker. New York: Dover, 1962.

Cocteau, Jean. *Le coq et l'arlequin: notes autour de la musique.* Paris: Stock, 1979.

Dümling, Albrecht. *Laßt euch nicht verführen: Brecht und die Musik.* Munich: Kindler, 1985.

Frisch, Werner, and K.W. Obermeier, eds. *Brecht in Augsburg: Erinnerungen, Texte, Fotos.* Frankfurt am Main: Suhrkamp, 1976.

Grimm, Reinhold, ed. *Episches Theater.* Cologne: Kiepenheuer, 1972.

Hecht, Werner, ed. *Brechts "Dreigroschenoper."* Frankfurt am Main: Suhrkamp, 1985.

Hinton, Stephen, ed. *Kurt Weill: The Threepenny Opera.* Cambridge: Cambridge University Press, 1990.

Hofmannsthal, Hugo von. *The Lord Chandos Letter.* In English and German. Translated into English by Russell Stockman. Marlboro, VT: Marlboro, 1986.

Honegger, Arthur. *Joan of Arc at the Stake*. Poem by Paul Claudel. Translated by Dennis Arundell. Paris: Salabert, 1947.

———. *King David: Symphonic Psalm in Three Parts after a Drama by René Morax*. Boston: Schirmer, 1925.

Kowalke, Kim H. *Kurt Weill in Europe*. Ann Arbor, MI: UMI Research Press, 1979.

Lucchesi, Joachim, and Ronald Shull, eds. *Musik bei Brecht*. Berlin: Henschel, 1988.

Milhaud, Darius. *Le boeuf sur le toit, ou, The Nothing Doing Bar Farce*. Conceived and arranged by Jean Cocteau. Paris: Sirène, 1920.

———. *Christophe Colomb. Vocal Score: German and French*. Libretto by Paul Claudel. Vienna: Universal, 1930.

———. *La création du monde: ballet de Blaise Cendrars*. New York: Associated Music Publishers, 1929.

———. *Notes without Music*. Translated by Donald Evans, edited by Rollo H. Myers. New York: Knopf, 1953.

Nietzsche, Friedrich Wilhelm. *The Portable Nietzsche*. Translated by Walter Kaufmann. New York: Viking, 1954.

Satie, Erik. *Parade: ballet realiste sur un thème de Jean Cocteau*. Paris: Salabert, 1917.

Stegmann, Vera Sonja. *Das epische Musiktheater bei Strawinsky und Brecht: Studien zur Geschichte und Theorie*. New York: Lang, 1991.

Stravinsky, Igor. *The Nightingale: Lyrical Poem in Three Acts. French, English, and German*. English translation by Robert Craft. London: Boosey, 1962.

———. *Oedipus Rex: Opera Oratorio in Two Acts after Sophocles*. Text by Jean Cocteau, translated into Latin by J. Danielou. New York: Boosey, 1949.

———. *The Soldier's Tale. English, French, and German*. Libretto by Charles Ferdinand Ramuz. New York: Kalmus, 1960.

———. *The Wedding: Ballet with Soli and Chorus*. English and German text. New York: Kalmus, 1923.

Wagner, Richard. *Opera and Drama*. Translated by William Ashton Ellis. New York: Broude, 1966.

Weill, Kurt. *Musik und Theater: Gesammelte Schriften*. Edited by Stephen Hinton and Jürgen Schebera. Berlin: Henschel, 1990.

Weisstein, Ulrich. "Cocteau, Stravinsky, Brecht, and the Birth of Epic Opera." *Modern Drama* 5 (1962): 142–53.

White, Eric Walter. *Stravinsky: The Composer and his Works*. Berkeley: University of California Press, 1979.

11

Brecht and His Musical Collaborators

Thomas R. Nadar

It was through his association with his composer-collaborators Kurt Weill, Hanns Eisler, and Paul Dessau that Bertolt Brecht participated in the musical life of his times and continues to speak to our own. To a far greater extent than most playwrights, Brecht has gained international renown through the musical settings of his works. Brecht's lyrics as performed by rock musicians such as David Bowie, Sting, and Jim Morrison and the Doors have helped a younger and wider American audience to become aware of Brecht, just as their parents were introduced to his lyrics by Lotte Lenya, Louis Armstrong, Frank Sinatra, Judy Collins, and Bobby Darin. Certainly nothing attests more to Brecht's status as a cultural icon in the United States than having his ''Mac the Knife'' pressed into service to market McDonald's Big Mac sandwich. *The Threepenny Opera* has survived sixty-five years through its songs. Indeed, it was only the popularity of the songs from his play *Happy End* that brought about a rediscovery of the original work.[1] *The Rise and Fall of the City of Mahagonny*, which was staged both on Broadway and at the Metropolitan Opera, is an extraordinarily innovative opera. The entire collection of learning/teaching plays (the *Lehrstücke*, including *The Mother*, *He Who Said Yes*, and *The Exception and the Rule*), occupies a unique position in the musical and theatrical activity of the period. Unsurprisingly, nearly all of Brecht's more than forty dramatic works contain songs and/or provide for instrumental music.[2] In addition, he worked on such serious musical forms as the opera, oratorio, ballet, and cantata.

Brecht collaborated with many composers over the years, among them Paul

Hindemith, Gottfried von Einem, Paul Burkhard, Simon Parmet, Rudolf Wagner-Regeny, Dimitri Shostakovich, Edmund Meisel, and Roger Sessions.[3] Moreover, he offered *The Trial of Lucullus* to Igor Stravinsky and to Hilding
Rosenberg and *The Caucasian Chalk Circle* to Carl Orff,[4] but none of these
composers was able to undertake the project because of other commitments.
Ultimately, it was with three men in particular, Weill, Eisler, and Dessau, that
Brecht enjoyed his closest and most successful collaborations during his migra-
tory career, first in Berlin; then in exile in Scandinavia, France, and California;
and finally back in Europe after World War II.

As is the case with other aspects of his stagecraft and dramatic art, Brecht's
attitudes and ideas about music within the theater can be observed not only in
the various works themselves but also in his numerous theoretical essays from
the mid-1920s until his death. To a great extent, he was influenced by the ideas
of his musical collaborators as well as by the traditions and movements they
represented. Yet Brecht also had many notions of his own on the subject. Each
composer adapted to Brecht's demands, made artistic demands of his own, and
collaborated in the creation of works for the musical stage. It follows that the
relationship between each composer and the playwright was unique.

KURT WEILL

Certainly the one composer who brought Brecht to the awareness of the
American public was Weill. His widow, Lotte Lenya, was responsible for the
successful renaissance of *The Threepenny Opera* in New York City in 1954.
Through her friends and associates in the recording industry, Brecht/Weill's
Mahagonny, The Seven Deadly Sins, Happy End, The Threepenny Opera, and
He Who Said Yes were recorded and given the exposure they deserved.[5] Weill
enjoyed a remarkable career in America as the composer of innovative and
highly regarded musical comedies that have proven their durability. Drama critic
Clive Barnes has referred to him as ''Broadway's greatest composer'' and characterizes Weill's style as follows: ''He took the street and cabaret music of his
native Berlin and mixed it with what he thought of as American jazz. The music
is often jaunty and with a bitter aftertaste to it and seems to have been written
more out of pain than pleasure'' (Barnes 43).

During his collaboration with Weill, Brecht was able to experiment in the
areas of the musical, opera, and the *Lehrstücke*.[6] Weill was interested in the
enormous possibilities of a musical theater, that is, in the various shapes and
forms musical drama could assume. Brecht, who insisted on the commitment of
art to a sociopolitical cause, was able to often overlook Weill's traditional conservative attitudes to see the formidable talent behind them. Throughout his stay
in America, Brecht planned several new collaborations with Weill, which were
unfortunately never completed when Brecht left America to return to Berlin.
Ironically, Brecht and Weill were nominated posthumously for the highest award

in American theater, the Tony Award, for their score to *Happy End*, first produced on Broadway in 1977.

One of the earliest collaborations between Brecht and Weill was their adaptation of John Gay's *The Beggar's Opera* (1728) for the opening of Ernst Josef Aufricht's Theater am Schiffbauerdamm. Despite many complications and problems, *The Threepenny Opera* was a strikingly innovative work. It featured singers who came from the dramatic stage and cabaret and had no formalized musical training, songs that deliberately interrupted the action of the play, catchy melodies, irresistible dance rhythms, and the accompaniment of a small cabaret-sized band.

Brecht and Weill tried the formula of *The Threepenny Opera* once again in their disastrous *Happy End*, which opened one year to the day after *The Threepenny Opera* in 1929. Set in an American milieu of gangsters, molls, and the Salvation Army, the play stands somewhere between Shaw's *Major Barbara* and Frank Loesser's musical comedy *Guys and Dolls*. As British scholar David Drew has pointed out, *Happy End* was as much an experiment as its predecessor, and once again its high points were its marvelous songs that Brecht and Weill used to different ends: "Whereas in *The Threepenny Opera* the music is an integral part of the dramatic structure, developing it or commenting upon it, the *Happy End* songs are purely decorative. With the exception of the 'Sailors' Tango' they are not essential to the development of the play, nor are they expressions of individual psychology" (Drew 85). Realizing that the play was very weak, Brecht withdrew his name from the playbill and substituted the pseudonym Dorothy Lane. According to Ernst Josef Aufricht, however, Weill insisted that Brecht at least keep his name as lyricist (Aufricht 85).

At the same time Brecht and Weill had been preparing *Happy End* for its opening, they had already begun to get involved in many of the avant-garde musical movements of the 1920s and 1930s. In 1930, Brecht and Weill premiered the *Schuloper* (school opera) *He Who Said Yes*, based on a Japanese No-drama, *Taniko* (The Valley-Hurling), by the fifteenth-century author Zenchiku. That the playwright was fascinated with the didacticism and epic structure, not to mention the sheer theatricality of Chinese and Japanese theater, is no revelation. In theory, the works for learning and teaching were aimed at educating not the audience but rather those participating in the performance itself. Whereas Brecht saw the pieces as teaching social attitudes by showing highly abstract formalized actions of representative individuals—in this case a young boy in his tradition-bound society—Weill regarded the work as technically instructive, that is, as a means of teaching musical technique in performance for amateur groups. In the case of their school opera, Brecht and Weill intended the piece for performance by school children. The central theme of *He Who Said Yes* is the concept of consent, that is, the individual's willingness to disregard his or her private feelings for the common good; Brecht would rework the material and adapt it with the title *The Measures Taken* with a new musical setting by Eisler for the workers' movement. The last collaboration of Brecht and Weill,

The Seven Deadly Sins, might well be regarded as a variation on this same theme. It is apparent that Weill viewed the sacrifices made by an individual for the good of society in terms of personal struggle, gain, and loss, rather than as a politically determined problem. Apart from Brecht, Weill continued to compose for amateur groups, but his emphasis was on enjoyment and entertainment rather than on a political platform.

The high point of their collaboration was the opera *Rise and Fall of the City of Mahagonny* (1930). It was indeed their most ambitious and controversial work, causing a famous theatrical riot in Leipzig at its first performance. Brecht and Weill continued to alter the opera for subsequent productions up to the stellar Berlin premiere on 21 December 1931, where it opened to rave reviews and ran continuously for over fifty performances, a record for a contemporary opera. Frederic Ewen calls the opera a "masterpiece" that "represents Brecht and Weill at their most original" (197). Martin Esslin regards the work as the artistic "culmination" (*Brecht* 44) of the team. Nevertheless, Michael Steinberg's reservations are perceptive: "[*Mahagonny* is] a troubled work, not like the casually thrown off (but perfectly aimed) *Threepenny Opera*, or the *Seven Deadly Sins*, the most successful of Brecht's and Weill's virtuosically calculated works, but [it is, nevertheless,] fascinating" (22).

Weill and his wife Lotte Lenya fled to Paris in March of 1933, when he received a commission to compose a ballet for choreographer George Balanchine's troupe Les Ballets 1933. The composer invited Brecht to Paris to write the libretto for this ballet-cantata, a daringly innovative work entitled *The Seven Deadly Sins*, and one of Weill's finest achievements. Brecht, however, underestimated its quality, withdrew his manuscript after the work flopped, and never published it. Nevertheless, he did not destroy the manuscript and added some verses that were published posthumously. During his tenure with the New York City Ballet, George Balanchine revived this work in 1958 with Lotte Lenya, and he was working on a new production at the time of his death in 1983 that was to star Bette Midler in the same role.

Weill came to America at the invitation of Max Reinhardt in 1935 to collaborate on the eminent director's production of Franz Werfel's biblical drama *The Eternal Road*. Following his decision to remain in the United States, Weill enjoyed an extremely successful career on Broadway, and to a lesser extent in Hollywood. His collaborators were the cream of the New York literary and theatrical world: Maxwell Anderson, Moss Hart, Ira Gershwin, Alan Jay Lerner, Paul Green, Langston Hughes, Ogden Nash, and Arnold Sundgaard. Weill's "Americanization" is evident from the fact that, angered and frustrated by the rise of the Nazi party in Germany, he refused to speak German anymore.

The same year Weill came to the United States, Brecht also came to New York to assist on a production of his own adaptation of Maxim Gorky's novel *The Mother*. The Theatre Union, the most famous of the American socialist workers' theaters, was producing the play and requested Brecht and Eisler's artistic help. Interestingly enough, Brecht was virtually unknown in the United

States, but Eisler, because of his extensive catalogue of popular songs for the workers' movement, was quite famous. When the Theatre Union initially proposed to do the play, the minutes of the Executive Board described it as ''Gorky's *Mother* in the Eisler operetta'' (quoted in Baxandall 70). Publicity for the production gave Eisler credit for *The Threepenny Opera* as well!

For nine years Brecht attempted without success to stage a production of one of his works on Broadway. He relied upon the reputation and royalties from *The Threepenny Opera* to support him during the lean years in exile. In 1942, MGM studios seriously considered filming the musical, while Clarence Muse wanted to produce an all-black version on Broadway. Needing Weill's permission, Brecht approached his former collaborator through an intermediary, Theodor Adorno, eminent critic and musicologist. Weill and Brecht had not parted on very amicable terms in Europe owing to their differences in aesthetic, ideological, and business matters. Not surprisingly, the composer was fairly hostile to Brecht's suggestions, and he was justifiably suspicious of his former collaborator's actual motives and how the project might affect his own future success in American theater. Brecht commented on Weill's ''nasty'' answer that was ''full of attacks on me and in praise of broadway [sic]'' in a letter to Adorno of April 1942 (*Journals* 222). Despite their animosity, Weill sent Brecht money anonymously to help him out (Baxandall 85, n. 23).

Although the Brecht/Weill partnership gradually drifted apart, there were several attempts, especially on the part of Brecht, to resume their collaboration. After all, this collaboration was based on, as Lenya observed, ''the most enormous respect'' the two men had ''for each other's opinion''—even if ''the relationship never deepened into a strong friendship (as it did between Kurt and Georg Kaiser and later between Kurt and Maxwell Anderson)'' (Lenya ix). Brecht also realized how important Weill could be for him in getting a play staged on Broadway, and he succeeded in obtaining an agreement from Weill to collaborate on an adaptation of the novel *The Good Soldier Švejk* by Jaroslav Hašek. In a letter to his friend Ferdinand Reyher, Brecht wrote that ''with [Weill's] name it will be easier to get a production'' (quoted in Lyon 199)—a hope that remained unfulfilled.

Because of his close ties with Brecht, Weill is accused of the same fundamental cynicism often associated with the playwright. Drew warns against such a perception: ''To believe this is to miss the whole point of his [Weill's] art, which is its humanity.'' Such humanity can be seen in many of the works Weill wrote for the American stage, including his opera *Street Scene*, based on Elmer Rice's 1929 drama, which treats the lives of working-class Americans in a New York tenement; and in his last play, *Lost in the Stars*, based on Alan Paton's novel *Cry, the Beloved Country*, which deals with the struggles of blacks and whites in South Africa and the dream of brotherhood among the races. In 1948 he completed *Down in the Valley*, written for performance by music and drama students on the college or university level.[7]

Brecht respected Weill for his talent and for his integrity. His final tribute to his collaborator was to paste the composer's obituary from *Time* magazine into his *Journals* as the last entry of 1950 (432).

THE BRECHT-WEILL LEGACY

No work has been more closely identified with Brecht in the United States than his early success *The Threepenny Opera* (1928), with music by Kurt Weill. American audiences have seen countless productions of this play with music, including the unsuccessful 1931 adaptation and the justly famous 1954 Off-Broadway version completed by Marc Blitzstein that ran for 2,611 performances. Blitzstein had met the playwright in New York in 1935 and discussed a song "Nickle under the Foot" with him. Brecht urged the writer to turn it into an evening's entertainment, and Blitzstein wrote *The Cradle Will Rock* in response. In late 1949 Blitzstein approached Weill with his own translation of the song "Pirate Jenny" from *The Threepenny Opera* that so impressed the composer and conductor Maurice Abravanel that he encouraged the young American to translate and adapt the entire *The Threepenny Opera* for Broadway (Sanders 400).

The 1954 Off-Broadway staging that used the Blitzstein translation was so popular that it has overshadowed other translations of the work. Mention should also be made of the 1976 Joseph Papp production of the Manheim/Willett translation (*CP* 2: 145–226) at Lincoln Center, and the 1989 disastrous Broadway revival with Sting as Macheath.

Weill's success on Broadway was instrumental in helping Brecht reach a wide circle of American theatrical talents. The popularity of the Lenya recordings of the Weill-Brecht songs from *Mahagonny*, *The Threepenny Opera*, and *Happy End* led to the creation of the deliberately imitative "Brecht-Weill" musical, *Cabaret* (1966), starring Lotte Lenya. Composer John Kander, lyricist Fred Ebb, and book author Joseph Stein concocted this fairly standard Broadway musical based loosely on Christopher Isherwood's *Berlin Stories* and John Van Druten's play *I Am a Camera*. Director Harold Prince added the concept of two levels of reality coexisting side by side: the real world of Nazi Germany and the artificial world of the cabaret with a master of ceremonies commenting on the action.

Prince, who has directed many operatic productions in the United States and in Europe, also directed the Andrew Lloyd Webber musical *Evita* (1979). Like Weill, Prince has consciously attempted to close the gap between the Broadway musical and the operatic stage. The composer's use of the chorus as a communal voice, as in *Lost in the Stars*, or as a witness to the action on stage while participating in the proceedings, as in *Street Scene*, prefigures a major trademark of Hal Prince musicals. But Prince has consistently denied any influence of Brecht or his collaborators: "I was flattered when the widow of Erwin Piscator said *Evita* was close in spirit to her husband's work, but in fact Russian theatre has influenced me far more than Brecht's tradition." He added an unflattering personal commentary: "I've been bored to death by Brecht-inspired productions" (quoted in Hirsch 15).

Prince's name has been most closely connected with that of Broadway musical composer Stephen Sondheim, including the latter's *Company* (1970), *Pacific Overtures* (1976), and *Sweeney Todd* (1979), all directed by Prince. While Sondheim has shown the influence of Brecht in many of his works, including the recent *Assassins* (1990), he is as reluctant as Prince to acknowledge any artistic debt to the controversial playwright: "I hate Brecht—all of Brecht. . . . You see, I find Brecht humorless and his points so obvious in the text itself that the songs have no surprise or wit for me" (quoted in Zadan 115). In a recent interview, Sondheim commented: "Brecht and Weill worked in a tradition of *Lehrstück*; my background is Broadway, and the two are very different. I like *Threepenny Opera* but not really anything else. Actually I prefer Weill's American to his European work" (quoted in Hirsch 15).

Choreographer Jerome Robbins, who "has a fascination with Brecht," staged the unsuccessful 1963 Broadway production of *Mother Courage and Her Children*. Robbins asked Sondheim to collaborate with Leonard Bernstein and him on an adaptation of *The Exception and the Rule*; Sondheim "put aside [his] prejudice against Brecht" (quoted in Zadan 115), but the project was never completed.

When composing his score for the musical *Company*, Sondheim needed to find a new form for the songs and used Brecht as his model: "All the songs had to be used, I'm sorry to say, in a Brechtian way as comment and counterpoint." The composer's justification was: "We tried to use the form, however, and improve on it" (quoted in Zadan 1989, 129). Certainly the two most Brechtian works of Sondheim's are *Pacific Overtures*, which takes a highly critical and extremely unemotional look at the American colonization of Japan in the nineteenth century, and *Sweeney Todd*, which places the murderous deeds of the title figure within the framework of the Industrial Revolution that ultimately motivates his criminal behavior. For example, in his opening aria, the title character defines the order of the world as utterly bleak and in terms he seems to have borrowed from Brecht.

When asked what she thought of this highly original musical, Lenya chuckled, "I never thought I'd live to see it. Brecht meets Max Reinhardt!" (x). Lenya was correct in seeing both the elements of Brechtian agit-prop social criticism, as well as the marvelous configurations of masses of people moving on stage, always maintaining dramatic focus in the manner of Reinhardt.

Sondheim's distaste for Brecht never deterred the composer from emulating this master theater practitioner. His closest collaborator, director Prince, was instrumental in the choice of styles and material. As Hirsch points out in his study of the director:

Evolving organically out of Marxist viewpoint, the Brecht-Weill of musical theater will always be temperamentally as well as politically at odds with the Broadway musical.

Nonetheless their work supplies an enticing model whose influence has filtered into the American mainstream primarily through the collaboration between Prince and Sondheim, even though neither the director nor his composer will admit any specific impact. Prince claims: "Unlike Brecht, my purpose is not to eliminate emotional response—it isn't by design that a show of mine is cold." (15)

Hirsch further argues: "It is my belief that both Prince and Sondheim have instincts in their approach to the musical theater that echo Brecht and Weill. Pure Brechtians, Marxist propagandists, they certainly are not; but in the kinds of statements they want the musical to make, and in the tone in which they have expressed their themes they have incorporated elements of the epic theater into a form that would seem to be its opposite number, the Broadway musical" (17).

HANNS EISLER

Of major importance in Brecht's theatrical career following Weill was his collaboration with composer Hanns Eisler (see Nadar). Like Weill, Eisler found it easy to participate in the American musical scene. Baxandall reports: "Arriving in New York in early 1935, Eisler had an enormous personal success. An interviewer for the *Daily Worker* found him a 'dynamic, powerfully expressive person inspiring confidence and trust.' Brecht was, on the contrary, disliked in New York" (70).

The presence of Eisler, and particularly of Brecht, at the rehearsals of *The Mother* was unhelpful. In fact, shortly before the premiere both men were finally forbidden to enter the theater on the grounds that they had disrupted the rehearsals too frequently (Eisler, *Brecht* 102–03).[8] Although the production would close after thirty-six performances, "the music of *The Mother* turned up again, performed at Steinway Hall by The New Singers in a farewell concert for Eisler on February 1 [1936], with the composer and Brecht as honored guests . . . the audience was overflow, and a repeat concert was offered on February 7" (Baxandall 80–81).[9]

Brecht enjoyed little success in America during the six years of his stay. Eisler, on the other hand, had more commitments than he could handle. He was in demand throughout the country as a lecturer, composer, and instructor. He ended up in Los Angeles as a lecturer at the University of California (UCLA) and worked for the movie industry. He was nominated for the Academy Award for two of his many film scores: *Hangmen also Die* (1943), for which Brecht collaborated on the screenplay, and *None but the Lonely Heart* (1944). If Weill helped Brecht leave an indelible mark on the American musical theater, it was through Eisler who composed background music for films that Brecht was to exert a certain influence on the Hollywood movie industry.

Eisler received a relatively major musical project when, along with musicologist Adorno, he was awarded $10,000 by the prestigious Rockefeller Foundation to complete the first major theoretical study of the aesthetics of film music.

The commission prompted Eisler to ask Brecht to jot down some informal thoughts on the topic. Brecht responded with his 1942 essay "Über Filmmusik" (*Werke* 23: 10–20; On Film Music). Eisler worked on his study from 1942 to 1947, and he incorporated many of Brecht's ideas into *Composing for the Films* (1947), a work that has remained an important and controversial contribution. This seminal work had a profound impact on an entire generation of film musicians, including Alex North, Jerome Moross, Jerry Goldsmith, and Elmer Bernstein. As the initial study for Eisler's volume, Brecht's essay has lost none of its relevance in the concerns it voices and the aesthetic concepts it presents.

In addition to his theoretical work on film music and his songs for the workers' movement, Eisler's music for Joseph Losey's 1947 production of *Galileo* in Los Angeles and New York, starring Charles Laughton, is well remembered. The play was subsequently filmed in 1975 with (Chaim) Topol in the title role.

Unfortunately, Eisler's stay in America came to a rather ignoble end. In September 1947 he was called before the House on Unamerican Activities Committee. Earlier that month, his brother Gerhart had been branded the number one Communist agent in the country and had been convicted on several technicalities. The committee now turned to Eisler and questioned him about his association with his brother, with the party in general, and with Brecht, with whom he had collaborated on *The Measures Taken*. Eisler's case created a minor national scandal when the hearing revealed that Eleanor Roosevelt had had something to do with the composer's acquisition of a visa (Bentley, "Insert"). Eisler was handed a deportation order, and the papers branded him the "Karl Marx of Music." A formal protest registered on his behalf by many celebrities, including Thomas Mann, Albert Einstein, Aaron Copland, Charlie Chaplin, Jean Cocteau, and Henri Matisse, was fruitless (Eisler, *Brecht* 307). Eisler left the United States in 1947, returned to Vienna and in 1950 joined Brecht in Berlin where he remained until the end of his life in 1962. Eisler was the most highly regarded composer in the German Democratic Republic, and the Music Academy in East Berlin bore his name until reunification.

PAUL DESSAU

Undoubtedly the composer who exerted the least influence on American music was Brecht's creative associate Paul Dessau. Coming to California in 1943, Dessau was able to find work in the Universal and Warner Brothers' studios as an orchestrator and arranger, with occasional minor assignments as a composer for such inferior films as *House of Frankenstein*. Consequently, Dessau never achieved the prominent status or reputation of Eisler in the movie industry. The most important of Dessau's compositions for Brecht include his incidental music and songs for *Mother Courage*, which he completed in 1946. He revised the music for productions at the Berliner Ensemble in 1949 and 1951; it was also used in the film version made by the East German state studio DEFA in 1961.

American audiences would hear his score in its entirety in the 1963 Broadway production of *Mother Courage* directed by choreographer Jerome Robbins.[10]

Dessau's most controversial collaboration with Brecht occurred with the opera *The Trial of Lucullus*; American composer Roger Sessions set to music a translation by H. R. Hays for a production by the University of California in Los Angeles on 18 April 1947. The Dessau/Brecht version was completed in 1950. It drew a great deal of criticism from the ministry of education of the GDR and underwent extensive alterations in its transformation from a radio play to its final form in 1951. The critical reception was disappointing, and after a few performances it was taken off the program. It was not until after Brecht's death that the opera was again produced, this time with great success. After running for a full season in Berlin and being presented at the Paris Festival in 1958, it was subsequently recorded and most recently reissued on compact disc. Not only in its original form as a radio play with music, but also in its final form as an opera, *Lucullus* represented the playwright's harkening back to certain principles of didacticism that had never lost their prominence in his drama. While Dessau, unlike Weill and Eisler, was never listed by Brecht as a collaborator and was never consulted during the planning stages of any of Brecht's dramatic works, his role in helping reshape and determine the final form of *Mother Courage* and *Lucullus* in the definitive Berlin productions should not be underestimated.

BRECHT'S MUSIC THEORY

Brecht was always extremely receptive to contacts with musicians and composers because his interest in music was deep-seated, extending back to early childhood. As a young man, Brecht performed his own works, accompanying himself on a guitar. In his early songs, Brecht seemed to create a deliberately vulgar and primitive style in order to give his music a pronounced strident sound and to make it more irritating and obnoxious. In part, this was Brecht's attempt to remove the element of aesthetic enjoyment from his art in order to make it appeal directly to the intellect and avoid emotional involvement, something Eisler called "Brecht's striving for reason, even in music" ("Brecht" 440–41).[11]

Brecht had little regard for any of the established composers in the pantheon of music, particularly Bach, Beethoven, or Brahms. He had no use for so-called absolute music. Brecht demanded that music, like literature, philosophy, and the sciences, express ideas and thereby take a stance toward society. By commenting on the social order of the world, music could actively participate in changing the existing society.

To be sure, Brecht regarded music, as he did every art form, from the perspective of a playwright and a poet. Nevertheless, his ideal remained the coordination of music with a text and/or dramatic situation. In this, he sought to overcome the inherent limitations and weaknesses of both the spoken word and music and to utilize their respective strengths as effectively as possible. Individually, each medium has a different and limited means of expression; when joined together they can augment each other's ability to take a stance on a subject through comment, evaluation, approval, or criticism. In this manner, music and the spoken word permit the intent or message of the work as a whole to be grasped more readily by the spectator or reader. Brecht carefully elaborated his ideas on this topic in a series of writings. Although Brecht's theoretical essays and writings are among his most widely read as well as translated publications, they alone are scarcely sufficient for anyone interested in gaining a deeper understanding of the playwright's stagecraft. The more one reads of Brecht, the more obvious it becomes that all of his ideas were worked out in practice as well as in theory. Moreover, we never lose sight of which of these two processes came first, as John Willett points out: "None of the main features of [Brecht's] work seems to be traceable back to purely theoretical considerations: again and again he appears to be intellectualizing a choice of methods or of models which had originally been made on half conscious aesthetic grounds" (*Brecht* 186).

Brecht may have rarely mentioned theory in productions at his Berliner Ensemble, but his theoretical writings fill seven volumes in *GW*. While we should not overestimate their importance, neither can we ignore their significance in documenting what Brecht attempted to accomplish in his various dramatic works.

Brecht first began to postulate his theories on the theater shortly after he moved to Berlin in 1924. By 1927, he was calling for the establishment of an epic theater, a term he used, according to Willett, "as the antithesis of 'dramatic' theatre" (*Brecht* 168). As such, his concept was clearly influenced by Erwin Piscator's "epic theater" with its use of music, stage machinery, film, transparencies, and extensive projections.[12] Brecht was almost instinctively drawn to the opera as the first stage of his epic theater. Attracted by its epic structure, the writer had little use for traditional opera, which Brecht termed "culinary," that is, designed to appeal to the palate of the dilettante theater-goer and to entertain. He was particularly repelled by what he perceived as the spectators' willing suspension of their disbelief and by their acceptance of the irrationality of musical theater. It was as if the audience had checked their minds along with their coats when entering the theater (*Theatre* 39). Brecht reasoned that if the spectators could be entertained and at the same time be provoked to thought, discussion, or criticism, rather than become a passive, emotionally responsive mass, they might become intellectually alive and consider how the problems depicted on the stage related to the society in which they lived.

Consequently, *The Threepenny Opera*, the first of the playwright's attempts to reform the opera, is intended as the prototype of a new genre, an amalgam of opera and drama. The next stage of Brecht's progressive experiments, was *Mahagonny*, an "epic opera" that does not abandon all elements of traditional opera but utilizes them for a new purpose. Brecht's attempts to reform the opera ended with *Mahagonny*. With his *Lehrstücke*, Brecht progressed one logical step beyond "epic opera." Brecht wanted to provoke the spectator who is conditioned to respond passively to a dramatic or musical work. To this end, he manipulated the performers so that they were forced to make the right decision when confronted with choices. Brecht also demanded that the participants discuss the piece before performing it. In the actual performance, the chorus presents a running commentary on the action, while participating in it in a limited way. However, in both *The Mother* and *The Exception and the Rule*, the last of the *Lehrstücke* written before he was forced to leave Berlin, Brecht intended to employ professional actors, and the chorus was relegated to a minor role. Once again, the playwright stressed the importance of the audience's participation and critical reaction. Brecht next turned to a form of epic drama that deals more realistically with human character, including *The Life of Galileo* (1937–1939) and *Mother Courage* (1938–1939). In theory, he reaffirmed the structure and principles set up for *The Threepenny Opera*, which in addition to having been a stage in the reformation of the opera, now reveals itself as the initial phase in his reformation of the drama and a stepping stone to further developments in the theater.

With his very first plays, from *Baal* (1918) through *A Man's a Man* (1924–1926)—all of which employ music in much the same manner as does traditional drama—Brecht had nevertheless taken steps toward what he would call epic theater, long before his attempts to reform the opera. Sensing in music an art form that could supplement what he felt was inherently lacking in theater, Brecht had been drawn to the operatic form on the basis of mechanics; subsequently he was drawn to the didactic cantata and oratorio as the optimal means of creating drama with an epic structure. Hence, music assumed a far more important role in the period from 1927–1933 than did the other elements of the production. From 1933 on, music again played a limited role and became an equal partner to the other theatrical arts as Brecht discovered the means to create epic drama with realistic, complex characters who must resolve distinct moral or social problems. But at none of these stages in his development did the playwright simply content himself with complete conformity in the use of music.

Just as Brecht rejected opera in its traditional form, he also rejected the traditional use of music for the stage. As he saw it, music fulfilled several functions in most dramas: it acted as a background by setting certain moods, and it was naturalistically motivated by the action: for example, a drinking song was called for in a tavern, a march was necessary for the entrance of soldiers, and a hymn was required in church. The most strikingly innovative feature of *The Threepenny Opera* was its clear separation of the songs from the dramatic action—the "separation of the elements" (*GW* 15: 473). While it was (and is) customary for a performer in operetta or musical comedy to burst suddenly into song when the spoken word is not adequate for the situation, Brecht stressed that this was not the case in *The Threepenny Opera*. He commented that the songs were not simply the culmination of a lyrical progression that began with an elevated monologue; there were also to be clear breaks or splits among the three levels of "normal speech, elevated speech and singing" (*GW* 17: 996). To separate the musical numbers from the dramatic action, Brecht insisted on projecting song titles onto a screen, on a change of stage lighting, on the use of emblems, and on the actor's changing his or her stance before beginning the song. This principle of separating music and text, which Brecht regarded as the most important innovation in the play, and which he set down on paper after the successful 1928 production, was to characterize all of his dramatic works.

The audience is "musically addressed" by songs (*Theatre* 203) that act as commentaries on the dramatic situation or on the characters. Through the songs, the singing character can communicate insights of which he or she, as a speaking character, is not capable. Because the dramatic character steps back into the action of the play after completing the song, he or she learns little or nothing from it. But it was not Brecht's purpose to make his characters understand themselves or their situations. On the contrary, he consistently demanded that the audience should realize these characters and situations are alterable. Since the song, as no other musical form, is particularly suited to act as a direct, straightforward commentary on characters and action or to serve as a narration, it was to remain Brecht's consistently favorite use of music in his dramatic works.

Brecht was also interested in the function of instrumental music within the drama as well as in motion pictures. At Eisler's behest he wrote the aforementioned essay on film music, a documentation of his ideas on dramatic music and melodrama. Brecht noted that composers in Hollywood could learn a great deal from his own experiments in musical theater, particularly from the "separation of the elements" that allowed music to make an important contribution to the overall quality and effectiveness of the entire work. Brecht spent most of his time in California discussing the possibilities that existed for music in his own epic theater.

It was not until after the end of World War II that Brecht published a reconsideration of his principles, "A Short Organum for the Theatre." For the most part, this essay reiterates many of the playwright's former principles, but it is significant that the term "epic theater" is conspicuously absent. In his last theoretical notes, "Dialectics in the Theatre" (*Theatre* 281–82) Brecht completely abandons the label on the grounds that it is inadequate. Yet he still maintained the necessity for audience detachment. His views on the role of music, however, remained consistent with his previous essays and statements. In notes of April 1956, he once again reduced the components of theater to three: the text, the music, and the set and costume design. Rather than drama incorporating elements of opera, or opera assuming properties of drama, Brecht stressed that there is to be an independence and separation of the arts within what he labels a "collective of independent arts" (*GW* 17: 1210).

VERFREMDUNG AND *VERFREMDUNGSEFFEKT*

If the main purpose of Brecht's theater was to stimulate and provoke a critical reaction on the part of the spectator, the most important device that facilitated this was what Brecht called the *Verfremdungseffekt*, or *V-Effekt*. Translated variously as "alienation" or "estrangement," Brecht suggests that it is a device that places his dramatic situations and characters in a new and unusual light or context and is designed to stimulate the critical and evaluative powers of the spectator.[13] *Verfremdung* could be created through dramatic content and structure, acting and directing techniques, set and costume design, language and music. In essence, what attracted Brecht to music in his earliest dramas was its ability to detach or estrange a text, character, or situation. Brecht often chose well-known melodies with certain associations for an audience.[14] When he collaborated with composers to create new music for his works, what generally resulted was written in antithesis or in contrast to the text or the situation. Numerous critics have been quick to label this a typically Brechtian device. Bentley notes that "just as Brecht inserts poems into his dialogue to alienate certain emotions, so he inserts music." Bentley characterizes this technique by contrasting it with standard theatrical practice: "Orthodox theatrical music duplicates the text. It is stormy in stormy scenes, quiet in quiet scenes. It adds A to A. In a Brecht play, the music is supposed to add B to A. Thus A is alienated and the texture of the work is enriched" (Bentley, "Stagecraft" 66). Reinhold Grimm comments: "Music, image and word mutually estrange one another; within a song, text and music function by contrast" (*Struktur* 72). And Esslin explains the function of this technique: "Brecht conceived of the use of music—as of other signifying systems of drama—as antithetic, in a dialectical relationship to each other. The tune [should] provide an ironic commentary on the words rather than 'expressing' their meaning" (Esslin, *Drama* 89).

These remarks may well be misleading in that we might be tempted to take a rather simplistic view of a complex problem. There may well be a contrasting relationship between text and music in Brecht's works that creates a *V-Effekt*, but it would be incorrect to generalize that music and text are diametrically opposed to one another. In addition to contrasting with a situation, music has the ability to reveal different aspects of that situation. This type of interaction must be understood as a vital part of Brecht's concept of *Verfremdung*. It strives not merely for a contrast that exists for its own sake, but for completeness through which the spectator gains additional information and arrives at critical judgments. Because of the ambiguous nature of musical forms and the different associations certain types of music may give rise to in different individuals, music is only one of several elements that contribute to the process of *Verfremdung* in the works of Brecht.[15]

NOTES

1. Brecht never published the text to *Happy End*, and Weill published only the three songs from the score. When Lotte Lenya recorded these songs in 1956, interest was generated for the lost work. An actor's copy was found and copyrighted by Felix Bloch Erben in Berlin in 1958. Universal Edition published the entire score from the composer's

manuscript. Much revised, the play was staged in Munich in February 1958; it has since received much exposure, particularly on Broadway in 1976–1977 in the adaptation by Michael Feingold.

2. On 21 November 1993 Brecht's "opera without music" *Prärie* (Prairie) but with a score by Austrian composer Wolfgang Floray was premiered in Rostock. Brecht based his 1919 work on a novella by Norwegian writer Knut Hamsun. This forty-five minute "opera" may well be the very last work by Brecht to be premiered.

3. Hindemith wrote the original setting for *The Flight over the Ocean* and *The Baden-Baden Cantata*; von Einem set the "Song of the Hours" from *Mother Courage* (*CP* 5: 164–65), on which Parmet began composition. Burkhard supplied a score for the Swiss premiere of this play. Wagner-Regeny wrote the music for *Trumpets and Drums*, Meisel the original score for *A Man's a Man*, and Sessions the first setting of the opera *Lucullus*. Shostakovich composed a musical setting for Brecht's late poem "Das Lied von den Flüssen" (*Werke* 15: 277–78; The Song of the Streams) in Joris Ivens's film of the same name.

4. With regard to Rosenberg, see *Journals* entry of 7 November 1939 (37–38); with regard to Stravinsky, see Willett (*Brecht* 139, n.). See also Hennenberg (492, n. 74). With regard to Orff, see *Letters* (711–12).

5. All of these recordings have been reissued on compact disc and are currently available.

6. See also Karl-Heinz Schoeps, "Brecht's *Lehrstücke*: A Laboratory for Epic and Dialectic Theater," in this volume.

7. The opera was first performed on the NBC radio network with a cast from the University of Michigan. Moreover, it became the first opera to be telecast on the popular NBC Opera Theatre in 1950. In composing for amateur performers and for the media, Weill was continuing a tradition he had begun with Brecht.

8. This episode was also related during an intermission interview on PBS of the Metropolitan Opera's broadcast of *Rise and Fall of the City of Mahagonny* in December 1979.

9. Incidentally, the two rehearsal pianists for the Theatre Union's production of *The Mother* were Jerome Moross and Alex North, two American composers who would later gain considerable prominence in Hollywood.

10. The first production in the United States was by the Actors' Workshop in San Francisco in 1956. The Jerome Robbins production, with Anne Bancroft in the lead role, was a prestigious failure. While the play closed after a mere fifty-two performances, it was selected for inclusion in *The Best Plays of 1962–1963* (Guernsey). Other productions of note include those of the Acting Company of the Juilliard School in New York City (1978), directed by Alan Schneider with Mary Lou Rosato as the title character; and the Boston Shakespeare Company (1984), with Linda Hunt as Mother Courage. All productions used the Dessau score and songs.

11. Brecht created a new name for this kind of music: *misuk* (Eisler, "Brecht" 440–41).

12. Innes (189–200) devotes an entire section to Brecht's artistic debt to Piscator. Most critics mention the influence of Piscator's activity on Brecht's formative years, but they tend to minimize his importance in the playwright's overall development. Innes (198) points out that Piscator's influence on Brecht's artistic development can be seen throughout the latter's entire career. In a March 1947 letter to Piscator, Brecht acknowledged his debt: "Let me go on record as saying that of all the people who have been

active in the theatre in the last twenty years, no one has been as close to me as you" (*Letters* 421).

13. See Reinhold Grimm, "Alienation in Context: On the Theory and Practice of Brechtian Theater," in this volume.

14. Brecht used well-known musical material to contrast with the action on the stage in *Drums in the Night* and *In the Jungle of Cities*. In the latter play, for example, while a nickelodeon plays Gounod's "Ave Maria," Garga talks to his sister Marie. Since the text of Gounod's work refers to Elizabeth's greeting to Mary, "Blessed be the fruit of thy womb," the immediate association is ironic, since Marie is pregnant out of wedlock. In the former play, Gounod's hymn is played on a phonograph while Kragler talks to his fiancée, who attempts to explain to him how she has become pregnant during his absence.

15. A good example of this ambiguity may be apparent in the following anecdote. When Brecht and Eisler became involved in a new Vienna production of *The Mother* in September 1953, Eisler had difficulty in finding a trumpeter for the orchestra. He abruptly gave up the search and told Brecht he was relieved, since now the jazz elements in his score would be subdued. Eisler had rejected jazz after 1933, and he wanted no part of it—owing partially to its association with American culture. But Brecht enjoyed this musical style that had different, highly positive associations for him. Without the jazz elements Brecht reasoned, "the music becomes a lament rather than an accusation" (*Journals* 456).

WORKS CITED (SEE ALSO REFERENCE GUIDE TO WORKS CITED IN ABBREVIATED FORM)

Aufricht, Ernst Josef. *Erzähle, damit du dein Recht erweist*. Munich: Deutscher Taschenbuch Verlag, 1969.

Barnes, Clive. "A Musical Voyage with Kurt Weill." *New York Times* (2 October 1972): 43.

Baxandall, Lee. "Brecht in America, 1935." *Drama Review* 12.1 (1967): 69–87. Rpt. in Munk, *Brecht* 33–60.

Bentley, Eric. "Insert Notes to *Brecht before the Un-American Activities Committee*." Folkways Recording FD 5531.

———. "The Stagecraft of Bertolt Brecht." 1953. In *Commentaries* 56–71.

Drew, David. "Liner Notes to *Happy End*." Columbia Recording OS–5630.

Eisler, Hanns. "Bertolt Brecht und die Musik." *Sinn und Form. 2. Sonderheft Bertolt Brecht*. Berlin: Rütten, 1957. 439–41.

Esslin, Martin. *The Field of Drama*. London: Methuen, 1987.

Ewen, Frederic. *Bertolt Brecht: His Life, His Art and His Times*. New York: Citadel, 1967.

Guernsey, Otis L., Jr. *The Best Plays of 1962–1963*. New York: Dodd, 1963.

Hennenberg, Fritz. *Dessau-Brecht: Musikalische Arbeiten*. Berlin: Henschelverlag, 1963.

Hirsch, Foster. *Harold Prince and the American Musical Theatre*. Cambridge: Cambridge University Press, 1989.

Innes, C.D. *Erwin Piscator's Political Theatre*. Cambridge: Cambridge University Press, 1972.

Lenya, Lotte. "That Was a Time." In *The Threepenny Opera*, by Bertolt Brecht.

Translated by Eric Bentley and Desmond I. Vesey. New York: Grove, 1964. v–xiv.

Lyon, James K. "Brecht's American Cicerone." *Brecht heute/Brecht Today: Brecht Yearbook* 2 (1972): 187–208.

Nadar, Thomas R. "Brecht's and Eisler's Impact on Film Music in America." *Brecht Unbound.* Edited by James K. Lyon and Hans-Peter Breuer. Newark: University of Delaware Press, 1995. 135–46.

Sondheim, Stephen, and Hugh Wheeler. *Sweeney Todd: The Demon Barber of Fleet Street.* New York: Dodd, 1979.

Sanders, Ronald. *The Days Grow Short: The Life and Music of Kurt Weill.* New York: Holt, 1980.

Steinberg, Michael. "Caldwell's Mahagonny." *High Fidelity Magazine* 23 (August 1973): 136–44.

Zadan, Craig. *Sondheim & Company.* 2nd ed. New York: Harper, 1989.

PART IV

MARXISM AND FEMINISM

12

Brecht's Marxist Aesthetic

DOUGLAS KELLNER

Brecht's relationship to Marxism is extremely important and highly complex. From the 1920s until his death in 1956, Brecht identified himself as a Marxist; when he returned to Germany after World War II, he chose the German Democratic Republic (GDR). There, his actress wife Helene Weigel and he formed their own theater troupe, the famed Berliner Ensemble, and were eventually given a state theater to run. Yet Brecht's relationship to orthodox Marxist officials and doctrine was often conflictual, and his own work and life were highly idiosyncratic. Possessing a strongly antibourgeois disposition even in his youth, the young Brecht also initially rejected Bolshevism. He experienced the German revolution of 1918 with some ambivalence and dedicated himself to literary and not political activity during the turbulent early years of the Weimar Republic. He recorded in his *Diaries*, for example, a negative response to a talk he heard on 1920 on the Soviet Union; he was repelled by the concept of socialist order that he had heard discussed. He indicated a negative impression of Bolshevism and concluded his entry by noting that he'd rather have a new car than socialism! (Diaries 45).

Yet from the beginning of his literary career, Brecht was an enemy of the established bourgeois society. He composed a strongly antibourgeois play, *Baal* (1918–1919), which had a complex relation to expressionism (Kellner, "Literature"), and in 1919 he wrote *Drums in the Night*, a play that dealt with the disillusionment after World War I and the German revolution. The returning soldier in the play, Kragler, turned his back on the revolution after the war in favor of going to bed with his girlfriend.

While in Berlin in the mid-1920s, Brecht began to show an interest in Marxism. He associated with a wide circle of distinguished leftist intellectuals and artists, and he became acquainted with Marxism through discussions with friends and collaborators such as Lion Feuchtwanger, Fritz Sternberg, John Heartfield, Wieland Herzfelde, Alfred Döblin, Hanns Eisler, and Erwin Piscator. As Brecht tells it, he needed information about economics for a play planned with Piscator for the 1926–1927 season about the Chicago grain market. The unfinished play, "Weizen" (Wheat), required knowledge about the sale and distribution of wheat. Brecht said that although he spoke extensively with grain brokers, they were not adequately able to explain the workings of the wheat market and that the grain market remained incomprehensible in standard economic and business discourse.

Although the planned drama remained fragmentary—it was later renamed "Joe Fleischhacker"—Brecht entered Marxist study groups at this time, including one run by Marxist heretic Karl Korsch. The man whom he later referred to as "my Marxist teacher" was one of the first Marxist intellectuals to be thrown out of the Communist party for "deviationism." Korsch also developed a strong early critique of Leninism and then Stalinism. In this article, I argue that Brecht's specific version of Marxism was highly influenced by his teacher Korsch and that indeed Korsch's version of Marxism shaped Brecht's aesthetic theory and practice. I will demonstrate that certain Marxist ideas were central not only to Brecht's world view but also to his very concept of political art. Accordingly, emphasis will be put on the ways that his political aesthetics, derived from Marxian ideas, helped shape the very form of his theater and writing. But first, I indicate how Brecht appropriated his concept of Marxism and what version of Marx's ideas so deeply influenced him.

KORSCH AND BRECHT

In the voluminous literature on Brecht, the impact on Brecht's work of the version of materialist dialectic advocated by Korsch has not been adequately clarified.[1] Not only did Korsch strongly influence Brecht's conception of Marxian dialectics; the Marxian ideas that became most fruitful for Brecht's aesthetic practice were precisely those shared by Brecht and Korsch in their conception of materialist dialectics and revolutionary practice. Brecht used the Korschian version of the Marxian dialectic in both his aesthetic theory and practice, in ways that are central—rather than incidental, as some critics have claimed—to his work.[2]

As noted, in the 1920s Brecht began serious study of Marxism while attempting to write a play on the grain market and shortly before working on *Saint Joan of the Stockyards*. During the late 1920s, Brecht became increasingly interested in both the Marxian theory of society and the dialectical method of analyzing society and history. He later wrote: "when I read Marx's *Kapital*, I understood my plays," (*GW* 20: 46) and he described Marx as "the only spectator for my plays" (*GW* 15: 129).

To help him in his study of Marxism, Brecht sought the acquaintance of people who could teach him its fundamental ideas and method. At the time, Korsch was one of the leading Marxist scholars in Germany and was also one of the most active militants in the Communist movement.[3] After the November revolution of 1918 and Germany's defeat in World War I, the Kaiser fled Germany, and the Social Democratic party was asked to form a government. They set up "socialization commissions" to study the socialization of industry, and Korsch served on such a commission that was charged with socializing the coal industry. But the Social Democrats soon lost power and nothing came of this work.

Fed up with the ineffective reformism of the Social Democrats, Korsch joined the Independent Socialist party (USPD) in 1919 and then the Communist party (KPD) in 1920. Korsch served as justice minister in a short-lived left coalition in Thuringia in 1923, became editor of the Communist journal *Internationale*, was on the Central Committee of the German Communist party, and represented the Communists in the Reichstag.

In 1926 Korsch was one of the first victims of Stalinism and was expelled from the movement to which he was deeply committed and which he had loyally served. Thereafter he moved into the forefront of the Left opposition and developed one of the sharpest critiques of the Stalinization of the Soviet Union, the Comintern, and the German Communist party. He worked with a variety of left oppositional groups and taught courses on Marxism at the Karl Marx School and in small study groups in Berlin. Brecht joined these courses and Korsch's study group and solidified a lifelong friendship with Korsch.

From the beginning of his involvement with the Communist movement in the early twenties, Korsch saw the Marxian dialectic as the theoretical core of Marxism. He characterized the Marxian dialectic by the principles of historical specification, critique, and revolutionary practice. The principle of historical specification articulates Marx's practice of comprehending all things social in terms of a definite historical epoch, of conceptualizing every society and phenomenon as historically specific as opposed to engaging in universalizing discourse and theory.

For Korsch, Marx's achievement was his analysis of historically distinct and specific features of capitalism and bourgeois society as well as his development of a method that enabled one to analyze distinct social formations critically and to transform them radically. Bourgeois political economy and theory, on the other hand, dealt with the forms of bourgeois society as if they were universal, eternal, and unchanging relationships rather than historical forms of a system that was full of contradictions and subject to radical transformation. According to Korsch, problems of economy, politics, and culture cannot be solved through a general abstract description of "economics as such," but they require "a detailed description of the definite relations which exist between definite economic phenomena on a definite historical level of development and definite phenomena which appear simultaneously or subsequently in every other field of political, juristic, and intellectual development" (Korsch, *Marx* 24).

For Korsch, the Marxian dialectic is a critical dialectic that aims at the critique and transformation of the existing bourgeois order (Korsch, "Marxist" 64–65). The Marxian dialectic sees reality as a process of continual change and is interested in those contradictions and antagonisms that make radical transformation possible. Above all, Marxian dialectic integrates critical theory with revolutionary practice as a prerequisite of the emancipation of the working class and the construction of socialism.

Korsch wrote his book *Karl Marx*, which summarizes his description of the basic principles of Marxism, when he was a guest of the Brecht family in exile in Denmark during 1935–1936. He and Brecht had daily discussions of the basic ideas of Marxism. They tended to agree on the basic principles, although they differed widely on their application. Korsch was highly critical of Leninism and the construction of socialism in the Soviet Union, while Brecht was more sympathetic. For Korsch and Brecht, Marxism provided "a new science of bourgeois society." It articulated the critical perceptions of the working class and attacked the views of the ruling bourgeois class. As a force of opposition to bourgeois society and its principles, it is "not a positive but a critical science." It is also a "practical theory" that aims at the revolutionary transformation of bourgeois society by investigating those tendencies visible in the current development of society that could lead to its overthrow. Thus, "it is not only a theory of bourgeois society but, at the same time, a theory of the proletarian revolution" (Korsch, *Marx* 36).[4]

Brecht's theoretical writings show that he agreed with Korsch on these issues and that he developed his conception of Marxian dialectics while working in Korsch's seminars and discussion groups. In the following, I shall accordingly delineate the parameters of Brecht's Marxist aesthetics, show the influence of Korsch, and then finally indicate the ambivalence and tensions in Brecht's relationship to Marxism.

EPIC THEATER: MATERIALIST DIALECTICS, THE *V-EFFEKT*, AND THE POLITICS OF SEPARATION

From the perspective of Korsch's version of Marxism, one could argue that Brecht's epic theater was built on the Marxian principles of historical specification and critique that he learned from Korsch. In his epic theater, Brecht sought to illuminate the historically specific features of an environment in order to show how that environment influenced, shaped, and often battered and destroyed the characters. Unlike dramatists who focused on the universal elements of the human situation and fate, Brecht was interested in the attitudes and behaviors that people adopted toward each other in specific historical situations.

Thus, in *Mahagonny* and *The Threepenny Opera*, Brecht was interested in how people related to each other in capitalist society; in *Mother Courage*, how tradespeople related to soldiers and civilians during war in an emerging market society; in *The Measures Taken*, Brecht depicted revolutionary relationships in the struggle in China. He called this practice "historicization" and believed that one could best adopt a critical attitude toward one's society if the present social arrangements and institutions were viewed as historical, transitory, and subject to change (*Theatre* 140). Brecht intended that epic theater should show emotions, ideas, and behavior as products of, or responses to, specific social situations and not as the unfolding of the human essence.

The primary theatrical device of epic theater, the *Verfremdungseffekt*, was intended to "estrange" or "distance" the spectator and thus prevent empathy and identification with the situation and characters and allow the adoption of a critical attitude toward the actions in the play (*Theatre* 91–99, 136–47, 191–96). By preventing empathetic illusion or a mimesis of reality, epic theater would expose the workings of societal processes and human behavior, and it would show the audience how and why people behaved a certain way in their society. For example, the greed in *Mahagonny* and *The Threepenny Opera*, the suffering of Mother Courage, or the persecution of Galileo were to be understood as historically specific constituents of a social environment, and the theater was to induce the spectator to reflect on *why* these events happened, thus providing the audience with better historical understanding and knowledge.

As Walter Benjamin stressed, the response to epic theater should be: "Things can happen this way, but they can also happen a quite different way" (8). The strategy was to produce an experience of curiosity, astonishment, and shock that gave rise to questions such as: "Is that the way things are? What produced this? It's terrible! How can we change things?" Such a critical and questioning attitude was also fostered by a "montage of images" and a series of typical social tableaux that Brecht called "gests" (*Theater* 42, 86–87, 104, 134, 139, 198–205). He wanted his spectators to work through these examples, to participate in an active process of critical thought that would provide insights into the workings of society, and to see the need for an implementation of radical social change.

Brecht's epic theater broke with the "culinary theater" that provided the spectator with a pleasant experience or moral for easy digestion. He rejected theater that tried to produce an illusion of reality, claiming that illusionist theater tended to reproduce the dominant ideology and induce the spectators to identify bourgeois ideologies with reality. Brecht appropriated Korsch's theory that ideology was a material force that served as an important tool of domination; they both saw ideology as a deluding force from which people should be emancipated, and both attempted to produce works that would break people's identification with bourgeois ideologies (Korsch, *Marxism* 70–73; *GW* 18: 156–58).

Hence Brecht's practice of ideology demolition and "intervening thought" is an application of Korsch's principle of ideology critique and intellectual action.

Brecht saw his plays as providing an alternative to the dominant bourgeois theater that would force his spectators to think and to look at the world more critically. He saw this as a form of critical intervention with bourgeois culture that would undermine it from within. Thus both Korsch and Brecht viewed intellectual action, as well as aesthetic and political theory, as important moments in revolutionary practice—along with economic and political action.

In order to produce a revolutionary theater, Brecht argued for a ''separation of the elements'' (Weber), or what MacCabe calls a ''politics of separation'' (46). In the important *Mahagonny* notes, Brecht distinguished his separation of words, music, and scene from the Wagnerian *Gesamtkunstwerk* that fused the elements into one seductive and overpowering whole so that words, music, and scene worked together to engulf the spectator in the aesthetic totality (*Theatre* 33–42).[5] Conversely, in his separation of the elements, each aesthetic component retains its autonomy and ''comments'' on the others, often in contradiction, to provoke thought and insight.

For instance, in *The Threepenny Opera*, first Mac and Polly, and then Mac and Jenny, sing of love and romance. But the scene in the first song is a warehouse full of stolen goods and in the second a brothel, and the plot is one of deception and betrayal. These scenes might shock one into reflecting on the bourgeois ideology of love and the context of exploitation and betrayal that, in Brecht's view, marked bourgeois relationships. In Brecht's film *Kuhle Wampe*, romantic organ music is played as a young unemployed youth returns home after another futile search for work, evoking a poignant contrast between music and image. Contradiction between the elements, Brecht believed, would prevent identification and passive immersion and would provoke critical reflection. Each aesthetic medium retains its separate identity, and the product is an aggregate of independent arts in provocative tension.

Brecht's theory of aesthetic production is congruent with Korsch's model of the workers' councils as the authentic organs of socialist practice.[6] For just as Korsch urged a democratic, participatory activity of collective production in the spheres of labor and politics, Brecht urged the same sort of collective participation in his aesthetic production.[7] Brecht worked whenever possible in collectives in which a team of coworkers collaborated on production. He was especially attracted to radio and film as both exemplary of the highest development of the forces of production and as involving a new kind of collective work.[8] He saw his coworkers as important participants in the creative process, all of whom were encouraged to contribute to the production of the work of art. Such a revolution in the concept of creation, which rejected the notion of the creator as the solitary genius, was intended to radically alter aesthetic production—just as the workers' councils were intended to revolutionize industrial and political organization—and to provide an anticipatory model for socialist cultural organization.

Both Brecht and Korsch stressed the primary importance of production in social life and saw socialism as a constant revolutionizing of the forces and relations of production. Thus, in opposition to such critics as Georg Lukács, Brecht defended the need to innovate, experiment, and produce new aesthetic forms.[9] In his 1930 essay, "The Modern Theatre Is the Epic Theatre: Notes to the Opera *Rise and Fall of the City of Mahagonny*," Brecht argued that since the apparatus of aesthetic production was not yet controlled by artists and did not work for the general good, revolutionary artists should strive to change the apparatus. One had to develop "the means of pleasure into an object of instruction, and to convert certain institutions from places of entertainment into organs of mass communication" (*Theatre* 42). Brecht's art thus aimed at a *radical pedagogy* that would provide political education, cultivate political instincts, and provoke revolutionary political practice.

THE LEARNING PLAYS AS THE MODEL OF BRECHTIAN REVOLUTIONARY THEATER

Parallel to his work on epic theater, which he feared might be as "culinary as ever" (*Theatre* 41), Brecht developed a new type of theater that he called *Lehrstück* or "learning play."[10] Here, too, Korsch's influence is pronounced, for, as Eisler has noted, these plays resemble political seminars (Eisler 132). Brecht described them as "a collective political meeting" in which the audience is to participate actively (*GW* 18: 132). One sees in this model a rejection of the concept of the bureaucratic elite party in which the theorists and functionaries are to issue directives and control the activities of the masses. In these plays, correct doctrine and practice are to be discovered and carried out through a participatory, collective practice rather than through hierarchical manipulation and domination; that is, the learning plays were to function as Korsch had envisioned the operation of the workers' councils.

The learning plays were conceived by Brecht as the model for the "theater of the future." They exemplified the principles of his political aesthetics that would create a new type of participatory culture intended to promote revolution. He now saw his epic dramas by contrast as "compromise forms." *Life of Galileo* he considered "technically a great step backwards" (*Journals* 23) that was necessitated by conditions of production in exile and then by the conditions prevailing in the early years of the GDR.[11] The learning plays were thus Brecht's most explicitly political plays and his most radical attempt to politicize art.

In his "theory of pedagogy" for a socialist future, Brecht argued that mere pleasure was harmful for cultivating appropriate social views and behavior. Rather, a socialist theater should attempt to be useful to the state and socialize individuals into appropriate socialist values (*GW* 17: 1023). The learning plays were superior to epic theater, in Brecht's view, because they were more effective pedagogically, both for the artistic producers and for the audience, who were to participate in more direct and creative ways in the aesthetic experience. The actors and audience were to distinguish social from asocial behavior by imitating ways of behaving, thinking, talking, and relating. Within a single play, the actors frequently exchanged roles so that they could experience situations from different points of view.

For example, the learning play *The Measures Taken* confronts the audience with basic questions of revolution: violence, discipline, the structure of the party, the relation to the masses, revolutionary justice, and so on. In the plot, revolutionaries are forced to sacrifice a comrade to advance the aims of the revolution, and he submits to the discipline. There is no "correct doctrine" set forth; the actors are to present a scene and then discuss it with the audience. Indeed, I saw a performance of this play in the 1970s and it elicited strenuous debate among the members of the audience—Stalinists, Trotskyites, members of the New Left, liberals, and hardcore anti-Communists—about politics and morality.

Brecht wanted such an occasion to elicit both audience participation and to produce political education. Like Korsch's model of the workers' councils, there is to be no established hierarchy in the production of the learning plays; rather there is to be democratic participation in collective production. Moreover, the audience is encouraged to suggest actions that should have been taken and to also participate as members of the chorus. As with Korsch's model of democratic socialism, it is the people who are to establish the principles of revolutionary practice, strategy, and tactics, and not the party elite theoreticians or bureaucrats. Moreover, the task of the revolutionary artist here is not to make the party doctrine palatable for easy assimilation, but to encourage revolutionary thought and critique. This stance was clearly a threat to bureaucratic party functionaries, and they have consistently opposed Brecht's work (Kurella; Völker, *Brecht* 146–47).

The learning plays confronted the audience with situations such as sacrificing oneself for the good of the public as in *The Flight Over the Ocean* and *The Baden-Baden Cantata*, or putting oneself egotistically above all the others, as in the fragments "Fatzer" and "Der böse Baal der asoziale" (Evil, Asocial Baal). There would often be contradictory models of service or exploitation as in *The Exception and the Rule*, social consent or refusal as in *He Who Said Yes* and *He Who Said No*, and effective or ineffective revolutionary practice as in *The Measures Taken*. Brecht called this practice of involving the producers and audience the "grand pedagogy" that would turn actors/audience into statesmen and philosophers. Whereas the "lesser pedagogy" of the epic theater merely "democratized the theater in the prerevolutionary period," the "grand pedagogy" completely transforms the role of the producers and "abolishes the system of performer and spectator" (*Werke* 21: 396; *GW* 17: 1022–24).

Brecht intended his learning plays for schools, factories, or political groups; actors and audiences could read, improvise, and alter the plays at will as Brecht himself had done in working on the plays with many different groups. Thus, in Brecht's concept of emancipatory pedagogy and revolutionary theater, the learning plays are to engage a small audience in a process of learning.

Brecht saw his learning plays as a series of "sociological experiments," as "limbering-up exercises" or "mental gymnastics" for dialecticians.[12] He thought that the learning plays would radically revolutionize the theater apparatus. Thus they should not be thought of as minor works, as many critics have suggested; rather, they should be viewed as important examples of Brecht's concept of political theater. Brecht did in fact return to epic theater with the advent of fascism and conditions of exile, for the learning plays were viable only in contexts where there were political groups who could perform them and an audience who could relate them to revolutionary practice. In his last years in the GDR after World War II, he again turned his attention to the learning play and suggested that *The Measures Taken* should be considered as the model for a revolutionary theater of the future (Steinweg, *Lehrstück* 102–103).

ME-TI: MATERIALIST DIALECTICS IN LITERATURE AND BRECHT'S POLITICAL CONTRADICTIONS

During the exile period, Brecht was forced to develop new aesthetic forms, since it was often difficult to find theaters to produce his work. Thus, I believe that the prose works of the exile period such as *Me-ti*, the "Anecdotes of Mr. Keuner," and the *Tui-Roman* (Tui Novel), as well as Brecht's *Journals*, can be seen as an extension of his aesthetic experiments to the realm of prose literature. One such experiment, *Me-ti*, embodies the principles of his political aesthetics in the prose domain while articulating the political conflicts of the times and, as I see it, unfolding the contradictions and ambiguities in Brecht's own political position.

The text was written in exile during the 1930s and 1940s and was deeply influenced by Brecht's collaboration with Korsch. Brecht began collecting fragments for a book on social ethics with the title "Büchlein mit Verhaltenslehren" (*GW* 12: 2* Booklet on Moral Teaching) that became the *Me-ti* collection. When Korsch stayed with Brecht in Denmark, he continued working on the project and expanded it from a book on social ethics based on the teaching of the ancient Chinese philosopher Mo Tse (in German: Me Ti or Me-ti) to an aphoristic reflection on the construction of socialism in the Soviet Union and a vehicle to play out in aphoristic form the debates of the era.

Me-ti is subtitled "Book of Changes," a concept influenced by the classical Chinese text the *I-Ching*, or book of changes. The text is especially valuable in articulating Brecht's complex position toward Marxism because it exhibits a dialogue between major Marxian theorists using Chinese pseudonyms for the classic Marxist theorists. Brecht himself was drawn at once to the ideas of democratic socialism espoused by Rosa Luxemburg and Korsch on the one hand and to the authoritarian communism of Lenin and Stalin on the other.[13] The tension between Brecht and orthodox Leninism in both politics and aesthetics surfaced in the hostility of the German Communist party toward his work and in his polemics with Lukács over the official aesthetic doctrine of Socialist Realism.[14] Although Brecht had an ambivalent position within the Communist movement, he presented himself as an orthodox Marxist, a fervent devotee of

Lenin, and publicly defended Communist orthodoxy in the Stalin period; the private Brecht was torn by ambivalence and doubts concerning Stalinism and developments in the Soviet Union. These doubts, which Brecht confided to Marxian heretics such as Korsch and Benjamin, found literary expression in *Me-ti*, one of the most important sources for measuring Korsch's influence on Brecht and Brecht's political contradictions.

There are formal similarities between the *Me-ti* novel and Brecht's learning plays. Both provoke thought and discussion of revolutionary theory and practice rather than simply promulgating ossified doctrines or a party line. The main topics of *Me-ti*, "the grand method" (dialectics) and "the grand order" or "the grand production" (socialism), are presented in the form of aphoristic debates in which Leninism, Stalinism, and the construction of socialism in the Soviet Union are measured against the ideas of Marx and Engels, Korsch, Luxemburg, and Trotsky. The reader is forced to think through the opposing positions of the Marxian classics and contemporary Marxian theorists and to evaluate for her/himself events in the Soviet Union. In addition, the reader is presented with fragments of political morality through which one can judge contemporary events.

Although Brecht inserts himself in the aphoristic dialogues, he does not represent a privileged point of view, nor does Me-ti, Mi-en-leh (Lenin), Master Ko (Korsch), or any of the other participants. The readers of this literary experiment are thus coworkers who contribute their own thoughts to produce revolutionary critique and reflection on Marxian theory and practice as well as on practical ethics. Indeed, Brecht sees ethics and politics as intertwined, and one of the goals of *Me-ti* is to make this connection explicit and convincing.

Throughout *Me-ti*, Brecht applies the materialist concept of history to the history of historical materialism, as Korsch did earlier. As I shall show, Brecht accepted much of Korsch's critique of Stalinism and took seriously Korsch's argument that workers' councils (the Soviets, or *Räte*) were the authentic organs of socialism and not the party bureaucracy.[15] Like Korsch, Brecht analyzes how later Marxian theories and practice realized or failed to realize Marx's ideas, which in turn were critically appraised in terms of the results they produced (or failed to produce). A passage in *Me-ti*, "The Opinion of Philosopher Ko concerning the Construction of the Order in Su," reveals the complexity of the situation Brecht was analyzing when he related Marxism to the developments in the Soviet Union. He indicates that Lenin "created a powerful state apparatus for the construction of the *grand order*, which must necessarily become a hindrance for the grand order in the foreseeable future"(*GW* 12: 537).

Here Brecht is referring to Marx's doctrine of the withering away of the state in the transition to a higher stage of socialism. The implication is that precisely the construction of a bureaucratic order such as the one in the Soviet Union will provide a deadly obstacle to the creation of a more democratic form of socialism—as indeed it did. Brecht then refers to Korsch's critique that "the *orderer* would be a hindrance to the order," in reference to Korsch's belief that the

Stalinist bureaucracy would prevent the development of an emancipatory socialism. Brecht also advanced Korsch's position that "actually the apparatus always functioned very badly and continually putrefied, throwing off a sharp stink"(*GW* 12: 537).

Further, Brecht cites Korsch's position that the power struggle between Stalin and Trotsky portended a surrender of Leninism, and that Trotsky merely "proposed rather doubtful reforms." The conclusion that "those principles proposed by Ko showed a clear weakness where Mi-en-leh's principles were strongest, but Ko characterized excellently the weaknesses of the principles of Mi-en-leh" (*GW* 12: 537) indicates that there are serious weaknesses in Leninism and suggests that there were sharp tensions in Brecht's political views. While Brecht did not accept all of Korsch's sharp attacks on the Soviet Union, Leninism, and Stalinism, he continually reflected on Korsch's views and frequently incorporated them into *Me-ti*.

For instance, an aphorism on "The Trials of Ni-En [Stalin]" is sharply critical of Stalin's trials and suppression of his opponents (*GW* 12: 538). Indeed, it is interesting that the Chinese character Brecht chooses for Stalin (Ni-En) signifies "no," a character of negation, thus implying that Stalin is a negative force, that he is a negation of authentic Marxian teaching. Yet Stalin is seen as "useful," in Brecht's phrase, for the construction of socialism because he has actually done something to construct socialism, unlike intellectuals (Brecht's Tuis) who merely talk and do not have the burden of making real decisions. Brecht also seems to imply that while it might be useful to remove the enemies of socialism, even through trials, the showcase trials run by Stalin did a disservice to the people. Brecht then presents a nuanced, though problematical, position toward Stalin's trials through which the latter eliminates his opponents and sets up a system of terror and death camps.

Yet in the aphorism "Autocratic Rule of Ni-en" (*GW* 12: 53), Brecht clearly chastises Stalin's autocratic rule and reversion to the authoritarian form of the emperor. Brecht points to the lineage between Lenin and Stalin, the achievement of Lenin in seizing power, and the regression of Stalin. Brecht suggests that the backwardness of the Soviet Union, stressed by Lenin, had helped produce a situation in which an autocrat like Stalin could wield absolute power in the absence of more developed democratic traditions.

Brecht continues his critique—strongly influenced by Korsch—in the aphorism on "Construction and Regression under Ni-en." Brecht praises here the advances in collectivizing industry and agriculture and suggests that all wisdom be directed toward economic construction and "chased out of politics" (*GW* 12: 539). For Brecht, socialism constituted a better mode of production, and he seemed to think that the Soviet Union had at least revolutionized production and could be commended from a strictly economic point of view. Yet in politics, the Soviet Union was developing a form of autocracy and not democracy. Following Korsch's criticism, Brecht also notes how Communist parties outside of the Soviet Union, and good but critical Communists inside, were harmed by the lack of political democracy. Yet Brecht criticizes Master Ko for turning away from the grand method. Although Korsch clearly rejected the form of communism developed in the Soviet Union, Brecht's criticism is only partially valid because Korsch continued to believe in the power of the dialectical method and democratic socialism that was based on workers' councils.

The *Me-ti* aphorisms may be regarded as merely an unfinished literary experiment; one might argue that the aphorisms conveyed points of view that Brecht was proposing for discussion and that did not express his own position. He never published *Me-ti*, which indicates a reluctance to attack Stalin and the Soviet Union openly. The same ambivalence toward Stalin and the Soviet Union, however, is found in his *Journals*, in which he considered Korsch's critiques with the utmost seriousness.[16] *Me-ti* represents Brecht's most comprehensive juxtaposition of Korsch's positions with ''official'' Marxian doctrines and shows that throughout the exile period he pondered questions of practical and theoretical Marxism. *Me-ti*, Brecht's letters, and his *Journals* show that he continued to reflect upon and to contrast his own views with the ideas of his teacher and friend Korsch, the theorist who helped provide the foundation for the playwright's Marxist aesthetic.

CONCLUSION

After World War II, Brecht left his exile in the United States and was invited to form a theater group in East Berlin; the Berliner Ensemble, headed by Weigel, which eventually was given a theater and became most influential. Although Brecht remained a somewhat orthodox Communist, he cannot really be considered an apologist of Stalinism. As I have demonstrated, he was deeply influenced by the heretical Marxism of Karl Korsch and was sharply critical of Stalin in his unpublished writings.[17] During the June 1953 workers' uprising in East Berlin against the Stalinist regime, Brecht made some cryptic comments that seemed to support the cause of the workers, but managed to keep his official position with the Berliner Ensemble.

Brecht's major work presents an important example of an aesthetic theory and practice influenced by Marxism, albeit of a critical nature. Indeed, in retrospect it appears that Brecht's faith in the construction of socialism in the Soviet Union was misplaced and that Korsch's criticism of Stalinism and the deformation of socialism in the Soviet bloc have turned out to be more accurate. Yet it was precisely Korsch's interpretation of Marxian theory that provided key impulses for Brecht's own aesthetic theory and production; despite the collapse of communism, many of those Marxian ideas remain useful today.

In view of the collapse of the entire Soviet socialist bloc in recent years, it is an irony of history that Marxian theory has proven more valuable than actual Marxian politics. Brecht found Marxism a productive source of ideas for both the understanding of works of art in particular and for the revolutionizing of art in general. It is then a further irony that, based in no small measure on Brecht's contributions, the Marxian revolution yielded more fruitful results in theory and cultural practice than in actual politics.

NOTES

This is a fully revised and updated version of my essay, "Brecht's Marxist Aesthetic: The Korsch Connection." In Weber/Heinen, *Brecht* 29–42.

1. Brecht's relationship to Korsch was first discussed by Rasch. Other contributions include Müller, Muenz-Koenen, Steinweg (Lehrslück), Brüggemann, Buono, and Mittenzwei. See also "Brecht/Korsch Diskussion."

2. Interpreters who downplay or denigrate Brecht's Marxism include Esslin (*Brecht*) and Bentley. The latter tries to dissociate Brecht from Marxism and to associate him with Beckett.

3. For a detailed reconstruction of Korsch's political activity and theory, see Kellner, "Korsch's Road."

4. Brecht consulted with Korsch on theoretical and aesthetic issues throughout the exile period. See "Briefwechsel Brecht-Korsch." Brecht's "Marxian Studies" are essentially a dialogue with Korsch: see the passages that summarize Korsch's works and set out theses developed in Korsch's seminars (*GW* 20: 68–72). Yet Brecht was also critical of Korsch, seeing him as an intransigent intellectual who refused to compromise with political realities; see "On My Teacher" (*GW* 20: 65–66). See also his critique of Korsch's *Karl Marx* as being too "formalistic," too much an abstract presentation of Marx's dialectics rather than a demonstration of dialectics in action that Brecht tried to provide (*Journals* 12).

5. See also Vera Stegmann, "Brecht contra Wagner: The Evolution of the Epic Music Theater," in this volume.

6. See Korsch, "Socialization?" and "Fundamentals."

7. Such issues would take us into biographical questions beyond the scope of this study, but one might argue that Brecht tended to exploit his coworkers, especially women, and did not live up to the democratic, participatory, and collective principles that he espoused. This position has been advanced recently by Fuegi, *Brecht*. Yet at many stages of his life, Brecht engaged in genuinely collective work, and the principles in Brecht's aesthetic practice remain consistent with a version of Korschian democratic Marxism, even if Brecht himself did not realize these principles in adequate fashion.

8. See Marc Silberman, "Brecht and Film," in this volume.

9. For Brecht's attack on Lukács and his argument that the revolutionary artist should revolutionize form as well content, see "Against Georg Lukács." On the aesthetic differences between Brecht and Lukács in the so-called expressionism controversy, see Gallas and Bronner.

10. See also Karl-Heinz Schoeps, "Brecht's *Lehrstücke*: A Laboratory for Epic and Dialectic Theater," in this volume.

11. In the same *Journals* entry of 25 February 1939, Brecht praises the learning play fragments "Fatzer" and "Der Brotladen" (The Breadshop) as technical models. My interpretation of the learning plays is much indebted to Steinweg (*Lehrstück*) and "Große und Kleine Pädagogik."

12. See Steinweg, *Lehrstück*.

13. Brecht admired the left-wing Communists Korsch and Luxemburg because of their

activism and adherence to the concept of the workers' councils that, they believed, contained the authentic institutions of socialist democracy. In Lenin, Brecht respected the ability to translate revolutionary theory into practice. Stalin—as *Me-ti*, the *Journals*, and unpublished manuscripts and clippings in the Brecht Archives attest—elicited an ambivalence in Brecht that has prevented consensus among critics on the subject of Brecht and Stalin. There is little evidence about his attitude toward Trotsky. During the period when Trotsky was heatedly debated within the international Communist movement, Brecht offered no substantive discussion of the "Trotsky question" in his *Journals*, although there are references to the debates in *Me-ti*.

14. Many commentators have stressed the tension between Brecht's communism and his aesthetic practice; however, most fail to see the tension and the ambiguities within Brecht's Marxism owing to the conflict between the democratic Marxism of Korsch and Western Marxism opposed to the authoritarian Marxism of Lenin and Stalin. The tension was played out in Brecht's ongoing dialogue within the Communist movement in the twenties and thirties and especially in his literary works.

15. Regarding Brecht's acceptance of Korsch's position that the workers' councils were indispensable to the construction of socialism, see Brecht's theses "On the Model R [*Räte*=workers' councils]" as a moment of the proletarian dictatorship (*GW* 20: 119), and his 1941 letter to Korsch in which he asks Korsch to write a historical account of the relationship of the councils to the party and to explain the suppression of the councils system ("Briefwechsel" 252).

16. For a more critical perspective on Brecht's Marxism and attitude toward Stalin, see Dahmer. Dahmer, however, neglects many passages in *Me-ti* and wrongly says that Korsch's views on the development of the Soviet Union are not included in *Me-ti* (67).

17. Völker (*Brecht* 354) points out that in addition to a rather cool obituary notice that Brecht penned on the occasion of Stalin's death in 1953, he only referred to Stalin twice in his works published during his lifetime.

WORKS CITED (SEE ALSO REFERENCE GUIDE TO WORKS CITED IN ABBREVIATED FORM)

Benjamin, Walter. *Understanding Brecht*. London: New Left, 1972.

Bentley, Eric. "Brecht Was a Lover, Too." *Village Voice* (3 May 1976).

Brecht, Bertolt. "Against Georg Lukács." Translated by Stuart Hood. *New Left Review* 84 (March-April 1974): 36–38.

"Brecht/Korsch Diskussion." *Alternative* 18.105 (1975).

"Briefwechsel Brecht-Korsch." *Alternative* 18.105 (1975): 242–58.

Bronner, Stephen Eric. "Expressionism and Marxism: Towards an Aesthetics of Emancipation." In *Passion and Rebellion: The Expressionist Heritage*. Edited by Stephen E. Bronner and Douglas Kellner. New York: Columbia University Press, 1989. 411–52.

Bronner, Stephen Eric, and Douglas Kellner, eds. *Passion and Rebellion: The Expressionist Heritage*. New York: Columbia University Press, 1989.

Brüggemann, Heinz. "Bertolt Brecht und Karl Korsch." *Über Karl Korsch*. Frankfurt am Main: Suhrkamp, 1973. 177–88.

———. *Literarische Technik und soziale Revolution*. Reinbek: Rowohlt, 1973.

Buono, Franco. *Zur Prosa Brechts*. Frankfurt am Main: Suhrkamp, 1973.

Dahmer, Helmut. "Brecht und Stalin." *Telos* 22 (1974–1975): 96–105.

Eisler, Hanns. "Das Lehrstück als politisches Seminar." *Alternative* 14.78/79 (1971): 132.

Gallas, Helga. *Marxistische Literaturtheorie.* Neuwied: Luchterhand, 1971.

"Große und Kleine Pädagogik: Brecht's Modell der Lehrstücke." *Alternative* 14.78/79 (1971).

Kellner, Douglas. "Expressionist Literature and the Dream of the 'New Man.' " In *Passion and Rebellion: The Expressionist Heritage.* Edited by Stephen E. Bronner and Douglas Kellner. New York: Columbia University Press, 1989. 166–200.

———. "Korsch's Road to Marxian Socialism." In *Revolutionary Theory*, by Karl Korsch. Edited by Douglas Kellner. Austin: University of Texas Press, 1977. 5–29.

———. "Fundamentals of Socialization." Translated by Roy Jameson and Douglas Kellner. In *Revolutionary Theory.* Edited by Douglas Kellner. Austin: University of Texas Press, 1977. 124–34.

———. *Karl Marx.* London: Chapman, 1938.

———. *Marxism and Philosophy.* London: New Left, 1970.

———. "The Marxist Dialectic." Translated by Karl-Heinz Otto. In *Revolutionary Theory.* Edited by Douglas Kellner. Austin: University of Texas Press, 1977. 135–40.

———. "On Materialist Dialectic." Translated by Karl-Heinz Otto. In *Revolutionary Theory.* Edited by Douglas Kellner. Austin: University of Texas Press, 1977. 140–44.

Korsch, Karl. *Revolutionary Theory.* Edited by Douglas Kellner. Austin: University of Texas Press, 1977.

———. "What Is Socialization?" *New German Critique* 6 (1975): 60–81.

———. "Why I Am a Marxist." *Three Essays on Marxism.* New York: Monthly Review Press, 1972.

Kurella, A[lfred]. "What Was He Killed for? Criticism of the Play *Strong Measures* [*The Measures Taken*] by Brecht, Dudov and Eisler." In Mews, *Critical Essays* 77–81.

MacCabe, Colin. "The Politics of Separation." *Screen* 16.4 (1976): 46–61.

Mittenzwei, Werner. "Nachwort: Der Dialektiker Brecht oder Die Kunst *Me-ti* zu lesen." In *Me-ti* 182–234.

Muenz-Koenen, Ingeborg. "Brecht in westdeutschen Publikationen." *Weimarer Beiträge* 15 (1969): 123–47.

Müller, Klaus-Detlef. *Die Funktion der Geschichte im Werk Bertolt Brechts.* Tübingen: Niemeyer, 1967.

Rasch, Wolfdietrich. "Bertolt Brechts marxistischer Lehrer." *Merkur* 17.188 (1963): 94–99.

Steinweg, Reiner. *Das Lehrstück.* Stuttgart: Metzler, 1972.

———. "Die Lehrstücke als Versuchsreihe." *Alternative* 14.78/79 (1971): 121–24.

Weber, Betty Nance. "Marxism, Brecht, Gesamtkunstwerk." *Brecht-Jahrbuch 1976*: 120–27.

13

The Evolution of the Feminine Principle in Brecht's Work: An Overview

LAUREEN NUSSBAUM

Looking at the images of women in Brecht's work is like viewing one of the periodic drawings by M. C. Escher, in which the spectator first observes, for example, a regular pattern of white fish before a shift of focus brings out complementary rows of black frogs (MacGillavry, plate 1b). Possibly, the Escher patterns with polychromatic symmetry, like the one with yellow bees, pink butterflies, blue mythical creatures, and white birds, offer an even better analogy to what we are facing when dealing with Brecht's characterization of the feminine (MacGillavry, plate 4). The first focus is clearly an important matter.

Sara Lennox, an acknowledged feminist critic, argues that Brecht tends to use women as "demonstration objects" ("Women" 91) and that "his drama fails to take concerns of women's liberation into account" ("Women" 93). This leads her to the conclusion that his "works . . . succeed in portraying only by means of the usual stereotypes, though somewhat modified by his wider political concerns" ("Women" 96). While Brecht's "works may urge us to perceive the changeability of society as far as capitalism is concerned . . . they are oblivious to the necessity or even possibility of a change in women's condition" ("Women" 96). Well aware that these charges against Brecht stem from her feminist perspective, Lennox allows for a complementary vision by acknowledging that "through the interstices" of Brecht's work "women . . . assert their refusal to participate" ("Women" 96) in his "productivist ethos" ("Women" 93).

This article draws attention to these "interstices" (i.e., the seemingly unstructured space in the perceived pattern), applying the "both/and" to Brecht's work rather than the "either/or," as Lennox has it ("Brecht" 18–19). Such a complementary approach is most promising in that it is consistent with Brecht's own dialectical practice; it will be adhered to in the following.

The women depicted in Brecht's earliest work are traditional mother figures, shown in relationship to their sons: mourning mothers of soldiers at the onset of World War I as in the poems "Moderne Legende" (*Werke* 13: 73–74; Modern Legend), "Mütter Vermißter" (*Werke* 13: 92–93; The Mothers of Missing [Soldiers]), and worrying mothers of licentious adventurer-sons a few years later as in "God's Evening Song," a psalm of 1920 (*Poems* 37–38).[1]

The psychological studies by Arnold Heidsieck and by Carl Pietzcker stress the central role of strong emotional ties between mother and son throughout Brecht's work. Heidsieck speaks of the ambivalence of these close ties and of the resulting distrust of the mother's power of seduction that dominates Brecht's early poetry and the original 1918 *Baal* version (36–38). Pietzcker stresses that it was Brecht's mother who urged upon him the typical, middle-class repression of sexuality (219–27), as evidenced by two "masturbation" poems, "Erinnerungen" (Memories) and "Die Bekenntnisse eines Erst-Kommunikanden" (Confessions of a Recipient of the First Holy Communion), both published posthumously (*Werke* 13: 184, 266–67).

Even without accepting Heidsieck's and Pietzcker's psychological interpretations in every detail, one can readily see how the ambivalent interrelationship between mother and son is thematic in Brecht's early work. Brecht's perception of this relationship distorts his women figures; rather than appearing as persons in their own right, they are projections of his struggle to come to terms with his own sexuality and to free himself from his middle-class milieu. This gives us a key to his early sweetheart figures. More often than not, they are just sex objects, particularly in the ballads of adventure and debauchery of 1918, which later found their place in Brecht's first volume of poetry, *Manual of Piety*.

The title figure of the 1917 poem, "The Legend of the Harlot Evelyn Roe" illustrates this point. Evelyn has piously set out on a pilgrimage to the Holy Land only to have the ship's entire crew force themselves on her. Thus, she becomes the sex object per se. The poet writes that Evelyn was spent after the summer's orgy and that subsequently the ocean washed her body clean (*Poems* 5–7). Since Brecht rejects Christian morality, there is neither salvation for her in heaven nor damnation in hell. It is fair to assume that young, promiscuous Brecht must have strongly identified with Evelyn. This is borne out by the later "Sonett No. 3," in which he reviews the legend of the pious maiden(s) and—speaking for himself—turns it into an indictment of God (*Werke* 13: 332). Most probably, projection takes place on yet another plane. Evelyn's legend can be read as an expression of the young poet's sexual anxieties, since it is also an inversion of the archetypal fertility myths in which the Mother Earth goddess annually uses and discards her youthful lover-son (Neumann 46–50).

Indeed, shortly after "Evelyn Roe," Brecht wrote his "Chorale of the Great Baal," in which the voluptuous "Woman Earth" is sweetheart and Mother Earth at the same time. As such she has archetypal qualities for the poet-lover, who invokes the immutable "father" sky, the masculine principle, in order to strengthen his resistance against its feminine counterpart: the life cycle of birth, growth, voluptuousness, decline, death, decay, and dissolution (*CP* 1: 2). Eventually, Brecht came to use the archetypal feminine principle in new creative and socially meaningful ways. As a young poet, however, he conveniently projected his own propensity to drift—expressed, for example, in "Of Swimming in Lakes and Rivers" (*Poems* 29–30)—upon abandoned sweetheart figures, who pay for the joys of making love by subsequently dissolving into nothingness.

Gaston Bachelard devotes a section of his study *L'eau et les rêves* (Water and Dreams) to male fantasies concerning a woman's death by drowning, which he calls "le complexe d'Ophélie" (109–25). It is a recurrent motif in Brecht's second and third *Baal* versions of 1919 and 1920 and in the poetry of the same years (Frenken 51–54). The young poet varies this theme in the "Ballad of the Death of Anna Cloudface," where he has the face of a former sweetheart amalgamate with the clouds (*Poems* 30–32). This ballad reads like a rough draft for the more famous "Remembering Marie A." of 1920, in which the transience of love is symbolized by a fleeting white cloud, even while the lyrical "I" is entering into a new intimate relationship (*Poems* 35–36).

There is a great deal of bravado in this poetry, quite common in Brecht's early writings. Renate Voris concludes in her exegesis of Brecht's *Diaries* that even there the young poet indulged in self-stylization to cover up his anxieties (Voris 82–93). Paula Banholzer, Brecht's first great love and the mother of his son Frank (born 1919), recalls in her memoirs the young playwright's basic timidity. Speaking of the play *Baal*, she says that Brecht would identify with the bashful poet-in-love, Johannes, rather than with the rapacious title figure (Banholzer 118). Although they never got married, Brecht stayed in touch with "Bi" Banholzer for many years and off and on supported their son.[2] Still, a growing fear of being tied down by a sweetheart, particularly after having made her pregnant, warps the image of woman in the successive *Baal* revisions and in much of Brecht's concurrent poetry.

New in Brecht's work and closely connected to these fears is a horror of bourgeois family life. No wonder, then, that in these same years Brecht created his first bourgeois fiancée and bride figures, Maria in *The Wedding* and Anna Balicke in *Drums in the Night*. He expresses little empathy with either of them. Anna's mother, insipid Mrs. Balicke, a bourgeois wife who is utterly dependent upon her husband and unmotherly toward her daughter, is a predecessor of several such middle-class figures of a later period. In 1919, in the one-act play *Lux in Tenebris*, Brecht also first introduces the madam-entrepreneur as a character. The wife in yet another one-act play of that year, *The Catch*, has some of the resolute, down-to-earth qualities that will be found time and again in Brecht's later woman figures, particularly in his indomitable mothers. In the early 1920s, however, the more conventional mother theme gradually recedes into the background, as is particularly evident in the three consecutive *Baal* versions. The poems of those years that concern Brecht's own mother, for instance, "Utterances of a Martyr" (*Poems* 15–16), express the tensions of their relationship. Brecht was at the point of breaking away when his mother died in 1920; yet there is great tenderness in the two poems dedicated to her shortly after her death (*Poems* 40–41, 49). For several years thereafter, mother-son relationships play a minor role in Brecht's work. In the struggle he was to wage and to depict in the years 1921–1929, each man had to survive on his own strength in a merciless, unmotherly world.

Brecht spent the early 1920s alternately in Munich, Berlin, and Augsburg. This was a period of transition in which he tried to detach himself from his time of youth and subjectivity while striving to conquer the Munich and Berlin theater worlds. A new trend toward objectivity is evident in Brecht's treatment of three young female figures in the poetry of these years.

"On the Infanticide Marie Farrar" deals with a deserted, pregnant woman (*Poems* 89–92). In marked contrast to a poem of three years earlier, "The Ship"—in which the vessel stands as a poetic metaphor for a pregnant woman (*Poems* 25–26)—Marie Farrar's story of despair is reported with detailed realism and deep concern. Here, Brecht indicts a society that drives an unwed mother to kill her newborn child.

In "Song of the Ruined Innocent Folding Linen," the girl—once she is no longer a virgin—develops into an independent woman, able to take life into her own hands (*Poems* 83–85). Brecht's depiction of a female who affirms her sexuality departs considerably from that of his earlier discarded, utterly passive sweetheart figures. The linen imagery he uses prefigures some of the lyrics of the widow Begbick in *A Man's a Man*, to be discussed later.

The "Ballad of Hannah Cash" is one of Brecht's first poems set in the big city (presumably Chicago, the locus of several of his later plays) (*Poems* 69–71). In this poem Brecht parodies the Sermon on the Mount as well as bourgeois marital bliss and family life (Wagenknecht 28). It is so subtly done that many critics have not perceived the irony. Hence, they interpret the ballad as a hymn in praise of a woman's lifelong devotion to an abusive man under the most dismal circumstances. On closer reading, however, Hannah Cash (note her surname!) turns out not to be a sucker but rather a precursor of the gritty Jenny figures of *The Threepenny Opera* and *Rise and Fall of the City of Mahagonny*.

Brecht's development toward greater objectivity and toward a critical social awareness is gradual and not necessarily linear. His two plays of the early 1920s, *In the Jungle of Cities* and *The Life of Edward the Second of England*, both depict homoerotic entanglements. In the female figures of these works, Brecht

expresses an existential despair that is only in part predicated upon socioeconomic circumstances. If the men of these two plays are depicted as largely at
the mercy of irrational forces, the women are placed in double jeopardy. They
are vulnerable to the same forces and also to their men. The fact that Brecht's
rather irrational and ahistorical dramatic figures of the years 1921–1924 lag
somewhat behind the more objective images he projects in his poetry proves
that the playwright, while openly critical of the expressionist theater of his day,
still could not quite avoid its pathos in his own work.

However, Mae, the mother of the dysfunctional Garga family in *Jungle*, is of
special interest as a link in the continuity of Brecht's developing image of
mother figures, even though her role is a minor one. Mae Garga is as devoted,
hardworking, sorrowful, understanding and, in many ways, traditional as
Brecht's earlier mother figures. But her decision to walk out on a hopeless family
situation is new in Brecht's work. It speaks for her good sense and vitality that
she does not want to remain a martyr for a cause she can no longer believe in,
and that she is willing to move on.[3] Concurrently with the Mae figure Brecht
also created his first poems about the vitality and spirited independence of elderly women, such as the ''Ballad of the Old Woman'' (*Poems* 92–93).

Given this gradual development of woman figures through the interstices of
Brecht's work, the analogy with Escher's static periodic drawings no longer
holds. The mature Escher, however, expanded his art into developmental wood-
cuts and lithographs, in which he allows interstitial spaces to evolve into more
and more independent three-dimensional figures that eventually lead a life of
their own. Dynamic Escher prints such as *Sky and Water* or *Liberation* provide
perfect analogies to the evolution of the image of woman in Brecht's *oeuvre*
(Escher, plates 13–17).

Brecht moved permanently to Berlin in the early fall of 1924. In his city
poetry, grouped in and around *Reader for Those Who Live in Cities* (1926–
1927), he describes a harsh reality in which men and women have to fend for
themselves. Relationships are temporary, and women—in order to survive or to
improve their socioeconomic status—often prostitute themselves (e.g., *Poems*
135). Of course, men also sell themselves in the city context, albeit not usually
for sexual exploitation. The few women occurring in the *Reader* poems exemplify the painful and indispensable adaptation required for survival in the me-
tropolis.

Concurrently with his city poetry, Brecht wrote some sonnets that are less
factually descriptive and more reflective than the *Reader* poems. ''Sonnet'' of
1925 is reminiscent of earlier sweetheart poetry. The woman in this poem is
nondescript and destined for oblivion (*Poems* 113–14). ''Discovery About a
Young Woman,'' however, deals with the male partner's sudden concern for
the woman's ephemerality and implicitly his own, as life is slipping by (*Poems*
114).[4]

In the stage work of the years 1924–1929, men and women are to a varying
degree participants in and victims of an exploitative system. The characters in

the stark comedy *A Man's a Man* and in the two satirical operas Brecht wrote with Kurt Weill, *The Threepenny Opera* and *Mahagonny*, are zestful and entertaining. The widow Leocadia Begbick in *A Man's a Man* exemplifies adaptability, that vitally necessary, yet morally questionable quality that the play—in line with the main theme of the city poetry of the same years—is all about. Begbick is the first major woman figure in Brecht's plays—rich, full of vitality, really the soul of the play. As a camp follower and entrepreneur she prefigures Mother Courage. An archetypal mother to the troops, she has nurturing as well as devastatingly asocial aspects, particularly with regard to Galy Gay, whom she helps transform from an innocuous porter into a human fighting machine. For the sergeant with the telling name "Fairchild," she is a real *Rabenmutter* (bad mother) when she provokes him to emasculate himself. Her interaction with both men illustrates the ambivalent mother-son relationship discussed earlier. But the main function of Begbick's role and of her theme song about the perpetual flux of all things is to exemplify a viable version of the "inexorable flexibility" Brecht speaks of admiringly in his poem, "Morning Address to a Tree Named Green" (*Poems* 93–94).

While the character of Begbick blends the roles of mother, entrepreneur, and prostitute, there is more differentiation between the exploiter and the exploited in Brecht's two caustic operas. Again, in the spirit of the city poetry, everybody is looking out for himself or herself. In *The Threepenny Opera*, the main female figures cover the entire spectrum of types discussed so far. Brecht combines in Mrs. Peachum some qualities of Begbick in *A Man's a Man* and features of Mrs. Balicke in *Drums in the Night*. As the partner-employee of her husband, the merchant of misery, Mrs. Peachum is both an entrepreneur and an unmotherly mother for their daughter, Polly. The latter is the sweetheart turned quasi-bourgeois bride in a most satirical wedding ceremony, after which she soon becomes the capable leader of her husband's gang of criminals. Jenny, finally, is the prostitute figure who is, however, more intractable than her predecessors. All three of them are somewhat overdrawn in the contemporaneous George Grosz cartoon style. However, Brecht's sympathy with some of his female figures finds expression in their lyrical interludes, including Polly's rendering of Pirate Jenny's rebellious and, at the same time, utopian song. In the main female characters, who range from power wielder to prostitute but who are all dependent on men, Brecht exposes a cross-section of a ruthlessly exploitative social order.

In the sardonic opera *Mahagonny*, the chief entrepreneur is again a widow named Leocadia Begbick. But of the many facets of her role in *A Man's a Man*, only that of the ruthless businesswoman remains. Jenny, the chief prostitute, is more heavily involved in the dramatic action—both as a victim and as a participant in the general exploitation—than her namesake in *The Threepenny Opera*. While the earlier Jenny exhibits touches of an operetta figure, Brecht emphasizes that *Mahagonny* Jenny—similar to Anna in *The Seven Deadly Sins* and Shen Teh in *The Good Person of Szechwan*—cannot afford to fall in love.

Both Begbick and Jenny underscore most effectively Brecht's devastating indictment of the evils of the society in which they are placed.

The vigorous women in Brecht's stage work of the late 1920s form an important link in the evolving feminine principle in Brecht's work. It is probably
not by chance that Brecht's major female stage figures came into being after
two important women had entered his life: the formidable actress Helene Weigel,
whom he married in 1929, and the writer-translator Elisabeth Hauptmann, who
was soon to be one of his most loyal and valuable collaborators. Starting with
A Man's a Man, Hauptmann coauthored several Brecht plays. She translated
John Gay's *Beggar's Opera*, brought the material to Brecht's attention, and
worked with him on its adaptation, *The Threepenny Opera*, Brecht's first great
success. Both Weigel and Hauptmann were members of the Communist party,
hence it is not surprising that from the late 1920s onward, Brecht took an increasing interest in Marxism.

It may be significant that the two dramatic works Brecht started in the depression year of 1929 remained fragments. Both "Der Brotladen" (The Breadshop) and "Untergang des Egoisten Johann Fatzer" (Demise of the Egotist
Johann Fatzer) are transitional works in which Brecht tried to come to grips
with the tensions between an individual's urge to survive at all cost and a new
social morality that is directed toward the greatest common good. In that same
year, Brecht also coauthored with Elisabeth Hauptmann the melodrama *Happy
End*. Except for the lyrics, the text is mostly Hauptmann's (Fuegi, *Brecht* 214–
15, 230–33). Yet, certainly the lady gangster leader, The Fly, is a worthy successor of Polly Peachum, while Hallelujah Lil is a rough draft of the complex
Saint Joan figure of Brecht's next great play.

In the *Lehrstücke* of the years 1929–1933, especially in *The Baden-Baden
Cantata* and in *The Measures Taken*, Brecht tries to create exemplary, com-
munity-directed figures who are ready to sacrifice their individuality, even their
lives, for the common good. Although there is one woman agitator in *The Measures Taken*, her womanhood is incidental. Probably, in Brecht's experience,
women were too much connected with the practical problems of survival to fit
the more theoretical framework of the learning plays. These practical problems
became momentous for the poor during the depression years. Parts of "Der
Brotladen" and several poems deal with a mother's struggle to provide food
and shelter for her too many children. In "The Ballad of Paragraph 218," the
desperate wife of an unemployed worker is seeking an abortion, but she is told
by a smug doctor that it is her duty to produce "fodder" for cannons and
factories (*Poems* 186–87). Brecht shows her helplessness; however, in other
poems of the time, he calls upon proletarian mothers to stop accepting the existing conditions of misery. This is most notable in the sixth part of *Die drei
Soldaten: Ein Kinderbuch* (The Three Soldiers: A Children's Book) of 1932
(*Werke* 14: 74–76).

The distress of the Great Depression also plays an important role in *Saint
Joan of the Stockyards* (1929–1931), a play that is both an end point and a new

beginning, as well as a travesty of Friedrich von Schiller. As a present-day counterfigure to Schiller's heroine in *The Maiden of Orleans*, however, Brecht's Joan lacks her predecessor's stature. She has the resourcefulness, compassion, and other admirable qualities of two of Bernard Shaw's figures, Major Barbara and Saint Joan. Yet Brecht makes his Joan fail her perceived mission because she is too set in her bourgeois thinking patterns to see the harsh realities of the class struggle. In many ways she stands for the progressive, well-meaning, but politically naive bourgeoisie that Brecht was addressing with this play. Joan's final call for leftist political activism as the only effective means for change expresses Brecht's main thrust of the last years of the Weimar Republic when he still hoped that his art could be instrumental in warding off the total ruin of his country.

Lennox regrets that Brecht did not take Joan's gender seriously, claiming rightly that the "Jeanne d'Arc figure itself seems to cry out for such treatment" ("Women" 93). Indeed, Shaw strikes a feminist chord when his heroine says in the Epilogue to *Saint Joan*: "Pity I was not a man: I should not have bothered you all so much then" (1004). Brecht's Joan has no such awareness, nor does she defy the existing order to the same extent as Shaw's heroic figure. Indeed, Brecht "alienates" the popular heroine for his own purposes ("Women" 92), and Lennox reproaches him for this special kind of exploitation of a female character. But does he really give his Joan figure "the typical features of the child-woman?" ("Women" 87). True, she is "young," "nurturing," and "idealistic," but she becomes "irresolute" ("Women" 87) only when she gives in to her very real subjective needs, that is, to hunger and cold (at the end of scene 9).

Joan is the first female title figure in Brecht's stage work. After her, most of Brecht's major plays have a woman as central character, and in some of the other future-directed works women occupy a much more important place than before. This is true for the film *Kuhle Wampe* (1931–1932), which addresses a proletarian audience. Young Anni Bonike, a skilled factory worker, is a novel kind of fiancée. Although she is pregnant, she walks out on her future husband rather than suffer indignity. Throughout his previous work Brecht had associated bourgeois society with male predominance. Now, working for change, he develops new, self-reliant, and politically conscious roles for proletarian women. These are often mothers who, for the love of their children, have a great stake in the future. Banking on the traditional mother-child relationship and particularly upon the archetypal bond between mother and son, Brecht wrote a stage adaptation of Maxim Gorky's novel, *The Mother*, in 1931 and shortly afterwards a cycle of poems, the "Lullabies" (*Poems* 188–91). Both works are powerful expressions of his hope that leftist activism spearheaded by mothers might yet avert disaster in Germany.[5] However, the rising tide of fascism was not stemmed. Within a year, after some 15,000 working-class women had seen the play and listened to its rousing songs that spoke directly to their plight, Hitler took over, and Brecht fled into exile.

Lennox has faulted the playwright for fashioning his Russian mother, Pelagea Vlassova, into a didactic "use object," underscoring "her willingness to serve others while ignoring her own subjective needs" ("Women" 86). However, that is tantamount to ignoring self-motivated activism on the part of women. In the early 1980s, the activists of Greenham Common in England and Women for Peace in Germany were hardly "use objects" when they protested on behalf of what they perceived as the common good: the prevention of nuclear war. In all fairness, activism on the stage as well as in reality can only be judged within the proper historical context. Other relevant examples of politicized women in the recent past are Rosa Parks, the black woman who—by boldly refusing to sit in the back of a Montgomery, Alabama bus—gave the impetus to the desegregation movement in the 1950s; and the two Irish peace activists, Mairead Corrigan and Betty Williams, who were awarded the Nobel Peace Prize of 1976.

It speaks for Brecht's determination and resilience that he continued to write prodigiously during his years in European exile (1933–1941), keeping a sharp eye on where his work could be performed or printed and on where he might be politically effective. In the spring of 1933, he wrote the libretto for *The Seven Deadly Sins* in Paris, where it was performed in June of that year with Weill's music. According to Klaus Völker, Brecht only wrote the lyrics to make some money (*Brecht* 180). Yet *The Seven Deadly Sins*, with its singer, Anna I, and its dancer, Anna II, dramatizes the theme of systematic self-exploitation as a particularly self-alienating outgrowth of capitalism. This is a theme which had been on Brecht's mind since the mid-1920s. It was to come to its fruition in the Shen Teh/Shui Ta constellation in *The Good Person*. In both instances the exploited individual is a woman. This is the elaboration of a motif Brecht used earlier in the poetry of his first city period. Because they can be physically reduced to a commodity, women stand paradigmatically for the uttermost mercantilization of bourgeois, capitalist society. The original working title for *The Good Person*, "Die Ware Liebe" (Love as a Commodity), is a pun on "die wahre Liebe" (true love). It emphasizes the commercialization of human relations. Brecht uses the same motif of "Ware unter den Waren" (commodity amongst commodities) for Nanna Callas, the Judith figure of *Round Heads and Pointed Heads*, a play he had just finished before leaving Berlin, but which he then reworked and updated politically during his first year of exile in Denmark.[6]

Life of Galileo (1938–1943) is one of the few major plays of the European exile years in which the female figures play minor roles in terms of Brecht's main concerns. Brecht's attention was focused on Galileo, the zestful scientist, who was willing to compromise himself as long as he could keep living and—surreptitiously—continue working and teaching. Some parallels between the Galileo figure and the exiled Brecht are obvious, others are more subtle, as Stern has pointed out so convincingly.

Young Virginia, Galileo's daughter, is just a foil for her father. Galileo neglects her education and disregards her feelings and her happiness because he is preoccupied with his research. The housekeeper, Mrs. Sarti, a mature woman in a subsidiary and rather traditional role, manages all the same to preserve a degree of dignity and self-esteem vis-à-vis the overpowering figure of Galileo. She rightly chides him: "you have no right to trample your daughter's happiness with your big feet!" (*CP* 5: 67). Yet this is exactly what Galileo does. At the end of the play, Virginia, now a middle-aged spinster, is her father's church-appointed warden. Being caught between her filial love and her devotion to the church, she sadly has to find fulfillment in mothering her wily, aging father, feeding, protecting, and chiding him in turn.

Critics such as Sue-Ellen Case take exception to the Virginia figure who, indeed, has no traits or function in the play that could seem positive to a feminist. But in looking for complementary images, we see that Brecht added to the play his own "subversive counter-discourse" (Lennox, "Brecht" 18). In the iconoclastic carnival scene, quite in keeping with Galileo's new insights, the old order is reversed and woman is no longer man's satellite (*CP* 5: 72).

There is again a father-daughter constellation in *Puntila and Matti, His Hired Man*, written 1940–1941 in Finland and based on folk tales Brecht first heard there from his hostess, the writer Hella Wuolijoki. Although, according to Fuegi, Brecht never shared with Wuolijoki the income he derived from *Puntila* (*Brecht* 492–93, *et passim*), she is acknowledged as coauthor of the play in which Eva, landowner Puntila's daughter, stands in her father's shadow, similarly to Virginia in *Galileo*. Eva's role, however, is more substantial than Virginia's, since she reflects her father's split personality. Her wholesome robustness and her erotic needs are in conflict with her place in society. Neither she nor Puntila can break out of the socioeconomic system they live in. Even though the mood of this Finnish *Volksstück* or popular play is quite different from that of the parable *The Good Person*, with which it was concurrently written, the main message is the same. The whole system will have to be changed if humaneness is to prevail and human needs are to be fulfilled. In *Puntila and Matti* Brecht underscores this basic conclusion with the delightful scenes "The League of Mr. Puntila's Fiancées" and "Finnish Tales." Against all odds, the four "early risers," hardworking, often abused, single women, are the most encouraging characters of the play (*CP* 6: 152–63). Brecht depicts them with special warmth, and he endows them with both a sense of humor and political insight. One defiant individual, he seems to say, can make a beginning in bringing about change. These four women, rather than Matti or even "red" Surkkala, the Communist farm hand, represent what is dearest to Brecht throughout his European exile years: vitality and tenacity, resilience and hope for the future.

Sharpened by his Marxist perspective, Brecht's earlier criticism of bourgeois marriage and sex relations is evident in several writings that originated around 1938, such as a number of sonnets, the poem "On the Decay of Love" (*Poems* 313), and the short treatise from *Der Tui-Roman* (The Tui Novel) "Über die Kunst des Beischlafs" (*GW* 12: 677–79; About the Art of Sexual Intercourse). Instead of the prevailing marital situation, which he defines with an ironic wink at Kant as "the contract for mutual use of property and sex organs" (*Werke*

11: 270), Brecht recommends in *Me-ti* nonpossessive partnerships based on mutual respect and on a common concern or task (*GW* 12: 555). However, he notices how these partnerships suffer under enormous stress caused by the developments in Nazi Germany. The plight of the female title figures in "The Ballad of Marie Sanders, the Jew's Whore" (*Poems* 251) and in the scene "The Jewish Wife" of *Fear and Misery of the Third Reich* exemplify this point.

Increasingly during the years of his European exile, Brecht created female characters as paradigms for what he saw as "productive" or "unproductive" responses to sociopolitical situations. His typical woman figures tend to stand alone as mothers or resistance fighters, and they are often endowed with special strength in order to persevere in dark times of crisis. In *Señora Carrar's Rifles*, a timely play set in Spain during the Civil War, neutrality and nonviolence as protective motherly attitudes are scrutinized and found ineffectual against the brute force of merciless aggressors. Señora Carrar, a wary widow, has to learn this lesson painfully. When at long last she joins the war effort against the fascist generals in her own down-to-earth way, she sets an example for other neutralists who have the future of their children at heart. Her development exemplifies a need-oriented learning process.

In some of his poetry and prose from the mid- to late 1930s, notably in "The Shopper" (*Poems* 225–26) and in "The Unseemly Old Lady" (*Stories* 178–82) Brecht again takes up the theme of spirited independence evinced by elderly women. In contrast to corresponding figures of the previous decade, however, these women are politicized. They exhibit more than personal vitality; they perform an educational function by the demonstrative character of their nonconventional actions. Part of the lesson they teach is that as long as there is life, change is possible. This lesson is evidently close to Brecht's heart during his exile.

Another figure of hope is the servant girl Anna, the central figure of the prose story, "The Augsburg Chalk Circle," of 1940 (*Stories* 188–200). In Anna, Brecht combines a number of life-fostering qualities, which he deemed necessary if there was to be a better future for mankind. Anna is brave, resourceful, tenacious, and independent minded but, above all, motherly. Although she is not the child's blood mother, she is lovingly concerned about his well-being and devoted to his social education. As such, she prefigures Grusha in *The Caucasian Chalk Circle*.

Among Brecht's last major works of the European exile years are *Mother Courage and Her Children*, his great antiwar chronicle, and *The Good Person*. Brecht uses Mother Courage and her daughter Kattrin to demonstrate two different responses to the calamities of war without making either persona flat or predictable. He shows how foolish it is of the clever merchant-mother to hope that she and her children could profit from the war. Mother Courage has the vitality, sensuousness, and strength of Leocadia Begbick in *A Man's a Man*, but, given the thrust of Brecht's work of the late 1930s, she cannot affirm the war and go unpunished the way Begbick did. Having lost her three children one by one, Mother Courage ends up the only survivor of her family. As the play closes, she trudges on, a mere shadow of her former zestful self.

Kattrin, by contrast, is an early victim of the war, having lost her voice as a child as a result of an act of violence. The suffering makes her compassionate, and compassion adds to her suffering. When, in the end, she arouses the inhabitants of the beleaguered city of Halle so as to save the children, she has to pay with her life for this heroic deed. Her firmness, however, sparks resistance in a young peasant. Although not a biological mother herself, she is much more motherly, in Brecht's terms, than Mother Courage. There is little justification for Lennox's description of Kattrin as a "child-woman" and an "untalented character" ("Women" 87). Kattrin is twenty at the beginning of the play and thirty at its end. She is alert and watches out for her two older brothers, and she is certainly much more intelligent than one of them, Swiss Cheese. Despite her muteness, she is attractive and intent on enhancing her charms. Whenever she demonstrates need-oriented behavior, she is her mother's bad conscience. In his notes to the play Brecht stresses the necessity of casting Kattrin from the beginning as an intelligent person (*CP* 5: 365). He had created that role for Helene Weigel so that language barriers would not keep her from playing mute Kattrin wherever fate would take the refugee Brecht family (Hecht 165).

The parallels between Kattrin and Anna in "The Augsburg Chalk Circle" are obvious. Kattrin, too, exemplifies the courageous, self-sacrificing, future-directedness in which Brecht saw the only hope during the dark years of his European exile. In the Mother Courage figure, he demonstrates that traditional middle-class motherliness will not do in times of war, since such times do not allow for individual happiness in the midst of general destruction.

The playwright wanted to convey similar insights with his parable *The Good Person*. The character of Shen Teh evolved only gradually over many years. Throughout the play Brecht gives her some of his finest lyrics as she develops from a prostitute to a woman in love and then to a nonbourgeois bride, who takes her life into her own hands after realizing that she is expecting a child. Her name, according to Tatlow, means "divine efficacy" ("China" 45). Yet in the end her generosity and her determined goodness are of as little avail as Mother Courage's mercantile cleverness. Nor does the increasingly agonizing process of self-alienation—as Shen Teh allows her ruthless "male cousin," Shui Ta, to take over for longer and longer periods of time—promise a lasting solution. Brecht suggests in the Epilogue that only "a changed world" will ensure a liveable future for Shen Teh's child, and the audience is called upon to bring about this other and better world (*CP* 6: 103–104).

Fuegi remarked twenty years ago that "the play is based very obviously on a series of societal clichés. . . . Brecht's poetic metaphor makes Shen Te[h] as a woman virtually a personification of feeling, while Shui Ta is made virtually a personification of reason and calculation" (Fuegi, "Alienated" 194). While Fuegi sees the play foremost as an indictment of sexism, Lennox claims that Brecht's "spectators again are left confirmed in their belief that such stereotypical male and female behavior is natural to the sexes'' (''Women'' 92). These critics' oversimplifications miss, for example, that Wang, the water vendor, is a mixed character. As a cheating merchant he is part of the calculating, mercantile system, albeit at the bottom of the ladder; in his unselfish concern for the gods and for Shen Teh as well as in his joy for the ''weeds and grasses''—when the nurturing rain falls and spoils his business (*CP* 6: 35)—he is an effusive, warm, and almost ''motherly'' individual. Conversely, Mrs. Mi Tzu, the house owner, apparently has no feeling. She is a hard-driving, exploitative woman, who looks out for her own advantage. In fact, she wants to ''buy'' young Sun, not just as a manager for her real estate business but also as a sex object. Mrs. Yang and Mrs. Shin turn into ''tigers'' when fighting for their children, especially the former. The latter is eventually capable of feeling for others, albeit in a context where she stands to gain from her compassion as Shen Teh/Shui Ta's confidante. The kindness of the old couple does not fit the male-female stereotype either. Hence, the play is multifaceted and in all fairness neither an indictment nor a confirmation of sexism. It is, however, a powerful denunciation of an exploitative system of which sexism is an integral part. The fact that Brecht split his Anna figure into two female parts and endowed his male Puntila figure with a split personality speaks against focusing too much attention on the male-female dichotomy in Shen Teh.

It has been shown that in the 1930s Brecht developed a number of memorable women figures. Foremost among them are the nurturing, indomitable mothers, whose main concern it is to provide enough food for their children (Knust 234–44).[7] But while love is all-inclusive for Pelegea Vlassova, Señora Carrar, the mother of the ''Lullabies,'' and both Kattrin and Anna, Mother Courage clings to an exclusive type of love for her children, as Kuplis has shown (227–29). This is illustrated by Mother Courage's intrepid theme song and by her telling variation of an old lullaby she sings for Kattrin in the last scene of the play.[8] Shen Teh, who started out so willing to give of herself to all who needed help, is reduced to the exclusive type of love when, as Shen Teh/Shui Ta, she faces the prospect of raising her child under the given socioeconomic conditions.

Beginning approximately in 1933, Brecht devoted a number of poems and short prose pieces to three of his most important female partners, all of whom were closely connected to his work: his actress-wife Helene Weigel, the polyglot writer Margarete Steffin, and the Danish actress and journalist Ruth Berlau. Little is known of what Brecht may have written for writer-translator Elisabeth Hauptmann, who brought him in touch with world literature and contributed significantly to many of his works (Fuegi, *Brecht* 144–46).

The accessible tributes to Weigel have a public rather than a private character. Brecht evokes her outstanding qualities as a superb actress, a politically conscious educator, a devoted mother, and, last but not least, a circumspect and wise partner, for example, in the poems ''The Actress'' (*Poems* 215–16); ''For Helene Weigel'' (*Poems* 415), and ''Weigel's Props'' (*Poems* 427–28). In an earlier poem, also entitled ''Die Requisiten der Weigel'' (*Werke* 15: 11; Weigel's Props), there is a subtle transition from the props Weigel handles on the stage to items she needs to feed her family during their life in exile.

Brecht's lyrical production for Steffin falls into three parts. The love poetry of around 1933 is closely connected to Brecht's erotic verses of the *Baal* years. He had met Steffin in Berlin when—unemployed during the Great Depression— she joined the *Kuhle Wampe* project. Soon she was to become his "little teacher from the working class" (*Werke* 15: 43). Steffin followed him into exile; intent on fleeing with Brecht and his family from Finland via the Soviet Union to California, she lost her long struggle against tuberculosis and died in Moscow at age thirty-three.

Of the early cycle of rather suggestive and often overbearing love sonnets Brecht wrote for her, only a few can be found in *Poems*, for instance, "The Fourth Sonnet," in which he deplores their lack of privacy, and "The Sixth Sonnet," in which the poet says that he cannot help but love her, even though he realizes that "unattached and free" he might have avoided "a lot of suffering" (*Poems* 213–14). A recent edition of Steffin's previously unpublished writings contains her early love poems for Brecht, whose sonnets of 1933 they complement. In her poetry, Steffin speaks of him as a consummate and irresistible lover, about whose faithfulness, however, she has few illusions (196–205).

In the poetry written for or about Steffin in 1937, Brecht celebrates a new equality between a male and a female partner. She must have become an almost indispensable sounding board and corrective for Brecht, as can be seen in his poem "The Good Comrade M.S." of 1937 (*Poems* 277–78). In the later "Sonnet No. 19," when war clouds are hanging over Europe, the poet demands that she stay and work with him. She is urgently needed, so no respite shall be given for her "to lick [her] wounds" and to recover (*Poems* 330; see Fuegi, *Brecht* 372–73).

In the group of six poems entitled "After the Death of My Collaborator M.S." (*Poems* 364–66), which Brecht wrote in 1941 upon his arrival in California, Steffin is addressed as "my pupil" and "my teacher," "my nurse" and "my nursling." From this cycle and from other poems, Steffin's image emerges as that of a partner of frail health but of an undaunted revolutionary fighting spirit. It is curious that in his fifth poem of mourning Brecht speaks of renaming the constellation of Orion "Steffin Constellation." In Greek mythology Orion was a mighty hunter who was killed by Artemis, the deity he worked for. Did Brecht draw parallels, although that would involve a reversal of gender? The third poem of this cycle, in which he tells how he had piled work upon her even while she was dying, points in that direction. In an earlier sonnet of 1937 the poet also expresses guilt feelings about the way he had treated Steffin (*Poems* 275). Over the years, Steffin certainly experienced their relationship as an unequal one, which she demonstrates in her autobiographical writings, for instance, in the prose piece "Vom Mädchen Ursula" (169; Of the Girl Ursula). Evidently, she kept trying to comply with his often unfair demands, under which she suffered greatly, in order to retain Brecht's love.

A third long-term partner in Brecht's life and work was Ruth Berlau, a beautiful and spirited woman, actress, journalist, and political activist, who arranged to meet Brecht in 1933 shortly after his arrival in Denmark and remained in his orbit until his death. As a Danish citizen, Berlau was of considerable practical help to Brecht during his eight years in Scandinavian exile. Brecht's poem "Ardens sed virens" (Burning yet still Intact) of 1939 is a tribute to Berlau's passionate nature, her courage, and her stamina (*Poems* 345). Almost from the outset, however, theirs was a problematic relationship. The tension is palpable in some of the "Lai-tu" stories, short prose pieces devoted to Berlau (*GW* 12: 570–85). Most of these reflections were written in the middle and late 1930s. While they are analytical or didactic in nature, they also reveal Brecht's jealousies and fears. Although Berlau was the one who originally took the initiative, Brecht describes Lai-tu as a satellite to "her brother" Kin-jeh, that is, Brecht's alter ego. In the closing sections written in 1950, we read that Kin-jeh had a sense of purpose, Lai-tu supported him in it; he produced, and she inspired him. In the end she is compared to an apple whose glory it is to be eaten. Thus Brecht adds insult to injury (*GW* 12: 585).

Berlau came with Brecht and his family to the United States and eventually became Brecht's de facto agent in New York, as can be read in Lyon's sensitive account of Brecht's and Berlau's eventful and often strained relationship during their six years of exile in the United States (*Brecht* 221–27). In her later years, Berlau contributed to Brecht's work most prominently as a photographer for his *Modellbücher* (model books) and for *Theaterarbeit* (Theater Work), the beautifully executed account of six stagings by the Berliner Ensemble. Yet, the image Brecht projects of Berlau is, all in all, that of a partner whom he did not see as his equal. In his eyes she lacked the memorable artistic skills, the resilience and the wisdom of Weigel and the revolutionary insight, training, and determined discipline of Steffin. Although Berlau had much to offer as an independent and courageous woman, she was trapped in a secondary and dependent role by her love for Brecht. After the war, he needed her less and less for his work. Soon his detachment became unbearable to her, causing her to make demands that were increasingly an irritant to him. In his poem "Veränderung, aber zum Schlechten" (Change, but for the Worse), the poet deplores that his friend's former cheerfulness and kindness have given way to harshness. Her personality change is epitomized in the two-line center stanza: Shen Teh was invited, but instead Shui Ta pays him a visit (*Werke* 15: 298–99). Frenken rightly remarks that Brecht seems to forget that in her desperate situation it was just as impossible for Berlau as for Shen Teh to remain kind and yet to live (235). Berlau's *Memoirs* have been published by Brecht student Hans Bunge and are available in translation under the title *Living for Brecht*. In his perceptive afterword Bunge tries to do justice to both Berlau and Brecht.

There is no glowing tribute to Elisabeth Hauptmann, Brecht's closest partner from the mid-1920s until 1933 and then again after Brecht's return to Berlin fifteen years later, with intermittent contacts during the American exile years.

Hauptmann was Brecht's invaluable translator from English to German and eventually became the editor of his collected works. Völker claims that the exhortatory poem beginning with "Du, der das Unentbehrliche" (You, Who [sees] the Indispensable) was directed to Hauptmann. This poem speaks of high Gexpectations that come with high respect and postulates that work has 83to go on without any special considerations (*Werke* 13: 364). Hauptmann had attempted suicide upon learning that Brecht had married Weigel in April 1929, and the poem may be considered Brecht's rather overbearing plea for her indulgence and continued cooperation while she was hurting from disappointed love (Völker, *Brecht* 129).

British Brecht expert John Willett has reason to believe that the "positively anaphrodisiac" poem of around 1939, called the "Song About the Good People," was also addressed to Hauptmann (*Poems* 337–39). "Against that," Willett writes, "she had clearly not only done a lot of the spadework for those plays, finished or unfinished, to which he put his name between 1924 and 1933; she had actually written parts of them—the Alabama and Benares songs in *Mahagonny*, the original translation of Gay's text for *The Threepenny Opera*, the bulk of *Der Jasager* (He, who says yes)" (Willett 122). Fuegi has claimed recently that Hauptmann wrote 80–90 percent of these "Brecht" works ("Zelda" 105, 112). In his sustained effort to cut Brecht down to size, Fuegi offers ample documentation of the vast array of major contributions Hauptmann, Steffin, Berlau, and others made to "Brecht's" collected works. Quite possibly he is right in attributing much of the "thematic orientation" around a central woman to Brecht's female co-authors (Fuegi, *Brecht* 144). The published poems and prose pieces devoted to the women who were of immeasurable importance in his life and work clearly demonstrate Brecht's dependence on the strength and forbearance of these partners and on their willingness to devote themselves totally to his pursuits for as long as he needed them.

After Brecht and his entourage arrived in the United States in July 1941, he was preoccupied with his struggle to find a place for himself in the New World's entertainment industry, first in California and later on Broadway. His efforts are reflected in the bitter-sad "Hollywood-Elegies" (1942) and other poetry from this period, in which he denounces the American marketplace for art, science, and literature. In the process, Brecht deals harshly with the society women of this mercenary New World in a vocabulary suggestive of common whores (*Poems* 380–81). He does the same with the venal intellectuals in his play *Turandot*, finished in 1954 but written mainly during his years in California. Taking issue with willing participants in a corrupt and exploitative society, Brecht does not accord them the sympathy that he formerly expressed for his common prostitute figures.

From Europe Brecht had brought with him a sketch for a new Saint Joan play that evolved into *The Visions of Simone Machard*. With his old Munich friend Lion Feuchtwanger, he worked on this play during his first two years in California. Alongside Kattrin in *Mother Courage*, young Simone is one of Brecht's few heroines. She, too, sacrifices herself in times of emergency in order to save others. Her actions, similar to Kattrin's, are an outcry against inhumanity. Like Shen Teh she is only out to help those she loves and those in need. But Simone acts in the context of occupied France in the early 1940s and becomes the initiator of the local resistance movement. She is the one ordinary person who makes a difference; again it is a woman who represents Brecht's hopes in those years.

Compared to the Simone figure, Brecht put fewer of his main concerns into Anna Kopecka, the innkeeper of his Jaroslav Hašek adaptation, *Schweyk in the Second World War* of 1943. Kopecka, whose name probably derives from the coin kopek, has the robust vitality, the sensuousness, and the resilience of Leocadia Begbick in *A Man's a Man* and of Mother Courage. She is also a good Czech citizen during the Nazi occupation. However, as an entrepreneur she thrives on the capitalist system. Not wanting to block his way to Broadway, Brecht alludes only very gently to her mercantile aspects, for instance, in her "Song of the Flagon" (*CP* 7: 127–28).

A second play with which Brecht hoped to make his entry on Broadway is *The Caucasian Chalk Circle*, written in 1944–1945. Except for the introductory *kolkhoz* (collective farm) scene, this is a seemingly unpolitical play. Yet, upon closer study, it turns out to be Brecht's most revolutionary one. With the subversive Azdak figure as an at least temporary savior, and with Grusha as a synthesis of all his positive woman figures, Brecht pointed the way toward a new social order that was to start with the needs of the children of this earth. In the first place, they require a good mother: robust, down to earth, able to provide food and shelter against all odds, and ready to sacrifice for the sake of the young. Grusha, who grew out of the Anna figure in the "The Augsburg Chalk Circle," develops all of these nurturing qualities. Brecht depicts her as a woman in love and as a fiancée, and he gives her some autonomy vis-à-vis her temporary husband, Jussuf. The new family she and Simon will eventually found is not based on bourgeois proprietorship, nor even on blood bonds, but on the needs of the child and on mutual love and respect. The revolutionary aspects of this play are evident in its apparent revision of Genesis 1 and 2. Brecht proposes implicitly that after the creation of heaven and earth, of light and dark, of flora and fauna, God first created a child, right in the Garden of Paradise. Because the little child needed nurturing, protection, and guidance, God gave him a mother. This mother took good care of the child and taught him kindness toward his fellow creatures and appreciation of nature. The motherly woman delighted in seeing the child grow and learn new things every day. Yet she longed for a companion. So God gave her a man to love and to have more children with, charging them to take good care of the new Garden of Eden.

With Grusha, Brecht created the mother-educator for a future in which all traditions are revised or replaced by kinder, more productive relationships between people. Since Grusha stands paradigmatically for Brecht's highest hopes, he gave her some of his finest lyrics. Tatlow rightly observes: "She also constitutes a passage for something more complex than the merely personal and private interests which some feminists accuse Brecht of ignoring. Her songs, and the words of the Singer, who speaks for her when emotion is too great for her to speak alone, are an expression of the social unconscious, just as the whole play demonstrates the frustration of those needs in her personal life" ("Way" 219). It seems that whatever Brecht wrote for the stage after *Chalk Circle* did not reach the height of this play in language, in dramatic richness, and in innovative ideas and characters.

In 1952, after his return to Berlin, Brecht coauthored with Anna Seghers *The Trial of Joan of Arc at Rouen, 1431*. Shaw's *Saint Joan* provided a model for the main character. Brecht and Seghers experimented with the idea of giving the populace a share of her glory by having Joan hear the voices of the common people rather than those of angels. She becomes a heroine in the contemporary class struggle, and her answers in the trial scene befit a twentieth-century resistance worker better than a fifteenth-century peasant girl. The net effect is quite ahistorical and therefore jarring.

Brecht wrote some beautiful poetry upon his return to Europe, particularly the *Buckow Elegies*. However, there is little in those lyrics that would add new insights into the evolution of the feminine principle in his work.[9] In such poems as "To My Countrymen," he continued to beseech mothers to avoid new wars, to see to it that their children would prosper, and to prevent the wrong people from returning to power (*Poems* 417–18). Among the "Five Children's Songs" of 1950 there is the "Little Song from Olden Times." It deals with male prerogatives that should henceforth be shared by women (*Poems* 421).

All of the above leads to the conclusion that while until 1920 the sweethearts in Brecht's work are almost exclusively sex partners and hence reflect only a limited, albeit vitally important aspect of life, Brecht soon uses figures of fiancées and brides as well as middle-class wives and prostitutes as vehicles for his criticism of the contemporaneous male-dominated bourgeois society. In the transition years, a passing existential despair is particularly strongly reflected by the female figures in Brecht's stage works, while in his city poetry the merciless struggle for survival also determines the ephemeral character of noncommittal relationships. Although generally women are the losers, they also can be exploitative, especially in the way they use sex to better themselves socioeconomically. Love binds and makes vulnerable, hence Brecht avoids this topic in his work for many years. Mothers, important for the security they give their sons in the earliest poetry, recede into the background during the Augsburg-Munich years, where they remain until Brecht's activist Marxist period.

Begbick in 1926 is Brecht's first creation of a major woman figure. Of her numerous qualities it is mainly her vitality, resilience, and self-reliance that make her the prototype of her many strong and fascinating successors. After Brecht had studied and embraced Marxism, his outlook on life became future-directed, as reflected in his Saint Joan figure of 1931. Joan Dark displays strength and resourcefulness as well as compassion for the poor; but she gains new insights only just before she succumbs. Her dying charge is that people of good will must work for change. Brecht will henceforth entrust his mother figures with this task. As the first teachers of the young, mothers are the ideal persons to pass on new ideas to posterity.

For Brecht as for Shaw, the female comes to represent productive vitality and the best guarantee for the improvement of mankind in her challenge of existing exploitation (Schoeps, *Shaw* 191), although Brecht's scope evidently is narrower than Shaw's. Brecht had particular faith in a mother's constructive influence on her son, a biased and limited perception that derives from archetypal, traditional, and/or sexist notions. He never worked out a productive mother-daughter relationship in the manner of Shaw's *Mrs. Warren's Profession* (1902). The interaction between Mother Courage and Kattrin can at best be considered an attempt to proceed in that direction. Moreover, unlike Shaw in *Candida* (1893), Brecht never put his theoretical ideas about a new kind of man-woman partnership to a convincing test. From Brecht's personal tributes it is clear that he had known productive working-loving cooperation with several women, but these relationships typically would become problematic—mainly owing to Brecht's personality. That might be the reason why there are no fruitful male-female partnerships depicted in his work: Brecht preferred time and again to entrust a single woman with his most pressing concerns.

Chalk Circle appears as a notable exception, since there is a certain balance between Grusha's and ''judge'' Azdak's contribution to the future of the child, while there is also a place for Simon in the renewed family. Although Azdak's supportive verdict is central, his interaction with Grusha is brief. As to Grusha and Simon, the audience has to assume that they will live happily ever after with the child. Brecht endows them with productive, future-oriented attitudes and qualities, but he does not show how they will manage. Will Simon's tertiary, subordinate role leave him free to come and go as he sees fit, since Grusha finds her main fulfillment in raising the child, whose survival has required all her resourcefulness and stamina? Is the new family in the end not all that new but merely a reflection of Brecht's own experience? He has, after all, more than once simultaneously played a tertiary role in several such ''families.''[10]

Brecht must have had a great affinity for the guiding and fostering principle and for the keen vitality with which he endowed so many of his motherly woman figures. As a stage director at the Berliner Ensemble, he is said to have been an unsurpassed master in nurturing the best in his young actors (*Theaterarbeit* 130–32). Moreover, in his poetry, the theme of fostering growth is repeatedly expressed by concern for a healthy environment for trees and by the motif of protecting and watering them and other plants.[11] Brecht was himself down to earth, tenacious, resourceful, and amazingly resilient. The early motif of ''inexorable flexibility'' recurs throughout his work and is expressed once again in the poem ''Iron'' (1953) that ends: ''But all that was of wood / Gave and held'' (*Poems* 442).

Even as a young man Brecht liked to assume the pose of a teacher, which is, for instance, reflected in the poem "Against Temptation" of 1920. Intended as the closing chapter of his *Manual of Piety*, he eventually incorporated it into *Mahagonny*, where this sermon of skeptical hedonism fits particularly well (*CP* 2: 110–11). Later, of course, he wrote *Lehrstücke*, the "Lehrgedicht von der Natur der Menschen" (*Werke* 15: 120–57; Didactic Poem Concerning Human Nature), and several treatises on theater practice.

It is therefore not surprising that motherly women are not the only educators in Brecht's work. There are several noteworthy male figures after 1933 who are mentors. These are foremost the theoreticians, Herr Keuner and Me-ti, who often speak for Brecht, the impassioned teacher-experimentalist Galileo, and the wise fool Azdak. However, these male teachers are never as ready to give of themselves and as prepared to sacrifice as are the mother-educators. In Brecht's poetry the two legendary teachers, Empedocles and Lao-Tsû (*Poems* 253, 314), both old and wise men, have some of the kindness and productive considerateness that brings them closer to Brecht's life-fostering mother figures. Lao-Tsû's attrition by "soft water" stands in part for persistent resistance against the Nazi power of the day. In a wider sense and in the original *Tao te Ching*, the gentle but irresistibly moving waters represent the feminine principle (Lao Tzû 45, 138, 140). Darko Suvin underscores this principle in Brecht's work and sees "matriarchal, liberating suppleness," as opposed to "patriarchal, authoritarian strength" in Brecht's dynamic, critical, and dialectical aesthetic attitude (Suvin 87).

Brecht clearly cherished these traits in the women who were close to him. He used their qualities creatively to promote the kind of friendliness between people who had become increasingly important to him. In the third part of "To Those Born Later" (1938), with which he closes his *Svendborg Poems*, Brecht expressed the dialectics of his own situation as he struggled in the dark exile years for a humane and responsive world: "Oh, we / Who wanted to prepare the ground for friendliness / Could not ourselves be friendly" (*Poems* 320). These dialectics are, of course, reflected in the Shen Teh/Shui Ta dichotomy of the same dark years. Even as the war clouds gathered over Europe, Brecht did not give up hope that if people only tried hard enough, the time would eventually come in which "man is a helper to man" (*Poems* 320). His future-directed female figures of the exile period all work toward that aim. Suvin's interpretation of Brecht's world view and aesthetic attitudes corresponds better with my findings than the opinion of Fritz Raddatz, who, based on his collage of some early poetry with samplings of biographical and psychological commentary, deems Brecht's women figures unerotic, nameless beings and purified *Ideenträger* (representatives of ideas). However, Raddatz does not include a discussion of Shen Teh, Grusha, or any other major woman character in Brecht's work, confining himself to some passing remarks about Mother Courage and a brief comparison of Brecht's Pelagea Vlassova with her Gorky model.

After settling in East Berlin, Brecht had the opportunity to work and to be productive in his own nurturing sense. In the poem "Pleasures" of 1954, he counts his blessings. Among the activities he enjoys are writing and planting. But the *summum bonum*, quite in keeping with the feminine principle that permeates much of his work, is "being friendly" (*Poems* 448). There remains the terrible dilemma that the world needs persons like Kattrin, Shen Teh, and Grusha in order to become a better place, but they in turn need a better world in order to thrive.

In looking at Brecht's early depiction of women, rather unattractive and traditional figures stand out. But, just as in Escher's art work, there are other, promising, complementary figures, who gradually develop from the interstices, come to the fore, and capture the eye.

NOTES

This is a revised and updated version of my essay, "The Evolution of the Feminine Principle in Brecht's Work: Beyond the Feminist Critique," *German Studies Review* 8 (1985): 217–44. For a more exhaustive study, see Nussbaum, "Image." The scope of the present contribution does not allow the inclusion of woman figures in Brecht's novels that have been rather neglected so far.

1. Preceding the mother figures in Brecht's works is "The Girl" in the one-act play *Die Bibel* (The Bible), written when he was fifteen and published in his school paper (*Werke* 1). "The Girl" was inspired by the apocryphal Judith figure, a figure that Brecht was to come back to in later works, most notably in *Roundheads and Pointed Heads* of 1931–1934.

2. John Fuegi amassed many details to bolster his view that Brecht was utterly callous vis-à-vis the needs of his first-born son (*Brecht* 61, 131, 137, 332, 415). Fuegi's treatise combines a great deal of well-known and some new information in such a fashion as to place Brecht—and by extension much of Brecht scholarship—in the most unfavorable light. The book appeared after the present essay was completed.

3. In Brecht's original *Jungle* version of 1921–1922 Mae Garga plays a more important role.

4. A number of pornographic poems—most of them belonging to the "Augsburger Sonette" (Augsburg Sonnets) of 1925–1927—have only been published posthumously. Brecht claimed that he wrote them as a diversion (see *Werke* 11: 325, n.). They will not be discussed here.

5. In a thorough study devoted to Brecht's double adaptation of the Pelegea Vlassova figure from Gorky's original, Thomas concludes that from the earlier more passive models, Brecht developed a very active and dynamic woman, truly the mother of the future (72–103).

6. For the successive versions, which began with an adaptation of Shakespeare's *Measure for Measure*, see Bahr.

7. See also Herbert Knust, "First Comes the Belly, then Morality," in this volume.

8. Lug, in her otherwise excellent article, is not aware of Brecht's subtle sarcasm in Mother Courage's lullaby for her dead daughter. In this bitterly ironic adaptation of a well-known cradle song, the bereft mother tries to justify her materialistic pursuits by her exclusive love. While Lug misreads it as an un-Brechtian "appeal to the emotion" (10, 12), this satirical lullaby, quite to the contrary, substantiates her valid thesis on Brecht's irreverent demystification of clichés.

9. Apparently, when under stress, writing sexist sonnets that border on pornography remained a diversion for Brecht. At the age of fifty he wrote, for instance, "Über die Verführung von Engeln" (About the Seduction of Angels) during a hectic sojourn in Zurich (*Werke* 15: 193). Even more disturbing, though, are the sentiments expressed in Brecht's "Song of a Loving Woman" of 1950, in which the lyrical "I" wishes she would die now while she is happy so that her lover would remember her in his old age as "a sweetheart that is still young" (*Poems* 430).

10. In 1925, Brecht had to provide for three children: Frank by Bi Banholzer; Hanne by Marianne Zoff, to whom he was then still married; and Stefan by Helene Weigel (Völker, *Brecht* 108). While Brecht was working on *Chalk Circle* in the summer of 1944, Berlau was expecting a child by him. Völker claims that the Grusha figure was meant as an example and encouragement for her (*Brecht* 304).

11. See, for instance, "The Plumtree" (*Poems* 243), "Thoughts on the Duration of Exile," and part I of "Spring 1938" (*Poems* 301–303), all written during the European exile, and the California poem "Of Sprinkling the Garden" (*Poems* 382).

WORKS CITED (SEE ALSO REFERENCE GUIDE TO WORKS CITED IN ABBREVIATED FORM)

Bachelard, Gaston. *L'eau et les rêves*. Paris: Corti, 1942.

Bahr, Gisela. "*Roundheads and Peakheads*: The Truth in Evil Times." In Mews/Knust, *Essays* 141–55.

Banholzer, Paula, Axel Poldner, and Willibald Eser, eds. *So viel wie eine Liebe: Der unbekannte Brecht*. Munich: Universitas, 1981.

Brecht, Bertolt. *Baal: Drei Fassungen*. Edited by Dieter Schmidt. Frankfurt am Main: Suhrkamp, 1966.

———. *Im Dickicht der Städte. Erstfassung und Materialien*. Edited by Gisela Bahr. Frankfurt am Main: Suhrkamp, 1968.

Case, Sue-Ellen. Contribution to discussion during the Sixth International Brecht Symposium in Portland, OR, May 1982.

Escher, M.C. *Grafiek en Tekeningen*. Zwolle: Tijl, 1959.

Frenken, Herbert. *Das Frauenbild in Brechts Lyrik*. Frankfurt am Main: Lang, 1993.

Fuegi, John. "The Alienated Woman: Brecht's *The Good Person of Setzuan*." In Mews/Knust, *Essays* 190–96.

———. "The Zelda Syndrom." In Thomson/Sacks, *Cambridge Companion* 104–16.

Hecht, Werner, ed. *Materialien zu Brechts "Mutter Courage und ihre Kinder."* Frankfurt am Main: Suhrkamp, 1964.

Heidsieck, Arnold. "Psychologische Strukturen im Werk Bertolt Brechts bis 1932." In *Ideologiekritische Studien zur Literatur: Essays 2*. Edited by Volkmar Sander. Berne: Lang, 1975. 31–71.

Knust, Herbert. "Brechts Dialektik vom Fressen und von der Moral." *Brecht heute/ Brecht Today. Brecht Yearbook* 3 (1973): 221–50.

Kuplis, Aija. "The Image of Woman in Bertolt Brecht's Poetry." Ph.D. diss., University of Wisconsin, 1976.

Lao Tzû. *Tao te Ching*. Translated and introduction by D.C. Lau. London: Penguin, 1963.

Lennox, Sara. "Brecht, Feminism and Form: Theses toward a Feminist Reutilization of

Brecht.'' *Communications from the International Brecht Society* 13.1 (1983): 16–19.

———. ''Women in Brecht's Works.'' *New German Critique* 14 (1978): 83–96.

Lug, Sieglinde. ''The 'Good' Woman Demystified.'' *Communications from the International Brecht Society* 14.1 (1984): 3–16.

MacGillavry, Caroline H., ed. *Symmetry Aspects of M.C. Escher's Periodic Drawings*. Utrecht: Oosthoek, 1965.

Neumann, Erich. *The Origins and History of Consciousness*. Translated by R.F.C. Hull. New York: Pantheon, 1954.

Nussbaum, Laureen. ''The Evolution of the Feminine Principle in Brecht's Work: Beyond the Feminist Critique.'' *German Studies Review* 8 (1985): 217–44.

———. ''The Image of Woman in the Work of Bertolt Brecht.'' Ph.D. diss., University of Washington, 1977.

Pietzcker, Carl. *Die Lyrik des jungen Brecht: Vom anarchischen Nihilismus zum Marxismus*. Frankfurt am Main: Suhrkamp, 1974.

Raddatz, Fritz J. ''Ent-weiblichte Eschatologie. Bertolt Brechts revolutionärer Gegenmythos.'' In *Text + Kritik* 2: 152–59.

Shaw, G. Bernard. *The Complete Plays*. London: Constable, 1931.

Steffin, Margarete. *Konfutse versteht nichts von Frauen*. Edited by Inge Gellert. Berlin: Rowohlt, 1991.

Stern, Guy. ''The Plight of the Exile: A Hidden Theme in Brecht's *Galileo Galilei*.'' *Brecht heute/Brecht Today: Brecht Yearbook* 1 (1971): 110–16.

Suvin, Darko. ''The Mirror and the Dynamo.'' In Munk, *Brecht* 80–98.

Tatlow, Antony. ''China oder Chima.'' *Brecht heute/Brecht Today: Brecht Yearbook* 1 (1971): 27–47.

———. ''The Way Ahead: 2. Brecht and Postmodernism.'' *Brecht-Jahrbuch/Brecht Yearbook* 12 (1983): 215–20.

Thomas, Emma. ''Brecht's Drama *Die Mutter*: A Case of Double Adaptation.'' Ph.D. diss., Indiana University, 1972.

Voris, Renate. ''Inszenierte Ehrlichkeit: Bertolt Brechts 'Weibergeschichten.' '' *Brecht-Jahrbuch/Brecht Yearbook* 12 (1983): 79–95.

Wagenknecht, Regine. ''Bertolt Brechts *Hauspostille*.'' In *Text + Kritik* 2: 20–29.

Willett, John. ''Bacon ohne Shakespeare?—The Problem of Mitarbeit.'' *Brecht-Jahrbuch/Brecht Yearbook* 12 (1983): 121–37.

PART V

TRANSLATION, RECEPTION, AND APPROPRIATION

Negotiating Meanings: Thoughts on Brecht and Translation

Michael Morley

> It seems to be the fate of the translator always to echo the cry of Rilke's
> *Ninth Elegy*: "Alas, but the other relation! What can be carried across?"
> and speculate mistrustfully: Are we, perhaps, here just for saying: House,
> Bridge, Fountain, Gate, Jug, Olive Tree, Window—possibly: Pillar, Tower?
> —Belitt, *Adam's Dream*[1]

> In the appreciation of a work of art or art form consideration of the receiver
> never proves fruitful.
> —Benjamin, *Illuminations*[2]

It is perhaps indicative of the problematic aspects of the links between translation theory and practice that, to take but two examples, Ben Belitt's *Adam's
Dream* is divided into two separate categories of theory and practice, and James
MacFarlane's elegantly argued classic essay on "Modes of Translation" no-
where provides instances of his own approach to translating Henrik Ibsen. Moreover, while MacFarlane canvasses a range of theories and approaches to
translation, his views of the relation between original text and its translation
would appear to be at odds with Benjamin's on several counts:

A Crocean aesthetic, for example, would insist that "works of art exist only in the minds
that create or re-create them" and it has been said that, "for art—and for aesthetics
generally—objects do not exist, but only experiences." Should we not then rather say
that a poem, being not a continuing *existent* but rather a permanent *possibility*, becomes

a poem only when it has been emotionally and synoptically experienced, and that any "meaning" that may attach to it is inseparably connected with the events leading up to and away from it, with the experiences of—to use Samuel Butler's terms—the sayer and the sayee. (MacFarlane 33)

The Brecht who kept the small donkey on his writing desk with the sign round its neck reading "I too must understand it" is clearly not an author who ignores the relationship between the articulation of meaning by the author and the making of meaning by the reader or listener. In fact, he goes even further in a passage from the prose work *Me-ti* where, speaking of the relationship between various registers of language, implied or expressed attitudes, and the means of linking these and conveying the result to an audience, he writes:

The writer Kin-jeh [a pen name for Brecht himself] . . . only incorporated attitudes into sentences and always saw that the attitudes were visible through the sentences. To this kind of language he gave the name "gestic," since it was just an expression of people's gestures. His sentences can best be read by carrying out at the same time certain physical movements which seem appropriate. . . . Often a particular *Gestus* (such as sadness) can encompass many other gestures as well (like calling on others to witness, restraining oneself, being unjust, etc.). The writer Kin recognized language as a tool of action and knew that even when someone is speaking to himself, he is also speaking to others. (*GW* 12: 458–59)

Theodore Savory, in his brief monograph on the problems of translation, discusses the divergence of views on what a translation should seek to achieve and traces the major reason for such divergence to "the neglect of the critic of the reader's point of view" (Savory 57). Yet the picture becomes complicated when, addressing the question of what might be described as a taxonomy of the reader, he postulates four types: the reader who knows nothing at all of the original language; the student; the reader who knew the language in the past; the scholar who knows it still. How can the translator address the perhaps differing, perhaps complementary requirements and expectations of these various readers? And if it is problematic enough—as a 1994 article by Andy Martin and ensuing correspondence in the *Guardian Weekly* suggest—in the case of dictionaries, where the range of available meanings can (or should) at least be listed, how much more complicated does it become when it is a question of the translation of dramatic or poetic texts?

While literary critics and translators may accept the proposition that "all writing is disguised translation, if not interlingual, then intralingual" (Martin 28), there will also be others of their number, perhaps sympathetic to the expectations of the first two categories on Savory's list, who would concur with the *Guardian* correspondent's proposition that dictionaries need to distinguish between "say, peacekeeping, peacemaking and peace enforcement." And not only dictionaries, for such "technical" terms have their analogies in Rilke's "Obstbaum," Brecht's *theatralische[r] Gedanke* (*GW* 17: 1117)—a "piece of stage business'' rather than a "theatrical thought,"—and Benjamin's view of "bad" translation as "an inaccurate transmission of an inessential content" (Benjamin, *Illuminations* 70). Yet the problem of definition implicit in the two epithets remain: who determines the degree of inaccuracy, who decides what is and is not essential?

In a brief note on "Some Factors in Translating Brecht 1967," John Willett, taking the poetry as his starting point, summed up what he saw as the essentials for any translator to keep in mind, as well as listing nine of the most common faults encountered in various translations of works by Brecht ("Factors" 245):

1. Germanisms
2. distortion of the characters
3. impossible verse (specially songs)
4. incongruous dialects, slang, etc. (They can be congruous)
5. wrong speech rhythms
6. failure to match Brecht's use of styles (e.g., his contrasting of heightened and ordinary speech)
7. tinkering with the tempo by breaking sentences up or stringing them together
8. flatness (result of 5, 6 and 7)
9. improvements

Broadly speaking, the available translations of Brecht's works can be divided into three categories: separate works consisting of prose, poetry or drama and translated during Brecht's lifetime or shortly after by figures such as Eric Bentley, H. R. Hays, and Desmond Vesey; translations that have appeared as part of the *Collected Works*—published by Methuen in the United Kingdom and by Random House in the United States—and that use different translators for the English and American editions; and individual plays which have been newly translated, and sometimes adapted, for stage performance. Yet it is ironic that over twenty-five years and several volumes of translations in the Random House/ Methuen editions later, the list's relevance has not diminished: rather it has become more acute because of the proliferation of a particular mode of translation criticized elsewhere by Willett—the "adaptation" or "version." These are, of course, specific to the dramatic *oeuvre*, rather than to the poetry or the fiction, and they represent the most extreme instance of a type of dual translation: first into another language and then, with suitable adjustments, into the "new" culture and a more "familiar" theatrical idiom.

THE DRAMA

To date, none of these "versions," whether they are the work of talented translators, like Ranjit Bolt, or of skilled dramatists in their own right, such as

Howard Brenton, commend themselves as alternatives to the texts published in the Random House/Methuen editions. Too often such versions display various combinations of the defects listed by Willett, together with thinly disguised attempts at providing an ''alternative performing text.'' It must be said that over the course of forty years, none of these ''versions'' could be considered either to have learned the lessons of the Brecht/Laughton *Galileo* or to have improved on it. This translation, still eminently playable, was arrived at in the course of Brecht's extensive and intensive sessions of close collaboration with Laughton himself—a process described by Brecht as one of the classic instances of collaboration between playwright and actor/translator. Reading Brecht's account of the course of a typical day's work on the text—the two men surrounded by dictionaries, thesauruses, copies of Shakespeare, and the Bible, among others, as reference points for style—we find a rehearsal/translation situation analogous to that described as the ideal by Vladimir Nabokov in his article on translating *Eugene Onegin*: ''I want translations with copious footnotes, footnotes reaching up like skyscrapers to the top of this or that page so as to leave only the gleam of one textual line between commentary and eternity. I want such footnotes and the absolutely literal sense, with no emasculation and no padding'' (Nabokov 502).

Unfortunately, few theaters nowadays can provide a workshop situation even remotely comparable to the process enjoyed by Brecht and Laughton. The combination of economic considerations and the reluctance of some translators to accept that the performer might have something useful to contribute on the question of translating the written word into both speech and action (while retaining some of the distinctive manner of the original) means that the version/adaptation—sometimes, though not always, arrived at from a newly prepared ''literal'' translation—is already in written form by the first day of rehearsals, with the result that only minor alterations are made in the course of rehearsal. The usual fate of such versions (and the case is not restricted to Brecht's dramas: something similar holds for those English versions of German dramatists like J.M.R. Lenz, Gerhart Hauptmann, or even Johann Wolfgang von Goethe) is that in the course of four or five weeks, the ''unfamiliar'' is made as ''familiar'' as possible—lest the audience find it too difficult to come to terms not only with a foreign text but also with an ''un-English'' manner of presenting character, milieu, and dramatic action. In such instances, the translator and director would be well advised to heed the comments of Rudolf Pannwitz, quoted approvingly by Benjamin toward the end of his essay: ''Our translations, even the best ones, proceed from a wrong premise. They wish to turn Indian, Greek, English into German instead of turning German into Indian, Greek, English. Our translators have a far greater reverence for the usage of their own language than for the spirit of the foreign works'' (Benjamin, *Illuminations* 80).

To illustrate some of the issues already outlined, let us consider four versions of a speech from *Life of Galileo*—the English adaptation by Laughton as reprinted in *Werke*, and the translations by Wolfgang Sauerlander and Manheim in *CP*, Willett in *Plays*, and Brenton. This speech could, in some respects, serve as a correlative to the process of establishing both meaning and its expression in translated form:

Galileo (*going to platform*): Thus we start the observation of these spots on the sun in which we are interested, at our own risk, not counting too much on protection from a problematical new Pope.

Andrea: But with every likelihood of dispelling Fabrizius' shadows and the vapours of Paris and Prague, and of establishing the rotation of the sun.

Galileo: And with some likelihood of establishing the rotation of the sun. My intention is not to prove that I was right but to find out whether I was right. "Abandon hope all ye who enter an observation." Before assuming these phenomena are spots, which would suit us, let us first set about proving that they are not fried fish. We crawl by inches. What we find today we wipe from the blackboard tomorrow and not keep it—unless it shows up again the day after tomorrow. And if we find anything which would suit us, that thing we will eye with particular distrust. In fact, we will approach this observation of the sun with the implacable determination to prove that the earth stands still and only if hopelessly defeated in this pious undertaking, can we allow ourselves to wonder if we may not have been right all the time; that the earth turns. (*Werke* 5: 159–60)

* * *

Galileo: And now let's start observing these spots in the sun which interest us—at our own risk, not counting too much on the protection of a new pope . . .

Andrea (*interrupting*): But fully confident of dispelling Mr. Fabricius' star shadows and the solar vapors of Prague and Paris, and proving that the sun rotates.

Galileo: Reasonably confident that the sun rotates. My aim is not to prove that I am right, but to find out whether or not I have been, I say: Abandon hope, all ye who enter upon observation. Maybe it's vapors, maybe it's spots, but before we assume that they're spots, though it would suit us if they were, we'd do better to assume they're fishtails. Yes, we shall start all over again from scratch. And we won't rush ahead with seven-league boots, but crawl at a snail's pace. And what we find today we'll wipe from the blackboard tomorrow, and not write it down again until we find it a second time. And if there's something we hope to find, we'll regard it with particular distrust when we do find it. Accordingly let us approach our observation of the sun with the inexorable resolve to prove that the earth *stands still!* Only after we have failed, after we have been totally and hopelessly defeated and are licking our wounds in utter dejection, only then shall we begin to ask whether the earth does not indeed move! (*CP* 5: 69–70)

* * *

Galileo: So let us embark on the examination of those spots on the sun in which we are interested, at our own risk and without banking too much on the protection of a new pope.

Andrea (*interrupting*): But fully convinced that we shall dispel Mr Fabricius's star shadows along with the sun vapours of Paris and Prague, and establish the rotation of the sun.

Galileo: Somewhat convinced that we shall establish the rotation of the sun. My object is not to establish that I was right but to find out if I am. Abandon hope, I say, all ye who enter on observation. They may be vapours, they may be spots, but before we assume that they are spots—which is what would suit us best—we should assume that they are fried fish. In fact we shall question everything all over again. And we shall go forward not in seven-league boots but at a snail's pace. And what we discover today we shall wipe off the slate tomorrow and only write it up again once we have again discovered it. And whatever we wish to find we shall regard, once found, with particular mistrust. So we shall approach the observation of the sun with an irrevocable determination to establish that the earth does *not* move. Only when we have failed, have been utterly and hopelessly beaten and are licking our wounds in the profoundest depression, shall we start asking if we weren't right after all, and the earth does go round. (*Plays* 3: 80–81).

* * *

Galileo: So. We begin our observation of the spots on the sun. They interest us. We do this at our own risk. We do not count too much on the protection of a new Pope.

Andrea (*interrupting*): But blithely confident of blowing away the star clouds of Signore Clavius and the sun vapours of Prague and Paris, and of proving the rotation of the sun.

Galileo: With some confidence of proving the rotation of the sun. I do not hope to prove I have been right up to now—but to find out if I have been. I say—abandon hope, all you who enter into an observation. Perhaps they're vapours. Perhaps they're spots. But before we say they are spots, let us say they are fishes tails. We'll question everything, everything, all over again. And we won't run at it in great big boots, we'll go at a snail's pace. And what we find today, we'll strike from the record tomorrow. And only when we find it once more will we write it in. And when we find something we want to find, we'll look at it with fierce suspicion. So—we will now start our observation of the sun with the determination to prove the earth STANDS STILL! And only when we fail, when we're beaten and licking our wounds, shattered and depressed, will we ask—were we right, does the earth go round the sun? (Brecht/Brenton 61–62)

In Brecht's original, Galileo's declaration of his belief in empirical science, his commitment to first principles, his constructive doubting, are expressed not in the brisk, clipped, simple sentences of Brenton's version, but in what Brecht himself referred to as ''aria form.'' The text of the play is dotted with such rhetorical passages, not all of them put into the mouth of the central character. And when Brecht describes approvingly how Laughton would bring in copies of varied literary texts in order to find an equivalent verbal *Gestus* for the original German, it suggests he has an expectation that any translation of the play must respond to and give a sense of its rhetorical expansiveness at moments when action is replaced by reflection and oratory.

When the Brenton version turns Galileo's opening—a somewhat oratorical prelude to the observation of sun spots—into a sequence of five short sentences, it turns Brecht's Galileo, pleased with his own command of language, into something akin to a Hemingway character speaking in terse headlines rather than in the style that reflects Galileo's literal and figurative expansiveness. Yet this expansiveness does not carry over into the absolute conviction that what he discovers is right; and the would-be translator might smile wryly at the gradations of confidence expressed in the opening phrase of Galileo's "aria." For where Andrea and Galileo in Brecht's original German (with Willett in *Plays*, Sauerlander/Manheim in *CP*, and Brenton following) speak of setting out on the scientific journey with varying degrees of confidence, in Laughton/Brecht's version pupil and mentor opt for every/some likelihood—which refers as much to the aims of the journey as to the state of mind of those undertaking it. Yet the expression seems neater and more apposite in English than the, strictly speaking, more literal translation; and perhaps the reader can do no better than echo the words of a reviewer of a recent translation of Enzensberger's poetry who, confronted with a translation such as "Blast the old days," suggested he found it "somewhat free . . . until [he] saw it was Enzensberger's own" (Lezard 28).

Of all the translations cited above, the Sauerlander/Manheim moves at a brisker pace than the others; it contains more elisions, opts for a more colloquial style. While this may allow the actor to feel more comfortable with the lines, it nevertheless works against the slightly grander, mock-rhetorical tone of the original. And it is perhaps symptomatic of the somewhat reductionist approach of the American Sauerlander/Manheim version that Galileo can begin his "aria" with the matter-of-fact statement that he is "reasonably confident that the sun rotates," whereas the original (and the other translations) emphasizes the link between confidence and *proof* of the rotation of the sun.

In some respects, the approach to the scientific task—founded on productive doubt, which Galileo describes in his monologue—could well apply, *mutatis mutandis*, to the translation of Brecht's drama into English. The first stage, in an ideal situation, would be to establish a workable hypothesis, in the form of a readable and playable translation, while the second would consist of seeking to establish not that it was right, but whether it was right—in other words, precisely the procedure followed by Brecht and Laughton. (And it is indicative of the problems of register confronting the translator that Brecht's original sentence ends with the pithy "but to find out whether," whereas the English translations all fill it out with a subordinate clause).

One could continue to contrast the respective alternative readings of all four translations: is "fierce suspicion" more "playable" than "particular mistrust"? Or "in the profoundest depression" (Willett) a worse state than "in utter dejection" (Sauerlander/Manheim), especially when the Laughton/Brecht speaks simply of "this pious undertaking"—which clearly is not in the German, but which equally clearly sounds the self-mocking note of the original which is hard to catch in the English? And yet, if it is accepted that the Brenton version is and was playable, it follows that the Galileo the audience saw and heard was a less complicated, more obvious figure than Brecht's original.

Common to the three other translations is at least the awareness that Brecht's play about the new age of science and the social responsibility of its practitioners combines instruction with entertainment; for this to be appropriately reflected in the English translation, the translator will need at times to employ a complex sentence structure and more elaborate syntax for those moments of scientific exposition or the expression of personal or philosophical beliefs. As Brecht himself put it: "The director must not for a moment forget that many of the actions and speeches are hard to understand" (*CP* 5: 237).

This is the same Brecht who, in a 1944 *Journals* entry prompted by Arthur Waley's *Translations from the Chinese*, noted with some dismay that the latter could not grasp the fact that there is no distinction between "didacticism" and "amusement" (335). This combination, a variation on Horace's "either to delight or to be useful" (*aut delectare aut prodesse*) finds its expression in all of Brecht's work from the late 1920s onwards, and as such represents a dialectic to which the translator must be responsive. Neatly turned epigrams and brisk, no-nonsense simple sentences may sound to the audience like a "sprightly translation"; but they are not always an appropriate rendering of Brecht's ideas and the various registers of language—rhetorical, matter-of-fact, expository, quasi-Biblical, mock-literary, and parodistic—he employs. It is better for the translator to aim at some equivalent of the various registers rather than to attempt to iron out the language so that it operates in one bland, unexceptionable register throughout. Brecht could have been sounding a cautionary note for such translators when he observed in 1944: "no wonder we find that learning, practised as the quick purchase of knowledge for resale purposes, arouses displeasure. in happier times learning meant a pleasurable absorption of the arts (in the baconian sense)" (*Journals* 335).

It is consequently mistaken for any translator to simplify the dialectic of instruction and entertainment (which informs all the plays from the 1930s onwards) and to seek to cut Brecht's thought, and the sentences that express it, down to size and package them as some form of easily marketable commodity. Auden's punchy rendition of the famous lines from *The Threepenny Opera* as "Grub first: Then ethics" (Auden 134) is both immediate and colorful; but it is some way from the deliberately precept-shaped and prescriptive tone of the German which also, of course, fits Kurt Weill's music.[3] Manheim/Willett's rendering of this epigram by "Food is the first thing, morals follow on" (*CP* 2: 202) reverses the order of the German in order to retain an equivalent to the balancing of the position of the two nouns, and allows the sentence to follow the shape of Weill's music. But as there is no direct English equivalent for the crudeness of *Fressen* ("stuff your faces" might correspond roughly to the sense of the German), the translator has to fall back on a more neutral term. The Manheim/Willett version opts for alliteration as an analogue to the assonance of the repeated "s" sounds, but it cannot offer an exact correlation to the balance of "Erst" (first) versus "dann" (then).

Michael Feingold is the latest in a long line of translators/adaptors to tackle *The Threepenny Opera*, and his version of the lines, though it provides an exact equivalent to the balanced syntax of the German original, with "First comes the feeding . . . then the moral code," suffers from over-politeness when compared with the German. So the task for any translator would be to find some amalgam of Auden's terseness, Manheim/Willett's clarity, Feingold's capturing of the German thought-sequence, and fit this precisely to Weill's music. It is, of course, impossible; and the series of compromises a translator must be ready to accommodate are significantly increased when there is the additional question of a musical setting.

It is also within this context of a discussion of differing performing texts of the plays that the question of the "English versus American version" needs addressing. As Willett points out in his notes, the imprimatur for establishing separate American and English translations is an influential one: "Stefan Brecht was very insistent that the Random House edition must use only American translations and the corresponding Methuen edition 'British' translations; this, he said, was because each theatre had its own modes of speech, and translations could not cross the Atlantic. I think he said it had also been his father's view" ("Factors" 242–43).

This response to the old cliché of two nations divided by a single language is, essentially, another variation on the "familiarizing" process outlined earlier. Yet it is hard to see how Brecht himself might have justified this differentiation, given the collaboration on *Galileo* with Laughton. For at the time Brecht began working on the text with the actor, Laughton had not appeared on stage (as distinct from screen) in America for many years, and his acting style, of which his vocal delivery and diction were an integral part, was frequently derided by some reviewers as "too English" and "old-fashioned," precisely because it still bore evidence of his origins. And although there are occasional nods in the direction of American usage in the text itself, it is difficult to see what set of criteria might be used to establish its "American" as opposed to its "British" qualities. Moreover, if one considers this question in a wider context—for instance, with reference to translations of Chekhov or Strindberg—the crude divisions between "American" and "British" versions disappear: Michael Frayn's translations of Chekhov have played in America, as have Michael Meyer's (though sometimes unacknowledged) of Strindberg. Similarly, translations done by American scholars of the same playwrights have been performed in the wider English-speaking world. Again, Willett's point is worth repeating: "all that's needed is for publisher or producer to change a word here and there, transmuting sidewalks to pavements and vice versa" (*Brecht* 244).

Yet it must be conceded that in the case of Brecht and Weill's most famous work, *The Threepenny Opera*, the question is particularly problematic. Because of the success in the 1950s of Marc Blitzstein's version, together with the hit parade fame of "Mac the Knife" in versions by Bobby Darin and Louis Armstrong, the work has come to occupy a position in the American musical theater somewhere between *The Cradle will Rock* and *Guys and Dolls*. Specifically, the Americanization of the work has meant that it is now difficult for any more faithful or idiomatic versions of the lyrics to songs like "Mac the Knife" or "Pirate Jenny" to establish themselves in the face of the earlier, more sanitized versions, which have by now become popular, if counterfeit, currency.

What is one to make of the opening lines of the former in the Blitzstein version—with its lame introduction of the two "dears" as an attempt to solve both the rhythmic problem and the *Gestus* of the ballad-singer—as he sets out both to ingratiate himself with, and instruct the audience? Or the register of the Blitzstein version of "Pirate Jenny," which turns a black and visionary account of rebellion and revenge as wish-fulfillment (though, of course, only somewhere under a pastel rainbow) into a downmarket and blandly Americanized cabaret number?

Perhaps the most egregious instance of how a nonliteral translation has contributed to a construction of meaning somewhat at odds with the original is Blitzstein's choice, in the same song, of the phrase "The ship, the black freighter" as a translation of Brecht's "ship with eight sails." It is a particularly problematic instance of the complexities of conveying meaning in translation, with the issue further complicated by the additional factors of rhythm, sound, and musical setting. To take the last two points together: given the shape of the musical phrase Weill chooses to underlay the text, with the fall over the two syllables of *Se-geln* in the German original, "freigh-ter" is a neat solution. The vowel sounds in both languages are similar, and breaking the English word the way he has, Blitzstein does not twist the syllables out of recognizable shape. Yet the connotations of "the black freighter" are altogether different from what the German indicates; and even if one might concede that a freighter may be powered by sail rather than steam, the choice of the ominous epithet "black" immediately makes crudely explicit what Brecht's neutral image, even by the second stanza, merely implies.

On the other hand, it might be debatable whether Manheim/Willett's literal translation is as happy a translation when sung, as his "See the shark with teeth like razors" (*CP* 2: 147) with its sense-and-sound equivalent for the German original shows. The juxtaposition of two identical diphthongs and the elongation of one syllable into two to fit the music ("eight sai-ls") is a problem; it might perhaps be less noticeable if the musical phrase rose rather than fell, though even then the tendency to sing the word as "say-els" would be hard to avoid.

This simple example could stand as a representative instance of the sense/sound, words/ideas style of the original/style of the translator dichotomies, as well as a gloss on the nature of the reader/listener/performer's contribution to the construction of meaning. On the page, no one can object to "ship with eight sails": the assonance might either slip by or be noted as "deliberate" and appreciated accordingly, while in performance, the awkward echoing of sounds tends to dominate over meaning—unless, that is, the performer finds a way around the problem. On the other hand, the Blitzstein version, while offering an effective solution to the problem of the sound of the phrase, provides a reconstructed (rather than deconstructed) answer to the question of meaning and, in so doing, also demonstrates how translation slides into adaptation.

Inevitably, the translator will occasionally encounter colorful or unusual images, pieces of folk wisdom, or pithy sayings that might require some creative modification in English. But when, for example, in the opening speech from *Mother Courage and Her Children* Manheim renders the recruiter's comment on the way one of his charges escapes from under his nose as "Sure enough, he's gone, like a fart out of a goose" (*CP* 5: 135), his choice of simile is neither creative nor apt. (Why not, for example, any other representative of farmyard poultry?) Willett's translation—"He's off like a flea with the itch" (*Plays* 2: 97)—alters the simile's focus by shifting the sense of the German which is, literally, "Like a louse from a scratch." Yet, even this is ambiguous, for "scratch" could be read (or, in the theater, heard) as meaning "abrasion," whereas what the German means is "The act of scratching." Where the translator of *Galileo* is confronted by the need to find equivalents for a dramatic language that is rich in rhetorical gesture and the eloquent expression of scientific and philosophical ideas, *Mother Courage*, with its mixture of the vernacular, its parodistic echoes of the Bible and folk tales, its invention of a dialect which combines elements from the German translation of Jaroslav Hašek's *The Good Soldier Švejk* with traces of Bavarian dialect, poses an even greater set of problems. Willett's choice of a "form of northern English . . . [as] a valid attempt to equate one provincial no-nonsense idiom with another" (Willett, "Introduction" xxxiv) worked well as a radio play, but would, unfortunately, not fit an American production.

However, when the American translation of one of Courage's speeches from scene nine renders the first three sentences thus: "Lamb, I'm sick of roaming around, myself. I feel like a butcher's dog that pulls the meat cart but doesn't get any for himself. I've nothing left to sell and the people have no money to pay for it" (*CP* 5: 196), it is hard to see what is specifically "American" about this blandly mid-Atlantic equivalent for the character's rough, clipped, and hardhitting language. The proliferation of verbs in the translation's second sentence (instead of participles, which would reflect the bluntness of the original) slows the sentence and the speech. The decision not to echo the four repeated "nix" of the German—"I am . . . getting nothing from it all. I've got nothing to sell, and people have got nothing left to pay for Nothing" (*Werke* 6: 73)—misses both the incongruity and the necessary emphases. And when one comes to *The Good Person of Szechwan* and *The Caucasian Chalk Circle*, a further set of problems arises, relating to the lyrical and poetic diction of the former, and the fairy-tale and fabulous elements of the latter. For all three plays, some latterday version of the poetic dramatic language of John Millington Synge, Sean O'Casey, or even Eugene O'Neill might be appropriate: what is certain is that without some attempt at sounding a poetic register, the plays become flat, banal, bathetic.

THE POETRY

Although Brecht's poetry does pose some, at times, insurmountable problems for the translator, there are enough idiomatic translations of songs from the plays and of many of the better-known poems to suggest that a readiness to respond to the poetic and metaphorical aspects of Brecht's dramatic language could yet yield more effective translations. When Bentley asserts that "In English, things have to be said more tersely than in German. Hence, English translations from German should always come out shorter than the original" ("Introduction" 12), he is offering a generalization which is not merely untenable (are the English translations of works by Hegel, Marx, Grass shorter than the original?) but reductive in its approach to translating Brecht's language and its manner of expression.

And while Bentley's essay suggests that Brecht was pragmatic in his attitude to cutting and changing the text of *The Good Person*, Willett's account of Brecht's objections to his translation of the concluding tercet of the Gods from the same play, namely, that Willett "missed its self-conscious, almost parodistic beauty" (Willett, "Englishman" 17) suggests that Brecht was vitally interested in tone and register—both crucial for the rendering of poetry in translation. Brecht himself, though he had comparatively little to say (and nothing particularly systematic) on the subject of translating poetry into another language, did make a number of isolated observations over the years that warrant consideration. When these are taken in conjunction with his own practice and response to translations, a suggestive if contradictory picture emerges. Writing in the 1930s he declares: "You usually inflict the worst damage on poems, when translating them into another language, by trying to translate too much. You should perhaps be satisfied with translating the thoughts and attitude of the original. You should try to translate what, in the rhythm of the original, is an element of the writer's attitude—no more than that" (*GW* 19: 404). When such remarks are considered in relation to the range of poetry in translation that he first read as an adolescent—especially the works of Rudyard Kipling, François Villon, and Arthur Rimbaud, who provided him with formal and thematic material for both *The Threepenny Opera* and his first collection of poems, *Manual of Piety*—it becomes clear that the question is a little more complicated than merely translating "attitude."

As Hanns Otto Münsterer points out in his memoir of the years between 1917 and 1922, a series of volumes of poetry, *Aus fremden Gärten* (From Distant Gardens), mostly translated by the Hungarian-born Otto Hauser, was well known to and widely read by Brecht and his circle (*Brecht* 27). Hauser, an extraordinary polymath, who himself translated from most of the European languages, was for, the most part, skillful at combining literal meaning with forms appropriate to both German and the original language. Brecht's early familiarity with French and English verse, together with his interest in Chinese poetry, are both traceable to his reading of such volumes in Hauser's collection. In the 1920s his collaborator Elisabeth Hauptmann drew his attention to Kipling translations by Lindau and Rosenzweig (Lyon, *Kipling* 54–55) while also translating some herself; and it is an indication of the accuracy of the various translators' attempts to reproduce Kipling's meter and rhythm in German that in one instance the English original can be set, without alteration, to Weill's musical underlay from the German translation. This is the case with "Polly's Song" at the end of the first scene of Act 2 in *The Threepenny Opera*. One of the more bizarre "translations" of this song is that by Feingold. It it is almost unsingable but provides a good illustration of how a translator with, apparently, little sense of the attitude of the speaker and the tone of the lines, can nullify the immediacy and colloquial directness of what he takes to be Brecht's original.[4]

While Brecht, in the comment cited above from the 1930s, argues for a relaxed and even unliteral approach to translation, it is clear from even a cursory comparison of Hauptmann's and his German versions of Kipling's English poems that his practice was to try and capture something of the rhythmic and formal structure of the original. The same approach holds for his translations/adaptations of Arthur Waley's translations of Chinese verse, where he rarely departs from the formal layout and syntactical structure of the English models that provided the starting point. On the other hand, when it is a case of poems or songs with a social or political function, Brecht's remarks, made on different occasions in the late 1920s and the 1930s, indicate that not only form but also function, meaning, and even aesthetic criteria were all questions that required consideration. In a sardonic yet informative 1927 letter to Erwin Piscator explaining why he had not completed a translation of a ballad of Upton Sinclair's for a German production of one of his dramas, he confesses that it was a lack of poetic and "revolutionary" qualities in the original which prevented him from finishing the task: "The poem, I believe, is not a good one. It's pretty, it's touching [it reads affectingly], the theme is objectively sound, but believe me, there's not an ounce of revolutionary feeling [effect] in it" (*Letters* 112).

In such instances, Brecht's pragmatic response to the issue suggests that both literary and political considerations prevailed. Similarly, when he tackles the question of translating songs of political struggle, he emphasizes that "the translator must not capitulate in the face of undoubted difficulties" (*GW* 19: 405) but should seek viable alternatives to what might be too specific or localized catch phrases or expressions. Songs of agitation, which are intended to have a role in the political struggle of the times, require of the translator a readiness to balance the general against the particular. The general are the large-scale, common goals, and to attain and express these the translator should be prepared to alter the specifics in terms of the needs of the particular situation. While each race, each group may express itself in specific ways, the translator, like the author of the original, must find appropriate, popular expressions for abstract phrases and formulations. Elsewhere, Brecht might assert that "A good expression is worth noting / So long as the occasion can recur / For which it is good" (*Poems* 195–96), but such an elastic approach to meaning and its expression is more suited to the translation of works for the stage than to providing fluent, intelligible, and idiomatic versions of the poetry.

Given Brecht's command of a wide range of poetic forms and techniques, the responsive and flexible translations of his poems—*Poems 1913–1956* (1976) and *Poems & Songs from the Plays* (1990), collected in the two volumes already published under Willett and Manheim's editorship—will remain definitive for some time to come. Rightly, as they indicate in their notes, they have opted in favor of rendering both the form and the sense of Brecht's poetry; and while there may always be, as Brecht noted in a letter to his American translator H.R. Hays, "implications which may escape the most ingenious student of language" (quoted in *Poems* 519), the various translators involved in the *Poems* have provided accurate, unforced, and lively versions that capture both Brecht's mastery of forms and his distinctive tone.

On the face of it, one might assume that the task of translating Brecht's "rhymeless verse with irregular rhythms" would be less demanding than rendering the early ballads, chorales, and songs in some English equivalent. Not so: for as the introduction notes, "[The editors] found, largely by a process of collaborative trial and error, that even in the unrhymed verse the rhythms, line breaks and order of thought (if not order of words) had as far as possible to be maintained" (*Poems* xxv). And though the editors cite Brecht's own unrhymed translation of Shelley's "Mask of Anarchy" as an instance of Brecht's not trying to translate too much, it is significant that he does follow the order of thought and, for the most part, the order of words in his line-for-line version of the original. But major difficulties arise when one seeks to observe all the points outlined above and fit a poem's words, sense, word order, and rhythm to an extant musical setting. If, for example, one compares Willett's translation of a number from *The Measures Taken* with an earlier translation that was not intended to fit Eisler's music, some revealing details emerge:

> The rice grows down the river
> The people in the upper provinces need that rice.
> If we leave the rice where it is
> Then rice will grow more expensive.
> The coolies who haul the rice-barges will get even less rice then.
> Then rice will be even less expensive for me.
> What is rice anyway?
> Do I know what rice is?
> How should I know who should know?
> I don't know what rice is.
> All I know is its price.
>
> (Brecht/Mueller 23–24)

> Rice can be had down the river.
> People in the remoter provinces need their rice.

If we can keep that rice off the market
Rice is bound to get dearer.
Then the men who pull the barges must go short of rice
And I shall get my rice for even less.
What is rice, anyhow?
Don't ask me what rice is.
Don't ask me my advice.
I've no idea what rice is.
All I have learnt is its price.

(Poems & Songs 100–101)

What is immediately obvious from a comparison of the two translations is the paradoxical fact that the restrictions imposed on the translator by the need to fit his version to Eisler's music has resulted in a more graphic, more direct, and ultimately more intelligible rendering of the German. Whereas Carl Mueller's opening two lines are bland and even vague (the temptation is to read his opening line as some oddly surreal image of rice growing down over or along the river), the Willett translation brings the antithetical and balanced structure of the original German into sharper focus. And where the German in lines three and four speaks of leaving the rice in the storehouses so that it will then become dearer for the people in the upper provinces, Willett's paraphrase, which relates the situation depicted in the song directly to the laws of the marketplace, drives home the point both through a new, colloquial image (keeping the rice off the market) and through the more conversational "bound to get dearer."

The echoing of "grow" in the first translation in line four is particularly unfortunate. In this case the (presumably intended) pun only serves to lessen the impact of the statement. At every turn, the Willett translation works more effectively: more succinct, more emphatic, it also demonstrates what Brecht means when he speaks of rhythmic elements in connection with attitude and manner and ties them both to his notion of *Gestus*. Moreover, even though the original German asks "Do I know what rice is?" Willett's English version is not only more immediate in terms of the *Gestus*, but is, as it happens, a more correct rendering of the German's rhetorical colloquialism. One might perhaps suggest "All that I know is its price" as closer to the German than Willett's version; but learning and knowing are related, and in this case the suggestion that the merchant has learned the laws of supply and demand is not at odds with the original.

While there will inevitably be occasions when a translation linked to its musical setting may miss elements to be found in a freer version, it is important to note that many of the Willett translations intended to fit settings by the various composers with whom Brecht worked (most notably Hanns Eisler) are more often than not clearer and more vivid than versions that ignore the musical setting.

OTHER WORKS

Apart from the poetry and the drama, there is currently a reasonable range of Brecht's theoretical and other writings available in English. Perhaps the most useful and influential of all the works has been Willett's 1964 edition of essays, notes, and comments entitled *Brecht on Theatre* (*Theatre*). The translations are accurate and readable, and Willett's notes, taking in details of first publication and relating the texts to the wider picture of Brecht's work and its political and cultural context, are exemplary. The reader seeking more detailed information and background on particular plays can be referred to the introductions and notes to individual dramas in both the American and English editions.

However, given the variety of material that has appeared over thirty years in both the Suhrkamp *GW* and later *Werke* editions, there is now a need for a supplementary volume of selected writings not only on the theater but also on art, literature, and politics. While the early *Diaries* (1979), the *Letters 1913–1956* (1990), and the recently published *Journals 1934–1955* (1993) provide both valuable insights into Brecht's working process and unsystematic though productive glosses on social, personal, and artistic issues that concerned him, there are still many important essays, articles, and commentaries that remain inaccessible to the English-speaking reader.

The same situation applies in the case of Brecht's narrative prose. The *Three-penny Novel* (reissued in 1956), the *Tales from the Calendar* (1961), and the *Short Stories 1921–1946* (1983) remain the only works available in English translation. While the merits of the unfinished novel *Die Geschäfte des Herrn Julius Caesar* (The Business Dealings of Mr. Julius Caesar) may remain a topic for critical debate, the fact that both it and the incomplete text complexes known as *Me-ti* (The Book of Twists and Turns) and the *Tui* novel are not yet translated into English, precludes not only an adequate appraisal of Brecht's importance as a prose-writer but also a fuller appreciation of the range of his responses to the central political and cultural questions of his age. In this respect, French and Italian readers, for example, are better served by the availability of a wider selection of Brecht's works.

It is not accidental that, in a letter to his friend Ferdinand Reyher in 1944, Brecht singled out the question of finding the right tone—in this case for the translation of his play *Schweyk in the Second World War*—as the main consideration for any translator. But it is not greatly reassuring for the prospective translator to find him one sentence later declaring that "it's a matter of luck" (*Letters* 376). Luck, perhaps, but also an attention to a series of basic details. At various times in his writings and conversations he suggests having available "a short list of words and phrases [from the original] . . . [which are] hard to translate, along with rough translations, which we will always be able to straighten out" (*Letters* 116); points out that Auden was not wrong, though to be blamed for using different meters for two poems from *The Caucasian Chalk Circle* instead of retaining the original German meter; and proves almost impossible to please when Bentley suggests alternative translations for the opening word of the poem "To Those Born Later." In his essay "Bad Language: Poetry, Swearing and Translation," which he describes as "deliberately inconclusive" (56), the English poet and critic Craig Raine, who concedes that he has no knowledge of German, devotes three pages to a consideration of the opening sections of this poem. He juxtaposes a version by the West Indian poet Derek Mahon, parts of which he considers an "inspired rendition" that "ends up as imitation" (49), and his own translation of the lines, which he describes as a "critique" of the Manheim/Willett version in *Poems*. But in his own translation of the opening three sections, there are phrases that seem to exemplify nothing so much as the smoothing out in keeping with the familiar idioms of the translator's language that Benjamin, through Pannwitz, criticizes in the essay cited above.

However, in the same way that Brecht's dramas are the result of a collaborative process, he is also convinced that translation, particularly for the stage, must not only "be revised with a view to production" (*Letters* 403) but also should draw on the responses and collaboration of others. Given the logistic and economic problems related to publishing translations, this may not always be a realizable objective. But, like the goal in "To Those Born Later," it is at least visible, and the committed translator(s) should continue to strive for it, aiming to capture what Friedrich Nietzsche in *Beyond Good and Evil* refers to as the most difficult quality to render in another language—"The tempo of its [i.e., the original's] style" (41).

NOTES

1. Significantly—and ironically—Rilke's original speaks not of an "olive tree," but a "fruit tree." Whether this is Belitt's mistranslation or an adaptation of the original is unclear.

2. Another translation of Benjamin's sentence (by Hynd and Valk)—"To know a work of art or a genre well, it is of little use to take heed of the audience, of the respondent"—might suggest, in view of its periphrastic style, that the translator has responded only too readily to Benjamin's assertion.

3. The original German runs: "Erst kommt das Fressen, dann kommt die Moral" (*GW* 2: 458). Literally, "First comes stuffing one's face, then come(s) morals (morality)." See also Herbert Knust, "First Comes the Belly, then Morality," in this volume.

4. The Hauptmann/Brecht translation (*GW* 2: 438) sticks closely to both the word order and meter/rhyme scheme of Kipling's original: "Nice while it lasted, an' now it is over / Tear out your 'eart an' good-bye to your lover! / What's the use o'grievin', when the mother that bore you/ (Mary, pity women!) knew it all before you?" (Kipling 231).

WORKS CITED (SEE ALSO REFERENCE GUIDE TO WORKS CITED IN ABBREVIATED FORM)

Auden, Wystan Hugh. *A Certain World. A Commonplace Book*. London: Faber, 1971.

Belitt, Ben. *Adam's Dream. A Preface to Translation*. New York: Grove, 1978.

Benjamin, Walter. "The Task of the Translator." Translated by Harry Zohn. In *Illuminations* 69–82.

———. "The Task of the Translator." Translated by James Hynd and E. M. Valk. *Delos* 2 (1968): 76–97.

Bentley, Eric. "Introduction." *The Caucasian Chalk Circle*, by Bertolt Brecht. New York: Grove, 1966. 5–14.

Brecht, Bertolt. *Life of Galileo*. Translated by Howard Brenton. London: Methuen, 1990.

———. *The Measures Taken*. In *The Measures Taken and other Lehrstücke*. Translated by Carl Mueller. London: Methuen, 1979.

———. *Vocal Selections from the The Threepenny Opera*. English adaptation of lyrics by Marc Blitzstein, music by Kurt Weill. New York: Warner, 1984.

———. *The Threepenny Opera*. Translated by Michael Feingold. Typescript. Valley Forge, PA: European American Music Corporation, 1989.

Kipling, Rudyard. *Verse. Definitive Edition*. New York: Doubleday, 1940.

Lezard, Nicholas. Review of *Selected Poems*, by Hans Magnus Enzensberger. *Guardian Weekly* (3 July 1994).

MacFarlane, James. "Modes of Translation." In *Ibsen and Meaning. Studies, Essays, and Prefaces 1953–1987*. Norwich: Norvik, 1989.

Martin, Andy. "Surf's up—but not in French." *Guardian Weekly* (21 August 1994): 228.

Nabokov, Vladimir. "Problems of Translation: *Onegin* in English." *Partisan Review* 22 (Autumn 1955): 496–512.

Nietzsche, Friedrich. *Complete Works*. 1909–1913. Edited by Oscar Levy. Vol. 12, *Beyond Good and Evil*. Translated by Helen Zimmern. New York: Russell, 1964.

Raine, Craig. "Bad Language: Poetry, Swearing and Translation." *Thumbscrew* 1 (Winter 1994–1995): 30–56.

Savory, Theodore. *The Art of Translation*. London: Cape, 1968.

Willett, John. "An Englishman Looks at Brecht." In *Brecht in Context* 9–20.

———. "Some Factors in Translating Brecht 1967." In *Brecht in Context* 242–45.

———. "Introduction." *Mother Courage and Her Children*, by Bertolt Brecht. Translated by John Willett, edited by Hugh Rorrison. London: Methuen, 1983. xvii–xxxv.

15

Brecht and the American Theater

CARL WEBER

In 1920, the twenty-two-year-old Bertolt Brecht began a prose poem in his collection "Psalms": "I am a band in Chicago. Niggers are drumming on the benches and applauding with their fat soles on the spit-covered floor, cigar butts stuck between their fangs. I'm playing the Marseillaise" (*Werke* 11: 19).

The young poet from the provincial Bavarian city of Augsburg was fascinated by an America he knew from the books that he voraciously read, for example, Upton Sinclair's *The Jungle*, and from the silent movies of Charlie Chaplin and other stars, many of whom he admired as exemplars of an acting style that he felt the German theater of his time was sorely lacking—as we know from his comments (Weber, "Vaudeville's Children" 55–57). He was equally impressed by the new kind of American music the Germans called *Yatss* (jazz), which became popular in the years right after World War I. His poem is an example of the wild and exotic fantasies in which many young European writers during the years before and after the war liked to indulge. Brecht, however, retained a fascination with America throughout his life, even if his view sobered somewhat after he eventually had to settle in the land of his youthful dreams and got to know it intimately.

In his first anthology of poetry, *Manual of Piety* (1927), eight poems out of forty-nine deal with American topics. For eight of the forty performance texts he completed, he elected America as the site of the action—an environment he placed more often on stage than any other one on the globe. Chicago—not Berlin or Paris or London—seems to have loomed as the archetypal modern big city in Brecht's mind; the plots of three of his major plays unfold in the Windy City—*In the Jungle of Cities*, *Saint Joan of the Stockyards*, and *The Resistible Rise of Arturo Ui*—as does the musical *Happy End* by his collaborator, Elisabeth Hauptmann, for which Brecht wrote the lyrics; he also contemplated a further play about Chicago, which he never completed. The American Revolution is a central topic in the last adaptation Brecht created with his team of collaborators at his theater in East Berlin; the comedy *Trumpets and Drums* was staged at the Berliner Ensemble one year before his death.[1] There is no other Central European poet or playwright who has so insistently portrayed the United States, or rather his own mythical version of it, as a paradigm of the modern world and a harbinger of its future.

How, then, were Brecht's plays about America as well as his thirty-two other dramas received in the country that so consistently engaged his interest? Did the society he repeatedly used as a model to demonstrate the quandaries of contemporary history embrace his theatrical projects? How has the American theater responded to Brecht's model of an epic and dialectic theater that tried to fuse entertainment with education—two activities the American tradition regards as mutually exclusive? And how did he himself fare in the country that once held such a powerful fascination for him when he was living there as an immigrant who had been banished from the culture and the language that were the roots of his talent and achievements?

When Brecht and his family arrived in California in July 1941, the playwright had to prepare for a long exile and a new career in the United States. Hitler's conquest of Europe appeared to be irrevocable at the time. The Soviet armies had disintegrated in hasty retreat before the advancing German troops, a weakened England remained the only country still fighting the Reich in the West, and America's entry into the war was by no means assured. Brecht, after a period of recuperation from the culture shock he suffered in his first encounter with Hollywood, set energetically to work, trying to establish himself as a screenwriter and—particularly on his trips to New York City—prospective author for the only professional American theater existing at the time; commercial Broadway. In Los Angeles he tried to activate all the connections he had in the large community of central European exiles in the film industry. Being the pragmatic man of theater he was throughout his life, he eagerly responded to any sign of interest in his work by star actors or well-known directors/producers and wrote several plays with a specific protagonist or interested producer in mind. Luise Rainer, Elisabeth Bergner, and Charles Laughton were among the stars for whom he created plays, as were former collaborators from Berlin, such as the composer Kurt Weill and the producer Ernst Josef Aufricht. Although he succeeded in selling several stories to the Hollywood studios, he certainly did not ''make it'' in the film industry; of his scripts, only *Hangmen also Die*, directed by Fritz Lang, was eventually produced. But little remained of Brecht's original text in the final product, and he was not even mentioned in the credits. Nor did he score on Broadway; none of his major plays were produced there, and only his adaptation of John Webster's *The Duchess of Malfi* had a brief run. The text had been commissioned by Bergner and had been badly mangled in rehearsals by its British director, who had dropped most of Brecht's text and returned to Webster's original work. Brecht was brought in to "doctor" the production during previews on the road but, after receiving poor notices, the show closed in New York after thirty-six performances. That was in 1946, a year after Germany's defeat, when Brecht was already preparing for his return to the country he had been forced to leave thirteen years earlier.

Nonetheless, Brecht's six American years were a truly creative period. He wrote four of his major theater texts (*The Visions of Simone Machard*, *Schweyk in the Second World War*, *The Caucasian Chalk Circle*, and the American version of *Life of Galileo*), close to two hundred poems, several short stories, numerous essays, and a number of film scenarios. He also worked on several texts that remained unfinished such as the versification of *The Communist Manifesto* under the title "Das Manifest," *Der Tui-Roman* (The Tui Novel), and *The Messingkauf Dialogues*. Still, the two professional productions he was able to achieve in the United States, *The Private Life of the Master Race* and *Galileo*, were shown in small houses and had only brief runs, although the *Galileo* production, with the great actor (and cotranslator) Charles Laughton in the title role, offered Brecht the first occasion to direct one of his plays since he had been banned from the German stage in 1933. There were also negotiations with several publishers who were interested in publishing his work, but only the translation *The Private Life of the Master Race* had been published by the time he left the country in late 1947.

Why, one might ask, did Brecht's work meet with such a resounding lack of interest? After all, a number of his fellow exiles enjoyed considerable success in their host country, among them three of Brecht's closest friends and collaborators, the writer Lion Feuchtwanger and the composers Kurt Weill and Hanns Eisler. Brecht's early "Psalm," with its naive notion of American culture, points at one of the reasons. In his writings for stage and screen, Brecht indeed happened to do something that amounted to playing the "Marseillaise." All of his texts contained a subversive element. Either in content matter or in their dramaturgy, they rejected the norms accepted by the American theater and film industry. They also questioned many values that were highly cherished by American society. It was not that Brecht did not try to accommodate the topics and formal patterns that were preferred in Hollywood and on Broadway. The plays he wrote or adapted during his American years offer evidence of a determined effort to do so. But Brecht was neither willing nor capable to suppress his disgust with a capitalist system that he regarded as a source of the evils besetting the modern industrial world. Nor would he force himself to lower his self-decreed artistic standards merely to please the powers that controlled the film and theater industry. While working on a film script he complained, for instance, that observing the "10,000 taboos" amounted to "hard labor" (Völker, *Chronicle* 115).

As to the young poet's other illusion, there were hardly any blacks participating in the American mainstream culture of the time, nor was there a black
audience who would have applauded Brecht's subversive texts. Actually, Brecht
did support an effort to get *The Threepenny Opera* produced with an all-black
cast. His old collaborator Weill who, unlike Brecht, had been remarkably successful on Broadway, was opposed and vetoed the project, convinced it would
thwart the musical's chance for an eventual Broadway production (*Letters* 627–
29).

Brecht met, however, a great number of writers, intellectuals, and theater
artists while living in the United States. By the time he returned to Europe, there
was a small but devoted circle of admirers who were enthusiastic about his work
and doing their best to make his writings known and have his plays produced.
Foremost among them were the stage designer Mordecai Gorelik, who prom-
ulgated Brecht's concept of the epic theater, and the critic Eric Bentley. Bentley
was the first translator of several plays as well as of some theoretical writings;
he also directed a number of stagings in the academic and professional theater.

In the late 1940s, when the first skirmishes of the Cold War took place and
the rise of McCarthyism was impending, the American political climate became
increasingly inhospitable to Brecht's kind of theater. Brecht himself had been
called before the House Un-American Activities Committee, which investigated
the alleged Communist infiltration of the Hollywood film industry, on 30 October 1947. Only his very circumspect performance—and a smart and funny
performance it was, as we can glean from the hearing's audio tape—saved him
from the kind of serious consequences that his friend Eisler had to suffer. The
day after the Washington hearing, Brecht took a plane to Paris. He did not have
occasion to see America again during the nine years that remained of his life.

His sojourn in the United States had been full of frustrations and disappoint-
ments for Brecht, who had been a celebrity in Europe at the time he was forced
into exile by the Nazis' accession of power. In America his efforts had not
achieved any impact to speak of. Still, he never entirely lost his sympathies for
the country that once had intrigued him and had stimulated his imagination as
no other one had done.

For the American mainstream theater, the Brecht who left in 1947 was the
same entity as the Brecht who had arrived in 1941, that is, an obscure writer
known only to a small coterie of Communist and other leftist liberals. There
had been a few productions of his plays, but none of them had attracted much
attention. In terms of a theater culture that rates everything as either a hit or a
flop, this hapless exile had been an unmitigated flop. His failure was probably
no surprise to most of the artists and producers active in the Broadway theater,
since the fate of Brecht's work in the years before he came to live in the United
States had hardly augured a more auspicious result.

The first documented presentation of a Brecht text in America took place in
a concert at the Philadelphia Academy of Music. On 4 April 1931 Leopold
Stokowski conducted a performance of Brecht's radio play *The Flight over the*

Ocean,[2] with music by Weill and Paul Hindemith. At the time, the triumphant 1928 Berlin production of *The Threepenny Opera* had initiated Brecht's international success in Europe; the Brecht/Weill musical had successfully played in Moscow, Paris, Prague, and Warsaw. A *Threepenny* movie, directed by G.W. Pabst, had been well received both in its German and French version, although Brecht had distanced himself from the film project and brought suit against the producing company.[3] We may assume that the Philadelphia concert did not pass unnoticed by East Coast intellectual, music, and theater circles.

By 1933, when Brecht was forced to leave Germany, *The Threepenny Opera* had been translated into eighteen languages and had scored more than 10,000 performances on European stages (*Werke* 2: 442). From the viewpoint of the commercial American theater, a Broadway production of Brecht's European hit musical must have seemed mandatory. On 12 April 1933 *The Threepenny Opera* had its American premiere at New York's Empire Theater. Of the two producers, Gifford Cochran was an experienced and successful old hand on Broadway, while John Krimsky was a young man who had been at Princeton at a time when the school's student theater was a hotbed of talent. After a brief career in banking, Krimsky decided to follow his inclination to become a theatrical producer. He had translated Brecht's text, and his decision to present it on the Broadway of the early 1930s deserved to be called courageous. On the other hand, he and Cochran surely reckoned on repeating the European success of a work that in its shape came so close to the popular American genre of musical comedy. The production, however, closed after twelve performances, a devastating flop that was to have its consequences. In the yearbook of the Broadway season, the names of Brecht and Weill do not even appear in the register. It took thirty years until Brecht's name would appear again on a Broadway marquee.

Two and a half years after the failure of *The Threepenny Opera* on Broadway, Brecht paid his first visit to the country that so profoundly intrigued him. He arrived in New York to attend the rehearsals of *The Mother*, his stage adaptation of Maxim Gorky's famous novel. The play had been optioned by the New York Theatre Union, a left-wing theater company, for a production at the Civic Repertory Theatre. Brecht had been invited, on his own insistence, to collaborate on the text's translation and to advise the director and other members of the production staff. During the weeks of rehearsal, Brecht became embroiled in an increasingly hapless struggle against the distortion of his text in translation and the director's willful ignorance of the concept of epic theater. It was Brecht's first encounter with a supposedly Stanislavsky-based understanding of the actor's art and its social function, which relies on empathy and identification with character and is still a dominant model in American theater training. The clash between this method and Brecht's own paradigm of epic theater has continued to be an important aspect of the American Brecht reception until the present.

After weeks of altercations during which Brecht did not behave all too diplomatically when venting his anger at work that he referred to as "absolute shit,''[4] he and his composer and comrade-in-arms, Eisler, were barred from rehearsals. There was nothing they could do but helplessly wait for the opening on 19 November 1935. It turned out to be an unqualified debacle. A deeply angered and frustrated Brecht wrote to his friend Erwin Piscator in Moscow:

The Mother has been badly butchered here (stupid mutilations, political ignorance, backwardness of all kinds etc.). . . . One thing I can tell you: steer clear of so-called left-wing theatres. They're run by small cliques dominated by hack playwrights who have the manners of the worst Broadway producers without their know-how, which doesn't amount to much, but even so. Even so, you're better off with Shubert, although of course you must read your contract very carefully. (*Letters* 223)

Brecht had learned a lesson he wearily tried to heed when ten years later he himself had to deal with Broadway producers.

Brecht and Eisler made good use of their New York sojourn in other ways. They went to Broadway theaters and, especially, to the movie houses around Times Square. As Eisler later recounted, they called their excursions, tongue-in-cheek, ''social studies'' (*Brecht* 103). Comparing the plays Brecht completed before his first visit to America with those he conceived afterwards, the impact these ''social studies'' had on his concept of theater is quite evident.

There was only one other documented American premiere of a Brecht text in the United States before World War II. The Green Street Theater in San Francisco presented *Señora Carrar's Rifles* in March 1939. The important port on the Pacific had a very active, radical trade union movement and also was home to many left-leaning intellectuals. There obviously was an audience for this agit-prop play about a fisherman's widow who decides to take up arms against the fascists when her husband and son are killed by Franco forces during the Spanish Civil War.

Brecht had already left the United States on a journey that eventually was going to take him to East Berlin, where he would obtain his own theater, when, on 7 December 1947, *Galileo* with Charles Laughton opened in New York after its brief run at the Coronet Theatre of Beverly Hills in the summer of 1947. The California opening had attracted an illustrious crowd of celebrities, among them Charlie Chaplin, Charles Boyer, Ingrid Bergman, Anthony Quinn, and other stars of the time. Yet the reviews were mixed (Houseman 228–42). The New York premiere at Maxine Elliott's Theatre did not fare much better, and the show had to close after three weeks. The most influential critic of the country, Brooks Atkinson of the *New York Times*, panned the play and set a trend that was to dominate the reception of Brecht's work by the critical establishment in the United States for many years to come. Atkinson later called the play one of ''the few devastatingly negative dramas that came from Europe. In form, they were dogmatic and ambitious. . . . In mood, they were savage and bleak'' (Atkinson 403). He commented at the time, ''Both as a play and performance, *Galileo* is fingertips playmaking. . . . Nothing the play says justified Mr. Brecht's

humble and fearful prayer for science in the epilogue'' (Higham 142). It seems
that America and its theater critics, in that victorious postwar euphoria, did not
like listening to Brecht's skeptical comment about a science that had created the
nuclear bomb. Thirty-three years later, the same Atkinson praised Brecht's text
on occasion of its second New York production at the Repertory Theater of
Lincoln Center, ''as a sharpwitted play of high ethics when Anthony Quayle
played it without egotism'' (404). Atkinson blamed Laughton's performance for
his former dismissal of the play, a stance that poorly hid his obvious embar-
rassment about his previous failure to appreciate a playwright who, by 1970,
had become widely accepted as a major figure of contemporary drama in America as well as in the rest of the world. Brecht himself had considered Laughton's
performance as an exemplar for the acting of his plays. He later devoted to
Laughton's Galileo a ''model book'' containing photos and analytic descriptions
of the actor's working process.

The American academic theater became interested in Brecht as soon as Bentley had published the first of his many translations, *The Private Life of the
Master Race*, in 1944. The play had its English-language premiere in 1945 at
the University of California at Berkeley, in 1948 *The Good Person of Szechwan*
premiered at Hamline University of St. Paul, and *Chalk Circle* had its world
premiere at Carlton College in Northfield, Minnesota, in 1948. The majority of
university theaters maintained their independence from political trends and cultural fashions; they presented plays rarely shown on stages that were dependent
on the box office and that therefore were sensitive to the country's political
climate. During the McCarthy period, the professional theater could not but
recoil from any contact with work that appeared to be contaminated by the
author's Marxist leanings.

In 1954, the year in which Senator McCarthy's strangle hold of public opinion
was finally broken, there appeared the first commercial production of a Brecht
play since *Galileo* had folded in 1947. *The Threepenny Opera*, in the effective
but in many ways reductive adaptation by the American composer Marc Blitzstein, opened at the Off-Broadway Theatre de Lys on 10 March 1954. Composer
Weill's widow, Lotte Lenya, played the role of Jenny, as she had in the Berlin
premiere of 1928. The production kept running for 2,611 performances over six
years and three months. The invested capital of $9,000 yielded a profit of
$3,000,000 and broke all records for the run of a musical in New York City
(Little 81–83). The play's theme song, ''Mac the Knife,'' quickly became a
popular hit after Louis Armstrong recorded it. The names of Brecht and Weill
soon were household words, at least among those who were interested in the
theater and popular music, and Brecht's work suddenly possessed distinct commercial viability.

During that same year, the Berliner Ensemble was invited to the first Théâtre
des Nations festival in Paris. Brecht's own staging of *Mother Courage* won the
festival's award for best performance. Several American theater artists saw the
company in Paris, among them Alan Schneider, a promoter of Beckett, who

was to become one of the most active pioneers of Brecht's work in the American theater. Soon, Americans began to arrive in East Berlin to attend performances and rehearsals at the Berliner Ensemble's house on Schiffbauerdamm, while others saw the company during its London season in the fall of 1956, among them Arthur Miller, Lee Strasberg of the Actors Studio, Herbert Blau of the San Francisco Actors Workshop, and many other leaders of the budding nonprofit theater movement. By the end of the 1950s Brecht had become a well-known author in American theater circles, if not yet a widely performed one.

The enormous success of *The Threepenny Opera* did not immediately lead to more productions of Brecht plays. The Cold War was still casting its chill, as the following obituary notice in *Time* of 27 August 1956 demonstrates: "Died Bertolt ('Bert') Brecht, 58, slight, bespectacled German playwright (librettist for Kurt Weill's *Threepenny Opera*) who, according to ex-Communist Arthur Koestler, sold Marxism 'with great brilliance and intellectual dishonesty' to 'the snobs and parlor Communists of Europe'; of a heart attack, in East Berlin'' (quoted in Mews 235).

The only other Brecht production in New York during the 1950s was Bentley's staging of *The Good Person of Szechwan* at the Phoenix Theatre on 18 December 1956. The Phoenix was an Off-Broadway house; indeed, Off-Broadway and, later, Off-off-Broadway theaters were, and still are, the houses where most of the Brecht productions in New York were presented. The producers as well as the founders of the nonprofit companies, whose amazing proliferation began in the late 1950s, shared in their majority a political and cultural agenda that was liberal and certainly not biased against Brecht's professed Marxism. His plays, several of his theoretical writings, and especially his directorial work at the Berliner Ensemble appeared to offer a viable model for a new kind of theater that rejected the commercialism of Broadway as well as the maudlin emotionalism that characterized much of American mainstream drama. This anti-Broadway movement presented, between 1960 and 1980, practically all of the forty plays and adaptations that Brecht completed, from *Baal* to *Trumpets and Drums*, at Off- and Off-off-Broadway houses and such nonprofit theaters as Circle in the Square, the New York Shakespeare Festival, the Living Theater, LaMama, Chelsea Theater Center, and the Repertory Theatre of Lincoln Center. Because of the print media's unreliable coverage of the numerous small New York theaters, it is impossible to obtain a complete list of all Brecht stagings. Many of his works had several productions such as did *A Man's a Man*. Two separate stagings of the play opened within two days at New York theaters in the 1962–1963 season. There were also compilations of texts from Brecht's poetry, prose writings, and plays such as George Tabori's *Brecht on Brecht*, which in 1962 had a successful run on the same stage on which eight years earlier *The Threepenny Opera* had initiated the American theater's discovery of Brecht. There is not another non-American author who has received as many productions in New York as Brecht received during the 1960s and 1970s.

The commercial moguls of Broadway were, of course, impressed by the spectacular profits *The Threepenny Opera* had earned. Not long after the show had successfully opened at the Theatre de Lys, feelers were put out to Brecht in East Berlin, proposing star actors and directors for a *Mother Courage* production.[5]

It would take seven years before the play opened on Broadway in 1963, with Anne Bancroft in the title role and Jerome Robbins as director. Robbins's staging was said to be faithfully based on Brecht's Berlin model production. Contrary to all expectations it failed—although the production boasted a leading actress and a director who were two of the biggest stars of the time. A year later, George Tabori's translation of *Arturo Ui* appeared on Broadway, with Christopher Plummer as Ui in Tony Richardson's staging. The producer, David Merrick, closed the show quickly in spite of its positive reception; he claimed the cost of the large cast made a run prohibitive. Brecht plays, with their numerous characters and serious ''message,'' were obviously not viable for a show business that is always watching the bottom line and trying to entertain but rarely dares to challenge its customers. It would take twenty-five years until another Brecht play opened on Broadway. In 1989, the British rock star Sting appeared as Mac the Knife in John Dexter's staging of *The Threepenny Opera*. This commercially promising effort had to close even before the announced run was supposed to end, since critics as well as audiences were clearly not impressed. If Brecht had become a losing proposition for Broadway producers, there were still successful productions of his work at Off-Broadway and nonprofit regional theaters that elicited their interest. As a consequence, stagings of *Arturo Ui* (1967, Guthrie Theater in Minneapolis) and *Happy End* (1977, Chelsea Theatre Center of Brooklyn) were brought to Broadway. The cost of Broadway productions increased dramatically during the 1980s, and eventually a capitalization of $5,000,000 or more was needed to launch any project that made substantial demands in cast size and production requirements, as most Brecht plays do. Brecht now shares the fate of Shakespeare and most other dramatists whose work is not strictly catering to the entertainment business and is consequently of little interest to America's big-time theater industry.

Off- and Off-off-Broadway, with their multitude of productions, remained Brecht's stronghold in the capital of the American theater. An even larger number of Brecht stagings, however, have been mounted at the nonprofit theaters in cities other than New York. The amazing increase in the number of such stages between 1960 and 1990, when the roster of companies increased from approximately twenty-five to more than two hundred, provided an ever-growing venue for serious, noncommercial drama. Of the nonprofit or regional theaters, as they were often called, the Arena Stage in Washington, DC, and the San Francisco Actors Workshop were the first to include Brecht in their repertoire in the late 1950s and early 1960s. By 1965, Brecht had become the most frequently presented and most hotly debated contemporary European playwright at the regional theaters.[6]

The Vietnam War quickly politicized the American theater, along with many other sections of society, and the Watergate affair added another impulse to this trend. Several plays by Brecht could easily be read in ways that responded to the history of the time, and they were as eagerly adopted by nonprofit theaters as they were emulated by young American playwrights who emerged during those years. Leading critic and Harvard professor Robert Brustein, who produced a remarkable number of Brecht productions as artistic director of the Yale Repertory Theatre and continued to do so as director of Harvard's American Repertory Theatre, concluded that Brecht's image of the Unites States

was hardly a view of our country reflected in the Broadway of *Oklahoma* and *Pal Joey*. ... But it would be articulated with increasing frequency in the sixties and seventies by Americans themselves, as the disillusionments associated with Vietnam began to stimulate perhaps the most ferocious critique of our social system in history. One suspects that the mordant, sardonic tone of this criticism owed a great deal to Brecht, as his style and attitudes gradually began to infiltrate American culture. (Brustein 20)

During the 1973–1975 seasons, there were twenty-six stagings of Brecht plays at one hundred regional theaters (*Theatre Profiles*, hereafter *TP*, 2: 206). *Arturo Ui* alone received six productions—presumably owing to several parallels that could be established between the text and Richard Nixon's "imperial presidency." During the subsequent years, after Nixon's presidency as well as the war had ended, the number of productions declined. For the seasons 1979–1981, however, twenty-six stagings were listed by the Theater Communications Group (T.C.G.), an umbrella organization of the regional theater movement, although this time for 158 companies (*TP* 5: 1201). Those were the years of the Iran hostage crisis and the rise of the Conservative Right that brought Ronald Reagan to the White House. American theater artists and their audiences again appeared to be interested in works that would take the social pulse of a highly politicized period or shed light on contemporary history. During the 1980s, the interest in a socially committed theater waned fast and with it the number of Brecht plays in the repertoire. For the years 1987–1989, T.C.G. statistics reported only seven productions at the 232 theaters covered (*TP* 9: 174). As the feminist theater historian and critic Sue-Ellen Case wrote in 1987:

In the late 1960s and 1970s ... Brecht's ideas of political theater were embraced by the experimental and political theaters of that time as directly related to their theatrical and political practices. ... The political strategies of the 1960s and 1970s were confrontational. ... The decade of the 1980s represents quite a different set of political realities, dramatic practices and critical strategies. Confrontational politics have been replaced by conservative ones, ethnic and feminist theaters are more concerned with the problems of survival and assimilation than those of innovation. (424)

With the recession and a growing awareness of social crisis at the beginning of the 1990s, however, the interest in Brecht appears to have been revived. The seasons of 1989–1991 and 1991–1993 are credited with seventeen and fifteen productions, respectively, in T.C.G.'s documentation (*TP* 10: 172; 11: 184). The connection between the political/social climate of the country and the theater community's interest in Brecht, which is generated by artists and audiences alike, has become quite evident. It might well have pleased the playwright who firmly believed in the theater's potential to change its spectators' perceptions of the world they live in.

Even during the slump of the 1980s, however, Brecht maintained his position as one of the four most frequently produced playwrights in translation, in company with Molière, Ibsen, and Chekhov. He also is the only German dramatist who has gained a permanent position in the American professional repertoire. Neither the German classics Lessing, Goethe, Schiller, Kleist, Büchner, nor any of their successors have achieved a comparable status. There were brief periods when one or another contemporary German dramatist achieved a fair number of productions for a couple of seasons, but then the name disappeared again from the repertoire.

In the academic theater the reception of Brecht's plays and of his theatrical model has surpassed by far his success in the professional arena. The study by Schmidt/Fromann (1987) shows that, between 1975 and 1986, there was a considerably greater number of Brecht productions presented by university theaters than by the numerous professional nonprofit companies. For instance, during the 1983–1984 season twenty-two plays were staged by academic theaters versus fourteen at regional companies.[7] The study by no means included all university productions in the country, but it proves the point. Its numbers support what Bentley wrote in 1964 in response to a questionnaire issued by the East German news agency ADN: "Brecht wrote me he preferred the college performances to those on Broadway, and in principle this preference was probably a wise one. In any case, it is certain that while Brecht plays no role in the Broadway, Hollywood, and television world, he had a firm place in college theaters—and in college courses" (Bentley, *Brecht Memoir* 305).

The academic theater has always been fighting a quite virulent, but rarely admitted, xenophobic tendency in the American theater culture that is evident, for example, in the conspicuous absence of foreign authors (i.e., authors from the non-English-speaking parts of the world) on Broadway. Academic theaters have established Brecht's work as a permanent part of their repertoire and have presented the American premieres of a number of his plays. Academic theater studies treat Brecht's paradigm of an epic theater, along with the theories of Stanislavsky and Artaud, as one of the fundamental contributions to the development of world theater in the twentieth century. Brecht's plays and writings on theater have been among the most frequently researched and discussed topics of performance studies in the United States since the 1960s.

The acceptance of Brecht's work and his theoretical paradigm by the American theater in its academic as well as its professional venues is remarkable for a number of reasons. In contrast to most European cultures, American society has traditionally perceived the theater as a business dealing in entertainment, an activity that is not to be taken seriously and that borders on frivolity. Only when substantial profits were created by the performing arts did these arts begin to attain a certain respect in a culture where profitability is regarded as the ultimate validation of any enterprise. Brecht profoundly disagreed with such a concept of theater, even if he did try to accommodate it while living in the United States. He kept questioning and criticizing a profit-based economic system in his writings—both in his plays and theoretical treatises. There has not been another major dramatist in the twentieth century who has attacked capitalism with similar insistence and stringency. There also has been no thinker and author of comparable stature who was equally willing to swallow his disgust over the excesses of a so-called socialist system. Brecht refused to abandon his conviction that socialism was the only feasible alternative to the destructive capitalism he had learned to despise, especially in its German incarnation that had brought a Hitler to power. While in America, he never quite forgot his youthful dream of performing a rabble-rousing "Marseillaise" for a black audience that would frenetically applaud his efforts.

These were not the dreams and ideas that would make a writer welcome in a society the majority of which believed in an unfettered market economy. As was to be expected, Brecht's reception by many of the leading critics and arbiters of the American cultural discourse was squarely negative. Beginning even before Atkinson's brusque dismissal of the social message of *Galileo* in 1947, a continuous current of negative criticism has been directed at Brecht's politics and writings. One of the more important instances was Hannah Arendt's 1966 attack on Brecht for his supposed defense of Stalinism (quoted in Mews 235). Often his plays received what a theatrical euphemism calls "mixed" reviews, not so much for their actual content or for any flaws in their performance but for Brecht's theories that, although barely read and habitually misunderstood, were used to dismiss his plays as tedious, hectoring, or merely Communist propaganda.

Brecht "can paradoxically be at his best when denying his own theory," wrote the critic of the *New York Post* on 15 March 1966 on the occasion of the New York premiere of *Chalk Circle* at the Repertory Theatre of Lincoln Center. Mr. Watts captioned his review "Brecht, Motherhood, and Justice," invoking these terms of American lore to herald his quite positive view of Brecht's text as an effective but rather corny melodrama (quoted in Mews 243–44). Most of the critics appear to have been completely unaware of the play's central intent, that is, the re-vision of a generally accepted concept of property that entailed "[a] complete reversal of the values by which our civilization has been living," as Bentley stated ("Un-American" 129).

A more recent attack on Brecht, or rather a sideswipe, appeared in Allan Bloom's widely acclaimed 1987 best-seller *The Closing of the American Mind*. The author cites the remarkable success of the song "Mac the Knife," by Brecht and Weill, as an example of the "astonishing Americanization" of Weimar-Germany's moral relativism. Bloom charges that the American public, along with the song, embraced "that ambiguous Weimar atmosphere . . . [where] any-

thing was possible for people who sang of the joy of the knife in cabarets''
(*Mind* 154). Aside from betraying an absurd ignorance of the song's dramatic
function in the context of *The Threepenny Opera*, where it is performed as an
indictment of the gangster Macheath, Bloom's moralistic condemnation of
Brecht's text and, implicitly, of the playwright's own morals, expresses a perception of Brecht that has been shared by many intellectuals, and not only by
those who belong to the conservative establishment (quoted in Mews 234–36).

Brecht's work succeeded, one might say, in spite of his ideology—despite
the likelihood that the American directors and producers, who discovered Brecht
and put his plays on stage in the 1950s, may have been attracted as much by
his critique of capitalism as they were by his poetry and theatrical imagination.
It is no coincidence that the American theater did not embrace Brecht until he
had died in 1956. His political agenda had become an item of past history by
then, and there was no longer any danger that he might upset the apple cart by
statements favoring the enemy in the Cold War. Even an often negative reception by the critics did not stop audiences from coming once they had seen his
plays, provided the productions were doing justice to the text. Bentley told me
once that in 1946 he had written to Brecht that in order "to promote him in the
USA, we'd have to set his Marxism-Leninism on one side." Brecht hardly
disagreed with Bentley's advice, since he was never overly concerned with the
ideological purity of those who staged his plays, as long as they did stage them
well.

Many critics have pointed out that the typical American Brecht production
emphasizes everything in his work that is familiar to American audiences at the
expense of Brecht's ideological concerns. Brustein, for instance, recounts that
"the highly successful, long-running off-Broadway revival of *The Threepenny
Opera* in the fifties—the first to expose Brecht to a wide American audience—
was performed in the style of *Pal Joey*" (Brustein 20). In the tradition of this
early and overwhelmingly successful production, Brecht's texts continued to
undergo interpretations that emulated current fashions of performance and tried
to make the plays palatable to the assumed taste of the respective audience.
They were "en-theatered" or *vertheatert*, to use a term Brecht once coined. The
critical intentions of his texts were played down, if not completely ignored, and
their evident entertainment value became the focus of the performance, at least
at a great number of professional theaters that had to rely on ticket sales.

In the universities, but also in many nonprofit theaters, there are directors,
actors, and designers who have faith in Brecht's idea of a socially committed,
politically active theater, and who present his works in stagings that aggressively
comment on the ills of contemporary society. They are adopting a position that
is quite close to Brecht's own, without necessarily embracing his Marxist
agenda. A look at the present repertory of the regional nonprofit theaters indicates that there may be a renewed interest in Brecht's project of a socially
engaged theater. From the late 1970s to the late 1980s *The Threepenny Opera*
appears to have been the play of choice when theaters were putting on a Brecht

production. During the 1987–1993 seasons, there were only two stagings of *The Threepenny Opera* listed in the T.C.G. statistics. The most often performed text was by far *Chalk Circle* (nine stagings), followed by *The Good Person* (four stagings), and *Saint Joan of the Stockyards* and *In the Jungle of Cities* (three productions each). *Arturo Ui*, *Puntila and Matti, His Hired Man*, *A Man's a Man*, *Galileo*, *Mother Courage*, and the musical *Happy End* achieved two productions each. Six other plays were staged one time only. The prevalence of texts with a socially critical thrust is evident.

A 1991 inquiry among prominent American directors, producers, and authors yielded answers that may help in defining Brecht's present status in the American theater culture. Brustein found that "Brecht is in a dip, after a period of extreme interest in his work, and of an influence radiating out in the American theater. . . . There is a political overtone because of the discrediting of the Soviet System and Communism's downfall. . . . Maybe we also got saturated with Brecht. . . . What we need now are new versions which treat Brecht as freely and cavalierly as he used to treat his own sources" (quoted in Weber, "Brecht" 183). In contrast, Richard Schechner—founder of the famous Performance Group in the late 1960s, professor of Performance Studies at New York University, and editor of the *Drama Review* regards Brecht as a classic. He claims: "There are, in my opinion, three classics of the Modern period: Chekhov, Brecht, and Genet. Being classics drains them of their immediate ideology. Brecht isn't anymore inherently ideological now than Shakespeare is. . . . He went through many periods, quite like Picasso. That sets him apart from other Modern playwrights who mainly wrote in one mode" (quoted in Weber, "Brecht" 184). Dan Sullivan, the artistic director of the Seattle Repertory Theater and a successful Broadway director (*I'm Not Rappaport*; *The Sisters Rosensweig*, and others), agreed: "The recent events in Eastern Europe make us look again at Brecht, and in a new way. . . . I always felt he's more interesting as a poet. . . . Marxism may be in disrepute, but I still have great respect for its thinking. . . . Brecht's work will still be important. He was the greatest of cynics, and his cynicism remains relevant: What man does to man (quoted in Weber, "Brecht" 182–83). Sullivan concluded, "Whenever you face a world crisis, you either do a Brecht or a Shakespeare."

Of course, in most instances the much more popular Shakespeare would be the choice—a choice facilitated by the fact that Brecht plays make intimidating demands on any theater's resources because of their huge casts and substantial scenic requirements. Schechner, however, dismisses this argument that so often is heard from artistic directors who try to defend their abstention from doing Brecht, "Brecht is a storyteller, his plays can be done in a storytelling technique, with six actors and some musicians. . . . The plays don't need lavish productions, we did *Mother Courage* with a few ropes" (quoted in Weber, "Brecht" 187).

There may be disagreements about the ideological, political, and economical aspects of presenting Brecht's work, but none of the artists and scholars questioned came to the conclusion that Brecht has outlived his "use value" or

Gebrauchswert—to use one of his favorite terms—for the American theater. Tony Kushner, the author of *Angels in America* and other successful plays, who is also a gifted director, summed up why Brecht's paradigm is attractive to Kushner's generation of writers and directors—now in their late twenties and thirties: "His theory and his art have much to teach us about the splendors, the necessities and the dangers of a genuine theater of political engagement. In the process of re-imagining this refugee, in making him uneasily at home in America, we have no choice but to invent a new Brecht—or rather new Brechts—ready to apply the hard won lessons of the past to the tumultuous complexities of the present" (Kushner 123). Kushner's own theater owes much to his long-standing examination of Brecht's theory and practice. In a recent interview he pointed out, "Because of Brecht I started to think of a career in the theater. It seemed the kind of thing one could do and still retain some dignity as a person engaged in society. . . . when I first read Benjamin's 'Understanding Brecht' . . . I decided I wanted to do theater" (Savran 23).

The influence of Brecht on a number of playwrights who have emerged in the 1990s is evident. Apart from Kushner, one ought to mention among others Robert Schenkkan (*The Kentucky Cycle*) and the African American playwright and director George C. Wolfe (*The Colored Museum*, *Spunk*, and *Jelly's Last Jam*). Anna Deavere Smith, the African American actor/author, has created the documentary solo performance pieces *Fires in the Mirror* and *Twilight: Los Angeles, 1992* that revitalize a model Brecht once proposed in his seminal essay "The Street Scene" (*Theatre* 121–29).

These writers, who often direct or perform in the manner of Brecht, are not merely emulating the models Brecht designed. They have adapted and developed his concepts in an age of the ever-present computerized electronic media, so that live performance again might stimulate its spectators to observe closely the events and persons presented on stage and then to rethink their own position. At the threshold of a century that will be dominated by electronic means of information, these authors are creating a theater that tries to prod audiences toward a reevaluation of past and present history. They are striving for a paradigm that Brecht believed to be the theater of the future, a theater that provokes doubt instead of affirming the current state of human affairs.

Brecht, the exile who once was hardly welcome in the United States, has, after all, found a firm place in the American theater. Brecht's plays and his thoughts have inspired artists who do not merely dream of playing the "Marseillaise" in the great cities of America. They do play their subversive tune, and they are playing it for audiences of all colors.

NOTES

1. Brecht had developed a method of collectively creating plays and film texts with his collaborators before he had to leave Germany in 1933. After his return to Berlin, he

resumed this mode of work again at the Berliner Ensemble, where he and a team of collaborators adapted several classical texts for the repertoire.

2. The original title of the piece was *Der Lindberghflug* (Lindbergh's Flight). See Karl-Heinz Schoeps, "Brecht's *Lehrstücke*: A Laboratory for Epic and Dialectic Theater," in this volume.

3. See Marc Silberman, "Brecht and Film," in this volume.

4. I owe this information to Albert Maltz, the playwright, screenwriter, and novelist, who was a member of the New York Theater Union's board in 1935. (See also Baxandall, "Introduction," 12).

5. In 1956 a prospective production of *Mother Courage* was negotiated. Helene Weigel informed me about the project and its probable director, Orson Welles, when we discussed my potential involvement as an assistant director. (See also Bentley, *Brecht* 79.)

6. As a result of Brecht's sudden popularity, I was invited to direct four of his plays in America during 1962–1964. Among them was the production of *Chalk Circle* for the San Francisco Actors Workshop, a company that had staged the first U.S. production of *Mother Courage* in 1956, directed by Herbert Blau. In the 1963 San Francisco production of *Chalk Circle* the prologue, entitled "The Dispute over the Valley," was presented for the first time in the United States. The prologue with its dispute about the ownership of a valley among the members of two collective farms in Soviet Georgia at the end of World War II and its unconventional settlement of the property dispute did not elicit any negative reaction and did not prove to be a "stumbling block for American audiences" (Bentley, "Un-American" 129). Quite to the contrary, this rejection of a concept of property cherished by Western civilization seemed to be perfectly acceptable to a San Francisco audience in the 1960s.

7. Schmidt/Fromann's extensive study demonstrates both the successes and problems that the Brecht reception has been facing during a decade of incisive political shifts.

WORKS CITED (SEE ALSO REFERENCE GUIDE TO WORKS CITED IN ABBREVIATED FORM)

Atkinson, Brooks. *Broadway*. New York: Macmillan, 1970.

Baxandall, Lee. "Introduction." *The Mother*, by Bertolt Brecht. Translated by Lee Baxandall. New York: Grove, 1965. 9–32.

Bentley, Eric. *The Brecht Memoir*. New York: PAJ Publications, 1985.

———. "An Un-American Chalk Circle?" *The Caucasian Chalk Circle*, by Bertolt Brecht. Revised edition. Edited by Eric Bentley. New York: Grove, 1966. 129–44.

Brustein, Robert. *Who Needs Theatre*. New York: Atlantic Monthly Press, 1987.

Case, Sue-Ellen. "Comment." *Theatre Journal* 39.4 (1988): 424.

Higham, Charles. *Charles Laughton: An Intimate Biography*. New York: Doubleday, 1976.

Houseman, John. *Front and Center*. New York: Simon, 1979.

Kushner, Tony. "American Brecht." *American Theatre* 6.6/7 (1989): 119–23.

Little, Stuart W. *Off-Broadway: The Prophetic Theatre*. New York: Coward, 1972.

Mews, Siegfried. " 'Brecht Motherhood, and Justice': The Reception of *The Caucasian Chalk Circle* in the United States." In *The Fortunes of German Writers in Amer-

ica: Studies in Literary Reception. Edited by Wolfgang Elfe, James Hardin, and
Gunther Holst. Columbia: University of South Carolina Press, 1992. 231–48.

Savran, David. "Tony Kushner Considers the Longstanding Problems of Virtue and
Happiness." *American Theatre* 11.8 (1994): 21–27, 100–104.

Schmidt, Klaus M., and Daniela Fromann. "Survey on Brecht Productions in the US
and Canada from 1975/76 to 1985/86 with Comparative Figures in the FRG,
GDR, and Austria." *Gestus: A Quarterly Journal of Brechtian Studies* 2.3 (1987):
237–50.

Theatre Profiles. vols. 2, 5, 9, 10, 11. New York: Theatre Communications Group, 1976–
1994.

Weber, Carl. "Vaudeville's Children and Brecht: The Impact of American Performance
Traditions on Brecht's Theory and Practice." *Brecht Jahrbuch/Brecht Yearbook*
15 (1990): 55–70.

———. "Brecht auf den Bühnen der USA: Ein Überblick—und Anmerkungen zur Re-
zeptionsgeschichte." *Brecht Jahrbuch/Brecht Yearbook* 18 (1993): 167–99.

16

Brecht in Latin America: Theater Bearing Witness

MARINA PIANCA

Brecht and Latin American theater are most closely intertwined when theater bears witness to injustice in defense of human rights. Theater and history are inextricably linked in Latin America; for this reason, Latin American theater created an ongoing narrative of witnessing based on the understanding that witnessing is a powerful social and psychological experience of great ethos and pathos. When so engaged, theater is involved in matters of life and death that contribute to creating the need and compulsion to bear witness in order to assure the existence and continuity of justice. In participating in this process, a feeling of personal and collective transcendence takes hold of those who bear witness to human suffering and injustice—Brecht's major concerns.

In the 1940s, the Argentine Yiddish Theater Front (IFT) staged *Mother Courage and Her Children* in Buenos Aires in Yiddish. This was probably the first production of Brecht in Latin America. Later, this same group presented *The Good Person of Szechwan* and *Schweyk in the Second World War*, both in Spanish. During the 1950s, a few Latin American theater groups and directors traveled to Europe—either because they had been invited to theater festivals or because they went on their own in search of new insights. In 1955, several Latin American theater groups were present at the Festival of Nations in Paris that was also attended by the Berliner Ensemble. This was a defining moment for many of the participants, among them Enrique Buenaventura, a director from Colombia who was to become one of Latin America's greatest theatrical minds. Others such as César Campodónico from Uruguay recall the impact of discovering Brecht in Italy at about the same time. They all returned to Latin America eager to stage Brecht's plays and to debate his theories.

In spite of Brecht's impact on some individuals and groups it was not until the 1960s that his influence was fully felt owing to the chronological proximity of Brecht's death in 1956 and the victory of the Cuban revolution in 1959. Brecht's death prompted a series of translations of his works into Spanish. The Cuban revolution became a catalyst for similar revolutionary movements throughout Latin America, and theater rapidly became the revolutionary movements' strongest cultural vehicle. Brecht's principles dovetailed perfectly with the needs of these urgent and insurgent movements, and his works rapidly became part of the struggle. In some cases, he was cannibalized and digested into new forms, in others he was internalized by some kind of osmosis. Brecht and Latin American theater formed a natural intercultural symbiosis in which Brecht was immersed in a dynamic, insurgent historical moment and was subject to constant change (see ATINT).

For this reason, the discussion of Brecht in Latin America cannot be restricted to focusing on the productions of his plays; his presence there is and was much more complex. Acting coaches, directors, actors, theater groups, and playwrights read and applied his theories, in many cases appropriating them or "nationalizing" them, so as to better suit local needs. It would be imposible to do justice to all the playwrights in Latin American countries who in one way or another have incorporated Brechtian ideas into their work. The same must be said of the directors who have staged Brecht's plays in Latin America. Hence I will mention the most important authors and directors, the most consequential trends in countries where Brecht's influence has been most strongly felt without in any way attempting to exhaust this subject (see also De Toro; Perales).

Often, during periods of military dictatorships, political repression, and censorship, Brecht's plays themselves were "nationalized" in order to offer a way of speaking out on current issues that could not be directly addressed by local playwrights. This kind of appropriation was not favored by local elites who preferred to see "pure" stagings of Brecht uncontaminated by local circumstances. They preferred plays that copied European productions. The *teatristas*—as they chose to call themselves—of the New Popular Theater movement opposed this elitist colonial mentality and were as irreverent as Brecht himself in their appropriations and transmutations.

Playwrights immersed in the urgency of their time either consciously applied Brecht's teachings or instinctively arrived at similar points. For some, the initial contact with Brecht became a hindrance, a straitjacket that undermined their own energy, but a straitjacket that they were eventually able to overcome by establishing a mutually enriching dialogic transculturation. Enrique Buenaventura speaks of this experience when he first tried to write a "Brechtian" play (Buenaventura 112).

During the early beginnings of Buenaventura's Teatro Experimental de Cali (TEC) in Cali, Colombia, the members researched paratheatrical forms of pop-

358 Translation, Reception, and Appropriation

ular expression that, after questioning their often oppressive, ideological content, could be used in stagings for the people. They began with a traditional Colombian nativity play in which the sacred family was depicted as a miserable local family, Herodes as a tropical dictator, and the massacre of the innocent as an indictment of government violence.

Later, they found Tomas Carrasquilla's short story, *A la diestra de Dios Padre* (On the Right Hand of God the Father), and adapted it for the theater. The first version was presented during the Second Bogota Theater Festival in 1958. TEC won all prizes. Critics hailed the play as the birth of a national theater. Buenaventura decided to rewrite the play following his discovery of Brecht (ca. 1959). According to Buenaventura, the second version of *A la diestra de Dios Padre* failed because he followed ("applied") Brecht too closely. In the third version of the play, he incorporated the *mojiganga*, a popular peasant theatrical form from Antioquia. In so doing, Buenaventura realized that, by questioning Brecht's "influence" and searching in his own Colombian roots, he was getting closer to Brecht in a deeper sense. He later was to become one of Latin America's most knowledgeable Brechtian theoreticians, and a *maestro* of Latin American theater.

Buenaventura, speaking of the relationship between theater and history, once said that history was written by the *terratenientes* (landowners), since only they knew how to write. He went on to argue that we could therefore speak of *historiotenientes* (owners of history), since they narrated history from a perspective that benefited their own interests. Given that ownership of history, the New Theater was to be part of the process of expropriating official history in order to create a version of history told from the people's perspective. The Latin American appropriation of Brecht, as well as that of the political theater of director and erstwhile collaborator of Brecht, Erwin Piscator, and post–World War II playwright Peter Weiss, were to serve the process of historical expropriation and bearing witness to a sense of truth.

In this process, popular theater traditions such as the *circo criollo* in Argentina, the *bumba meu boi* in Brazil, the *teatro bufo* in Cuba, the *mojiganga* in Colombia were incorporated. These popular traditions, which often brought new ingredients to a Brechtian aesthetic in Latin America, are just a few examples of what could be considered the Latin American equivalents of the *commedia dell'arte*.

In order to better understand Brecht's place in Latin American theater, it is important to place him within the context of the developing movements for a new Latin American popular theater—movements that tended to be highly politicized endeavors and were closely tied to revolutionary, emancipatory, and anti-imperialist social projects. The tension arising from the struggle for an internal autonomous development, which respected the heterogeneity and integrity of the individual nations, and the opposing model of liberal or neoliberal economics and politics, which neither defended nor respected that sovereignty, forms the undercurrent of the cultural and intellectual history of Latin America.

All facets of life have been galvanized by the force of these polarized perspectives for a collective destiny. The New Latin American Popular Theater movement of the 1970s was also inspired by the ideals of nineteenth-century Cuban patriot and essayist José Martí who sought to promote the theatrical language of *Nuestra América* (Our America), a decolonized language capable of entering into nonsubaltern dialogues with any country in the world.

From the late 1960s to the mid-1970s, when Brecht's presence was most strongly felt, the search for a specific theatrical language of *Nuestra América* became the focal point of a conscious, concerted, and international effort that included the Chicano/Latino theater in the United States (see Pianca, *El teatro*). No longer did it suffice to think only in terms of developing a national dramaturgy; rather, the movement strove for an articulation of its efforts on the entire continent. This concerted effort led to the restructuring and redefinition of the theatrical paradigm, a paradigm previously based on European traditions. The questioning of the methods and modes of production turned out to be crucial in that it became one of the richest sources of innovation. The structures of organization, production, and distribution were questioned and modified. This new theater movement wished to transform the modes rather than just the contents of artistic production. It redefined the idea of form, author, and artistic product itself by questioning the social relations of producers and consumers of artistic products. The adherents of the movement believed that production not only creates an object for the subject but also a subject for the object.

The theater group, with its emphasis on collective creation and the search for a popular audience beyond the limits of established cultural spaces, became central to the process. Factories, schools, churches, fields, parks, streets, peasant communities—all became part of that new cultural space. These theater groups questioned the vertical line of authority in theater consisting of playwright, director, actor, and audience and endeavored to abandon it in favor of a horizontal linkage that potentially included all voices. The creation of a Latin American theater was viewed as a collective project that was closely tied to a larger historical social project. Latin American theater then took Brecht's theories and enriched them with new nonhierarchical practices.

From the mid-1970s to the mid-1980s, the New Latin American Popular Theater movement was subjected to a process of atomization and restructuring as a result of the intensification of political repression throughout the region. The need to bear witness and the search for a historically rooted Latin American expression continued in the most extreme circumstances: in exile, under dictatorial rules, in concentration camps, and in prisons. Many of those who struggled for the social project of *Nuestra América* were once again victims of exile and death. Brecht continued to be present during these dark times as his plays often offered a way of speaking out in a culture of silence and fear.

BRECHT AND PAULO FREIRE: CONFLUENT PEDAGOGIES
FOR LATIN AMERICAN THEATER

The transnational, transdisciplinary character of cultural production is evident in the "cooperation" of German playwright Bertolt Brecht and Brazilian educator Paulo Freire, both of whose works were widely adopted in Latin American theater.

History and war make any other teacher superfluous, Piscator once remarked (5). Nevertheless, the interpretation of history, the determination never to repeat its horrors, and, above all, the commitment to change the world in which those horrors happen, gave birth to a very special breed of intellectual: the pedagogues for liberation. As early as 1936 Brecht placed himself among those pedagogues: "The stage began to be instructive. . . . The theater became an affair for philosophers, but only for such philosophers as wished not just to explain the world but also to change it. So we had philosophy, and we had instruction" (*Theatre* 72). In 1929, Brecht had remarked: "A new art does not exist without a new objective. Pedagogy is that new objective" (*Werke* 21: 303–304). The common root of Brecht and Freire's views on pedagogy is presumably attributable to the fact that both developed their work with objectives derived from a Marxist interpretation of reality. But both were also humanists who avoided the pitfalls of dogmatism owing to their strong belief in permanent rereadings and reinterpretations of the world and our role within it.

Upon studying the respective theories that were at the base of Brecht's and Freire's work, interesting parallels appear. Brecht speaks of *Gestus*, Freire speaks of *codificação* (codification). *Verfremdung* has its counterpart in the idea of *conscientização* (conscientization).[1] This parallelism could be attributed to chance, but if we think of Freire's objectives for a literacy campaign in Brazil and of Brecht's theater work in the Berliner Ensemble, the element of chance is overshadowed by the fact that both intended to teach in order to provoke the need to change the future course of history in those they reached with their work. Similar techniques were the result of similar objectives. The similarities of their premises and methods displaces the notion of "influence" and replaces it with the confluential transnational character of cultural products that are based on shared objectives for political change.

As early as 1960, barely one year after its revolution, Cuba launched its "year of education" in which millions were taught how to read as they learned to implement revolutionary changes. It is obvious that the impact of the Cuban revolution went far beyond the boundaries of the island and that it had profound effects on all levels. In many cases, the teachings that emerged from Cuba were enriched with experiences elsewhere and vice versa. This was particularly true in theater and education.

The need for a popular theater, whose objective was to contribute to the revolutionary process, soon manifested itself. Just as Freire evolved a theory for the education of illiterates based on the conviction that every human being can learn to break the "culture of silence" if provided with the proper tools for a dialogical encounter with his world, so *teatristas* were convinced of the need to make theater techniques available to the oppressed for the same purpose. In this way many *teatristas* became theater teachers who in turn educated other teachers dedicated to the transmission and creation of knowledge through theater in the vein of both Brecht and Freire.

For Brecht theater involves not only watching but also seeing with new eyes, and for Freire learning how to read is not restricted to the simple act of deciphering linguistic symbols. A central theme in Freire's work is his insistence on the need for readers to adopt a critical attitude. Freire conceives of education and literacy in terms of a practice geared toward liberation, a practice that dispenses with the verticality of the educational process and replaces it with the horizontal relationship between those involved. In this way teacher and student learn from each other as they learn to decode their world together. The stress on the horizontal, dialogic relationship was a key element in the development of collective creations in Latin American theater and its drive to establish a dialogue with the audiences they reached through public *foros* (forums) after each performance.

Freire's methodology went through a historic confrontation in Brazil from 1962 to 1964, in which an extremely rapid politicization of the masses resulted from a literacy campaign that gave rise to the *conscientização* of large numbers of peasants and unskilled urban workers. This process was rapidly stopped by the military *coup d'état* of 1964 that overthrew President João Goulart. At that time, Freire was imprisoned and, after his release, went into exile.

In 1968 Freire published his book, *Pedagogy of the Oppressed*. Six years later, renowned Brazilian playwright and director Augusto Boal's *Theater of the Oppressed*, which was based on both Brecht and Freire, appeared. Boal recounts his experiences in Peru during a literacy campaign in which Freire's techniques as well as Brechtian theater techniques were employed. He also speaks of his own experiences with non-Aristotelian theater in his Teatro Arena. And he finally presents his *sistema comodín* or *sistema coringa* (joker system), a practice according to which plays are written and/or performed including a "joker" or "wild-card character" whose role it is to assure the pedagogical nature of the play by interrupting it to underline contradictions, mystifications, and so on in such a way as to promote *conscientização*.

In 1969, Buenaventura introduced the "Method of Collective Creation" that he had developed with TEC based on the group's practice as well as on both Brecht and Freire. Buenaventura's method reconfigures the traditional theater paradigm by doing away with its vertical structure—especially the hierarchical role of the director and the author—with the aim of creating a dialogical relationship among all members of the team, whose role it is to decode reality in non-Manichean theatrical terms. The new horizontal paradigm also introduces an important new element by including the audience in the dialogical relationship as a determining factor in the development and writing of works. The audience thus becomes one more member of the collective production team. This method was widely adopted and was instrumental in the development of a theater of collective creation in Latin America.

Similar experiences are to be found throughout Latin America. Each group or individual adopted from Brecht, Freire, Boal, Buenaventura, and others whatever best served their objectives. Whether their theoretical pronouncements spoke of *Gestus* or *codificação*, of *Verfremdung* or *conscientização*, of culture circles or collective creations, the tools these groups offered opened the door to seeking new realities by embarking upon alternate historical courses. In such a sense, we can safely say that Latin American theater has been shaped by the new pedagogues for liberation and their reinterpretation of history.

ARGENTINA

Argentina in general—and Buenos Aires in particular—has always had a very active, highly productive, and intellectually sophisticated theatrical milieu. As mentioned before, in the 1940s the Jewish theater IFT in Buenos Aires presented *Mother Courage* in Yiddish. Later, it produced *The Good Person* and *Schweyk* in Spanish. IFT was instrumental in making Brecht available to Argentine audiences in that among its highly successful theater school graduates were several actors and directors who went on to produce Brecht's plays in Argentina. Many authors in Argentina were in dialogue with Brecht early on, among them Osvaldo Dragún who began doing realistic theater in the 1950s and who, because of Brecht's influence, modified his style in his early work *Historias para ser contadas* (Stories to Be Told). In 1966, Dragún's play *Heroica de Buenos Aires*, inspired by *Mother Courage*, received the highly coveted Cuban Casa de las Américas prize, but the play was not staged in Argentina until 1984.

In the 1950s, the Teatro de los Independientes (Theater of the Independents) presented *The Threepenny Opera* and *Life of Galileo*. The unforgettable version of *The Caucasian Chalk Circle* directed by Uruguayan Atahualpa del Cioppo, one of Latin America's legendary Brechtian directors, was presented by his group El Galpón in Buenos Aires in the late 1950s. It so dazzled Omar Grasso, an Argentine director, that he followed the group to Montevideo, Uruguay, where he remained for eighteen years and brought several of Brecht's works to the stage. Upon his return to Argentina, Grasso directed great works with provocative messages during the so-called Dirty War (1976–1983). After 1981, during the Teatro Abierto (Open Theater) movement, which was directed against the military dictatorship and its role in the Dirty War, Grasso became the director most sought after by Argentine playwrights.

In 1960, Jaime Kogan's first work as a director was *Fear and Misery of the Third Reich*, produced by IFT. In the period 1964–1969, Inda Ledesma founded the Teatro Argentino and directed *Puntila and Matti, His Hired Man*. It was the first professional Brecht work to be presented in Argentina. The memorable productions of *Schweyk* and *Puntila and Matti* demonstrated Ledesma's technical mastery of Brecht. In 1974, upon the return to democracy after many years of military dictatorship, the San Martin Theater was able to present *Chalk Circle* in a version by Manuel Iedvabni. Fernández identifies the production as the "reappearance of Brecht" in Argentina ("Peronismo" 148).

Towards the end of the 1960s, a kind of Artaudian realism arose in the Argentine theater. It was a mixture of the theater of cruelty with a sociopolitical testimonial, one that included Brechtian influences. It seemed to aspire to a theatrical language that would break with the old theatrical traditionalism as well as with the "new" irrationalism. One example is *El avión negro* (The Black Airplane) by Roberto Cossa, Ricardo Rozenmacher, Alberto Somigliana, and Ricardo Talesnik, a play about Juan Domingo Peron's return to Argentina in 1973.

Andrés Lizarraga used Brecht's methods in his historical trilogy *Alto Perú* (High Peru), *Tres jueces para un largo silencio* (Three Judges for a Long Silence), and *Santa Juana de América* (Saint Joan of America). Ricardo Halac, David Viñas, Oscar Viale, among others, were also aware of Brecht's techniques in structuring their work. Viñas considers the present through the past; Viale uses Brechtian distancing methods in his documentary theater.

In 1984, Brecht once again returned to the stage after years of dictatorship and censorship, when *Galileo*, directed by Jaime Kogan (in a version by Kogan and Gerardo Fernández), was staged in the San Martin Theater. It drew the largest audience—160,000—in the theater's history, and the production was considered the theater happening of 1984. The ideas it expressed were a clear reaction to the years of imposed silence (Fernández, *Veinte espectáculos* 1: 166). As a result, a new interest in Brecht took hold, and *Galileo, Saint Joan of the Stockyards, Señora Carrar's Rifles, The Resistible Rise of Arturo Ui, The Exception and the Rule, The Seven Deadly Sins, The Tutor*, and various compilations and versions of Brecht's texts were presented to eager audiences. Though the presentations were of varying quality, Brecht's works allowed the return of political discourse that had been muzzled during the dictatorship.

Despite economic hardship and massive inflation that led to a crisis for many theaters that lacked a sufficient number of paying customers, Kogan's 1984 staging of the opera *Rise and Fall of the City of Mahagonny* in the legendary Teatro Colón of Buenos Aires was enormously successful—to the extent that tickets sold on the black market for five times the box office price (Cosentino 1: 157).

URUGUAY

It would be impossible to speak of Brecht in Latin America without emphasizing the immense role played by the above-mentioned theater group El Galpón and its founder and director Atahualpa del Cioppo, a *maestro* of Latin American theater who for more than sixty years showed an unrelenting, passionate commitment to theater, to Latin America, and to Brecht. In many Latin American countries, del Cioppo's stagings of Brecht have become paradigmatic; in Costa Rica, for example, his version of *Arturo Ui* (1976) is considered a "paradigm of perfection" and remains "in every way a myth" of Costa Rican theater (Mora 1: 400).

In the early years of its existence, El Galpón staged several of Brecht's works such as *Chalk Circle* (1955) and the prize-winning *The Threepenny Opera* (1957), directed by del Cioppo. In 1969, it inaugurated its new theater with *Puntila and Matti, His Hired Man*, directed by César Campodónico, and in 1972 *Arturo Ui*, directed by Rubén Yáñez, was staged.

A fierce military dictatorship took hold of the nation in 1973. In 1976, the dictatorship dissolved El Galpón by a presidential decree that was published on the front page of the country's newspapers—evidence of the political importance of theater in Latin America. El Galpón's building, which housed both the theater and the school, was confiscated, and several actors were jailed and tortured. The majority of the cast sought exile in Mexico.

In 1984, the dictatorship finally fell and El Galpón returned to Uruguay where it was able to recapture its theater, its school, and its audience. In 1986, it staged *Chalk Circle* directed by Amanecer Dotta, but the play met with a mixed reception. Its lack of success was perhaps owing to the fact that the nation, exhausted by the horrors of the dictatorship, did not wish to see them reproduced on stage at that time. But some critics considered the play a "dream-like proposal, without any naturalistic characteristics which often put words aside in a performance that disconcerted many" (Pons 195). The staging of this work marked the beginning of an aesthetic debate within the group regarding the proper place of their work in the new, emerging historical context.

In 1982, while Uruguay was still being ruled by a military dictatorship, Héctor Manuel Vidal directed *Galileo*. The production was awarded the much coveted Florencio, a theater prize. Despite the prevailing censorship, audiences filled each performance. The theater thus became a center for alternative communication within a culture of fear and silence. Galileo—seen both as a rejection of authoritarianism and as the man of science who astutely ridicules obscurantism—incarnated the audience's own rebellious thoughts against its own authoritarian rulers. These thoughts could only be expressed by being present in that theatrical event—an instance in which a language of complicity broke the culture of silence. In 1983, the Teatro Circular (Circular Theater) continued this line of work by staging *Del pobre B.B.* (From/by the Poor B.B.), written by Mercedes Rein and Jorge Curi, directed by Curi. In 1987, Héctor Manuel Vidal once again directed one of Brecht's plays, this time *The Seven Deadly Sins*, to great success and with a renewed Uruguayan touch. It was presented to great acclaim also at the Cádiz Theater Festival in Spain.

CHILE

Brecht's ideas began circulating in Chilean theater at the beginning of the 1960s. By the second half of the 1960s, the theater of the University of Chile

developed a repertoire related to the political realities of the moment and premiered *Puntila and Matti*. By that time, several authors had begun to incorporate
Brechtian techniques in their theater, among them Fernando Debesa and Isidora
Aguirre. Debesa used Brecht's methods in his historical theater. His work *Mel-
garejo* (1967) was a type of epic drama. Aguirre's *Los papeleros* (1963; The
Paper Collectors), the story of a group of trash collectors, used posters and songs
to facilitate the transition from one scene to another in order to show the consequences of the lack of solidarity and unity in the struggle for justice. Aguirre's
Los que van quedando en el camino (1969; Those Who Are Left by the Way-
side) also shows this didactic tendency in its defense of revolutionary ideology
in conflict with the status quo.

A prolific author, Aguirre has appropriated Brechtian techniques as well as
the language and methods of the New Latin American Popular Theater. After
the fall of Augusto Pinochet's bloody military regime, Aguirre was commissioned by a theater group in Yumbel, Chile, to write about their "disappeared"
loved ones during Pinochet's dictatorship. Aguirre traveled to Yumbel, where
she did exhaustive research on the subject as well as on the region's religion,
beliefs, and history in collaboration with experts in different disciplines. In this
way, she contributed to the expropriation of "official history" in the vein of
Latin American theaters' new practice. The result of Aguirre's labors was *El
retablo de Yumbel* (The Yumbel Altar), a rich tableau of local life and history
from the times of Saint Sebastian to the present, that is seen through different
prisms, including those of the theology of liberation and revolutionary struggles.
The weaving of past and present in a metatheatrical context makes this a
uniquely powerful play.

During the years of Salvador Allende's Popular Unity government (1971–
1973), which was the first socialist, democratically elected government of Latin
America, theater played an extremely important role in the struggle for revolutionary change. The theaters of the *poblaciones* (shanty towns) as well as
professional and university theaters engaged in a rich period of experimentation
and political commitment closely tied to Brechtian principles.

After the fall in 1973 of the Popular Unity government, there began a new
reign of terror and a culture of silence. As in Argentina and Uruguay, the independent Chilean theater groups tried to allude to the horrors of the current
situation through the "nationalization" and appropriation of classic authors.
Brecht once again became a useful tool in times of repression. *Mahagonny* was
staged as an attempt at indirect social criticism. But, recognizing Brecht's subversive role, the authorities forbade the staging of his works.

Members of groups such as El Aleph, directed by Oscar Castro, attempted to
continue their previous line of work during the dictatorship, but they were soon
imprisoned, tortured, and then "disappeared." Because of international pressure,
Castro, who had been sent from concentration camp to concentration camp, was
allowed to leave the country. He had survived, even though his mother and
brother-in-law "disappeared" after visiting him. The theater—produced under
extreme circumstances, in prisons, concentration camps, war zones, occupied

zones, and exile—also owes something to Brechtian ideas. In *Testimonios de Teatro Latinoamericano* (1991; Latin American Theater Testimonies) I document these experiences as narrated by the protagonists themselves, among them Castro.

BRAZIL

As part of the modernization of Brazilian theater from 1940 to 1960, there was some experimentation with Brecht's theories. Ironically, the "golden period" of Brazilian revolutionary theater began in 1964, the year the military coup against president João Goulart brought a new dictatorial regime to power. This regime began as a *dictablanda* (a "soft" dictatorship) that allowed some freedom to theatrical cultural spaces. Nevertheless, after the passing of Institutional Act 5 in 1968, constitutional rights were eradicated. Full power was placed into the hands of the military government that was not held accountable, and the citizenry was left without recourse—a process not uncommon in Latin America.

Between 1968 and 1979, censorship was arbitrary, and its severity varied according to changes within the military power structure. Ignorant censors, unaware of his nationality—or his death—searched for Brecht to have him give a police deposition about the content of his plays. He was in good company; Sophocles was also sought for the same purpose. In the end, the dictatorship in Brazil prohibited various works by Brecht, Sophocles, Tennessee Williams, Max Frisch, Edward Albee, and others.

From the late 1950s to the 1964 coup, there was a pervasive sense of imminent revolution in Brazil. Brecht was already a part of the Brazilian theatrical tradition by this time; and beginning with the 1964 coup until the 1970s, when many theater groups were dissolved, Brecht and the application of his theories became a sign of mobilization and protest.

As we have seen, the role of theater groups is of particular importance in the development of theater in Latin America. In the case of Brazil, Teatro Oficina (Theater Workshop) directed by José Celso Martínez Correia, Teatro Arena (Arena Theater) directed by Boal, and Teatro Opinião (Opinion Theater) have contributed greatly to Brechtian theater in Brazil. In this vein, in 1970 Teatro Oficina in cooperation with the Argentine Teatro Lobo made an abortive attempt to jointly produce a play with the Living Theater from the United States.

Correia and his group Teatro Oficina first "cannibalized" Constantin Stanislavsky, then Brecht, and later Jerzy Grotowski and Antonin Artaud. In the 1960s, Teatro Oficina appropriated Brecht more freely than other groups by adapting his works in that the group considered him an influential dramatist rather than a theorist or aesthetician. The group's presentations of *In the Jungle of Cities* and *Galileo* emphasized "the texts' rebellious and anarchical content" (De Lima 261) as well as their own existential views that considered rebellion an essential human trait: "Distinct from the Left's mode of operation, which was struggling to clarify consciences, Oficina directed itself at the darkest zones of the psyche, where vital impulses agitate'' (De Lima 262). The group dissolved in 1973 after enduring a long debate with Teatro Arena, directed by Boal, which accused Teatro Oficina of having lost its combative position in its desire to transcend a strictly political and didactic framework.

Teatro Oficina articulated its autochthonous ''cannibalistic aesthetics,'' which dated from the 1920s, in its theater of aggression, reminiscent of Living Theater techniques, in which Brazilian cultural stereotypes were deconstructed through Brechtian techniques. Teatro Oficina also made Brechtian techniques suitable for the tropics in characteristic fashion. The rendering of *Galileo* is legendary in this respect. Faced with Fernando Peixoto's attempts to ''bring Brecht back to Brecht,'' the adherents of tropicalization in Teatro Oficina argued that this process would have elated Brecht. To this day Caca Rosset, director of the famous Ornitorrinco group, continues to ''tropicalize'' Brecht, as his staging of *Mahagonny* during the 1984 New York Joseph Papp Latino Theater Festival demonstrated.

Upon Boal's return to Brazil in 1956 from the United States, where he studied theater at Columbia University, he became a key figure in Teatro Arena (founded in 1953) and soon took over its direction. Boal brought with him Stanislavskian Method acting and that of the Actors Studio. At that time, Teatro Arena privileged political content and did not focus as much on the work of the actor. Oduvaldo Vianna, one of its founders, objected to this neglect, and Boal began to pay particular attention to the developmental needs of the actor.

In the 1960s, Teatro Arena began leaving behind the Stanislavskian approach of its first presentations and embraced Brechtian expression because it ''treats dramatic conflict as an expression of social antagonisms and eliminates character psychology in favor of *gestus*'' (De Lima 258).

In 1971, the dictatorship, which had begun in 1964 and resulted in a succession of increasingly repressive military presidencies, perceived Teatro Arena as threatening, and it was not allowed to continue its work. Boal was imprisoned and tortured, but he was then allowed to leave the country and live in exile. While in Peru, Boal undertook a series of very unique experiments during a literacy campaign in which he applied Brechtian and Freirian techniques. Later, he moved on to Paris, where he resided for many years as director of the Théâtre de l'Opprimé (Theater of the Oppressed).

In view of the debate between the members of Teatro Arena, who had abandoned a psychological approach, and Teatro Oficina, referred to above, it is ironic that Boal, according to Bernard Dort, ''brought psychology galloping back'' (quoted in Navarro 84) in his version of ''The Jewish Wife'' that was presented in Paris in 1981. Dort argues that Boal violated Brecht's most basic principles in questioning the characters rather than the social system.

Teatro Opinião originated from the reorganization of the theater of the Centro Popular de Cultura (CPC; Popular Culture Center) which was burned down in a repressive attack the night after the 1964 coup. Both CPC and Teatro Opinião believed in mobilizing revolution around Brechtian theater, a tradition that reverberates today. In 1964, almost immediately after the coup, Teatro Opinião presented *Show Opinião* at Teatro Arena's theater in Rio de Janeiro. The first major theatrical response to the dictatorship, *Show Opinião* was a musical show that featured three popular musical artists representing *bossa nova* and *samba*. Written by Oduvaldo Vianna Filho (Vianninha) (see Damasceno), Armando Costa, and Paulo Pontes, the text was based on taped interviews with these singers. It interwove their personal testimonies that underscore their divergent class, race, and regional backgrounds and thus provided a commentary on the state of democracy and the prospects for social change in Brazil at that time. It is a protest musical in which the authors intentionally used Brechtian techniques to confront the repressive situation in their country.

Vianninha and Ferreira Goullar, both of whom were very active with CPC and Teatro Opinião, also wrote together *Si correr o bicho pega, si ficar o bicho come* (If You Run, the Beast Gets You, If You Stay, He Eats You), a farce in verse about absentee landlords that was not far from Brecht in either intention or spirit.

Among the authors who incorporated Brecht's ideas into their plays, Vianninha was directly influenced by Brecht. Well known for his varied works that apply both Brechtian principles and autochthonous theatrical traditions, Vianninha's two masterpieces are *Papa Highirte* (Father Highirte) and *Rasga Coração* (Torn Heart). Vianninha denounced the capitalist system while at the same time following the line of psychological theater as represented by Tennessee Williams. *Cuatro Cuadras de Tierra* (Four Acres of Land) is indicative of his stage of pronounced didactic-political theater, a theater that continued his Brechtian social criticism—albeit with an admixture of analyzing individual insecurities and communicating his own personal doubts.

It should also be noted that Brechtian techniques and theories have been studied as part of the Popular Theater Movement of the Northeast of Brazil from the 1950s to the present. In particular, Hermilo Borba Filho noted correspondences between Brazilian popular theater deriving from the Middle Ages and Brechtian theories.

COLOMBIA

Perhaps no other country in Latin America has done more than Colombia to promote a new theatrical language born of new modes of production and inserted in the struggle for a new culture. A new breed of *teatristas* came forth who were capable of filling all roles in the theater and who did not separate what was done on stage from daily life. El Nuevo Teatro (The New Theater) became a way of life in which the aesthetics of participation in theater was indivisible from the ethics of participation in all struggles for liberation. In the 1950s *teatristas* such as Buenaventura, Santiago García, Carlos José Reyes, Ricardo Camacho, Gilberto Martínez, and Jorge Alí Triana went beyond the experimental theater of groups like El Buho (The Owl) to further develop Brecht's ideas in their work. Notably, Buenaventura published widely read articles about Brecht in which he opposed the experimental, ahistorical theater of groups such as El Buho.

The most unique aspect of Colombian theater after 1960 has been its questioning of the concept of the playwright who works in isolation. Playwrights were often members of groups and were involved in the collective writing and staging of plays. These plays often underwent several revisions on the basis of a dialogue with the audience and among the members of the group. A particular historical event or issue would be thoroughly researched by the theater group through archival and field work as well as through in-depth interviews and collaborative work with specialists in various fields such as sociology and anthropology. Once this part of the work was complete, the improvisational work began; it was based on the results of the group's research and often incorporated historical speeches and other documents. As the work progressed, scenes were written out, and slowly the whole play emerged as a genuine collective effort. In this way, the actor became central to the process in what Buenaventura once called "La dramaturgia del actor" (the dramaturgy of the actor). Although this way of producing theater was widespread throughout Latin America, it was most fully developed in Colombia.

Particularly in the case of Brechtian productions, the plays were subject to the processes of nationalization and appropriation and yielded unique, dynamic, and collective products. Many of those who promoted Brecht had the opportunity to travel and study abroad and to acquire firsthand experience with the staging of his work. At the beginning of the 1960s, García studied theater in France and in the German Democratic Republic; Triana worked a few months at the Berliner Ensemble after having studied theater in Czechoslovakia; and Buenaventura stayed in France after participating in the Festival of Nations in 1960 and studied directing in Paris.

After their return to Colombia, these *teatristas* presented works that reflected the experiences they had gathered both in Europe and in their own countries. During the 1960 Festival of Nations in Paris, the Teatro Experiemental de Cali (TEC), directed by Buenaventura, obtained second place in an opinion poll by the French magazine *Partisans* and was only surpassed by the Berliner Ensemble. TEC performed *A la diestra de Dios Padre* by Buenaventura and *Historias para ser contadas* by Argentine Dragún. In 1971, the TEC participated (together with the Casa de la Cultura and LaMama) in the Eighth World Theater Festival in Nancy, France. Respected critics such as Bernard Dort, Emile Copferman, Denis Bablet, and Françoise Kourilsky recognized "the wise and creative application of Brecht's thesis embedded in *Soldados*," the play TEC presented (Domínguez, "Camino" 328).

The first work by Brecht staged in Colombia was *The Trial of Lucullus* (1957). By the beginning of the 1960s, Brecht's influence began to be felt in Colombia. By the mid-1960s, Colombian university theaters—a powerful cultural presence that extended beyond the confines of academia—adopted Brecht's ideas. Numerous works of "collective creation" provided a new reading of history that revealed the ideological mechanisms underlying official history and put a different emphasis on each event. The traditional heroic character in plays was replaced by a collective entity. The critical rereading of history and of the dominant ideology through Brecht enabled Colombian theater to acquire a powerful means of revolutionary expression. However, dogmatism and a rigidly applied definition of political theater coexisted with the more lucid, successful search for a new theatrical language that could accompany an ever more urgent and insurgent revolutionary process.

At this point it is important to emphasize the importance of the university theaters in Latin America in general and in Colombia in particular. The relationship between the university theaters and independent theaters has been complex and often problematic. University theater groups exist in virtually all institutions of higher learning, but they are usually not attached to theater departments—for the simple reason that such departments often do not exist. These groups were formed with specific objectives that were mostly of a political nature. Many of the group members did not continue their work in theater once they had finished their university studies. Nevertheless, while involved in theater, they had a voice in the ongoing debates about their country that was shaped by their theater experience—even if this experience bordered on problematic agit-prop. Among some of the younger members of the rapidly growing theater movement, an elementary and reductive appropriation of Brecht developed that only aspired to produce revolutionary theses. It was a theater that rejected everything that was subjective and psychological as "bourgeois" (Gómez 338). It was at this point that the rigidity of an ill-conceived Brechtian "orthodoxy" began to do more harm than good. This process of dogmatization in theater paralleled similar processes in cultural, political, and social contexts. By the late 1960s and 1970s, an extreme "culture of dogmatism" seemed to emerge among those inspired by revolutionary zeal. They viewed society in binary, highly polarized terms and fell victim to the dangers of Manichean thought. Others, although true to revolutionary principles, avoided the pitfall of Manicheanism and confronted the "culture of dogmatism" with the richness of their works.

Works such as *Guadalupe, años sin cuenta* (Guadalupe, Unaccounted Years), directed by García with the group La Candelaria; are indicative of the emerging new dramaturgy that has undogmatically appropriated Brecht and, at the same time, rediscovered its own popular, traditional theatrical as well as musical forms. Brechtian ideas can be discerned in *Guadalupe*: autonomous scenes, songs that link the scenes and support a critical narrative function by underscoring key issues, actors who portray class prototypes, narrative "jump cuts," and so on. In 1964, García presented *Galileo* for only thirteen performances in a memorable version with the Teatro Estudio of the National University. Owing to the growing repression within the universities, many theater practitioners, among them García, had to leave the academic context and become part of the

Independent Theater movement. García then founded La Candelaria and produced *Yo, Bertolt Brecht* (I, Bertolt Brecht) in 1969 as well as *The Good Person*.
The second, collectively produced work of the group La Candelaria, *La ciudad
dorada* (The Golden City), dealt with peasant migration to the cities and the
subsequent conflicts that result from the emergence of the shanty towns surrounding the urban centers. La Candelaria under the direction of García became
a highly influential theater group along with, among others, Buenaventura's
Teatro Experimental de Cali and Triana's Teatro Popular de Bogotá (TPB). In
1971, Triana directed *Señora Carrar's Rifles* in the TPB and in so doing brought
modern political theater to that institution. In 1974, the TPB presented a play
with the English title *I Took Panamá*, also directed by Triana, who placed
special emphasis on the actor by aspiring to a synthesis between Stanislavsky
and Brecht. In 1976, TBP presented *The Threepenny Opera*.

In the 1960s, Buenaventura wrote a series of five short plays under the title
Los papeles del infierno (Papers from Hell) based on *Fear and Misery of the
Third Reich*. In "Apuntes para un método de creación colectiva" (1969; Notes
on a Method of Collective Creation), first circulated in mimeographed form,
Buenaventura and TEC went beyond their ideological and aesthetic affinities
with Brecht to outline the essential "method" of collective creation that was to
have considerable impact on Latin American theater. Buenaventura, an established playwright, for many years subordinated his individual talent to the collective process. With his prolific drama production, theoretical treatises, work
as a director, promoter of theater, and painter, Buenaventura ranks with del
Cioppo, García, and Boal as a *teatrista* the impact of whose work can be felt
throughout Latin America.

PERU

In 1960, Histrión Teatro de Arte in Lima staged Julio Ramón Ribeyro's *Vida
y pasión de Santiago el pajarero* (The Life and Passion of Santiago the Bird
Keeper), directed by Hernando Cortés. It was the first Brechtian epic staged in
Peru inspired by *Galileo*. But in order to evaluate Brecht's presence in Peru it
is necessary to take into account del Cioppo's work at the theater school of the
University of Engineering in Lima during the 1960s. There he staged *The Threepenny Opera*, the high point of Brecht's reception in Peru. The reader may have
already discerned that *maestros* such as del Cioppo, Buenaventura, Boal, and
García fulfilled their role as *teatristas* not only by promoting the development
of their own national theaters but also by working in different countries in
solidarity with the development of theater throughout Latin America. Del
Cioppo was exemplary in this respect in that he continued his work in different
countries well into his eighties. Often, the repercussions of a production or a
seminar by one of these *maestros* could be felt for years to come in the countries
they visited. Such was the case of del Cioppo in Peru.

Brecht's arrival in Peru must also be framed in the context of the 1960s, a time of political upheaval in the universities that galvanized the theater movement and polarized its members. The Peruvian theater participated in the general "counterculture attitude" of the time as expressed by hippies, rock music, and the like; it was aware of representative groups such as the Living Theater and the Bread and Puppet Theater, and produced plays inspired by Peter Brook, Grotowski, Stanislavsky, and Artaud. But by the mid-1960s, given the politically charged atmosphere, the phenomenon of Brecht exploded in Peru in particular and in Latin America in general.

By the 1970s, social, political, and collectively created theater influenced by Brecht dominated the scene. Just as in other Latin American countries, a clear tendency toward group theater took hold in Peru, with groups constituting themselves as theatrical communities that privileged "the work place, the home and daily life as their referents" (Del Alcázar, *1968–1988* 307). The groups Cuatrotablas, Yuyachkani, Raíces, Magia, Maguey, and Villa El Salvador are representative examples of this communal drive in theater. In the following, Cuatrotablas, Yuyachkani, and Villa El Salvador will be briefly discussed.

Hugo Salazar Del Alcázar notes that Cuatrotablas in *El sol bajo las patas de los caballos* (1974; The Sun beneath the Horses' Hoofs) "deepens its sociopolitical reflection." Later he notes a stage of ritualization that reached its climax in *La noche larga* (The Long Night), a play by Cuatrotablas produced in 1975, that "marks the cancellation of the social epic's explicit discourse in order to try to speak theatrically about an existential ethic" (Del Alcázar, *Cuatrotablas* 310). But one can also speak of a Brechtian, political stage in groups like Cuatrotablas and Yuyachkani. The 1972 productions of *Oye* (Listen) by Cuatrotablas, directed by Mario Delgado, and *Puño de cobre* (Copper Fist) by Yuyachkani, directed by Miguel Rubio, proposed a new version of Peruvian history. In 1973, Cuatrotablas came into contact with Grotowski and with Eugenio Barba, who was promoting an anthropological "Third Theater" in Latin America. This was to drastically change Cuatrotablas's aesthetic tendencies in the direction of ritualized productions.

Initially, Yuyachkani's ideological mentors were Brecht and Boal, and the paradigm was an epic theater of agitation. *Mother Courage* was produced by Yuyachkani in 1976, at a time when leftist political activity was prohibited and groups like Yuyachkani filled the function of an agit-prop press. Although in *Los músicos ambulantes* (1983; The Roaming Musicians) by Yuyachkani some of Brecht's methods seem to have been articulated with a renewed ethnoanthropological interest, this work marked a high point in that the group took it beyond political agit-prop theater.

Another turning point occurred when members of Yuyachkani—urban middle class in their origins—were confronted with Andean indigenous cultures. The confrontation with a new language, Quechua, and with unfamiliar ancestral cultural practices began to fracture the utopia of progress and of Brechtian, Piscatorian poetics. Yuyachkani's members endeavored to learn the language as they researched the new reality they had come into contact with, a reality that was ultimately a part of their own heterogeneous country and being. They did not "abandon" Brecht, they simply incorporated their own reality in a deeper sense. Faced with Andean life, the binary opposition of oppressors and oppressed needed to be enriched with a broader cultural and anthropological perspective. The body, rhythms, music, movements, gestures, language, needed to be "andeanized" and internalized in a different manner if Yuyachkani was to reach that indigenous community and a deeper sense of itself.

In 1985, Yuyachkani staged *Baladas del bienestar* (Ballads of Well-being), a work for one actor, by Teresa Ralli. It constituted a rereading of Brecht that was "heterodox, manipulated, and even postmodern. It allowed itself to ironize with its own artifice: alienation. It stated it in order to dilute it" (Del Alcázar, *Cuatrotablas* 313).

Tensions between apparent binary oppositions such as ritual versus political theater, Brecht versus Grotowski, prevailed for some time. At present, these oppositions are in a process of synthesis on account of the questioning of the dogmatization of culture that began during the 1960s and 1970s. Nevertheless, the ethical and political dimension of Yuyachkani and other theaters tends to persist.

The theater group of Villa El Salvador owes much to Brechtian theater. The theater originated in a community that was created by an invasion of land by the urban poor who founded a "pueblo nuevo" or new town in Lima with its own internal laws and cultural production. Brecht served as the starting point for their theater, which was enriched by specific national contexts and traditions.

MEXICO

Lola Bravo introduced Brecht to the Mexican theater in the 1950s. The renaissance of Mexican theater that occurred between 1959 and 1975 was very much linked to the art of playwright Héctor Mendoza, to his creative freedom, and to the principles of improvisation. He broke with the established rules in order to search for his own personal artistic path. His stagings of Brecht (in 1959 and 1964) were related to his heterodox attitude in interpretating the classics and in dealing with theater in general (De Ita 141).

In 1959, Héctor Mendoza and his Club de Teatro (Theater Club) staged *Fear and Misery of the Third Reich*; in 1964, he directed *The Good Person*. In both works, Mendoza incorporated elements of Mexican popular culture in the structure of the plays. *The Good Person* exemplified the high point of Mendoza's maturity as a director. Previously, Brecht's *The Threepenny Opera* had been staged in Mexico with little success. His pop staging in 1966 of *Don Gil de las calzas negras* (Don Gil with the Black Britches), based on Tirso de Molina's play, is considered a vanguard attempt at adapting classical Spanish theater to the theories of Brecht—although Grotowski and Artaud must also be counted as influences (Peralta 137–38). The classical verses were accompanied by tango rhythms, mariachi music, and twist beats.

In the early 1960s, the Mexican director Rafaél López Miarnau also began to concentrate on the social content of his works and defined himself as a ''Brechtian director.'' In a somewhat similar vein, the theater of Luis de Tavira, acknowledged as one of Mexico's preeminent directors, has a ritual quality that reaches its greatest success when combined with a Brecht-inspired epic. Tavira's ideas were influenced by Brecht but also by Grotowski, Stanislavsky, and the Living Theater. His theater, like that of Yuyachkani in Peru, unites political concerns and an anthropological vision as a way of realizing the connection between theater and society.

In 1975, Marta Luna directed *The Threepenny Opera*, a production that marked the revitalization of Mexican theater. It was ''a very special moment of cohesion and passion'' (Harmony 166). For the first time, members of the then recently created Sindicato de Actores Independientes (Independent Actors' Union) were involved in the production. At that time, the country was making a very difficult transition from the riches of its earlier oil boom to an economic crisis that was reaching all sectors of society and resulting in highly politicized cultural productions. In 1980, the theater department of the University of Veracruz presented *The Seven Deadly Sins*, directed by Raúl Zermeño. The work was adapted to Mexican reality and was considered to be among the most notable plays of the decade.

CUBA

Cuba is perhaps the country with the highest number of productions of Brecht's plays. Between 1959 and 1988, more than thirty of Brecht's plays were staged by some of the most outstanding Cuban and Latin American directors. But even before the revolution, interest in Brecht was apparent. As early as 1957, the magazine *Nuestro tiempo* (Our Time), on the occasion of Brecht's death in 1956, published fragments of ''A Short Organum for the Theatre'' and the text of *He Who Said Yes*. In 1958 Vicente Revuelta announced the premiere of *The Good Person* by Teatro Estudio, but he was only able to present it in 1959 upon the triumph of the revolution and the departure of dictator Batista, with Raquel Revuelta in the leading role.

From 1960 to 1963, Brecht's theater as well as his theories and aesthetic principles were actively promoted in Cuba and abroad, his works were published in Spanish, and a number of his plays were staged. The Uruguayan director Hugo Ulive premiered *Chalk Circle*, and Revuelta presented *Mother Courage* with Raquel Revuelta in the role of the protagonist. Other directors also premiered works by Brecht. All of these activities contributed to Brecht's impact not only in Cuba but also in those Latin American countries where Cuban journals and publications were distributed. After the revolution, students of theater had the opportunity to study in East Germany and to expand their knowledge of Brecht—a development that contributed to extending the influence of Brecht, who was placed in the service of the revolution when, in 1969, Grupo Escambray produced a freely adapted version of *Señora Carrar's Rifles* that reflected the conflicts between the counterrevolutionaries and the revolutionaries in the Escambray region. Even though it is true that Cuba's cultural and political processes influenced the rest of Latin America, it is also important to remember that Cuban theater was greatly affected by the input of those roving *maestros* mentioned above, notably del Cioppo, Buenaventura, García, and Boal.

In 1974, Vicente Revuelta, an exquisite barometer of his society, premiered *Galileo* at a time when dogmatism was rising in Cuba. In 1985, within the Cuban Process of Rectification (a process initiated by Fidel Castro that called for criticism and self-criticism within the revolution), Revuelta staged his third version of *Galileo* in which he appeared as Galileo. He mixed professional actors and students from the Instituto Superior de Arte (Advanced Art Institute) and left the stage open to improvisation so that each night the actors confronted unexpected situations in their theater in the round. At one point, Galileo/Revuelta asked if this attempt to have an open, social dialogue was not preaching in the desert. *Galileo*, part of Revuelta's trilogy dealing with "human destiny," appeared at a time in which Cuban theater insistently showed images of alienation and of the distortion of previous ideals.

The current intellectual climate is characterized by the struggle between the old and the new, the need for a synthesis, and the need for an end to the culture of dogmatism that stifles the true revolutionary spirit. Brechtian principles are strongly rooted in this new Cuban theatrical quest that is based on an intercultural drive aiming for the incorporation of all facets of Cuban history and reality.

PUERTO RICO

Puerto Rico's long history of political upheaval as well as its ongoing and often questioned status in the United States have made political theater highly visible on the island. As in the rest of Latin America, Brechtian principles have contributed to the politicization of theater. Specifically, in 1967, the university theater group El Tajo de Alacrán, directed by Lydia Milagros González, presented the play *Brecht de Brecht* (Brecht by Brecht) as politically committed theater. In the 1970s, the Teatro de Guerrilla (Guerrilla Theater) of the University of Puerto Rico staged *Mother Courage*.

In 1980, *La verdadera historia de Pedro Navajas* (The True/Real Story of Pedro Navajas) by Pablo Cabrera was a big success in that it had the longest run in Puerto Rican theater history. Staged by Teatro del '60 (Theater of the 60s), it played to full houses for more than a year. For many the play represents the epic theater of Brecht transposed to the Caribbean environment. Based on the song by Rubén Blades by the same title, it was based on *The Beggar's Opera* by John Gay (the model for *The Threepenny Opera*) and featured songs, *salsa* music, dance, and critical as well as incisive dialogue about Puerto Rican reality.

CENTRAL AMERICA

A few cursory remarks here may suffice. Perhaps less readily received than in other countries, Brechtian ideas were not completely absent from the region. In Nicaragua, for example, Brechtian theater was a strong component of the Sandinista revolution that used theater as a vehicle for education and the promotion of revolutionary ideals. Conversely, the simple act of staging Brecht could lead to repressive measures. In 1979, at the Quinta Muestra Nacional de Teatro (Fifth National Theater Show) in El Salvador, *The Exception and the Rule* was presented. The right-wing government of General Fernando Romeo Lucas initiated an investigation of the festival because of the political repercussions that the staging of the work had caused. The actors received anonymous death threats and, between 1980 and 1981, several had to go into hiding or exile (Molina 35).

CONCLUSION

As the foregoing discussion has shown, Brecht's presence and impact in Latin America is undeniable. At the same time, Latin America's cannibalization of his ideas is very much in evidence. The intercultural products that result from this process are and have been unique renderings of the images of a highly galvanized reality. Specifically, participatory, dialogic, and nonhierarchical collective principles seem to be Latin America's genuine contribution to the further development of the Brechtian theater.

NOTE

1. See also Michael Bodden, "Brecht in Asia," in this volume.

WORKS CITED (SEE ALSO REFERENCE GUIDE TO WORKS CITED IN ABBREVIATED FORM)

"ATINT Symposium: Brecht in Latin America." Edited by Maria H. Lima, et al. *Brecht-Jahrbuch/Brecht Yearbook* 13 (1984): 91–142.

Boal, Augusto. *Theater of the Oppressed.* 1974. Translated by Charles A. and Maria-Odilia Leal McBride. New York: Urizen, 1979.

Buenaventura, Enrique. "El arte no es un lujo." *Teatro y política.* Buenos Aires: Ediciones de la Flor, 1969.

Cosentino, Olga. "1984–1987: La democracia, un avance lento e inseguro." In *Escenarios de dos mundos: Inventario teatral iberoamericano.* Edited by Moisés Pérez-Coterillo. Madrid: Centro de Documentación Teatral, 1990. 1: 152–57.

Damasceno, Leslie. *Cultural Space and Theatrical Conventions in the Work of Oduvaldo Vianna Filho.* Detroit: Wayne State University Press, 1996.

De Ita, Fernando. "De Seki Sano a Luis de Tavira: Itineraio de la puesta en escena." In *Escenarios de dos mundos: Inventario teatral iberoamericano.* Edited by

Moisés Pérez-Coterillo. Madrid: Centro de Documentación Teatral, 1990. 3: 139–42.

De Toro, Fernando. *Brecht en el teatro hispanoamericano contemporáneo*. Buenos Aires: Editorial Galerna, 1987.

Del Alcázar, Hugo Salazar. "1968–1988: Modernidad, eclecticismo y ruptura." In *Escenarios de dos mundos: Inventario teatral iberoamericano*. Edited by Moisés Pérez-Coterillo. Madrid: Centro de Documentación Teatral, 1990. 3: 297–308.

———. "Cuatrotablas y Yuyachkani, los heterodoxos del teatro peruano." In *Escenarios de dos mundos: Inventario teatral iberoamericano*. Edited by Moisés Pérez-Coterillo. Madrid: Centro de Documentación Teatral, 1990. 3: 309–313.

De Lima, Mariángela. "1960–1988: De la dictadura militar a la democracia." In *Escenarios de dos mundos: Inventario teatral iberoamericano*. Edited by Moisés Pérez-Coterillo. Madrid: Centro de Documentación Teatral, 1990. 1: 256–70.

Démange, Camille. *Brecht*. Paris: Seghers, 1967.

Domínguez, Carlos Espinoza. "Por el camino del TEC." In *Escenarios de dos mundos: Inventario teatral iberoamericano*. Edited by Moisés Pérez-Coterillo. Madrid: Centro de Documentación Teatral, 1990. 1: 326–31.

———. "La Candelaria: Vivir para el teatro." In *Escenarios de dos mundos: Inventario teatral iberoamericano*. Edited by Moisés Pérez-Coterillo. Madrid: Centro de Documentación Teatral, 1990. 1: 332–37.

Fernández, Gerardo. "1949–1983: Del Peronismo a la dictadura militar." In *Escenarios de dos mundos: Inventario teatral iberoamericano*. Edited by Moisés Pérez-Coterillo. Madrid: Centro de Documentación Teatral, 1990. 1: 135–51.

———. "Veinte espectáculos en la memoria." In *Escenarios de dos mundos: Inventario teatral iberoamericano*. Edited by Moisés Pérez-Coterillo. Madrid: Centro de Documentación Teatral, 1990. 1: 162–67.

Ferrer, Edgar H. Quiles. "1960–1987: La voluntad de existir." In *Escenarios de dos mundos: Inventario teatral iberoamericano*. Edited by Moisés Pérez-Coterillo. Madrid: Centro de Documentación Teatral, 1990. 4: 108–122.

George, David. *The Modern Brazilian Stage*. Austin: University of Texas Press, 1992.

Gómez, Eduardo. "Los veinte años del TPB." In *Escenarios de dos mundos: Inventario teatral iberoamericano*. Edited by Moisés Pérez-Coterillo. Madrid: Centro de Documentación Teatral, 1990. 1: 338–42.

Harmony, Olga. "Espectáculos para la memoria." In *Escenarios de dos mundos: Inventario teatral iberoamericano*. Edited by Moisés Pérez-Coterillo. Madrid: Centro de Documentación Teatral, 1990. 3: 166–71.

Molina, Manuel Fernández. "1944–1988: Un desarrollo lento pero continuado." In *Escenarios de dos mundos: Inventario teatral iberoamericano*. Edited by Moisés Pérez-Coterillo. Madrid: Centro de Documentación Teatral, 1990. 3: 25–37.

Mora, Arnoldo. "Diez espectáculos en la memoria." In *Escenarios de dos mundos: Inventario teatral iberoamericano*. Edited by Moisés Pérez-Coterillo. Madrid: Centro de Documentación Teatral, 1990. 1: 399–401.

Navarro, Felipe. "Augusto Boal: El teatro como detonador político." In *Escenarios de dos mundos: Inventario teatral iberoamericano*. Edited by Moisés Pérez-Coterillo. Madrid: Centro de Documentación Teatral, 1990. 1: 81–84.

Peixoto, Fernando. "The Good Soul of Brecht in Brazil." Translated and edited by Leslie Damasceno. *Communications from the International Brecht Society* 17.1 (1987): 50–52.

Perales, Rosalina. *Teatro hispanoamericano contemporáneo*. 2 vols. Mexico City: Grupo Editorial Gaceta, S.A., 1989–1993.

Peralta, Braulio. "Hector Mendoza: Todo un estilo." In *Escenarios de dos mundos: Inventario teatral iberoamericano*. Edited by Moisés Pérez-Coterillo. Madrid: Centro de Documentación Teatral, 1990. 3: 134–138.

Pianca, Marina. *El teatro de Nuestra América: Un proyecto continental (1959–1989)*. Minneapolis, MN: Institute for the Studies of Ideologies and Literatures, 1990.

———. *Testimonios de Teatro Latinoamericano*. Buenos Aires: Grupo Editor Latinoamericano, 1991.

Pons, Juan Estrades. "1985–1988: Una difícil recuperación." In *Escenarios de dos mundos: Inventario teatral iberoamericano*. Edited by Moisés Pérez-Coterillo. Madrid: Centro de Documentación Teatral, 1990. 4: 191–200.

17

Brecht in Asia: New Agendas, National Traditions, and Critical Consciousness

MICHAEL BODDEN

The last two decades have witnessed the growth of a remarkable interest in the dramas and theories of Bertolt Brecht in a wide variety of Asian countries. Antony Tatlow has eloquently refuted one line of reasoning that seeks to explain this phenomenon by assigning Brecht to a stage of cultural development long outgrown by the West but still relevant to the "backward" East. In a series of articles, he demonstrates that, contrary to the opinions of those critics who see Brecht's work as suited to Asian theater and society because of its presumed simplicity, both Brecht's works and ideas and the cultural forms and political situations of Asia are incredibly complex.

Furthermore, the arguments of such critics ignore the real intricacies of historical development by assuming that Asian countries must go through precisely the same stages of cultural (and economic) development as the countries of the West and North America, when in fact Asian countries are modernizing under conditions markedly different from those prevailing in the West during the late nineteenth and early twentieth centuries. While Europe and the United States still exercise considerable cultural and economic hegemony over much of the rest of the world, and while there are likely to be some similarities, there will also be crucial differences in the courses of development pursued by Asian countries.

All of this is to suggest that the reception of Brecht's works and ideas in Indonesia or China, for example, will end in the creation of a Brecht different from the Brecht known to Weimar audiences in the 1920s and 1930s and different from the Brecht who subsequently became familiar to European and North American audiences in the immediate postwar decades. The connection between Brecht's work and contemporary Asian theater is, in fact, better described as one of "cross-cultural appropriation" rather than "influence." This appropriation is a creative, dynamic process of reinterpreting and retooling certain of Brecht's ideas or techniques rather than a stiff imitation of a transparent model by groups that "lag behind" the times aesthetically due to a "backward" state of social and cultural development. Such a dynamic process is perhaps easier to imagine if we remember that Brecht himself selectively appropriated elements of the Japanese *No* and Kabuki theaters, as well as the traditional Chinese theater, in order to enlarge the creative possibilities of his own, continually changing approach. At no point did Brecht simply copy features of such Asian forms; rather he attempted to "transport" (refunction) them according to his own needs (Tatlow, *Mask*).

What, then, is similar, and what is different? Of course, the answer will again vary depending on whether we are speaking about Japan or Bengal, and whether we are discussing the 1960s or the 1980s. There are some major trends, however, that will allow us to gain a general understanding of how Asian theater practitioners are appropriating Brecht. Briefly, these trends include the adaptation of Brecht's plays to local political situations and theater forms; the appropriation of Brechtian theories and techniques as part of the construction of discourses and practices of "national" cultures; the refunctioning or integration of certain Brechtian ideas and techniques into original, local dramatic creations; and the mobilization of Brechtian ideas of theater as an educational institution for new grassroots theater movements.

Certainly, throughout Asia, many dramatists and groups are attracted to Brecht's work because he developed plays and techniques that they have found useful in articulating a critique of existing power structures on behalf of the disenfranchised and marginalized. Critiques of this nature by Asian theater practitioners are, however, never undertaken from the same ideological position as that occupied by Brecht during his life. In many instances, oppositional or dissident groups have used Brecht to attack military dictatorships and authoritarian regimes of varying stripes in the name of "democratic" reform. In the Philippines, for instance, a 1980 performance of *Life of Galileo* focused opposition to the Marcos dictatorship on the issues of authoritarian control of knowledge and the social responsibility of the scientist. In this case, the play specifically raised issues associated with a contemporary campaign opposing the construction of a controversial nuclear power plant in the Philippines. This plant, while promising to provide power for many newly located foreign multinational subsidiaries, was seen by the opposition as both ecologically unsound and threatening to a Filipino national industrial sector that stood to lose much in the face of competition from the multinationals.

Indonesian productions of *The Caucasian Chalk Circle* in 1976 and 1980 inserted topical references to the frustrations of the Indonesian intelligentsia under the military-bureaucratic New Order government. One of contemporary Indonesia's most important director/dramatists, W.S. Rendra, used his 1976 production, *Linkaran Kapur Putih* (The Chalk Circle), to suggest that the military authorities were unwilling to engage in a dialogue with their civilian critics, a situation that could eventually lead to more severe troubles (Bujono, "Astaga," 15). A 1980 staging directed by Basuki Rachmat took advantage of student dissatisfaction with the government's Campus Normalization program (an attempt to ban student activism from campus areas) and included graffiti found on the Yogyakarta university campus in the text of the play (Bujono, Brecht 24).

In China, there are indications that Brecht's plays *Galileo* (1979) and *Schweyk in the Second World War* (1986) were chosen for performance and succeeded with the public precisely because they were regarded as an attack, in the name of greater individual freedom, on the despotic ideological authority of the Communist party (Schlenker, "Paradigmenwechsel" 75). A reading of *Galileo* by one of its codirectors, Chen Yong, is quite revealing of another possible, though related, interpretation. Staged shortly after the end of the Cultural Revolution, Chen frames the play's significance in relation to both the end of the Cultural Revolution and the reign of the Gang of Four, and the subsequent initiation of the Four Modernizations campaign. He suggests that Brecht's play, via the character of Galileo, warns that any new age will still be full of difficulties, setbacks, contradictions, and even "betrayals among the vanguard" (Chen, "Beijing" 90). Li Jianming has suggested that staging Brecht's works in China in the 1980s and 1990s has become more difficult because the contemporary atmosphere is moving theater in the direction of exploring "human nature" and the individual "personality" rather than the great social events and the relationship of man to society (Li 64–65). However, Chen Yong still praises Brecht for opening up more creative choices for the Chinese stage by offering an alternative to a "strictly naturalistic, outward imitation of life." According to Chen, Brecht helped creative dramatists maneuver their own and the audience's imaginative power to overcome the regimentation of everyday life (Chen, "Brecht" 48–49).

The appropriation of Brecht in Japan followed a rather different course than that in China, though in both countries the beginnings of substantial interest in Brecht's work coincided with attempts to counter the artistic domination of Stanislavskian acting and Socialist Realism, currents that had developed simultaneously with Brecht's theater in the European context of the 1930s. The popularity of Brecht's works, with the support of Senda Korea's Haiyuza Theater Company, reached a peak in the late 1950s and early 1960s during the broad left-progressive campaign against the extension of the Japanese government's security pact with the United States. Haiyuza performed three Brecht plays in 1960: *The Mother*, *The Good Person of Szechwan*, and *The Exception and the Rule*. Shortly thereafter, serious rifts within the Communist party, coupled with the party's ensuing bureaucratization, resulted in a fragmentation of the left. This fragmentation was accompanied by an impulse to question the party's authority. The relationship between the individual and the community was critically examined in such a context, and *The Measures Taken* was staged and discussed intensively as part of this process (Iwabuchi, "Ändert Brecht" 68–69).

As can be seen from the foregoing examples, one of the most frequent ways in which Asian practitioners come to grips with Brechtian theater is through the staging of his plays. In the majority of cases these stagings do not simply seek to imitate the "proper" method of staging Brecht as he himself might have done in his own time. Rather they are most frequently attempts to reconstruct his plays in accordance with local settings, issues, and styles. Such "translations" often take on different meanings and connote different things for their Asian audiences than do the texts as originally performed in Europe.

The Pakistani group, Ajoka, for example, performed a version of *The Threepenny Opera* in January of 1989 in both Urdu and Punjabi. The play was set in Lahore's officially nonexistent red-light district, Polly was played as a caricature of Benazir Bhutto, and the members of Mac the Knife's gang, who objected to Polly's takeover of their affairs, were portrayed as fundamentalists and upper-class businessmen (van Erven, *Revolution* 170).

In the Philippines, the prologue of *Chalk Circle*, as performed by the Philippine Educational Theater Association (PETA) in late 1977, replaced the debate between neighboring collectives in the original with a discussion among residents of an urban squatter community over the vast social disparities existing in Philippine society (Labad "PETA" 8). This brought the play much closer to home for Philippine audiences than did the original Caucasus setting of the play's frame would have done for East Germans in 1954—although in terms of the construction of socialism the 1954 production was most likely relevant. Such a change also committed the central tale to a much more visceral, direct relationship with the conditions prevailing during the Philippine martial law era. The coup of the central tale, in which the soldiers of the council of princes seize state power from the Georgian governor, could scarcely help but remind Filipino audiences of Ferdinand E. Marcos's declaration of martial law only five years earlier. Similarly, the play's theme of utopian justice, introduced through the character of Azdak and his climactic legal decision, was given particular emphasis in a situation where broad social campaigns were underway against random arrests, torture, and the summary justice so prevalent under Marcos (Wurfel 125–29).

In Indonesia, Teater Koma's 1983 adaptation of Brecht's *The Threepenny Opera* (retitled *Opera Ikan Asin* or The Salted-Fish Opera) chose to stress and elaborate upon themes of governmental corruption, crony capitalism, and the government's penchant for evading its own laws. The change in resonance of the final pardoning scene as played by Teater Koma is illustrative of this point. In the original the pardon serves to underscore the fact that the play is only a play and that the poor can almost never expect such happy endings; in the Indonesian version the pardon reinforces a sense of government corruption. In

Opera Ikan Asin, the bond between the police and criminals, as represented by the Macheath-Tiger Brown relationship, is raised to a national level when the pardon becomes a case of the president of Indonesia forgiving a morally and legally compromised veteran of the Indonesian revolution against Dutch rule, while simultaneously giving him a substantial sum for monthly maintenance and a house in a wealthy section of South Jakarta (Riantiarno/Tjie 65). Such a change indeed echoed actual cases from Indonesia's recent past. There is also a tendency to expand, always in a sarcastic and derogatory vein, references to the general transformation of the base of economic power from mercantile and petty trade capitalism to industrial and finance capital (as illustrated by Macheath's final speech in Brecht's version). This particular reworking hints again at the rather general frustration of the Indonesian urban intelligentsia, including many of its theater workers and creative artists, with their exclusion from effective power in the changing politico-economic structure of New Order Indonesia. One example is the additions Teater Koma's adapters made to the song "Concerning the Insecurity of the Human State" (*CP* 2: 177–79)—which became "Dunia Yang Kejam" (The Cruel World) in Indonesian. In the original, the Peachums agree with Polly that it would be nice if we could be happy and do good, but forbid her to marry Mac the Knife because happiness and good deeds are simply not realistic goals in this wicked, cutthroat sort of world. The Indonesian version stresses that human rights are unattainable and that people just have to suffer in the name of "national development," as symbolized by government program acronyms.[1] In this climate, the song concludes, only "corruptors" can survive (Riantiarno/Tjie 24–25). The term "corruptor", quite common at the time of the play's performance, is a reference to government military-bureaucrats who engaged in massive corruption schemes and dominated modern economic development in league with Chinese-Indonesian businessmen.

In Thailand, a radical theater group aligned to the Literature for Life movement performed *The Exception and the Rule* in 1976. In its Bangkok performance, the troupe juxtaposed scenes from the Brecht play with improvised scenes from the life of a contemporary Thai factory worker. Chetana Nagavajara has written that the Thai scenes seemed inserted into the play precisely to heighten its emotional impact (52).

These examples confirm a trend by many Asian practitioners to reemotionalize Brecht's work by effacing the distanciation of time and place that Brecht built into his plays. In many such instances, it seems, groups appropriating Brecht attempt to combine Brecht's desire for promoting critical thinking with a need for immediate relevance and engagement in pressing issues. The preceding examples, to varying degrees, succeeded in interesting and arousing their audiences through a synthesis of such objectives. In some instances, however, as Rustam Barucha has suggested for a number of stagings in Bengal, the adaptation of Brecht's works did not get beyond an "indiscriminate alteration of details and characters." In such cases, the adaptation of Brecht, though clothed in local costume, does not necessarily make connections with the actual contradictions of the local political situation (Barucha 80).

One of the key features of many Asian adaptations is the conscious combination of Brecht with local theater genres. In Southeast Asia, there is a tendency to stage Brecht's plays in ways that are familiar to local audiences in order to facilitate communication of the play's themes. In Indonesia for instance, Basuki Rachmat, directing a team composed of members of Bengkel Muda Surabaya and Grup Teater Surabaya from East Java, staged *Chalk Circle* according to the styles of Javanese theater forms such as *Ketoprak*, *Ludruk*, and *Wayang Orang* in 1980.[2] In addition, musical accompaniment was provided by a Javanese Gamelan orchestra. The result, according to one reviewer, was a play full of folk humor, joking, and spontaneity (Bujono, ''Brecht'' 24). The same play, performed in the southernmost region of the Philippine island of Mindanao in 1985, utilized the local Kambayoka performance style in which the actors use their bodies and traditional Malong cloths to form all the scenery. Incorporated into the performance as well were the use of local musical instruments and a traditional Sagayan war dance (Millado 41). In Pakistan, a 1985 production of *Chalk Circle* by the Ajoka theater group used a local narrative form called Bandh, which worked as a distancing device through the informal dialogues of two Punjabi storytellers (van Erven, *Revolution* 165).

In China, there has been great interest in combining Brechtian theater with traditional Chinese theater in order to create a new national style. Experiments toward that end began prior to the Cultural Revolution with the work of Huang Zuolin (Hsia 47–62), and have continued both in the subsequent work of Huang and in that of his collaborator on the 1979 production of *Galileo*, Chen Yong (Chen, ''Brecht'' 47–50). A similar situation can be seen in the efforts of a number of Vietnamese scholars and theater workers to combine Brecht with the Vietnamese traditional peasant theater form, *Cheo*. Nguyen Dinh Quang, in arguing for the integration of the musical, highly sentimentalized *Cheo* with Brechtian elements, stated that though the traditional musical theater was widely esteemed, it needed to be more than simply a fossilized bit of national heritage. Nguyen, citing the Communist party's own statements, argued that one must know the past in order to be able to create something new, and that new advances were absolutely necessary (Nguyen 101).

These examples indicate that in a number of Asian countries, the issues of national identity and national culture have emerged to become key foci of public discourse. Such discursive strands can in themselves have extremely complex histories. In the Vietnamese case, for instance, the determination of the Communist party to rescue and develop traditional forms into modern national idioms may well have been based in part on its long strategic connection with the peasants. However, the party was also committed to such forms based on its opposition to political rivals among the local elite whose cultural inclinations tended toward Western models at the expense of folk forms, considered to be intransigent, reactionary, outmoded, and unsalvageable for contemporary needs by the elite (Nguyen 99–101). Huang and Chen's efforts in China to fuse Brecht with classical Chinese theater forms so as to create a new Chinese style are also a result of a search for a kind of theater that can handle contemporary themes and topics but that does not abandon the broad narrative scope and expressive gestural vocabulary of traditional theater. Such a combination was seen by Huang and others in the wake of the Cultural Revolution as a way out of a decades-long social and creative impasse in which the favored theater style of Socialist Realism was assigned the task of conveying contemporary themes deemed appropriate, while the traditional theater was relegated to being a stylistically and thematically ossified bit of "national heritage" (Tatlow, "Paradigm" 16–17).

In much of India, Brecht's work and ideas became quite popular in the 1960s and 1970s among urban theater groups. Many of these groups had been performing realistic plays based on Western models or direct translations of works by Ibsen, Chekhov, Pirandello, Sartre, Camus, and Beckett. This activity took place primarily under the influence of the Indian People's Theater Association (IPTA), the 1940s cultural movement that had grown up around the independence struggle. Following independence, the movement lost its focus and a split in the Indian Communist party in the late 1950s created an acute crisis within the predominantly left-leaning urban theater movement. During the 1960s, according to Dalmia-Lüderitz, Indian theater practitioners increasingly turned toward the use of traditional forms, enlivened with contemporary relevance, in an effort to create a national theatrical idiom. Increasing engagement with the work of Brecht, given his interest in folk theater as manifested in plays such as *Puntila and Matti, His Hired Man* and *Chalk Circle*, thus provided a modern, politically and aesthetically defensible model that left-wing theater workers could point to as a justification for utilizing folk theater in an urban setting. Such a development endowed folk theater with contemporary relevance and seemed to offer a link between urban intellectuals and the masses. This option was pursued with particular energy in Bengal, where a leftist government was elected for the first time in 1967.

PETA and other groups in the Philippines have also had occasion to use Brechtian techniques as a part of their attempt to create a critical yet militantly nationalist theater. As early as the late 1960s, radical nationalist groups began appropriating some of Brecht's techniques and ideas in order to create an anti-illusionistic street theater that would goad mass audiences to think critically about their lives as well as about contemporary Philippine politics. PETA has continued this legacy in its own way, applying Brechtian techniques in traditional theater forms such as the Filipino nativity play, *Panunuluyan*. The modern version of this genre, written by Rody Vera, Alan Glinoga, and Al Santos and given the title *Panunuluyan* (1979) had Joseph and Mary looking for an inn in present-day Manila. A Brechtian approach was also brought to bear in creating the musical score of Nicanor Tiongson's 1982 attempt to modernize the Zarzuwela form, *Pilipinas Circa 1907*. Additionally, PETA's use of Brechtian elements contributed to the overall creation of a sociocritical modern Filipino theater. Through working with Fritz Bennewitz, the company's composers studied Brecht's notions regarding the use of music in his theater, then proceeded to adapt key ideas for their own practice. PETA's music is thus frequently geared toward stressing the words and argumentation of a particular song as well as toward bringing out the contradictions in those lyrics. PETA members felt such changes in musical style to be a distinct advance from sentimental traditional Filipino musical theater.

PETA's designers also learned from their productions with Bennewitz and further developed their own concept for Philippine theater design, "The Aesthetics of Poverty," by appropriating aspects of Brechtian practice. Beginning with a rather limited budget not uncommon to many third-world theater groups, PETA's designers had long tried to make a virtue out of their relative poverty. Relying on their own resourcefulness, they frequently constructed sets from commonly used, recycled, and found materials. This led them to an appreciation of the aesthetic qualities of even impoverished surroundings. Eventually, they came to produce sets that expressed the most salient qualities and contradictions of a social ambience. Such an aesthetic approach came to parallel that of Brecht to scenic design; following their work with Bennewitz on Philippine versions of *Chalk Circle* (1978) and *Galileo* (1980), in an interview Brenda Fajardo and her colleagues began to describe the kinds of sets they constructed with the term "scenic gestus."[3] The resulting style seemed, to PETA's designers and many others, both politically and economically appropriate for a radical national theater (Fajardo, *Aesthetics* 3).

Many Asian theorists have attempted to grapple with Brecht's concepts within similar contexts of nationalist concerns. For example, Indra Nath Chouduri has endeavored to use Brecht to validate the notion of a national tradition of Indian theater that is artistically and theoretically equal, if not superior, to anything found in Europe or North America. Chouduri's argument posits that Brecht drew upon Asian traditions, and that *Verfremdung* and other techniques of Brechtian theater were in fact long present in some of the traditional regional forms of Indian theater. Furthermore, he attempts to show that the ancient Sanskrit aesthetician, Bharata, had produced in his *Natyasastra* a theory of drama (the *Rasa* theory) that far surpassed Brecht's theories in profundity, while matching many of the specific effects of Brechtian theater (Chouduri 281–87). Chouduri is not alone in making such claims. Others, including noted Filipino scholar and critic Bienvenido Lumbera, while avoiding the kinds of hierarchical aesthetic evaluations in which Chouduri engages, suggest that techniques resembling those of Brecht were already available to Filipino cultural activists in forms of traditional nonrealistic theater such as the Komedya.

Conversely, critics such as Nagavajara, Dalmia-Lüderitz, Barucha, and Maria Luisa Torres-Reyes have analyzed the appropriations of Brecht in a historically specific manner. They have noted not only the similarities but also the crucial differences that make traditional theaters similar rather than identical to Brecht's theater. Dalmia-Lüderitz provides a useful comparison of Brechtian theater and the Hindi folk genre, *Svang*. Though the action of *Svang* is frequently interrupted by songs and a narrator, these events do not create critical distance; rather they serve to deepen and reinforce the audience's identification with the action and with the good characters in a way completely opposite to the intentions of Brechtian theater (Dalmia-Lüderitz 115–16).

A number of contemporary Asian playwrights have appropriated Brechtian techniques for their own creative work. A brief examination of two such re-functionings may serve to better inform us of the ways in which Brecht's techniques and concepts are taken up and resituated in Asian contexts. Malou Jacob's *Juan Tamban* (first staged in 1979) was written and performed for Philippine audiences only a year after PETA had performed its version of *Chalk Circle*. Briefly stated, the play is about the struggle of a destitute street child (Juan) to survive in contemporary Manila. A social worker, Marina, attempts to understand and help this child. In the process she realizes that society is so constructed as to benefit only certain of its citizens. Those less well off, like Juan, are divested of all rights and comforts. Marina's growing involvement in Juan's case leads to her eventual alienation from all the social institutions that have previously supported her life and sense of identity: family, marriage, a university career, and the justice system.

Several PETA members have commented on the ways in which the Brecht performance helped develop or clarify concepts that were in turn mobilized for the production of *Juan Tamban*. Fajardo has described the way in which the scenic design for the play put into practice the concept of scenic gestus, an idea first clearly articulated by PETA as a result of the staging of *Chalk Circle* in Tagalog under the title *Ang Hatol ng Guhit na Bilog*. Furthermore, Lutgardo Labad notes that both of the central characters, Juan and Marina, like Grusha in *Chalk Circle*, embody the sum total of processes and contradictions present in the society depicted. Similarly, Labad maintains that the story and dramaturgical motif of the Brecht play–the travails of a woman confronted with different sectors of society—contributed to the shape of *Juan Tamban* in which a woman struggles to protect a child against the travails of various sectors of contemporary Filipino society (Labad, "PETA" 11).

In addition, the play was composed in a collective fashion. Its author rewrote the original scenario several times after receiving comments and suggestions from the director, improvising actors, and Lutgardo Labad (Jacob 10, 141–50). Such a process allowed for ample input by PETA members who had been involved in the Brecht performance. Certainly, *Juan Tamban* does contain a number of devices that are similar to those found in *Chalk Circle* and other Brecht plays. It features a chorus that supplies commentary on the events being portrayed, poses questions to the audience and characters, and articulates the feelings of several characters at key moments. The play is structured as a montage-like juxtaposition of scenes, and the knots of the plot are made more visible at several instances. A number of other devices such as courtroom scenes and innocent or ignorant characters questioning the logic of the established order are deployed skillfully to undercut the audience/reader's expectations much as in Brecht's concept of *Verfremdung*.

Yet, in interviews with members of PETA such as Apolonio Bayani Chua and playwright Malou Jacob, it became clear that some members did not consider these devices specifically Brechtian. During the late 1970s, when the company mounted its performance of *Chalk Circle*, it was also deeply involved in the creation of a new, militant grassroots theater practice that combined improvisational theater techniques with the problem-posing educational system of Paulo Freire. Freire's system of education was intended to develop the critical consciousness of the students by presenting their own codes for understanding the world as a problem to be solved. Freire called this process of increasing critical awareness "conscientization" (Freire, *Pedagogy*). The forms developed and utilized in PETA's workshops, building upon the techniques of Freirian pedagogy, resulted in a number of theater practices that ran parallel to those of Brechtian theater and were later reappropriated by PETA for its own urban stage practice. Thus the role of the chorus (Koro) in *Juan Tamban* springs from the function of the Koro in the "dramatized poem" (Dula-tula) segments of PETA's grassroots workshops, and not directly from Brecht, although there are parallel uses of a chorus in *Chalk Circle*. Similarly, the atmosphere of examination, of critical questioning that pervades the play was a result of the company's increasing political commitment to and engagement with grassroots groups. The Freirian concept of conscientization had, by 1978, long been integrated into church-led grassroots theater workshops in Mindanao, a fact of which PETA was certainly conscious. Such an overlap of techniques and interests was therefore a key stimulus for heightened interest in Brecht's works in the Philippines at about this time, and it may well have been the crucial factor that led to PETA's decision to stage *Chalk Circle* in the first place.

Still, there is a major difference between most of Brecht's plays and *Juan Tamban*. The character of Marina, a young middle-class professional, is clearly intended to elicit an empathic identification from the Manila audience, most of whom would have come from a similar background. The audience is therefore positioned to identify with Marina at the same time as they are urged to question, along with her, her basic initial assumptions—that is, those of the society that has produced and conditioned her. As in a Freirian educational dialogue, the audience's own codes for understanding the world are mobilized in order to be challenged. Such a tactic deepens the emotional impact of the questioning and learning that occurs in the play, but it is quite different from Brechtian theater, in which major characters are rarely, if ever, created with an eye toward inducing such a close, emotional bond between character and audience—*The Mother* and *Señora Carrar's Rifles* are partial exceptions.

There is another difference as well. Most of Brecht's plays are set in distant, strange, even mythicized locales so as to aid in emotionally distancing the audience. *Juan Tamban*, like most other Philippine plays that have appropriated aspects of Brechtian theater, presents a number of current problems set in a contemporary context. Thus situated, the final scene, in which Marina commits herself to working for and with the urban poor against an intransigent system, is transformed into a more vigorous plea for a specific and immediate audience commitment than can be found in most of Brecht's plays.

Another example of the ways in which Brechtian theater is appropriated by Asian practitioners can be found in Indonesian playwright/director N. Riantiarno's *Opera Kecoa* (1985; *Cockroach Opera*), written a little over a year after he had adapted and staged Brecht's *The Threepenny Opera*. Riantiarno is a great admirer of the Weill/Brecht songs as well as of Brecht's language, which he regards as remarkable for its accessibility as well as its power to cut to the bone of the matter. Riantiarno reads Brecht as creating a mood in his plays that is highly appropriate for Indonesian conditions and that hovers between despair and hope. In *Opera Kecoa* Riantiarno has taken elements of Brechtian theater and refitted them for his own use. Like *Juan Tamban*, *Opera Kecoa* is set in a contemporary locale that is familiar to the audience—in this case, Jakarta—and deals with pressing social issues. Its language is the lively, slangy jargon of the Jakarta streets, full of sexual humor, puns, and play with language. In its thirty scenes, fragments of Brecht are combined with a sentimental love-triangle plot, burlesque comedy, and reform-minded social criticism. The play is about the lives of a group of urban slum dwellers—prostitutes, bandits, transvestites, and displaced farmers—all of whom are seeking a way to make ends meet. While we follow the efforts of two of the slum dwellers, petty gangster Roima and his transvestite lover/prostitute Julini, to survive, a government official is trying to close a deal guaranteeing foreign funding to develop the land on which the slum is located. If the deal goes through, the slum will have to be demolished in order to make way for development projects. The entire play revolves around the efforts of the little people, called cockroaches, to eke out a paltry living for themselves amid a brutal urban environment, and the schemes of government officials less concerned about the well-being of the urban and rural poor than about personally enriching themselves by carrying out huge development projects and erecting monuments that demonstrate the nation's culture.

Riantiarno has adapted several elements of *The Threepenny Opera* for use in his play. First, the existence of the petty gangsters under the leadership of Kumis is reminiscent of Mac the Knife's gang. Kumis himself, however, is more like an amalgam of Mac and Peachum—he is still working on a petty level, but he is concerned with management, screening for potentially good employees, and getting into a bigger scale of operations. Yet unlike the criminals and thieves of Brecht's play, Kumis and his gang have no connection with the official establishment. One of the reasons Kumis has turned to crime is because his low-level position as a neighborhood security guard was phased out, and he himself was replaced with a more sophisticated security operative. Like the residents of the slum, Kumis, Bleki, and their gang are seen as victims of a skewed economic system.

Perhaps the main feature of the play suggestive of Brechtian theater is a number of songs that indeed convey Riantiarno's sense of Brecht's work—a mood between despair and hope. The song Roima sings after Julini has been shot, "Jula-Juli Kodok Marah" (Song of the Angry Frog) offers a clear example. Roima declares that it is probably the useless song of a dreamer, but the world must be changed immediately so that there are no longer any poor (Riantiarno, *Opera Kecoa* 45). The song "Jula-Juli Anjing Beringas" (The Wild Dogs), sung by the gangsters in scene thirteen, also reflects this mood, albeit in a darker vein: happiness has to be stolen and prayers are ineffective for achieving respect when only power and wealth are heeded. The gangsters are determined, however, to seize wealth and fortune and survive (Riantiarno, *Opera Kecoa* 23–24). Their song echoes parts of the "First Threepenny Finale," the aforementioned "Concerning the Insecurity of the Human State." Julini's song of scene fourteen, "Jula-Juli Tiga Kenikmatan" (The Three Pleasures) states, with saddened resignation, that the three pleasures most sought after by people— sex, speech, and thought—must all be paid for, for nothing is free in this world (Riantiarno, *Opera Kecoa* 25). Other songs, apparently more given over to sentiments of love-sorrow, such as "Jula-Juli Kumbang Merana" (The Song of the Miserable Bumblebee), are also followed by dialogue that suggests that the circumstances in which the poor find themselves do not allow much time for such emotion: Julini, after singing out his/her refusal to take money given to "her" (instead of the affection she desires) by Roima, ends by picking up the money she has thrown to the ground and saying: "And yet, money is still necessary" (Riantiarno, *Opera Kecoa* 33).

Despite these similarities, *Opera Kecoa* is, like *Juan Tamban*, different from Brecht's dramas. Most of the songs are not all as full of biting commentary on the action or on the underlying attitude of the characters as those just discussed—many are quite sentimental and flow directly from the immediate, surface actions or moods of the characters who sing them. In this sense, they are at odds with Brecht's notion of music—a music that should indicate its own separateness from the action while commenting on that action (Willett, *Brecht* 132–34). Such a difference reflects both Riantiarno's sense of his audience and his admiration of Broadway as well as traditional Indonesian theater—both of which often strive for fairly predictable, romantic, or lighthearted emotional effects. Furthermore, the cynicism voiced in the songs mentioned above is not really directed at laying bare the basic contradictions of Indonesian society but, rather, to drive home quite effectively the plight of society's marginalized to its theatergoing elites. In fact, *Opera Kecoa* is more concerned with reforming the system than with overturning it and with including the poor in middle-class/elite society than in creating a totally new society. This is obvious in the number of times we hear prostitutes justifying their profession as just another means of making a living or dreaming of eventually saving enough money to start a real business and get out of the sex trade. Julini, the transvestite, also desires a normal life like others, impossibly hoping for marriage and children. Even the gangster captain, Kumis, expresses a longing for a pure love that other, more legitimate citizens presumably have access to—despite the fact that we hear of many divorces and many husbands coming to the prostitutes! Finally, Julini, having been chased from public plazas where national monuments stand, from urban slums, and from the golf courses of the wealthy, desperately complains that he/she too has a valid identity card that confirms his being a citizen of Indonesia. Julini's statement, which relies on the notion of national identity, is the work's most obvious plea for inclusion.

The play's ending, in which Julini is killed and the slum burned down, seems to demonstrate that there is little hope, given present circumstances, of reform from above. Yet the sinister presence of the ubiquitous *tukang sulap* (magician, medicine seller), hawking "anticockroach" poison and warning of the danger of a revolution of the cockroaches in an increasingly shrill voice, indicates that *Opera Kecoa* is an alarmed plea to the Jakartan middle class, government bureaucrats, and wealthy developers to heed the plight of the poor and to work on eradicating poverty before the "cockroaches" take matters into their own hands. Attempting to recreate in his own play the critical, desperate, yet hopeful edge that he found in Brecht, Riantiarno succeeds in constructing a sense of tension between the seemingly unstoppable momentum of an unrepentantly corrupt elite's plans for personal enrichment within the development process that they direct, and the possibility of reform so necessary to avert social disaster and upheaval from below. Such a tension does not allow a completely comfortable feeling at the play's end, which significantly features a reprise of the dark Wild Dogs song, despite the preceding joking riposte of a transvestite making light of the threatening situation.

Ultimately, both *Juan Tamban* and *Opera Kecoa* represent different ways of combining Brecht with local needs, issues, and forms to create new, vital theater. In the former, the audience's own middle-class codes for understanding the world are foregrounded and then challenged through a process of emotional identification with a principal character. In the latter, hard-edged lyrics in the style of Brecht, which attempt to penetrate to the underlying social attitudes of characters, are deployed in order to convey the desperation of urban slum dwellers fighting for survival, and, it is hoped, to awaken Indonesian elites to the seriousness of the problem before time runs out.[4] Although the plays are quite different in many ways, both aim at calling on urban elites and professional groups to engage with the problems of the large underclass of urban poor. Neither presents a case of influence in which ideas emanating from a master such as Brecht simply exercise an effect on a receiving subject. Rather, both demonstrate the active agency of the groups that created them through a process of reappropriation, of consciously adopting and refunctioning Brechtian concepts to fit specific local situations and needs.

The grassroots theater practices developed in the Philippines, Indonesia, Bangladesh, India, and Thailand can also, in part, trace their roots back to Brechtian notions of the role of theater in society. However, here again the conditions of their emergence are quite different from those of Brecht's own attempts to pioneer a new kind of popular theater, the *Lehrstücke*. They are often targeted at different kinds of audiences than Brecht imagined in 1930. Similarly, the kind of learning upon which the grassroots theater workshops are premised is substantially different from that which Brecht theorized about.

In the Philippines, PETA's founder Cecilia Guidote valued Brecht's notions that theater could be an educational institution—that it could stimulate the pleasure of knowing and that it must be both entertaining and instructive. Theater activists of the First Quarter Storm era of political protest against the premartial law Marcos government and United States' hegemony in the Philippines also sought to appropriate Brecht's notions of *Verfremdung* and an "anti-illusionistic" theater for their radical street theater performances. Reacting to what they perceived to be the overly melodramatic emotionalism of traditional theater forms, these activists also wanted to instruct the audience by urging them to critically appraise the play's story and, by implication, contemporary Philippine society (Patajo-Legasto 227–40). After martial law was declared, activists within PETA and other theater groups, though having to maintain a lower profile, still continued to look for means to apply such notions of theater's role in society.

In the southern Philippine island of Mindanao, for example, Catholic activists, interested in organizing Basic Christian Communities, began to use theater as an alternative means of evangelizing. Organizing peasants in remote rural districts, they often became aware of the difficulties such peasants faced in holding onto their land and surviving in the face of land appropriation by large landowners and multinational corporations. Eventually, the theater practice they pioneered became the basis not only for religious education but also for Freirian-style "conscientization" about social issues such as land rights and agricultural political economy. However, in addition to Freire's educational methodology and the teachings of the Vatican II Council, such theater practitioners also incorporated into their manual a passage from Brecht's essay "On Experimental Theater" (*Theatre* 130–35) in order to stress that theater was a valid means for social education. The passage chosen emphasized the need for people to use the models of human life that a theater could project in order to understand and master their own social environment.

This type of theater was also being developed, almost simultaneously, by teams of PETA facilitators, and by the late 1970s such efforts had resulted in the beginnings of a national grassroots theater network that reached a peak of about four hundred groups in the mid-1980s. Those who participate in grassroots theater workshops and form a majority of these cultural groups are most frequently peasant groups, workers, students, urban slum dwellers, and indigenous tribal groups. Such workshops use theater productions to stress critical evaluation of one's social environment, collective work and creation, and the power of organized self-expression. Productions of plays created by the participants themselves, using techniques learned in the workshops, are often, though not always, the springboard to the creation of a new cultural group.[5]

These workshops and the plays they produce contain both similarities to and interesting differences from Brecht's concept of the *Lehrstück*. Both Philippine grassroots theater and Brecht's *Lehrstücke* extol the potential of theater as a pedagogical tool. Both allow for modifications of plays (or texts) based upon postperformance discussions of the participants and audience. Both are intended to stimulate the desire of performers (and, in the case of the Philippines, the audience) to transform the world. Similarly, each practice emphasizes collectivity, although on this point some differences become apparent.

For Brecht, the collective experience is achieved through the individual singing a role and enacting motions in unison with other members of the chorus. There is great stress placed on the discipline and subordination of the singer/performers to the text (*Theatre* 34). In addition, the *Lehrstücke* are stubbornly devoted to examining the theme of negating the individual in service to the collective, as well as to the ever-changing momentum of history. PETA's grassroots workshops also underscore the value of collective work through practical exercises—group tasks and games to break the social ice. Yet in this instance, the emphasis is not so much on discipline and subordination as it is on supportive, critical creation and sensitive group dynamics.

Further differences can also be pinpointed. Whereas for Brecht the classics of Marxism and notions about what attitudes workers needed to learn to carry out class struggle formed the point of departure for most of his *Lehrstücke* (Brooker, *Dialectics* 191; Mueller, *Media* 37–38), PETA's approach differs markedly. PETA's writings and practice stress the importance of the participants' own life experiences as the "most authentic sources" for creative expression (Fajardo/Topacio 4). In a Freirian sense, such an approach leads to a codification of the participants' own themes that can then be posed as a problem for reflection. Similarly, while Brecht and one or two collaborators usually produced the *Lehrstücke* texts to be performed by student or worker groups, Philippine grassroots plays are produced by the workshop participant/performers themselves. These differences are related to a further difference in educational approach between Brecht and PETA. Brecht follows Bekhterev's behavioralist notions of the importance of imitation in that participants must learn the texts and the attitudes that go with them before criticizing them (Mueller, *Media* 40, 42; Guttsman 172–73). Conversely, PETA developed the problem-posing, cointentional methods of Freire in order to break down the barriers between workshop facilitators and participants. This produced the potential for more egalitarian relations in the production of both text and knowledge.

One consequence of these differences can be found in the nature of the subject matter of both groups of plays. Since the texts of PETA's grassroots workshop plays are produced by the participants themselves based upon their own life experiences, such plays tend to be much more immediate and topical in a way that only the most urgent of Brecht's *Lehrstücke*, for example *The Mother*, can aspire to. On the whole, Brecht's learning/teaching plays are fashioned around much more abstract, philosophical, or tactical issues and set, again, in distant locales.

Finally, the grassroots work of PETA and other Philippine groups has developed a more democratic organizational dimension than Brecht was able to effect in his work. This is apparent in the decentralization of workshop training and in PETA's ability to adjust its methods in response to criticism from the grassroots. One such problem involved the very approach of the workshops that introduced modern, Euro-American, and urban Philippine concepts to groups of participants who had virtually no prior contact with these forms. PETA was criticized by cultural workers from the Central Philippines Visayas area for relying too heavily on the Manila/Tagalog area-based *Dula-tula* (dramatized poem) form in its workshops. This resulted in Visayan participants simply mimicking what they had been taught. They were unable to add anything of their own cultural traditions that would have allowed them to improvise much more comfortably. PETA and the Philippines Theater Network acknowledged this shortcoming and now try to research local cultural traditions before attempting a workshop in an unfamiliar area (Carunungan, "Culture" 7).

In Indonesia, Thailand, and Bangladesh, similar grassroots theater practices have developed. Indonesian practices have little direct connection with Brecht's work, yet strong indirect links do exist in the case of the Arena Teater of Yogyakarta. By appropriating certain aspects of the work of PETA, Augusto Boal, and Ross Kidd (who had each reworked Brechtian concepts), Arena Teater constructed its own grassroots workshop format stressing that peasants, workers, scavengers, and other socially disadvantaged groups create their own dramas in order to better understand their situations and how to alter them. In addition, Arena Teater, like the Bangladeshi group Proshika, attempts to link theater workshop "conscientization" (or animation) efforts with the activities of nongovernment organizations (NGOs) promoting grassroots development and rights-mobilization projects. Arena Teater holds that it is not enough for workshop participants to mount a play dramatizing their situation, despite the immediate benefits that increased self-confidence, dialogue, and group solidarity may bring. According to the experiences of organizations like Proshika, Arena, and PETA, the momentum from such workshops needs to be sustained and cultural work nurtured through partnerships with NGOs (Bodden 307–13).

In conclusion, then, the scope of the Brecht reception in Asia is wide and varied, ranging from the staging of Brecht plays in local idioms, to combining Brechtian ideas of theater as an educational institution with Freirian critical-consciousness-raising pedagogy and grassroots development initiatives. Asian practitioners generally tend consciously to resituate Brechtian plays and ideas in local contexts. Often such appropriations attempt to fuse Brecht's critical stance toward his material, with demands for immediate relevance, local authenticity, and commitment to action. Equally often, Brecht's plays are used by dissident groups endeavoring to stake out a critique of an oppressive regime and its problems in the name of some manner of reform. Certain implications of Brecht's efforts to actively engage the audience in judging the play have been expanded upon by Asian grassroots theater practitioners who insist that the audience become the performers and that theater be a part of democratic mobilization and economic development. All of these processes indicate the tremendous creativity that Asian practitioners are bringing to bear in their attempts to create dynamic new forms of theater that are at the same time profoundly social.

NOTES

1. In this case the caricatural acronym is *poleksosbud*, which in an all-encompassing manner amalgamates development concerns in the areas of politics (*politik*), economy (*ekonomi*), social matters (*sosial*), and culture (*budaya*).

2. *Ketoprak* is a form that was first developed in Central Java in the early decades of the twentieth century; its material is mainly drawn from old historical legends and court chronicles. *Ludruk* is an urban, East Javanese form created in the 1930s, which combines elements of comedy and melodrama to create stories that urge adaptation to new, modern, urban ways of life. All roles, including those of female characters, are traditionally played by men. *Wayang Orang* is a form that originated in the courtly culture of the last great Central Javanese kingdoms, and whose dancers performed stories based on the Indian epics, the *Mahabharata* and the *Ramayana* in 1980.

3. For more information about how PETA's practice of scenic design incorporated Brechtian elements, see Fajardo (*Aesthetics* 10).

4. *Opera Kecoa* was published with *Bom Waktu* (*Time Bomb*) in an English translation. The title of the latter play underscores the perceived urgency of the problems dealt with in these works.

5. Van Erven (*Revolution* 28) contains a good outline description of how a typical workshop is conducted.

WORKS CITED (SEE ALSO REFERENCE GUIDE TO WORKS CITED IN ABBREVIATED FORM)

Banerjee, Arundhati. "Brecht Adaptations in Modern Bengali Theater: A Study in Reception." *Asian Theater Journal* 7.1 (1990): 1–28.

Barucha, Rustam. "Beyond Brecht: Political Theatre in Calcutta." *Brecht-Jahrbuch/ Brecht Yearbook* 11 (1983): 72–90.

Bodden, Michael H. "Imagining The Audience as Agent of its Own History: Brecht, Grassroots Theater and Representations of Interclass Alliance in the Phillippines and Indonesia." Ph.D. diss., University of Wisconsin–Madison, 1993.

Bujono, Bambang. "Astaga! Kurang Ajar!" *Tempo* (28 February 1976): 15.

———. "Brecht yang Penuh Tawa." *Tempo* (29 March 1980): 24.

Carunungan, Maria. "To Build a People's Culture: The Visayan Experience." *Makiisa* 1.4 (1988–1989): 2–9.

———. Personal interview. 20 June 1991.

Chatterjee, Sekhar. "Brecht in West Bengal." In *Brecht and East Asian Theatre*. Edited by Antony Tatlow and Tak Wai-Wong. Hong Kong: University of Hong Kong Press, 1982. 138–44.

Chen, Yong. "Brecht and the Current Transformation of the Theater in China." *Brecht-Jahrbuch/Brecht Yearbook* 14 (1989): 47–53.

———. "The Beijing Production of *Life of Galileo*." In *Brecht and East Asian Theatre*. Edited by Antony Tatlow and Tak Wai-Wong. Hong Kong: University of Hong Kong Press, 1982. 88–95.

Chouduri, Indra Nath. "Bharata and Brecht and the Relevance of Rasa as a Critical Idiom of the Theater." In *Proceedings of the Xth Congress of the International Comparative Literature Association*. Edited by Anna Balakian, James J. Wilhelm, Douwe W. Fokkema, and Edward C. Smith III. New York: Garland, 1985. 281–87.

Chua, Apolonio Bayani. Personal interview. 5 July 1991.

Chua, Apolonio Bayani, and Manny Pambid. Personal interview. 28 June 1991.

Dalmia-Lüderitz, Vasudha. "Brecht in Hindi: The Poetics of Response." *Brecht-Jahrbuch/Brecht Yearbook* 14 (1989): 107–21.

Fajardo, Brenda. *The Aesthetics of Poverty: A Rationale in Designing for the Philippine Theater*. PETA Theater Studies 5. Quezon City: Philippines Educational Theater Assoc., n.d.

———, and Socrates Topacio. *BITAW: Basic Integrated Theater Arts Workshop*. Quezon City: Philippines Educational Theater Assoc., 1989.

Glinoga, Alan, Al Santos, and Rody Vera. *Ang Panunuluyan*. PETA Kalinangan Ensemble Script Series 4. Quezon City: Philippines Educational Theater Assoc., 1983.

Guidote, Cecilia Reyes. "A Prospectus for the National Theatre of the Philippines." M.A. thesis, Trinity University, San Antonio, TX, 1967.

Guttsman, W.L. *Workers' Culture in Weimar Germany*. New York: Berg, 1990.

Horfilla, Nestor. "Theater in Mindanao 1983." In *The Politics of Culture: The Philippine Experience*. Manila: Philippines Educational Theater Assoc. and People's Resource Collection—Philippine Assistance for Rural and Urban Development, 1984.

Hsia, Adrian. "The Reception of Bertolt Brecht in China and its Impact on Chinese Drama." In *Brecht and East Asian Theatre*. Edited by Antony Tatlow and Tak Wai-Wong. Hong Kong: University of Hong Kong Press, 1982. 46–64.

Iwabuchi, Tatsuji. "Ändert Brecht dann, wenn ihr Brecht ändern könnt!: Brecht-Rezeption in Japan aus der Sicht der Theaterpraxis." *Zeitschrift für Germanistik* 9.1 (1988): 64–70.

———. "Brecht Reception in Japan: The Perspective of Theatrical Practice." In *Brecht and East Asian Theatre*. Edited by Antony Tatlow and Tak Wai-Wong. Hong Kong: University of Hong Kong Press, 1982. 111–29.

Jacob, Marilou Leviste. *Juan Tamban*. PETA Kalinangan Ensemble Script Series 1. Quezon City: Philippines Educational Theater Assoc., 1984.

———. Personal interview. 5 July 1991.

Kinne, Warren. *A People's Church? The Mindanao-Sulu Church Debacle*. Frankfurt am Main: Lang, 1990.

Kulturang Atin Foundation Inc., ed. *Community Theater: The Mindanao Experience*. Davao City, Philippines: Kulturang Atin Foundation Inc., 1983.

Labad, Lutgardo. "Composer's Notes." In *Pilipinas Circa 1907*. PETA KE Script Series 7. Quezon City: Philippines Educational Theater Assoc., 1985. 16–20.

———. *PETA and Brecht: The Story of a Friendship*. PETA Theater Studies 4. Quezon City: Philippines Educational Theater Assoc., 1983.

———. Personal interview. 25 June 1991.

Li, Jianming. "Brecht and the Chinese Theater in the 1980s." *Brecht-Jahrbuch/Brecht Yearbook* 14 (1989): 60–68.

Lumbera, Bienvenido. Personal interview. 29 July 1991.

Millado, Chris. "Text and Context: From *Caucasian Chalk Circle* to *Hukom Sang Badlis Nga Lingin*." *Makiisa* 1.1 (1988): 16–41.

Mindanao-Sulu Pastoral Conference Secretariat Drama Team, eds. *MPCS Creative Dramatics Training Kit*. Davao City, Philippines: MSPCS, 1978.

Nagavajara, Chetana. "Brecht's Reception in Thailand: The Case of *Die Ausnahme und die Regel*." *Monatshefte* 75 (1983): 46–54.

Nguyen Dinh Quang. "Das vietnamesische Theater in der Epoche des nationalen Befreiungskampfes und seine Perspektive unter besonderer Berücksichtigung der Integration der Arbeitsweise Bertolt Brechts in das vietnamesische Theater." In *Brecht und Cheo: Integration zweier epischer Theaterformen*. Berlin: Brecht Zentrum der DDR, 1988. 17–179.

Patajo-Legasto, Priscelina. "Philippine Contemporary Theater, 1946–1985: A Materialist Approach." Ph.D. diss., University of the Philippines, Quezon City, 1988.

Riantiarno, N[ano]. *Bom Waktu*. Jakarta: Teater Koma, 1986.

———. *Opera Kecoa*. Jakarta: Teater Koma, 1985.

———. Personal interview. 8 August 1991.

———. *Time Bomb & Cockroach Opera: Two Plays*. *Time Bomb* translated by Barbara Hatley, *Cockroach Opera* by John H. McGlynn, edited by John H. McGlynn, introduction by Barbara Hatley. Jakarta: Lontar Foundation, c1992.

Riantiarno, N[ano], and Tjie Tjin Siang. "Opera Ikan Asin." Typescript, 1983.

Schlenker, Wolfram. "Brecht in Asia—The Chinese Contribution." In *Brecht and East Asian Theatre*. Edited by Antony Tatlow and Tak Wai-Wong. Hong Kong: University of Hong Kong Press, 1982. 186–208.

———. "Paradigmenwechsel—Auch in China: Neue Chancen für Brecht auf chinesischen Bühnen?" *Brecht-Jahrbuch/Brecht Yearbook* 14 (1989): 69–79.

Tatlow, Antony. "Analyis and Transference." *Brecht-Jahrbuch/Brecht Yearbook* 17 (1992): 124–33.

———. "Brecht and the Paradigm Change." *Brecht-Jahrbuch/Brecht Yearbook* 14 (1989): 13–29.

———. "Brecht Seminar in Singapore, December 1989." *Communications from the International Brecht Society* 19.2 (1990): 14–18.

———. "Brecht's Position in World Theatre." *Communications from the International Brecht Society* 19.2 (1990): 20–29.

Tiongson, Nicanor. *Pilipinas Circa 1907*. PETA Kalinangan Ensemble Script Series 7. Quezon City: Philippines Educational Theater Assoc., 1985.

———. Personal interview. 5 July 1991.

Torres [-Reyes], Marisa Luisa F. "Brecht and the Philippines: Anticipating Freedom in Theater." *Brecht-Jahrbuch/Brecht Yearbook* 14 (1989): 134–51.

van Erven, Eugène. *The Playful Revolution: Theatre and Liberation in Asia*. Bloomington: Indiana University Press, 1992.

———. *Stages of People Power: The Philippines Educational Theater Association*. Verhandelingen No. 43. The Hague: Centre for the Study of Education in Developing Countries (CESO), 1989.

Wurfel, David. *Filipino Politics: Development and Decay*. Ithaca: Cornell University Press, 1988.

Annotated Bibliography

SIEGFRIED MEWS

The Bibliography is essentially confined to titles in English and does not aspire to complete inclusiveness. For further details, see both Reference Guide to Works Cited in Abbreviated Form (pp. xi–xvi) and the Works Cited sections of the individual contributions.

WORKS BY BRECHT IN GERMAN

Gesammelte Werke in 20 Bänden. 20 vols. Frankfurt am Main: Suhrkamp, 1967. Also published in seven volumes. Cited as *GW*. Supplementbände I–II: *Texte für Filme*. Edited by Wolfgang Gersch and Werner Hecht. 1969. Supplementbände III–IV: *Gedichte aus dem Nachlaß*. Edited by Herta Ramthun. Frankfurt am Main: Suhrkamp, 1982.

Werke. Große kommentierte Berliner und Frankfurter Ausgabe. 30 vols. Edited by Werner Hecht, Jan Knopf, Werner Mittenzwei, and Klaus-Detlef Müller. Frankfurt am Main: Suhrkamp/Berlin: Aufbau, 1988–. The standard edition that upon completion is going to supersede *GW*. Cited as *Werke*.

WORKS BY BRECHT IN ENGLISH TRANSLATION: PLAYS

Collected Plays. 9 vols. Edited by Ralph Manheim and John Willett. New York: Vintage, 1971– . This is the American edition of the plays in *Bertolt Brecht: Plays, Poetry and Prose*. Edited by Ralph Manheim and John Willett. Cited as *CP* and used as the standard edition in this volume. However, not all volumes have appeared and those that have appeared are out of print. In addition to the texts listed below, the volumes include notes by Brecht, editorial notes, and variants:

Vol. 1: *Baal, Drums in the Night*; *In the Jungle of Cities*; *The Life of Edward the Second of England*; Five One-Act Plays—*The Wedding, The Beggar, or The Dead Dog, He Drives Out a Devil, Lux in Tenebris, The Catch*.

Vol. 2: *A Man's a Man, Rise and Fall of the City of Mahagonny, The Threepenny Opera*.

Vol. 5: *Life of Galileo, The Trial of Lucullus, Mother Courage and Her Children*.

Vol. 6: *The Good Person of Szechwan*; *Puntila and Matti, His Hired Man*; *The Resistible Rise of Arturo Ui, Dansen*; *How Much Is Your Iron?*; Practice Pieces for Actors—*The Murder in the Porter's Lodge (Macbeth), The Battle of the Fish-wives (Maria Stuart), Ferry Scene (Hamlet), The Servants (Romeo and Juliet)*.

Vol. 7: *The Visions of Simone Machard, Schweyk in the Second World War, The Caucasian Chalk Circle, The Duchess of Malfi*.

Vol. 9: Adaptations—*The Tutor* (J.M.R. Lenz), *Coriolanus* (Shakespeare), *The Trial of Joan of Arc at Rouen, 1431* (Anna Seghers), *Don Juan* (Molière), *Trumpets and Drums* (George Farquhar).

Collected Plays. 8 vols. London: Eyre Methuen, 1970–. This is the English edition of the plays in *Bertolt Brecht: Plays, Poetry and Prose*. Edited by John Willett and Ralph Manheim. It is more inclusive than the American edition, but the two editions of *Collected Plays* are not identical—they differ primarily with regard to the choice of translators. A listing of titles published through 1994 may be found in Thomson/Sacks, *Cambridge Companion* 288–89.

Complete Dramatic Work of Bertolt Brecht. New York: Arcade, 1993–. The Arcade edition is based on the English edition of *Collected Plays*; plays are published both in omnibus volumes, which include introductions and brief chronologies of life and work, and issues of individual plays in random order. Only the issues of individual plays reprint the critical apparatus of *Collected Plays*. The following volumes have appeared through 1995 (or their publication has been announced):

Vol. 1: *The Threepenny Opera. Baal. The Mother*. Cited as *Plays* 1.

Vol. 2: *The Good Person of Szechwan. Mother Courage and Her Children. Fear and Misery of the Third Reich*. Cited as *Plays* 2.

Vol. 3: *Life of Galileo. The Resistible Rise of Arturo Ui. The Caucasian Chalk Circle*. Cited as *Plays* 3.

Single editions of plays: *The Caucasian Chalk Circle, The Good Person of Szechwan, Life of Galileo, Mother Courage and Her Children, Mr. Puntila and His Man Matti, The Rise and Fall of the City of Mahagonny, The Seven Deadly Sins, The Threepenny Opera*.

Seven Plays. Edited and introduction by Eric Bentley. New York: Grove, 1961. The first American edition of several plays in one volume that served as a kind of predecessor to the edition below. It includes: *In the Swamp* [*In the Jungle*], *A Man's a Man, Saint Joan of the Stockyards, Mother Courage, Galileo, The Good Woman of Setzuan, The Caucasian Chalk Circle*.

Works of Bertolt Brecht. New York: Grove Press Edition. General Editor: Eric Bentley. A series of plays in paperbacks in translations by Bentley and others with introductions and some additional texts by Brecht and others. Several titles of translations differ from those of the American *Collected Plays*. Several of the volumes have been reprinted repeatedly (in most instances the date of publication is that of the most recent issue as of 1995):

Baal, A Man's a Man, and The Elephant Calf. 1989.

The Caucasian Chalk Circle. 1987.

Edward II. A Chronicle Play. 1970.

Galileo. 1966.

The Good Woman of Setzuan. 1966.

The Jewish Wife and Other Short Plays: "The Jewish Wife," "In Search of Justice," "The Informer," "The Elephant Calf," *The Measures Taken, The Exception and the Rule*, "Salzburg Dance of Death." 1965. Cited as *Jewish Wife.*

Jungle of Cities and Other Plays: Jungle of Cities, Drums in the Night, Roundheads and Peakheads. 1966.

The Mother. 1989.

Mother Courage and Her Children. 1987.

The Threepenny Opera. 1983.

The Visions of Simone Machard (with Lion Feuchtwanger). 1965.

WORKS BY BRECHT IN ENGLISH: POETRY

Manual of Piety/Die Hauspostille. A Bilingual Edition. Translated by Eric Bentley, notes by Hugo Schmidt. 1966. New York: Grove, 1991. A translation based on the German text as published in 1927. Cited as *Manual of Piety.*

Poems 1913–1956. Edited by John Willett and Ralph Manheim with the co-operation of Erich Fried. 1976. 2nd ed. New York: Methuen, 1987. The most extensive collection of poems in English with editorial notes and notes by Brecht. Cited as *Poems.*

Poems & Songs from the Plays. Edited and translated by John Willett. London: Methuen, 1990. Contains 171 poems and songs with editorial comments and notes that were not included in *Poems* but, for the most part, were published as part of plays in *CP.* Cited as *Poems & Songs.*

Selected Poems. Translated and introduction by H.R. Hays. 1947. Rpt. New York: Grove, 1959. The first substantial selection of poems in English, a bilingual edition.

Songs of Bertolt Brecht and Hanns Eisler. 42 Songs in German and English. Edited, with singable English translations and introductory notes by Eric Bentley. Music edited by Earl Robinson. New York: Oak Publications [1967].

WORKS BY BRECHT IN ENGLISH: PROSE

Diaries 1920–1922. Edited by Herta Ramthun, translated by John Willett. New York: St. Martin's Press, 1979. Cited as *Diaries.*

Journals 1934–1955. Translated by Hugh Rorrison, edited by John Willett. New York: Routledge, 1993. Cited as *Journals.*

Letters 1913–1956. Translated by Ralph Manheim, edited by John Willett. New York: Routledge, [1990]. Cited as *Letters.*

Short Stories 1921–1946. Edited by John Willett and Ralph Manheim. London: Methuen, 1983. Cited as *Stories.*

Tales from the Calendar. Translated by Yvonne Kapp and Michael Hamburger. London: Methuen, 1961. Cited as *Tales.*

Threepenny Novel. Translated by Desmond Vesey and Christopher Isherwood. New York: Grove, 1956. Reissue of *A Penny for the Poor* (London: Hale, 1937).

WORKS BY BRECHT IN ENGLISH: THEORY OF THEATER

Brecht on Theatre. The Development of an Aesthetic. Edited and translated by John Willett. New York: Hill, 1964. An influential selection of theoretical writings, including "A Short Organum for the Theatre," with editorial notes. Cited as *Theatre*.
The Messingkauf Dialogues. Translated by John Willett. London: Methuen, 1965. Probably Brecht's most important theoretical treatise—albeit less well known than "Short Organum."

WORKS ON BRECHT AND HIS WORKS: BIOGRAPHIES, CHRONOLOGY, SCRAPBOOK

Bertolt Brecht's Berlin. A Scrapbook of the Twenties. Edited by Wolf von Eckardt and Sander L. Gilman. Garden City, NY: Anchor Books, 1975.
Cook, Bruce. *Brecht in Exile*. New York: Holt, 1983.
Esslin, Martin. *Brecht: A Choice of Evils. A Critical Study of the Man, His Work and His Opinions*. 1959. 4th, rev. ed. London: Methuen, 1984. Cited as Esslin, *Brecht*. First American edition published under the title, *Brecht: The Man and His Work*. New York: Doubleday, 1960.
Ewen, Frederic. *Bertolt Brecht. His Life, His Art and His Times*. New York: Citadel Press, 1967.
Fuegi, John. *Brecht and Company: Sex, Politics, and the Making of the Modern Drama*. New York: Grove, 1994. Cited as Fuegi, *Brecht*.
Hayman, Ronald. *Brecht. A Biography*. New York: Oxford University Press, 1983.
Lyon, James K. *Bertolt Brecht in America*. Princeton, NJ: Princeton University Press, 1980. Cited as Lyon, *Brecht*.
Völker, Klaus. *Brecht. A Biography*. Translated by John Nowell. New York: Seabury, 1978. Cited as Völker, *Brecht*.
————. *Brecht Chronicle*. Translated by Fred Wieck. New York: Seabury, 1975. Cited as Völker, *Chronicle*.

WORKS ON BRECHT: MEMOIRS

Bentley, Eric. *The Brecht Memoir*. New York: PAJ Publications, 1985.
Berlau, Ruth. *Living for Brecht: The Memoirs*. Edited by Hans Bunge, translated by Geoffrey Skelton. New York: Fromm, 1987. Cited as Berlau, *Memoirs*.
Canetti, Elias. "Brecht." In *The Torch in My Ear*. Translated by Joachim Neugroschel. New York: Farrar, 1982. 272–78.
Münsterer, Hanns Otto. *The Young Brecht*. Translated and introduction by Tom Kuhn and Karen J. Leeder. London: Libris, 1992. Cited as Münsterer, *Brecht*.
Witt, Hubert, ed. *Brecht as They Knew Him*. Translated by John Peet. London: Lawrence, 1975.

WORKS ON BRECHT: CRITICAL STUDIES

Benjamin, Walter. *Understanding Brecht*. 1973. London: New Verso, 1983.

Bentley, Eric. *The Brecht Commentaries: 1943–1980*. New York: Grove, 1981. Cited as Bentley, *Commentaries*.

Brooker, Peter. *Bertolt Brecht. Dialectics, Poetry, Politics*. London: Croom, 1988. Cited as Brooker, *Dialectics*.

Brown, H.M. *Leitmotiv and Drama: Wagner, Brecht, and the Limits of "Epic" Theatre*. Oxford: Clarendon Press, 1991.

Calabro, Tony. *Bertolt Brecht's Art of Dissemblance*. Wakefield, NH: Longwood Academic, 1990.

Dickson, Keith. *Towards Utopia. A Study of Brecht*. Oxford: Clarendon Press, 1978.

Fuegi, John. *Bertolt Brecht. Chaos, According to Plan*. Cambridge: Cambridge University Press, 1987.

———. *The Essential Brecht*. Los Angeles, CA: Hennessey, 1972.

Gilbert, Michael. *Bertolt Brecht's Striving for Reason, Even in Music: A Critical Assessment*. New York: Lang, 1976.

Gray, Ronald. *Brecht the Dramatist*. Cambridge: Cambridge University Press, 1976.

Hill, Claude. *Bertolt Brecht*. Boston: Twayne, 1975.

Hinton, Stephen, ed. *Kurt Weill: The Threepenny Opera*. Cambridge: Cambridge University Press, 1990.

Kiebuzinska, Christine Olga. *Revolutionaries in the Theater: Meyerhold, Brecht, and Witkiewicz*. Ann Arbor, MI: UMI Research Press, 1988.

Kleber, Pia. *Exceptions and Rules: Brecht, Planchon, and "The Good Person of Szechwan."* New York: Lang, 1987.

Lyon, James K. *Bertolt Brecht and Rudyard Kipling*. The Hague: Mouton, 1975. Cited as Lyon, *Kipling*.

Mueller, Roswitha. *Bertolt Brecht and the Theory of Media*. Lincoln: University of Nebraska Press, 1989. Cited as Mueller, *Media*.

Murphy, G. Ronald, S.J. *Brecht and the Bible*. Chapel Hill: University of North Carolina Press, 1980.

Needle, Jan, and Peter Thompson. *Brecht*. Chicago: University of Chicago Press, 1981.

Parmalee, Patty. *Brecht's America*. Columbus: Ohio State University Press, 1981.

Pike, David. *Lukács and Brecht*. Chapel Hill: University of North Carolina Press, 1985.

Schoeps, Karl H. *Bertolt Brecht*. New York: Ungar, 1977.

Speirs, Ronald. *Brecht's Early Plays*. Atlantic Highlands, NJ: Humanities Press, 1982.

Suvin, Darko. *To Brecht and Beyond. Soundings in Modern Dramaturgy*. Totowa, NJ: Barnes, 1984.

Tatlow, Antony. *The Mask of Evil. Brecht's Response to the Poetry, Theatre and Thought of China and Japan: A Comparative and Critical Evaluation*. Berne: Lang, 1977. Cited as Tatlow, *Mask*.

Taylor, John Russell. *Strangers in Paradise: The Hollywood Emigrés 1933–1950*. New York: Holt, 1983.

Thomson, Philip J. *The Poetry of Bertolt Brecht: Seven Studies*. Chapel Hill: University of North Carolina Press, 1989.

Whitaker, Peter. *Brecht's Poetry. A Critical Study*. Oxford: Clarendon Press, 1985.

White, Alfred, D. *Bertolt Brecht's Great Plays*. New York: Barnes, 1978.

Willett, John. *Brecht in Context: Comparative Approaches*. London: Methuen, 1984.
    Cited as Willett, *Brecht in Context*.
———. *The Theatre of Bertolt Brecht: A Study from Eight Aspects*. 1959. 3rd, rev. ed.
    New York: New Directions, 1968. Cited as Willett, *Brecht*.
Wright, Elizabeth. *Postmodern Brecht. A Re-Presentation*. London: Routledge, 1989.
    Cited as Wright, *Brecht*.

WORKS ON BRECHT: COLLECTIONS OF ESSAYS BY SEVERAL AUTHORS

Bartram, Graham, and Anthony Waine, eds. *Brecht in Perspective*. London: Longman,
    1982.
Demetz, Peter, ed. *Brecht*. Englewood Cliffs, NJ: Prentice-Hall, 1962.
Kleber, Pia, and Colin Visser, eds. *Re-interpreting Brecht: His Influence on Contempo-
    rary Drama and Film*. Cambridge: Cambridge University Press, 1990. Cited as
    Kleber/Visser, *Re-interpreting Brecht*.
Lyon, James K., and Hans-Peter Breuer, eds. *Brecht Unbound. Presented at the Inter-
    national Bertolt Brecht Symposium Held at the University of Delaware February
    1992*. Newark: University of Delaware Press, 1995.
Mews, Siegfried, ed. *Critical Essays on Bertolt Brecht*. Boston: Hall, 1989. Cited as
    Mews, *Critical Essays*.
———, and Herbert Knust, eds. *Essays on Brecht: Theater and Politics*. Chapel Hill:
    University of North Carolina Press, 1974. Cited as Mews/Knust, *Essays*.
Munk, Erika, ed. *Brecht*. New York: Bantam, 1972. Cited as Munk, *Brecht*.
Thomson, Peter, and Glendyr Sacks, eds. *The Cambridge Companion to Brecht*. Cam-
    bridge: Cambridge University Press, 1994. Cited as Thomson/Sacks, *Cambridge
    Companion*.
Weber, Betty Nance, and Hubert Heinen, eds. *Bertolt Brecht. Political Theory and Lit-
    erary Practice*. Athens: University of Georgia Press, 1980. Cited as Weber/Hei-
    nen, *Brecht*.

WORKS ON BRECHT: PERIODICAL PUBLICATIONS

Brecht-Jahrbuch/Brecht Yearbook. Published since 1971 under varying titles, the year-
    book publishes scholarly articles (most of them in English) on all facets of Brecht
    research as well as book reviews.
Communications from the International Brecht Society. The semiannual publication fea-
    tures shorter articles on productions of plays by Brecht and on related events.

WORKS ON BRECHT: FICTION AND DRAMA

Feinstein, Elaine. *Loving Brecht*. 1992. London: Sceptre, 1993.
Grass, Günter. *The Plebeians Rehearse the Uprising. A German Tragedy*. Translated by
    Ralph Manheim. New York: Harcourt, 1966.
Hampton, Christopher. *Tales from Hollywood*. London: Faber, 1983.

General Index

Abravanel, Maurice, 266
Adorno, Theodor W., 21, 60, 222, 265, 268
Actors Studio, 346, 367
Aesthetics of Poverty, 386
Agit-prop theater, 48, 57, 79, 85, 208, 267, 344, 370, 372
Ajoka (theater group), 382
Albee, Edward, 366
Alexander of Macedonia, 181
Alienation. *See Verfremdung*
Allende, Salvador, 365
Allio, René, 223; *La vieille dame indigne*, 223
American Repertory Theatre, 348
Ammer, K. L., 10, 255
Anbruch, 240
Anderson, Maxwell, 264–65
Angewandte Musik, 80
Anschluß (of Austria), 20
Appetites, 89, 90, 91, 92, 93, 94, 95, 96, 98, 99, 100, 101, 102, 107, 109, 110
Aragon, Louis, 27
Arena Stage (Washington, DC), 347

Arena Teater, 394
Arendt, Hannah, 27, 350
Argentine Yiddish Theater Front, 356, 362, 364
Aristotle, 38, 39, 40, 63; *Poetics*, 38, 39
Armstrong, Louis, 11, 261, 329, 345
Artaud, Antonin, 35, 49, 349, 366, 369, 372, 373
Atkinson, Brooks, 344, 345, 350
Auden, Wystan Hugh, 328, 329, 336, 338
Aufbau (publisher), 29
Aufricht, Ernst Josef, 254, 263, 340
Augsburger Neueste Nachrichten, 3
Auric, Georges, 242–43
Authorship, 153–54

Bach, Johann Sebastian, 240–41; *St. Matthew Passion*, 80
Bachelard, Gaston, 298
Bacon, Francis, 182; *Essayes*, 36; *Novum organum scientiarum*, 25, 44
Baden-Baden music festival, 71, 72, 73, 79, 84
Bahn, Roma, 255

Balanchine, George, 264

Balázs, Béla, 204

Bancroft, Anne, 347

Bandh (narrative form), 394

Barucha, Rustam, 383, 386

Basic Christian Communities, 392

Bauhaus, 84

Bakhtin, Mikhail, 48

Balzac, Honoré de, 62

Banholzer, Paula (Bi or Bie), 4, 8, 26, 298

Bänziger, Hans, 107

Barthes, Roland, 49, 52, 54, 66, 148, 153

Becher, Johannes R., 27

Beckett, Samuel, 1, 36, 385

Bekhterev, Vladimir Mikhailovich, 393

Belitt, Ben, 321, 337

Bengkel Muda Surabaya (theater group), 384

Benjamin, Walter, 17, 19, 48, 60, 61, 63, 65, 83, 142–46, 154, 170, 171, 172, 248, 250, 285, 321, 323, 334, 337, 353; "Kleine Geschichte der Photographie" (Short History of Photography), 145, 154; "The Work of Art in the Age of Mechanical Reproduction,"143

Benn, Gottfried, 5

Bennewitz, Fritz, 386

Bentley, Eric, 15, 16, 17, 48, 323, 332, 337, 342, 345, 346, 349, 350, 351

Berghahn, Klaus, 170

Bergman, Ingmar, 221

Bergman, Ingrid, 344

Bergner, Elisabeth, 340, 341

Berlau, Ruth 8, 15, 21, 22, 25, 26, 149, 308, 310–11; Living for Brecht, 28, 310

Berliner Ensemble, 10, 25, 26, 27, 28, 30, 63, 64, 66, 133, 212, 213, 222, 227, 253, 269, 271, 281, 292, 340, 345, 346, 356, 360, 369

Berlin Wall, 1, 26, 28, 29, 234

Bernstein, Elmer, 269

Bernstein, Leonard, 267

Besson, Benno, 26

Betz, Albrecht, 75, 80

Bharata Muni: Natyasastra, 386

Bhutto, Benazir, 382

The Bible, 2, 3, 77, 93, 99, 100, 107, 180

Bidermann, Jakob: Cenodoxus, 84

Biha, Otto, 78

Bismarck, Otto von, 243, 248

Blau, Herbert, 49, 58, 346

Blitzstein, Marc, 11, 266, 329, 330, 345; The Cradle Will Rock, 266, 329

Bloch, Ernst, 170, 258

Bloom, Allan, 11; The Closing of the American Mind, 350

Boal, Augusto, 361, 362, 366, 367, 371, 372, 375, 394; Theater of the Oppressed, 361

Bolt, Ranjit, 323

Bond, Edward, 49

Borges, Jorge Louis, 59

Bowie, David, 261

Boyer, Charles, 344

Brecht, Bertolt: and capitalism (see Capitalism); and dialectical thinking (see Dialectics); and film, 197–219 (see also DEFA; Hollywood); and Marxism (see Marx, Karl); and musical collaborators (see Burkhard, Paul; Dessau, Paul; Einem, Gottfried von; Eisler, Hanns; Hindemith, Paul; Meisel, Edmund; Parmet, Simon; Sessions, Roger; Shostakovich, Dimitri; Wagner-Regeny, Rudolf; Weill, Kurt); and politics (see Cold War; Communism; Hitler, Adolf; House Un-American Activities Committee; Lenin, V. I.; Socialism; Stalin, J. V.); and theater (see Agit-prop theater; Berliner Ensemble; Broadway; Epic theater; Gestus; Lehrstück; Montage; No theater; Non-Aristotelian drama; Parable play; Socialist Realism; Stanislavsky, Constantin; Verfremdung); and women (see Banholzer, Paula; Berlau, Ruth; Fleißer, Marieluise; Hauptmann, Elisabeth; Neher, Carola; Steffin, Margarete; Weigel, Helene; Zoff, Marianne); authorship of (see Collective mode of production); history, concept of (see History); in exile (see Exile); reception/ appropriation in: Argentina, 362–63;

Asia, 379–98; Brazil, 366–68; Central
America, 376; Chile, 364–66; Colombia, 368–71; Mexico, 373–74; Peru,
371–73; Puerto Rico, 375; Uruguay,
363–64; United States, 339–55; works:
appetites in (*see* Appetites); culinarism
in (*see* Culinarism); humor in (*see* Hu-
mor); irony in (*see* Irony); pedagogy in
(*see* Pedagogy); sensuality in (*see* Sen-
suality); women and mother figures in,
296–317
Brecht fatigue, 29
Brecht, Frank (son), 4, 8
Brecht industry, 29
Brecht, Stefan (son), 8, 14, 25, 329
Brecht Prize, 29
Brecht-Schall, Barbara (daughter), 8, 25
Brenton, Howard, 324, 325, 326
Broadway, 22, 23, 49, 144, 261, 262,
263, 264, 265–67, 268, 270, 311, 312,
340, 341, 342, 243–48, 352, 390
Bronnen, Arnolt, 7, 48, 201; *Vatermord*
(Patricide), 7
Bruckner, Ferdinand, 227; *Krankheit der
Jugend*, 227
Brückner, Jutta, 228; *Lieben Sie Brecht?*,
228
Bruinier, Franz, 258
Bruno, Giordano, 181
Brustein, Robert, 58, 348, 351
Büchner, Georg, 53, 58, 349
Buenaventura, Enrique, 356, 357, 358,
361, 362, 368, 369, 371, 375
Bunge, Hans, 313
Buonaparte, Napoleon, 15
Burkhard, Paul, 262, 275
Burri, Emil, 81
Busch, Ernst, 78
Busoni, Ferruccio: *Arlecchino*, 74, 239–
42; *Sketch of a New Esthetic of Music*,
241
Butler, Samuel, 322

Caesar, Julius, 226
Campodónico, César, 356, 364
Camus, Albert, 385
Canetti, Elias, 5, 10
Capitalism, 1, 2, 10, 11, 12, 13, 15, 20,
21, 39, 42, 45, 46, 61, 72, 82, 93, 94,
95, 100, 116, 118, 125, 132, 133, 134,
137, 149, 203, 204, 206, 207, 278,
280, 296, 304, 312, 341, 350, 351,
368, 382, 383
Capitalist. *See* Capitalism
Capone, Al, 20
Carrasquilla, Tomas: *A la diestra de Dios
Padre*, 358
Carow, Heiner, 222
Case, Sue-Ellen, 305, 348
Castro, Fidel, 375
Cavalcanti, Alberto, 213–14
Césaire, Aimé, 27
Chaplin, Charlie, 21, 50, 55, 201, 213,
269, 339, 344; *City Lights*, 213; *The
Face on the Barroom Floor*, 201;
Goldrush, 201
Chaucer, Geoffrey, 1
Chekhov, Anton, 35, 329, 349, 352, 385
Chelsea Theater Center, 346, 347
Chen Yong, 381
Cheo (peasant theater form), 384
Chiang Kai-shek, 76
Chouduri, Indra Nath, 386
Chua, Apolonio Bayani, 388
Churchill, Winston, 133–34
Cinema: acting in, 226; actors in, 232,
233; avant-garde, 221, 222, 229, 233;
counter, 229; documentary, 225, 226,
227, 228, 231, 233, 234; essay, 226;
expressionist, 198, 201, 203; feminism
in, 234, 235; feminist theory of, 220,
221, 229–31; "formalism" in, 221,
223, 225, 229; fragmentation of narrative in, 223, 225, 226, 231, 232; Neo-
Realism in, 222, 224, 230; nôvo, 224;
political modernism in, 221, 222, 223,
235; politics of the new left and, 222,
223, 224, 227, 229, 230, 231, 234–35;
psychoanalysis and, 229–31; representation in, 223, 225, 228, 231, 233–34;
silent, 200, 203; social function of,
224, 225, 229, 234. *See also* Hollywood; New German cinema; New
Latin American cinema; New wave
cinema; Soviet cinema; Third World
cinema

Circle in the Square, 346
Cochran, Gifford, 343
Cocteau, Jean, 239, 243–44, 269; *Le coq et l'arlequin*, 242
Cold War, 1, 27, 79, 117, 133, 213, 222, 342, 346, 351
Collective mode of production, 3, 8, 9, 10, 13, 26, 48, 54, 73, 75, 153–54, 206, 207, 208, 210, 211, 286, 287, 288, 359, 361, 393
Collins, Judy, 261
Communism, 1, 2, 12, 13, 24, 27, 28, 32, 33, 45, 46, 50, 59, 60, 66, 76, 77, 78, 79, 90, 101, 122, 124, 125, 129, 131, 137, 208, 234, 269, 278, 283, 284, 285, 287, 305, 342, 346, 350, 352
Communist. *See* Communism
Communist party, 50, 59, 60, 64, 77, 79, 173, 208, 277, 278, 284, 286, 302, 381, 384, 385. *See also* Communism
Confucius, 175, 176
Confucianism. *See* Confucius
Copland, Aaron, 269
Cuatrotablas (theater group), 372
Cuban revolution, 357, 360, 374
Culinarism, 88, 94, 95, 96, 98, 99, 102, 103, 104, 107, 110, 111
Cultural Revolution (in China), 381, 384–85

Dalmia-Lüderitz, Vasudha, 385, 386–87
Dante Alighieri, 1
Darin, Bobby, 261, 329
De Molina, Tirso, 373
Debussy, Claude, 244
DEFA, 213, 269
Defamiliarization. *See* Verfremdung
Del Cioppo, Atahualpa, 362, 363, 364, 371, 375
Deleuze, Gilles, 154
Derrida, Jacques, 154
Dessau, Paul, 27, 81, 244, 261–62, 269–70
Der deutsche Rundfunk, 239–40, 244
Dexter, John, 347
Dialectic theater. *See* Epic theater
Dialectical structure. *See* Dialectics
Dialectical thinking. *See* Dialectics

Dialectics, 18, 41, 42, 43, 45, 46, 50, 57, 58, 59, 71, 75, 80, 83, 91, 99, 103, 105, 107, 109, 117, 118, 121, 122, 124, 126, 129, 137, 169, 170, 175, 177, 178, 184, 185, 187, 188, 189, 192, 281–92, 297, 315, 328, 340
Dialogue, 170, 173, 174, 178, 184
Didactic play. *See* Lehrstück
Diderot, Denis, 27, 38, 64, 65, 66; *Jacques le Fataliste et son maître*, 20, 65, 178; *Le Neveu de Rameau*, 178
Diderot Society, 64
Diebold, Bernhard, 94
Dietrich, Marlene, 48
Distanciation. *See* Verfremdung
Döblin, Alfred, 282
Dort, Bernard, 367, 369
Dragún, Osvaldo, 362, 369; *Heroica de Buenos Aires*, 362; *Historias para ser contadas*, 362
Dudov (Dudow), Slatan, 72, 77, 78, 203, 207–8
Dula-tula (dramatized poem), 388, 394
Duncan, Isadora, 48
"Dunia Yang Kejam" (song), 383
Durey, Louis, 242
Dziga-Vertov group, 223; *British Sounds*, 223; *Luttes en Italie*, 223; *Vent d'Est*, 223, 224; *Vladimir et Rosa*, 223. *See also* Godard, Jean-Luc, and Gorin, Jean-Pierre

Eagleton, Terry, 52, 61
Ebb, Fred, Kander, John, and Stein, Joseph: *Cabaret*, 266
Einem, Gottfried von, 26, 262, 275
Einstein, Albert, 36, 63, 269
Eisenstein, Sergei, 48, 51, 56, 57, 221
Eisler, Gerhart, 269
Eisler, Hanns, 15, 17, 24, 48, 51, 70, 74, 75, 76, 77, 78, 79, 80, 81, 83, 85, 208, 222, 246, 261–65, 268–70, 273, 282, 334, 335, 341, 344; *Composing for the Films*, 222, 269; *None but the Lonely Heart* (film music), 268; *Tagebuch (Opus 9)*, 79; *Tempo der Zeit*, 80
El Galpón (theater group), 362, 363, 364

Empedocles, 315
Engel, Erich, 6, 7, 201, 213; *Mysterien eines Frisiersalons*, 201
Engels, Friedrich, 176. *See also* Marx, Karl
Enlightenment tradition, 180
Enzensberger, Hans Magnus, 327
Epic dramaturgy. *See* Epic theater
Epic music theater. *See* Epic theater
Epic style. *See* Epic theater
Epic theater, 7, 9, 12, 18, 40, 50, 52, 53, 55, 56, 60, 61, 63, 65, 80, 95, 199, 202, 205, 209, 222, 225, 228, 231 284–87, 340, 342, 343, 349, 365, 371, 372, 374, 375
Epigram(s), 116, 127, 139, 140, 149, 150, 152, 155–61, 238–59
Erpenbeck, Fritz, 25
Escher, M. C., 296, 300, 316
Esslin, Martin, 5, 9, 23, 24, 26, 58, 66
Estrangement. *See* Verfremdung
Emigration. *See* Exile
Exile, 14, 21, 60, 63, 82, 116, 117, 122, 126, 127, 132, 133, 134, 135, 136, 140, 151, 154, 157, 165, 169, 170, 178, 179, 210–12, 244, 248, 262, 265, 279, 282, 284, 287, 302, 304, 305, 306, 307, 309, 310, 315, 340, 341, 342, 353
Expressionism, 61, 62, 281

Fajardo, Brenda, 386, 387
Farocki, Harun, 233, 234–35; *Zwischen zwei Kriegen*, 234
Fassbinder, Rainer Werner, 221, 222, 227–28, 232; *Der amerikanische Soldat*, 227; *Die Ehe der Maria Braun*, 228; *Götter der Pest*, 227; *Katzelmacher*, 227, 232
Fascism. *See* Nazism
Feingold, Michael, 328, 329, 333
Feinstein, Elaine: *Loving Brecht*, 9
Feuchtwanger, Lion, 6, 48, 151, 212, 282, 311, 341; *Erfolg* (Success), 7; *The Visions of Simone Machard*, 22
Feuchtwanger, Martha, 21
Filho, Oduvaldo Vianna (Vianninha), 368
Film. *See* Brecht, Bertolt; Cinema

First Quarter Storm (in the Philippines), 392
Fischer, Ruth, 12, 79
Fleißer, Marieluise, 9, 48; "Der Tiefseefisch," 9
Floray, Wolfgang, 275
Flusser, Vilém, 143, 155
Ford, John, 221
Forke, Alfred, 175
Formalism, 42, 43, 64, 65
Formalism/realism debate, 18, 171. *See also* Formalism; Realism; Socialist Realism
Foucault, Michel, 67
Four Modernizations campaign (in China), 381
Franco, Francisco, 16
Frankfurt School, 221, 230, 231
Frayn, Michael, 329
Frederick the Great, 181
Freire, Paulo 360–62, 388, 392–94; *codificação*, 360, 362; *conscientização*, 360, 361, 362, 380; *Pedagogy of the Oppressed*, 361
Frenken, Herbert, 298, 310
Friedrich, Ernst, 144
Frisch, Max, 25, 28, 366
Fromann, Daniela, 349, 354
Fuegi, John, 4, 8, 10, 16, 30, 48, 55, 302, 305, 307–9, 311; *Brecht and Company*, 2, 29

Galilei, Galileo, 24, 44, 63; *Discorsi*, 37, 102, 103
Gamelan (Javanese orchestra), 384
Gang of Four, 381
Garbe, Hans, 84
García, Santiago, 372, 373, 374, 375, 379
Gardner, Herb: *I'm Not Rappaport*, 352
Gay, John, 10, 52, 94; *The Beggar's Opera*, 10, 94, 254, 256–57, 263, 302, 375
Gebrauchsmusik, 51, 73, 74, 84
GDR. *See* German Democratic Republic
Gemeinschaftsmusik, 74
Genet, Jean, 352
George, Heinrich, 7
George, Stefan, 148

German Democratic Republic, 222, 227, 281, 287
German Revolution (1918), 281, 283
Gershwin, Ira, 264
Gesamtkunstwerk, 44, 238, 240, 247–48, 250–51. *See also* Wagner, Richard
Gestic acting. *See Gestus*
Gestus, 49, 50, 51, 55–56, 58, 65, 173, 176, 201, 203, 205, 252–53, 257, 322, 326, 335, 330, 360, 362, 367, 386, 387
Gilbert, Robert, 80
Gide, André, 243
Glinoga, Alan: *Panunuluyan*, 385
Godard, Jean-Luc, 221, 222, 223, 224; *Le mépris*, 222, 223; *Vivre sa vie*, 223. *See also* Dziga-Vertov group
Godard, Jean-Luc, and Gorin, Jean-Pierre: *Tout va bien* (with Gorin), 223, 229
Godard, Jean-Luc, and Miéville, Anne-Marie: *Ici et ailleurs* 223; *Six fois deux*, 223
Goethe, Johann Wolfgang von, 324, 349; *Unterhaltungen deutscher Ausgewanderten*, 178
Goldsmith, Jerry, 269
Gorelik, Mordecai, 342
Gorin, Jean-Pierre, 223, 224; *Tout va bien* (with Godard), 223, 229. *See also* Dziga-Vertov group; Godard, Jean-Luc
Gorky, Maxim, 264, 315, 343; *The Mother* 13, 122, 303
Goulart, João, 361, 366
GPU, 79
Grabbe, Christian Dietrich, 4
Granach, Alexander, 78
Grand Method, 18, 175, 176, 177, 285, 287. *See also* Dialectics
Grand Order, 18, 175, 285. *See also* Marxism
Grass, Günter, 27, 28; *The Plebeians Rehearse the Uprising*, 27, 28
Grasso, Omar, 362
Great Depression, 11, 77
Green, Paul, 264
Greene, Graham, 30
Greek drama, 77
Gropius, Walter, 48
Grosz, George, 48, 57, 301

Große Methode. See Grand Method
Große Ordnung. See Grand Order
Grotowski, Jerzy, 366, 372, 373, 374
Grup Teater Surabaya, 384
Guattari, Felix, 154
Guidote, Cecelia, 392
Guthrie Theater, 347

Händel, Georg Friedrich, 254, 256–57
Häußler, Inge, 173
Haltung. See Gestus
Haiyuza Theater, 381
Hammerstein, Oscar. *See* Rodgers, Richard
Hampton, Christopher: *Tales from Hollywood*, 29
Hamsun, Knut, 53, 275
Handke, Peter, 29
Harrer, Johann, 246
Hart, Moss, 264
Hašek, Jaroslav, 312, 331; *The Good Soldier Švejk*, 20, 22, 265, 331
Hauptmann, Elisabeth, 8, 10, 26, 28, 35, 48, 71, 72, 74, 75, 81, 253–54, 256, 302, 308, 310–11, 333, 340
Hauptmann, Gerhart, 324; *The Beaver Coat*, 48, 54; *Drayman Henschel*, 94
Hauser, Otto, 332
Hays, H. R., 270, 323, 324
Hayman, Ronald, 24, 26
Hegel, Georg Wilhelm Friedrich, 9, 24, 42, 43, 58, 59, 60, 172, 177, 178, 190, 191, 195, 332; *Aesthetics*, 59; *Phenomenology*, 42
Heidsieck, Arnold, 297
Heraclitus, 45, 184
Hermsdorf, Klaus, 170
Herzfelde, Wieland, 118, 282
Heydrich, Reinhard, 21
Heartfield, John, 139, 143, 282
Hindemith, Paul, 48, 51, 70, 72, 73, 74, 78, 79, 85, 242–43, 262, 275; *Hin und Zurück*, 74
Hiob, Hanne (Brecht's daughter), 8, 228
History, 24, 41, 42, 45, 53, 54, 58, 62, 67, 91, 115, 116, 117, 121, 122, 125, 127, 129, 130, 180, 181, 183, 189, 226, 228, 248, 278, 285, 287, 360

Hitler, Adolf, 11, 13, 14, 15, 18, 20, 21, 22, 109, 116, 122, 125, 127, 133, 140, 144, 152, 159, 160, 162, 164, 165, 169, 172, 170, 172, 211, 248–49, 258, 303, 340, 350
Hitler/Stalin pact, 20
Hölderlin, Friedrich: *Antigone*, 25
Hofmannsthal, Hugo von: "Lord Chandos Letter," 241
Hollywood, 21, 22, 29, 199, 204, 211–13, 220, 221, 222, 224, 225, 227–28, 233, 340, 341, 342, 349
Homer: *Iliad*, 91
Honecker, Erich, 129, 137
Honegger, Arthur, 242–43; *Joan of Arc at the Stake*, 243; *King David*, 243
Horace, 3, 38, 328
Horkheimer, Max, 21
Horváth, Ödön von, 29
House Un-American Activities Committee, 12, 17, 79, 212, 269, 342
House of Frankenstein, 269
HUAC. *See* House Un-American Activities Committee
Huang Zuolin, 384–85
Hubalek, Claus, 26
Hughes, Langston, 264
Huillet, Danièle, 221, 225–27. *See also* Straub, Jean-Marie
Humor, 19, 178, 199, 200, 205, 213, 248, 267, 305
Humperdinck, Engelbert, 240

I-Ching. *Book of Changes*, 175, 289
Ibsen, Henrik, 1, 321, 349, 385
Icarus, 182
Ideology. *See* Marxism
IFT. *See* Argentine Yiddish Theater Front
Ihering, Herbert, 5, 10
Indian People's Theater Association, 385
Internationale Literatur, 82, 83
IPTA. *See* Indian People's Theater Association
Irony, 19, 116, 134, 146, 148, 165, 173, 174, 175, 179, 189, 200, 202, 246, 248, 249, 251, 258, 274, 299, 305
Isherwood, Christopher, 48; *Berlin Stories*, 266

Jacob, Malou, 387–88; *Juan Tamban*, 387–89, 391
Jannings, Emil, 48
Jauss, Hans Robert, 67
Jazz, 239–40, 244–45, 256, 258
Jesus Christ, 77, 80, 94, 107, 110
Joan of Arc, 100
Johst, Hanns, 48; *Der Einsame* (The Lonely One), 4, 89
Joyce, James, 1
Jugendmusikbewegung, 85
Junge Bühne, 7

Kabuki theater, 380
Kafka, Franz: *Metamorphosis*, 201
Kaiser, Georg, 57, 265. *See also* Weill, Kurt
Kambayoka (performance style), 384
Kander, John. *See* Ebb, Fred
Kant, Immanuel, 190, 305
Kerr, Alfred, 10, 94, 255
Ketoprak (theater form), 384
Khruschev, Nikita, 66
Kidd, Ross, 394
Kipling, Rudyard, 8, 6, 53, 81, 332, 333, 337
Kivi, Aleksis, 178
Klabund (Henschke, Alfred), 254
Kleist, Heinrich von, 349; *Michael Kohlhaas*, 15
Knopf, Jan, 5, 169, 170, 171
Koestler, Arthur, 346
Kogan, Jaime, 362, 363
Komedya (theater form), 386
Korea, Senda, 381
Korsch, Karl, 17, 45, 48, 59, 176, 277–87
Kortner, Fritz, 211, 2271
Kott, Jan, 53
KPD. *See* Communist party
Kracauer, Siegfried, 170
Kraus, Karl, 57
Krimsky, John, 343
Kristeva, Julia, 54
Kroetz, Franz Xaver, 30
Kuomintang, 76
Kuplis, Aija, 308
Kurella, Alfred, 12, 18, 78, 86

Kushner, Tony: *Angels in America*, 353
Kutscher, Artur, 3

Labad, Lutgardo, 387
Lacis, Asja, 48, 57, 60
Laienspielbewegung, 85
LaMama, 346, 369
Lang, Fritz, 22, 201, 211–12; *Hangmen
    also Die*, 21, 197, 340; *Metropolis*,
    201
Lania, Leo, 203, 205, 210
Lao-tse, 127, 184, 315
Lao-tsû (Lao tzû). *See* Lao-tse
Laughton, Charles, 23, 24, 244, 269, 324,
    326, 327, 329, 340, 341, 344
Learning play. *See Lehrstück*
Lehrstück, 10, 12, 13, 43, 60, 70–86,
    122, 169, 173, 186, 287–89, 392–94.
    See also Pedagogy
Leitmotiv, 238, 240. *See also* Wagner,
    Richard
Lenin, V. I., 9, 45, 80, 115, 117, 121,
    160, 176, 177, 277, 284, 285, 286,
    288, 289–90, 351
Leninism. *See* Lenin, V. I.
Lennox, Sara, 296–97, 303–4, 307–8
Lenya, Lotte, 9, 11, 48, 254–55, 261–62,
    264–67, 274, 276, 279, 345
Lenz, Jakob Michael Reinhold, 52, 324;
    The Tutor, 54
Lerner, Alan Jay, 264
Lessing, Gotthold Ephraim, 38, 66, 349;
    *Ernst und Falk: Gespräche für Frei-
    mäurer*, 178
Lezar, Nicholas, 327
Li Jianming, 381
Lindbergh, Charles, 71, 72
Living Theater, 346, 366, 367, 372, 374
Lodge, David, 30
Losey, Joseph, 269
Loesser, Frank: *Guys and Dolls*, 263
Lorre, Peter, 48
Lubitsch, Ernst: *To Be or Not to Be*, 213
Ludruk (theater form), 384
Luftwaffe, 157, 162
Lukács Georg, 18, 60, 61, 62, 63, 64,
    221, 222, 287, 289
Lumbera, Bienvenido, 386

Luther, Martin, 2, 98. *See also* The Bible
Luxemburg, Rosa, 176, 289, 290
Lyons, James, 310

MacCabe, Colin, 286
MaFarlane, James, 321, 322
Mackeben, Theo, 254
Mahon, Derek, 337
Malik Verlag, 82
Maltz, Albert, 354
Manheim, Ralph, 324, 327, 328, 329,
    330, 331, 334, 337
Mann, Heinrich, 48
Mann, Thomas, 5, 6, 62, 269
Marcos, Ferdinand, 380, 382, 392
Marcuse, Herbert, 21
Marlowe, Christopher: *Edward II*, 7, 52,
    54, 55
Martí, José, 359
Martin, Andy, 322
Marx, Karl, 2, 4, 9, 10, 11, 16, 24, 28,
    42, 43, 45, 58, 59, 60, 62, 70, 71, 72,
    77, 78, 79, 96, 99, 100, 101, 115, 117,
    121, 122, 125, 130, 140, 148, 169,
    170, 176, 177, 188, 189, 204, 228,
    229, 230, 240, 244, 247, 255, 267,
    268, 269, 276–80, 284–88, 302, 305,
    313, 332, 345, 346, 351, 352, 360, 393;
    Das Kapital, 17, 58, 100, 283
Marx, Karl, and Engels, Friedrich: *The
    Communist Manifesto*, 341
Marxian. *See* Marx, Karl
Marxism. *See* Marx, Karl
Marxism-Leninism. *See* Leninism; Marx-
    ism
Marxist. *See* Marx, Karl
Matisse, Henri, 269
Mayakovsky, Vladimir, 42
McCarthy, Eugene, 342, 345
Mei Lan-fang, 17, 38, 44
Meisel, Edmund, 239, 262, 275
Merrick, David, 347
Me-ti. *See* Mo-tzu
Me-tse. *See* Mo-tzu
Mews, Siegfried, 169
Meyer, Michael, 329
MGM Studios, 212, 265
Midler, Bette, 264

Milhaud, Darius, 242–43; *Le boeuf sur le toit* 243; *Christophe Colomb*, 243; *La création du monde*, 243; *Der arme Matrose*, 74

Mendelsohn, Erich, 148; *Amerika*, 144–45

Mendes, Lothar: *SOS. Die Insel der Tränen*, 201

Meyerhold, Vsevolod, 56, 57, 56, 66

Michaelis, Karin, 14

Milfull, John, 83

Miller, Arthur, 346

Milton, John, 1

Mittenzwei, Werner, 30

Mo Tse. *See* Mo-tzu

Mo-tzu, 175, 176, 289

Moholy-Nagy, László, 142

Molière, 35, 349; *Don Juan*, 26

Moross, Jerome, 269, 275

Morrison, Jim, 261

Moscow Art Theater, 35, 56, 64, 66

Moscow show trials, 12, 17, 18, 81, 291. *See also* Stalin, J. V.

Mozart, Wolfgang Amadeus, 240–41

Mueller, Carl, 334, 335

Müller, Heiner; *Der Lohndrücker*, 84

Müller, Klaus-Detlev, 169, 170, 175, 181

Münsterer, Hanns Otto, 3, 246, 332

Mukařovsky, Jan, 50

Muse, Clarence, 265

Musil, Robert, 170

Nabokov, Vladimir, 324

Nagavajara, Chetana, 383, 386

Nash, Ogden, 264

National Socialism. *See* Nazism

Nazism, 3, 13, 14, 15, 16, 18, 19, 20, 21, 22, 26, 41, 72, 78, 82, 85, 117, 122, 124, 125, 128, 132, 133, 135, 151, 153, 157, 159, 162, 170, 172, 178, 179, 228, 239, 248–49, 258, 265, 266, 306, 312, 315, 342. *See also* Hitler, Adolf

Neher, Carola, 20, 18, 48, 254

Neher, Caspar, 3, 6, 25, 48, 72, 200, 203, 254

Neruda, Pablo, 27

New German cinema, 225–28

New Latin American cinema, 224

New Latin American Popular Theater movement, 359, 365

New Testament. *See* The Bible

New York Shakespeare Festival, 346

New wave cinema, 220–21, 222–23, 224, 225, 227

Nguyen Dinh Quang, 384

Nietzsche, Friedrich, 11, 45, 246, 337; *Beyond Good and Evil*, 337; *The Case of Wagner*, 244, 246; *Nietzsche Contra Wagner*, 246

Nixon, Richard, 29, 348

No play(s). *See No* theater

No theater, 75, 263, 380

Non-Aristotelian drama, 36, 38, 39, 40, 44, 55, 63, 65, 250, 252, 361

Noske, Gustav, 133, 151

North, Alex, 269, 275

O'Casey, Sean, 331

Odysseus, 172

O'Neill, Eugene, 331

Oppenheimer, Julius Robert, 63

Orff, Carl, 262, 275

Ottwalt, Ernst, 208

Pabst, Georg Wilhelm (G. W.), 48, 203, 205, 343

Palitzsch, Peter, 26

Pannwitz, Rudolf, 324

Papp, Joseph, 266

Parable, 127, 132, 170, 174, 181

Parable play, 15, 16, 39, 82, 105, 115, 305, 307

Parmet, Simon, 262, 275

Patera, Paul, 79

Paton, Alan: *Cry, the Beloved Country*, 265

Paulsen, Harald, 255

Pavis, Patrice, 49, 52, 54, 55, 56

Pedagogy, 70, 74, 84, 140, 170, 178, 186, 187, 192, 282, 283, 360–62, 393, 394. *See also Lehrstück*

Péladan, Joséphin, 243

Pepusch, Johann Christoph, 254–55. *The Beggar's Opera*, 254. *See also* Gay, John

Peron, Juan Domingo, 362
PETA. *See* Philippines Educational Theater Association
Philip of Spain, 181
Philippines Educational Theater Association, 382, 385–86, 387–89, 392–94; *Ang Hatol ng Guhit na Bilog*, 387
Phoenix Theater, 346
Photogram, 142
Pianca, Marina: *Testimonios de Teatro Latinoamericano*, 366
Picasso, Pablo, 243, 352
Pietzcker, Carl, 297
Pinochet Augusto, 365
Pirandello, Luigi, 385; *Six Characters in Search of an Author*, 57
Piscator, Erwin, 10, 48, 54, 64, 202, 203, 208, 210, 266, 271, 282, 333, 344, 358, 360, 372; *Schweyk* (production of), 22, 57; *The Political Theatre*, 35
Platonic dialogues, 177
Plummer, Christopher, 347
Pollet, Jean-Daniel: *Méditerranée*, 223
Ponto, Erich, 255
Potter, Sally, 231; *Thriller*, 231
Poulenc, Francis, 242
Pozner, Vladimir, 214
Prague Linguistic Circle, 50
Prince, Hal (Harold), 266–68
Proshika (theater group), 394

Quayle, Anthony, 345
Quinn, Anthony, 344

Rachmat, Basuki, 381, 384
Raddatz, Fritz, 315
Raine, Craig, 337
Rainer, Louise, 340
Rainer, Yvonne, 221, 321–34, 235; *Film about a Woman Who . . .* , 232; *Journeys from Berlin/1971* 232; *The Man Who Envied Women*, 232–33; *Privilege*, 232
Ramuz, Charles, 245
Rankl, Karl, 78
Rasa theory (of drama), 386
Reagan, Ronald, 348

Realism, 18, 42, 43, 44, 53, 59, 61, 62, 63, 64, 65, 66, 98, 213, 289, 299, 381
Reformpädagogik, 85
Reich, Bernhard, 48
Reichstag, 13, 14, 20, 140, 210, 278
Reinhardt, Max, 48, 57, 48, 254, 264, 267
Renaissance, 25, 62, 183
Rendra, W. S., 380–81; *Linkaran Kapur Putih*, 381
Remarque, Erich Maria: *All Quiet on the Western Front*, 119
Renoir, Jean, 222, 226
Repertory Theatre of Lincoln Center, 346, 347
Resnais, Alain, 222; *Nuit et brouillard*, 222
Reyher, Ferdinand, 265, 336
Riantiarno, N., 383, 388–91; *Opera Kecoa*, 389–91
Richardson, Tony, 347
Rice, Elmer: *Street Scene*, 265–66
Riefenstahl, Leni, 48
Rilke, Rainer Maria, 5, 148, 241, 321, 322, 337
Rimbaud, Arthur, 6, 53, 89, 332
Robbins, Jerome, 267, 347
Rocha, Glauber, 221, 224–25; *Antonio das Mortes*, 224, 225; *Deus e o Diabo na Terra do Sol*, 224, 225; *Der Leone Have Sept Cabecas*, 224
Rockefeller Foundation, 268
Rodgers, Richard, and Hammerstein, Oscar: *Oklahoma!*, 348
Roosevelt, Eleanor, 269
Rosenberg, Hilding, 262, 275
Rosler, Martha, 231; *Vital Statistics of a Citizen, Simply Obtained*, 231
Rote Fahne, 78, 79
Russian Formalists, 42, 43

Sacks, Glendyr. *See* Thomson, Peter
Sagayan war dance, 384
Samson-Körner, Paul, 48, 51
San Francisco Actors Workshop, 346, 347, 354
Sander, Helke, 233, 234–35; *Die allseitig*

reduzierte Persönlichkeit-Redupers, 234;
    BeFreier und Befreite, 234
Sanders-Brahms, Helma, 228, 231;
    Deutschland bleiche Mutter, 228
Santos, Al. *See* Glinoga, Alan
Sartre, Jean-Paul, 385; *Huis clos*, 40
Satie, Eric, 239, 243–44; *Parade*, 242–44;
    Les Six, 239, 242–43
Sauerlander, Wolfgang, 324, 327
Savory, Theodore, 322
Schechner, Richard, 353
Schenkkan, Robert: *The Kentucky Cycle*,
    353
Scherchen, Hermann, 72
Scherler, Gerhart, 85, 86
Schiller, Friedrich von, 100, 349; *The
    Maiden of Orleans*, 303; *The Robbers*,
    54
Schmidt, Klaus M., 349
Schneider, Alan, 345
Schoenberg, Arnold, 48, 73, 74, 78, 79
Schulmusikbewegung, 72
Schuloper, 74
Schulstück, 83
Schwaen, Kurt, 83
Screen, 229, 230
Seattle Repertory Theater, 352
Seghers, Anna: *The Trial of Joan of Arc
    at Rouen, 1431*, 313
Sensuality, 88, 89, 90, 91, 96, 98, 101
    102, 103, 112
Sessions, Roger, 262, 270, 275
Shakespeare, William, 1, 35, 47, 52, 53,
    56, 94, 352; *Coriolanus*, 27, 54; *King
    Lear*, 99; *King Richard III*, 94; *Mea-
    sure for Measure*, 15
Shaw, George Bernard, 36, 47, 53, 51,
    263; *Candida*, 313; *Major Barbara*,
    13, 263, 303; *Mrs. Warren's Profes-
    sion*, 313–14; *Saint Joan*, 13, 303
Shelley, Percy Bysshe, 334; *The Cenci*,
    35
Shklovsky, Viktor, 42, 57, 189; "Art as
    Technique," 43; *ostranenie*, 43, 56
Shostakovich, Dimitri, 262, 275
Silberman, Marc, 49
Sinclair, Upton, 333; *The Jungle*, 6, 13,
    100, 339

Sinatra, Frank, 261
Sirk, Douglas, 222, 227
Smith, Anna Deavere; *Fires in the Mir-
    ror*, 353; *Twilight: Los Angeles, 1992*
    353
Social Democratic Party, 282
Social Democracy, 184
Socialism/communism. *See* Communism;
    Socialism
Socialism, 2, 9, 25, 45, 46, 59, 125, 133,
    176, 178, 276, 279, 281, 283–87, 350,
    382
Socialist Realism, 18, 25, 61–66, 222,
    284, 381, 385
Socrates, 177, 181
Sollers, Philippe. *See* Pollet, Jean-Daniel
Sondheim, Stephen: *Company*, 267; *Pa-
    cific Overtures*, 267; *Sweeney Todd*,
    267
Sophocles, 35, 366; *Antigone*, 25
Soviet cinema, 209
Soviet Union, 18, 20, 25, 28, 57, 59, 61,
    63, 132, 136, 137, 164, 176, 276, 279,
    281, 284–87, 309
Spanish Civil War, 16
Spartacus uprising, 5, 90
SPD. *See* Social Democratic Party
Stalin, J. V., 18, 20, 27, 42, 43, 45, 66,
    79, 125, 137, 176, 177, 223, 279, 281,
    288, 289, 290, 291, 293, 350
Stalinism. *See* Stalin, J. V.
Stanislavsky, Constantin, 35, 55, 56, 64,
    66, 343, 349, 366, 367, 371, 372, 374,
    381
Stanislavsky Method, 64, 65, 66, 367
Stanzel, F. K. 40
Staudte, Wolfgang, 213
Steffin, Margarete, 8, 13, 14, 15, 20, 48,
    82, 116, 228, 308–9, 310–11
Stein, Joseph. *See* Ebb, Fred
Stendhal, 62
Stern, Guy, 304
Sternberg, Fritz, 19, 58, 282
Sternberg, Josef von, 48
Sting, 261, 266
Stokowski, Leopold, 342
Strasberg, Lee, 346
Straub, Jean-Marie, 221, 225–27

Straub, Jean-Marie, and Huillet, Danièle,
   221, 225–27; *Der Bräutigam, die Ko-
   mödiantin und der Zuhälter*, 227; *Ge-
   schichtsunterricht*, 226, 231
Strauss, Richard, 240
Stravinsky, Igor, 48, 239, 243–45, 262;
   The Nightingale, 245; *Oedipus Rex*,
   244–45; *The Soldier's Tale*, 245; *The
   Wedding*, 245
Strindberg, August, 4, 36, 329
Stuckenschmidt, Heinz, 78
Suhrkamp (publisher), 29
Suhrkamp, Peter, 85, 118
Sullivan, Dan, 352
Sundgaard, Arnold, 264
Surina, Tamara, 66
Suvin, Darko, 64
Svang (Hindi folk genre), 387
Swift, Jonathan, 66, 315
Syberberg, Hans Jürgen, 225, 227; *Hitler–
   Ein Film aus Deutschland*, 227; *Lud-
   wig–Requiem für einen jungfräulichen
   König*, 227; *Nach meinem letzten
   Umzug*, 227
Synge, J. M., 331

Tabori, George, 346, 347; *Brecht on
   Brecht*, 346
Tailleferre, Germaine, 242
Tairov, Alexander, 57
Taniko, 74, 75, 263
Tao te Ching, 184, 315
Taoism, 184
Tatlow, Antony, 307, 312
Teater Koma, 382; *Opera Ikan Asin*, 382–
   83
Teatristas, 357, 361, 368, 369, 371
Teatro Arena, 361, 362, 366, 367–68
Teatro Experimental de Cali, 357–58,
   361, 369, 371
TEC. *See* Teatro Experimental de Cali
Theatre Communications Group, 348
Theatre de Lys, 345, 346
Théâtre des Nations festival, 345
Theatre Union, New York, 17, 21, 264–
   65, 343
Third World cinema, 224

Thomson, Peter, and Sacks, Glendyr: *The
   Cambridge Companion to Brecht*, 1
Tiongson, Nicanor: *Pilipinas Circa 1907*,
   385
Titus Livius, 82
Toch, Ernst, 242
Toller, Ernst, 57
Tolstoy, Leo, 4
Topol, Chaim, 269
Torres-Reyes, Maria Luisa, 386
Tretyakov, Sergei, 18, 20, 43, 48, 66, 81;
   Roar China, 57
Trotsky, Leon, 176, 177, 288, 290, 291
Tunney, Gene, 51

Ulbricht, Walter, 27, 129, 137
Unseld, Siegfried, 85

Vaida, Ladislav, 204
Valentin, Karl, 6, 50, 201
Van Druten, John: *I Am a Camera*, 266
Vera, Rody. *See* Glinoga, Alan
Verfremdung, 9, 10, 36, 38, 41, 42, 43,
   44, 49, 50, 55, 57, 58, 65, 175, 188,
   192, 199, 200, 205, 214, 222, 226,
   232, 233, 242, 244, 247, 250–53, 273–
   74, 284–87, 360, 362, 386, 388, 392
Verfremdungseffekt. See Verfremdung
Verhoeven, Michael, 228; *Das schreck-
   liche Mädchen*, 228
Verlaine, Paul, 53, 89
Vertov, Dziga, 221
Vesey, Desmond, 323
Vianninha. *See* Filho, Oduvaldo Vianna
Villa El Salvador (theater group), 372,
   373
Villon, François, 10, 47, 53, 255, 332
Virilio, Paul: *War and Cinema*, 162
Völker, Klaus, 9, 304, 311
Voltaire, 66
Voris, Renate, 298

Wagenknecht, Regina, 299
Wagner, Richard, 12, 238–59; *The Flying
   Dutchman*, 240, 258; *Lohengrin*, 246,
   248, 258; *The Mastersingers of Nurem-
   berg*, 246; *Opera and Drama*, 245, 247;
   Parsifal, 245–46, 248; *Ring of the Ni-*

belung, 240, 246; *Tannhäuser*, 240; *Tristan and Isolde*, 246
Wagner-Regeny, Rudolf, 262, 275
Waley, Arthur, 74, 328, 333
Wallace, Edgar, 53, 52
Wasserstein, Wendy: *The Sisters Rosensweig*, 352
Wayang Orang (theater form), 384
Wayne, John, 136–37
Webber, Andrew Lloyd: *Evita*, 266
Webern, Anton, 74
Webster, John: *The Duchess of Malfi*, 22, 341
Wedekind, Frank, 3, 53, 54, 57, 58, 89
Weigel, Helene, 8, 10, 14, 15, 16, 25, 26, 28, 48, 64, 78, 255, 281, 292, 302, 307, 308–9, 310
Weill, Kurt, 10, 11, 12, 14, 22, 51, 73, 74, 75, 79, 85, 36, 48, 70, 71, 72, 73, 74, 75, 79, 85, 203, 205, 222, 239–44, 247, 249, 252, 253–59, 261–66, 267, 268, 270, 328, 329, 330, 333, 340, 341, 342, 345, 346, 350, 389; *Down in the Valley*, 265, 275; *Lost in the Stars*, 265–66; *Street Scene*, 265–66
Weill, Kurt, and Kaiser, Georg: *The Czar Has His Photograph Taken*, 254; *Protagonist*, 254
Weimar Republic, 13, 76, 84, 85, 122,

125, 140, 203, 209, 222, 227, 258, 281, 303
Weiss, Peter, 358
Welles, Orson, 354
Werfel, Franz, 148; *The Eternal Road*, 264
Wexley, John, 22, 211
Wiene, Robert, 199; *The Cabinet of Dr. Caligari*, 199
Willett, John, 5, 17, 27, 66, 73, 311, 323, 324, 328, 329, 330, 331, 332, 334, 335
Williams, Tennessee, 366, 367
Wirth, Andrzej, 49
Wolf, Friedrich, 25
Wolf, Konrad, 222; *Ich war, 19*, 222
Wolfe, George C.: *The Colored Museum*, 353; *Jelly's Last Jam*, 353; *Spunk*, 353
Wright, Elizabeth, 61
Wuolijoki, Hella, 19, 305

Yale Repertory Theatre, 348
Yuyachkani (theater group), 372, 373, 374

Zarzuwela (theater form), 385
Zhdanov, A. A., 42, 61
Zinnemann, Fred: *The Seventh Cross*, 213
Zoff, Marianne, 8, 26, 246
Zuckmayer, Carl, 3, 7, 8, 25, 48

Title Index of Works by Brecht

Collected Works:

Collected Works, 323
Gesammelte Werke (*GW*), 28, 36, 150, 169, 170, 172, 336
Malik edition of works, 83, 117
Versuche, 83, 183
Werke, 29, 36, 118, 324, 336

Plays: Collections, Individual Plays, "Operas," Adaptations, Fragments/Projects:

Antigone, 25
Antigone-Modell, 226
Arturo Ui. See *The Resistible Rise of Arturo Ui*
Baal, 4, 5, 9, 53, 58, 70, 83, 88, 89, 90, 91, 119, 120, 246, 272, 281, 288, 297, 298,
    299, 309, 346
The Baden-Baden Cantata, 70, 72, 75, 97, 275, 288, 302
"Die Bibel" (The Bible), 2, 88
"Der böse Baal, der asoziale" (Evil, Asocial Baal), 70, 288
"Der Brotladen" (The Breadshop), 84, 99, 302
The Catch, 299
The Caucasian Chalk Circle, 23, 40, 90, 99, 103, 104, 106, 107–9, 115, 183, 191,
    251, 262, 306, 314–16, 312–13, 331, 336, 362, 363, 364, 374, 380–81, 382,
    384, 385, 386, 387–88
Chalk Circle. See *The Caucasian Chalk Circle*
Collected Plays (*CP*), 325

The Condemnation of Lucullus, 26, 27, 98, 99, 101, 104, 244, 262, 270, 369

Coriolanus, 27, 54

The Days of the Commune, 99

Demise of the Egotist Johann Fatzer. *See* "Untergang des Egoisten Johann Fatzer"

Don Juan, 26

Drums in the Night, 4, 5, 59, 90, 91, 243, 246, 276, 281, 298, 301

The Duchess of Malfi, 22, 341

The Exception and the Rule, 43, 70, 81, 82, 97, 104, 261, 267, 272, 288, 363, 371, 376, 381, 383

"Fatzer." *See* "Untergang des Egoisten Johann Fatzer" (Demise of the Egotist Johann Fatzer)

Fear and Misery of the Third Reich, 15, 16, 99, 306, 362, 371, 375, 377. *See also The Private Life of the Master Race*

The Flight over the Ocean, 70, 71, 72, 239, 279, 288, 343

Der Flug der Lindberghs (The Flight of the Lindberghs), 71, 85. *See also Der Lindberghflug*

Galileo. *See Life of Galileo*

Goliath, 246

The Good Person of Szechwan, 14, 16, 17, 39, 51, 70, 82, 97, 99, 105, 107, 191, 301, 304–5, 307–8, 312, 315–17, 331, 332, 345, 346, 356, 363, 381

Happy End, 239, 261–63, 274, 302, 340, 347, 352

He Who Said No, 70, 75, 82, 288

He Who Said Yes, 70, 74, 75, 76, 77, 82, 173, 239, 261–63, 288, 374

The Horatii and the Curiatii, 70, 82, 83, 97

In the Jungle of Cities, 6, 20, 58, 59, 91, 100, 101, 276, 299–300, 340, 352, 366

"In Search of Justice," 16

"The Informer," 16

"The Jewish Wife," 16, 367

The Jewish Wife and Other Short Plays, 16

"Joe Fleischhacker," 9, 254, 282

The Life of Edward the Second of England, 7, 54, 55, 57, 91–92, 97, 299–300

Life of Galileo, 16, 23, 39, 45, 84, 99, 101–103, 109, 115, 244, 269, 272, 287, 304–5, 315, 324, 325–28, 331 341, 344, 345, 350, 362, 364, 380, 381, 386

Der Lindberghflug (Lindbergh's Flight), 71, 72, 74, 80. *See also Der Flug der Lindberghs*

Lucullus. *See The Condemnation of Lucullus*

Lux in Tenebris, 298

Mahagonny. *See Rise and Fall of the City of Mahagonny*

A Man's a Man, 8, 59, 73, 92, 239, 272, 299, 301–302, 306, 312, 313, 346, 352

The Measures Taken, 12, 13, 59, 70, 71, 75, 76, 77, 78, 79, 80, 82, 84, 96, 97, 122, 124, 173, 227, 263, 269, 285, 288–89, 302, 334, 382

The Mother, 13, 16, 17, 21, 70, 97, 99, 122, 124, 202, 208, 211, 261, 264–65, 268, 272, 303–4, 308, 343, 344, 381, 388, 394

Mother Courage and Her Children, 16, 17, 25, 39, 62, 99, 103, 105, 107, 191, 249, 267, 269–70, 272, 285, 306–8, 311–12, 314–17, 331, 345, 347, 352, 354, 356, 362, 372, 374, 375

The Private Life of the Master Race, 16, 341, 345. *See also Fear and Misery of the Third Reich*

Puntila and Matti, His Hired Man, 16, 19, 25, 26, 39, 51–52, 65, 90, 97, 99, 105, 106, 107, 132, 305, 308, 352, 362, 364, 365, 385

Rise and Fall of the City of Mahagonny, 12, 36, 37, 70, 95, 96, 223, 239, 246–47, 252, 261–62, 264, 270, 275, 285, 286, 299–301, 311, 315, 363, 365, 367

The Resistible Rise of Arturo Ui, 20, 30, 99, 116, 340, 347, 348, 352, 363, 364, 365

Roundheads and Peakheads. See Roundheads and Pointed Heads

Roundheads and Pointed Heads, 15, 98, 99, 104, 304

Saint Joan of the Stockyards, 13, 20, 94, 97, 99, 100–101, 254, 282, 302–3, 313–14, 340, 352, 363

Schweyk in the Second World War, 22, 99, 107–8, 109, 312, 336, 341, 356, 362, 381

Señora Carrar's Rifles, 16, 99, 313, 344, 363, 371, 375, 388

The Seven Deadly Sins, 14, 36, 39, 222, 239, 262, 264, 301, 304, 308, 363, 364, 374

Songspiel Mahagonny, 239, 242–43

The Threepenny Opera, 10, 11, 14, 28, 36, 53, 70, 74, 88, 93–94, 95, 96, 100, 101, 104, 106, 142, 197, 203–4, 205, 207, 211, 213, 239, 245, 251, 253–59, 261–67, 271–72, 285, 286, 299, 301, 311, 328, 329–30, 332, 333, 336, 342, 343, 345, 346, 347, 351–52, 362, 364, 371, 373, 374, 375, 382–83, 389

The Trial of Lucullus. See The Condemnation of Lucullus

The Trial of Joan of Arc at Rouen, 1431, 313

Trumpets and Drums, 340, 346

The Tutor, 54, 363

Turandot, or The Whitewashers' Congress, 21, 88, 133, 311

"Untergang des Egoisten Johann Fatzer" (Demise of the Egotist Johann Fatzer), 70, 83, 84, 173, 288, 302

The Visions of Simone Machard, 22, 99, 212, 311–12

The Wedding, 6, 90, 298

"Weizen" (Wheat), 282

Poetry: Collections, Poems, Songs:

"About the Way to Construct Enduring Works," 126

"The Actress," 308

"After the Death of My Collaborator M. S.," 309

"Against Temptation," 315

"Ardens sed virens," 310

"At Ulm, 1592," 182, 183, 189

"Bad Time for Poetry," 14

"Ballad of the Dead Soldier." *See* "Legend of the Dead Soldier"

"Ballad of Hannah Cash," 299

"The Ballad of Mac the Knife," 255, 261, 329, 330, 345, 350

"The Ballad of Marie Sanders, the Jew's Whore," 306

"Ballad of the Old Woman," 300

"The Ballad of Paragraph 218," 302

"Ballad of the Death of Anna Cloudface," 298

"Die Bekenntnisse eines Erst-Kommunikanden" (Confessions of a Recipient of the First Holy Communion), 297

Buckow Elegies, 27, 28, 115, 133, 134–37, 157, 313

"Burial of the Trouble-Maker in a Zinc Coffin," 122–24

"The Carpet-Weavers of Kuyan-Bulak Pay Tribute to Lenin," 186

"Chorale of the Great Baal," 298
"Concerning the Insecurity of the Human State," 383, 390
"Deutsche *Kriegsfibel*" (German War Primer), 127, 158, 159
"Discovery About a Young Woman," 300
"Dream of a Great Grumbler," 248
Die drei Soldaten: Ein Kinderbuch (The Three Soldiers: a Children's Book), 302
"Du, der das Unentbehrliche" (You, Who [sees] the Indispensable), 311
"Erinnerungen" (Memories), 297
"Die Erziehung der Hirse" (The Education of the Millet), 115
"Finnish Landscape," 132
"The Flower Garden," 134, 137
"For Helene Weigel," 308
"The Fourth Sonnet," 309
"German Satires," 155
German War Primer. *See* "Deutsche *Kriegsfibel*"
"Germany," 122, 134, 228
"God's Evening Song," 297
"The Good Comrade M. S.," 309
Hauspostille. See *Manual of Piety*, 118, 119
"Hollywood," 21, 222
"Hollywood Elegies," 134, 311
"Hot Day," 135–36
"The House-Painter Speaks of Great Times to Come," 127
Hundert Gedichte (A Hundred Poems), 117, 129, 133
"In Praise of Dialectics," 124–25, 129
"Iron," 314
"Is the People Infallible?" 18
Kriegsfibel (War Primer), 117, 118, 133–34, 139–66
"Kurzer Bericht über 400 (Vierhundert) junge Lyriker" (Short Report on 400 [Four Hundred] Young Poets), 148, 156
"Legend of the Dead Soldier," 3, 119–20, 122
"The Legend of the Harlot Evelyn Roe," 297–98
"Legend of the Origin of the Book Tao-Tê-Ching on Lao-Tsû's Road into Exile," 127–28, 184, 186, 315
"Lehrgedicht von der Natur der Menschen" (Didactic Poem Concerning Human Nature), 315
"Lied der Lyriker" (The Poets' Song), 155
"Das Lied vom Anstreicher Hitler" (The Song of Hitler, the House Painter), 159
Lieder, Gedichte, Chöre (Songs, Poems, Choruses), 117, 122, 124, 125
"Little Song from Olden Times," 313
"Lullabies," 303
"Das Manifest" (*The Communist Manifesto*), 341
Manual of Piety, 2, 5, 117, 118, 119, 120, 121, 122, 147–48, 180, 239, 297, 315, 332, 339
"The Mask of Evil," 191
"Moderne Legende" (Modern Legend), 297
"Morning Address to a Tree Named Green," 301, 314
"Mütter Vermißter" (The Mothers of Missing [Soldiers]), 297

"Nasty Morning," 28
"1940," 20, 117
"Of Poor B. B.," 2, 7
"Of Sprinkling the Garden," 130–31
"Of Swimming in Lakes and Rivers," 298
"On the Decay of Love," 305
"On the Infanticide Marie Farrar," 299
"On Kant's Definition of Marriage," 190
"Paddling, Talking," 135, 136
"Pirate Jenny," 255, 257, 258, 266, 301, 330
"Pleasures," 315–16
Pocket Manual. *See Taschenpostille*
Poems 1913–1956, 5, 334
Poems & Songs from the Plays, 334
Poems in Exile, 129
"Prohibition of Theatre Criticism," 248
"Psalm," 339, 341
"Questions from a Worker Who Reads," 181
Reader for Those Who Live in Cities, 7, 147, 300
"Reading a Soviet Book," 115, 136, 137
"Reading the Paper while Brewing the Tea," 129
"Remembering Marie A.," 298
"Die Requisiten der Weigel" (Weigel's Props), 308–9
"The Ship," 299
"The Shoe of Empedocles," 315
"The Shopper," 306
"The Sixth Sonnet," 309
"The Smoke," 135
"Soldier of the Revolution," 13
"The Solution," 28, 191
"Song About the Good People," 311
"Song of Chaos," 108
"Song of the Flagon," 312
"The Song of the Moldau," 22, 109
"Song of the Ruined Innocent Folding Linen," 299
Die Songs der Dreigroschenoper (The Songs of *The Threepenny Opera*), 10
"Sonnet" (1925), 300
"Sonnet No. 19," 309
Steffin Collection, 131–32, 157, 160
"Still at It," 134
Svendborg Poems, 17, 117, 127–29, 134, 154, 157, 158, 159, 160, 248, 315
Taschenpostille (Pocket Manual), 117, 118
"Thoughts on the Duration of Exile," 14
"To My Countrymen," 313
"To Those Born Later," 19, 117, 128–29, 134, 315, 337
"Die unbesiegliche Inschrift" (The Undefeatable Inscription), 160
"Utterances of a Martyr," 299
"Veränderung, aber zum Schlechten" (Change, but for the Worse), 310

"Weigel's Props," 308
"Wenn der Anstreicher durch die Lautsprecher über den Frieden redet" (As the House
    Painter Talks over the Loudspeakers about Peace), 159
"What Keeps Mankind Alive?", 103
"When the Fascists Kept Getting Stronger," 14
"Why Should My Name Be Mentioned?", 153

Prose: Theater, Art, Politics:

"Alienation Effects in Chinese Acting," 9, 17, 37, 64–65
Brecht on Theatre, 336
Der Dreigroschenprozeß (The Threepenny Trial), 142, 147, 201, 202, 203, 206–7, 210
"Dialectics in the Theatre," 273
"Fotografie," 146
The Messingkauf Dialogues, 25, 37, 36, 41, 178, 341
"The Modern Theatre Is the Epic Theatre." *See* "Notes to the Opera *Rise and Fall of
    the City of Mahagonny*"
"Notes to the Opera *Rise and Fall of the City of Mahagonny*," 12, 37, 63, 244, 247,
    252, 286, 287
"On Experimental Theater," 37, 38, 392
"On Gestic Music," 252
"On Rhymeless Verse with Irregular Rhythms," 155, 255
"On Stage Music," 248
"On the Use of Music in an Epic Theatre," 56, 242, 252, 256
"A Short Organum for the Theatre," 25, 36, 45–46, 49, 55, 56, 63, 64, 226, 251, 273,
    374
Theaterarbeit, 26, 310
"Theatre for Pleasure or Theatre for Instruction?", 37
"Über Photographie" (On Photography), 145–46
"The Street Scene," 353
"Über den Film" (On Film), 201
"Über Filmmusik" (On Film Music), 269
"Underrating the Formal Aspect," 155
"Weite und Vielfalt der realistischen Schreibweise" (Breadth and Abundance of the
    Realistic Mode of Writing), 18
"Writing the Truth: Five Difficulties," 165

**Prose: Diaries, Fiction (Novels/Fragments, Short Stories, Anecdotes), Journals,
    Letters**:

"Anecdotes of Mr. Keuner," 83–84, 168, 169, 170, 171, 172–75, 178, 179, 180, 181,
    185, 289
"The Augsburg Chalk Circle," 23, 183, 306–77, 312
"Bargan Gives Up," 4
"Büchlein mit Verhaltenslehren" (Booklet on Moral Teaching), 289
Diaries, 276, 281, 298, 336
"Eßkultur" (Dining Culture), 99
"The Exertions of the Best People," 191
"The Experiment," 44, 181, 182, 186

Flüchtlingsgespräche (Refugee Conversations), 19, 26, 59, 164, 171, 172, 177–80,
        181, 187, 190, 191
Die Geschäfte des Herrn Julius Caesar (The Business Dealings of Mr. Julius Caesar),
        18, 211, 226, 336
''Geschichten von Lai-tu'' (Stories about Lai-tu), 28
''The Heretic's Coat,'' 181
Journals 1934–1955, 64, 84, 116, 131, 140, 142, 158, 266, 289, 292, 328, 336
Kalendergeschichten. See Tales from the Calendar
Lai-tu stories, 310
Letters 1913–1956, 333, 336
Me-ti. Buch der Wendungen (Me-ti. The Book of Twists and Turns), 17, 28, 164, 170,
        171, 172, 175–77, 178, 181, 185, 187, 190, 289–92, 322, 336
''The Monster,'' 202
''On Meeting Again,'' 189
A Penny for the Poor. See Threepenny Novel
''The Question, Is There a God,'' 190
''Die Rolle der Gefühle'' (The Role of Emotions), 185
Short Stories 1921–1946, 336
''Socrates Wounded,'' 181
Tales from the Calendar, 23, 164, 169, 170, 172, 180–84, 336
Threepenny Novel, 14, 15, 169, 203, 336
Der Tui-Roman (The Tui Novel), 21, 168, 176, 177, 289, 305, 336, 341
''The Unseemly Old Lady,'' 183, 223, 306
''Who Knows Whom,'' 187

Film: Projects, Scripts:

Die Beule (The Bruise), 203–4, 206, 213
''Der Brillantenfresser'' (The Jewel Eater), 200
''Drei im Turm'' (Three in the Tower), 200
''Der Gallische Krieg oder Die Geschäfte des Herrn J. Caesar'' (The Gallic War or
        The Business Affairs of Mr. J. Caesar), 211
Hangmen also Die, 21, 197, 211–12, 208, 268, 340
Herr Puntila und sein Knecht Matti (*Puntila and Matti, His Hired Man*), 213–14
Kuhle Wampe, 122, 197, 207–10, 229, 234, 286, 303, 309
''Lohengrin,'' 248
Mutter Courage (Mother Courage), 213
''Das Mysterium der Jamaika-Bar'' (The Mystery of the Jamaica Bar), 200
Mysterien eines Frisiersalons (Mysteries of a Hairdressing Salon), 201
''Robinson in Assuncion'' (Robinson in Assuncion), 201
The Threepenny Opera, 205, 343
The Visions of Simone Machard, 212

About the Editor and Contributors

SIEGFRIED MEWS is professor of German at the University of North Carolina at Chapel Hill. He served as editor of the monograph series University of North Carolina Studies in the Germanic Languages and Literatures and the quarterly *South Atlantic Review*. He has published widely on nineteenth- and twentieth-century German and comparative literature; his edition of *Collected Essays on Bertolt Brecht* appeared in 1989.

MICHAEL BODDEN is assistant professor of Indonesian Language and Southeast Asian Literature at the University of Victoria, British Columbia. His dissertation dealt with Brecht in contemporary Philippine and Indonesian theater. He is currently working on issues of theater and censorship in Indonesia as well as on issues of nationalism and gender in Philippine and Indonesian literature.

CHRISTIANE BOHNERT is an independent scholar and translator. She has published articles on eighteenth-century literature, E.T.A. Hoffmann, and the literature of the former German Democratic Republic (GDR). Her book on Brecht's poetry, *Brechts Lyrik im Kontext: Zyklen und Exil*, appeared in 1982; a volume on the theory and practice of satire in different cultures with an emphasis on the eighteenth century is forthcoming.

BARTON BYG is associate professor of German at the University of Massachusetts, Amherst. He teaches German and film studies, is cofounder of the interdepartmental program in film studies, and has authored *Landscapes of Resistance: The German Films of Danièle Huillet and Jean-Marie Straub* (1995).

REINHOLD GRIMM is professor of German and Comparative Literature at the University of California at Riverside. A former president of the American Association of Teachers of German and editor of the *German Quarterly*, he received an honorary doctorate from Georgetown University and is a member of the international PEN. He has published numerous monographs, editions, articles, and essays, mainly on nineteenth- and twentieth-century German and comparative literature. His most recent publication is *Versuche zur europäischen Literatur* (1994).

SABINE GROSS is assistant professor of German at the University of Wisconsin–Madison. Her research interests are literary theory, reader response theory, twentieth-century literature, theater, and film and media studies. She has published on literary canon formation, the media, the reading process, and twentieth-century German literature.

DOUGLAS KELLNER is professor of philosophy at the University of Texas at Austin. He is the author of numerous books on social theory, politics, history, and culture, including *Critical Theory, Marxism, and Modernity* (1989), *Jean Baudrillard: From Marxism to Postmodernism and Beyond* (1989), *Media Culture: Cultural Studies, Identity, and Politics between the Modern and the Postmodern* (1995). With Steven Best he coauthored *Postmodern Theory: Critical Interrogations* (1991).

CHRISTINE KIEBUZINSKA is associate professor of English at Virginia Polytechnic and State University. She is the author of *Revolutionaries in the Theater: Meyerhold, Brecht, and Witkiewicz* (1988), and her articles and reviews have appeared in *Comparative Literature Studies, Comparatist, Brecht-Jahrbuch/ Brecht Yearbook, Modern Language Studies, South Atlantic Review, Slavic and East European Arts*, and *Theatre Journal*.

HERBERT KNUST is professor of German and Comparative Literature at the University of Illinois at Urbana-Champaign. His research has focused on modern literature, especially drama, literary thematics, literature and the other arts, travel literature, and the literature of the Weimar Republic. He has made numerous contributions to Brecht scholarship, including *Materialien zu Bertolt Brechts "Schweyk im zweiten Weltkrieg"* (1974) and *Bertolt Brecht: "Leben des Galilei"* (6th, enlarged edition, 1993).

MICHAEL MORLEY is professor of Drama at Flinders University in Adelaide, South Australia. He has published studies of Brecht's poetry and drama as well as on Brecht's musical collaborators. He has also translated poems by Brecht for *Poems*.

THOMAS R. NADAR is associate professor of German at Auburn University in Alabama. He has published on German drama, film, language pedagogy, and Brecht and music. He has directed three NEH Summer Institutes for the study of German and Austrian literature at the University of Oregon; in May 1991 he was the recipient of the Outstanding Teacher in the Humanities Award at Auburn University.

LAUREEN NUSSBAUM is professor *emerita* of German at Portland State University. She wrote her dissertation on women in the work of Brecht and published several articles on that topic. Further publications deal with *littérature engagée* and documentary theater. Recently her research has focused on German literature in Dutch exile; her publications in this area include articles on the German/Dutch writer Anne Frank.

MARINA PIANCA is associate professor of Spanish and Chair of the Latin American Studies Program at the University of California at Riverside. She has done extensive work on Latin American theater and cultural studies and is founder and editor, since 1984, of *Díogenes: Anuario Crítico del Teatro Latino-americano*. Among her publications are *El Teatro de Nuestra América: Un proyecto continental (1959–1989)* (1990), *Testimonios de Teatro Latinoamericano* (1991), and (with Judith Weiss and others) *Popular Theater in Latin America* (1994).

KARL-HEINZ SCHOEPS is professor of German at the University of Illinois at Urbana-Champaign. He has published articles on twentieth-century authors, the East German novel, and Gruppe 47. His publications on Brecht include *Bertolt Brecht und Bernard Shaw* (1974), *Bertolt Brecht* (1977), and *Bertolt Brecht: Life, Work, and Criticism* (1989).

MARC SILBERMAN is professor of German at the University of Wisconsin–Madison where he teaches German literature, culture, and cinema. He has published on the East German novel, German cinema, and the dramatist Heiner Müller. From 1990 to 1995 he served as managing editor of *Brecht-Jahrbuch/ Brecht Yearbook*, the annual publication of the International Brecht Society (IBS). His latest, book-length study is entitled *German Cinema: Texts in Contexts* (1995).

STEFAN SOLDOVIERI is an advanced graduate student at the University of Wisconsin–Madison. He has published on the political rhetoric of Günter Grass and translated from the German. Currently he is working on a research project on the cinema of the former German Democratic Republic (GDR).

VERA STEGMANN is associate professor of German at Lehigh University. She is the author of *Das epische Musiktheater bei Strawinsky und Brecht: Studien zur Geschichte und Theorie* (1991) and several articles on twentieth-century literature and music. From 1991 to 1995 she served as editor of the semiannual publication, *Communications from the International Brecht Society*.

CARL WEBER is professor of Directing and Dramaturgy at Stanford University. A collaborator of Bertolt Brecht and actor, director, and dramaturg at the Berliner Ensemble from 1952 to 1961, he has since directed for major theaters in Europe, North America, and India. He has edited and translated works by French and German playwrights, among them those by Heiner Müller and other contemporary dramatists. His essays have appeared in journals such as *Theatre Journal*, *Drama Review*, *Brecht-Jahrbuch/Brecht Yearbook*, and *Performing Arts Journal*; he is coeditor of the two last-mentioned publications.

ISBN 0-313-29266-3

9 780313 292668

HARDCOVER BAR CODE